W9-BZV-977

Fundamentals of Computer Graphics

Fundamentals of Computer Graphics

Peter Shirley
School of Computing
University of Utah

A K Peters
Natick, Massachusetts

Editorial, Sales, and Customer Service Office

A K Peters, Ltd.
63 South Avenue
Natick, MA 01760
www.akpeters.com

Library of Congress Cataloging-in-Publication Data

Shirley, P. (Peter), 1963-
Fundamentals of computer graphics / Peter Shirley.
p. cm.
ISBN 1-56881-124-1
1. Computer graphics. I. Title.

T385 .S434 2002
006.6--dc21

2002070370

Printed in Canada
06 05 04 03 10 9 8 7 6 5 4 3 2

Contents

Preface xi

1 Introduction 1

1.1 Graphics Areas 1
1.2 Major Applications 2
1.3 Graphics APIs 3
1.4 3D Geometric Models 4
1.5 Graphics Pipeline 4
1.6 Numerical Issues 5
1.7 Efficiency 7
1.8 Software Engineering 8
1.9 A Short History of Computer Graphics 12

2 Miscellaneous Math 15

2.1 Sets and Mappings 15
2.2 Solving Quadratic Equations 19
2.3 Trigonometry 20
2.4 Vectors 23
2.5 2D Implicit Curves 29
2.6 2D Parametric Curves 36
2.7 3D Implicit Surfaces 38
2.8 3D Parametric Curves 40
2.9 3D Parametric Surfaces 41

2.10 Linear Interpolation 42
2.11 Triangles 42

3 Raster Algorithms 49
3.1 Raster Displays 49
3.2 Monitor Intensities and Gamma 50
3.3 RGB Color 52
3.4 The Alpha Channel 54
3.5 Line Drawing 55
3.6 Triangle Rasterization 60
3.7 Simple Antialiasing 64
3.8 Image Capture and Storage 65

4 Linear Algebra 69
4.1 Determinants 69
4.2 Matrices 71

5 Transformation Matrices 85
5.1 Basic 2D Transforms 85
5.2 Basic 3D Transforms 97
5.3 Translation 101
5.4 Inverses of Transformation Matrices 104
5.5 Coordinate Transformations 104

6 Viewing 109
6.1 Drawing the Canonical View Volume 110
6.2 Orthographic Projection 111
6.3 Perspective Projection 116
6.4 Some Properties of the Perspective Transform 122
6.5 Field-of-View 123

7 Hidden Surface Elimination 127
7.1 BSP Tree 127
7.2 Z-Buffer 135

8 Surface Shading 141
8.1 Diffuse Shading 141
8.2 Phong Shading 144
8.3 Artistic Shading 147

9 Ray Tracing 151
9.1 The Basic Ray Tracing Algorithm 152
9.2 Computing Viewing Rays 153
9.3 Ray-Object Intersection 154
9.4 A Ray Tracing Program 159

9.5 Shadows 161
9.6 Specular Reflection 161
9.7 Refraction 162
9.8 Instancing 165
9.9 Sub-Linear Ray-Object Intersection 167
9.10 Constructive Solid Geometry 182
9.11 Distribution Ray Tracing 183

10 Texture Mapping 191
10.1 3D Texture Mapping 192
10.2 2D Texture Mapping 198
10.3 Tessellated Models 199
10.4 Texture Mapping for Rasterized Triangles 201
10.5 Bump Textures 204
10.6 Displacement Mapping 204
10.7 Environment Maps 205
10.8 Shadow Maps 206

11 A Full Graphics Pipeline 209
11.1 Clipping 209
11.2 Location of Clipping Segment of the Pipeline 210
11.3 An Expanded Graphics Pipeline 214
11.4 Backface Elimination 215
11.5 Triangle Strips and Fans 216
11.6 Preserved State 217
11.7 A Full Graphics Pipeline 217

12 Data Structures for Graphics 221
12.1 Triangle Meshes 221
12.2 Winged-Edge Data Structure 222
12.3 Scene Graphs 224
12.4 Tiling Multidimensional Arrays 225

13 Curves and Surfaces 231
13.1 Bilinear Patches 231
13.2 Quadratic Bézier Curves 232
13.3 Higher-Order Bézier Curves 234
13.4 Properties of Bézier Curves 235

13.5 Bézier Surfaces . . . 236
13.6 Hermite and Catmull-Rom Curves . . . 238
13.7 B-Splines . . . 240
13.8 Loop Subdivision Surfaces . . . 245

14 Measure and Sampling 249
14.1 Integrals and Measure . . . 249
14.2 Continuous Probability . . . 254
14.3 Monte Carlo Integration . . . 258
14.4 Choosing Random Points . . . 260

15 Antialiasing 271
15.1 Filtering . . . 271
15.2 Implementing Filtering . . . 276

16 Light 279
16.1 Radiometry . . . 279
16.2 Transport Equation . . . 288
16.3 Photometry . . . 289

17 Human Vision 293
17.1 Overview of Vision . . . 293
17.2 Makeup of the Eyes . . . 295
17.3 Adaptation . . . 296
17.4 Dimensions of the Low-Level Visual Experience . . . 298

18 Color 301
18.1 Light and Light Detectors . . . 302
18.2 Tristimulus Color Theory . . . 302
18.3 CIE Tristimulus Values . . . 304
18.4 Chromaticity . . . 305
18.5 Scotopic Luminance . . . 308
18.6 RGB Monitors . . . 308
18.7 Approximate Color Manipulation . . . 309
18.8 Opponent Color Spaces . . . 310
18.9 Tone Mapping . . . 311

19 Global Illumination 317
19.1 Particle Tracing for Lambertian Scenes . . . 317
19.2 Path Tracing . . . 321

20 Accurate Direct Lighting 327
20.1 Mathematical Framework . . . 327
20.2 Direct Lighting from Many Luminaires . . . 331

21 Reflection Models 337
21.1 Real-World Materials 337
21.2 Implementing Reflection Models 339
21.3 Specular Reflection Models 341
21.4 Smooth Layered Model 342
21.5 Rough Layered Model 345

22 Image-Based Rendering 353
22.1 The Light Field 354
22.2 Creating a Novel Image from a Set of Images 355

23 Visualization 359
23.1 2D Scalar Fields 359
23.2 3D Scalar Fields 360

Index 371

Preface

This book is a product of several graphics courses I have taught at Indiana University and the University of Utah. All graphics books must choose between teaching the low-level details "under the hood" of graphics programs, or teaching how to use modern graphics APIs such as OpenGL, Direct3D, and Java3D. This book chooses the former approach. I do not have a good justification for this choice other than that I have taught both styles of courses, and the students in the "low-level" courses seemed to understand the material better than the other students, and even seemed to use the APIs more effectively. There are many reasons this might be true, and the effect may not transfer to other teachers or schools. However, I believe that teaching the fundamentals is usually the right approach, whether in graphics, another academic discipline, or a sport.

How to Use this Book

The book begins with eight chapters that roughly correspond to a one-semester course which takes students through the graphics pipeline and basic ray tracing. It has students implement everything—i.e., it is not a "learn OpenGL" style text. However, the pipeline presented is consistent with the real thing, and students who have used the book should find OpenGL or other common APIs familiar in many ways. The second part of the book is a series of advanced topics that are not highly ordered. This would allow a variety of second-semester courses, and a few weeks of advanced topics in a first semester course.

For the first semester, I would suggest the following as a possible outline of initial assignments:

1. Math homework at the end of Chapter 2 followed by at least one in-class exam.

2. Line rasterization.

3. Triangle rasterization with barycentric color interpolation

4. Orthographic wireframe drawing

5. Perspective wireframe drawing

6. BSP-tree with flat-shaded triangles and wireframe edges with only trivial z-clipping and with mouse-driven viewpoint selection

7. Finite-precision z-buffer implementation with only trivial z-clipping

Following these assignments the instructor could do assignments on ray tracing, or could have the students add shadow-maps, Phong lighting, clipping, and textures to their z-buffers, or could move the students into programming with a 3D API.

In the second semester, almost any sequence could be followed, but I think advanced students should be exposed to at least global illumination and subdivision surfaces.

About the Cover

The cover image is from *Tiger in the Water* by J. W. Baker (brushed and airbrushed acrylic on canvas, 16" by 20", www.jbwart.com).

The subject of a tiger is a reference to a wonderful talk given by Alain Fournier (1943–2000) at the Cornell Workshop in 1998. His talk was an evocative verbal description of the movements of a tiger. He summarized his point:

> Even though modelling and rendering in computer graphics have been improved tremendously in the past 35 years, we are still not at the point where we can model automatically a tiger swimming in the river in all its glorious details. By automatically I mean in a way that does not need careful manual tweaking by an artist/expert.
>
> The bad news is that we have still a long way to go.
>
> The good news is that we have still a long way to go.

Acknowledgements

The following people have provided helpful comments about the book: Josh Andersen, Zeferino Andrade, Michael Ashikman, Adam Berger, Stephen Chenney, Greg Coombe, Michael Gliecher, Chuck Hansen, Andy Hanson, Vicki Interrante, Ray Jones, Steve Marschner, Keith Moreley, Micah Neilson, Blake Nelson, Steve Parker, Matt Pharr, Peter Poulos, Nate Robins, Richard Sharp, Peter-Pike Sloan, Tony Tahbaz, Bruce Walter, and Amy Williams. Ching-Kuang Shene and David Solomon allowed me to borrow examples from their works. Kenneth Joy's online notes on modeling were extremely useful, and the presentation of that topic was based on his treatment. Henrik Jensen, Eric Levin, Matt Pharr, and Jason Waltman generously provided images.

Brandon Mansfield was very helpful in improving the content of the discussion of hierarchical bounding volumes for ray tracing.

I am extremely thankful to J. W. Baker helping me get the cover I envisioned. In addition to being a talented artist, he was a great pleasure to work with personally.

Many works were helpful in preparing this book, and most of them appear in the notes for the appropriate chapters. However, a few pieces that influenced the content and presentation do not, and I list them here. I thank the authors for their help. These include the two classic computer graphics I first learned the basics from as a student: *Computer Graphics: Principles & Practice* by Foley et al., and *Computer Graphics* by Hearn and Baker. Other include all of Alan Watt's excellent books, Hill's *Computer Graphics Using OpenGL*, Angel's *3D Computer Graphics with openGL*, Hughes Hoppe's University of Washington dissertation, and Rogers' two classic graphics texts.

This book was written using the *Latex* document preparation software on an Apple Powerbook. The figures were made by the author using the *Adobe Illustrator* package. I would like to thank the creators of those wonderful programs.

I'd like to thank the University of Utah for allowing me to work on this book during sabbatical.

I would like to especially thank Alice and Klaus Peters for encouraging me to write this book, and for their great skill in making the process of writing a book a pleasure for the author.

Peter Shirley
Salt Lake City
March 2002

Introduction

The term *Computer Graphics* describes any use of computers to create or manipulate images. This book takes a slightly more specific view and deals mainly with algorithms for image generation. Doing computer graphics inevitably requires some knowledge of specific hardware, file formats, and usually an API[1] or two. The specifics of that knowledge are a moving target due to the rapid evolution of the field, and therefore such details will be avoided in this text. Readers are encouraged to supplement the text with relevant documentation for their software/hardware environment. Fortunately the culture of computer graphics has enough standard terminology and concepts that the discussion in this book should map nicely to most environments. This chapter defines some basic terminology, and provides some historical background as well as information sources related to computer graphics.

1.1 Graphics Areas

It is always dangerous to try to categorize endeavors in any field, but most graphics practitioners would agree on the following major areas, and that they are part of the field of computer graphics:

- **Modeling** deals with the mathematical specification of shape and appearance properties in a way that can be stored on the computer.

[1] An *application program interface* (API) is a software interface for basic operations such as line drawing. Current popular APIs include OpenGL, Direct3D, and Java3D.

For example, a coffee mug might be described as a set of ordered 3D points along with some interpolation rule to connect the points, and a reflection model that describes how light interacts with the mug.

- **Rendering** is a term inherited from art and deals with the creation of shaded images from 3D computer models.
- **Animation** is a technique to create an illusion of motion through sequences of images. Here, modeling and rendering are used, with the handling of time as a key issue not usually dealt with in basic modeling and rendering.

There are many other areas that involve computer graphics, and whether they are core graphics areas is a matter of opinion. These will all be at least touched on in the text. Such related areas include:

- **User interaction** deals with the interface between input devices such as mice and tablets, the application and feedback to the user in imagery and other sensory feedback. Historically this area is associated with graphics largely because graphics researchers had some of the earliest access to the input/output devices that are now ubiquitous.
- **Virtual reality** attempts to *immerse* the user into a 3D virtual world. This typically requires at least stereo graphics and response to head motion. For true virtual reality, sound and force feedback should be provided as well. Because this area requires advanced 3D graphics and advanced display technology, it is often closely associated with graphics.
- **Visualization** attempts to give users insight via visual display. Often there are graphic issues to be addressed in a visualization problem.
- **Image processing** deals with the manipulation of 2D images and is used in both the fields of graphics and vision.
- **3D scanning** uses range-finding technology to create measured 3D models. Such models are useful for creating rich visual imagery, and the processing of such models often requires graphics algorithms.

1.2 Major Applications

Almost any endeavor can make some use of computer graphics, but the major consumers of computer graphics technology include the following industries:

- **Video games** increasingly use sophisticated 3D models and rendering algorithms.
- **Cartoons** are often rendered directly from 3D models. Many traditional 2D cartoons use backgrounds rendered from 3D models which allows a continuously moving viewpoint without huge amounts of artist time.
- **Film special effects** use almost all types of computer graphics technology. Almost every modern film uses digital compositing to superimpose backgrounds with separately filmed foregrounds. Many films use computer-generated foregrounds with 3D models.
- **CAD/CAM** stand for *computer-aided design* and *computer-aided manufacturing.* These fields use computer technology to design parts and products on the computer and then, using these virtual designs, to guide the manufacturing procedure. For example, many mechanical parts are now designed in a 3D computer modeling package, and are then automatically produced on a computer-controlled milling device.
- **Simulation** can be thought of as accurate video gaming. For example, a flight simulator uses sophisticated 3D graphics to simulate the experience of flying an airplane. Such simulations can be extremely useful for initial training in safety-critical domains such as driving, and for scenario training for experienced users such as specific fire-fighting situations that are too costly or dangerous to create physically.
- **Medical imaging** creates meaningful images of scanned patient data. For example, a magnetic resonance imaging (MRI) dataset is composed of a 3D rectangular array of density values. Computer graphics is used to create shaded images that help doctors digest the most salient information from such data.
- **Information visualization** creates images of data that do not necessarily have a "natural" visual depiction. For example, the temporal trend of the price of ten different stocks does not have an obvious visual depiction, but clever graphing techniques can help humans find patterns in such data.

1.3 Graphics APIs

A key part of using graphics libraries is dealing with an *application program interface* (API). An API is a software interface that provides a model for how an application program can access system functionality, such as drawing an image into a window. Typically, the two key issues in designing graphics programs are dealing with graphics calls such as "draw triangle" and handling user interaction such as a button press.

Most APIs have a user-interface toolkit of some kind that uses *callbacks.* Callbacks refer to the process of using function pointers or virtual functions to pass a reference to a function. For example, to associate an action with a button press, an underlying function is dynamically associated with the button press. In this way, the user-interface toolkit can process the event of the button press, and any action can be associated with it by the programmer.

There are currently two dominant paradigms for APIs. The first is the integrated approach of Java where the graphics and user-interface toolkits are integrated and portable *packages* that are fully standardized and supported as part of the language. The second is represented by Direct3D and OpenGL, where the drawing commands are part of a software library tied to a language such as C++, and the user-interface software is an independent entity that might vary from system to system. In this latter approach, it is problematic to write portable code, although for simple programs it may be possible to use a portable library layer on top of the system specific event-handling.

Whatever your choice of API, the basic graphics calls will be largely the same, and the concepts of this book will apply.

1.4 3D Geometric Models

A key part of graphics programs is using 3D geometric models. These models describe 3D objects using mathematical primitives such as spheres, cubes, cones, and polygons. The most ubiquitous type of model is composed of 3D triangles with shared vertices, which is often called a *triangle mesh.* These meshes are sometimes generated by artists using an interactive modeling program and sometimes by range scanning devices. In either case, these models usually contain many triangles, most of them small, so your programs should be optimized for such datasets.

1.5 Graphics Pipeline

Almost all modern computers now have an efficient 3D *graphics pipeline.* This is a special software/hardware subsystem that efficiently draws 3D primitives in perspective. Usually these systems are optimized for processing 3D triangles with shared vertices. The basic operations in the pipeline map the 3D vertex locations to 2D screen positions, and shade the triangles so that they both look realistic and that they appear in proper back-to-front order.

Although drawing the triangles in valid back-to-front order was once the most important research issue in computer graphics, it is now almost always solved using the *z-buffer* which uses a special memory-buffer to solve the problem in a brute-force manner.

It turns out that the geometric manipulation used in the graphics pipeline can be accomplished almost entirely in a 4D coordinate space composed of three traditional geometric coordinates and a fourth *homogeneous* coordinate that helps us handle perspective viewing. These 4D coordinates are manipulated using 4 by 4 matrices and 4-vectors. The graphics pipeline, therefore, contains much machinery for efficiently processing and composing such matrices and vectors. This 4D coordinate system is one of the most subtle and beautiful constructs used in computer science, and it is certainly the biggest intellectual hurdle to jump when learning computer graphics. A big chunk of the first part of every graphics book deals with these coordinates.

The speed of most modern graphics pipelines is roughly proportional to the number of triangles being drawn. Because interactivity is typically more important to applications than visual quality, it is worthwhile to minimize the number of triangles used to represent a model. In addition, if the model is viewed in the distance, fewer triangles are needed than when the model is viewed from a closer distance. This suggests that it is useful to represent a model with a varying *level-of-detail* (LOD).

1.6 Numerical Issues

Many graphics programs are really just 3D numerical codes. Numerical issues are often crucial in such programs. In the "old days," it was very difficult to handle such issues in a robust and portable manner because machines had different internal representations for numbers, and even worse, handled exceptions in many incompatible fashions. Fortunately, almost all modern computers conform to the *IEEE floating point* standard. This allows the programmer to make many convenient assumptions about how certain numeric conditions will be handled.

Although IEEE floating point has many features that are valuable when coding numeric algorithms, there are only a few that are crucial to know for most situations encountered in graphics. First, and most important, is to understand that there are three "special" values for real numbers in IEEE floating point:

infinity (∞) This is a valid number that is larger than all other valid numbers.

minus infinity ($-\infty$) This is a valid number that is smaller than all other valid numbers.

not a number (NaN) This is an invalid number that arises from an operation with undefined consequences such as zero divided by zero.

The designers of IEEE floating point made some decisions that are extremely convenient for programmers. Many of these relate to the three special values above in handling exceptions such as division by zero. In these cases an exception is logged, but in many cases the programmer can ignore that. Specifically, for any positive real number a, the following rules involving division by infinite values hold:

$$+a/(+\infty) = +0$$
$$-a/(+\infty) = -0$$
$$+a/(-\infty) = -0$$
$$-a/(-\infty) = +0$$

Note that IEEE floating point distinguishes between -0 and $+0$. In most graphics programs this distinction does not matter, but it is worth keeping in mind for more classical numeric algorithms.

Other operations involving infinite values behave the way one would expect. Again for positive a, the behavior is:

$$\infty + \infty = +\infty$$
$$\infty - \infty = \text{NaN}$$
$$\infty \times \infty = \infty$$
$$\infty/\infty = \text{NaN}$$
$$\infty/a = \infty$$

Another way to get the *not a number* value are:

$$\infty/0 = \text{NaN}$$
$$0/0 = \text{NaN}$$

The rules in a Boolean expression involving infinite values are as expected:

1. All finite valid numbers are less than $+\infty$.

2. All finite valid numbers are greater than $-\infty$.

3. $-\infty$ is less than $+\infty$.

The rules involving expressions that have NaN values are simple:

1. Any arithmetic expression that includes NaN results in NaN.
2. Any Boolean expression involving NaN is false.

Perhaps the most useful aspect of IEEE floating point is how divide-by-zero is handled; for any positive real number a, the following rules involving division by zero values hold:

$$+a/0 = +\infty$$
$$-a/0 = -\infty$$

There are many numeric codes that become much simpler if the programmer takes advantage of IEEE floating point. For example, consider the expression:

$$a = \frac{1}{\frac{1}{b} + \frac{1}{c}}.$$

Such expressions arise with resistors and lenses. If divide-by-zero resulted in a program crash (as was true in many systems before IEEE floating point), then two *if* statements would be required to check for small or zero values of b or c. Instead, with IEEE floating point, if b or c are zero, we will get a zero value for a as desired. Another common technique to avoid special checks is to take advantage of the Boolean properties of NaN. Consider the following code segment:

$a = f(x)$
if $(a > 0)$ ***then***
  do something

Here, the function f may return "ugly" values such as ∞ or NaN. Because the *if* statement is false for $a =$ NaN or $a = -\infty$ and true for $a = +\infty$, no special checks are needed. This makes programs smaller, more robust, and more efficient.

1.7 Efficiency

There are no magic rules for making code more efficient. Efficiency is achieved through careful tradeoffs, and these tradeoffs are different for different architectures. However, for the foreseeable future, a good heuristic is that programmers should pay more attention to memory access patterns than to operation counts. This is the opposite of the best heuristic of a decade ago. This switch has occurred because the speed of memory has not kept pace with the speed of processors. Since that trend continues, the importance of limited and coherent memory access for optimization should only increase.

A reasonable approach to making code fast is to proceed in the following order, taking only those steps which are needed:

1. Write the code in the most straightforward way possible. Compute data as needed on the fly without storing it.
2. Compile in optimized mode.
3. Use whatever profiling tools exist to find critical bottlenecks.
4. Examine data structures to look for ways to improve locality. If possible, make data unit sizes match the cache/page size on the target architecture.
5. If profiling reveals bottlenecks in numeric computations, examine the assembly code generated by the compiler for missed efficiencies. Rewrite source code to solve any problems you find.

The most important of these steps is the first one. Most "optimizations" make the code harder to read without speeding things up. In addition, time spent upfront optimizing code is usually better spent correcting bugs or adding features. Also, beware of suggestions from old texts; some classic tricks such as using integers instead of reals no longer yield speed because many modern CPUs can usually perform floating point operations just as fast as they perform integer operations.

1.8 Software Engineering

A key part of any graphics program is to have good classes or routines for geometric entities such as vectors and matrices, as well as graphics entities such as RGB colors and images. These routines should be made as clean and efficient as possible. Most graphics programmers use C++, so some discussion of that language is in order. A critical issue is whether locations and displacements should be seperate classes because they have different operations, e.g., a location multiplied by one-half makes no geometric sense while one-half of a displacement does. This is a personal decision, but I believe strongly in the KISS ("keep it simple, stupid") principle, and in that light the argument for two classes is not compelling enough to justify the added complexity. This implies that some basic classes that should be written:

- *vector2*: A 2D vector class that stores an x and y component. It should store these components in a length-2 array so that an indexing operator can be well supported. You should also include operations for vector addition, vector subtraction, dot product, cross product, scalar multiplication, and scalar division.
- *vector3*: A 3D vector class analogous to vector2.
- *hvector*: A homogeneous vector with four components (see Chapter 6).

- *rgb*: An RGB color that stores three components. You should also include operations for RGB addition, RGB subtraction, RGB multiplication, scalar multiplication, and scalar division.

- *transform*: A four-by-four matrix for transformations. You should include a matrix multiply and member functions to apply to locations, directions, and surface normal vectors. As shown in Chapter 5 these are all different.

- *image*: A 2D array of RGB pixels with an output operation.

In addition, you might or might not want to add classes for intervals, orthonormal bases, and coordinate frames. You might also consider unit-length vectors, although I have found them more pain than they are worth. There are several basic decisions to be made which are outlined in the following sections.

1.8.1 Float versus Double

Modern architecture suggests that keeping memory use down and maintaining coherent memory access are the keys to efficiency. This suggests using single-precision data. However, avoiding numerical problems suggests using double-precision arithmetic. The trade-offs depend on the program, but it is nice to have a default in your class definitions. I suggest using doubles for geometric computation and floats for color computation. Where memory usage is high, as it is for triangle meshes, I suggest storing float data, but converting to double when data is accessed through member functions.

1.8.2 Inlining

Inlining is a key to efficiency for utility classes such as RGB. Almost all RGB and vector functions should be inlined. Be sure to profile your code to make sure that things are actually being inlined. Non-utility code and other large functions should not be inlined unless the profiler shows them to be hogging runtime. Even then be sure making them inline does not slow the code further. Note, that on most systems, the inline function definitions must be in the header files. For member functions, these can be linked to the declarations, for example:

```
class vector3 {
     .
     .
     .
   double lengthSquared { return x()*x()+y()*y()+z()*z(); }
};
```

1.8.3 Member Functions versus Non-Member Operators

For operators such as the addition of two vectors we can make them either a member of a vector class or an operator that exists outside of the class. I suggest that such operators always exist outside of a class. This is because it is the only solution for something like the multiplication operator for a double and a vector (as opposed to vector times double). Since we have to make it a non-member in such cases, we may as well be consistent and always make it a non-member. We should make such operators as compact as possible, for example:

```
inline vector3 operator+(vector3 a, vector3 b) {
    return vector3( a.x() + b.x(), a.y() + b.y(), a.z() + b.z() );
}
```

Note that for non-inlined operators and for some compilers, using a `const` reference for argument passing avoids some data copying:

```
inline vector3 operator+(const vector3& a, const vector3& b) {
    return vector3( a.x() + b.x(), a.y() + b.y(), a.z() + b.z() );
}
```

1.8.4 Include Guards

All classes should have include guards surrounding the class declarations. The names of these guards should follow some simple naming convention. For example:

```
#ifndef VECTOR3H
#define VECTOR3H

class vector3 {
      .
      .
      .

};

#endif
```

This prevents problems when a header file is included more than once which is almost unavoidable in practice. Note that when `VECTOR3H` is already defined, the header file is still opened and one line is read. For large libraries, this file opening can dominate compilation time. In such cases, an ugly, but effective, solution is to add a check when the include is made:

```
#ifndef VECTOR3H
#include <vector3.h>
#endif
```

1.8.5 Using assert() Effectively

You should generously sprinkle asserts throughout your code. An assert is a macro that stops the program if the Boolean statement it contains is false. For example:

```
#include <assert.h>
    .
assert( fabs( v.length() - 1 ) < 0.00001 );
```

makes sure that v is close to unit length. Asserts are excellent to add during debugging as well as during development. If you ever add one, leave it in. You might well add a bug later that triggers it again. Note that in an optimized run, you need do define the preprocessor variable NDEBUG to turn off the asserts. This is typically accomplished with the compiler flag -DNDEBUG.

1.8.6 Experimental Debugging

If you ask around, you may find that as programmers become more experienced, they use traditional debuggers less and less. One reason for this is that using such debuggers is more awkward for complex programs than for simple programs. Another reason is that the most difficult errors are conceptual ones where the wrong thing is being implemented, and it is easy to waste large amounts of time stepping through variable values without detecting such cases.

In graphics programs there is an alternative to traditional debugging that is often very useful. The downside to it is that it is very similar to what computer programmers are taught not to do early in their careers, so you may feel "naughty" if you do it: we create an image, and observe what is wrong with it. Then we develop a hypothesis about what is causing the problem, and test it. For example, in a ray tracing program we might have many somewhat random looking dark pixels. This is the classic "shadow acne" problem that most people run into when they write a ray tracer. Traditional debugging is not helpful here; instead we must realize that the shadow rays are hitting the surface being shaded. We might notice that the color of the dark spots is the ambient color, so the direct lighting is what is missing. Direct lighting can be turned off in shadow, so you might hypothesize that these points are incorrectly being tagged as in shadow when they are not. To test this hypothesis, we could turn off the shadowing check and recompile. This would indicate that these are false shadow tests, and we could continue our detective work. The key reason this method can sometimes be good practice is that we never had to spot a false value or really determine our conceptual error. Instead, we just narrowed in on our conceptual error experimentally. Typically only a few trials are needed to track things down, and this type of debugging is enjoyable.

In the cases where the program crashes, a traditional debugger is useful for pinpointing the site of the crash. You should then start backtracking in the program, using asserts and recompiles, to find where the program went wrong. These asserts should be left in the program for potential future bugs you will add. This again means the traditional step-though process is avoided, because that would not be adding the valuable asserts to your program.

1.9 A Short History of Computer Graphics

The core technology of rendering and homogeneous coordinates was developed in the 1960s and 1970s mainly at MIT, Harvard, and the University of Utah. The modern graphical user interface was foreshadowed to a remarkable extent by Ivan Sutherland at MIT in his 1962 *Sketchpad* system that included direct manipulation of 2D graphics using a lightpen. Around the same time, Larry Roberts at Harvard, who also was the father of the packet-switching network and the large-scale internet, developed homogeneous coordinates to efficiently draw 3D wireframe images viewed in perspective. Sutherland then moved to Harvard and made an interactive 3D display in a head-mounted display that he developed with the help of Chuck Seitz of MIT. This was the first sophisticated example of *virtual reality*. In 1968, Sutherland moved to the University of Utah to work with Dave Evans. Over the next seven years, researchers at Utah developed the frame buffer, the z-buffer, texture mapping, 3D shading, and then applied that technology in an interactive flight simulator in the spinoff company Evans&Sutherland. Many researchers from Utah moved on to NYIT to develop the first major computer animation project, and later to industry to produce many of the modern products that are now ubiquitous. The first 3D computer graphics to appear in commercial film was the wireframe head done by Frank Crow for the 1973 film *Westworld*. The first full-length computer-generated film was the 1994 *Toy Story*.

While these rendering advances were being made, progress on modeling was going on mainly in the automotive industry. The computer modeling of cars required the representation of smooth free-form surfaces. A number of researchers, notably Coons and Bézier developed most of the modern smooth-surface technology during the 1960s and 1970s.

Notes

The discussion of software engineering is influenced by the *Effective C++* series by Brad Meyer, the *Extreme Programming* movement, and by discussions with Kenneth Chiu, Steven Parker and Brian Smits. The use of extra include guards in source files for large programs, as well as other strategies for dealing with big C++ projects can be found in *Large-Scale C++ Software Design* (Lakos, Addison-Wesley, 1996). There are many places to gain more information about computer graphics, and many good books on the subject. Readers interested in more details about IEEE floating point can find detailed information in *Numerical Computing with IEEE Floating Point Arithmetic* (Overton, SIAM Press, 2001). There are a number of annual conferences related to computer graphics, and these can be found by doing web searches by their title:

- ACM SIGGRAPH Conference
- Graphics Interface Conference
- Game Developers' Conference (GDC)
- EUROGRAPHICS Conference
- Pacific Graphics Conference
- EUROGRAPHICS Workshop on Rendering
- Solid Modeling Conference
- IEEE Visualization Conference

Miscellaneous Math

Much of graphics is just translating math directly into code. The cleaner the math, the cleaner the resulting code. Thus, much of this book concentrates on using just the right math for the job. This chapter reviews various tools from high school and college mathematics, and is designed to be used more as a reference than as a tutorial. It may appear to be a hodge-podge of topics, and indeed it is; each topic is chosen because it is a bit unusual in "standard" math curricula, because it is of central importance in graphics, or because it is not typically treated from a geometric standpoint. In addition to establishing a review with the notation used in the book, the chapter also emphasizes a few points that are sometimes skipped in the standard undergraduate curricula, such as barycentric coordinates on triangles. This chapter is not intended to be a rigorous treatment of the material; instead intuition and geometric interpretation are emphasized. A discussion of linear algebra is deferred until Chapter 4 just before transformation matrices are discussed. Readers are encouraged to skim this chapter to familiarize themselves with the topics covered, and to refer back to it as needed. The exercises at the end of the chapter may be useful in determining which topics need a refresher.

2.1 Sets and Mappings

Mappings, also called *functions*, are basic to mathematics and programming. Like a function in a program, a mapping in math takes an argument of one *type* and maps it (returns) to an object of a particular type. In a program we say "type;" in math we would identify the set. When we have an object that is a member of a set, we use the $\in$ symbol. For example:

$$a \in \mathbf{S},$$

can be read "a is a member of set $\mathbf{S}$." Given any two sets $\mathbf{A}$ and $\mathbf{B}$, we can create a third set by taking the *Cartesian product* of the two sets, denoted $\mathbf{A} \times \mathbf{B}$. This set $\mathbf{A} \times \mathbf{B}$ is composed of all possible ordered pairs (a, b) where $a \in \mathbf{A}$ and $b \in \mathbf{B}$. As a shorthand, we use the notation $\mathbf{A}^2$ to denote $\mathbf{A} \times \mathbf{A}$. We can extend the Cartesian product to create a set of all possible ordered triples from three sets, and so on for arbitrarily long ordered tuples from arbitrarily many sets.

Common sets of interest include:

- $\mathbb{R}$: the real numbers.
- $\mathbb{R}^+$: the non-negative real numbers (includes zero).
- $\mathbb{R}^2$: the ordered pairs in the real plane, i.e., the points in the 2D plane.
- $\mathbb{R}^n$: the points in n-dimensional Cartesian space.
- $\mathbb{Z}$: the integers.
- S^2: the set of 3D points (points in $\mathbb{R}^3$) on the unit sphere.

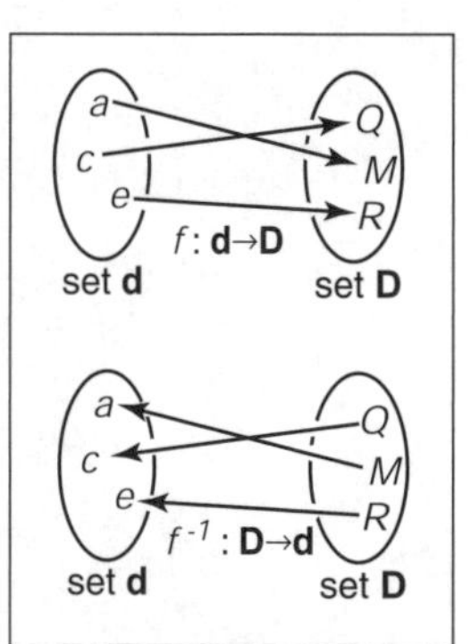

Figure 2.1. A bijection f and the inverse function f^{-1}. Note that f^{-1} is also a bijection.

Note that although S^2 is composed of points embedded in three-dimensional space, they are on a surface that can be parameterized with two variables, so it can be thought of as a 2D set. Notation for mappings uses the arrow and a colon, for example:

$$f : \mathbb{R} \mapsto \mathbb{Z},$$

which you can read: "There is a function called f that takes a real number as input and maps it to an integer." Here, the set that comes before the arrow is called the *domain* of the function, and the set on the righthand side is called the *target*. The subset of the target that contains all image points under the function (i.e., points in $\mathbb{Z}$ so that there exists a point in $\mathbb{R}$) is called the *range* of the function. Computer programmers might be more comfortable with the equivalent language: "There is a function called f which has one real argument and returns an integer". In other words, the set notation above is equivalent to the common programming notation:

$$\text{integer } f(\text{real}) \quad \leftarrow \text{equivalent} \rightarrow \quad f : \mathbb{R} \mapsto \mathbb{Z}.$$

So the colon-arrow notation can be thought of as a programming syntax. It's that simple.

2.1.1 Inverse Mappings

If we have a function $f : \mathbf{A} \mapsto \mathbf{B}$, there may exist an *inverse function* which is defined by the rule $f^{-1}(b) = a$ where $b = f(a)$. This definition only works if each $b \in B$ is an image point under f and if there is only one point a such that $f(a) = b$. Such mappings or functions are called *bijections*.. A bijection maps every $a \in \mathbf{A}$ to a unique $b \in \mathbf{B}$, and for every $b \in \mathbf{B}$, there is exactly one $a \in \mathbf{A}$ such that $f(a) = b$ (Figure 2.1). A bijection between a group of riders and horses indicates that everybody rides a single horse, and every horse is ridden. The two functions would be *rider(horse)* and *horse(rider)*. These are inverse functions of each other. Functions that are not bijections have no inverse (Figure 2.2).

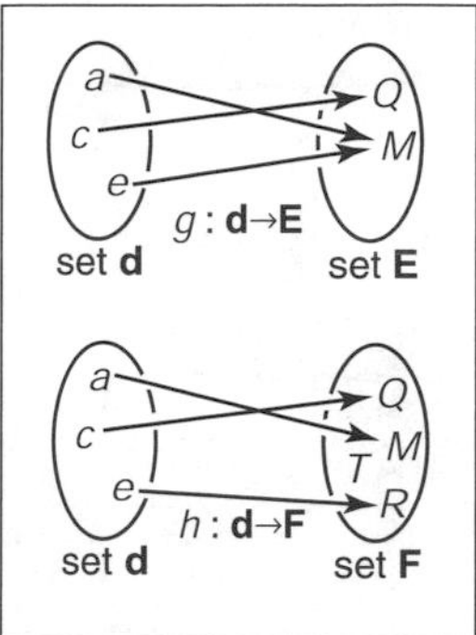

Figure 2.2. The function g does not have an inverse because two elements of $\mathbf{d}$ map to the same element of $\mathbf{E}$. The function h has no inverse because element T of $\mathbf{F}$ has no element of $\mathbf{d}$ mapped to it.

An example of a bijection is $f : \mathbb{R} \mapsto \mathbb{R}$,with $f(x) = x^3$. The inverse function is $f^{-1}(x) = \sqrt[3]{x}$. This example shows that the standard notation can be somewhat awkward because x is used as a dummy variable in both f and f^{-1}. It is sometimes more intuitive to use different dummy variables, with $y = f(x)$ and $x = f^{-1}(y)$. This yields the more intuitive $y = x^3$ and $x = \sqrt[3]{y}$. A function that does not have an inverse is $sqr : \mathbb{R} \mapsto \mathbb{R}$, where $sqr(x) = x^2$. This is for two reasons: first $x^2 = (-x)^2$, and second no members of the domain map to the negative portions of the target. Note that we can define an inverse if we restrict the domain and range to $\mathbb{R}^+$. Then $\sqrt{x}$ is a valid inverse.

2.1.2 Intervals

Often we would like to specify that a function deals with real numbers that are restricted in value. One such constraint is to specify an *interval*. An example of an interval is the real numbers between zero and one, not including zero or one. We denote this $(0, 1)$. Because it does not include its endpoints, this is referred to as an *open interval*. The corresponding *closed interval* is denoted with square brackets: $[0, 1]$. This notation can be mixed, i.e., $[0, 1)$ includes zero but not one. In general when writing an inteval $[a, b]$, we assume that $a \leq b$. The three common ways to represent an interval are shown in Figure 2.3. The Cartesian products of intervals are used often. For example, to indicate that a point $\mathbf{x}$ is in the unit cube in 3D, we say $\mathbf{x} \in [0, 1]^3$.

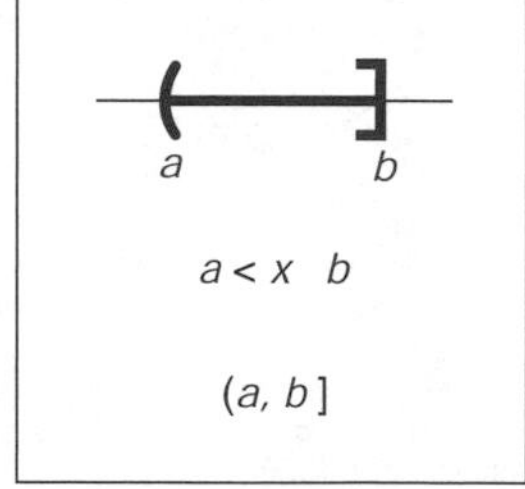

Figure 2.3. Three equivalent ways to denote the interval from a to b that includes b but not a.

Intervals are particularly useful in conjunction with set operations: *intersection*, *union*, and *difference*. For example, the intersection of two intervals is the set of points they have in common. The symbol $\cap$ is used for intersection. For example, $[3, 5) \cap [4, 6] = [4, 5)$. For unions, the symbol $\cup$ is used to denote points in either interval. For example, $[3, 5) \cup [4, 6] = [3, 6]$. Unlike for the first two operators, the difference operator produces different results depending on argument order. The minus sign is used for the differ-

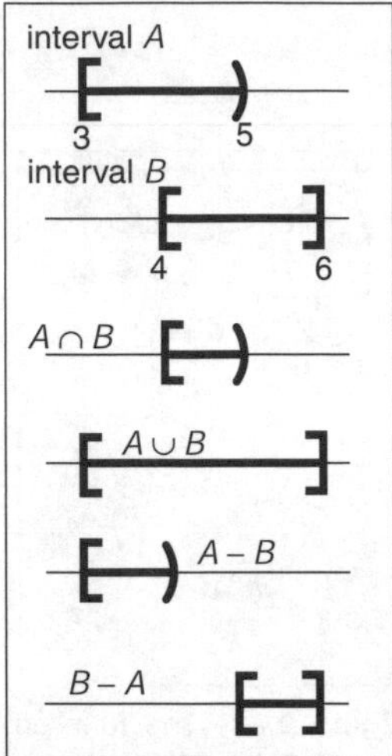

Figure 2.4. Interval operations on [3,5) and [4,6].

ence operator, which returns the points in the left interval that are not also in the right. For example, $[3, 5) - [4, 6] = [3, 4)$ and $[4, 6] - [3, 5) = [5, 6]$. These operations are particularly easy to visualize using interval diagrams (Figure 2.4).

2.1.3 Logarithms

Although not as prevalent as they were before calculators, *logarithms* are often useful in problems where equations with exponential terms arise. By definition, every logarithm has a *base a*. The "log base a" of x is written $\log_a x$, and is defined as "the exponent to which a must be raised to get x," i.e.,

$$y = \log_a x \quad \Leftrightarrow \quad a^y = x.$$

Note that the logarithm base a and the function that raises a to a power are inverses of each other. This basic definition has several consequences:

$$\begin{aligned} a^{\log_a(x)} &= x. \\ \log_a(a^x) &= x. \\ \log_a(xy) &= \log_a x + \log_a y. \\ \log_a(x/y) &= \log_a x - \log_a y. \\ \log_a x &= \log_a b \, \log_b x. \end{aligned}$$

When we apply calculus to logarithms, the special number $e = 2.718\ldots$ turns out to be helpful. The logarithm with base e is called the *natural logarithm*. The natural logarithm arises so often we adopt the common shorthand ln to denote it:

$$\ln x \equiv \log_e x.$$

Note that the "$\equiv$" symbol can be read "is equivalent by definition." Like π, the special number e arises in a remarkable number of contexts. Many fields use a particular base in addition to e for manipulations and omit the base in their notation, i.e., $\log x$. For example, astronomers often use base 10 and theoretical computer scientists often use base 2. Because computer graphics borrows technology from many fields we will avoid this shorthand.

The derivatives of logarithms and exponents illuminate why the natural logarithm is "natural":

$$\begin{aligned} \frac{d}{dx} \log_a x &= \frac{1}{x \ln a}. \\ \frac{d}{dx} a^x &= a^x \ln a. \end{aligned}$$

The constant multipliers above are unity only for $a = e$.

2.2 Solving Quadratic Equations

A *quadratic equation* has the form:

$$Ax^2 + Bx + C = 0,$$

where x is a real unknown, and A, B, and C are known constants. If you think of a 2D xy plot with $y = Ax^2 + Bx + C$, the solution is just whatever x values are "zero crossings" in y. Because $y = Ax^2 + Bx + C$ is a parabola, there will be zero, one, or two real solutions depending on whether the the parabola misses, grazes, or hits the x axis (Figure 2.5).

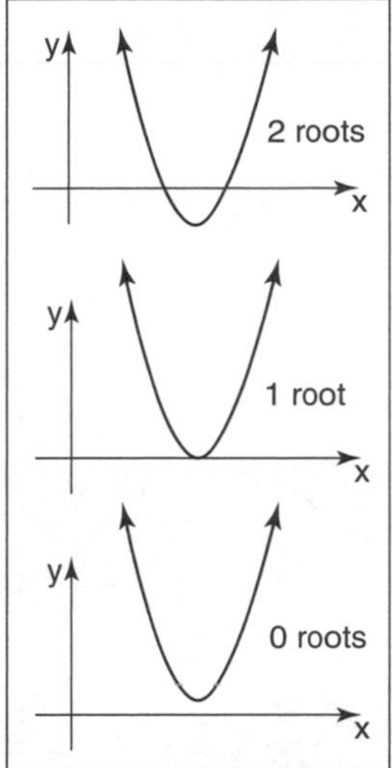

Figure 2.5. The geometric interpretation of the roots of a quadratic equation is the intersection points of a parabola with the *x*-axis.

To solve the quadratic equation analytically, we first divide by A:

$$x^2 + \frac{B}{A}x + \frac{C}{A} = 0.$$

Then we "complete the square" to group terms:

$$\left(x + \frac{B}{2A}\right)^2 - \frac{B^2}{4A^2} + \frac{C}{A} = 0.$$

Moving the constant portion to the righthand side and taking the square root gives:

$$x + \frac{B}{2A} = \pm\sqrt{\frac{B^2}{4A^2} - \frac{C}{A}}.$$

Subtracting $B/(2A)$ from both sides and grouping terms with the denominator $2A$ gives the familiar form:

$$x = \frac{-B \pm \sqrt{B^2 - 4AC}}{2A}. \tag{2.1}$$

Here the "$\pm$" symbol means there are two solutions, one with a plus sign and one with a minus sign. Thus 3 ± 1 equals "two or four". Note that the term which determines the number of real solutions is:

$$D \equiv B^2 - 4AC,$$

which is called the *discriminant* of the quadratic equation. If $D > 0$, there are two real solutions (also called *roots*). If $D = 0$, there is one real solution (a "double" root). If $D < 0$, there are no real solutions.

For example, the roots of $2x^2 + 6x + 4 = 0$ are $x = -1$ and $x = -2$, and the equation $x^2 + x + 1$ has no real solutions. The discriminants of these equations are $D = 4$ and $D = -3$ respectively, so we expect the number of solutions given. In programs, it is usually a good idea to evaluate D first, and return "no roots" without taking the square root if D is negative.

2.3 Trigonometry

In graphics we use basic trigonometry in many contexts. Usually, it is nothing too fancy, and it often helps to remember the basic definitions.

2.3.1 Angles

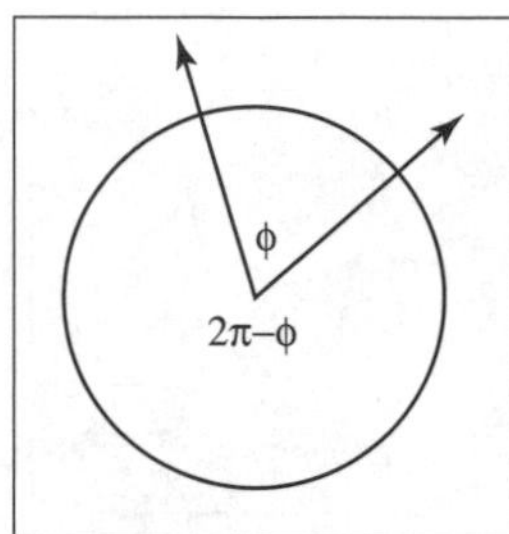

Figure 2.6. Two half-lines cut the unit circle into two arcs. The length of either arc is a valid angle "between" the two half-lines. Either we can use the convention that the smaller length is the angle, or that the two half-lines are specified in a certain order and the arc that determines angle θ is the one swept out counterclockwise from the first to second half-line.

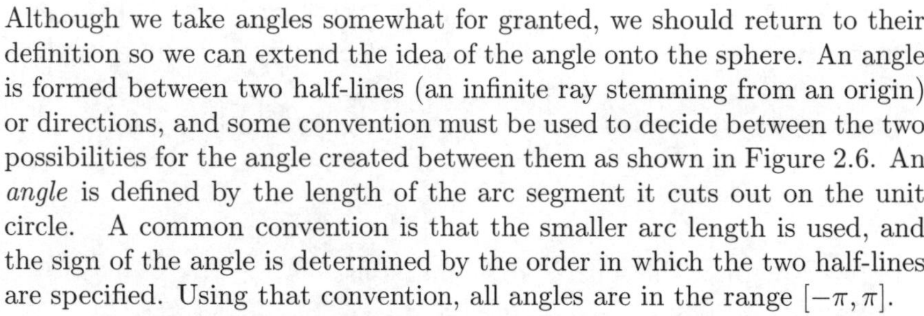

Although we take angles somewhat for granted, we should return to their definition so we can extend the idea of the angle onto the sphere. An angle is formed between two half-lines (an infinite ray stemming from an origin) or directions, and some convention must be used to decide between the two possibilities for the angle created between them as shown in Figure 2.6. An *angle* is defined by the length of the arc segment it cuts out on the unit circle. A common convention is that the smaller arc length is used, and the sign of the angle is determined by the order in which the two half-lines are specified. Using that convention, all angles are in the range $[-\pi, \pi]$.

Each of these angles is *the length of the arc of the unit circle that is "cut" by the two directions.* Because the perimeter of the unit circle is 2π, the two possible angles sum to 2π. The unit of these arc lengths is *radians.* Another common unit is degrees, where the perimeter of the circle is 360 degrees. Thus, an angle that is π radians is 180 degrees, usually denoted 180°. The conversion between degrees and radians is:

$$\text{degrees} = \frac{180}{\pi}\text{radians}$$

$$\text{radians} = \frac{\pi}{180}\text{degrees}$$

2.3.2 Trigonometric Functions

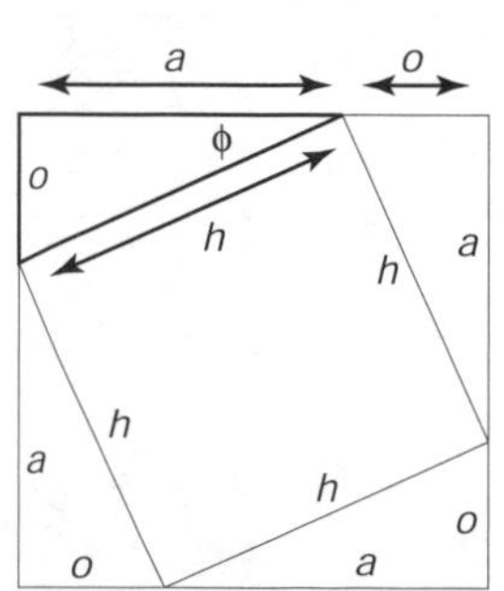

Figure 2.7. A geometric demonstration of the Pythagorean theorem.

Given a right triangle with sides of length a, o, and h, where h is the length of the longest side (which is always opposite the right angle), or *hypotenuse*, an important relation is described by the *Pythagorean theorem*:

$$a^2 + o^2 = h^2.$$

You can see that this is true from Figure 2.7, where the big square has area $(a + o)^2$, the four triangles have the combined area $2ao$, and the center square has area h^2.

Because the triangles and inner square subdivide the larger square evenly, we have $2ao + h^2 = (a + o)^2$, which is easily manipulated to the form above. We define *sine* and *cosine* of ϕ, as well as the other ratio-based trigonometric expressions:

$$\begin{aligned}
\sin\phi &\equiv o/h,\\
\csc\phi &\equiv h/o,\\
\cos\phi &\equiv a/h,\\
\sec\phi &\equiv h/a,\\
\tan\phi &\equiv o/a,\\
\cot\phi &\equiv a/o.
\end{aligned}$$

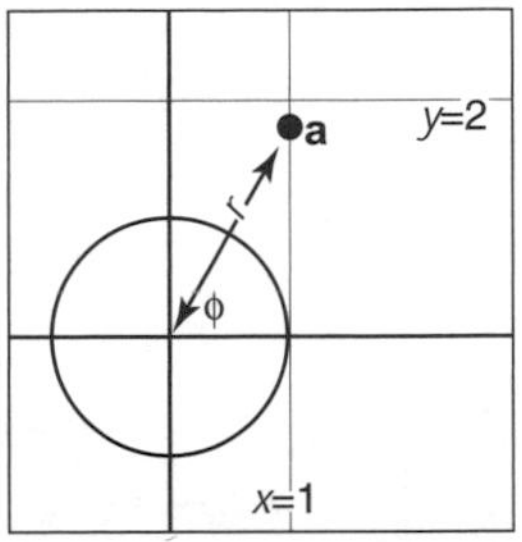

These defintions allow us to set up *polar coordinates*, where a point is coded as a distance from the origin and a signed angle relative to the positive x-axis (Figure 2.8). Note the convention that angles are in the range $\phi \in (-\pi, \pi]$, and that the positive angles are counter-clockwise from the positive x-axis. This convention that counter-clockwise maps to positive numbers is arbitrary, but it is used in many contexts in graphics so it is worth committing to memory.

Figure 2.8. Polar coordinates for the point $(x_a, y_a) = (1, \sqrt{3})$ is $(r_a, \phi_a) = (2, \pi/3)$.

Trigonometric functions are periodic amd can take any angle as an argument. For example $\sin(A) = \sin(A + 2\pi)$. This means the functions are not invertible when considered with the domain $\mathbb{R}$. This problem is avoided by restricting the range of standard inverse functions, and this is done in a standard way in almost all modern math libraries. The domains and ranges are:

$$\begin{aligned}
\text{asin} &: [-1, 1] \mapsto [-\pi/2, \pi/2],\\
\text{acos} &: [-1, 1] \mapsto [0, \pi],\\
\text{atan} &: \mathbb{R} \mapsto [-\pi/2, \pi/2],\\
\text{atan2} &: \mathbb{R}^2 \mapsto [-\pi, \pi].
\end{aligned} \tag{2.2}$$

The last function, $\text{atan2}(s, c)$ is often very useful. It takes an s value proportional to $\sin A$ and a c value that scales $\cos A$ by the same factor, and returns A. The factor must be positive. One way to think of this is that it returns the angle of a 2D Cartesian point (s, c) in polar coordinates (Figure 2.9).

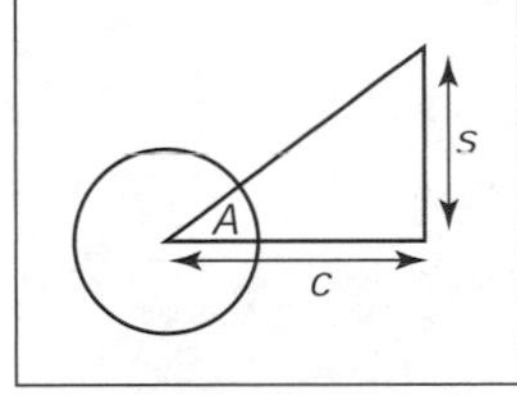

Figure 2.9. The function atan2(s,c) returns the angle A and is often very useful in graphics.

2.3.3 Useful Identities

This section lists without derivation a variety of useful trigonometric identities.

Shifting identities:

$$\begin{aligned}
\sin(-A) &= -\sin A\\
\cos(-A) &= \cos A\\
\tan(-A) &= -\tan A\\
\sin(\pi/2 - A) &= \cos A\\
\cos(\pi/2 - A) &= \sin A\\
\tan(\pi/2 - A) &= \cot A
\end{aligned}$$

Pythagorean identities:

$$\sin^2 A + \cos^2 A = 1$$
$$\sec^2 A - \tan^2 A = 1$$
$$\csc^2 A - \cot^2 A = 1$$

Addition and subtraction identities:

$$\begin{aligned}
\sin(A+B) &= \sin A\cos B + \sin B\cos A\\
\sin(A-B) &= \sin A\cos B - \sin B\cos A\\
\sin(2A) &= 2\sin A\cos A\\
\cos(A+B) &= \cos A\cos B - \sin A\sin B\\
\cos(A-B) &= \cos A\cos B + \sin A\sin B\\
\cos(2A) &= \cos^2 A - \sin^2 A\\
\tan(A+B) &= \frac{\tan A + \tan B}{1 - \tan A\tan B}\\
\tan(A-B) &= \frac{\tan A - \tan B}{1 + \tan A\tan B}\\
\tan(2A) &= \frac{2\tan A}{1 - \tan^2 A}
\end{aligned}$$

Half-angle identities:

$$\sin^2(A/2) = (1 - \cos A)/2$$
$$\cos^2(A/2) = (1 + \cos A)/2$$

Product identities:

$$\begin{aligned}
\sin A\sin B &= -(\cos(A+B) - \cos(A-B))/2\\
\sin A\cos B &= (\sin(A+B) + \sin(A-B))/2\\
\cos A\cos B &= (\cos(A+B) + \cos(A-B))/2
\end{aligned}$$

The following identities are for arbitrary triangles with sidelengths a, b, and c, each with an angle opposite it given by A, B, C respectively (Figure 2.10).

$$\frac{\sin A}{a} = \frac{\sin B}{b} = \frac{\sin C}{c} \qquad \text{(Law of sines)}$$

$$c^2 = a^2 + b^2 - 2ab\cos C \qquad \text{(Law of cosines)}$$

$$\frac{a+b}{a-b} = \frac{\tan\left(\frac{A+B}{2}\right)}{\tan\left(\frac{A-B}{2}\right)} \qquad \text{(Law of tangents)}$$

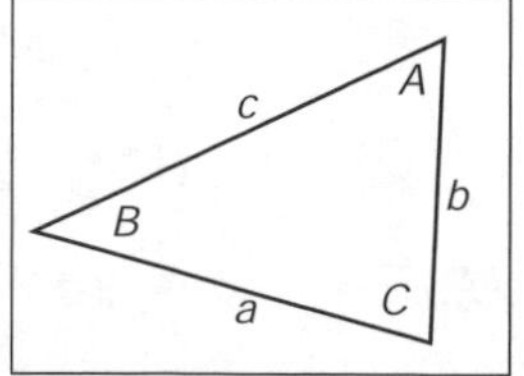

Figure 2.10. Geometry for triangle laws.

The area of a triangle can also be computed in terms of these side lengths:

$$\text{triangle area} = \frac{1}{2}\sqrt{(a+b+c)(-a+b+c)(a-b+c)(a+b-c)}.$$

2.4 Vectors

A *vector* describes a length and a direction. It can be usefully represented by an arrow. Two vectors are equal if they have the same length and direction even if we think of them as being located in different places (Figure 2.11). As much as possible, you should think of a vector as an arrow and not as coordinates or numbers. At some point we will have to represent vectors as numbers in our programs, but even in code they should be manipulated as objects and only the low-level vector operators should know about their numeric representation. Vectors will be represented as bold characters, e.g., **a**. A vector's length is denoted $\|\mathbf{a}\|$. A *unit vector* is any vector whose length is one. The *zero vector* is the vector of zero length. The direction of the zero vector is undefined.

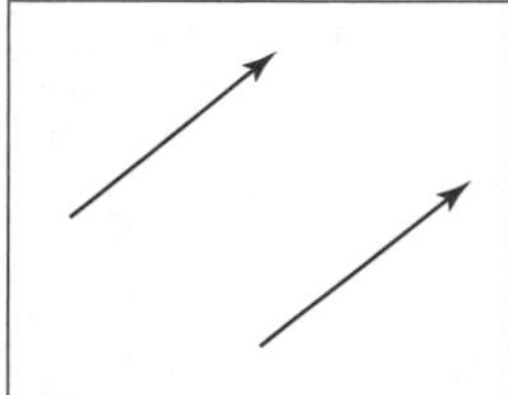

Figure 2.11. These two vectors are the same because they have the same length and direction.

Vectors can be used to represent many different things. For example, they can be used to store an *offset*, also called a *displacement*. If we know "the treasure is buried two paces east and three paces north of the secret meeting place," then we know the offset, but we don't know where to start. Vectors can also be used to store a *location*, another word for *position* or *point*. Locations can be represented as a displacement from another location. Usually there is some understood *origin* location from which all other locations are stored as offsets. Note that locations are not vectors. As we shall discuss, you can add two vectors. However, it usually does not make sense to add two locations. Adding two offsets does make sense, so that is one reason why offsets are vectors. But this emphasizes that a location is not a offset; it is an offset from a specific origin location. The offset by itself is not the location.

2.4.1 Vector Operations

Vectors have most of the usual arithmetic operations that we associate with real numbers. Two vectors are equal if and only if they have the same length and direction. Two vectors are added according to the *parallelogram rule*. This rule states that the sum of two vectors is found by placing the tail of either vector against the head of the other (Figure 2.12). The sum vector is the vector that "completes the triangle" started by the two vectors. The parallelogram is formed by taking the sum in either order. This emphasizes that vector addition is commutative:

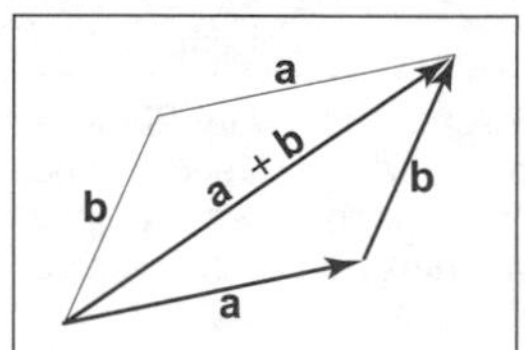

Figure 2.12. Two vectors are added by arranging them head to tail. This can be done in either order.

$$\mathbf{a} + \mathbf{b} = \mathbf{b} + \mathbf{a}$$

Note that the parallelogram rule just formalizes our intuition about displacements. Think of walking along one vector, tail to head, and then walking along the other. The net displacement is just the parallelogram diagonal. You can also create a *unary minus* for a vector: $-\mathbf{a}$ (Figure 2.13).

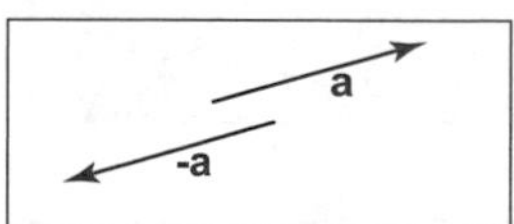

Figure 2.13. The vector **-a** has the same length but opposite direction of the vector **a**.

This is just a vector with the same length but opposite direction. This allows us to also define subtraction:

$$\mathbf{b} - \mathbf{a} \equiv -\mathbf{a} + \mathbf{b}$$

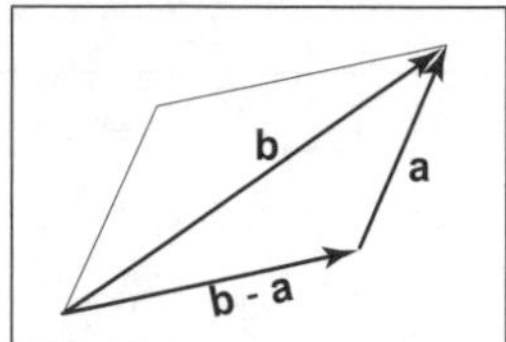

Figure 2.14. Vector subtraction is just vector addition with a reversal of the second argument.

You can visualize vector subtraction with a parallelogram (Figure 2.14). We can write:

$$\mathbf{a} + (\mathbf{b} - \mathbf{a}) = \mathbf{b}$$

Vectors can also be multiplied. In fact, there are many ways we can take products involving vectors. First, we can *scale* the vector by multiplying it by a real number k. This just multiplies the vector's length without changing its direction. For example, $3.5\mathbf{a}$ is a vector in the same direction as $\mathbf{a}$ but it is 3.5 times as long as $\mathbf{a}$. There are several ways to take the product of two vectors. We later discuss two of them, the dot and cross products. We will also discuss determinants as the products of vectors later in this chapter.

2.4.2 Cartesian Coordinates of a Vector

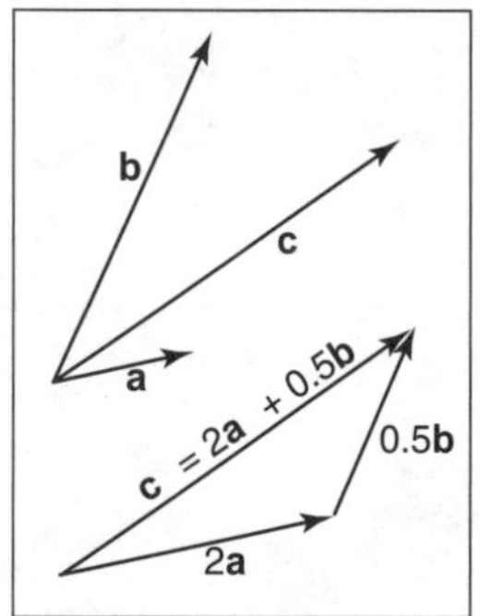

Figure 2.15. Any 2D vector ***c*** can be represented by a weighted sum of any two nonparallel 2D vectors **a** and **b**.

A 2D vector can be written as a combination of any two non-zero vectors which are not parallel. This property of the two vectors is called *linear independence.* Two such vectors which are linearly independent form a 2D *basis*, and the vectors are thus referred to as *basis vectors*. For example, a vector $\mathbf{c}$ may be expressed as a combination of two basis vectors $\mathbf{a}$ and $\mathbf{b}$ (Figure 2.15):

$$\mathbf{c} = a_c\mathbf{a} + b_c\mathbf{b}. \tag{2.3}$$

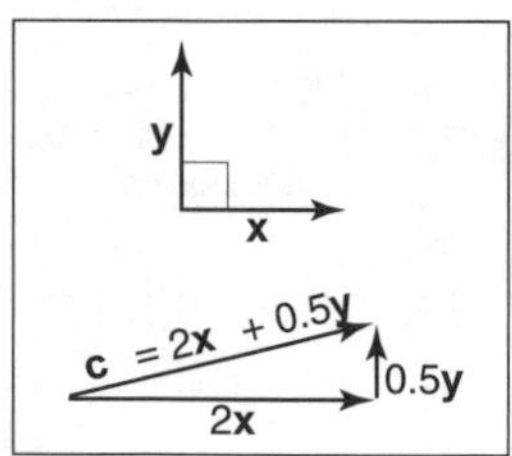

Figure 2.16. A 2D Cartesian basis for vectors.

Note that the weights a_c and b_c are unique. This is especially useful if the two vectors are *orthogonal*, i.e., they are at right angles to each other. It is even more useful if they are also unit vectors in which case they are *orthonormal*. If we assume two such "special" vectors $\mathbf{x}$ and $\mathbf{y}$ are known to us, then we can use them to represent all other vectors in a *Cartesian* coordinate system, where each vector is represented as two real numbers. For example, a vector $\mathbf{a}$ might be represented as:

$$\mathbf{a} = x_a\mathbf{x} + y_a\mathbf{y},$$

where x_a and y_a are the real Cartesian coordinates of the 2D vector $\mathbf{a}$ (Figure 2.16). Note that this is not really any different conceptually from Equation 2.3, where the basis vectors were not orthonormal. But there is an advantage to a Cartesian coordinate system; by the Pythagorean theorem, the length of $\mathbf{a}$ is:

$$\|\mathbf{a}\| = \sqrt{x_a^2 + y_a^2}.$$

By convention we write the coordinates of **a** either as an ordered pair (x_a, y_a) or a column matrix:

$$\mathbf{a} = \begin{bmatrix} x_a \\ y_a \end{bmatrix}.$$

Which we use will depend on typographic convenience. We will also occasionally write the vector as a row matrix, which we will indicate as $\mathbf{a}^T$:

$$\mathbf{a}^T = \begin{bmatrix} x_a & y_a \end{bmatrix}.$$

We can also represent 3D, 4D, etc., vectors in Cartesian coordinates. For the 3D case we use a basis vector **z** which is orthogonal to both **x** and **y**.

2.4.3 Dot Product

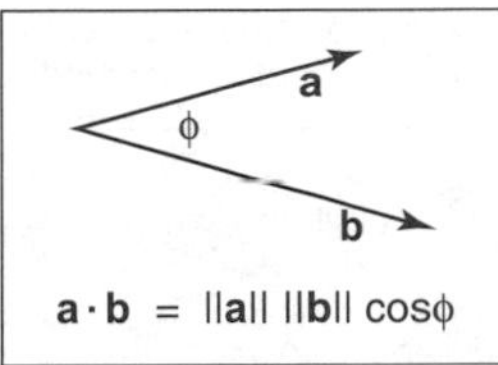

Figure 2.17. The dot product is related to length and angle and is one of the most important formulas in graphics.

The simplest way to multiply two vectors is the *dot* product. The dot product of **a** and **b** is denoted $\mathbf{a} \cdot \mathbf{b}$ and is often called the *scalar product* because it returns a scalar. The dot product returns a value related to its arguments' length and the angle ϕ between them (Figure 2.17):

$$\mathbf{a} \cdot \mathbf{b} = \|\mathbf{a}\| \; \|\mathbf{b}\| \; \cos\phi, \tag{2.4}$$

The most common use of the dot product in graphics programs is to compute the cosine of the angle between two vectors.

The dot product can also be used to find the *projection* of one vector onto another. This is the length $\mathbf{a}{\rightarrow}\mathbf{b}$ of a vector **a** that is projected at right angles onto a vector **b** (Figure 2.18):

$$\mathbf{a}{\rightarrow}\mathbf{b} = \|\mathbf{a}\| \; \cos\phi = \frac{\mathbf{a} \cdot \mathbf{b}}{\|\mathbf{b}\|}. \tag{2.5}$$

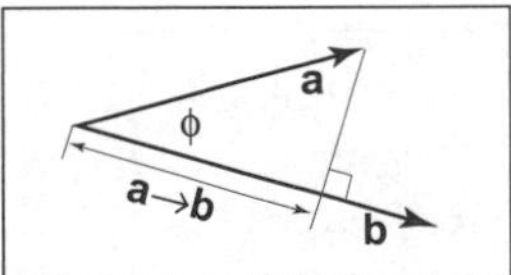

Figure 2.18. The projection of **a** onto **b** is a length found by Equation 2.5.

The dot product obeys the familiar associative and distributive properties we have in real arithmetic:

$$\begin{aligned} \mathbf{a} \cdot \mathbf{b} &= \mathbf{b} \cdot \mathbf{a}, \\ \mathbf{a} \cdot (\mathbf{b} + \mathbf{c}) &= \mathbf{a} \cdot \mathbf{b} + \mathbf{a} \cdot \mathbf{c} \\ (k\mathbf{a}) \cdot \mathbf{b} &= \mathbf{a} \cdot (k\mathbf{b}) = k\mathbf{a} \cdot \mathbf{b}. \end{aligned} \tag{2.6}$$

If 2D vectors **a** and **b** are expressed in Cartesian coordinates, we can take advantage of $\mathbf{x} \cdot \mathbf{x} = \mathbf{y} \cdot \mathbf{y} = 1$ and $\mathbf{x} \cdot \mathbf{y} = 0$ to derive that their dot product is:

$$\begin{aligned} \mathbf{a} \cdot \mathbf{b} &= (x_a \mathbf{x} + y_a \mathbf{y}) \cdot (x_b \mathbf{x} + y_b \mathbf{y}) \\ &= x_a x_b (\mathbf{x} \cdot \mathbf{x}) + x_a y_b (\mathbf{x} \cdot \mathbf{y}) + x_b y_a (\mathbf{y} \cdot \mathbf{x}) + y_a y_b (\mathbf{y} \cdot \mathbf{y}) \\ &= x_a x_b + y_a y_b. \end{aligned}$$

Similarly in 3D we can find:

$$\mathbf{a} \cdot \mathbf{b} = x_a x_b + y_a y_b + z_a z_b.$$

2.4.4 Cross Product

The cross product $\mathbf{a} \times \mathbf{b}$ is usually used only for three-dimensional vectors; generalized cross products are discussed in references given in the chapter notes. The cross product returns a 3D vector that is perpendicular to the two arguments of the cross product. The length of the resulting vector is related to $\sin\theta$:

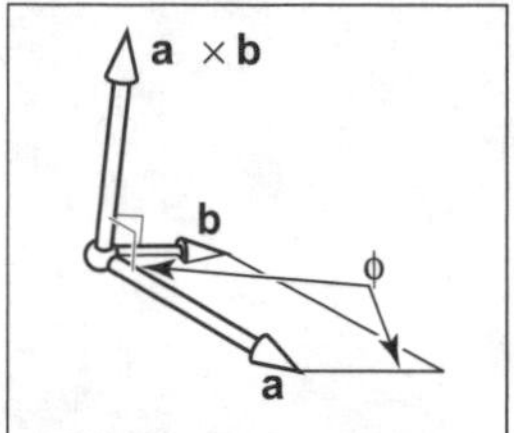
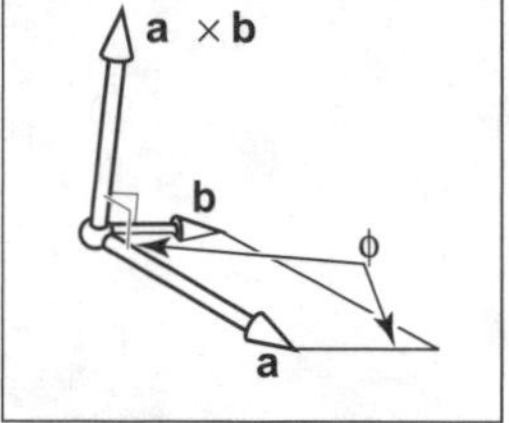

Figure 2.19. The cross product $\mathbf{a} \times \mathbf{b}$ is a 3D vector perpendicular to both 3D vectors **a** and **b**, and its length is equal to the area of the parallelogram shown.

$$\|\mathbf{a} \times \mathbf{b}\| = \|\mathbf{a}\| \, \|\mathbf{b}\| \sin\theta.$$

The magnitude $\|\mathbf{a} \times \mathbf{b}\|$ is equal to the area of the parallelogram formed by vectors **a** and **b**. In addition, $\mathbf{a} \times \mathbf{b}$ is perpendicular to both **a** and **b** (Figure 2.19). Note that there are only two possible directions for such a vector. By definition the vectors in the direction of the x-, y- and z-axes are given by:

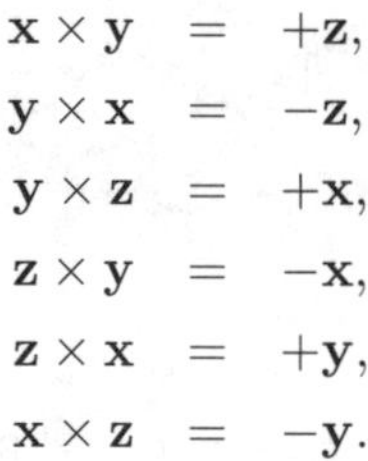

$$\begin{aligned} \mathbf{x} &= (1,0,0), \\ \mathbf{y} &= (0,1,0), \\ \mathbf{z} &= (0,0,1), \end{aligned}$$

and we set as a convention that $\mathbf{x} \times \mathbf{y}$ must be in the plus or minus **z** direction. The choice is somewhat arbitrary, but it is standard to assume that:

$$\mathbf{z} = \mathbf{x} \times \mathbf{y}.$$

All possible permutations of the three Cartesian unit vectors are:

$$\begin{aligned} \mathbf{x} \times \mathbf{y} &= +\mathbf{z}, \\ \mathbf{y} \times \mathbf{x} &= -\mathbf{z}, \\ \mathbf{y} \times \mathbf{z} &= +\mathbf{x}, \\ \mathbf{z} \times \mathbf{y} &= -\mathbf{x}, \\ \mathbf{z} \times \mathbf{x} &= +\mathbf{y}, \\ \mathbf{x} \times \mathbf{z} &= -\mathbf{y}. \end{aligned}$$

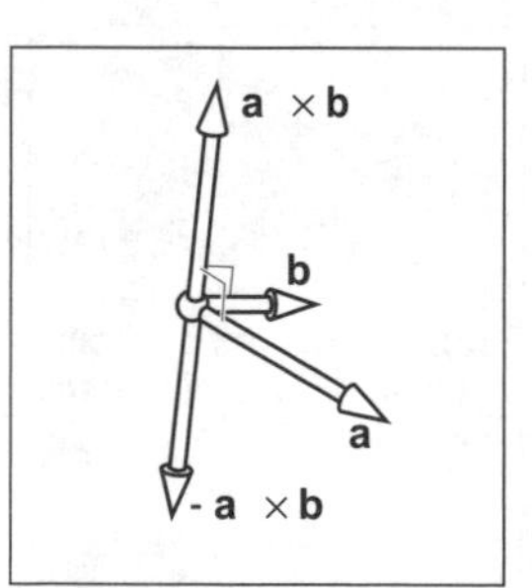

Figure 2.20. The "right hand rule" for cross products. Imagine placing the base of your right palm where **a** and **b** join at their tails, and pushing the arrow of **a** toward **b**. Your extended right thumb should point toward $\mathbf{a} \times \mathbf{b}$.

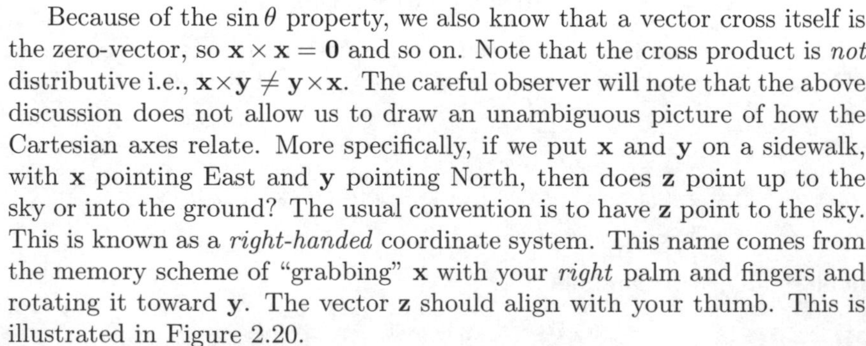

Because of the $\sin\theta$ property, we also know that a vector cross itself is the zero-vector, so $\mathbf{x} \times \mathbf{x} = \mathbf{0}$ and so on. Note that the cross product is *not* distributive i.e., $\mathbf{x}\times\mathbf{y} \neq \mathbf{y}\times\mathbf{x}$. The careful observer will note that the above discussion does not allow us to draw an unambiguous picture of how the Cartesian axes relate. More specifically, if we put **x** and **y** on a sidewalk, with **x** pointing East and **y** pointing North, then does **z** point up to the sky or into the ground? The usual convention is to have **z** point to the sky. This is known as a *right-handed* coordinate system. This name comes from the memory scheme of "grabbing" **x** with your *right* palm and fingers and rotating it toward **y**. The vector **z** should align with your thumb. This is illustrated in Figure 2.20.

The cross product has the nice property that:

$$\mathbf{a} \times (\mathbf{b} + \mathbf{c}) = \mathbf{a} \times \mathbf{b} + \mathbf{a} \times \mathbf{c},$$

and

$$\mathbf{a} \times (k\mathbf{b}) = k(\mathbf{a} \times \mathbf{b}).$$

However, a consequence of the right hand rule is:

$$\mathbf{a} \times \mathbf{b} = -(\mathbf{b} \times \mathbf{a}).$$

In Cartesian coordinates, we can use an explicit expansion to compute the cross product:

$$\begin{aligned}
\mathbf{a} \times \mathbf{b} &= (x_a\mathbf{x} + y_a\mathbf{y} + z_a\mathbf{z}) \times (x_b\mathbf{x} + y_b\mathbf{y} + z_b\mathbf{z}) \\
&= x_a x_b \mathbf{x} \times \mathbf{x} + x_a y_b \mathbf{x} \times \mathbf{y} + x_a z_b \mathbf{x} \times \mathbf{z} \\
&\quad + y_a x_b \mathbf{y} \times \mathbf{x} + y_a y_b \mathbf{y} \times \mathbf{y} + y_a z_b \mathbf{y} \times \mathbf{z} \\
&\quad + z_a x_b \mathbf{z} \times \mathbf{x} + z_a y_b \mathbf{z} \times \mathbf{y} + z_a z_b \mathbf{z} \times \mathbf{z} \\
&= (y_a z_b - z_a y_b)\mathbf{x} + (z_a x_b - x_a z_b)\mathbf{y} + (x_a y_b - y_a x_b)\mathbf{z}.
\end{aligned} \tag{2.7}$$

So in coordinate form:

$$\mathbf{a} \times \mathbf{b} = (y_a z_b - z_a y_b, z_a x_b - x_a z_b, x_a y_b - y_a x_b). \tag{2.8}$$

2.4.5 Orthonormal Bases and Coordinate Frames

Any set of two 2D vectors $\mathbf{u}$ and $\mathbf{v}$ form an *orthonormal basis* provided they are orthogonal (at right angles) and are each of unit length. Thus:

$$\|\mathbf{u}\| = \|\mathbf{v}\| = 1,$$

and

$$\mathbf{u} \cdot \mathbf{v} = 0.$$

In 3D, three vectors $\mathbf{u}$, $\mathbf{v}$, and $\mathbf{w}$ form an orthonormal basis if:

$$\|\mathbf{u}\| = \|\mathbf{v}\| = \|\mathbf{w}\| = 1,$$

and

$$\mathbf{u} \cdot \mathbf{v} = \mathbf{v} \cdot \mathbf{w} = \mathbf{w} \cdot \mathbf{u} = 0.$$

This orthonormal basis is *right-handed* provided:

$$\mathbf{w} = \mathbf{u} \times \mathbf{v},$$

and otherwise it is left-handed.

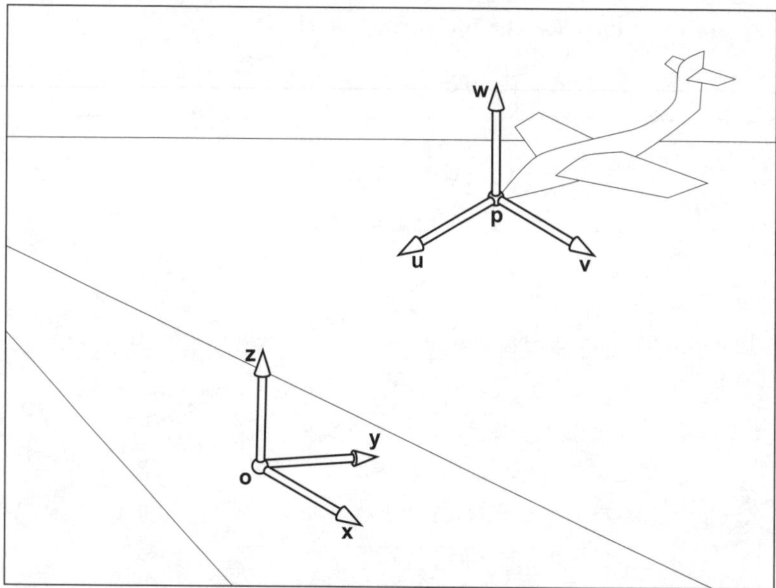

Figure 2.21. There is always a master or "canonical" coordinate system with origin **o** and orthonormal basis **x, y**, and **z**. This coordinate system is usually defined to be aligned to the global model and is thus often called the "global" or "world " coordinate system. This origin and basis vectors are never stored explicitly. All other vectors and locations are stored with coordinates that relate them to the global frame. The coordinate system associated with the plane are explicitly stored in terms of global coordinates.

Note that the Cartesian canonical orthonormal basis is just one of infinitely many possible orthonormal bases. What makes it special is that it and its implicit origin location are used for low-level representation within a program. Thus, the vectors **x**, **y**, and **z** are never explicitly stored, and neither is the canonical origin location **o**. The global model is typically stored in this canonical coordinate system, and it is thus often called the *global coordinate system*. However, if we want to use another coordinate system with origin **p** and orthonormal basis vectors **u**, **v**, and **w**, then we *do* store those vectors explicitly. Such a system is called a *frame of reference* or *coordinate frame*. For example, in a flight simulator, we might want to maintain a coordinate system with the origin at the nose of the plane, and the orthonormal basis aligned with the airplane. Simultaneously we would have the master canonical coordinate system (Figure 2.21). The coordinate system associated with a particular object, such as the plane, is usually called a *local coordinate system*.

At a low level, the local frame is stored in canonical coordinates. For example:

$$\mathbf{u} = (x_u, y_u, z_u) \equiv x_u\mathbf{x} + y_u\mathbf{y} + z_u\mathbf{z}.$$

A location implicitly includes an offset from the canonical origin:

$$\mathbf{p} = (x_p, y_p, z_p) \equiv \mathbf{o} + x_p\mathbf{x} + y_p\mathbf{y} + z_p\mathbf{z}$$

Note that if we store a vector $\mathbf{a}$ with respect to the uvw frame, we store a triple (u_a, v_a, w_a) which we can interpret geometrically as:

$$(u_a, v_a, w_a) \equiv u_a\mathbf{u} + v_a\mathbf{v} + w_a\mathbf{w}.$$

To get the canonical coordinates of a vector $\mathbf{a}$ stored in the $\mathbf{u}\,\mathbf{v}\,\mathbf{w}$ coordinate system, simply recall that $\mathbf{u}$, $\mathbf{v}$, and $\mathbf{w}$ are themselves stored in terms of Cartesian coordinates, so the expression $u_a\mathbf{u} + v_a\mathbf{v} + w_a\mathbf{w}$ is already in Cartesian coordinates if evaluated explicitly. Using matrices to manage changes of coordinate systems is discussed in Sections 5.2.1 and 5.5.

2.4.6 Constructing a Basis from a Single Vector

Often we must construct an orthonormal basis from a single vector, i.e., given a vector $\mathbf{a}$, we want an orthonormal $\mathbf{u}$, $\mathbf{v}$, and $\mathbf{w}$ such that $\mathbf{w}$ points in the same direction as $\mathbf{a}$. This cannot be done uniquely, but typically all we need is a robust procedure to find any one of the possible bases. This can be done as follows:

$$\mathbf{w} = \frac{\mathbf{a}}{\|\mathbf{a}\|}$$

To get $\mathbf{u}$ and $\mathbf{v}$, we need to find a vector $\mathbf{t}$ that is not collinear with $\mathbf{w}$. To do this, simply set $\mathbf{t}$ equal to $\mathbf{w}$ and change the smallest magnitude component of $\mathbf{t}$ to one. For example, if $\mathbf{w} = (1/\sqrt{2}, -1/\sqrt{2}, 0)$ then $\mathbf{t} = (1/\sqrt{2}, -1/\sqrt{2}, 1)$. The $\mathbf{u}$ and $\mathbf{v}$ follow easily:

$$\mathbf{u} = \frac{\mathbf{t} \times \mathbf{w}}{\|\mathbf{t} \times \mathbf{w}\|}$$

$$\mathbf{v} = \mathbf{w} \times \mathbf{u}$$

2.5 2D Implicit Curves

Intuitively , a *curve* is a set of points that can be drawn on a piece of paper without lifting the pen. A common way to describe a curve is using an *implicit equation* . An implicit equation in two dimensions has the form:

$$f(x, y) = 0.$$

The function $f(x, y)$ returns a real value. Points (x, y) where this valuethere may exist an *inverse function* is zero are on the curve, and points where the value is non-zero are not on the curve. For example, let's say that $f(x,y)$ is:

$$f(x,y) = (x - x_c)^2 + (y - y_c)^2 - r^2, \tag{2.9}$$

where (x_c, y_c) is a 2D point and r is a non-zero real number. If we take $f(x,y) = 0$, the points where this equality hold are on the circle with center (x_c, y_c) and radius r. The reason that this is called an "implicit" equation is that the points (x,y) on the curve cannot be immediately calculated from the equation, and instead must be determined by plugging (x,y) into f and finding out whether it is zero or by solving the equation. Thus, the points on the curve are not generated by the equation *explicitly*, but they are buried somewhere *implicitly* in the equation.

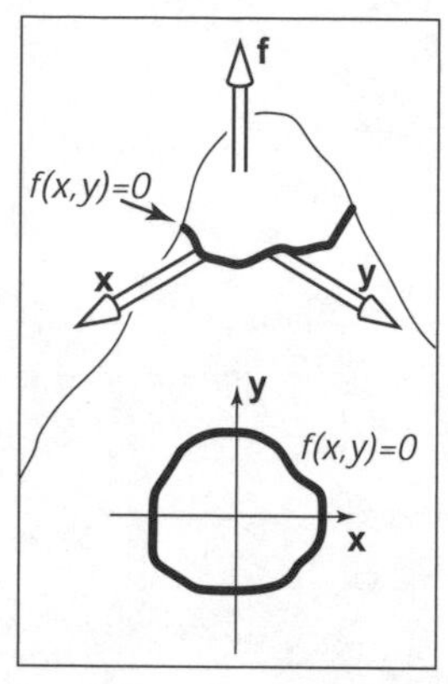

Figure 2.22. An implicit function *f(x,y) = 0* can be thought of as a height field where *f* is the height (top). A path where the height is zero is the implicit curve (bottom).

It is interesting to note that f does have values for all (x,y). We can think of f as a terrain, with sea-level at $f = 0$ (Figure 2.22). The shore is the implicit curve. The value of f is the altitude. Another thing to note is that the curve partitions space into regions where $f > 0$, $f < 0$ and $f = 0$. So you evaluate f to decide whether a point is "inside" a curve. Note that $f(x,y) = c$ is a curve for any constant c, and $c = 0$ is just used as a convention. For example if $f(x,y) = x^2 + y^2 - 1$, varying c just gives a variety of circles centered at the origin (Figure 2.23).

We can compress our notation using vectors. If we have $\mathbf{c} = (x_c, y_c)$ and $\mathbf{p} = (x,y)$, then our circle with center $\mathbf{c}$ and radius r is defined by those position vectors that satisfy:

$$(\mathbf{p} - \mathbf{c}) \cdot (\mathbf{p} - \mathbf{c}) - r^2 = 0.$$

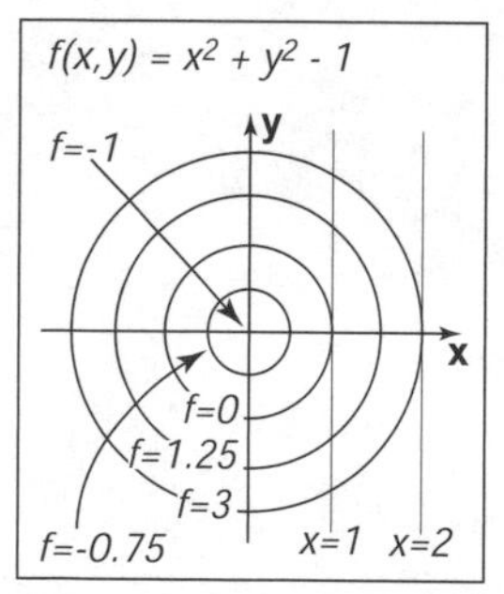

Figure 2.23. An implicit function *f(x,y) = 0* can be thought of a a height field where *f* is the height (top). A path where the height is zero is the implicit curve (bottom).

This equation, if expanded algebraically, will yield Equation 2.9, but it is easier to see that this is an equation for a circle by "reading" the equation geometrically. It reads, "points $\mathbf{p}$ on the circle have the following property: the vector from $\mathbf{c}$ to $\mathbf{p}$ when dotted with itself has value r^2." It is also easier to implement vector equations than implementing fully expanded equations if you implement a vector type in your code; the cut-and-paste errors involving x, y, and z will go away. Because a vector dotted with itself is just its own length squared, we could also read the equation as, "points $\mathbf{p}$ on the circle have the following property: the vector from $\mathbf{c}$ to $\mathbf{p}$ has squared length r^2."

Even better, is to observe that the squared length is just the squared distance from $\mathbf{c}$ to $\mathbf{p}$, which suggests the equivalent form:

$$\|\mathbf{p} - \mathbf{c}\|^2 - r^2 = 0,$$

and, of course, this suggests:

$$\|\mathbf{p} - \mathbf{c}\| - r = 0.$$

The above could be read "the points $\mathbf{p}$ on the circle are those a distance r from the center point $\mathbf{c}$," which is as good a definition of circle as any.

This illustrates that the vector form of an equation often suggests more geometry and intuition than the equivalent full-blown Cartesian form with xs and ys. For this reason, it is usually advisable to use vector forms when possible. In addition, you can support a vector class in your code; the code is cleaner when vector forms are used. It takes a little while to get used to vectors in these equations, but once you get the hang of it, the payoff is large.

2.5.1 The 2D Gradient

If we think of the function $f(x, y)$ as a height field with height $= f(x, y)$, the *gradient* vector points in the direction of maximum upslope, i.e., straight uphill. The gradient vector $\nabla f(x, y)$ is given by:

$$\nabla f(x, y,) = \left(\frac{\partial f}{\partial x}, \frac{\partial f}{\partial y} \right).$$

The gradient vector evaluated at a point on the implicit curve $f(x, y) = 0$ is perpendicular to the *tangent* vector of the curve at that point. This perpendicular vector is usually called the *normal vector* to the curve. In addition, since the gradient points uphill, it indicates the direction of the $f(x, y) > 0$ region.

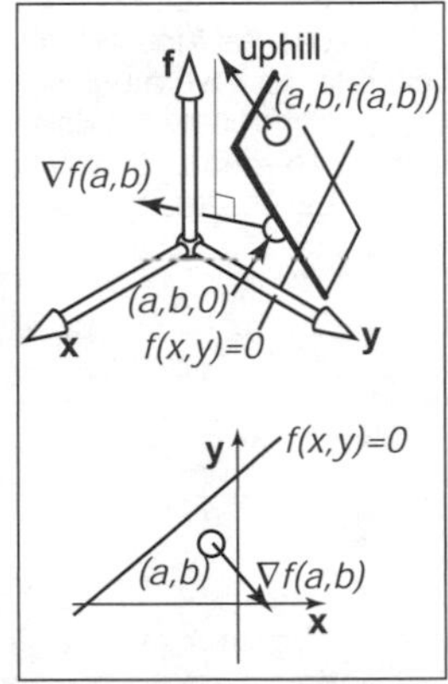

Figure 2.24. A surface height = *f(x,y)* is locally planar near *(x,y) = (a,b)*. The gradient is a projection of the uphill direction onto the height = 0 plane.

In the context of height fields, the geometric meaning of partial derivatives and gradients is more visible than usual. Suppose that near the point (a, b), $f(x, y)$ is a plane (Figure 2.24). There is a specific uphill and downhill direction. At right angles to this direction is a direction that is level with respect to the plane. Any intersection between the plane and the $f(x, y) = 0$ plane will be in the direction that is level. Thus the uphill/downhill directions will be perpendicular to the line of intersection $f(x, y) = 0$. To see why the partial derivative has something to do with this, we need to visualize its geometric meaning. Recall that the conventional derivative of a 1D function $y = g(x)$ is:

$$\frac{dy}{dx} \equiv \lim_{\Delta x \to 0} \frac{\Delta y}{\Delta x} = \lim_{\Delta x \to 0} \frac{g(x + \Delta x) - g(x)}{\Delta x}. \quad (2.10)$$

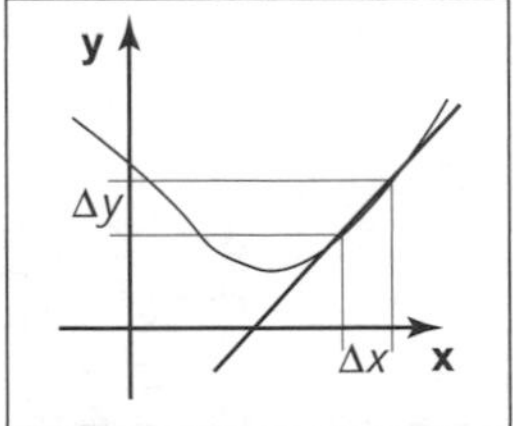

Figure 2.25. The derivative of a 1D function measures the slope of the line tangent to the curve.

What this measures is is the *slope* of the *tangent* line to g (Figure 2.25).

The partial derivative is a generalization of the 1D derivative. For a 2D function $f(x, y)$, we can't take the same limit for x as in Equation 2.10, because f can change in many ways for a given change in x. However, ifwe hold y constant, we can define an analog of the derivative, called the *partial derivative* (Figure 2.26):

$$\frac{\partial f}{\partial x} \equiv \lim_{\Delta x \to 0} \frac{f(x + \Delta x, y) - f(x, y)}{\Delta x}.$$

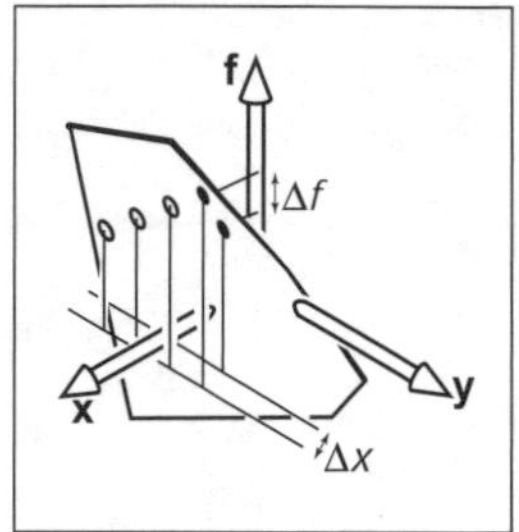

Figure 2.26. The partial derivative of a 2D function with respect to *f* must hold *y* constant to have a unique value, as shown by the dark point. The hollow points show other values of *f* that do not hold *y* constant.

Why is it that the partial derivatives of x and y are the components of the gradient vector? Again, there is more obvious insight in the geometry than in the algebra. In Figure 2.27, we see the vector $\mathbf{a}$ travels along a path where $\mathbf{f}$ does not change. Note that this is again at a small enough scale that the surface height$(x, y) = f(x, y)$ can be considered locally planar. From the figure, we see that the vector $\mathbf{a} = (\Delta x, \Delta y)$.

Because the uphill direction is perpendicular to $\mathbf{a}$, we know the dot product is equal to zero:

$$(\nabla f) \cdot \mathbf{a} \equiv (x_\nabla, y_\nabla) \cdot (x_a, y_a) = x_\nabla \Delta x + y_\nabla \Delta y = 0. \tag{2.11}$$

We also know that the change in f in the direction (x_a, y_a) is zero:

$$\Delta f = \frac{\partial f}{\partial x}\Delta x + \frac{\partial f}{\partial y}\Delta y \equiv \frac{\partial f}{\partial x}x_a + \frac{\partial f}{\partial y}y_a = 0. \tag{2.12}$$

Given any vectors (x, y) and (x', y') that are perpendicular, we know the angle between them is ninety degrees, and thus their dot product is zero (recall that the dot product is proportional to the cosine of the angle between the two vectors). Thus we have $xx' + yy' = 0$. Given (x, y), it is easy to construct valid vectors whose dot product with (x, y) equals zweo, the two most obvious being $(y, -x)$ and $(-y, x)$; you can verify that these vectors give the desired zero dot product with (x, y). A generalization of this observation is that $(x, y) = k(x, -y)$ where k is any non-zero constant. This implies that:

$$(x_a, y_a) = k\left(\frac{\partial f}{\partial y}, -\frac{\partial f}{\partial x}\right). \tag{2.13}$$

Combining Equations 2.12 and 2.13 gives:

$$(x_\nabla, y_\nabla) = k'\left(\frac{\partial f}{\partial x}, \frac{\partial f}{\partial y}\right),$$

where k' is any non-zero constant. By definition, "uphill" implies a positive change in f, so we would like $k' > 0$, and $k' = 1$ is a perfectly good convention.

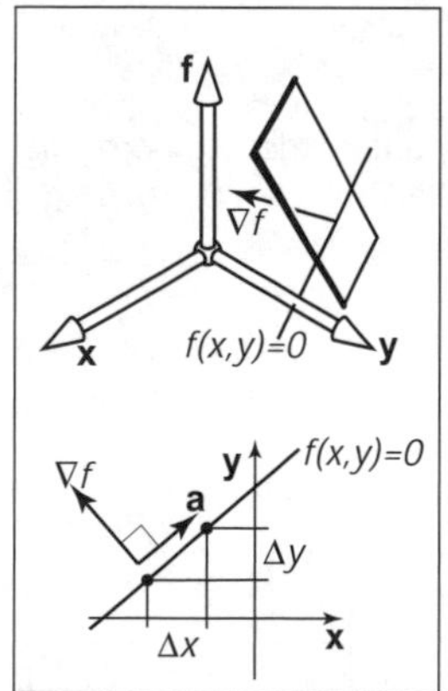

Figure 2.27. The vector **a** points in a direction where *f* has no change and is thus perpendicular to the gradient vector ∇ *f*.

As an example of the gradient, consider the implicit circle $x^2+y^2-1=0$ with gradient vector $(2x, 2y)$, indicating that the outside of the circle is the positive region for the function $f(x, y) = x^2 + y^2 - 1$. Note that the length of the gradient vector can be different depending on the multiplier in the implicit equation. For example, the unit circle can be described by $Ax^2 + Ay^2 - A = 0$ for any non-zero A. The gradient for this curve is $(2Ax, 2Ay)$. This will be normal (perpendicular) to the circle, but will have a length determined by A. For $A > 0$, the normal will point outward from the circle, and for $A < 0$, it will point inward. This switch from outward to inward is as it should be, since the positive region switches inside the circle. In terms of the height-field view, $h = Ax^2 + Ay^2 - A$, the circle is the zero altitude point. For $A > 0$, the circle encloses a depression and for $A < 0$, the circle encloses a bump. As A becomes more negative, the bump increases in height, but the $h = 0$ circle doesn't change. The direction of maximum uphill doesn't change, but the slope increases. The length of the gradient reflects this change in degree of the slope. So intuitively, you can think of the gradient's direction as pointing uphill, and its magnitude as measuring how uphill the slope is.

2.5.2 Implicit 2D Lines

The familiar "slope-intercept" form of the line is:

$$y = mx + b. \tag{2.14}$$

This can be converted easily to implicit form (Figure 2.28):

$$y - mx - b = 0. \tag{2.15}$$

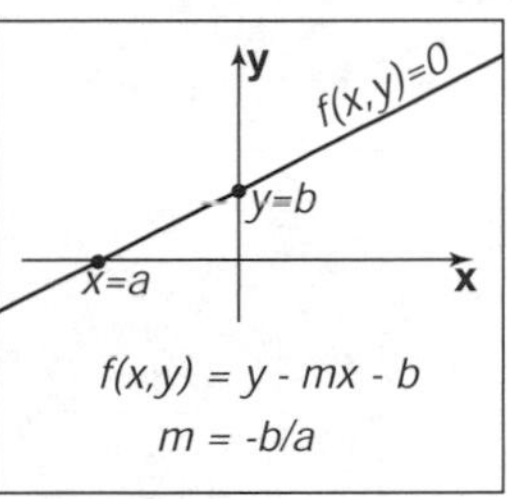

Figure 2.28. A 2D line can be described by the equation $y - mx - b = 0$.

Here m is the "slope" (ratio of rise to run) and b is the y value where the line crosses the y axis, usually called the *y-intercept* . The line also partitions the 2D plane, but here "inside" and "outside" might be more intuitively called "over" and "under."

Because we can multiply an implicit equation by any constant without changing the points where it is zero, $kf(x, y) = 0$ is the same curve for any non-zero k. This allows several implicit forms for the same line, for example:

$$2y - 2mx - 2b = 0.$$

One reason the slope-intercept form is sometimes awkward is that it can't represent some lines such as $x = 0$ because m would have to be infinite. For this reason, a more general form is often useful:

$$Ax + By + C = 0, \tag{2.16}$$

for real numbers A, B, C. Suppose we know two points on the line (x_0, y_0) and (x_1, y_1). Because these points lie on the line, they must both satisfy Equation 2.16:

$$Ax_0 + By_0 + C = 0,$$
$$Ax_1 + By_1 + C = 0.$$

Unfortunately we have two equations and *three* unknowns: A, B, C. This problem arises because of the arbitrary multiplier we can have with an implicit equation. We could set $C = 1$ for convenience:

$$Ax + By + 1 = 0,$$

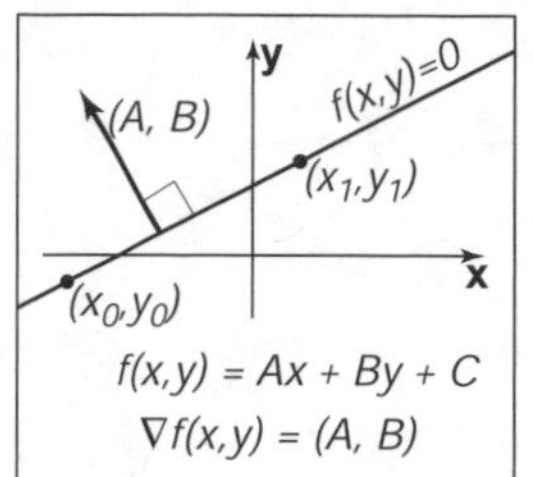

Figure 2.29. The gradient vector *(A,B)* is perpendicular to the implicit line *Ax + By + C = 0.*

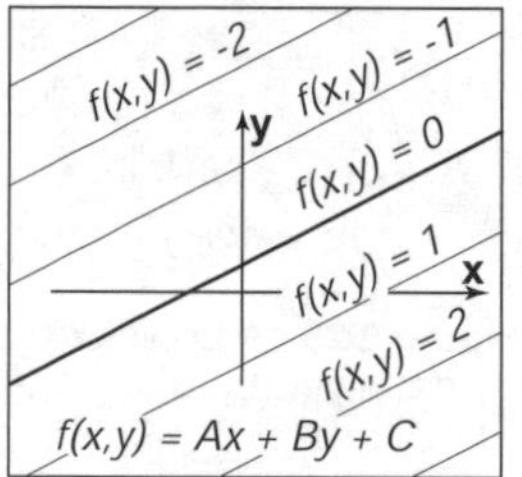

Figure 2.30. The value of the implicit function *f(x,y) = Ax + By + C* is a constant times the signed distance from *Ax + By +C = 0.*

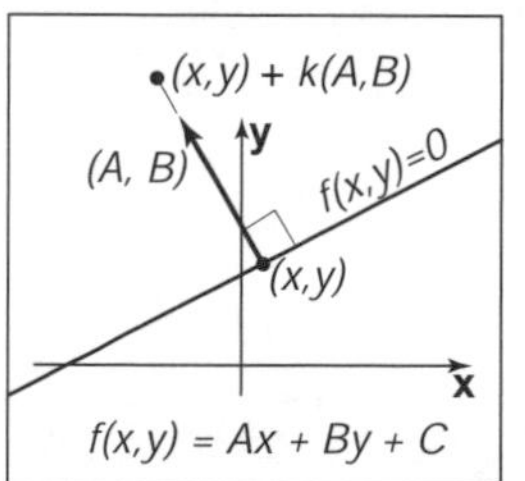

Figure 2.31. The vector *k(A,B)* connects a point *(x,y)* on the line closest to a point not on the line. The distance is proportional to *k.*

but we have a similar problem to the infinite slope case in slope-intercept form: lines through the origin will have $A(0) + B(0) + 1 = 0$ so A or B has to be infinite. For example, the equation for a forty-five degree line through the origin can be written $x - y = 0$, or equally well $y - x = 0$, or even $17y - 17x = 0$, but it cannot be written in the form $Ax + By + 1 = 0$.

Whenever we have such pesky algebraic problems, try to solve the problems using geometric intuition as a guide. One tool we have, as discussed in Section 2.5.1, is the gradient. For the line $Ax + By + C = 0$ the gradient vector is (A, B). This vector is perpendicular to the line (Figure 2.29), and points to the side of the line where $Ax + By + C$ is positive. Given two points on the line (x_0, y_0) and (x_1, y_1), we know that the vector between them points in the same direction as the line. This vector is just $(x_1 - x_0, y_1 - y_0)$, and because it is parallel to the line, it must also be perpendicular to the gradient vector (A, B). Recall that there are an infinite number of (A, B, C) that describe the line because of the arbitrary scaling property of implicits. We want any one of the valid (A, B, C).

We can start with a valid (A, B), which is any (A, B) perpendicular to $(x_1 - x_0, y_1 - y_0)$. We can get a valid (A, B) perpendicular to the vector $(x_1 - x_0, y_1 - y_0)$ and thus parallel to the line whose equation we seek.Such a vector is just $(A, B) = (y_0 - y_1, x_1 - x_0)$ by the same reasoning as in Section 2.5.1. This means the equation of the line through (x_0, y_0) and (x_1, y_1) is

$$(y_0 - y_1)x + (x_1 - x_0)y + C = 0. \qquad (2.17)$$

Now we just need to find C. Because (x_0, y_0) and (x_1, y_1) are on the line, they must satisfy Equation 2.17. We can plug either in and solve for C. Doing this for (x_0, y_0) yields $C = x_0 y_1 - x_1 y_0$, and thus the full equation for the line is

$$(y_0 - y_1)x + (x_1 - x_0)y + x_0 y_1 - x_1 y_0 = 0. \qquad (2.18)$$

Again, this is one of infinitely many valid implicit equations for the line through two points, but this form has no division operation, and thus no numerically degenerate cases for points with finite Cartesian coordinates. A nice thing about Equation 2.18 is that we can always convert to slope-intercept form by moving the non-y terms to the righthand side of the equation, and dividing by the multiplier of the y term:

$$y = \frac{x_1 - x_0}{y_1 - y_0} x + \frac{x_1 y_0 - x_0 y_1}{x_1 - x_0}.$$

An interesting property of the implicit line equation is that it can be used to find the signed distance from a point to the line. The value of $Ax + By + C$ is proportional to the distance from the line (Figure 2.30). As shown in Figure 2.31, the distance from a point to the line is the length of the vector

$k(A, B)$, which is:

$$\text{distance} = k\sqrt{A^2 + B^2}. \quad (2.19)$$

For the point $(x, y) + k(A, B)$, the value of $f(x, y) = Ax + By + C$ is:

$$\begin{aligned} f(x + kA, y + kB) &= Ax + kA^2 + By + kB^2 + C \\ &= k(A^2 + B^2). \end{aligned} \quad (2.20)$$

The simplification in that equation is a result of the fact that we know (x, y) is on the line, so $Ax + By + C = 0$. From Equations 2.19 and 2.20, we can see that the signed distance from line $Ax + By + C = 0$ to a point (a, b) is:

$$\text{distance} = \frac{f(a, b)}{\sqrt{A^2 + B^2}}.$$

Here "signed distance" means that its magnitude (absolute value) is the distance, but it may be positive or negative. On one side of the line, distances are positive, and on the other they are negative. Note that if (A, B) is a unit vector, then $f(a, b)$ is the signed distance. We can multiply Equation 2.18 by a constant that ensures (A, B) is a unit vector:

$$\begin{aligned} f(x, y) = \frac{y_0 - y_1}{\sqrt{(x_1 - x_0)^2 + (y_0 - y_1)^2}} x &+ \frac{x_1 - x_0}{\sqrt{(x_1 - x_0)^2 + (y_0 - y_1)^2}} y \\ &+ \frac{x_0 y_1 - x_1 y_0}{\sqrt{(x_1 - x_0)^2 + (y_0 - y_1)^2}} = 0. \end{aligned} \quad (2.21)$$

Note that evaluating $f(x, y)$ in Equation 2.21 directly gives the signed distance, but does require a square root to set up the equation. Note also that although distances on one side of the line are positive, those on the other side of the line are negative. You can choose between the equally valid representations $f(x, y) = 0$ and $-f(x, y) = 0$ if your problem has some reason to prefer a particular side being positive. This will turn out to be very useful for triangle rasterization (Section 3.6). Other forms for 2D lines are discussed in Chapter 14.

2.5.3 Implicit Quadratic Curves

For 2D quadric curves, i.e., ellipses, and parabolas, as well as the special cases of hyperbolas, circles, and lines, we have the general implicit form:

$$Ax^2 + Bxy + Cy^2 + Dx + Ey + F = 0.$$

The equation for the circle with center (x_c, y_c) and radius r is:

$$(x - x_c)^2 + (y - y_c)^2 - r^2 = 0.$$

Equations for parabolas include:

$$y - k(x - x_c)^2 = 0,$$

where k is a non-zero constant and x_c is the axis of symmetry for the parabola. There is an analogous form for parabolas with horizontal axes of symmetry. An axis-aligned ellipse is:

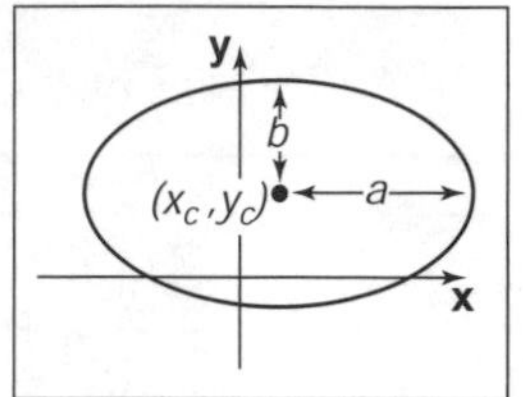

Figure 2.32. The ellipse with center (x_c, y_c) and semi-axes of length a and b.

$$\frac{(x - x_c)^2}{a^2} + \frac{(y - y_c)^2}{b^2} - 1 = 0,$$

where (x_c, y_c) is the center of the ellipse, and a and b are the minor and major semi-axes (Figure 2.32).

2.6 2D Parametric Curves

A *parametric* curve is controlled by a single *parameter* that can be considered a sort of index that moves continuously along the curve. Such curves have the form:

$$\begin{bmatrix} x \\ y \end{bmatrix} = \begin{bmatrix} g(t) \\ h(t) \end{bmatrix}.$$

Here (x, y) is a point on the curve, and t is the parameter that influences the curve. For a given t, there will be some point determined by the functions g and h. For continuous g and h, a small change in t will yield a small change in x and y. Thus, as t continuously changes, points are swept out in a continuous curve. This is a nice feature because we can use the parameter t to explicitly construct points on the curve. Often we can write a parametric curve in vector form:

$$\mathbf{p} = f(t),$$

where f is a vector valued function: $f : \mathbb{R} \mapsto \mathbb{R}^2$. Such vector functions can generate very clean code, so they should be used when possible. Note that we can think of the curve with a position as a function of time. The curve can go anywhere, and could loop and cross itself. We can also think of the curve as having a velocity at any point. For example, the point $\mathbf{p}(t)$ is travelling slowly near $t = -2$ and quickly between $t = 2$ and $t = 3$. This type of "moving point" vocabulary is often used when discussing parametric curves even when the curve is not describing a moving point.

2.6.1 2D Parametric Lines

A parametric line in 2D that passes through points $\mathbf{p}_0 = (x_0, y_0)$ and $\mathbf{p}_1 = (x_1, y_1)$ can be written:

$$\begin{bmatrix} x \\ y \end{bmatrix} = \begin{bmatrix} x_0 + t(x_1 - x_0) \\ y_0 + t(y_1 - y_0) \end{bmatrix}.$$

Because the formulas for x and y have such similar structure, we can use the vector form for $\mathbf{p} = (x, y)$ (Figure 2.33):

$$\mathbf{p}(t) = \mathbf{p}_0 + t(\mathbf{p}_1 - \mathbf{p}_0).$$

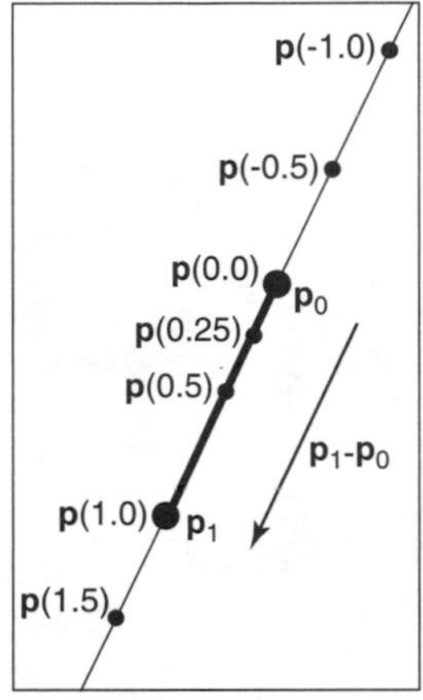

Figure 2.33. A 2D parametric line through $\mathbf{p}_0$ and $\mathbf{p}_1$. The line segment defined defined by $t \in [0,1]$ is shown in bold.

You can read this in geometric form as: "start at point $\mathbf{p}_0$ and go some distance toward $\mathbf{p}_1$ determined by the parameter t." A nice feature of this form is that $\mathbf{p}(0) = \mathbf{p}_0$, and $\mathbf{p}(1) = \mathbf{p}_1$. Since the point changes linearly with t, the value of t between $\mathbf{p}_0$ and $\mathbf{p}_1$ measures the fractional distance between the points. Points with $t < 0$ are to the "far" side of $\mathbf{p}_0$, and points with $t > 1$ are to the "far" side of $\mathbf{p}_1$.

Parametric lines can also be described as just a point $\mathbf{o}$ and a vector $\mathbf{d}$:

$$\mathbf{p}(t) = \mathbf{o} + t(\mathbf{d}).$$

When the vector $\mathbf{d}$ has unit length, the line is *arc-length parameterized.* This means t is an exact measure of distance along the line. Any parametric curve can be arc-length parameterized which is obviously a very convenient form, but not all can be converted analytically.

2.6.2 2D Parametric Circles

A circle with center (x_c, y_x) and radius r has a parametric form:

$$\begin{bmatrix} x \\ y \end{bmatrix} = \begin{bmatrix} x_c + r\cos\phi \\ y_c + r\sin\phi \end{bmatrix}.$$

To ensure that there is a unique parameter ϕ for every point on the curve, we can restrict its domain: $\phi \in [0, 2\pi)$ or $\phi \in (-\pi, \pi]$ or any other half open interval of length 2π.

An axis-aligned ellipse can be constructed by scaling the x and y parametric equations separately:

$$\begin{bmatrix} x \\ y \end{bmatrix} = \begin{bmatrix} x_c + a\cos\phi \\ y_c + b\sin\phi \end{bmatrix}.$$

2.7 3D Implicit Surfaces

Implicit equations *implicitly* define a set of points that are on the surface

$$f(x, y, z) = 0.$$

Any point (x, y, z) that is on the surface returns zero when given as an argument to f. Any point not on the surface returns some number other than zero. This is called implicit rather than explicit because you can check whether a point is on the surface by evaluating f, but you cannot always explicitly construct a set of points on the surface. As a convenient shorthand, I will write such functions of $\mathbf{p} = (x, y, z)$ as

$$f(\mathbf{p}) = 0.$$

2.7.1 Surface Normal to an Implicit Surface

A surface normal, which is needed for lighting computations, is a vector perpendicular to the surface. Each point on the surface may have a different normal vector. The surface normal at the intersection point $\mathbf{p}$ is given by the gradient of the implicit function

$$\mathbf{n} = \nabla f(\mathbf{p}) = \left(\frac{\partial f(\mathbf{p})}{\partial x}, \frac{\partial f(\mathbf{p})}{\partial y}, \frac{\partial f(\mathbf{p})}{\partial z} \right).$$

The gradient vector may point "into" the surface or may point "out" from the surface. If the particular form of f creates inward facing gradients and outward facing gradients are desired, the surface $-f(\mathbf{p}) = 0$ is the same as surface $f(\mathbf{p}) = 0$ but has directionally reversed gradients, i.e., $\nabla f(\mathbf{p}) = -\nabla(-f(\mathbf{p}))$.

2.7.2 Implicit Planes

As an example, consider the infinite plane through point $\mathbf{a}$ with surface normal $\mathbf{n}$. The implicit equation to describe this plane is given by

$$(\mathbf{p} - \mathbf{a}) \cdot \mathbf{n} = 0. \tag{2.22}$$

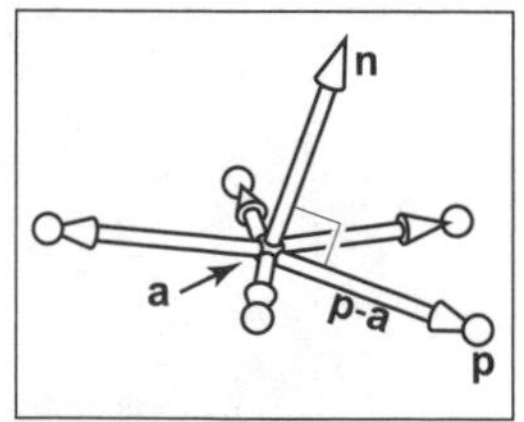

Figure 2.34. Any of the points **p** shown are in the plane with normal vector **n** that includes point **a** if Equation 2.22 is satisfied.

Note that $\mathbf{a}$ and $\mathbf{n}$ are known quantities. The point $\mathbf{p}$ is any unknown point that satisfies the equation. In geometric terms this equation says "the vector from $\mathbf{a}$ to $\mathbf{p}$ is perpendicular to the plane normal." If $\mathbf{p}$ were not in the plane, then $(\mathbf{p} - \mathbf{a})$ would not make a right angle with $\mathbf{n}$ (Figure 2.34).

Sometimes we want the implicit equation for a plane through points $\mathbf{a}$, $\mathbf{b}$, and $\mathbf{c}$. The normal to this plane can be found by taking the cross product of any two vectors in the plane. One such cross product is:

$$\mathbf{n} = (\mathbf{b} - \mathbf{a}) \times (\mathbf{c} - \mathbf{a}).$$

This allows us to write the implicit plane equation:

$$(\mathbf{p}-\mathbf{a})\cdot((\mathbf{b}-\mathbf{a})\times(\mathbf{c}-\mathbf{a}))=0.$$

A geometric way to read this equation is that the volume of the parallelepiped defined by $\mathbf{p}-\mathbf{a}$, $\mathbf{b}-\mathbf{a}$, and $\mathbf{c}-\mathbf{a}$ is zero, i.e., they are coplanar. This can only be true if $\mathbf{p}$ is in the same plane as $\mathbf{a}$, $\mathbf{b}$, and $\mathbf{c}$. The full blown Cartesian representation for this is given by the determinant (this is discussed in more detail in Section 4.2.3):

$$\begin{vmatrix} x-x_a & y-y_a & z-z_a \\ x_b-x_a & y_b-y_a & z_b-z_a \\ x_c-x_a & y_c-y_a & z_c-z_a \end{vmatrix}=0. \tag{2.23}$$

The determinant can be expanded (see Section 4.2.3 for the mechanics of expanding determinants) to the somewhat bloated form:

$$\begin{aligned}(z_c(y_b-y_a)-y_c(z_b-z_a))\,x \\ +\,(x_c(z_b-z_a)-z_c(x_b-x_a))\,y \\ +\,(y_c(x_b-x_a)-x_c(y_b-y_a))\,z \\ +\,(x_c(y_az_b-y_bz_a)+y_c(x_az_b-x_bz_a)+z_c(x_by_a-x_ay_c)))=0.\end{aligned} \tag{2.24}$$

Equations 2.22–2.24 are all equivalent, and comparing them is instructive. Equation 2.22 is easy to interpret geometrically and will yield efficient code. In addition, it is relatively easy to avoid a typographic error that compiles into incorrect code if it takes advantage of debugged cross and dot product code. Equation 2.23 is also easy to interpret geometrically and will be efficient provided an efficient 3 by 3 determinant function is implemented. It is also easy to implement without a typo provided a call of the type *determinant*$(\mathbf{a},\mathbf{b},\mathbf{c})$ exists. It will be especially easy for others to read your code if you rename the *determinant* function *volume*. So both Equations 2.22 and 2.23 map well into code. Equation 2.24, however, maps poorly into code. It is not very readable geometrically, and is prone to hard-to-find typos such as a switched subscript. Such typos are likely to compile, and thus be especially pesky. This is an excellent example of clean math generating clean code, and bloated math generating bloated code.

2.7.3 3D Curves from Implicit Surfaces

One might hope that an implicit 3D curve could be created with the form $f(\mathbf{p})=0$. However, all such curves are just degenerate surfaces and are rarely useful in practice. 3D curves can be constructed from the intersection of two simultaneous implicit equations:

$$\begin{aligned} f(\mathbf{p})&=0,\\ g(\mathbf{p})&=0.\end{aligned}$$

For example, a 3D line can be formed from the intersection of two implicit planes. Typically, it is more convenient to use 3D parametric curves, which are straightforward extensions of 2D parametric curves.

2.8 3D Parametric Curves

A 3D parametric curve operates much like a 2D parametric curve:

$$\begin{aligned} x &= f(t), \\ y &= g(t), \\ z &= h(t). \end{aligned}$$

For example, a spiral around the z axis is:

$$\begin{aligned} x &= \cos t, \\ y &= \sin t, \\ z &= t. \end{aligned}$$

In this chapter we only discuss 3D parametric lines in detail. General 3D parametric curves are discussed more extensively in Chapter 13.

2.8.1 3D Parametric Lines

A 3D parametric line can be written as a straightforward extension of the 2D parametric line, e.g.,

$$\begin{aligned} x &= 2 + 7t, \\ y &= 1 + 2t, \\ z &= 3 - 5t. \end{aligned}$$

This is cumbersome and does not translate well to code variables, so we will write it in vector form:

$$\mathbf{p} = \mathbf{o} + t\mathbf{d},$$

where, for this example, $\mathbf{o}$ and $\mathbf{d}$ are given by

$$\begin{aligned} \mathbf{o} &= (2, 1, \quad 3), \\ \mathbf{d} &= (7, 2, -5). \end{aligned}$$

Note that this is very similar to the 2D case. The way to visualize this is to imagine that the line passes though $\mathbf{o}$ and is parallel to $\mathbf{d}$. Given any value of t, you get some point $\mathbf{p}(t)$ on the line. For example, at $t = 2$, $p(t) = (2, 1, 3) + 2(7, 2, -5) = (16, 5, -7)$. This general concept is the same as for two dimensions (Figure 2.30).

As in 2D, a *line segment* can be described by a 3D parametric line and an interval $t \in [t_a, t_b]$. The line segment between two points $\mathbf{a}$ and $\mathbf{b}$ is given by $\mathbf{p}(t) = \mathbf{a} + t(\mathbf{b} - \mathbf{a})$ with $t \in [0, 1]$. Here $\mathbf{p}(0) = \mathbf{a}$, $\mathbf{p}(1) = \mathbf{b}$, and $\mathbf{p}(0.5) = (\mathbf{a} + \mathbf{b})/2$, the midpoint between $\mathbf{a}$ and $\mathbf{b}$.

A *ray*, or *half-line*, is a 3D parametric line with a half-open interval, usually $[0, \infty)$. From now on we will refer to all lines, line segments, and rays as "rays." This is sloppy, but corresponds to common usage, and makes the discussion simpler.

2.9 3D Parametric Surfaces

Another way to specify 3D surfaces (surfaces in 3D space) is with 2D *parameters*. These surfaces have the form:

$$x = f(u, v),$$
$$y = g(u, v),$$
$$z = h(u, v).$$

2.9.1 Parametric Spheres

A point on the surface of the earth is given by the two parameters, longitude and latitude. For example, if we put a polar coordinate system on a radius r sphere with center at the origin (Figure 2.35), we get the parametric equations

$$\begin{aligned} x &= r \cos\phi \sin\theta, \\ y &= r \sin\phi \sin\theta, \\ z &= r \cos\theta. \end{aligned} \tag{2.25}$$

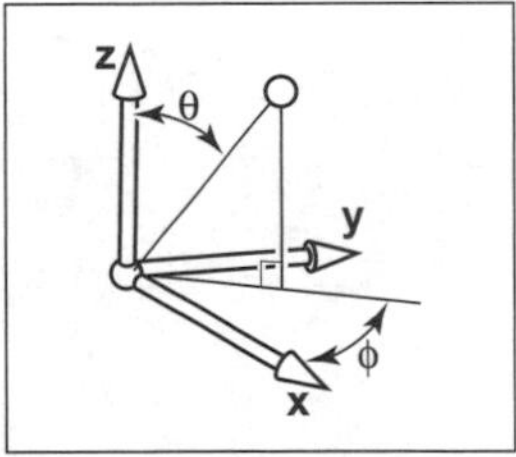

Figure 2.35. The geometry for spherical coordinates.

Ideally, we'd like to write this in vector form, but it isn't feasible for this particular parametric form. This use of θ and ϕ may or may not be backwards depending upon the reader's background. Unfortunately there is no standard for which angle uses which symbol across disciplines. Anyone who dismisses the importance of such standards should try to manipulate an equation of the form $\mathbf{bA} = \mathbf{x}$ where $\mathbf{b}$ is a square matrix and the other variables are column vectors, rather than the usual $\mathbf{Ax} = \mathbf{b}$. The more familiar they are with linear algebra, the worse their confusion will be. In graphics, we will always assume the meaning of θ and ϕ given in Equation 2.25. We will return to this equation when we texture map a sphere.

We would also like to be able to find the (θ, ϕ) for a given (x, y, z). If we assume that $\phi \in (-\pi, \pi]$ this is easy to do using the *atan2* function from

Equation 2.2:

$$\begin{aligned}\theta &= \operatorname{acos}(z/\sqrt{x^2+y^2+z^2}),\\ \phi &= \operatorname{atan2}(y,x).\end{aligned} \tag{2.26}$$

2.10 Linear Interpolation

Perhaps the most common mathematical operation in graphics is *linear interpolation* . We have already seen an example of linear interpolation of position to form line segments in 2D and 3D, where two points $\mathbf{a}$ and $\mathbf{b}$ are associated with a parameter t to form the line $\mathbf{p} = (1-t)\mathbf{a} + t\mathbf{b}$. This is *interpolation* because $\mathbf{p}$ goes through $\mathbf{a}$ and $\mathbf{b}$ exactly at $t = 0$ and $t = 1$. It is *linear* interpolation because the weighting terms t and $1-t$ are linear polynomials of t.

Another common linear interpolation is among a set of positions on the x-axis: x_0, x_1, ..., x_n, and for each x_i we have an associated height, y_i. We want to create a continuous function $y = f(x)$ that interpolates these positions, so that f goes through every data point, i.e., $f(x_i) = y_i$. For linear interpolation, the points (x_i, y_i) are connected by straight line segments. It is natural to use parametric line equations for these segments. The parameter t is just the fractional distance between x_i and x_{i+1}:

$$f(x) = y_i + \frac{x - x_i}{x_{i+1} - x_i}(y_{i+1} - y_i). \tag{2.27}$$

Because the weighting functions are linear polynomials of x, this is linear interpolation.

The two examples above have the common form of linear interpolation. Create a variable t that varies from 0 to 1 as we move from data item A to data item B. Intermediate values are just the function $(1-t)A + tB$. Notice that Equation 2.27 has this form with,

$$t = \frac{x - x_i}{x_{i+1} - x_i}.$$

2.11 Triangles

Triangles in both 2D and 3D are the fundamental modeling primitive in most graphics programs. Often information such as color is tagged onto triangle vertices, and this information is interpolated across the triangle. The coordinate system that makes such interpolation straightforward is called *barycentric coordinates*, and we will develop these from scratch. We will also discuss 2D triangles, which must be understood before we can draw their pictures on 2D screens.

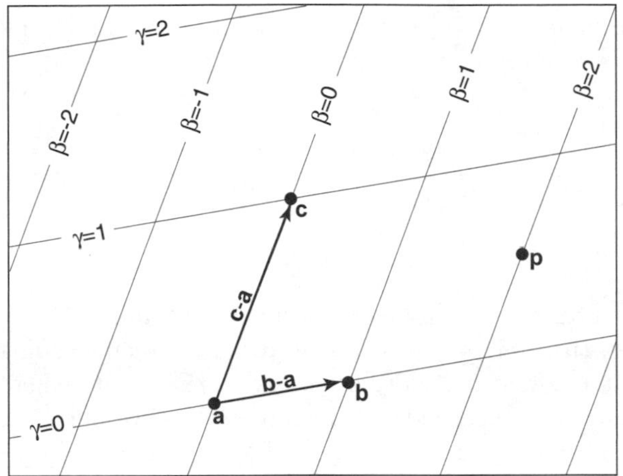

Figure 2.36. A 2D triangle with vertices **a**, **b**, **c** can be used to set up a non-orthogonal coordinate system with origin **a** and basis vectors (**b** - **a**) and (**c** - **a**). A point is then represented by an ordered pair (β, γ). For example, the point **p** = (2.0, 0.5), i.e., **p** = **a** + 2.0 (**b**- **a**) + 0.5 (**c**- **a**).

2.11.1 2D Triangles

If we have a 2D triangle defined by 2D points **a**, **b**, and **c**, we can first find its area:

$$\begin{aligned} \text{area} &= \frac{1}{2}\begin{vmatrix} x_b - x_a & x_c - x_a \\ y_b - y_a & y_c - y_a \end{vmatrix} \\ &= \frac{1}{2}\left(x_a y_b + x_b y_c + x_c y_a - x_a y_c - x_b y_a - x_c y_b\right). \end{aligned} \tag{2.28}$$

The derivation of this formula can be found in Section 4.2.3. This area will have a positive sign if the points **a**, **b**, and **c** are in counter-clockwise order, and a negative sign otherwise.

Often in graphics, we wish to assign a property such as color at each triangle vertex and smoothly interpolate the value of that property across the triangle. There are a variety of ways to do this, but the simplest is to use *barycentric* coordinates. One way to think of barycentric coordinates is as a non-orthogonal coordinate system as was discussed briefly in Section 2.4.2. Such a coordinate system is shown in Figure 2.36, where the coordinate origin is **a** and the vectors from **a** to **b** and **c** are the basis vectors. With that origin and those basis vectors, any point **p** can be written:

$$\mathbf{p} = \mathbf{a} + \beta(\mathbf{b} - \mathbf{a}) + \gamma(\mathbf{c} - \mathbf{a}). \tag{2.29}$$

Note that we can reorder the terms in Equation 2.29 to get:

$$\mathbf{p} = (1 - \beta - \gamma)\mathbf{a} + \beta\mathbf{b} + \gamma\mathbf{c}.$$

Often people define a new variable α to improve the symmetry of the equations:

$$\alpha \equiv 1 - \beta - \gamma,$$

which yields the equation:

$$\mathbf{p}(\alpha, \beta, \gamma) = \alpha\mathbf{a} + \beta\mathbf{b} + \gamma\mathbf{c}, \tag{2.30}$$

with the constraint that

$$\alpha + \beta + \gamma = 1. \tag{2.31}$$

Barycentric coordinates seem like an abstract and unintuitive construct at first, but they turn out to be powerful and convenient. You may find it useful to think of how street addresses would work in a city where there were two sets of parallel streets, but where those sets were not at right angles. The natural system would essentially be barycentric coordinates, and you would quickly get used to them. Barycentric coordinates are defined for all points on the plane. A particularly nice feature of barycentric coordinates is that a point $\mathbf{p}$ is inside the triangle formed by $\mathbf{a}$, $\mathbf{b}$, and $\mathbf{c}$ if and only if

$$\begin{aligned} 0 &< \alpha < 1, \\ 0 &< \beta < 1, \\ 0 &< \gamma < 1. \end{aligned}$$

If one of the coordinates is zero and the other two are between zero and one, then you are on an edge. If two are zero, then the other is one, and you are at a vertex. Another nice property of barycentric coordinates is that Equation 2.30 in effect mixes the the coordinates of the three vertices in a smooth way. The same mixing coefficients (α, β, γ) can be used to mix other properties such as color, as we will see in the next chapter.

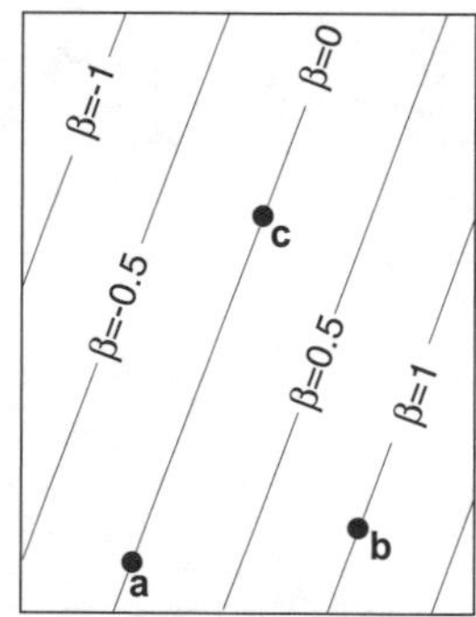

Figure 2.37. The barycentric coordinate β is the signed scaled distance from the line through **a** and **c**.

Given a point $\mathbf{p}$, how do we compute its barycentric coordinates? One way is to write Equation 2.29 as a linear system with unknowns β and γ, solve, and set $\alpha = 1 - \beta - \gamma$. That linear system is:

$$\begin{bmatrix} x_b - x_a & x_c - x_a \\ y_b - y_a & y_c - y_a \end{bmatrix} \begin{bmatrix} \beta \\ \gamma \end{bmatrix} = \begin{bmatrix} x_p - x_a \\ y_p - y_a \end{bmatrix}. \tag{2.32}$$

Although it is straightforward to solve Equation 2.32 algebraically, it is often fruitful to compute a direct geometric solution.

One geometric property of barycentric coordinates is that they are the signed scaled distance from the lines through the triangle sides, as is shown for β in Figure 2.37. Recall from Section 2.5.2 that evaluating the equation $f(x, y)$ for the line $f(x, y) = 0$ returns the scaled signed distance from (x, y) to the line. Also recall that if $f(x, y) = 0$ is the equation for a particular line, so is $kf(x, y) = 0$ for any non-zero k. Changing k scales the distance and controls which side of the line has positive signed distance, and which negative. We would like to choose k such that, for example, $kf(x, y) = \beta$.

Since k is only one unknown, we can force this with one constraint, namely that at point $\mathbf{b}$ we know $\beta = 1$. So if the line $f_{ac}(x, y) = 0$ goes through both $\mathbf{a}$ and $\mathbf{c}$, then we can compute β for a point (x, y) as follows:

$$\beta = \frac{f_{ac}(x, y)}{f_{ac}(x_b, y_b)}, \tag{2.33}$$

and we can compute γ and α in a similar fashion. For efficiency, it is usually wise to compute only two of the barycentric coordinates directly and to compute the third using Equation 2.31.

To find this "ideal" form for the line through $\mathbf{p}_0$ and $\mathbf{p}_1$, we can first use the technique of Section 2.5.2 to find *some* valid implicit lines through the vertices. Equation 2.18 gives us:

$$f_{ab}(x, y) \equiv (y_a - y_b)x + (x_b - x_a)y + x_a y_b - x_b y_a = 0.$$

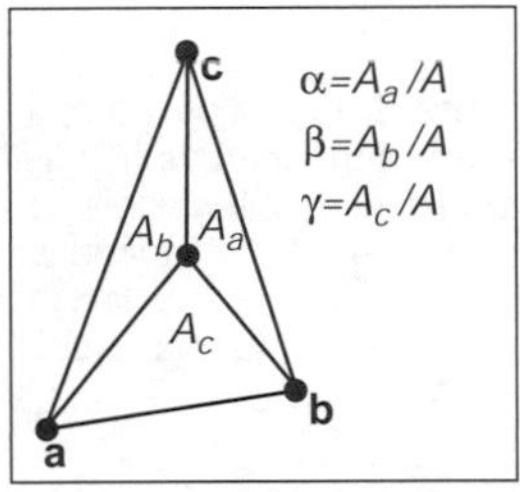

Figure 2.38. The barycentric coordinates are proportional to the areas of the three subtriangles shown.

Note that $f_{ab}(x_c, y_c)$ probably does not equal one, so it is probably not the ideal form we seek. By dividing through by $f_{ab}(x_c, y_c)$ we get:

$$\gamma = \frac{(y_a - y_b)x + (x_b - x_a)y + x_a y_b - x_b y_a}{(y_a - y_b)x_c + (x_b - x_a)y_c + x_a y_b - x_b y_a}.$$

The presence of the division might worry us because it introduces the possibility of divide-by-zero, but this cannot occur for triangles with areas that are not near zero. There are analogous formulas for α and β, but typically only one is needed:

$$\beta = \frac{(y_a - y_c)x + (x_c - x_a)y + x_a y_c - x_c y_a}{(y_a - y_c)x_b + (x_c - x_a)y_b + x_a y_c - x_c y_a},$$
$$\alpha = 1 - \beta - \gamma.$$

Another way to compute barycentric coordinates is to compute the areas A_a, A_b, and A_c, of subtriangles as shown in Figure 2.38. Barycentric coordinates obey the rule

$$\begin{aligned} \alpha &= A_a/A, \\ \beta &= A_b/A, \\ \gamma &= A_c/A, \end{aligned} \tag{2.34}$$

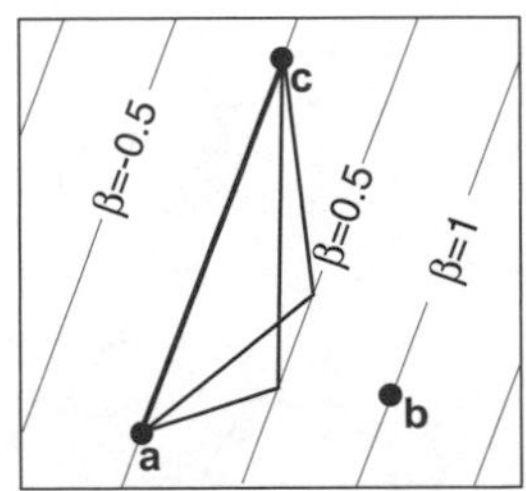

Figure 2.39. The area of the two triangles shown is base times height and are thus the same, as is any triangle with a vertex on the $\beta = 0.5$ line. The height and thus the area is proportional to β.

where A is the area of the triangle. Note that $A = A_a + A_b + A_c$, so it can be computed with two additions rather than a full area formula. This rule still holds for points outside the triangle if the areas are allowed to be signed. The reason for this is shown in Figure 2.39. Note that these are signed areas, and will be computed correctly as long as the same signed area computation is used for both A and the subtriangles A_a, A_b and A_c.

2.11.2 3D Triangles

One wonderful thing about barycentric coordinates is that they extend almost transparently to 3D. If we assume the points **a**, **b**, and **c** are 3D, then we can still use the representation:

$$\mathbf{p} = (1 - \beta - \gamma)\mathbf{a} + \beta\mathbf{b} + \gamma\mathbf{c}.$$

Now as we vary β and γ we sweep out a plane.

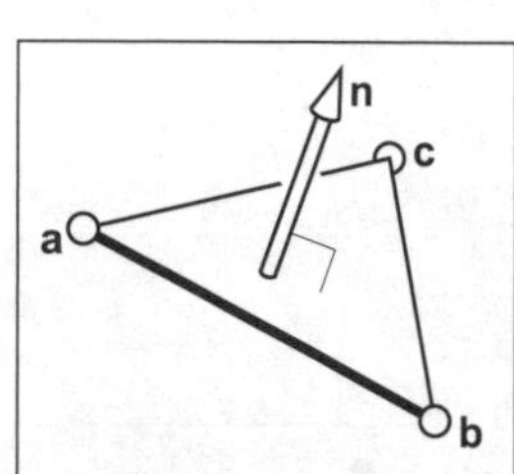

Figure 2.40. The normal vector of the triangle is perpendicular to all vectors in the plane of the triangle, and thus perpendicular to the edges of the triangle.

The normal vector to a triangle can be found by taking the cross product of any two vectors in the plane of the triangle (Figure 2.40). It is easiest to use two of the three edges as these vectors, for example:

$$\mathbf{n} = (\mathbf{b} - \mathbf{a}) \times (\mathbf{c} - \mathbf{a}). \tag{2.35}$$

Note that this normal vector is not necessarily of unit length, and it obeys the right hand rule of cross products.

The area of the triangle can be found by taking the length of the cross product:

$$\text{area} = \frac{1}{2}\|(\mathbf{b} - \mathbf{a}) \times (\mathbf{c} - \mathbf{a})\|. \tag{2.36}$$

Note that this is *not* a signed area, so it cannot be used directly to evaluate barycentric coordinates. However, we can observe that a triangle with a "clockwise" vertex order will have a normal vector that points in the opposite direction to the normal of a triangle in the same plane with a "counter-clockwise" vertex order. Recall that

$$\mathbf{a} \cdot \mathbf{b} = \|\mathbf{a}\| \; \|\mathbf{b}\| \; \cos\phi,$$

where ϕ is the angle between the vectors. If **a** and **b** are parallel, then $\cos\phi = \pm 1$, and this gives a test of whether the vectors point in the same or opposite directions. This, along with Equations 2.34, 2.35, and 2.36 suggest the formulas:

$$\alpha = \frac{\mathbf{n} \cdot \mathbf{n}_a}{\|\mathbf{n}\|^2},$$

$$\beta = \frac{\mathbf{n} \cdot \mathbf{n}_b}{\|\mathbf{n}\|^2},$$

$$\gamma = \frac{\mathbf{n} \cdot \mathbf{n}_c}{\|\mathbf{n}\|^2}$$

where **n** is Equation 2.35 evaluated with vertices **a**, **b**, and **c**; $\mathbf{n}_a$ is Equation 2.35 evaluated with vertices **b**, and **c**, and **p**, and so on, i.e.,

$$\begin{aligned}
\mathbf{n}_a &= (\mathbf{c} - \mathbf{b}) \times (\mathbf{p} - \mathbf{b}), \\
\mathbf{n}_b &= (\mathbf{a} - \mathbf{c}) \times (\mathbf{p} - \mathbf{c}), \\
\mathbf{n}_c &= (\mathbf{b} - \mathbf{a}) \times (\mathbf{p} - \mathbf{a}).
\end{aligned} \tag{2.37}$$

Frequently Asked Questions

- Why isn't there vector division?

It turns out that there is no "nice" analogy of division for vectors. However, it is possible to motivate the quaternions by examining this questions in detail (see Hoffman's book referenced in the chapter notes).

- Is there something as clean as barycentric coordinates for polygons with more than three sides?

Unfortunately there is not. Even convex quadrilaterals are much more complicated. This is one reason triangles are such a common geometric primitive in graphics.

- Is there an implicit form for 3D lines?

No. However, the intersection of two 3D planes defines a 3D line, so a 3D line can be described by two simultaneous implicit 3D equations.

Notes

The history of vector analysis is particularly interesting. It was largely invented by Grassman in the mid-1800s but was ignored and reinvented later as discussed in Crowe's *A History of Vector Analysis: The Evolution of the Idea of a Vectorial System* (Dover, 1994). Grassman now has a following in the graphics field of researchers who are developing *Geometric Algebra* based on some of his ideas. Readers interested in why the particular scaler and vector products are in some sense the right ones, and why we do not have a commonly-used vector division, will find enlightenment in Hoffman's concise *About Vectors* (Dover, 1977).

Exercises

1. The *cardinality* of a set is the number of elements it contains. Under IEEE floating point representation (Section 1.6), what is the cardinality of the *floats*?

2. Is it possible to implement a function that maps 32-bit integers to 64-bit integers that has a well defined inverse? Do all functions from 32-bit integers to 64-bit integers have well defined inverses?

3. Specify the unit cube (x, y, and z coordinates all between 0 and 1 inclusive) in terms of the Cartesian product of three intervals.

4. If you have access to the natural log function $\ln(x)$, specify how you could use it to implement a $\log(b, x)$ function where b is the base of the log. What should the function do for negative b values? Assume an IEEE floating point implementation.

5. Solve the quadratic equation $4x^2 - 6x + 9 = 0$.

6. Implement a function that takes in coefficients A, B, and C for the quadratic equation $Ax^2+By+C = 0$ and computes the two solutions. Have the function return the number of valid (not NaN) solutions and fill in the return arguments so the smaller of the two solutions is first.

7. Show by brute-force computation that for 3D vectors $\mathbf{a}$, $\mathbf{b}$, and $\mathbf{c}$, $a \times (b \times c) = (a \times b) \times c$.

8. Show that for three 3D vectors $\mathbf{a}$, $\mathbf{b}$, $\mathbf{c}$, the following identity holds: $|\mathbf{abc}| = (\mathbf{a} \times \mathbf{b}) \cdot \mathbf{c}$.

9. Given the non-parallel 3D vectors $\mathbf{a}$ and $\mathbf{b}$, compute a right-handed orthonormal basis such that $\mathbf{u}$ is parallel to $\mathbf{a}$ and $\mathbf{c}$ is normal to the planes defined by $\mathbf{a}$ and $\mathbf{b}$.

10. What is the gradient of $f(x, y, z) = x^2 + y - 3z^3$?

11. What is a parametric form for the axis-aligned 2D ellipse?

12. What is the implicit equation of the plane through 3D points $(1, 0, 0)$, $(0, 1, 0)$, and $(0, 0, 1)$? What is the parametric equation? What is the normal vector to this plane?

13. Given four 2D points $\mathbf{a}_0$, $\mathbf{a}_1$, $\mathbf{b}_0$, and $\mathbf{b}_1$, design a robust procedure to determine whether the line segments $\mathbf{a}_0\mathbf{a}_1$ and $\mathbf{b}_0\mathbf{b}_1$ intersect.

14. Design a robust procedure to compute the barycentric coordinates of a 2D point with respect to three 2D non-colinear points.

Raster Algorithms

Most computer graphics images are presented to the user on a *raster* display. Such systems show images as rectangular arrays of *pixels*, which is short for "picture elements." These pixels are set using RGB (red-green-blue) color. In this chapter, we discuss the basics of raster displays, emphasizing the RGB color system and the non-linearities of standard image display.

3.1 Raster Displays

There are a variety of display technologies for desktop and projected display. These displays vary in *resolution* (the number of pixels) and physical size. Programmers can usually assume that the pixels are laid out in a rectangular array, also called a *raster*.

3.1.1 Pixels

Each displayable element in a raster display is called a *pixel*. Displays usually index pixels by an ordered pair (i, j) indicating the row and column of the pixel. If a display has n_x columns and n_y rows of pixels, the bottom-left element is pixel $(0, 0)$ and the top-right is pixel $(n_x - 1, n_y - 1)$.[1]

[1] In many APIs the rows of an image will be addressed in the less intuitive manner from the top-to-bottom, so the top-left pixel has coordinates $(0, 0)$. This convention is common for historical reasons; it is the order that rows come in a standard television transmission.

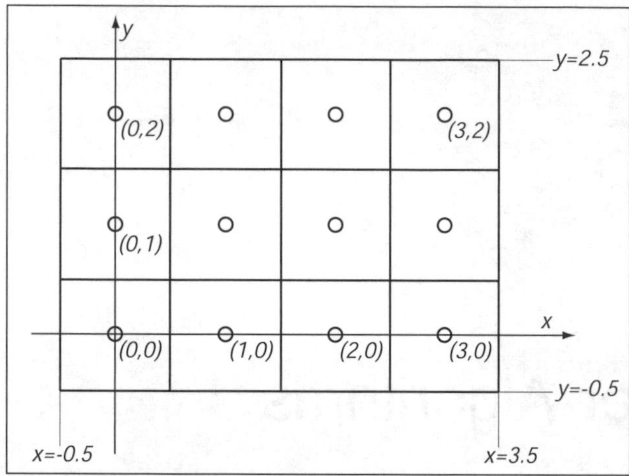

Figure 3.1. Coordinates of a four pixel by three pixel screen. Note that in some APIs the *y*-axis will point downwards.

We need 2D real screen coordinates to specify pixel positions. The details of such systems vary among APIs, but the most common is to use the integer lattice for pixel centers, as shown by the 4 by 3 screen in Figure 3.1. Because pixels have finite extent, note the 0.5 unit overshoot from the pixel centers.

Physical pixels, i.e., the actual displayed elements in hardware, will vary in shape from system to system. In *CRTs* (cathode ray systems) , the pixel is associated with a patch of phosphor in the CRT, and this phosphor glows based on how much an electron beam stimulates the phosphor. The shape of the pixel depends both on the details of how the electron beam sweeps the pixel, as well as the details of how the phosphor is distributed in the monitor. As a first approximation, we can assume the phosphor will have a "blobby" shape on the screen, with the highest intensity in the center, and a gradual falloff toward the sides of the pixel. On an LCD (liquid crystal display) system, the pixels are approximately square filters which vary their opacity to darken a backlight. These pixels are almost perfect squares, and there is a small gap between squares to allow the control circuitry to get to the pixels. Most display systems other than CRTs or LCDs will behave somewhat like these two, with either blobby or square pixels.

3.2 Monitor Intensities and Gamma

All modern monitors take digital input for the "value" of a pixel and convert this to an intensity level. Real monitors have some non-zero intensity when they are off because the screen reflects some light. For our purposes we can consider this "black" and the monitor fully on as "white." We assume a numeric description of pixel color that ranges from zero to one. Black is zero, white is one, and a grey halfway between black and white is 0.5. Note that here "halfway" refers to the physical amount of light coming from the pixel, rather than the appearance. The human perception of intensity is non-linear, and will not be part of the present discussion.

There are two key issues that must be understood to produce images on monitors. The first is that monitors are non-linear with respect to input. For example, if you give a monitor 0, 0.5, and 1.0 as inputs for three pixels, the intensities displayed might be 0, 0.25, and 1.0 (i.e., zero, one-quarter fully on, and fully on). As an approximate characterization of this non-linearity, most monitors are characterized by a γ ("gamma") value. This value is the degree of freedom in the formula:

$$\text{displayed intensity} = (\text{maximum intensity})a^{\gamma}, \tag{3.1}$$

where a is the input intensity between zero and one. For example, if a monitor has a gamma of 2.0, and we input a value of $a = 0.5$, the displayed intensity will be one fourth the maximum possible intensity because $0.5^2 = 0.25$. Note that $a = 0$ maps to zero intensity and $a = 1$ maps to the maximum intensity regardless of the value of γ. Describing a display's non-linearity using γ is just a first-order approximation; we do not need a great deal of accuracy in estimating the γ of a device. A nice visual way to gauge the non-linearity is to find what value of a gives an intensity halfway between black and white. This a will be:

$$0.5 = a^{\gamma}.$$

If we can find that a, we can deduce γ by taking logs of both sides which yields:

$$\gamma = \frac{\ln 0.5}{\ln a}.$$

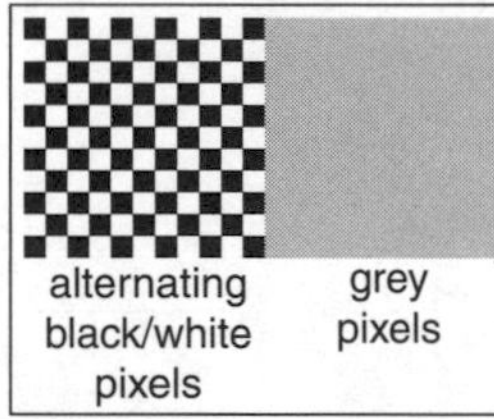

Figure 3.2. Alternating black and white pixels viewed from a distance are halfway between black and white. The gamma of a monitor can be inferred by finding a grey value that appears to have the same intensity as the black and white pattern.

We can find this a by a standard technique where we display a checkerboard pattern of black and white pixels next to a square of grey pixels with input a (Figure 3.2). When you look at this image from a distance (or without glasses if you are nearsighted), the two sides of the image will look about the same when a is halfway between black and white. This is because the blurred checkerboard is mixing even numbers of white and black pixels so the overall effect is a uniform color halfway between white and black. To make this work, we must be able to try many values for a until one matches. This can be done by giving the user a slider to control a, or using many different gray squares simultaneously against a large checkered region. Note that for CRTs, which have difficulty rapidly changing intensity along the horizontal direction, horizontal black and white stripes will work better than a checkerboard.

Once we know γ, we can *gamma correct* our input so that a value of $a = 0.5$ is displayed with intensity halfway between black and white. This is done with the transformation:

$$a = a^{\frac{1}{\gamma}}.$$

When this formula is plugged into Equation 3.1 we get:

$$\begin{aligned} \text{displayed intensity} &= \left(a^{\frac{1}{\gamma}}\right)^{\gamma} (\text{maximum intensity}) \\ &= a(\text{maximum intensity}). \end{aligned}$$

Another important characteristic of real displays is that they usually take quantized input values. So while we can manipulate intensities in the floating point range $[0, 1]$, the detailed input to a monitor is usually a fixed-size non-negative integer. The most common range for this integer is 0–255 which can be held in 8 bits of storage. This means that the possible values for a are not any number in $[0, 1]$ but instead:

$$\text{possible values for } a = \left\{ \frac{0}{255}, \frac{1}{255}, \frac{2}{255}, \ldots, \frac{254}{255}, \frac{255}{255} \right\}$$

This means the possible displayed intenity values are approximately:

$$\left\{ M\left(\frac{0}{255}\right)^{\gamma}, M\left(\frac{1}{255}\right)^{\gamma}, M\left(\frac{2}{255}\right)^{\gamma}, \ldots, M\left(\frac{254}{255}\right)^{\gamma}, M\left(\frac{255}{255}\right)^{\gamma} \right\},$$

where M is the maximum intensity. In applications where the exact intensities need to be controlled, we would have to actually measure the 256 possible intensities, and these intensities might be different at different points on the screen, especially for CRTs. They might also vary with viewing angle. Fortunately few applications require such accurate calibration.

3.3 RGB Color

Most computer graphics images are defined in terms of red-green-blue (RGB) color. RGB color is a simple space that allows straightforward conversion to the controls for most computer screens. In this section RGB color is discussed from a user's perspective, and operational facility is the goal. A more thorough discussion of color is given in Chapter 18, but the mechanics of RGB color space will allow us to write most graphics programs. The basic idea of RGB color space is that the color is displayed by mixing three *primary* lights, one red, one green, and one blue. The lights mix in an *additive* manner. Additive color mixing is fundamentally different from the more familiar *subtractive* color mixing that governs the mixing of paints and crayons. In those familiar media, red, yellow, and blue are the primaries, and they mix in familiar ways, such as yellow mixed with blue is green. In RGB additive color mixing we have (Figure 3.3):

$$\begin{aligned} \text{red} + \text{green} &= \text{yellow} \\ \text{green} + \text{blue} &= \text{cyan} \\ \text{blue} + \text{red} &= \text{magenta} \\ \text{red} + \text{green} + \text{blue} &= \text{white}. \end{aligned}$$

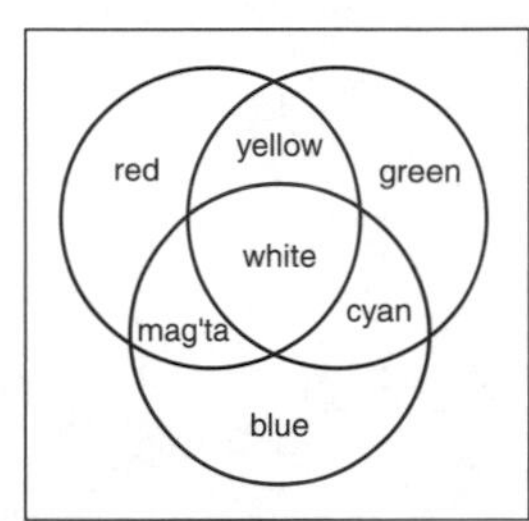

Figure 3.3. The additive mixing rules for colors red/green/blue.

The color "cyan" is a blue-green, and the color "magenta" is a purple.

If we are allowed to dim the primary lights from fully off to fully on, we can create all the colors that can be displayed on an RGB monitor. By convention, we write a color as the fraction of "fully on" it is for each monitor. This creates a three-dimensional *RGB color cube* that has a red, a green, and a blue axis. Allowable coordinates for the axes range from zero to one. The color cube is shown graphically in Figure 3.4.

The RGB coordinates of familiar colors are:

$$\begin{aligned} \text{black} &= (0,0,0) \\ \text{red} &= (1,0,0) \\ \text{green} &= (0,1,0) \\ \text{blue} &= (0,0,1) \\ \text{yellow} &= (1,1,0) \\ \text{magenta} &= (1,0,1) \\ \text{cyan} &= (0,1,1) \\ \text{white} &= (1,1,1). \end{aligned}$$

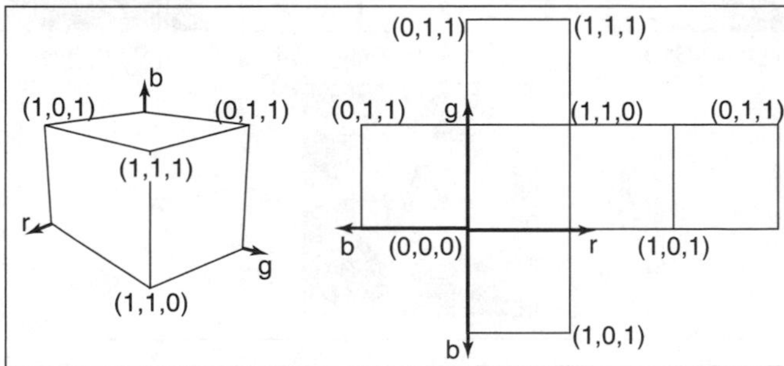

Figure 3.4. The RGB color cube in 3D and its faces unfolded. Any RGB color is a point in the cube. (See also Plate VII.)

Actual RGB levels are often given in quantized form, just like the greyscales discussed in Section 3.2. Each component is specified with an integer. The most common size for these integers in one byte each, so each of the three RGB components is an integer between 0 and 255. The three integers together take up three bytes, which is 24 bits. Thus a system that has "24 bit color" has 256 possible levels for each of the three primary colors. Issues of gamma correction discussed in Section 3.2 also apply to each RGB component separately.

3.4 The Alpha Channel

Often we would like to only partially overwrite the contents of a pixel. A common example of this occurs in *compositing*, where we have a background and want to insert a foreground image over it. For opaque pixels in the foreground, we just replace the background pixel. For entirely transparent foreground pixels, we do not change the background pixel. For *partially* transparent pixels, some care must be taken. Partially transparent pixels can occur when the foreground object has partially transparent regions such as glass, or when there are sub-pixel holes in the foreground object such as in the leaves of a distant tree. To blend foreground and background in the case of holes, we want to measure the fraction of the pixel that should be foreground. We can call this fraction α. If we want to

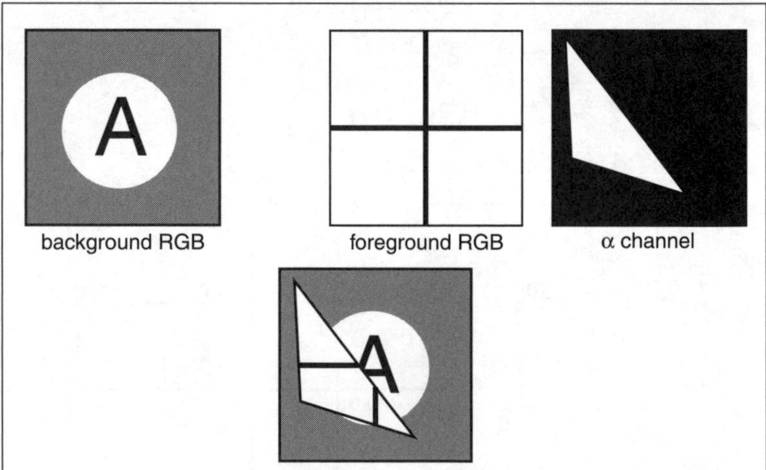

Figure 3.5. An example of compositing using Equation 3.2. The foreground image is in effect cropped by the α channel before being put on top of the background image. The resulting composite is shown on the bottom.

composite a foreground color $\mathbf{c}_f$ over background color $\mathbf{c}_b$, and the fraction of the pixel covered by foreground is α, then we can use the formula:

$$\mathbf{c} = \alpha\mathbf{c}_f + (1-\alpha)\mathbf{c}_b \tag{3.2}$$

An example of using Equation 3.2 is shown in Figure 3.5. Note that the α image might be stored with the RGB image, or might be stored as a separate greyscale (single channel) image.

Although Equation 3.2 is what is usually used, there are a variety of situations where α is used differently. See the chapter notes for the classic reference on compositing by Porter and Duff.

3.5 Line Drawing

Most graphics packages contain a line drawing command that takes two endpoints in screen coodinates (Figure 3.1) and draws a line between them. For example, the call for endpoints (1,1) and (3,2) would turn on pixels (1,1) and (3,2) and fill in one pixel between them. For general screen coordinate endpoints (x_0, y_0) and (x_1, y_1), the routine should draw some "reasonable" set of pixels that approximate a line between them. The values x_0, x_1, y_0, y_1 are usually restricted to be integers (pixel centers) for simplicity, and because the lines themselves are coarse enough entities that subpixel accuracy is not appropriate. If you are implementing an API which calls for real number endpoint coordinates, rounding them to the nearest integer is usually a reasonable strategy that application programmers are unlikely to notice. Because the endpoint coordinates are integers, care should be taken to understand implicit conversions when these integers interact with floating point variables. Drawing such lines is based on line equations, and we have two types of equations to choose from: implicit and parametric. This section describes the two algorithms that result from these two types of equations.

3.5.1 Line Drawing Using Implicit Line Equations

The most common way to draw lines using implicit equations is the *midpoint* algorithm. The midpoint algorithm ends up drawing the same lines as the *Bresenham algorithm* but is somewhat more straightforward.

The first thing to do is find the implicit equation for the line as discussed in Section 2.5.2:

$$f(x,y) \equiv (y_0 - y_1)x + (x_1 - x_0)y + x_0y_1 - x_1y_0 = 0. \tag{3.3}$$

We assume that $x_0 \leq x_1$. If that is not true, we swap the points so that it is true. The slope m of the line is given by:

$$m = \frac{y_1 - y_0}{x_1 - x_0}.$$

The following discussion assumes $m \in (0, 1]$. Analogous discussions can be derived for $m \in (-\infty, -1]$, $m \in (-1, 0]$, and $m \in (1, \infty)$. The four cases cover all possibilities.

For the case $m \in (0, 1]$, there is more "run" than "rise", i.e., the line is moving faster in x than in y. If we have an API where the y-axis points downwards, we might have a concern about whether this makes the process harder, but, in fact, we can ignore that detail. We can ignore the geometric notions of "up" and "down," because the algebra is exactly the same for the two cases. Cautious readers can confirm that the resulting algorithm works for the y-axis downwards case. The key assumption of the midpoint algorithm is that we draw the thinnest line possible that has no gaps. A diagonal connection between two pixels is not considered a gap.

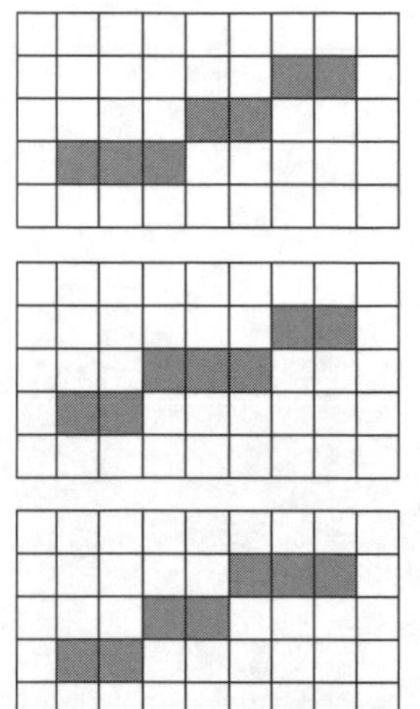

Figure 3.6. Three "reasonable" lines that go seven pixels horizontally and three pixels vertically.

As the line progresses from the left endpoint to the right, there are only two possibilities: draw a pixel at the same height as the pixel drawn to its left, or draw a pixel one higher. There will always be exactly one pixel in each column of pixels between the endpoints. Zero would imply a gap, and two would be too thick a line. There may be two pixels in the same row for the case we are considering; the line is more horizontal than vertical so sometimes it will go right, and sometimes up. This concept is shown in Figure 3.6, where three "reasonable" lines are shown, each advancing more in the horizontal direction than in the vertical direction.

The midpoint algorithm for $m \in (0, 1]$ first establishes the leftmost pixel and the column number (x-value) of the rightmost pixel and then loops horizontally establishing the row (y-value) of each pixel. The basic form of the algorithm is:

$y = y_0$
for $x = x_0$ *to* x_1 ***do***
  draw(x, y)
  if (*some condition*) ***then***
    $y = y + 1$

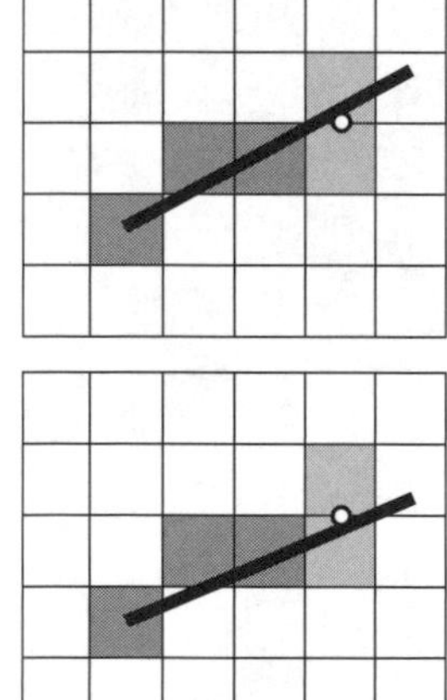

Figure 3.7. Top: the line goes above the midpoint so the top pixel is drawn. Bottom: the line goes below the midpoint so the bottom pixel is drawn.

Note that x and y are integers. In words this says, "keep drawing pixels from left-to-right and sometimes move upwards in the y direction while doing so." The key is to establish efficient ways to make the decision in the *if* statement.

An effective way to make the choice is to look at the *midpoint* of the line between the two potential pixel centers. More specifically, the pixel just drawn is pixel (x, y) whose center in real screen coordinates is at (x, y). The candidate pixels to be drawn to the right are pixels $(x + 1, y)$ and $(x+1, y+1)$.The midpoint between the centers of the two candidate pixels is $(x+1, y+0.5)$. If the line passes below this midpoint we draw the bottom pixel, and otherwise we draw the top pixel (Figure 3.7).

To decide whether the line passes above or below $(x + 1, y + 0.5)$, we evaluate $f(x, y+0.5)$ in Equation 3.3. Recall from Section 2.5 that $f(x, y) =$

0 for points (x, y) on the line, $f(x, y) > 0$ for points on one side of the line, and $f(x, y) < 0$ for points on the other side of the line. Because $-f(x, y) = 0$ and $f(x, y) = 0$ are both perfectly good equations for the line, it is not immediately clear whether $f(x, y)$ being positive indicates that (x, y) is above the line, or whether it is below. However, we can figure it out; the key term in Equation 3.3 is the y term $(x_1 - x_0)y$. Note that $(x_1 - x_0)$ is definitely positive because $x_1 > x_0$. This means that as y increases, the term $(x_1 - x_0)y$ gets larger (i.e., more positive or less negative). Thus, the case $f(x, +\infty)$ is definitely positive, and definitely above the line, implying points above the line are all positive. Another way to look at it is that the y component of the gradient vector is positive. So above the line, where y can increase arbitrarily, $f(x, y)$ must be positive. This means we can make our code more specific by filling in the *if* statement:

```
if f(x + 1, y + 0.5) < 0 then
   y = y + 1
```

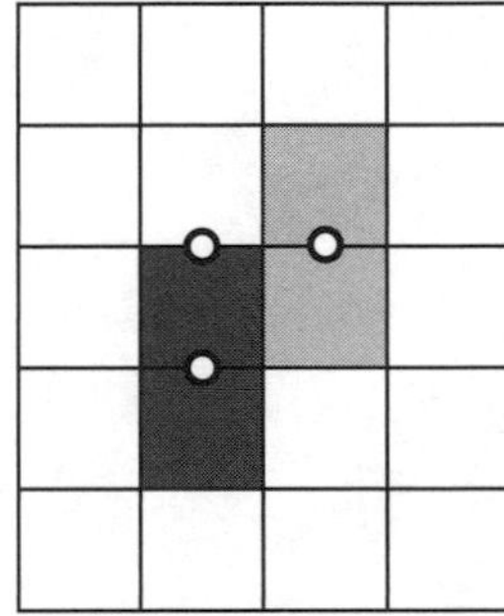

Figure 3.8. When using the decision point shown between the two light grey pixels, we just drew one of the dark grey pixels, so we evaluated f at one of the two left points shown.

The above code will work nicely for lines of the appropriate slope (i.e., between zero and one). The reader can work out the other three cases which differ only in small details.

If greater efficiency is desired, using an *incremental* method can help. An incremental method tries to make a loop more efficient by reusing computation from the previous step. In the midpoint algorithm as presented, the main computation is the evaluation of $f(x+1, y+0.5)$. Note that inside the loop, after the first iteration, either we already evaluated $f(x-1, y+0.5)$ or $f(x-1, y-0.5)$ (Figure 3.8). Note also this relationship:

$$f(x + 1, y) = f(x, y) + (y_0 - y_1)$$
$$f(x + 1, y + 1) = f(x, y) + (y_0 - y_1) + (x_1 - x_0).$$

This allows us to write an incremental version of the code:

```
y = y0
d = f(x0 + 1, y0 + 0.5)
for x = x0 to x1 do
   draw(x, y)
   if d < 0 then
      y = y + 1
      d = d + (x1 − x0) + (y0 − y1)
   else
      d = d + (y0 − y1)
```

This code should run faster since it has little extra setup cost compared to the non-incremental version (that is not always true for incremental algorithms), but it may accumulate more numeric error because the evaluation of $f(x, y + 0.5)$ may be composed of many adds for long lines. However, given that lines are rarely longer than a few thousand pixels, such error is unlikely to be critical. Slightly longer setup cost, but faster loop execution, can be achieved by storing $(x_1 - x_0) + (y_0 - y_1)$ and $(y_0 - y_1)$ as variables. We might hope a good compiler would do that for us, but if the code is critical, it would be wise to examine the results of compilation to make sure.

In some cases, it is faster if an algorithm uses only integer operations. Because we have imposed the constraint that x_0, x_1, y_0, y_1 are all integers, the algorithm above is almost an integer-only algorithm. However, it does require the initialization $d = f(x_0 + 1, y_0 + 0.5)$. Note that this can be expanded as:

$$f(x_0 + 1, y_0 + 0.5) = (y_0 - y_1)(x_0 + 1) + (x_1 - x_0)(y_0 + 0.5) + x_0 y_1 - x_1 y_0.$$

The $y_0 + 0.5$ is not an integer operation, and results in a non-integer multiplier. But we can fix this: if $f(x, y) = 0$ is the equation of the line, then $2f(x, y) = 0$ is also a valid equation for the same line. So if we use $2f(x, y)$ instead of $f(x, y)$, the expression for d becomes:

$$\begin{aligned} 2f(x_0 + 1, y_0 + 0.5) = {} & 2(y_0 - y_1)(x_0 + 1) + (x_1 - x_0)(2y_0 + 1) \\ & + 2x_0 y_1 - 2x_1 y_0, \end{aligned}$$

which has all integer terms. The resulting code is:

```
y = y0
d = 2(y0 − y1)(x0 + 1) + (x1 − x0)(2y0 + 1) + 2x0y1 − 2x1y0
for x = x0 to x1 do
  draw(x, y)
  if d < 0 then
    y = y + 1
    d = d + 2(x1 − x0) + 2(y0 − y1)
  else
    d = d + 2(y0 − y1)
```

The careful reader will note that before we can execute the all-integer code above, we must check whether $m \in [0, 1)$, and explicitely computing m requires a divide. However, the following code, which is equivalent to the explicit slope check, can be used:

$$((y_1 \geq y_0) \text{ and } (x_1 - x_0 > y_1 - y_0)) \quad \equiv \quad (m \in [0, 1))$$

3.5.2 Line Drawing Using Parametric Line Equations

As derived in Section 2.6.1 a parametric line in 2D that goes through points $\mathbf{p}_0 = (x_0, y_0)$ and $\mathbf{p}_1 = (x_1, y_1)$ can be written:

$$\begin{bmatrix} x \\ y \end{bmatrix} = \begin{bmatrix} x_0 + t(x_1 - x_0) \\ y_0 + t(y_1 - y_0) \end{bmatrix},$$

or equivalently in vector form:

$$\mathbf{p}(t) = \mathbf{p}_0 + t(\mathbf{p}_1 - \mathbf{p}_0).$$

If the slope of the line $m \in [-1, 1]$ then the "for" loop can advance in x and we get remarkably compact code. A similar algorithm results for m outside $[-1, 1]$, so only two cases are needed. Because t progresses constantly along the distance of the line, so do the x and y components of the line; thus, we can compute t as a function of x:

$$t = \frac{x - x_0}{x_1 - x_0}.$$

The resulting code is:

$$
\begin{aligned}
&\textbf{\textit{for}}\ x = x_0\ \textit{to}\ x_1\ \textbf{\textit{do}}\\
&\quad t = (x - x_0)/(x_1 - x_0)\\
&\quad y = y_0 + t(y_1 - y_0)\\
&\quad \textit{draw}(x, \textit{round}(y))
\end{aligned}
$$

A nice property of this algorithm is that it works whether or not $x_1 > x_0$. So the code for parametric lines turns out to be very simple. However, it cannot be made integer-only as we shall see. In many computer languages, conversion from float to integer is implemented as truncation, so the term round(y) can be implemented as an integer conversion of $(y + 0.5)$.

This code can also be made incremental because t and therefore y change by a constant amount in each iteration:

$$
\begin{aligned}
&\Delta y = (y_1 - y_0)/(x_1 - x_0)\\
&y = y_0\\
&\textbf{\textit{for}}\ x = x_0\ \textit{to}\ x_1\ \textbf{\textit{do}}\\
&\quad \textit{draw}(x, \textit{round}(y))\\
&\quad y = y + \Delta y
\end{aligned}
$$

Sometimes lines are specified with RGB colors $\mathbf{c}_0$ and $\mathbf{c}_1$ at either end, and we would like to change the color smoothly along the line. If we can parameterize the line segment in terms of a $t \in [0, 1]$, we can use the formula

$$\mathbf{c} = (1 - t)\mathbf{c}_0 + t\mathbf{c}_1.$$

This allows us to compute a color at each pixel. An example of such a colored line which shifts from red to green is shown in Figure 3.9. Note that the expression for $\mathbf{c}$ and for t can also be computed incrementally if desired. The code for this would be:

$$
\begin{aligned}
&\Delta y = (y_1 - y_0)/(x_1 - x_0)\\
&\Delta r = (r_1 - r_0)/(x_1 - x_0)\\
&\Delta g = (g_1 - g_0)/(x_1 - x_0)\\
&\Delta b = (b_1 - b_0)/(x_1 - x_0)
\end{aligned}
$$

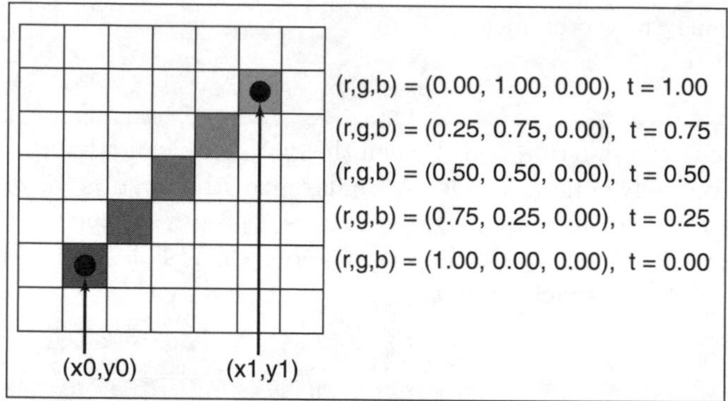

Figure 3.9. A colored line switching from red to green. The middle pixel is half red and half green which is a "dark yellow". (See also Plate V.)

$y = y_0$, $r = r_0$, $g = g_0$, $b = b_0$
for $x = x_0$ *to* x_1 ***do***
  $draw(x, round(y), r, g, b)$
  $y = y + \Delta y$
  $r = r + \Delta r$
  $g = g + \Delta g$
  $b = b + \Delta b$

A similar change can be made to the midpoint (implicit) algorithm, but it would be difficult to do using only integer operations. In infrastructures where floating point division is expensive, the four divides above can be replaced by one divide and four multiplies.

3.6 Triangle Rasterization

We often want to draw a 2D triangle with 2D points $\mathbf{p}_0 = (x_0, y_0)$, $\mathbf{p}_1 = (x_1, y_1)$, and $\mathbf{p}_2 = (x_2, y_2)$ in screen coordinates. This is similar to the line drawing problem, but it has some of its own subtleties. It will turn out that there is no advantage to integer coordinates for endpoints, so we will allow the (x_i, y_i) to have floating point values. As with line drawing, we may wish to interpolate color or other properties from values at the vertices. This is straightforward if we have the barycentric coordinates (Section 2.11). For example, if the vertices have colors $\mathbf{c}_0$, $\mathbf{c}_1$, and $\mathbf{c}_2$, the color at a point in the triangle with barycentric coordinates (α, β, γ) is:

$$\mathbf{c} = \alpha\mathbf{c}_0 + \beta\mathbf{c}_1 + \gamma\mathbf{c}_2$$

This type of interpolation of color is known in graphics as *Gouraud* interpolation after its inventor.

Another subtlety of rasterizing triangles is that we are usually rasterizing triangles that share vertices and edges. This means we would like to rasterize adjacent triangles so there are no holes. We could do this by using the midpoint algorithm to draw the outline of each triangle, and then fill in the interior pixels. This would mean adjacent triangles both draw the same pixels along each edge. If the adjacent triangles have different colors, the image will depend on the order in which the two triangles are drawn. The most common way to rasterize triangles that avoids the order problem and eliminates holes is to use the convention that pixels are drawn if and only if their centers are inside the triangle, i.e., the barycentric coordinates of the pixel center are all in the interval $(0, 1)$. This raises the issue of what to do if the center is exactly on the edge of the triangle. There are several ways to handle this as will be discussed later in this section. The key observation is that barycentric coordinates allow us to decide whether to draw a pixel, and what color that pixel should be if we are interpolating colors from the vertices. So our problem of rasterizing the triangle boils down to efficiently finding the barycentric coordinates of pixel centers. The brute-force rasterization algorithm is:

for** all x **do
    for** all y **do
        compute (α, β, γ) *for* (x, y)
        if $(\alpha \in [0, 1]$ *and* $\beta \in [0, 1]$ *and* $\gamma \in [0, 1])$ ***then***
            $\mathbf{c} = \alpha\mathbf{c}_0 + \beta\mathbf{c}_1 + \gamma\mathbf{c}_2$
            drawpixel (x, y) *with color* $\mathbf{c}$

The rest of the algorithm limits the outer loops to a smaller set of candidate pixels and makes the barycentric computation efficient.

We can add a simple efficiency by finding the bounding rectangle of the three vertices and only looping over this rectangle for candidate pixels to draw. We can compute barycentric coordinates using Equation 2.33. This yields the algorithm:

$x_{min} =$ *floor* (x_i)
$x_{max} =$ *ceiling* (x_i)
$y_{min} =$ *floor* (y_i)
$y_{max} =$ *ceiling* (y_i)
for $y = y_{min}$ *to* y_{max} ***do***
    for $x = x_{min}$ *to* x_{max} ***do***
        $\alpha = f_{12}(x, y)/f_{12}(x_0, y_0)$
        $\beta = f_{20}(x, y)/f_{20}(x_1, y_1)$
        $\gamma = f_{01}(x, y)/f_{01}(x_2, y_2)$
        if $(\alpha > 0$ *and* $\beta > 0$ *and* $\gamma > 0)$ ***then***
            $\mathbf{c} = \alpha\mathbf{c}_0 + \beta\mathbf{c}_1 + \gamma\mathbf{c}_2$
            drawpixel (i, j) *with color* $\mathbf{c}$

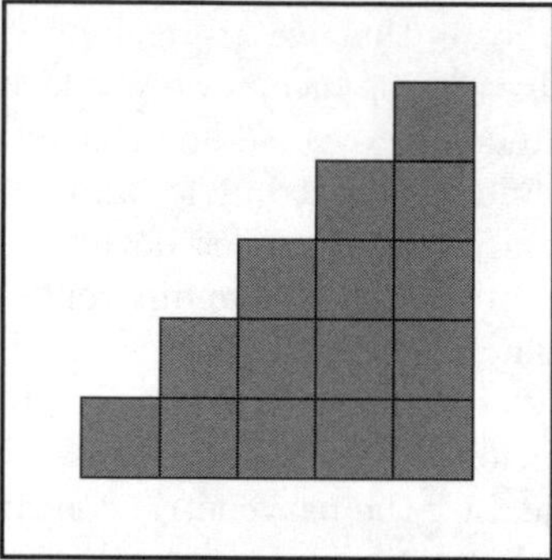

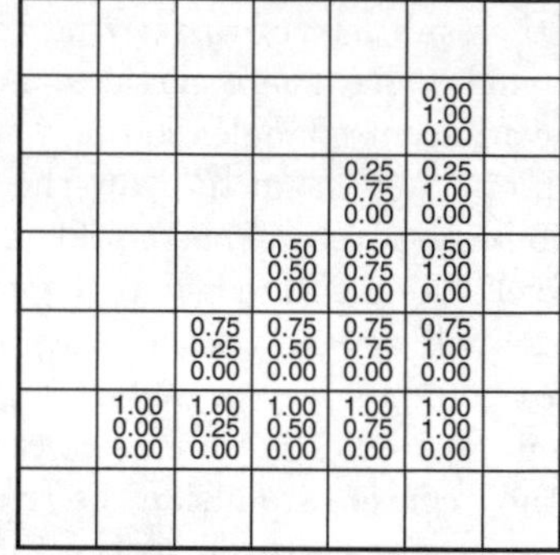

Figure 3.10. A colored triangle with barycentric interpolation. Note that the changes in color components are linear in each row and column as well as along each edge. In fact it is constant along every line, such as the diagonals, as well. (See also Plate VI.)

Here f_{ij} is the line given by Equation 3.3 with the appropriate vertices:

$$\begin{aligned} f_{01}(x, y) &= (y_0 - y_1)x + (x_1 - x_0)y + x_0 y_1 - x_1 y_0, \\ f_{12}(x, y) &= (y_1 - y_2)x + (x_2 - x_1)y + x_1 y_2 - x_2 y_1, \\ f_{20}(x, y) &= (y_2 - y_0)x + (x_0 - x_2)y + x_2 y_0 - x_0 y_2. \end{aligned}$$

Note that we have exchanged the test $\alpha \in (0, 1)$ with $\alpha > 0$ etc., because if all of α, β, γ are positive, then we know they are all less than one because $\alpha + \beta + \gamma = 1$. We could also compute only two of the three barycentric variables and get the third from that relation, but it is not clear that this saves computation once the algorithm is made incremental, which is possible as in the line drawing algorithms; each of the computations of α, β, and γ does an evaluation of the form $f(x, y) = Ax + By + C$. In the inner loop, only x changes, and it changes by one. Note that $f(x + 1, y) = f(x, y) + A$. This is the basis of the incremental algorithm. In the outer loop, the evaluation changes for $f(x, y)$ to $f(x, y+1)$, so a similar efficiency can be achieved. Because α, β, and γ change by constant increments in the loop, so does the color $\mathbf{c}$. So this can be made incremental as well. For example, the red value for pixel $(x + 1, y)$ differs from the red value for pixel (x, y) by a constant amount that can be precomputed. An example of a triangle with color interpolation is shown in Figure 3.10.

3.6.1 Dealing With Pixels on Triangle Edges

We have still not discussed what to do for pixels whose centers are exactly on the edge of a triangle. If a pixel is exactly on the edge of a triangle, then it is also on the edge of the adjacent triangle if there is one. There is no obvious way to award the pixel to one triangle or the other. The worst decision would be to not draw the pixel because a hole would result between the two triangles. Better, but still not good, would be to have both triangles draw the pixel. If the triangles are transparent, this will result in a double-coloring. We would really like to award the pixel to exactly one of the triangles, and we would like this process to be simple; which triangle is chosen does not matter as long as the choice is well defined.

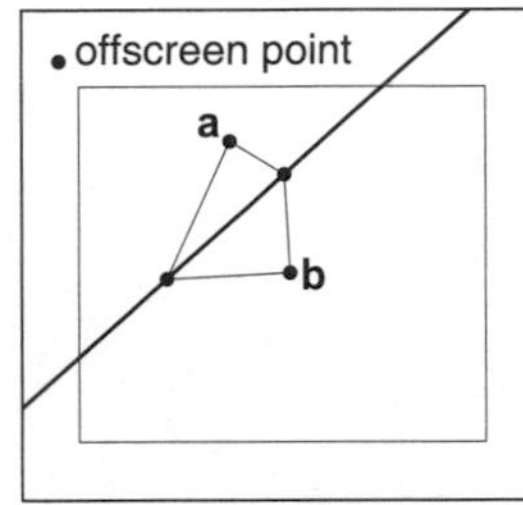

Figure 3.11. The offscreen point will be on one side of the triangle edge or the other. Exactly one of the non-shared vertices **a** and **b** will be on the same side.

One approach is to note that any off-screen point is definitely on exactly one side of the shared edge and that is the edge we will draw. For two non-overlapping triangles, the vertices not on the edge are on opposite sides of the edge from each other. Exactly one of these vertices will be on the same side of the edge as the off-screen point (Figure 3.11). This is the basis of the test. The test if numbers a and b have the same sign can be implemented as the test $ab > 0$, which is very efficient in most environments. Note that the test is not perfect because the line through the edge may also go through the offscreen point, but we have at least greatly reduced the number of problematic cases. Which off-screen point is used is arbitrary, and $(x, y) = (-1, -1)$ is as good a choice as any. We will need to add a check for the case of a point exactly on an edge. We would like this check not to be reached for common cases, which are the completely inside or outside tests. This suggests:

$x_{min} = \mathit{floor}\ (x_i)$
$x_{max} = \mathit{ceiling}\ (x_i)$
$y_{min} = \mathit{floor}\ (y_i)$
$y_{max} = \mathit{ceiling}\ (y_i)$
$f_\alpha = f_{12}(x_0, y_0)$
$f_\beta = f_{20}(x_1, y_1)$
$f_\gamma = f_{01}(x_2, y_2)$
for $y = y_{min}$ *to* y_{max} **do**
  for $x = x_{min}$ *to* x_{max} **do**
    $\alpha = f_{12}(x, y)/f_\alpha$
    $\beta = f_{20}(x, y)/f_\beta$
    $\gamma = f_{01}(x, y)/f_\gamma$
    if $(\alpha \geq 0$ *and* $\beta \geq 0$ *and* $\gamma \geq 0)$ **then**
      if $(\alpha > 0$ *or* $f_\alpha f_{12}(-1, -1) > 0)$ *and* $(\beta > 0$ *or* $f_\beta f_{20}(-1, -1) > 0)$ *and* $(\gamma > 0$ *or* $f_\gamma f_{01}(-1, -1) > 0)$ **then**
        $\mathbf{c} = \alpha \mathbf{c}_0 + \beta \mathbf{c}_1 + \gamma \mathbf{c}_2$
        drawpixel (i, j) *with color* $\mathbf{c}$

We might expect that the above code would work to eliminate holes and double-draws only if we use exactly the same line equation for both triangles. In fact, the line equation is the same only if the two shared vertices have the same order in the draw call for each triangle. Otherwise the equation might flip in sign. This could be a problem depending on whether the

Figure 3.12. A jaggy and a antialiased line viewed at close range so individual pixels are visible.

compiler changes the order of operations. So if a robust implementation is needed, the details of the compiler and arithmetic unit may need to be examined. The first four lines in the pseudocode above must be coded carefully to handle cases where the edge exactly hits the pixel center.

In addition to being amenable to an incremental implementation, there are several potential early exit points. For example, if α is negative, there is no need to compute β or γ. While this may well result in a speed improvement, profiling is always a good idea; the extra branches could reduce pipelining or concurrency and might slow down the code. So as always, test any attractive looking optimizations if the code is a critical section.

Another detail of the above code is that the divisions could be divisions by zero for degenerate triangles, i.e., if $f_\gamma(-1,-1) = 0$. Either the floating point error conditions should be accounted for properly, or another test will be needed.

3.7 Simple Antialiasing

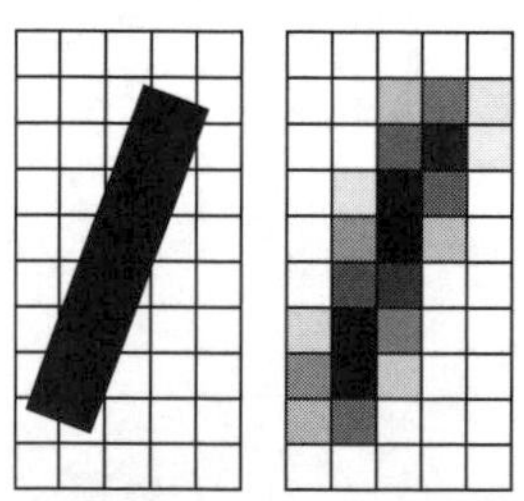

Figure 3.13. An antialiased line can be created by using an underlying rectangle.

One problem with the line and triangle drawing algorithms presented earlier is that they have fairly jaggy appearances. We can lessen this visual artifact by allowing a pixel to be "partially" on. For example, if the center of a pixel is *almost* inside a black triangle on a white background, we can color it halfway between white and black. The top line in the figure is drawn this way. In practice this form of blurring helps visual quality, especially in animations. This is shown as the bottom line of Figure 3.12.

The most straightforward way to create such "unjaggy" images is to use a *box filter*, where the pixel is set to the average color of the regions inside it. This means we have to think of all drawable entities as having well-defined areas. For example, a line is just a rectangle as shown in Figure 3.13. More sophisticated methods of blurring for visual quality are discussed in Chapter 15. Jaggy artifacts, like the sawtoothed lines the midpoint algorithm generates, are a result of *aliasing*, a term from signal processing. Thus, the general technique of carefully selecting pixel values to avoid jaggy artifacts is called *antialiasing*. The box filter will suffice for most applications that do not have extremely high visual quality requirements.

The easiest way to implement box-filter antialiasing is to create images at very high resolutions and then downsample. For example, if our goal is a 256 by 256 pixel image of a line with width 1.2 pixels, we could rasterize a rectangle version of the line with width 4.8 pixels on a 1024 by 1024 screen, and then average 4 by 4 groups of pixels to get the colors for each of the 256 by 256 pixels in the "shrunken" image. This is an approximation of the actual box-filtered image, but works well when objects are not extremely small relative to the distance between pixels.

3.8 Image Capture and Storage

Almost all graphics software deals with some "real" images that are captured using digital cameras or flatbed scanners. This section deals with the practicalities of acquiring, storing and manipulating such images.

3.8.1 Scanners and Digital Cameras

Scanners and digital cameras use some type of light-sensitive chip to record light. The dominant technologies are *CCD* and *CMOS* arrays. These devices are sensitive to light intensity across all wavelengths. To get color images, either the light is split into three components and then filtered through red, green, and blue filters (so three chips are needed), three passes are made with different filters and the same chip, or the sensors on the chip are individually coated with different colored filters.

In most current digital cameras, a single light-sensitive CCD is used with colored filters in the *Bayer mosaic* (Figure 3.14). This pattern devotes half of the sensors to the green channel, and a quarter each to red and blue. The pattern makes the green channels a regular array at a forty-five degree angle to the chip lattice. For natural scenes this pattern works well in practice, but for some man-made scenes color aliasing can result. Camera manufacturers have different proprietary algorithms for creating a single RGB image from an image captured using the Bayer mosaic that are somewhat more complicated than the obvious strategy of linear interpolation in each separate channel.

G	B	G	B	G	B	G
R	G	R	G	R	G	R
G	B	G	B	G	B	G
R	G	R	G	R	G	R
G	B	G	B	G	B	G
R	G	R	G	R	G	R

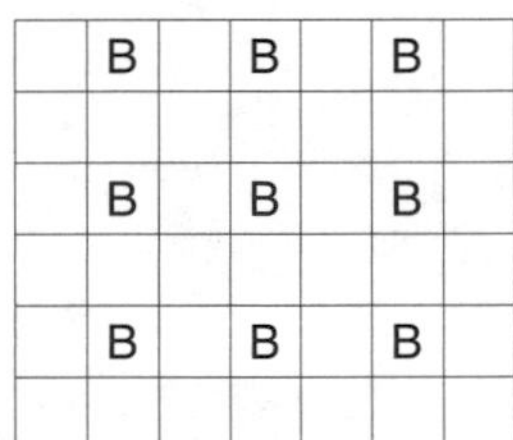

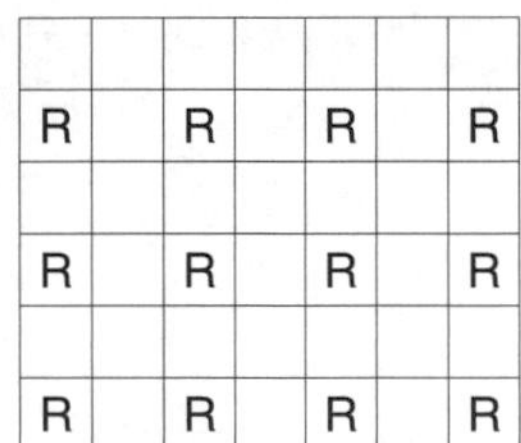

R		R		R		R
R		R		R		R
R		R		R		R

Figure 3.14. The top image shows the mosaic of RGB sensors in a typical digital camera. The bottom three images show the same pattern with individual colors highlighted.

3.8.2 Image Storage

Most RGB image formats use eight bits for each of the red, green, and blue channels. This results in approximately three megabytes of raw information for a single million-pixel image. To reduce the storage requirement, most image formats allow for some kind of compression. At a high level, such compression is either *lossless* or *lossy*. No information is discarded in lossless compression, while some information is lost unrecoverably in a lossy system. Popular image storage formats include:

gif This lossy format indexes only 256 possible colors. The quality of the image depends on how carefully these 256 colors are chosen. This format typically works well for natural diagrams.

jpeg This lossy format compresses image blocks based on thresholds in the human visual system. This format works well for natural images.

tiff This lossless format is usually a compressed 24-bit per pixel although many other options exist.

ppm This lossless format is typically a 24-bit per pixel uncompressed format although many options exist.

Because of compression and variants, writing input/output routines for images can be involved. For non-commercial applications it is advisable to just use raw ppm if no read/write libraries are readily available.

Frequently Asked Questions

- **Why don't they just make monitors linear and avoid all this gamma business?**

Ideally the 256 possible intensities of a monitor should *look* evenly spaced as opposed to being linearly spaced in energy. Because human perception of intensity is itself non-linear, a gamma between 1.5 and 3 (depending on viewing conditions) will make the intensities approximately uniform in a subjective sense. In this way gamma is a feature. Otherwise the manufacturers would make the monitors linear.

- **How are polygons that are not triangles rasterized?**

These can either be done directly scan-line by scan-line, or they can be broken down into triangles. The latter appears to be the more popular technique.

• Is it always better to antialias?

No. Some images look crisper without antialiasing. Many programs use unantialiased "screen fonts" because they are easier to read.

Notes

Incremental scan conversion was introduced by J. Bresenham in the mid-1960s. The midpoint formulation was presented in *Curve-drawing Algorithms for Raster Displays* (Van Aken and Novak, ACM Transactions on Graphics, 4(2), 1985). The triangle scan conversion using barycentric coordinates is based on *A Parallel Algorithm for Polygon Rasterization* (Pineda, SIGGRAPH 88 Proceedings). The classic reference for digital compositing is *Compositing Digital Images* (Porter and Duff, SIGGRAPH 84 Proceedings).

Exercises

1. Derive the incremental form of the midpoint line drawing algorithm with colors at endpoints for $0 < m \leq 1$.

2. Modify the triangle drawing algorithm so that it will draw exactly one pixel for points on a triangle edge which goes through $(x, y) = (-1, -1)$.

3. Simulate an image acquired from the Bayer mosaic by taking a natural image (preferably a scanned photo rather than a digital photo where the Bayer mosaic may already have been applied) and creating a greyscale image composed of interleaved red/green/blue channels. This simulates the raw output of a digital camera. Now create a true RGB image from that output and compare with the original.

Linear Algebra

Perhaps the most universal tool of graphics programs are the matrices that change or *transform* points and vectors. In the next chapter, we will see how a vector can be represented as a matrix with a single column, and how the vector can be represented in a different basis via multiplication with a square matrix. We will also describe how we can use such multiplications to accomplish changes in the vector such as scaling, rotation, and translation. In this chapter, we review basic linear algebra from a geometric perspective. This chapter can be skipped by readers comfortable with linear algebra. However, there may be some enlightening tidbits even for such readers, such as the development of determinants and the discussion of singular and eigenvalue decomposition.

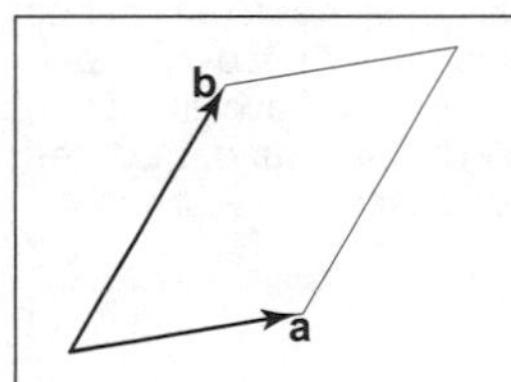

Figure 4.1. The signed area of the parallelogram is $|\mathbf{ab}|$, and in this case the area is positive.

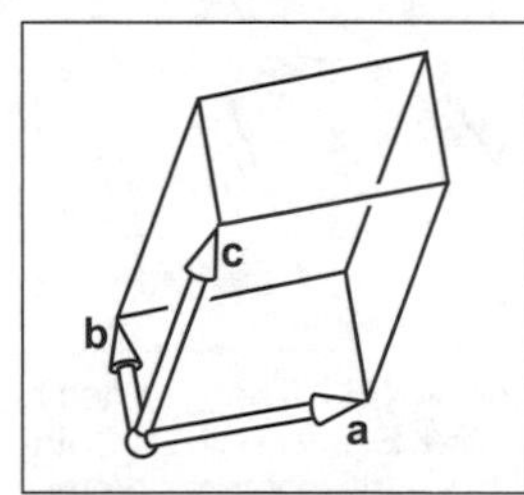

Figure 4.2. The signed volume of the parallel-epiped shown is denoted by the determinant $|\mathbf{abc}|$, and in this case the volume is positive because the vectors form a right-handed basis.

4.1 Determinants

We usually think of determinants as arising in the solution of linear equations. However, for our purposes, we will think of determinants as another way to multiply vectors. For 2D vectors $\mathbf{a}$ and $\mathbf{b}$ the determinant $|\mathbf{ab}|$ is the area of the parallelogram formed by $\mathbf{a}$ and $\mathbf{b}$ (Figure 4.1). This is a signed area, and the sign is positive if $\mathbf{a}$ and $\mathbf{b}$ are right-handed, and negative if they are left-handed. This means $|\mathbf{ab}| = -|\mathbf{ba}|$. In 2D we can interpret "right-handed" as meaning we would rotate the first vector counterclockwise to close the smallest angle to the second vector. In 3D the determinant must be taken with three vectors at a time. For three 3D vectors, $\mathbf{a}$, $\mathbf{b}$ and

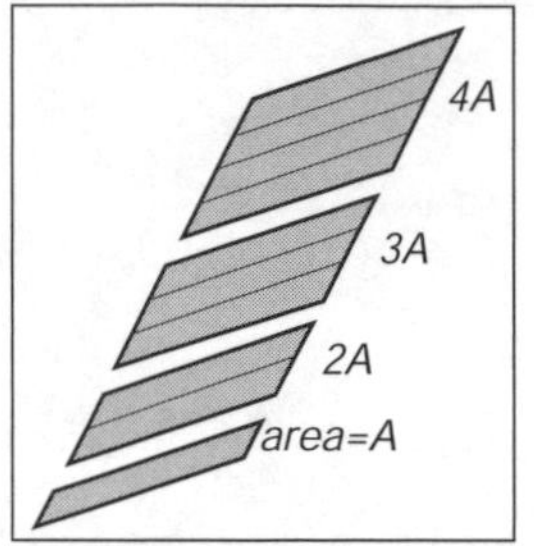

Figure 4.3. Scaling a parallelogram along one direction changes the area in the same proportion.

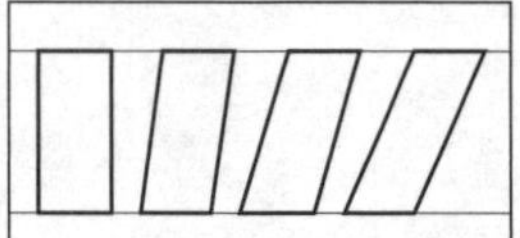

Figure 4.4. Shearing a parallelogram does not change its area. These four parallelograms have the same length base and thus the same area.

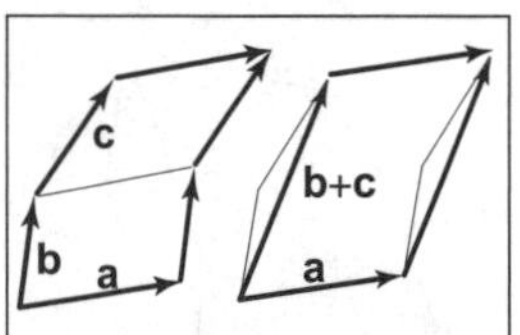

Figure 4.5. The geometry behind Equation 4.1. Both of the parallelograms on the left can be sheared to cover the single parallelogram on the right.

$\mathbf{c}$, the determinant $|\mathbf{abc}|$ is the signed volume of the parallelepiped (3D parallelogram; a sheared 3D box) formed by the three vectors (Figure 4.2). To compute a 2D determinant, we first need to establish a few properties of the determinant. We note that scaling one side of a parallelogram scales its area by the same fraction (Figure 4.3):

$$|(k\mathbf{a})\mathbf{b}| = |\mathbf{a}(k\mathbf{b})| = k|\mathbf{ab}|.$$

Also, we note that "shearing" a parallelogram does not change its area (Figure 4.4):

$$|(\mathbf{a} + k\mathbf{b})\mathbf{b}| = |\mathbf{a}(\mathbf{b} + k\mathbf{a})| = |\mathbf{ab}|.$$

Finally, we see that the determinant has the following property:

$$|\mathbf{a}(\mathbf{b} + \mathbf{c})| = |\mathbf{ab}| + |\mathbf{ac}|, \tag{4.1}$$

because as shown in Figure 4.5 we can "slide" the edge between the two parallelograms over to form a single parallelogram without changing the area of either of the two original parallelograms.

Now let's assume a Cartesian representation for $\mathbf{a}$ and $\mathbf{b}$:

$$\begin{aligned}
|\mathbf{ab}| &= |(x_a\mathbf{x} + y_a\mathbf{y})(x_b\mathbf{x} + y_b\mathbf{y})| \\
&= x_a x_b|\mathbf{xx}| + x_a y_b|\mathbf{xy}| + y_a x_b|\mathbf{yx}| + y_a y_b|\mathbf{yy}| \\
&= x_a x_b(0) + x_a y_b(+1) + y_a x_b(-1) + y_a y_b(0) \\
&= x_a y_b - y_a x_b.
\end{aligned}$$

This simplification uses the fact that $|\mathbf{vv}| = 0$ for any vector $\mathbf{v}$, because the parallelograms would all be collinear with $\mathbf{v}$, and thus without area.

In three dimensions, the determinant of three 3D vectors $\mathbf{a}$, $\mathbf{b}$, and $\mathbf{c}$ is denoted $|\mathbf{abc}|$. With Cartesian representations for the vectors, there are analogous rules for parallelepipeds as there are for parallelograms, and we can do an analogous expansion as we did for 2D:

$$\begin{aligned}
|\mathbf{abc}| &= |(x_a\mathbf{x} + y_a\mathbf{y} + z_a\mathbf{z})(x_b\mathbf{x} + y_b\mathbf{y} + z_b\mathbf{z})(x_c\mathbf{x} + y_c\mathbf{y} + z_c\mathbf{z})| \\
&= x_a y_b z_c - x_a z_b y_c - y_a x_b z_c + y_a b_z c_x + z_a x_b y_c - z_a y_b x_c.
\end{aligned}$$

As you can see, the computation of determinants in this fashion gets uglier as the dimension increases. We will discuss less error-prone ways to compute determinants in Section 4.2.3.

Determinants arise naturally when computing the expression for one vector as a linear combination of two others. For example, if we wish to express a vector $\mathbf{c}$ as a combination of vectors $\mathbf{a}$ and $\mathbf{b}$:

$$\mathbf{c} = a_c\mathbf{a} + b_c\mathbf{b},$$

we can see from Figure 4.6 that

$$|(b_c\mathbf{b})\mathbf{a}| = |\mathbf{ca}|,$$

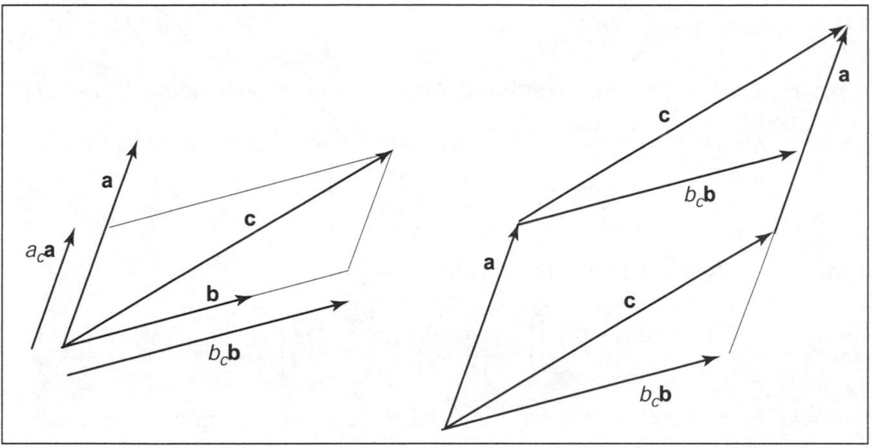

Figure 4.6. On the left the vector **c** can be represented using two basis vectors as $a_c\mathbf{a}+b_c\mathbf{b}$. On the right we see that the parallelogram formed by **a** and **c** is a sheared version of the parallelogram formed by $b_c\mathbf{b}$ and **a**.

because these parallelograms are just sheared versions of each other. Solving for b_c yields:

$$b_c = \frac{|\mathbf{ca}|}{|\mathbf{ba}|}.$$

An analogous argument yields:

$$a_c = \frac{|\mathbf{bc}|}{|\mathbf{ba}|}.$$

This is the two-dimensiona version of *Cramer's Rule* which we will revisit in Section 4.2.5.

4.2 Matrices

A matrix is an array of numeric elements that follow certain arithmetic rules. An example of a matrix with two rows and three columns is:

$$\begin{bmatrix} 1.7 & -1.2 & 4.2 \\ 3.0 & 4.5 & -7.2 \end{bmatrix}$$

Matrices are frequently used in computer graphics for a variety of purposes including representation of spatial transforms. For our discussion, we assume the elements of a matrix are all real numbers. This chapter describes both the mechanics of matrix arithmetic and the *determinant* of "square" matrices, i.e., matrices with the same number of rows as columns.

4.2.1 Matrix Arithmetic

A matrix times a constant results in a matrix where each element has been multiplied by that constant, e.g.,

$$2\begin{bmatrix}1 & -4\\ 3 & 2\end{bmatrix} = \begin{bmatrix}2 & -8\\ 6 & 4\end{bmatrix}.$$

Matrices also add element by element, e.g.,

$$\begin{bmatrix}1 & -4\\ 3 & 2\end{bmatrix} + \begin{bmatrix}2 & 2\\ 2 & 2\end{bmatrix} = \begin{bmatrix}3 & -2\\ 5 & 4\end{bmatrix}.$$

For matrix multiplication, we "multiply" rows of the first matrix with columns of the second matrix:

$$\begin{bmatrix}a_{11} & \dots & a_{1m}\\ \vdots & & \vdots\\ \boxed{a_{i1} \ \dots \ a_{im}} & & \\ \vdots & & \vdots\\ a_{r1} & \dots & a_{rm}\end{bmatrix}\begin{bmatrix}b_{11} & \dots & \boxed{b_{1j}} & \dots & b_{1c}\\ \vdots & & \vdots & & \vdots\\ b_{m1} & \dots & b_{mj} & \dots & b_{mc}\end{bmatrix} = \begin{bmatrix}p_{11} & \dots & p_{1j} & \dots & p_{1c}\\ \vdots & & \vdots & & \vdots\\ p_{i1} & \dots & \boxed{p_{ij}} & \dots & p_{ic}\\ \vdots & & \vdots & & \vdots\\ p_{r1} & \dots & p_{rj} & \dots & p_{rc}\end{bmatrix}$$

So the element p_{ij} of the resulting product is:

$$p_{ij} = a_{i1}b_{1j} + a_{i2}b_{2j} + \cdots + a_{im}b_{mj}.$$

Note that taking a product of two matrices is only possible if the number of columns of the left matrix is the same as the number of rows of the right matrix. For example,

$$\begin{bmatrix}0 & 1\\ 2 & 3\\ 4 & 5\end{bmatrix}\begin{bmatrix}6 & 7 & 8 & 9\\ 0 & 1 & 2 & 3\end{bmatrix} = \begin{bmatrix}0 & 1 & 2 & 3\\ 12 & 17 & 22 & 27\\ 24 & 33 & 42 & 51\end{bmatrix}.$$

Matrix multiplication is *not* communitive in most instances:

$$\mathbf{AB} \neq \mathbf{BA}. \tag{4.2}$$

Also, if $\mathbf{AB} = \mathbf{AC}$ it does not necessarily follow that $\mathbf{B} = \mathbf{C}$. Fortunately, matrix multiplication is associative and distributive:

$$\begin{aligned}(\mathbf{AB})\mathbf{C} &= \mathbf{A}(\mathbf{BC}),\\ \mathbf{A}(\mathbf{B}+\mathbf{C}) &= \mathbf{AB}+\mathbf{AC},\\ (\mathbf{A}+\mathbf{B})\mathbf{C} &= \mathbf{AC}+\mathbf{BC}.\end{aligned}$$

In graphics, we use a square matrix to transform a vector represented as a matrix. For example if you have a 2D vector $\mathbf{a} = (x_a, y_a)$ and want to "reflect" it about the y axis to form vector $\mathbf{a}' = (-x_a, y_a)$, you can use a product of a two by two matrix and a two by one matrix, often called a "column vector". The operation in matrix form is:

$$\begin{bmatrix} -1 & 0 \\ 0 & 1 \end{bmatrix} \begin{bmatrix} x_a \\ y_a \end{bmatrix} = \begin{bmatrix} -x_a \\ y_a \end{bmatrix}.$$

We can get the same result by "premultiplying" with a "row vector":

$$\begin{bmatrix} x_a & y_a \end{bmatrix} \begin{bmatrix} -1 & 0 \\ 0 & 1 \end{bmatrix} = \begin{bmatrix} -x_a & y_a \end{bmatrix}.$$

These days, postmultiplication using column vectors is fairly standard, but in many older books and systems you will run across row vectors and premultiplication. The only difference is that the transform matrix must be replaced with its *transpose*. The transpose $\mathbf{A}^T$ of a matrix A is one whose rows are switched with its columns, e.g.,

$$\begin{bmatrix} 1 & 2 \\ 3 & 4 \\ 5 & 6 \end{bmatrix}^T = \begin{bmatrix} 1 & 3 & 5 \\ 2 & 4 & 6 \end{bmatrix}.$$

Note that in the previous reflection example, the transpose of the matrix is the same as the matrix. Such matrices are called *symmetric*. Note that the transpose of a product of two matrices obeys:

$$(\mathbf{AB})^T = \mathbf{B}^T \mathbf{A}^T.$$

We would like a matrix analog of the inverse of a real number. We know the inverse of a real number x is $1/x$ and that the product of x and its inverse is 1. We need a matrix $\mathbf{I}$ that we can think of as a "matrix one." This exists only for square matrices and is know as the *identity matrix*; it consists of ones down the "diagonal" and zeroes elsewhere. For example, the four by four identity matrix is:

$$\mathbf{I} = \begin{bmatrix} 1 & 0 & 0 & 0 \\ 0 & 1 & 0 & 0 \\ 0 & 0 & 1 & 0 \\ 0 & 0 & 0 & 1 \end{bmatrix}$$

The identity matrix is a special case of a *diagonal matrix*, where all non-zero elements are along the diagonal. The diagonal are those elements whose column index equals the row index counting from the upper left. The *inverse matrix* $\mathbf{A}^{-1}$ of a matrix $\mathbf{A}$ is the matrix that ensures $\mathbf{A}\mathbf{A}^{-1} = \mathbf{I}$. For example:

$$\begin{bmatrix} 1 & 2 \\ 3 & 4 \end{bmatrix}^{-1} = \begin{bmatrix} -2.0 & 1.0 \\ 1.5 & -0.5 \end{bmatrix} \quad \text{because} \quad \begin{bmatrix} 1 & 2 \\ 3 & 4 \end{bmatrix}\begin{bmatrix} -2.0 & 1.0 \\ 1.5 & -0.5 \end{bmatrix} = \begin{bmatrix} 1 & 0 \\ 0 & 1 \end{bmatrix}$$

Note that the inverse of $\mathbf{A}^{-1}$ is $\mathbf{A}$. So $\mathbf{A}\mathbf{A}^{-1} = \mathbf{A}^{-1}\mathbf{A} = \mathbf{I}$. Also note that the inverse of a product of two matrices is:

$$(\mathbf{AB})^{-1} = \mathbf{B}^{-1}\mathbf{A}^{-1}.$$

We will return to inverses later in the chapter.

4.2.2 Vector Operations in Matrix Form

We can use matrix formalism to encode vector operations for vectors when using Cartesian coordinates; if we consider the result of the dot product a one by one matrix, it can be written:

$$\mathbf{a} \cdot \mathbf{b} = \mathbf{a}^T\mathbf{b}.$$

For example, if we take two 3D vectors we get:

$$\begin{bmatrix} x_a & y_a & z_a \end{bmatrix} \begin{bmatrix} x_b \\ y_b \\ z_b \end{bmatrix} = \begin{bmatrix} x_a x_b + y_a y_b + z_a z_b \end{bmatrix}.$$

4.2.3 Matrices and Determinants

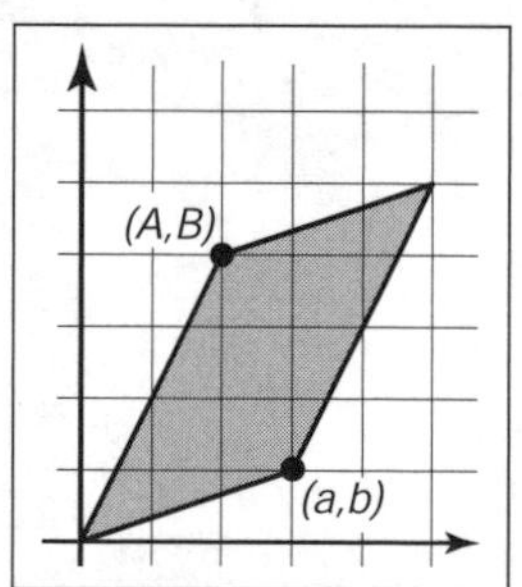

Figure 4.6. The 2D determinant in Equation 4.3 is the area of the parallelogram formed by the 2D vectors.

Recall from Section 4.1 that the determinant takes n n-dimensional vectors and combines them to get a signed n-dimensional volume of the n-dimensional parallelepiped defined by the vectors. For example, the determinant in 2D is the area of the parallelogram formed by the vectors. We can use matrices to handle the mechanics of computing determinants.

If we have 2D vectors $\mathbf{r}$ and $\mathbf{s}$, we denote the determinant $|\mathbf{rs}|$; this value is the signed area of the parallelogram formed by the vectors. Suppose we have two 2D vectors with Cartesian coordinates (a, b) and (A, B) (Figure 4.6). The determinant can be written in terms of column vectors or as a shorthand:

$$\left| \begin{bmatrix} a \\ b \end{bmatrix} \begin{bmatrix} A \\ B \end{bmatrix} \right| \equiv \begin{vmatrix} a & A \\ b & B \end{vmatrix} = aB - Ab. \tag{4.3}$$

Note that the determinant of a matrix is the same as the determinant of its transpose:

$$\begin{vmatrix} a & A \\ b & B \end{vmatrix} = \begin{vmatrix} a & b \\ A & B \end{vmatrix} = aB - Ab.$$

This means that for any parallelogram in 2D there is a "sibling" parallelogram that has the same area but a different shape (Figure 4.7). For example the parallelogram defined by vectors (3, 1) and (2, 4) has area 10, as does the parallelogram defined by vectors (3, 2) and (1, 4).

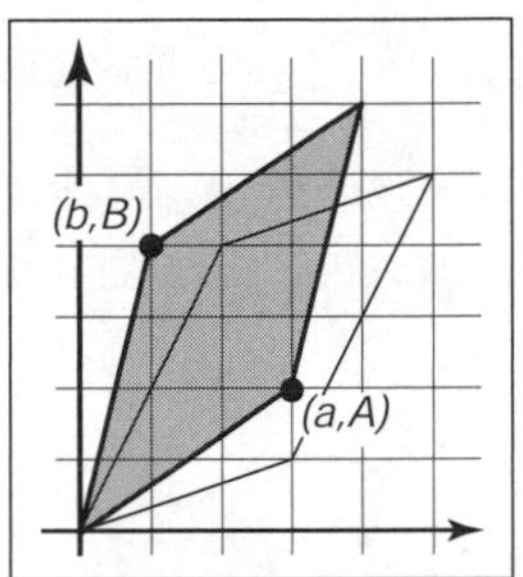

Figure 4.7. The sibling parallelogram has the same area as the parallelogram in Figure 4.6.

The geometric meaning of the 3D determinant is helpful in seeing why certain formulas make sense. For example, the equation of the plane through the points (x_i, y_i, z_i) for $i = 0, 1, 2$ is:

$$\begin{vmatrix} x - x_0 & x - x_1 & x - x_2 \\ y - y_0 & y - y_1 & y - y_2 \\ z - z_0 & z - z_1 & z - z_2 \end{vmatrix} = 0.$$

Each column is a vector from point (x_i, y_i, z_i) to point (x, y, z). The volume of the parallelepiped with those vectors as sides is zero only if (x, y, z) is coplanar with the three other points. Almost all equations involving determinants have similarly simple underlying geometry.

As we saw earlier, we can compute determinants by a brute force expansion where most terms are zero and there is a great deal of bookkeeping on plus and minus signs. The standard way to manage the algebra of computing determinants is to use a form of *Laplace's expansion*. The key part of computing the determinant this way is to find *cofactors* of various matrix elements. Each element of a square matrix has a cofactor which is the determinant of a matrix with one fewer row and column possibly multiplied by minus one. The smaller matrix is obtained by eliminating the row and column that the element in question is in. For example, for a 10 by 10 matrix, the cofactor of a_{82} is the determinant of the 9 by 9 matrix with the 8th row and 2nd column eliminated. The sign of a cofactor is positive if the sum of the row and column indices is even, and negative otherwise. This can be remembered by a checkerboard pattern:

$$\begin{bmatrix} + & - & + & - & \cdots \\ - & + & - & + & \cdots \\ + & - & + & - & \cdots \\ - & + & - & + & \cdots \\ \vdots & \vdots & \vdots & \vdots & \ddots \end{bmatrix}$$

So for a four by four matrix:

$$\mathbf{A} = \begin{bmatrix} a_{11} & a_{12} & a_{13} & a_{14} \\ a_{21} & a_{22} & a_{23} & a_{24} \\ a_{31} & a_{32} & a_{33} & a_{34} \\ a_{41} & a_{42} & a_{43} & a_{44} \end{bmatrix}$$

The cofactors of the first row are:

$$a_{11}^c = \begin{vmatrix} a_{22} & a_{23} & a_{24} \\ a_{32} & a_{33} & a_{34} \\ a_{42} & a_{43} & a_{44} \end{vmatrix} \quad a_{12}^c = - \begin{vmatrix} a_{21} & a_{23} & a_{24} \\ a_{31} & a_{33} & a_{34} \\ a_{41} & a_{43} & a_{44} \end{vmatrix}$$

$$a_{13}^c = \begin{vmatrix} a_{21} & a_{22} & a_{24} \\ a_{31} & a_{32} & a_{34} \\ a_{41} & a_{42} & a_{44} \end{vmatrix} \quad a_{14}^c = - \begin{vmatrix} a_{21} & a_{22} & a_{23} \\ a_{31} & a_{32} & a_{33} \\ a_{41} & a_{42} & a_{43} \end{vmatrix}$$

The determinant of a matrix is found by taking the sum of products of the elements of any row or column with their cofactors. For example, the determinant of the four by four matrix above taken about its second column is:

$$|\mathbf{A}| = a_{12}a_{12}^c + a_{22}a_{22}^c + a_{32}a_{32}^c + a_{42}a_{42}^c.$$

We could do a similar expansion about any row or column and they would all yield the same result. Note the recursive nature of this expansion.

A concrete example for the determinant of a particular three by three matrix by expanding the cofactors of the first row is:

$$\begin{aligned} \begin{vmatrix} 0 & 1 & 2 \\ 3 & 4 & 5 \\ 6 & 7 & 8 \end{vmatrix} &= 0 \begin{vmatrix} 4 & 5 \\ 7 & 8 \end{vmatrix} - 1 \begin{vmatrix} 3 & 5 \\ 6 & 8 \end{vmatrix} + 2 \begin{vmatrix} 3 & 4 \\ 6 & 7 \end{vmatrix} \\ &= 0(32 - 35) - 1(24 - 30) + 2(21 - 24) \\ &= 0. \end{aligned}$$

We can deduce that the volume of the parallelepiped formed by the vectors defined by the columns (or rows since the determinant of the transpose is the same) is zero. This is equivalent to saying that the columns (or rows) are not linearly independent. Note that the sum of the first and third rows is twice the second row, which implies linear dependence.

4.2.4 Computing Inverses

Determinants give us a tool to compute the inverse of a matrix. It is a very inefficient method for large matrices, but often in graphics our matrices are small. A key to developing this method is that the determinant of a matrix with two identical rows is zero. This should be clear because the volume of the n-dimensional parallelepiped is zero if two of its sides are the same. Suppose we have a four by four matrix $\mathbf{A}$ and we wish to find its inverse $\mathbf{A}^{-1}$. The inverse is:

$$\mathbf{A}^{-1} = \frac{1}{|\mathbf{A}|}\begin{bmatrix} a^c_{11} & a^c_{21} & a^c_{31} & a^c_{41} \\ a^c_{12} & a^c_{22} & a^c_{32} & a^c_{42} \\ a^c_{13} & a^c_{23} & a^c_{33} & a^c_{43} \\ a^c_{14} & a^c_{24} & a^c_{34} & a^c_{44} \end{bmatrix}.$$

Note that this is just the transpose of the matrix where elements of $\mathbf{A}$ are replaced by their respective cofactors multiplied by the leading constant(1 or -1). This matrix is called the *adjoint* of $\mathbf{A}$. The adjoint is the transpose of the *cofactor* matrix of $\mathbf{A}$. We can see why this is an inverse. Look at the product $\mathbf{AA}^{-1}$ which we expect to be the identity. If we multiply the first row of $\mathbf{A}$ by the first column of the adjoint matrix we need to get $|\mathbf{A}|$ (remember the leading constant above divides by $|\mathbf{A}|$:

$$\begin{bmatrix} a_{11} & a_{12} & a_{13} & a_{14} \\ \cdot & \cdot & \cdot & \cdot \\ \cdot & \cdot & \cdot & \cdot \\ \cdot & \cdot & \cdot & \cdot \end{bmatrix}\begin{bmatrix} a^c_{11} & \cdot & \cdot & \cdot \\ a^c_{12} & \cdot & \cdot & \cdot \\ a^c_{13} & \cdot & \cdot & \cdot \\ a^c_{14} & \cdot & \cdot & \cdot \end{bmatrix} = \begin{bmatrix} |\mathbf{A}| & \cdot & \cdot & \cdot \\ \cdot & \cdot & \cdot & \cdot \\ \cdot & \cdot & \cdot & \cdot \\ \cdot & \cdot & \cdot & \cdot \end{bmatrix}.$$

This is true because the first row of $\mathbf{A}$ is multiplied exactly by their cofactors in the first column of the adjoint matrix which is exactly the determinant. The other values along the diagonal of the resulting matrix are $|\mathbf{A}|$ for analogous reasons. The zeros follow a similar logic:

$$\begin{bmatrix} \cdot & \cdot & \cdot & \cdot \\ a_{21} & a_{22} & a_{23} & a_{24} \\ \cdot & \cdot & \cdot & \cdot \\ \cdot & \cdot & \cdot & \cdot \end{bmatrix}\begin{bmatrix} a^c_{11} & \cdot & \cdot & \cdot \\ a^c_{12} & \cdot & \cdot & \cdot \\ a^c_{13} & \cdot & \cdot & \cdot \\ a^c_{14} & \cdot & \cdot & \cdot \end{bmatrix} = \begin{bmatrix} \cdot & \cdot & \cdot & \cdot \\ 0 & \cdot & \cdot & \cdot \\ \cdot & \cdot & \cdot & \cdot \\ \cdot & \cdot & \cdot & \cdot \end{bmatrix}.$$

Note that this product is a determinant of *some* matrix:

$$a_{21}a^c_{11} + a_{22}a^c_{12} + a_{23}a^c_{13} + a_{24}a^c_{14}.$$

The matrix in fact is:

$$\begin{bmatrix} a_{21} & a_{22} & a_{23} & a_{24} \\ a_{21} & a_{22} & a_{23} & a_{24} \\ a_{31} & a_{32} & a_{33} & a_{34} \\ a_{41} & a_{42} & a_{43} & a_{44}. \end{bmatrix}.$$

Because the first two rows are identical, the matrix is singular and thus its determinant is zero.

The argument above does not apply just to four by four matrices; using that size just simplifies typography. For any matrix, the inverse is the adjoint matrix divided by the determinant of the matrix being inverted. The adjoint is the transpose of the cofactor matrix, which is just the matrix whose elements have been replaced by their cofactors. For example, the inverse of a three by three matrix whose determinant is 6 is:

$$\begin{bmatrix} 1 & 1 & 2 \\ 1 & 3 & 4 \\ 0 & 2 & 5 \end{bmatrix}^{-1} = \frac{1}{6} \begin{bmatrix} \begin{vmatrix} 3 & 4 \\ 2 & 5 \end{vmatrix} & -\begin{vmatrix} 1 & 2 \\ 2 & 5 \end{vmatrix} & \begin{vmatrix} 1 & 2 \\ 3 & 4 \end{vmatrix} \\ -\begin{vmatrix} 1 & 4 \\ 0 & 5 \end{vmatrix} & \begin{vmatrix} 1 & 2 \\ 0 & 5 \end{vmatrix} & -\begin{vmatrix} 1 & 2 \\ 1 & 4 \end{vmatrix} \\ \begin{vmatrix} 1 & 3 \\ 0 & 2 \end{vmatrix} & -\begin{vmatrix} 1 & 1 \\ 0 & 2 \end{vmatrix} & \begin{vmatrix} 1 & 1 \\ 1 & 3 \end{vmatrix} \end{bmatrix}$$

$$= \frac{1}{6} \begin{bmatrix} 7 & -1 & -2 \\ -5 & 5 & -2 \\ 2 & -2 & 2 \end{bmatrix}.$$

You can check this yourself by multiplying the matrices and making sure you get the identity.

4.2.5 Linear Systems

We often encounter linear systems in graphics with "n equations and n unknowns". For example ($n = 3$),

$$\begin{aligned} 3x + 7y + 2z &= 4, \\ 2x - 4y - 3z &= -1, \\ 5x + 2y + z &= 1. \end{aligned}$$

Here x, y and z are the "unknowns" for which we wish to solve. We can write this in matrix form:

$$\begin{bmatrix} 3 & 7 & 2 \\ 2 & -4 & -3 \\ 5 & 2 & 1 \end{bmatrix} \begin{bmatrix} x \\ y \\ z \end{bmatrix} = \begin{bmatrix} 4 \\ -1 \\ 1 \end{bmatrix}.$$

A common shorthand for such systems is $\mathbf{Ax} = \mathbf{b}$ where it is assumed that $\mathbf{A}$ is a square matrix with known constants, $\mathbf{x}$ is an unknown column vector (with elements x, y, and z in our example), and $\mathbf{b}$ is a column matrix of known constants.

There are many ways to solve such systems, but for small systems we will use *Cramer's rule* as we saw earlier in 2D from a geometric standpoint.

Here, we show this algebraically. The solution to the above equation is:

$$x = \frac{\begin{vmatrix} 4 & 7 & 2 \\ -1 & -4 & -3 \\ 1 & 2 & 1 \end{vmatrix}}{\begin{vmatrix} 3 & 7 & 2 \\ 2 & -4 & -3 \\ 5 & 2 & 1 \end{vmatrix}} \quad y = \frac{\begin{vmatrix} 3 & 4 & 2 \\ 2 & -1 & -3 \\ 5 & 1 & 1 \end{vmatrix}}{\begin{vmatrix} 3 & 7 & 2 \\ 2 & -4 & -3 \\ 5 & 2 & 1 \end{vmatrix}} \quad z = \frac{\begin{vmatrix} 3 & 7 & 4 \\ 2 & -4 & -1 \\ 5 & 2 & 1 \end{vmatrix}}{\begin{vmatrix} 3 & 7 & 2 \\ 2 & -4 & -3 \\ 5 & 2 & 1 \end{vmatrix}}$$

The rule here is to take a ratio of determinants, where the denominator is $|\mathbf{A}|$ and the numerator is the determinant of a matrix created by replacing a column of $\mathbf{A}$ with the column vector $\mathbf{b}$. The column replaced corresponds to the position of the unknown in vector $\mathbf{x}$. For example, y is the second unknown and the second column is replaced. Note that if $|\mathbf{A}| = 0$, the division is undefined and there is no solution. This is just another version of the rule that if $\mathbf{A}$ is singular (zero determinant) then there is no unique solution to the equations.

4.2.6 Eigenvalues and Matrix Diagonalization

Square matrices have *eigenvalues* and *eigenvectors* associated with them. The eigenvectors are those *non-zero* vectors whose directions do not change when multiplied by the matrix. For example, suppose for a matrix $\mathbf{A}$ and vector $\mathbf{a}$, we have:

$$\mathbf{Aa} = \lambda\mathbf{a}. \tag{4.4}$$

This means we have stretched or compressed $\mathbf{a}$, but its direction has not changed. The scalefactor λ is called the eigenvalue associated with eigenvector $\mathbf{a}$. Knowing the eigenvalues and eigenvectors of matrices is helpful in a variety of practical applications. We will describe them to gain insight into geometric transformation matrices, and as a step toward singular values and vectors described in the next section.

If we assume a matrix has at least one eigenvector, then we can do a standard manipulation to find it. First, we make both sides the product of a square matrix and a vector:

$$\mathbf{Aa} = \lambda\mathbf{Ia}, \tag{4.5}$$

where $\mathbf{I}$ is an identity matrix. This can be rewritten

$$\mathbf{Aa} - \lambda\mathbf{Ia} = 0. \tag{4.6}$$

Because matrix multiplication is distributive, we can group the matrices:

$$(\mathbf{A} - \lambda\mathbf{I})\,\mathbf{a} = 0. \tag{4.7}$$

This equation can only be true if the matrix $(\mathbf{A} - \lambda\mathbf{I})$ is singular, and thus its determinant is zero. The elements in this matrix are the numbers in $\mathbf{A}$ except along the diagonal. For example, for a 2 by 2 matrix the eigenvalues obey:

$$\begin{vmatrix} a_{11} - \lambda & a_{12} \\ a_{21} & a_{22} - \lambda \end{vmatrix} = \lambda^2 - (a_{11} + a_{22})\lambda + (a_{11}a_{22} - a_{12}a_{21}) = 0. \qquad (4.8)$$

Because this is a quadratic equation, we know there are exactly two solutions for λ. These solutions may or may not be unique or real. A similar manipulation for an n by n matrix will yield an nth degree polynomial in λ. Because it is not possible, in general, to find exact explicit solutions of polynomial equations of degree greater than four, we can only be guaranteed to find eigenvalues of matrices 4 by 4 or smaller by analytic methods. For larger matrices, numerical methods are the only option.

An important special case is eigenvalues of symmetric matrices (where $\mathbf{A} = \mathbf{A}^T$). Here, it is known that the eigenvalues are real. If they are also distinct, their eigenvectors are mutually orthogonal. Such matrices can be put into *diagonal form*:

$$\mathbf{A} = \mathbf{RDR}^T, \qquad (4.9)$$

where $\mathbf{R}$ is an orthogonal matrix and $\mathbf{D}$ is a diagonal matrix. Recall that an orthogonal matrix might be better called an orthonormal matrix; its columns are mutually orthogonal and the sum of the squares of the elements of each column are one. The columns of $\mathbf{R}$ are the eigenvectors of $\mathbf{A}$ and the non-zero elements of $\mathbf{D}$ are the eigenvalues of $\mathbf{A}$. For example, given the matrix

$$\mathbf{A} = \begin{bmatrix} 2 & 1 \\ 1 & 1 \end{bmatrix},$$

the eigenvalues of $\mathbf{A}$ are the solutions to

$$\lambda^2 - 3\lambda + 1 = 0.$$

We approximate the exact values for compactness of notation:

$$\lambda = \frac{3 \pm \sqrt{5}}{2}, \approx \begin{bmatrix} 2.618 \\ 0.382 \end{bmatrix}.$$

Now we can find the associated eigenvector. The first is the nontrivial (not $x = y = 0$) solution to the homogeneous equation:

$$\begin{bmatrix} 2 - 2.618 & 1 \\ 1 & 1 - 2.618 \end{bmatrix} \begin{bmatrix} x \\ y \end{bmatrix} = \begin{bmatrix} 0 \\ 0 \end{bmatrix}.$$

This is approximately $(x, y) = (0.8507, 0.5257)$. Note that there are infinitely many solutions parallel to that 2D vector, and we just picked the one of unit length. Similarly the eigenvector associated with λ_2 is $(x, y) = (-0.5257, 0.8507)$. This means the diagonal form of $\mathbf{A}$ is (within some precision due to our numeric approximation):

$$\begin{bmatrix} 2 & 1 \\ 1 & 1 \end{bmatrix} = \begin{bmatrix} 0.8507 & -0.5257 \\ 0.5257 & 0.8507 \end{bmatrix} \begin{bmatrix} 2.618 & 0 \\ 0 & 0.382 \end{bmatrix} \begin{bmatrix} 0.8507 & 0.5257 \\ -0.5257 & 0.8507 \end{bmatrix}.$$

We will revisit the geometry of this matrix as a transform in the next chapter.

4.2.7 Singular Value Decomposition

We saw in the last section that any symmetric matrix can be "diagonalized". However, most matrices we encounter in graphics are not symmetric. Fortunately, these matrices can be decomposed using *singular value decomposition* (SVD). We take the matrix $\mathbf{M}$ and represent it as

$$\mathbf{M} = \mathbf{USV},$$

where $\mathbf{U}$ and $\mathbf{V}$ are orthogonal and $\mathbf{S}$ is diagonal. The diagonal elements of $\mathbf{S}$ are the *singular values* of $\mathbf{M}$. There is a standard trick to computing the SVD. First we define $\mathbf{A} = \mathbf{MM}^T$. We assume that we can perform a SVD on $\mathbf{M}$:

$$\mathbf{A} = \mathbf{MM}^T = (\mathbf{USV})(\mathbf{USV})^T = \mathbf{USVV}^T\mathbf{SU}^T = \mathbf{US}^2\mathbf{U}^T.$$

The substitution is based on the fact that $(\mathbf{BC})^T = \mathbf{C}^T\mathbf{B}^T$, that the transpose of an orthogonal matrix is its inverse, and the transpose of a diagonal matrix is the matrix itself. The beauty of this new form is that $\mathbf{A}$ is symmetric, and $\mathbf{US}^2\mathbf{U}^T$ is its eigenvalue diagonal decomposition, where $\mathbf{S}^2$ contains the eigenvalues. Thus, we find that the singular values of a matrix are the square roots of the eigenvalues of that matrix times its transpose. We now make this concrete with an example:

$$\mathbf{M} = \begin{bmatrix} 1 & 1 \\ 0 & 1 \end{bmatrix} \quad \mathbf{A} = \mathbf{MM}^T = \begin{bmatrix} 2 & 1 \\ 1 & 1 \end{bmatrix}.$$

We saw the eigenvalue decomposition for this matrix in the previous section. We observe immediately

$$\begin{bmatrix} 1 & 1 \\ 0 & 1 \end{bmatrix} = \begin{bmatrix} 0.8507 & -0.5257 \\ 0.5257 & 0.8507 \end{bmatrix} \begin{bmatrix} \sqrt{2.618} & 0 \\ 0 & \sqrt{0.382} \end{bmatrix} \mathbf{V}.$$

We can solve for $\mathbf{V}$ algebraically:

$$\mathbf{V} = \mathbf{S}^{-1}\mathbf{U}^T\mathbf{A}.$$

The inverse of $\mathbf{S}$ is a diagonal matrix with the reciprocals of the diagonal elements of $\mathbf{S}$. This yields:

$$\begin{bmatrix} 1 & 1 \\ 0 & 1 \end{bmatrix} = \mathbf{U} \begin{bmatrix} \sigma_1 & 0 \\ 0 & \sigma_2 \end{bmatrix} \mathbf{V}$$

$$= \begin{bmatrix} 0.8507 & -0.5257 \\ 0.5257 & 0.8507 \end{bmatrix} \begin{bmatrix} 1.618 & 0 \\ 0 & 0.618 \end{bmatrix} \begin{bmatrix} 0.5257 & 0.8507 \\ -0.8507 & 0.5257 \end{bmatrix}.$$

This form used the standard symbol σ for a singular value. Note that for a symmetric matrix, the eigenvalues and the singular values are the same ($\sigma_i = \lambda_i$). Also note that the eigenvalue diagonalization and the SVD are the same. We will examine the geometry of SVD more in Section 5.1.6.

Frequently Asked Questions

• Why is matrix multiplication defined the way it is rather than just element by element?

Element by element multiplication is a perfectly good way to define matrix multiplication, and indeed it has nice properties. However, in practice it is not very useful. Ultimately most matrices are used to transform column vectors, e.g., in 3D you might have:

$$\mathbf{b} = \mathbf{M}\mathbf{a}$$

where $\mathbf{a}$ and $\mathbf{b}$ are vectors and $\mathbf{M}$ is a three by three matrix. To allow geometric operations such as rotation, combinations of all three elements of $\mathbf{a}$ must go into each element of $\mathbf{b}$. That requires us to either go row-by-row or column-by-column through $\mathbf{M}$. That choice is made based on composition of matrices having the desired property:

$$\mathbf{M}_2(\mathbf{M}_1\mathbf{a}) = (\mathbf{M}_2\mathbf{M}_1)\mathbf{a}$$

which allows us to use one composite matrix $\mathbf{C} = \mathbf{M}_2\mathbf{M}_1$ to transform our vector. This is valuable when many vectors will be transformed by the same composite matrix. So in summary, the somewhat weird rule for matrix multiplication is engineered to have these desired properties.

• Sometimes I hear that eigenvalues and singular values are the same thing and sometimes that one is the square of the other. Which is right?

If a real matrix $\mathbf{M}$ is symmetric, then its eigenvalues and singular values are the same. If $\mathbf{M}$ is not symmetric, the matrix $\mathbf{A} = \mathbf{M}\mathbf{M}^T$ is symmetric and has real eignenvalues. The singular values of $\mathbf{M}$ and $\mathbf{M}^T$ are the same, and are the square roots of the singular/eigenvalues of $\mathbf{A}$. Thus, when the square root statement is made, it is because two different matrices (with a very particular relationship) are being talked about: $\mathbf{A} = \mathbf{M}\mathbf{M}^T$.

Notes

The discussion of determinants as volumes is based on *A Vector Space Approach to Geometry* (Hausner, Dover, 1998). Hausner has an excellent discussion of vector analysis and the fundamentals of geometry as well. The geometric derivation of Cramer's rule in 2D is taken from *The Geometry Toolbox for Graphics and Modeling* (Farin and Hansford, A K Peters, 1998). That book also has geometric interpretations of other linear algebra operations such as Gaussian elimination. The discussion of eigenvalues and singular values is based primarily on *Linear Algebra and its Applications* (Strang, Harcourt Brace College Publishers, 1998). The example of SVD of the shear matrix is based on a discussion in *Computer Graphics and Geometric Modeling* (Solomon, Springer Verlag, 1999).

Exercises

1. Write an implicit equation for the 2D line through points (x_0, y_0) and (x_1, y_1) using a 2D determinant.

2. Show that if the rows of a matrix are orthonormal, then so are the columns.

3. Show that the eigenvalues of a diagonal matrix are its diagonal elements.

4. Show that for a square matrix $\mathbf{A}$, $\mathbf{A}\mathbf{A}^T$ is a symmetric matrix.

Transformation Matrices

In this chapter we describe how we can use matrix multiplications to accomplish changes in a vector such as scaling, rotation, and translation. We also discuss how these transforms operate differently on locations (points), displacement vectors, and surface normal vectors.

We will show how a set of points transform if they are represented as offset vectors from the origin. So think of the image we shall use (a clock) as a bunch of points which are the ends of vectors whose tails are at the origin.

5.1 Basic 2D Transforms

We can use matrices to change the components of a 2D vector. For example:

$$\begin{bmatrix} a_{11} & a_{12} \\ a_{21} & a_{22} \end{bmatrix} \begin{bmatrix} x \\ y \end{bmatrix} = \begin{bmatrix} a_{11}x + a_{12}y \\ a_{21}x + a_{22}y \end{bmatrix}.$$

Such a transformation can change vectors in a variety of ways which are useful. In particular it can be used to scale, rotate, and shear. We will introduce more general transformations later, but the basics of transformation is embodied in the simple formula above. For our purposes, consider moving along the x-axis a horizontal move, and the y-axis, a vertical move.

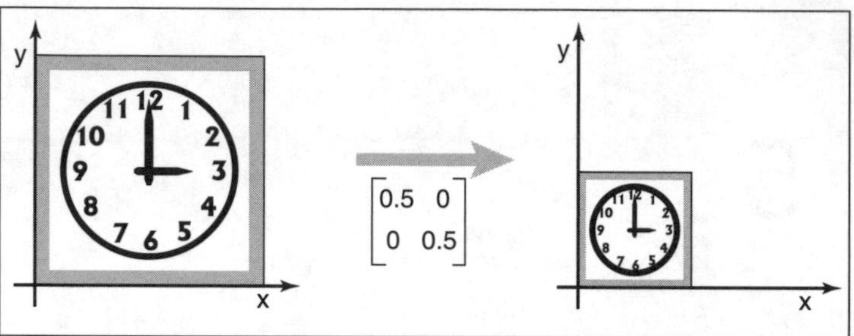

Figure 5.1. Scaling uniformly by half for each axis. The scale matrix has the proportion of change in each of the diagonal elements, and zeroes in the off-diagonal elements.

5.1.1 Scaling

The most basic transform is a *scale*. This transform can change length and possibly direction.

$$\text{scale}(s_x, s_y) = \begin{bmatrix} s_x & 0 \\ 0 & s_y \end{bmatrix}.$$

Note what this matrix does to a vector with Cartesian components (x, y):

$$\begin{bmatrix} s_x & 0 \\ 0 & s_y \end{bmatrix} \begin{bmatrix} x \\ y \end{bmatrix} = \begin{bmatrix} s_x x \\ s_y y \end{bmatrix}.$$

For example, the matrix that shrinks x and y uniformly by a factor of two is (Figure 5.1):

$$\text{scale}(0.5, 0.5) = \begin{bmatrix} 0.5 & 0 \\ 0 & 0.5 \end{bmatrix}.$$

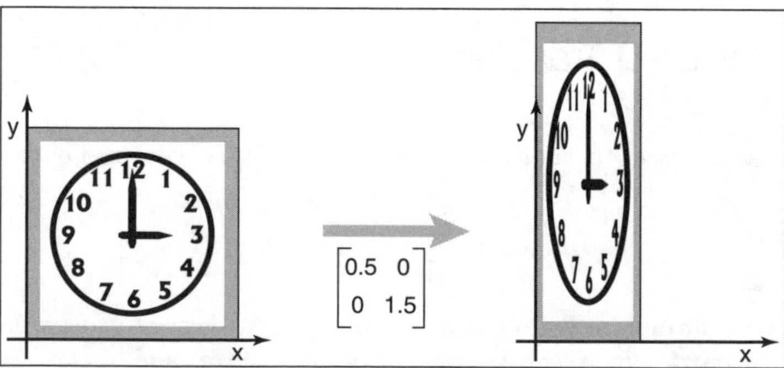

Figure 5.2. Scaling non-uniformly in *x* and *y*. The scaling matrix is diagonal with non-equal elements. Note that the square outline of the clock becomes a rectangle and the circular face becomes an ellipse.

A matrix which halves in the horizontal and increases to three-halves in the vertical is (see Figure 5.2):

$$\text{scale}(0.5, 1.5) = \begin{bmatrix} 0.5 & 0 \\ 0 & 1.5 \end{bmatrix}.$$

5.1.2 Shearing

A shear is something that pushes things sideways, producing something like a deck of cards across which you push your hand; the bottom card stays put and cards move more the closer they are to the top of the deck. The horizontal and vertical shear matrices are:

$$\text{shear-x}(s) = \begin{bmatrix} 1 & s \\ 0 & 1 \end{bmatrix}, \quad \text{shear-y}(s) = \begin{bmatrix} 1 & 0 \\ s & 1 \end{bmatrix}.$$

For example, the transform that shears horizontally so that vertical lines become 45° lines leaning towards the right is (see Figure 5.3):

$$\text{shear-x}(1) = \begin{bmatrix} 1 & 1 \\ 0 & 1 \end{bmatrix}.$$

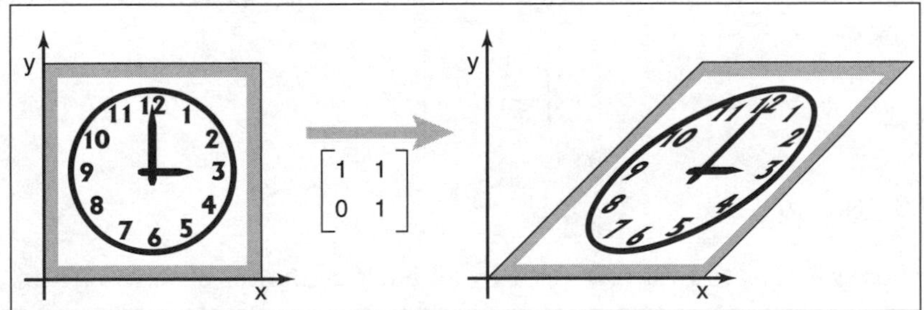

Figure 5.3. An *x* shear matrix moves points to the right in proportion to their *y* coordinate. Now the square outline of the clock becomes a parallelogram and, as with scaling, the circular face of the clock becomes an ellipse.

An analogous transform vertically is (see Figure 5.4):

$$\text{shear-y}(1) = \begin{bmatrix} 1 & 0 \\ 1 & 1 \end{bmatrix}.$$

Note that the square outline of the sheared clock becomes a parallelogram. Also, note that the circular face of the sheared clock looks like it could be an ellipse. In fact it is, as will be evident when we discuss SVD.

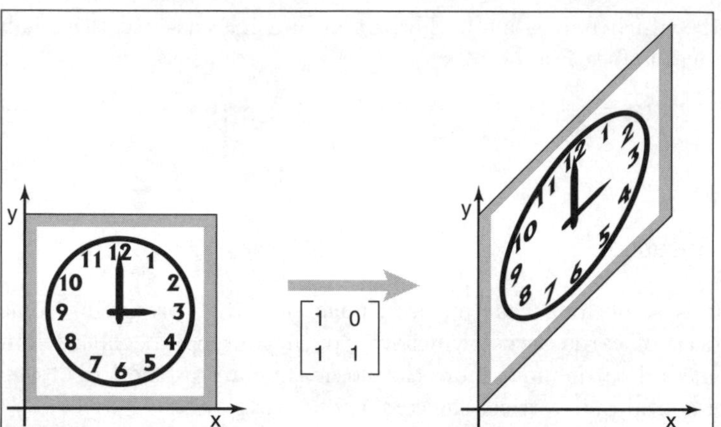

Figure 5.4. A *y* shear matrix moves points up in proportion to their *x* coordinate.

Another way to think of a shear is in terms of rotation of only the vertical (or horizontal) axes. The shear transform that takes a vertical axis and tilts it clockwise by an angle ϕ is:

$$\begin{bmatrix} 1 & \tan\phi \\ 0 & 1 \end{bmatrix}.$$

Similarly, the shear matrix which rotates the horizontal axis counter-clockwise by angle ϕ is:

$$\begin{bmatrix} 1 & 0 \\ \tan\phi & 1 \end{bmatrix}.$$

5.1.3 Rotation

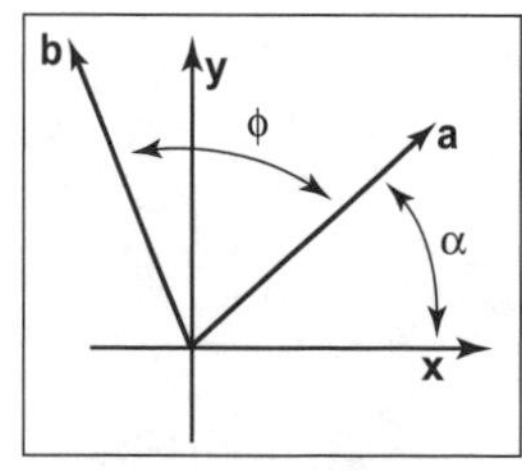

Figure 5.5. The geometry for Equation 5.1.

Suppose we want to rotate a vector by an angle ϕ counter-clockwise. First, suppose we have a vector $\mathbf{a} = (x_a, y_a)$, and we want to rotate it by an angle ϕ to get to vector $\mathbf{b} = (x_b, y_b)$. If the vector $\mathbf{a}$ makes an angle α with the x-axis, and its length is $r = x_a^2 + y_a^2$, then we know that by definition:

$$\begin{aligned} x_a &= r\cos\alpha, \\ y_a &= r\sin\alpha. \end{aligned}$$

Because $\mathbf{b}$ is a rotation of $\mathbf{a}$, it also has length r. Because it is rotated an angle ϕ from $\mathbf{a}$, the angle $\mathbf{b}$ makes with the x-axis is $(\alpha + \phi)$ (Figure 5.5). From basic trigonometry we know:

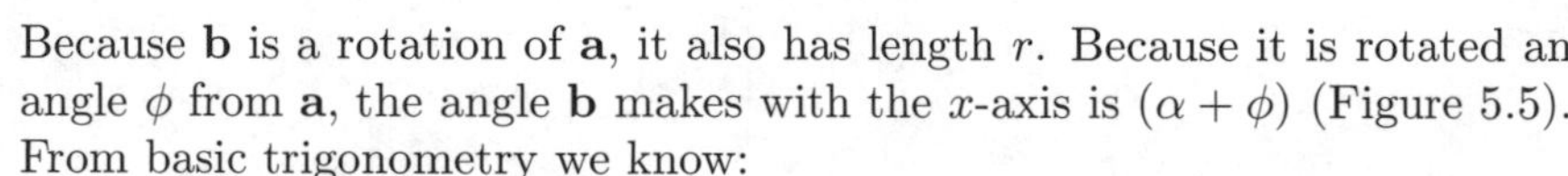

$$\begin{aligned} x_b &= r\cos(\alpha + \phi) = r\cos\alpha\cos\phi - r\sin\alpha\sin\phi, \\ y_b &= r\sin(\alpha + \phi) = r\sin\alpha\cos\phi + r\cos\alpha\sin\phi. \end{aligned} \tag{5.1}$$

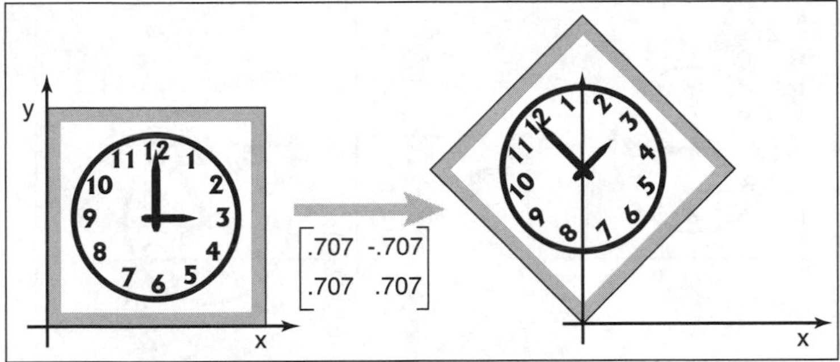

Figure 5.6. A rotation by 45 degrees. Note that the rotation is counter-clockwise, and that cos(45°) = sin(45°) ≈ .707.

Substituting the components in $x_a = \cos\alpha$ and $y_a = \sin\alpha$ gives:

$$x_b = x_a \cos\phi - y_a \sin\phi,$$
$$y_b = y_a \cos\phi + x_a \sin\phi.$$

In matrix form, the equivalent transformation that takes **a** to **b** is:

$$\text{rotate}(\phi) = \begin{bmatrix} \cos\phi & -\sin\phi \\ \sin\phi & \cos\phi \end{bmatrix}.$$

For example, a matrix which rotates vectors by $\pi/4$ radians (45 degrees) is (see Figure 5.6):

$$\begin{bmatrix} \cos\frac{\pi}{4} & -\sin\frac{\pi}{4} \\ \sin\frac{\pi}{4} & \cos\frac{\pi}{4} \end{bmatrix} = \begin{bmatrix} 0.707 & -0.707 \\ 0.707 & 0.707 \end{bmatrix}.$$

A matrix which rotates by $\pi/6$ radians (30 degrees) in the *clockwise* direction is a rotation by $-\pi/6$ radians in our framework (see Figure 5.7):

$$\begin{bmatrix} \cos\frac{-\pi}{6} & -\sin\frac{-\pi}{6} \\ \sin\frac{-\pi}{6} & \cos\frac{-\pi}{6} \end{bmatrix} = \begin{bmatrix} 0.866 & 0.5 \\ -0.5 & 0.866 \end{bmatrix}.$$

Because the norm of each row of a rotation matrix is one ($\sin^2\phi + \cos^2\phi = 1$), and the rows are orthogonal ($\cos\phi(-\sin\phi) + \sin\phi\cos\phi = 0$), we see that rotation matrices are orthogonal matrices (i.e., orthogonal rows each of length one).

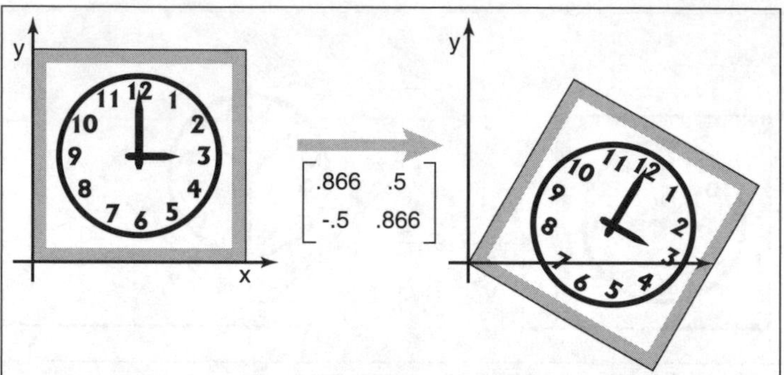

Figure 5.7. A rotation by minus thirty degrees. Note that the rotation is clockwise, and that cos(-30°) $\approx$ .866 and sin(-30°) = -.5.

5.1.4 Reflection

We can reflect a vector around either of the coordinate axes (see Figures 5.8 and 5.9):

$$\text{reflect-x}(s) = \begin{bmatrix} -1 & 0 \\ 0 & 1 \end{bmatrix}, \quad \text{reflect-y}(s) = \begin{bmatrix} 1 & 0 \\ 0 & -1 \end{bmatrix}.$$

While one might expect that the matrix with -1 in both elements of the diagonal is also a reflection, in fact it is just a rotation by π radians.

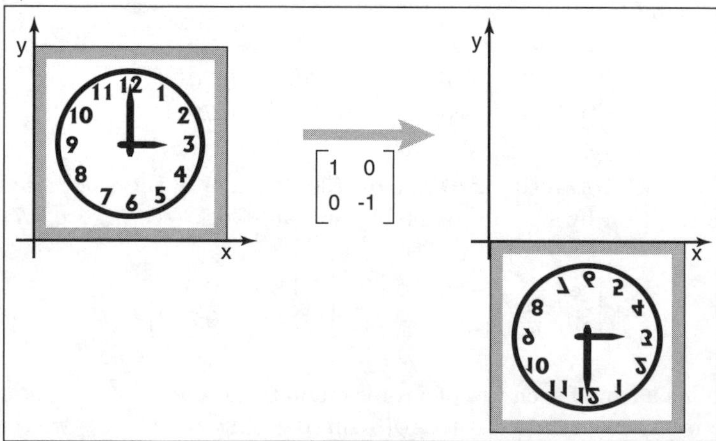

Figure 5.8. A reflection about the *x*-axis is achieved by multiplying all *y* coordinates by -1.

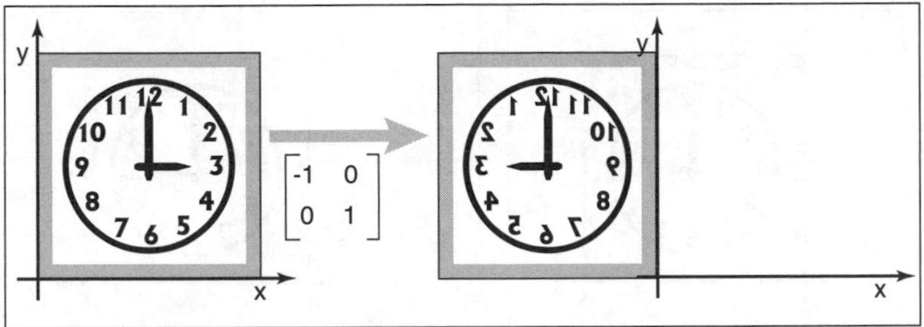

Figure 5.9. A reflection about the *y*-axis is achieved by multiplying all *x* coordinates by -1.

5.1.5 Composition of 2D Transforms

It is common for graphics programs to apply more than one transformation to an object. For example, we might want to first apply a scale $\mathbf{S}$, and then a rotation $\mathbf{R}$. This would be done in two steps on a 2D vector $\mathbf{v}_1$:

$$\text{first,}\mathbf{v}_2 = \mathbf{S}\mathbf{v}_1, \text{ then,}\mathbf{v}_3 = \mathbf{R}\mathbf{v}_2.$$

Another way to write this is:

$$\mathbf{v}_3 = \mathbf{R}(\mathbf{S}\mathbf{v}_1).$$

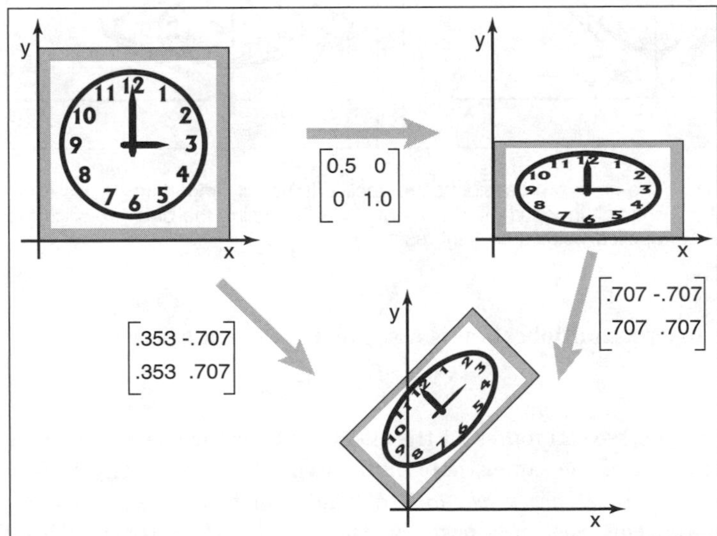

Figure 5.10. Applying the two transform matrices in sequence is the same as applying the product of those matrices once. This is a key concept that underlies most graphics hardware and software.

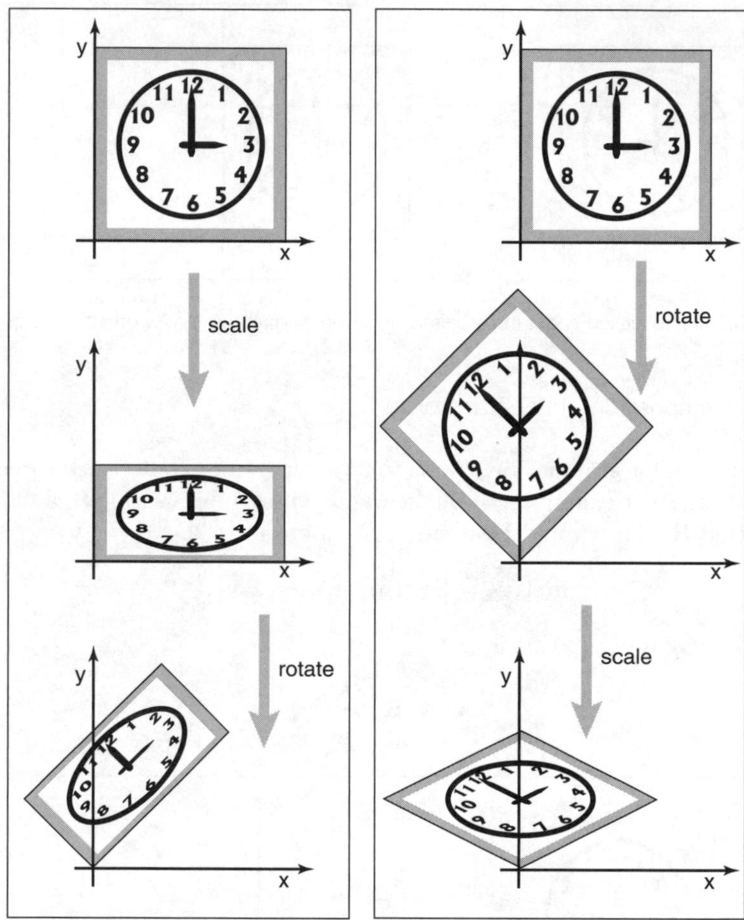

Figure 5.11. The order two transforms are applied is usually important. In this example we do a scale by one-half in *y* and then rotate by 45°. Reversing the order in which these two transforms are applied yields a different result.

Because matrix multiplication is associative, we can also write:

$$\mathbf{v}_3 = (\mathbf{RS})\,\mathbf{v}_1.$$

In other words, we can represent the effects of transforms by two matrices in a single matrix of the same size by multiplying the two matrices: $\mathbf{M} = \mathbf{RS}$ (Figure 5.10). It is *very important* to remember that these transforms are applied from the *right side first.* So the matrix $\mathbf{M} = \mathbf{RS}$ first applies $\mathbf{S}$ and then $\mathbf{R}$.

As an example, suppose we want to scale by one-half in the vertical direction and then rotate by $\pi/4$ radians (45 degrees). The resulting matrix is:

$$\begin{bmatrix} 0.707 & -0.707 \\ 0.707 & 0.707 \end{bmatrix} \begin{bmatrix} 0.5 & 0 \\ 0 & 1 \end{bmatrix} = \begin{bmatrix} 0.353 & -0.707 \\ 0.353 & 0.707 \end{bmatrix}$$

It is important to always remember that matrix multiplication is not commutative. So the order of transforms *does* matter. For example, scaling then rotating is usually different than rotating then scaling (see Figure 5.11).

5.1.6 Decomposition of 2D Transforms

For any given transformation matrix $\mathbf{M}$, we can decompose it into various matrix products $\mathbf{M} = \mathbf{M}_1\mathbf{M}_2$, $\mathbf{M} = \mathbf{M}_3\mathbf{M}_4\mathbf{M}_5$, and so on.

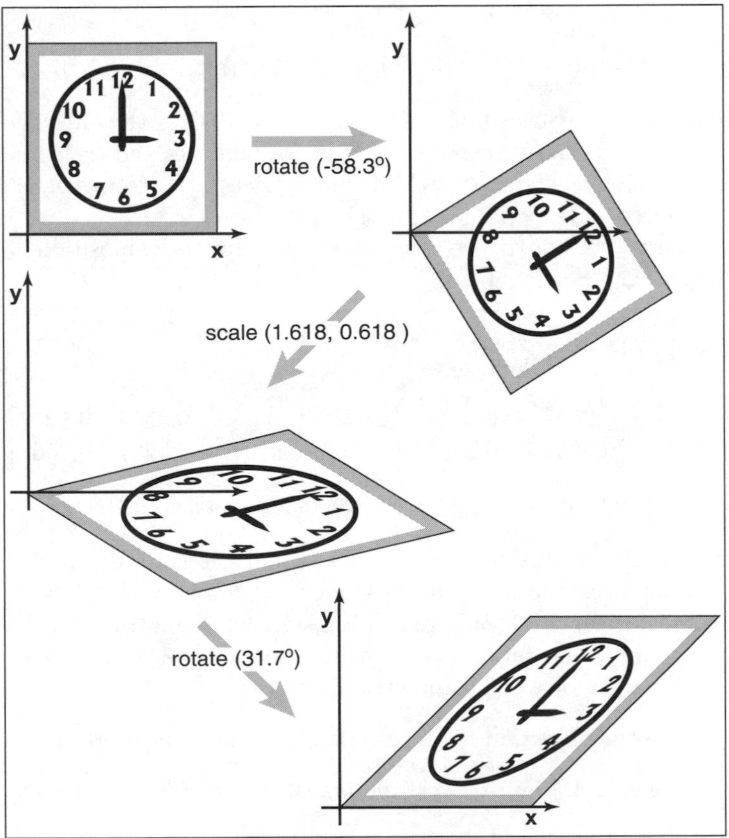

Figure 5.12. Singular Value Decomposition (SVD) for a shear matrix. Any 2D matrix can be decomposed into a product of rotation, scale, rotation. Note that the circular face of the clock must become an ellipse because it is just a rotated and scaled circle.

An interesting result is that any 2D transform can be decomposed into the product of a rotation, a scale, and a rotation, with the caveat that the scale may have minus signs in it (i.e., it may include a reflection). This observation follows from the existence of the *singular value decomposition* (SVD) discussed in Section 4.2.7. As shown there, a matrix is a product $\mathbf{M} = \mathbf{R}_2\mathbf{S}\mathbf{R}_1$, where $\mathbf{R}_1$ and $\mathbf{R}_2$ are rotation matrices, and $\mathbf{S}$ is a scale matrix. The example used in Section 4.2.7 is in fact a shear matrix (Figure 5.12):

$$\begin{aligned}\begin{bmatrix}1 & 1\\ 0 & 1\end{bmatrix} &= \mathbf{R}_2 \begin{bmatrix}\sigma_1 & 0\\ 0 & \sigma_2\end{bmatrix} \mathbf{R}_1\\ &= \begin{bmatrix}0.8507 & -0.5257\\ 0.5257 & 0.8507\end{bmatrix} \begin{bmatrix}1.618 & 0\\ 0 & 0.618\end{bmatrix} \begin{bmatrix}0.5257 & 0.8507\\ -0.8507 & 0.5257\end{bmatrix}\\ &= \text{rotate}\ (31.7^\circ)\ \text{scale}\ (1.618, 0.618)\ \text{rotate}\ (-58.3^\circ).\end{aligned}$$

An immediate consequence of the existence of SVD is that all 2D basic transform matrices can be made from rotation matrices and scale matrices (with negative elements allowed). Shear matrices are a convenience, but are not required for expressing potential transforms.

For a symmetric matrix, we can do an eigenvalue decomposition. Recall the example from Section 4.2.6:

$$\begin{aligned}\begin{bmatrix}2 & 1\\ 1 & 1\end{bmatrix} &= \mathbf{R} \begin{bmatrix}\lambda_1 & 0\\ 0 & \lambda_2\end{bmatrix} \mathbf{R}^T\\ &= \begin{bmatrix}0.8507 & -0.5257\\ 0.5257 & 0.8507\end{bmatrix} \begin{bmatrix}2.618 & 0\\ 0 & 0.382\end{bmatrix} \begin{bmatrix}0.8507 & 0.5257\\ -0.5257 & 0.8507\end{bmatrix}\\ &= \text{rotate}\ (31.7^\circ)\ \text{scale}\ (2.618, 0.382)\ \text{rotate}\ (-31.7^\circ).\end{aligned}$$

Note that this is exactly the product we would get if we did SVD; SVD and eigenvalue decomposition are the same for symmetric matrices. Again, the diagonal form $\mathbf{R}\mathbf{S}\mathbf{R}^T$ only exists for symmetric matrices, so SVD is certainly the more general tool. The geometric interpretation of the transformation by a diagonalized symmetric matrix is:

1. Rotate some direction to the x-axis (the transform by $\mathbf{R}^T$);
2. Scale in x and y by (λ_1, λ_2) (the transform by $\mathbf{S}$);
3. Rotate the y-axis back to the original direction (the transform by $\mathbf{R}$).

These three transforms together have the effect of a scale in an arbitrary direction (Figure 5.13). For example, the matrix above, according to its

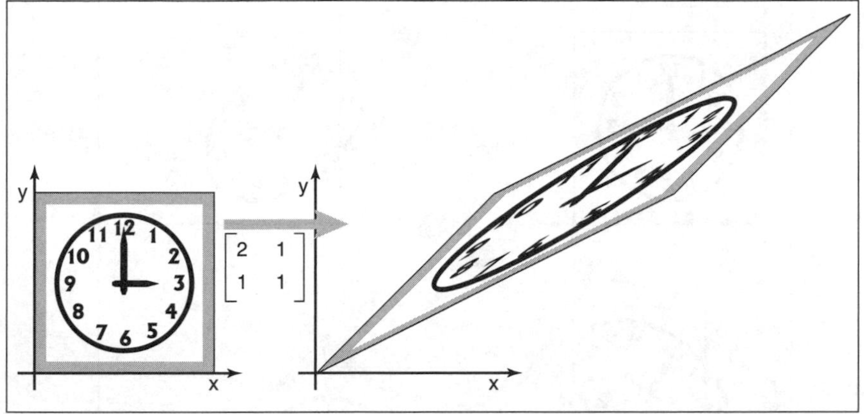

Figure 5.13. A symmetric matrix is always a scale along some axis. In this case it is along the ϕ = 31.7° direction which means the real eigenvector for this matrix is in that direction.

eigenvalue decomposition, scales in a direction 31.7° counter-clockwise from three o'clock (the x-axis). This is a touch before 2pm on the clockface as is confirmed by the figure. We can also reverse the diagonalization process; to scale by (λ_1, λ_2) with the scaling by λ_1 in angle ϕ we have:

$$\begin{bmatrix} \cos\phi & \sin\phi \\ -\sin\phi & \cos\phi \end{bmatrix} \begin{bmatrix} \lambda_1 & 0 \\ 0 & \lambda_2 \end{bmatrix} \begin{bmatrix} \cos\phi & -\sin\phi \\ \sin\phi & \cos\phi \end{bmatrix} = \begin{bmatrix} \lambda_1 \cos^2\phi + \lambda_2 \sin^2\phi & (\lambda_2 - \lambda_1)\cos\phi\sin\phi \\ (\lambda_2 - \lambda_1)\cos\phi\sin\phi & \lambda_2 \cos^2\phi + \lambda_1 \sin^2\phi \end{bmatrix}.$$

We should take heart that this is a symmetric matrix as we know must be true since we constructed it assuming an eigenvalue diagonalization was possible.

In summary, every matrix can be decomposed via SVD into a rotation times a scale times another rotation. Only symmetric matrices can be decomposed via eigenvalue diagonalization into a rotation times a scale times the inverse-rotation, and such matrices are a simple scale in an arbitrary direction. The SVD of a symmetric matrix will yield the same triple product as eigenvalue decomposition via a slightly more complex algebraic manipulation.

Another decomposition uses shears to represent non-zero rotations. The following identity allows this:

$$\begin{bmatrix} \cos\phi & -\sin\phi \\ \sin\phi & \cos\phi \end{bmatrix} = \begin{bmatrix} 1 & \frac{\cos\phi - 1}{\sin\phi} \\ 0 & 1 \end{bmatrix} \begin{bmatrix} 1 & 0 \\ \sin\phi & 1 \end{bmatrix} \begin{bmatrix} 1 & \frac{\cos\phi - 1}{\sin\phi} \\ 0 & 1 \end{bmatrix}.$$

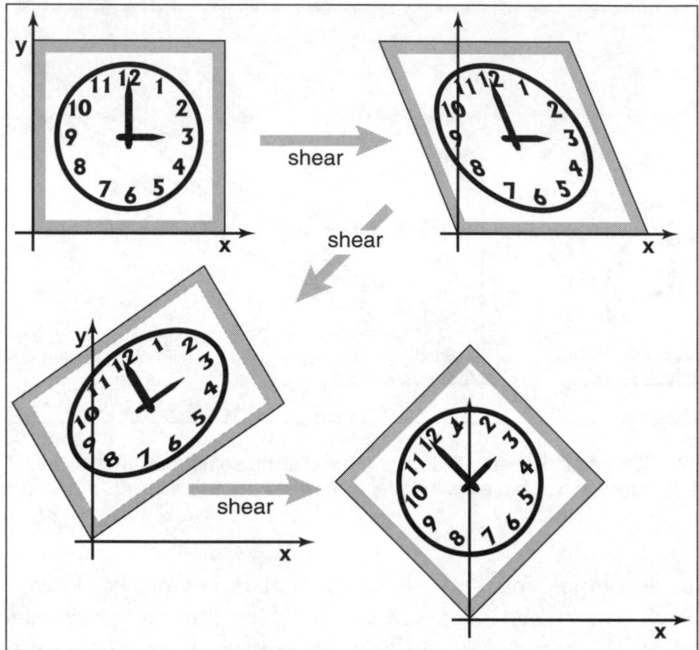

Figure 5.14. Any 2D rotation can be accomplished by three shears in sequence. In this case a rotation by 45° is decomposed as shown in Equation 5.2.

For example, a rotation by $\pi/4$ (45 degrees) is (see Figure 5.14):

$$\text{rotate}(\frac{\pi}{4}) = \begin{bmatrix} 1 & 1-\sqrt{2} \\ 0 & 1 \end{bmatrix} \begin{bmatrix} 1 & 0 \\ \frac{\sqrt{2}}{2} & 1 \end{bmatrix} \begin{bmatrix} 1 & 1-\sqrt{2} \\ 0 & 1 \end{bmatrix}. \tag{5.2}$$

This particular transform is useful for raster rotation because shearing is a very efficient raster operation for images; it introduces some jagginess, but will leave no holes. The key observation is that if we take a raster position (i, j) and apply a horizontal shear to it, we get

$$\begin{bmatrix} 1 & s \\ 0 & 1 \end{bmatrix} \begin{bmatrix} i \\ j \end{bmatrix} = \begin{bmatrix} i + sj \\ j \end{bmatrix}.$$

If we round sj to the nearest integer, this amounts to taking each row in the image and moving it sideways by some amount—a different amount for each row. Because it is the same displacement within a row, this allows us to rotate with no gaps in the resulting image. A similar action works for a vertical shear. Thus, we can implement a simple raster rotation easily.

5.2 Basic 3D Transforms

The basic 3D transforms are an extension of the 2D transforms. For example, a scale along Cartesian axes is:

$$\text{scale}(s_x, s_y, s_z) = \begin{bmatrix} s_x & 0 & 0 \\ 0 & s_y & 0 \\ 0 & 0 & s_z \end{bmatrix}. \tag{5.3}$$

Rotation is somewhat more complicated because there are now more possible axes of rotation. However, if we simply want to rotate about the z-axis, which will only change x and y coordinates, we can use the 2D rotation matrix with no operation on z:

$$\text{rotate-z}(\phi) = \begin{bmatrix} \cos\phi & -\sin\phi & 0 \\ \sin\phi & \cos\phi & 0 \\ 0 & 0 & 1 \end{bmatrix}.$$

Similarly we can construct matrices to rotate about the x-axis and the y-axis:

$$\text{rotate-x}(\phi) = \begin{bmatrix} 1 & 0 & 0 \\ 0 & \cos\phi & -\sin\phi \\ 0 & \sin\phi & \cos\phi \end{bmatrix},$$

$$\text{rotate-y}(\phi) = \begin{bmatrix} \cos\phi & 0 & \sin\phi \\ 0 & 1 & 0 \\ -\sin\phi & 0 & \cos\phi \end{bmatrix}.$$

We will discuss rotations about arbitrary axes in the next section.

As in two dimensions, we can shear along a particular axis, for example:

$$\text{shear-x}(d_y, d_z) = \begin{bmatrix} 1 & d_y & d_z \\ 0 & 1 & 0 \\ 0 & 0 & 1 \end{bmatrix}.$$

As with 2D transforms, any 3D transformation matrix can be decomposed using SVD into a rotation, scale, and another rotation. Any symmetric 3D matrix has an eigenvalue decomposition into rotation, scale, and inverse-rotation. Finally, a 3D rotation can be decomposed into a product of 3D shear matrices.

5.2.1 Arbitrary 3D Rotations

As in 2D, 3D rotations are *orthonormal* matrices. Geometrically, this means the three rows of the matrix are the Cartesian coordinates of three mutually-orthogonal unit vectors as discussed in Section 2.4.5. The columns are three potentially different mutually-orthogonal unit vectors. There are an infinite number of such rotation matrices. Let's write down such a matrix:

$$\mathbf{R}_{uvw} = \begin{bmatrix} x_u & y_u & z_u \\ x_v & y_v & z_v \\ x_w & y_w & z_w \end{bmatrix}$$

Here, $\mathbf{u} = x_u\mathbf{x} + y_u\mathbf{y} + z_u\mathbf{z}$ and so on for $\mathbf{v}$ and $\mathbf{w}$. Since the three vectors are orthonormal we know:

$$\begin{aligned} \mathbf{u}\cdot\mathbf{u} = \mathbf{v}\cdot\mathbf{v} = \mathbf{w}\cdot\mathbf{w} = 1, \\ \mathbf{u}\cdot\mathbf{v} = \mathbf{v}\cdot\mathbf{w} = \mathbf{w}\cdot\mathbf{u} = 0. \end{aligned}$$

We can infer some of the behavior of the rotation matrix by applying it to the vectors $\mathbf{u}$, $\mathbf{v}$ and $\mathbf{w}$. For example,

$$\mathbf{R}_{uvw}\mathbf{u} = \begin{bmatrix} x_u & y_u & z_u \\ x_v & y_v & z_v \\ x_w & y_w & z_w \end{bmatrix} \begin{bmatrix} x_u \\ y_u \\ z_u \end{bmatrix} = \begin{bmatrix} x_u x_u + y_u y_u + z_u z_u \\ x_v x_u + y_v y_u + z_v z_u \\ x_w x_u + y_w y_u + z_w z_u \end{bmatrix}.$$

Note that those three rows of $\mathbf{R}_{uvw}\mathbf{u}$ are all dot products:

$$\mathbf{R}_{uvw}\mathbf{u} = \begin{bmatrix} \mathbf{u}\cdot\mathbf{u} \\ \mathbf{v}\cdot\mathbf{u} \\ \mathbf{w}\cdot\mathbf{u} \end{bmatrix} = \begin{bmatrix} 1 \\ 0 \\ 0 \end{bmatrix} = \mathbf{x}.$$

Similarly, $\mathbf{R}_{uvw}\mathbf{v} = \mathbf{y}$, and $\mathbf{R}_{uvw}\mathbf{w} = \mathbf{z}$. So $\mathbf{R}_{uvw}$ takes the basis $\mathbf{uvw}$ to the corresponding Cartesian axes via rotation.

If $\mathbf{R}_{uvw}$ is a rotation matrix with orthonormal rows, then $\mathbf{R}_{uvw}^T$ is also a rotation matrix with orthonormal columns, and in fact is the inverse of $\mathbf{R}_{uvw}$ (the inverse of an orthogonal matrix is always its transpose). An important point is that for transformation matrices, the algebraic inverse is also the geometric inverse. So if $\mathbf{R}_{uvw}$ takes $\mathbf{u}$ to $\mathbf{x}$, then $\mathbf{R}_{uvw}^T$ takes $\mathbf{x}$ to $\mathbf{u}$. The same should be true of $\mathbf{v}$ and $\mathbf{y}$ as we can confirm:

$$\mathbf{R}_{uvw}^T\mathbf{y} = \begin{bmatrix} x_u & x_v & x_w \\ y_u & y_v & y_w \\ z_u & z_v & z_w \end{bmatrix} \begin{bmatrix} 0 \\ 1 \\ 0 \end{bmatrix} = \begin{bmatrix} x_v \\ y_v \\ z_v \end{bmatrix} = \mathbf{v}.$$

So we can always create rotation matrices from orthonormal bases.

If we wish to rotate about an arbitrary vector $\mathbf{a}$, we can form an orthonormal basis with $\mathbf{w} = \mathbf{a}$, rotate that basis to the canonical basis $\mathbf{xyz}$, rotate about the z-axis, and then rotate the canonical basis back to the $\mathbf{xyz}$ basis. In matrix form, to rotate about the w-axis by an angle ϕ:

$$\begin{bmatrix} x_u & x_v & x_w \\ y_u & y_v & y_w \\ z_u & z_v & z_w \end{bmatrix} \begin{bmatrix} \cos\phi & -\sin\phi & 0 \\ \sin\phi & \cos\phi & 0 \\ 0 & 0 & 1 \end{bmatrix} \begin{bmatrix} x_u & y_u & z_u \\ x_v & y_v & z_v \\ x_w & y_w & z_w \end{bmatrix}.$$

Here we have $\mathbf{w}$ a unit vector in the direction of $\mathbf{a}$ (i.e. $\mathbf{a}$ divided by its own length). But what are $\mathbf{u}$ and $\mathbf{v}$? A method to find reasonable $\mathbf{u}$ and $\mathbf{v}$ is given in Section 2.4.6.

Note that if we have a rotation matrix and we wish to know in which direction it is rotating, we can compute the one real eigenvalue (which will be $\lambda = 1$), and the corresponding eigenvector is the "pole" of the rotation. This is the one axis that is not changed by the rotation.

5.2.2 Transforming Normal Vectors

While most 3D vectors we use represent positions (offset vectors from the origin) or directions, such as where light comes from, some vectors represent *surface normals*. Surface normal vectors are perpendicular to the tangent plane of a surface. These normals do not transform the way we would like when the underlying surface is transformed. For example, if the points of a surface are transformed by a matrix $\mathbf{M}$, a vector $\mathbf{t}$ that is tangent to the surface and is multiplied by $\mathbf{M}$ will be tangent to the transformed surface. However, a surface normal vector $\mathbf{n}$ that is transformed by $\mathbf{M}$ may not be normal to the transformed surface (Figure 5.15).

We can derive a transform matrix $\mathbf{N}$ which does take $\mathbf{n}$ to a vector perpendicular to the transformed surface. One way to attack this issue is to note that a surface normal vector and a tangent vector are perpendicular, so their dot product is zero, which is expressed in matrix form as:

$$\mathbf{n}^T\mathbf{t} = \mathbf{0}. \qquad (5.4)$$

If we denote the desired transformed vectors as $\mathbf{t}_M = \mathbf{Mt}$ and $\mathbf{n}_N = \mathbf{Nn}$, our goal is to find $\mathbf{n}$ such that $\mathbf{n}_N^T\mathbf{t}_M = \mathbf{0}$. We can find $\mathbf{N}$ by some algebraic tricks. First, we can sneak an identity matrix into the dot product, and

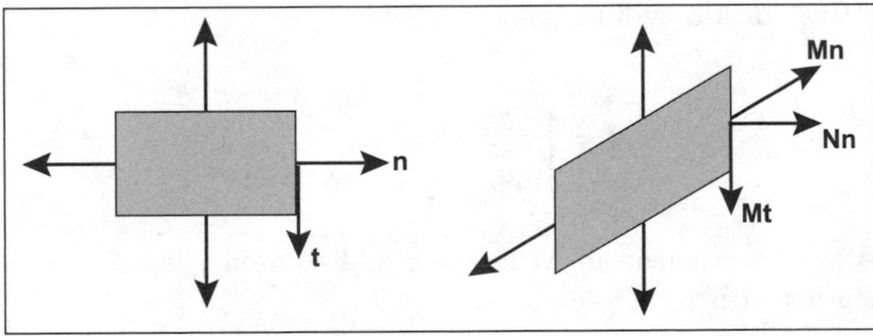

Figure 5.15. When a normal vector is translated using the same matrix that transforms the points on an object, the resulting vector may not be perpendicular to the surface as is shown here for the sheared rectangle. The tangent vector, however, does transform to a vector tangent to the transformed surface.

then take advantage of $\mathbf{M}^{-1}\mathbf{M} = \mathbf{I}$:

$$\mathbf{n}^T\mathbf{t} = \mathbf{n}^T\mathbf{I}\mathbf{t} = \mathbf{n}^T\mathbf{M}^{-1}\mathbf{M}\mathbf{t} = \mathbf{0}.$$

Although the manipulations above don't obviously get us anywhere, note that we can add parentheses that make the above expression more obviously a dot product:

$$\left(\mathbf{n}^T\mathbf{M}^{-1}\right)(\mathbf{M}\mathbf{t}) = \left(\mathbf{n}^T\mathbf{M}^{-1}\right)\mathbf{t}_M = \mathbf{0}.$$

This means that the row vector that is perpendicular to $\mathbf{t}_M$ is the left part of the expression above. This expression holds for any of the tangent vectors in the tangent plane. Since there is only one direction in 3D (and its opposite) that is perpendicular to all such tangent vectors, we know that the left part of the expression above must be the row vector expression for $\mathbf{n}_N$, i.e., it is $\mathbf{n}_M^T$, so this allows us to infer $\mathbf{N}$:

$$\mathbf{n}_M^T = \mathbf{n}^T\mathbf{M}^{-1},$$

so we can take the transpose of that to get:

$$\mathbf{n}_M = \left(\mathbf{n}^T\mathbf{M}^{-1}\right)^T = \left(\mathbf{M}^{-1}\right)^T\mathbf{n}, \tag{5.5}$$

Therefore, we can see that the matrix which correctly transforms normal vectors so they remain normal is $\mathbf{N} = (\mathbf{M}^{-1})^T$, i.e., the transpose of the inverse matrix. Since this matrix may change the length of $\mathbf{n}$, we can multiply it by an arbitrary scalar and it will still produce $\mathbf{n}_N$ with the right direction. Recall from Section 4.2.3 that the inverse of a matrix is the transpose of the cofactor matrix divided by the determinant. Because we don't care about the length of a normal vector, we can skip the division and find that for a 3 by 3 matrix:

$$\mathbf{N} = \begin{bmatrix} m_{11}^c & m_{12}^c & m_{13}^c \\ m_{21}^c & m_{22}^c & m_{23}^c \\ m_{31}^c & m_{32}^c & m_{33}^c \end{bmatrix}.$$

This assumes the element of $\mathbf{M}$ in row i and column j is m_{ij}. So the full expression for $\mathbf{M}$ is:

$$\mathbf{N} = \begin{bmatrix} m_{22}m_{33} - m_{23}m_{32} & m_{23}m_{31} - m_{21}m_{33} & m_{21}m_{32} - m_{22}m_{31} \\ m_{13}m_{32} - m_{12}m_{33} & m_{11}m_{33} - m_{13}m_{31} & m_{12}m_{31} - m_{11}m_{32} \\ m_{12}m_{23} - m_{13}m_{22} & m_{13}m_{21} - m_{11}m_{23} & m_{11}m_{22} - m_{12}m_{21} \end{bmatrix}.$$

5.3 Translation

We have been looking at methods to change vectors using a matrix $\mathbf{M}$. In two dimensions, these transforms have the form:

$$\begin{aligned} x' &= m_{11}x + m_{12}y, \\ y' &= m_{21}x + m_{22}y. \end{aligned}$$

We cannot use such transforms to *move* locations we have represented as offset vectors from the origin. Recall that for directions and offset vectors without an origin, it does not make sense to talk about moving them; we are only talking about locations here. To move a location, we need a transform of the form:

$$\begin{aligned} x' &= x + x_t, \\ y' &= y + y_t. \end{aligned}$$

There is just no way to do that by multiplying (x, y) by a two by two matrix. It would be feasible to just keep track of scales and rotations as a matrix and keep track of translations (moves) separately, but doing that would involve fairly painful bookkeeping. Instead, we can use a technique to move the computation into a higher dimension. This technique has become standard in almost every graphics program, and especially in every graphics hardware chip.

They key observation is that when we do a 3D shear based on the z-coordinate we get this transform:

$$\begin{bmatrix} 1 & 0 & x_t \\ 0 & 1 & y_t \\ 0 & 0 & 1 \end{bmatrix} \begin{bmatrix} x \\ y \\ z \end{bmatrix} = \begin{bmatrix} x + x_t z \\ y + y_t z \\ z \end{bmatrix}.$$

Note that this almost has the form we want in x and y for a 2D translation, but has a z hanging around that doesn't have a meaning in 2D. Now comes the key decision: we will add a coordinate $z = 1$ to all 2D locations. This gives us:

$$\begin{bmatrix} 1 & 0 & x_t \\ 0 & 1 & y_t \\ 0 & 0 & 1 \end{bmatrix} \begin{bmatrix} x \\ y \\ 1 \end{bmatrix} = \begin{bmatrix} x + x_t \\ y + y_t \\ 1 \end{bmatrix}.$$

By associating a $z = 1$ coordinate with all 2D points, we now can encode translations into matrix form. For example, to first translate in 2D by (t_x, t_y) and then rotate by angle ϕ we would use the matrix:

$$\mathbf{M} = \begin{bmatrix} \cos\phi & -\sin\phi & 0 \\ \sin\phi & \cos\phi & 0 \\ 0 & 0 & 1 \end{bmatrix} \begin{bmatrix} 1 & 0 & x_t \\ 0 & 1 & y_t \\ 0 & 0 & 1 \end{bmatrix}.$$

Note that the 2D rotation matrix is now three by three with zeros in the "translation slots." With this type of formalism, which uses shears along $z = 1$ to encode translations, we can represent any number of 2D shears, 2D rotations, and 2D translations as one composite 3D matrix. Interestingly, the bottom row of that matrix will always be $(0, 0, 1)$, so we even don't really have to store it. We just need to remember it is there when we multiply two matrices together.

A problem with this new formalism is that we do not want direction or arbitrary offset vectors to move when we apply a translation. Fortunately, we can do this by making their third coordinate zero. This gives:

$$\begin{bmatrix} 1 & 0 & x_t \\ 0 & 1 & y_t \\ 0 & 0 & 1 \end{bmatrix} \begin{bmatrix} x \\ y \\ 0 \end{bmatrix} = \begin{bmatrix} x \\ y \\ 0 \end{bmatrix}.$$

This is exactly the behavior we want for vectors. So the third coordinate in 2D will be either 1 or 0 depending on whether we are encoding a position or a direction. This coordinate is usually called the *homogeneous* coordinate. We actually do need to store the homogeneous coordinate so we can distinguish between locations and other vectors. For example,

$$\begin{bmatrix} 3 \\ 2 \\ 1 \end{bmatrix} \text{ is a location} \quad \text{and} \quad \begin{bmatrix} 3 \\ 2 \\ 0 \end{bmatrix} \text{ is a displacement or direction.}$$

Later, when we do perspective viewing, we will see that it is useful to allow the homogeneous coordinate to be some value other than one or zero.

In 3D, the same technique works: we can add a fourth coordinate, a homogeneous coordinate, and then we have translations:

$$\begin{bmatrix} 1 & 0 & 0 & x_t \\ 0 & 1 & 0 & y_t \\ 0 & 0 & 1 & z_t \\ 0 & 0 & 0 & 1 \end{bmatrix} \begin{bmatrix} x \\ y \\ z \\ 1 \end{bmatrix} = \begin{bmatrix} x + x_t \\ y + y_t \\ z + z_t \\ 1 \end{bmatrix}.$$

Again, for a vector, the fourth coordinate is zero and the vector is thus unaffected by translations.

It is interesting to note that if we multiply an arbitrary matrix composed of shears and rotations with a simple translation, (translation comes second) we get:

$$\begin{bmatrix} 1 & 0 & 0 & x_t \\ 0 & 1 & 0 & y_t \\ 0 & 0 & 1 & z_t \\ 0 & 0 & 0 & 1 \end{bmatrix} \begin{bmatrix} a_{11} & a_{12} & a_{13} & 0 \\ a_{21} & a_{22} & a_{23} & 0 \\ a_{31} & a_{32} & a_{33} & 0 \\ 0 & 0 & 0 & 1 \end{bmatrix} = \begin{bmatrix} a_{11} & a_{12} & a_{13} & x_t \\ a_{21} & a_{22} & a_{23} & y_t \\ a_{31} & a_{32} & a_{33} & z_t \\ 0 & 0 & 0 & 1 \end{bmatrix}.$$

Thus we can look at any matrix and think of it as a scaling/rotation part and a translation part because the components are nicely separated from each other.

An important class of transforms are *rigid-body* transforms. These are composed only of translations and rotations, so they have no stretching or shrinking of the objects. Such transforms will have a pure rotation for the a_{ij} above.

5.3.1 Windowing Transforms

Often in graphics we need to create a transform matrix that takes points in the rectangle $[a, A] \times [b, B]$ to the rectangle $[c, C] \times [d, D]$. This can be accomplished with a single scale and translate in sequence. However, it is more intuitive to create the transform from a sequence of three operations (Figure 5.16):

1. Move the point (a, b) to the origin.

2. Scale the rectangle to be the same size as the target rectangle.

3. Move the origin to point (c, d).

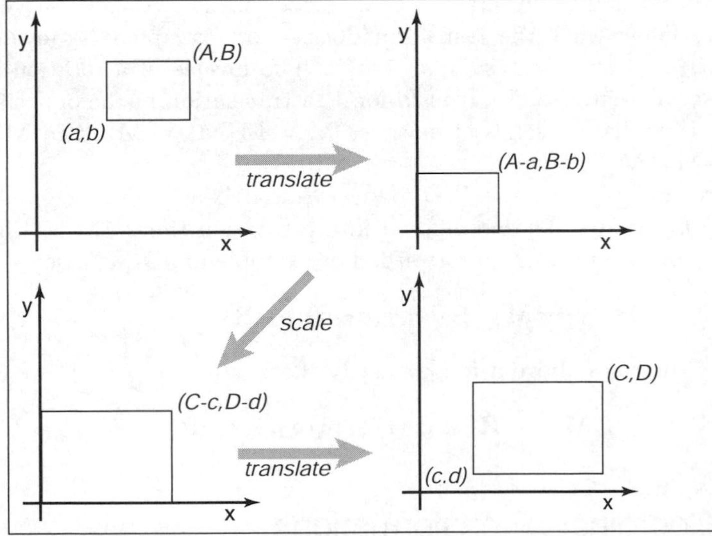

Figure 5.16. To take one rectangle (window) to the other, we first shift the lower-left corner to the origin, then scale it to the new size, and then move the origin to the lower-left corner of the target rectangle.

Remembering that the right-hand matrix is applied first, we can write:

$$\text{window} = \text{translate}\ (c, d)\ \text{scale}\left(\frac{C-c}{A-a}, \frac{D-d}{B-b}\right)\ \text{translate}\ (-a, -b)$$

$$= \begin{bmatrix} 1 & 0 & c \\ 0 & 1 & d \\ 0 & 0 & 1 \end{bmatrix} \begin{bmatrix} \frac{C-c}{A-a} & 0 & 0 \\ 0 & \frac{D-d}{B-b} & 0 \\ 0 & 0 & 1 \end{bmatrix} \begin{bmatrix} 1 & 0 & -a \\ 0 & 1 & -b \\ 0 & 0 & 1 \end{bmatrix}$$

$$= \begin{bmatrix} \frac{C-c}{A-a} & 0 & \frac{cA-Ca}{A-a} \\ 0 & \frac{D-d}{B-b} & \frac{dB-Db}{B-b} \\ 0 & 0 & 1 \end{bmatrix}. \tag{5.6}$$

It is perhaps not surprising to some readers that the resulting matrix has the form it does, but the constructive process with the three matrices leaves no doubt as to the correctness of the result.

5.4 Inverses of Transformation Matrices

While we can always invert a matrix algebraically, we can use geometry if we know what the transform does. For example, the inverse of scale(s_x, s_y, s_z) is scale$(1/s_x, 1/s_y, 1/s_z)$. The inverse of a rotation is its transpose. The inverse of a translation is a translation in the opposite direction. If we have a series of matrices $\mathbf{M} = \mathbf{M}_1\mathbf{M}_2 \cdots \mathbf{M}_n$ then $\mathbf{M}^{-1} = \mathbf{M}_n^{-1} \cdots \mathbf{M}_2^{-1}\mathbf{M}_1^{-1}$.

Interestingly, we can use SVD to invert a matrix as well. Since we know that any matrix can be decomposed into a rotation times a scale times a rotation, inversion is straightforward. For example in 3D we have:

$$\mathbf{M} = \mathbf{R}_1 \text{scale}(\sigma_1, \sigma_2, \sigma_3)\mathbf{R}_2,$$

and from the rules above it follows easily that:

$$\mathbf{M}^{-1} = \mathbf{R}_2^T \text{scale}(1/\sigma_1, 1/\sigma_2, 1/\sigma_3)\mathbf{R}_1^T.$$

5.5 Coordinate Transformations

All of the previous discussion has been in terms of using transformation matrices to move points around. We can also think of them as simply

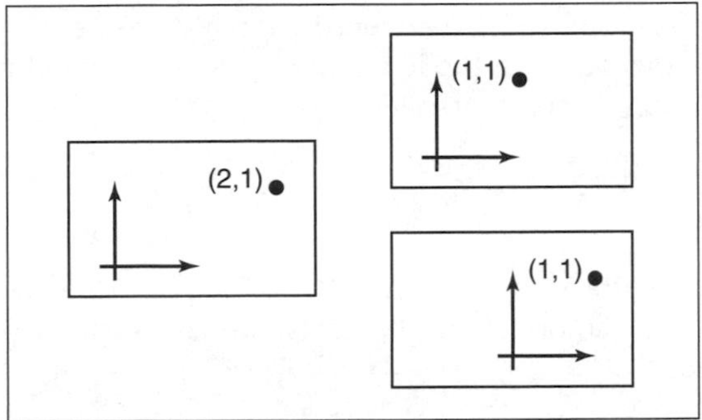

Figure 5.17. The point (2,1) has a transform "translate by (-1,0)" applied to it. On the top right is our mental image if we view this transformation as a physical movement, and on the bottom right is our mental image if we view it as a change of coordinates (a movement of the origin in this case). The artificial boundary is just an artifice, and the relative position of the axes and the point are the same in either case.

changing the coordinate system in which the point is represented. For example, in Figure 5.17, we see two ways to visualize a movement. In different contexts, either interpretation may be more suitable. For example, suppose we have the model of a city and a car. We can provide an illusion of motion as long as the relative coordinates of the car and city change in an appropriate manner. This can be accomplished by changing either car or city coordinates. Intuitively, we should probably think in terms of moving the car; however, we could think in terms of changing the city coordinates as well. It is not really important how one chooses to think about these things, provided the thinking is consistent and documented.

Often we need to manage multiple Cartesian-style coordinate systems, each having its own basis vectors and origins. Typically there is a "global" or "canonical" coordinate system. In 2D the usual convention is is to use the point $\mathbf{o}$ for the origin, and $\mathbf{x}$ and $\mathbf{y}$ for the right-handed orthonormal basis vectors $\mathbf{x}$ and $\mathbf{y}$ (Figure 5.18). Another coordinate system might have an origin $\mathbf{e}$ and right-handed orthonormal basis vectors $\mathbf{u}$ and $\mathbf{y}$. Note that typically the canonical data $\mathbf{o}$, $\mathbf{x}$, and $\mathbf{y}$ are never stored explicitly. They are

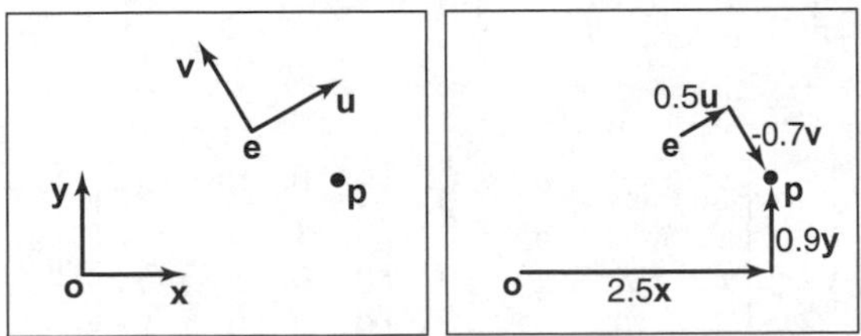

Figure 5.18. The point **p** can be represented in terms of either coordinate system.

the frame-of-reference for all other coordinate systems. In that coordinate system, we often write down the location of $\mathbf{p}$ as an ordered pair, which is shorthand for a full vector expression:

$$\mathbf{p} = (x_p, y_p) \equiv \mathbf{o} + x_p\mathbf{x} + y_p\mathbf{y}.$$

For example, in Figure 5.18, $(x_p, y_p) = (2.5, 0.9)$. Note that the pair (x_p, y_p) implicitly assumes the origin $\mathbf{o}$. Similarly, we can express $\mathbf{p}$ in terms of another equation:

$$\mathbf{p} = (u_p, v_p) \equiv \mathbf{e} + u_p\mathbf{u} + v_p\mathbf{v}. \tag{5.7}$$

In Figure 5.18, this has $(u_p, v_p) = (0.5, -0.7)$. Again, the origin $\mathbf{e}$ is left as an implicit part of the coordinate system associated with $\mathbf{u}$ and $\mathbf{v}$. We can use the simple matrix machinery of this chapter to move back and forth between coordinate systems:

$$\begin{bmatrix} x_p \\ y_p \\ 1 \end{bmatrix} = \begin{bmatrix} 1 & 0 & x_e \\ 0 & 1 & y_e \\ 0 & 0 & 1 \end{bmatrix} \begin{bmatrix} x_u & x_v & 0 \\ y_u & y_v & 0 \\ 0 & 0 & 1 \end{bmatrix} \begin{bmatrix} u_p \\ v_p \\ 1 \end{bmatrix}.$$

Note that this assumes we have the point $\mathbf{e}$ and vectors $\mathbf{u}$ and $\mathbf{v}$ stored in canonical coordinates; the xy coordinate system is the first among equals. To go in the other direction we have:

$$\begin{bmatrix} u_p \\ v_p \\ 1 \end{bmatrix} = \begin{bmatrix} x_u & y_u & 0 \\ x_v & y_v & 0 \\ 0 & 0 & 1 \end{bmatrix} \begin{bmatrix} 1 & 0 & -x_e \\ 0 & 1 & -y_e \\ 0 & 0 & 1 \end{bmatrix} \begin{bmatrix} x_p \\ x_p \\ 1 \end{bmatrix}.$$

Analogously, in 3D we have:

$$\begin{bmatrix} x_p \\ y_p \\ z_p \\ 1 \end{bmatrix} = \begin{bmatrix} 1 & 0 & 0 & x_e \\ 0 & 1 & 0 & y_e \\ 0 & 0 & 1 & z_e \\ 0 & 0 & 0 & 1 \end{bmatrix} \begin{bmatrix} x_u & x_v & x_w & 0 \\ y_u & y_v & y_w & 0 \\ z_u & z_v & z_w & 0 \\ 0 & 0 & 0 & 1 \end{bmatrix} \begin{bmatrix} u_p \\ v_p \\ w_p \\ 1 \end{bmatrix} \tag{5.8}$$

and

$$\begin{bmatrix} u_p \\ v_p \\ w_p \\ 1 \end{bmatrix} = \begin{bmatrix} x_u & y_u & w_u & 0 \\ x_v & y_v & w_v & 0 \\ x_w & y_w & w_w & 0 \\ 0 & 0 & 0 & 1 \end{bmatrix} \begin{bmatrix} 1 & 0 & 0 & -x_e \\ 0 & 1 & 0 & -y_e \\ 0 & 0 & 1 & -z_e \\ 0 & 0 & 0 & 1 \end{bmatrix} \begin{bmatrix} x_p \\ y_p \\ z_p \\ 1 \end{bmatrix} \tag{5.9}$$

Frequently Asked Questions

- **Can't I just hardcode transforms rather than use the matrix formalisms?**

Yes, but in practice it is harder to derive, harder to debug, and not any more efficient. Also, all current graphics APIs use this matrix formalism so it must be understood even to use graphics libraries.

- **The bottom row of the matrix is always (0,0,0,1). Do I have to store it?**

You do not have to store it unless you include perspective transforms (Chapter 6).

Notes

Rotations as shears were first presented in *A Fast Algorithm for General Raster Rotation* (Paeth, Graphics Gems, Academic Press, 1990). The derivation of the transformation properties of normals is based on *Properties of Surface Normal Transformations* (Turkowski, *Graphics Gems*, Academic Press, 1990). The matrix representation of transformations was introduced in Roberts' Ph.D. dissertation (Harvard, 1966). In it and many treatments through the mid-1990s, vectors were represented as row vectors and premultiplied, e.g., $\mathbf{b} = \mathbf{a}\mathbf{M}$. In our notation this would be $\mathbf{b}^T = \mathbf{a}^T\mathbf{M}^T$. If you want to find a rotation matrix $\mathbf{R}$ that takes one vector $\mathbf{a}$ to a vector $\mathbf{b}$ of the same length: $\mathbf{b} = \mathbf{R}\mathbf{a}$ you could use two rotations constructed from orthonormal bases. A more efficient method is given in *Efficiently Building a Matrix to Rotate One Vector to Another* (Möller and Hughes, journal of graphics tools 4(4), 1999).

Exercises

1. Show that the inverse of of a rotation matrix is its transpose.
2. Write down the 4 by 4 3D matrix to move by (x_m, y_m, z_m).
3. Write down the 4 by 4 3D matrix to rotate by an angle θ about the y axis.
4. Write down the 4 by 4 3D matrix to scale an object by 50% in all directions.
5. Write the 2D rotation matrix that rotates by 90 degress clockwise.

6. Write the matrix from Problem 5 as a product of three shear matrices.

7. Describe in words what this 2D transform matrix does:

$$\begin{bmatrix} 0 & -1 & 1 \\ 1 & 0 & 1 \\ 0 & 0 & 1 \end{bmatrix}$$

8. Write down the 3 by 3 matrix that rotates a 2D point by angle θ about a point $\mathbf{p} = (x_p, y_p)$.

9. Write down the 4 by 4 rotation matrix matrix that takes the orthonormal 3D vectors $\mathbf{u} = (x_u, y_u, z_u)$, $\mathbf{v} = (x_v, y_v, z_v)$ and $\mathbf{w} = (x_w, y_w, z_w)$, to orthonormal 3D vectors $\mathbf{a} = (x_a, y_a, z_a)$, $\mathbf{b} = (x_b, y_b, z_b)$ and $\mathbf{c} = (x_c, y_c, z_c)$, So $M\mathbf{u} = \mathbf{a}$, $M\mathbf{v} = \mathbf{b}$, and $M\mathbf{w} = \mathbf{c}$.

10. What is the inverse matrix for the answer to the previous problem?

Viewing

The transform tools developed in the last chapter will make it straightforward for us to create images of 3D line segments. In this chapter, we develop the methods to produce 3D orthographic and perspective views of line segments in space with no "hidden-line" removal (Figure 6.1). Note that in the orthographic projection, the parallel lines in 3D are parallel in the image, while in the perspective projection they may not be parallel in the image. For the entire chapter, we assume that 3D line segments are specified by two end points, each of the form (x, y, z). In the next chapter we use BSP trees and z-buffers to allow opaque objects with hidden-line and hidden-surface removal, and we will use triangle faces rather than triangle edges.

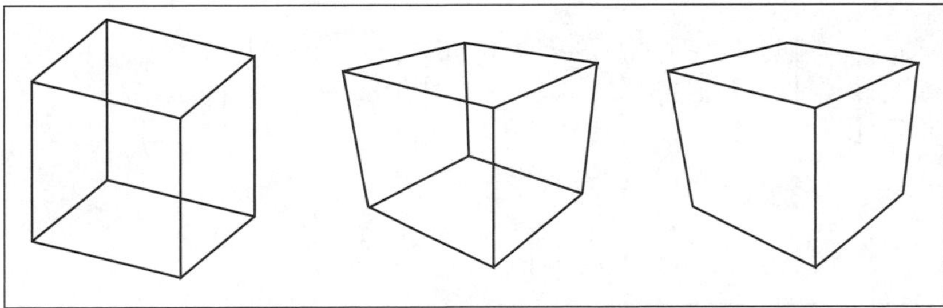

Figure 6.1. Left: orthographic projection. Middle: perspective projection. Right: perspective projection with hidden lines removed.

6.1 Drawing the Canonical View Volume

We begin with a problem whose solution will be reused for any viewing condition. We want to map lines to the screen along the z-axis in the positive direction. We will limit this projection to objects within the *canonical*[1] *view volume*. This is the volume defined by all 3D points whose Cartesian coordinates are between -1 and +1. This cube can be specified as $(x, y, z) \in [-1, 1]^3$ (Figure 6.2). If we have a screen made up of n_x by n_y pixels, we project $x = -1$ to the left side of the screen, $x = +1$ to the right half of the screen, $y = -1$ to the bottom of the screen, and $y = +1$ to the top of the screen. Note that this is mapping the square $[-1, +1]^2$ to a potentially non-square rectangle. That is not a problem; x and y will just have different scaling parameters when they are converted to pixel coordinates. For now we will assume that all line segments to be drawn are completely inside the canonical view volume. Later we will relax that assumption when we discuss *clipping*.

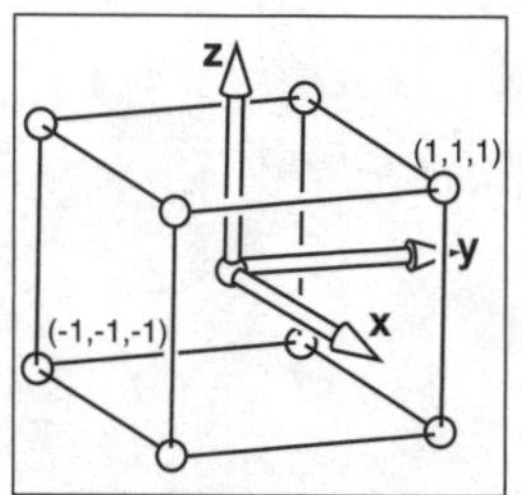

Figure 6.2. The canonical view volume is a cube with side of length two centered at the origin.

Recall from Chapter 3 that pixels have a finite square extent, the coordinates have a 0.5 unit overshoot from the pixel centers, and the smallest pixel center coordinates are $(0, 0)$; an n_x by n_y screen has integer centers and boundaries defined by $[-0.5, n_x - 0.5] \times [-0.5, n_y - 0.5]$. This is called a windowing transform and is given by Equation 5.6:

$$\begin{bmatrix} x_{\text{pixel}} \\ y_{\text{pixel}} \\ 1 \end{bmatrix} = \begin{bmatrix} \frac{n_x}{2} & 0 & \frac{n_x-1}{2} \\ 0 & \frac{n_y}{2} & \frac{n_y-1}{2} \\ 0 & 0 & 1 \end{bmatrix} \begin{bmatrix} x_{\text{canonical}} \\ y_{\text{canonical}} \\ 1 \end{bmatrix}. \tag{6.1}$$

Also recall that in some APIs the y-axis points *downward*. We'll examine this case because it makes a nice exercise. It creates the somewhat odd transform where the y values need to be flipped. The transform to convert points in the canonical view volume to such pixel coordinates is a variant of the windowing transform (Equation 5.6), but because of the flip, we will derive it from scratch. It can be accomplished as shown in Figure 6.3, which yields:

$$\begin{aligned} \begin{bmatrix} x_{\text{pixel}} \\ y_{\text{pixel}} \\ 1 \end{bmatrix} &= \begin{bmatrix} 1 & 0 & \frac{n_x-1}{2} \\ 0 & 1 & \frac{n_y-1}{2} \\ 0 & 0 & 1 \end{bmatrix} \begin{bmatrix} \frac{n_x}{2} & 0 & 0 \\ 0 & \frac{n_y}{2} & 0 \\ 0 & 0 & 1 \end{bmatrix} \begin{bmatrix} 1 & 0 & 0 \\ 0 & -1 & 0 \\ 0 & 0 & 1 \end{bmatrix} \begin{bmatrix} x_{\text{canonical}} \\ y_{\text{canonical}} \\ 1 \end{bmatrix} \\ &= \begin{bmatrix} \frac{n_x}{2} & 0 & \frac{n_x-1}{2} \\ 0 & -\frac{n_y}{2} & \frac{n_y-1}{2} \\ 0 & 0 & 1 \end{bmatrix} \begin{bmatrix} x_{\text{canonical}} \\ y_{\text{canonical}} \\ 1 \end{bmatrix}. \end{aligned} \tag{6.2}$$

[1]The word "canonical" crops up in many contexts and usually refers to some customary variable or shape that is in some way "nice." For example, if we were to define a "canonical circle," it would likely be of unit radius and centered at the origin.

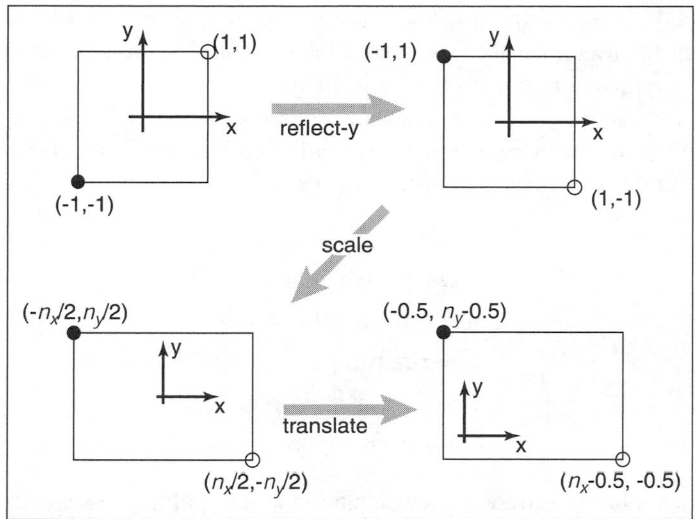

Figure 6.3. When the *y* screen coordinates increase from the top of the screen to the bottom, the transform from the *xy* components of the canonical view-volume to the screen coordinates involve a flip.

Note that there is no allowance for z values here. Since we are projecting along the z-axis, those values don't matter. After the transform, you can take $(x_{\text{pixel}}, y_{\text{pixel}})$ and issue 2D line drawing commands. Note that ignoring z-values means we will have "see through" graphics when we issue line-drawing commands. Later we will cover hidden surface methods which will allow polygon drawing commands as well.

We save a lot of pain by doing transforms using more than one matrix as we derive things. For example, there is no reason not to implement Equation 6.1 as a product of three simple matrices. If you implement a matrix library with reflection, scale, and translate initialization routines for matrices, these can be re-used in many situations. Also, the resulting code is easier to debug; note how much easier it is to relate the expanded form of Equation 6.2 to Figure 6.3. If we expand the full-blown algebra by hand, we might make mistakes and the equations would be less informative; we can see by looking at the matrix product that we scale/flip and then move. That would be much harder to see with the expanded product. So let the matrix multiplication handle the algebra in your implementation. No efficiency is lost except for a small preprocessing time, and your code is more modifiable and more likely to be correct.

6.2 Orthographic Projection

We usually want to render lines in some region of space other than the canonical view volume. The basic step is to take each line with 3D endpoints **a** and **b** and to use a matrix **M** to take these points to **Ma** and **Mb** which can be drawn in the canonical view volume. The matrix **M** encodes all the nasty geometry of viewing and projection.

The simplest case occurs when this volume is the axis-aligned box $[l, r] \times [b, t] \times [n, f]$ shown in Figure 6.4. We call this box the *orthographic view volume* , and refer to the bounding planes as:

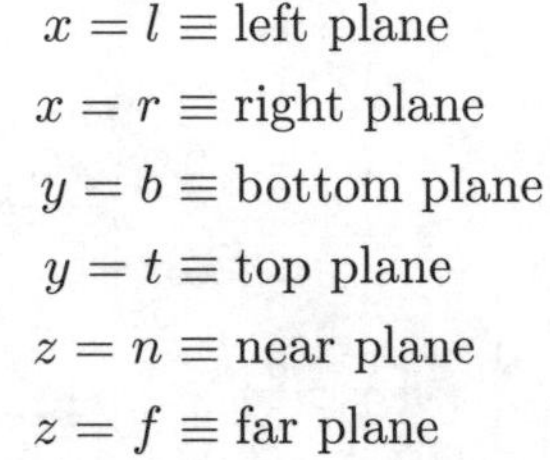

$$
\begin{aligned}
x = l &\equiv \text{left plane} \\
x = r &\equiv \text{right plane} \\
y = b &\equiv \text{bottom plane} \\
y = t &\equiv \text{top plane} \\
z = n &\equiv \text{near plane} \\
z = f &\equiv \text{far plane}
\end{aligned}
$$

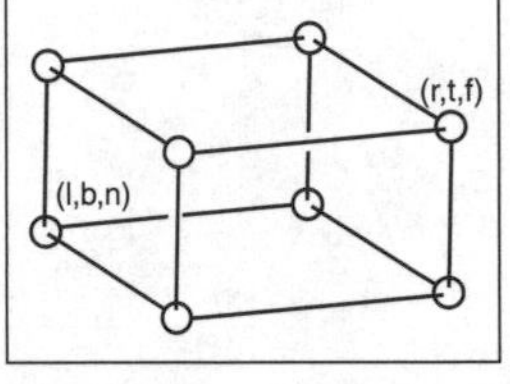

Figure 6.4. The orthographic view volume.

That vocabulary assumes a viewer who is looking along the *minus* z-axis with his head pointing in the y direction.[2] This implies that $n > f$ which may be unintuitive, but if you assume the entire orthographic view-volume has negative z values then the $z = n$ "near" plane is closer to the viewer if and only if $n > f$; here f is a smaller number than n, i.e., a negative number of larger absolute value than n. This concept is shown in Figure 6.5. The transform from orthographic view volume to the canonical view volume is really just a 3D version of the 2D windowing transform presented in Section 5.3.1.

This transformation that takes $y = b$ to $y = -1$, $y = t$ to $y = +1$, $x = l$ to $x = -1$, $z = n$ to $z = 1$, and $z = f$ to $z = -1$ can be encoded as a scale and then a move, or a move and then a scale. Note that with this choice for

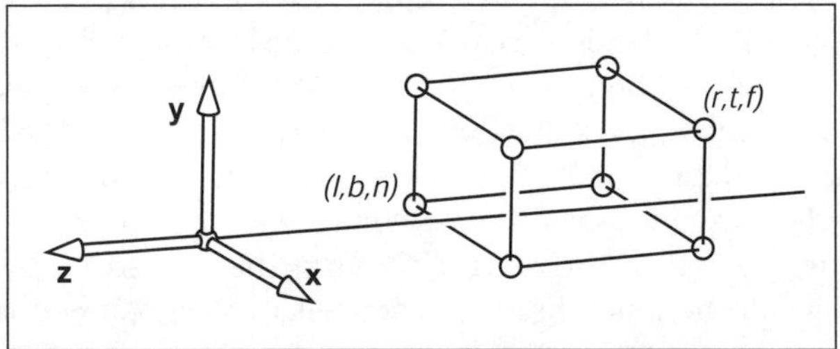

Figure 6.5. The orthographic view volume is along the negative z-axis, so f is a more negative number than n, thus $n > f$.

[2]Most programmers find it intuitive to have the x-axis pointing right and the y-axis pointing up. In a right-handed coordinate system, this implies that we are looking in the $-z$ direction. Some systems use a left-handed coordinate system for viewing so that the gaze direction is along the $+z$ direction. Which is the best compromise is a matter of taste, and this text assumes a right-handed coordinate system. A reference that argues for the left-handed system instead is given in the notes at the end of the chapter.

$[n, f]$, f is a more negative number than n in z. Here n stands for "near plane" and f stands for "far plane". Many programs flip them at this point as we will discuss later. Moving to the origin first is somewhat more intuitive for most people:

$$\begin{bmatrix} x_{\text{canonical}} \\ y_{\text{canonical}} \\ z_{\text{canonical}} \\ 1 \end{bmatrix} = \begin{bmatrix} \frac{2}{r-l} & 0 & 0 & 0 \\ 0 & \frac{2}{t-b} & 0 & 0 \\ 0 & 0 & \frac{2}{n-f} & 0 \\ 0 & 0 & 0 & 1 \end{bmatrix} \begin{bmatrix} 1 & 0 & 0 & -\frac{l+r}{2} \\ 0 & 1 & 0 & -\frac{b+t}{2} \\ 0 & 0 & 1 & -\frac{n+f}{2} \\ 0 & 0 & 0 & 1 \end{bmatrix} \begin{bmatrix} x \\ y \\ z \\ 1 \end{bmatrix}. \tag{6.3}$$

Note that we have gone to 4 by 4 transformation matrices because z is also being manipulated here, and because $n - f$ is a positive number.

To draw 3D line segments in the orthographic view volume, we project them into screen xy coordinates, and ignore z coordinates. We do this by combining Equations 6.1 and 6.3. Because Equation 6.1 is 2D, we add a "do nothing" operation on z to get:

$$\mathbf{M}_o = \begin{bmatrix} \frac{n_x}{2} & 0 & 0 & \frac{n_x-1}{2} \\ 0 & \frac{n_y}{2} & 0 & \frac{n_y-1}{2} \\ 0 & 0 & 1 & 0 \\ 0 & 0 & 0 & 1 \end{bmatrix} \begin{bmatrix} \frac{2}{r-l} & 0 & 0 & 0 \\ 0 & \frac{2}{t-b} & 0 & 0 \\ 0 & 0 & \frac{2}{n-f} & 0 \\ 0 & 0 & 0 & 1 \end{bmatrix} \begin{bmatrix} 1 & 0 & 0 & -\frac{l+r}{2} \\ 0 & 1 & 0 & -\frac{b+t}{2} \\ 0 & 0 & 1 & -\frac{n+f}{2} \\ 0 & 0 & 0 & 1 \end{bmatrix} \tag{6.4}$$

Note that in a program we multiply the three square matrices together to form one matrix $\mathbf{M}_o$, and then manipulate points as follows:

$$\begin{bmatrix} x_{\text{pixel}} \\ y_{\text{pixel}} \\ z_{\text{canonical}} \\ 1 \end{bmatrix} = \mathbf{M}_o \begin{bmatrix} x \\ y \\ z \\ 1 \end{bmatrix}$$

The z coordinate will now be in $[-1, 1]$. We don't take advantage of this now, but it will be useful when we examine z-buffer algorithms.

Note that we could also derive Equation 6.4 as just a 3D windowing transform. It is straightforward to generalize Equation 5.6 to 3D; to take the 3D box $[a, A] \times [b, B] \times [c, C]$ to the 3D box $[d, D] \times [e, E] \times [f, F]$ we have:

$$\text{window3D} = \begin{bmatrix} \frac{D-d}{A-a} & 0 & 0 & \frac{dA-Da}{D-a} \\ 0 & \frac{E-e}{B-b} & 0 & \frac{eB-Eb}{E-b} \\ 0 & 0 & \frac{F-f}{C-c} & \frac{fC-Fc}{F-c} \\ 0 & 0 & 0 & 1 \end{bmatrix} \tag{6.5}$$

Equation 6.4 takes $[l,r] \times [t,b] \times [n,f]$ to $[-0.5, n_x - 0.5] \times [-0.5, n_y - 0.5] \times [-1, 1]$, which can be plugged into Equation 6.5 to get the matrix we want.

The code to draw many 3D lines with endpoints $\mathbf{a}_i$ and $\mathbf{b}_i$ thus becomes both simple and efficient:

compute $\mathbf{M}_o$
for *each line segment* $(\mathbf{a}_i, \mathbf{b}_i)$ ***do***
  $\mathbf{p} = \mathbf{M}_o \mathbf{a}_i$
  $\mathbf{q} = \mathbf{M}_o \mathbf{b}_i$
  drawline(x_p, y_p, x_q, y_q)

This is a first example of how matrix transformation machinery makes graphics programs clean and efficient.

6.2.1 Arbitrary View Positions

We'd like to able to change the viewpoint in 3D and look in any direction. There are a multitude of conventions for specifying viewer position and orientation. We will use the following one (see Figure 6.6):

- the eye position $\mathbf{e}$,
- the gaze direction $\mathbf{g}$,
- the view-up vector $\mathbf{t}$.

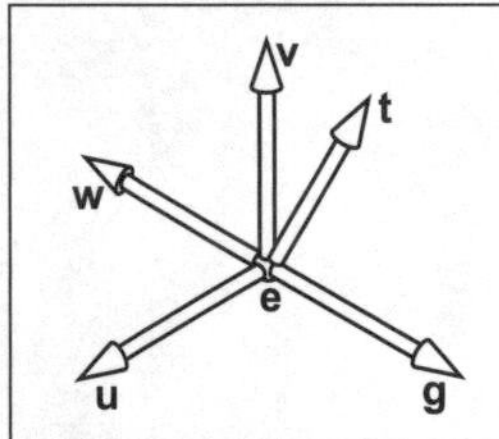

Figure 6.6. The user specifies viewing as an eye position **e**, a gaze direction **g**, and an up vector **t**. We construct a right-handed basis with **w** pointing opposite to the gaze, and **v** being in the same plane as **g** and **t**.

The eye position is a location that the eye "sees from." If you think of graphics as a photographic process, it is the center of the lens. The gaze direction is any vector in the direction that the viewer is looking. The view-up vector is any vector in the plane that both bisects the viewer's head into right and left halves and points "to the sky" for a person standing on the ground. These vectors provide us with enough information to set up a coordinate system with origin $\mathbf{e}$ and a uvw basis:

$$\mathbf{w} = -\frac{\mathbf{g}}{\|\mathbf{g}\|},$$

$$\mathbf{u} = \frac{\mathbf{t} \times \mathbf{w}}{\|\mathbf{t} \times \mathbf{w}\|},$$

$$\mathbf{v} = \mathbf{w} \times \mathbf{u}.$$

Note that our job would be done if all points we wished to transform were stored in coordinates with origin $\mathbf{e}$ and uvw axes, but as shown in Figure 6.7, they are stored with the canonical origin $\mathbf{o}$ and xyz axes. To use the machinery we have already developed, we just need to convert the

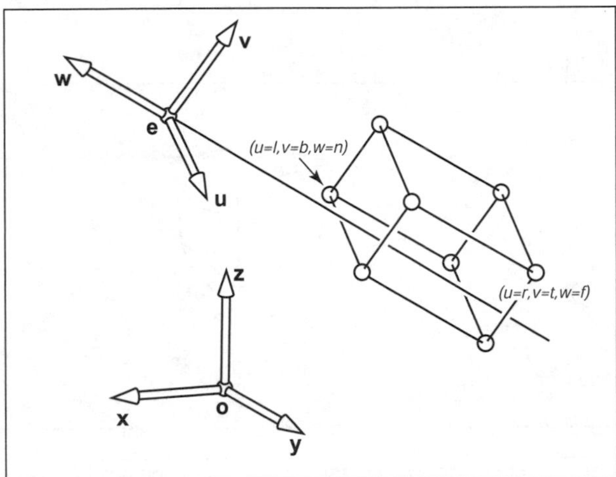

Figure 6.7. For arbitrary viewing, we need to change the points to be stored in the "appropriate" coordinate system. In this case it has origin **e** and offset coordinates in terms of axes **uvw**.

coordinates of the line segment endpoints we wish to draw into (u, v, w) coordinates offset from origin $\mathbf{e}$. Alternatively (the math is the same), we can think of the transform as moving $\mathbf{e}$ to the origin and aligning $\mathbf{uvw}$ to $\mathbf{xyz}$. This view transformation is:

$$\mathbf{M}_v = \begin{bmatrix} x_u & y_u & z_u & 0 \\ x_v & y_v & z_v & 0 \\ x_w & y_w & z_w & 0 \\ 0 & 0 & 0 & 1 \end{bmatrix} \begin{bmatrix} 1 & 0 & 0 & -x_e \\ 0 & 1 & 0 & -y_e \\ 0 & 0 & 1 & -z_e \\ 0 & 0 & 0 & 1 \end{bmatrix}$$

If we multiply a point $\mathbf{p}$ by $\mathbf{M}_v$, we will have "aligned" it to the coordinate axes. This allows us to make a very minor change to the z axis viewing algorithm we saw earlier:

compute $\mathbf{M}_v$
compute $\mathbf{M}_o$
$\mathbf{M} = \mathbf{M}_o\mathbf{M}_v$
for *each line segment* $(\mathbf{a}_i, \mathbf{b}_i)$ ***do***
  $\mathbf{p} = \mathbf{M}\mathbf{a}_i$
  $\mathbf{q} = \mathbf{M}\mathbf{b}_i$
  drawline(x_p, y_p, x_q, y_q)

This illustrates the remarkable power we gain when using transformation matrices to implement algorithms. Almost no code is needed once the matrix infrastructure is in place.

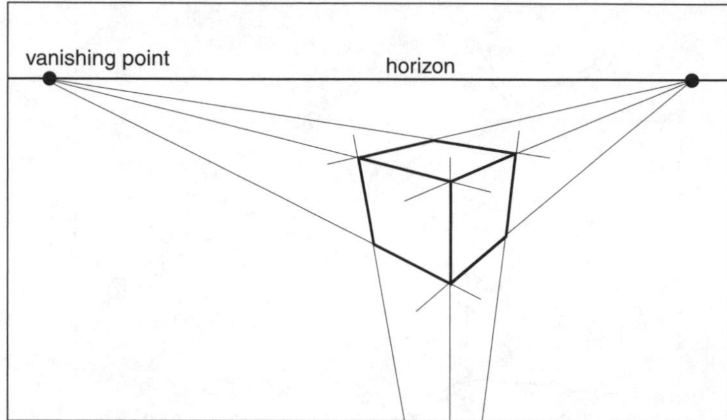

Figure 6.8. In three-point perspective, an artists picks "vanishing points" where parallel lines meet. Parallel horizontal lines will meet at a point on the horizon. Every set of parallel lines has its own vanishing points. These rules are followed automatically if we implement perspective based on the correct geometric principles.

6.3 Perspective Projection

To capture the effects of *perspective*, we need to draw line segments that are farther from the viewer smaller than similar line segments that are closer to the viewer. While one might expect to automate the artistic conventions of *three-point perspective* (Figure 6.8), in fact all such rules will be followed automatically if we follow the simple mathematical rule underlying perspective: objects are projected directly toward the eye and they are drawn where they meet a view-plane in front of the eye.

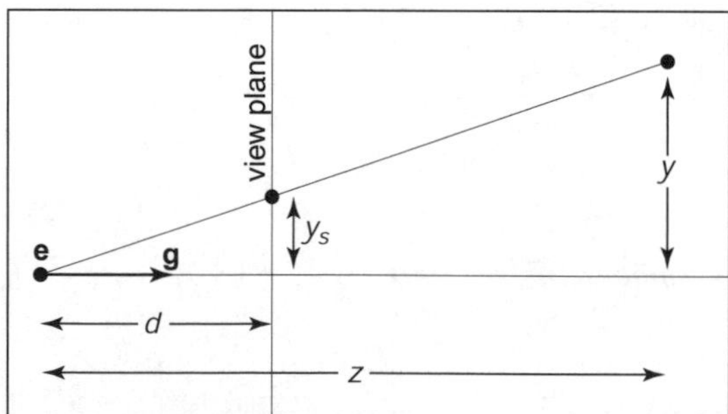

Figure 6.9. The geometry for Equation 6.6. The viewer's eye is at **e** and the gaze direction **g** (the minus *z*-axis). The view-plane is a distance *d* from the eye. A point is projected toward **e** and where it intersects the view-plane is where it is drawn.

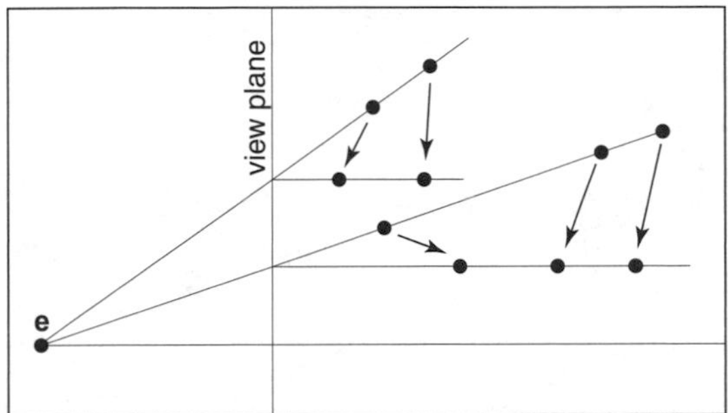

Figure 6.10. The perspective projection can be obtained by an orthographic projection provided lines through the eye are all parallel to the gaze direction. The spacing of the resulting lines should intersect the view-plane wherever the lines through the eye do.

In fact, the size of an object on the screen is proportional to $1/z$ for an eye at the origin looking up the negative z-axis. This can be expressed more precisely in an equation for the geometry in Figure 6.9:

$$y_s = \frac{d}{z}y, \tag{6.6}$$

where y is the distance of the point along the y axis, and y_s is where the point should be drawn on the screen.

We would really like to use the matrix machinery we developed for orthographic projection to draw perspective images; we could then just multiply another matrix into our composite matrix and use the algorithm we already have. The geometric operation that allows us to do that is the tranformation of the points along a line through the eye to a line parallel to the z-axis. This is shown in Figure 6.10. Note that it does not matter *where* the points are transformed in z because the orthographic projection will ignore z anyway. If we want to have the transform work seamlessly with the orthographic projection, then we want to set the view-plane to be at $z = n$, and then the portion of the viewplane with $(u, v) \in [l, r] \times [b, t]$ will be displayed. Such a transform is shown in Figure 6.11. One property of that transform is that lines through the eye are made parallel in such a way that their intersections with the $z = n$ plane are unchanged (Figure 6.12).

We would like it if we could write down a matrix that would accomplish the above transformation, but it cannot be done; the divide by z in Equation 6.6 is not an operation that the matrix machinery we have seen so far can accomplish. However, there is a beautiful and simple extension to this technology that makes such a "perspective z divide" possible. The key is to use the fourth coordinate of the points, which have been one so far, and allow them to take values other than one. We refer to this fourth coordinate (for 3D locations) as the *homogeneous* coordinate h. This coordinate really encodes how much the other three coordinates have been

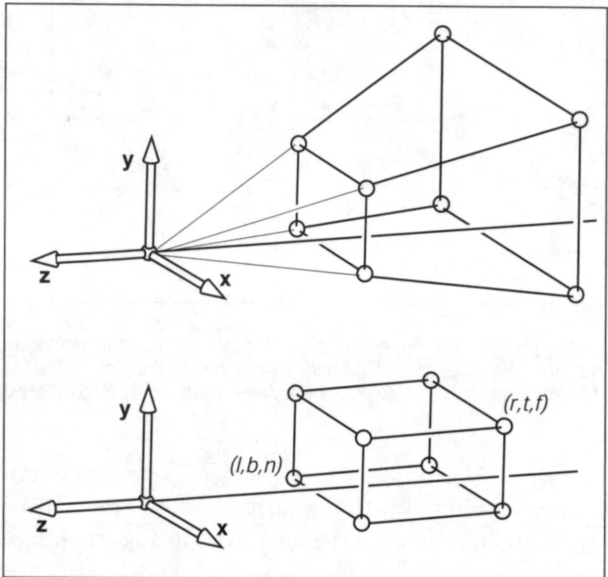

Figure 6.11. The perspective projection leaves points on the $z = n$ plane unchanged and maps the large $z = f$ rectangle at the back of the perspective volume to the small $z = f$ rectangle at the back of the orthographic volume.

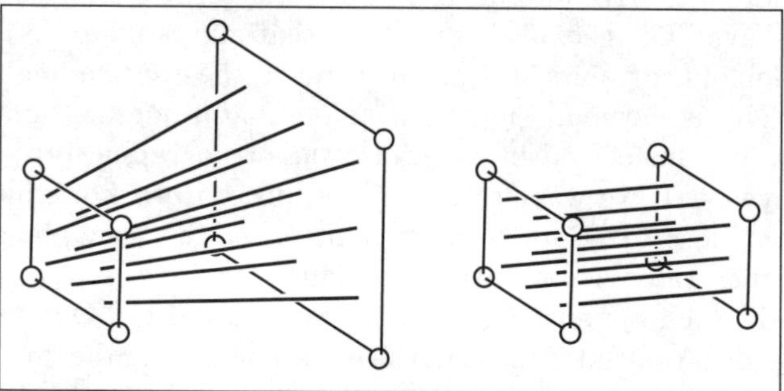

Figure 6.12. The perspective projection maps any line through the origin/eye to a line parallel to the z-axis and without moving the point on the line at $z = n$.

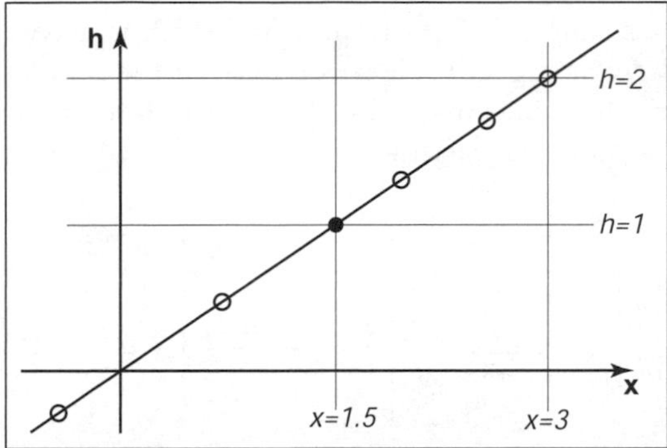

Figure 6.13. The homogeneous value $x = 1.5$ is represented by any point on the line $x = 1.5h$, such as points at the hollow circles. However, before we interpret x as a conventional Cartesian coordinate, we first divide by h to get $(x,h) = (1.5,1)$ as shown by the black point.

scaled. Since in the end we only care about (x, y, z), we define the following somewhat strange equivalence:

$$\begin{bmatrix} hx \\ hy \\ hz \\ h \end{bmatrix} \equiv \begin{bmatrix} x \\ y \\ z \\ 1 \end{bmatrix}.$$

Thus, we can compute with points whose fourth (homogeneous) coordinate h is not one, but we must divide the other three coordinates by h before interpreting them as traditional Cartesian coordinates. For example, the x coordinate is the same for all points on the homogeneous 4D "line" $x = 1.5h$ as shown in Figure 6.13. For example,

$$\begin{bmatrix} 6 \\ -2 \\ 8 \\ 2 \end{bmatrix} \xrightarrow{\text{homogenize}} \begin{bmatrix} 3 \\ -1 \\ 4 \\ 1 \end{bmatrix}.$$

With this *homogenization* procedure, where we get the "real" location by dividing by the fourth coordinate h, we can construct the *perspective* matrix:

$$\mathbf{M}_p = \begin{bmatrix} 1 & 0 & 0 & 0 \\ 0 & 1 & 0 & 0 \\ 0 & 0 & \frac{n+f}{n} & -f \\ 0 & 0 & \frac{1}{n} & 0 \end{bmatrix}.$$

There are many matrices which can function as perspective matrices, and all of them non-linearly distort the z coordinate. This specific matrix has the nice properties shown in Figures 6.11 and 6.12; it leaves points on the $z = n$ plane entirely alone, and it leaves points on the $z = f$ plane at $z = f$ while "squishing" them in x and y by the appropriate amount. The effect of the matrix on a point (x, y, z) is:

$$\mathbf{M}_p \begin{bmatrix} x \\ y \\ z \\ 1 \end{bmatrix} = \begin{bmatrix} x \\ y \\ z\frac{n+f}{n} - f \\ \frac{z}{n} \end{bmatrix} \xrightarrow{\text{homogenize}} \begin{bmatrix} \frac{nx}{z} \\ \frac{ny}{z} \\ n + f - \frac{fn}{z} \\ 1 \end{bmatrix}.$$

As you can see, x and y are scaled and, more importantly, divided by z. Because both n and z (inside the view volume) are negative, there are no "flips" in x and y. Although it is not obvious (see the exercise at the end of the chapter), the transform also preserves the relative order of z values between $z = n$ and $z = f$, allowing us to do depth ordering after this matrix is applied. This will be important later when we do hidden surface elimination.

For homogeneous points, $\mathbf{p} = h\mathbf{p}$, or more explicitly $(x, y, z, 1) = (hx, hy, hz, h)$; thus, we can take any transformation matrix $\mathbf{M}$ and multiply it by an arbitrary constant because $\mathbf{M}(h\mathbf{p}) = (h\mathbf{M})\mathbf{p} = \mathbf{M}\mathbf{p}$. For this reason, we can multiply the perspective matrix by n to make it a little prettier:

$$\mathbf{M}_p = \begin{bmatrix} n & 0 & 0 & 0 \\ 0 & n & 0 & 0 \\ 0 & 0 & n+f & -fn \\ 0 & 0 & 1 & 0 \end{bmatrix}.$$

Sometimes we will want to take the inverse of $\mathbf{P}$, for example to bring a screen coordinate plus z back to the original space, as we might want to do for picking. The inverse is:

$$\mathbf{M}_p^{-1} = \begin{bmatrix} \frac{1}{n} & 0 & 0 & 0 \\ 0 & \frac{1}{n} & 0 & 0 \\ 0 & 0 & 0 & 1 \\ 0 & 0 & -\frac{1}{fn} & \frac{n+f}{fn} \end{bmatrix}.$$

As mentioned earlier, the effect of a homogeneous transformation matrix does not change if we multiply it by a constant. The same applies to an inverse matrix; a matrix and its inverse need only produce any diagonal matrix with identical values along the diagonal. So the inverse matrix above is the inverse of any of our perspective matrices. An alternative inverse matrix is found by multiplying by nf:

$$\mathbf{M}_p^{-1} = \begin{bmatrix} f & 0 & 0 & 0 \\ 0 & f & 0 & 0 \\ 0 & 0 & 0 & fn \\ 0 & 0 & -1 & n+f \end{bmatrix}.$$

The beauty of the perspective matrix is, that once we apply it, we can use an orthographic transform to get to the canonical view volume. Thus, all of the orthographic machinery applies and all that we have added is one matrix and one divide operation. It is also heartening that we are not "wasting" the bottom row of our four by four matrices!

One issue, however, is how are l,r,b,t determined for perspective? They identify the "window" through which we look. Since the perspective matrix does not change the values of x and y on the $z = n$ plane, we can specify (l, r, b, t) on that plane.

We would like to integrate the perspective matrix into our orthographic infrastructure. A key point is that the perspective matrix assumes we are looking up the $-z$ axis, so it cannot be applied until after the viewing matrix $\mathbf{M}_v$ has been applied. So the full set of matrices for perspective viewing is:

$$\mathbf{M} = \mathbf{M}_o \mathbf{M}_p \mathbf{M}_v.$$

The resulting algorithm is:

compute $\mathbf{M}_o$
compute $\mathbf{M}_v$
compute $\mathbf{M}_p$
$\mathbf{M} = \mathbf{M}_o \mathbf{M}_p \mathbf{M}_v$
for *each line segment* $(\mathbf{a}_i, \mathbf{b}_i)$ ***do***
  $\mathbf{p} = \mathbf{M}\mathbf{a}_i$
  $\mathbf{q} = \mathbf{M}\mathbf{b}_i$
  drawline$(x_p/h_p, y_p/h_p, x_q/h_q, y_q/h_q)$

Note that the only change other than the additional matrix is the divide by the homogeneous coordinate h.

You might have the misgiving that the perspective matrix changes the value of the homogeneous coordinate, so the move and scale might no longer work properly. However, note that for a move on a homogeneous point we have:

$$\begin{bmatrix} 1 & 0 & 0 & t_x \\ 0 & 1 & 0 & t_y \\ 0 & 0 & 1 & t_z \\ 0 & 0 & 0 & 1 \end{bmatrix} \begin{bmatrix} hx \\ hy \\ hz \\ h \end{bmatrix} = \begin{bmatrix} hx + ht_x \\ hy + ht_y \\ hz + ht_z \\ h \end{bmatrix} \xrightarrow{\text{homogenize}} \begin{bmatrix} x + t_x \\ y + t_y \\ z + t_z \\ 1 \end{bmatrix}.$$

Similar effects are true for other transforms (see the exercise at the end of the chapter).

The matrix product $\mathbf{M}_o\mathbf{M}_p$ is commonly called the *projection* matrix. Multiplying $\mathbf{M}_o$ times $\mathbf{M}_p$ yields:

$$\mathbf{M}_{\text{projection}} = \begin{bmatrix} \frac{2n}{r-l} & 0 & \frac{l+r}{l-r} & 0 \\ 0 & \frac{2n}{t-b} & \frac{b+t}{b-t} & 0 \\ 0 & 0 & \frac{f+n}{f-n} & \frac{2fn}{n-f} \\ 0 & 0 & 1 & 0 \end{bmatrix}.$$

This or similar matrices often appear in documentation, and they are less mysterious when one realizes that they are usually the product of a few simple matrices.

Many APIs such as *OpenGL* use the same canonical view volume as presented here. They also usually have the user specify the absolute values of n and f. The projection matrix for *OpenGL* is:

$$\mathbf{M}_{\text{OpenGL}} = \begin{bmatrix} \frac{2|n|}{r-l} & 0 & \frac{r+l}{r-l} & 0 \\ 0 & \frac{2|n|}{t-b} & \frac{t+b}{t-b} & 0 \\ 0 & 0 & \frac{|n|+|f|}{|n|-|f|} & \frac{2|f||n|}{|n|-|f|} \\ 0 & 0 & -1 & 0 \end{bmatrix}.$$

Other APIs set n and f to 0 and 1, respectively. Blinn recommends making the canonical view volume $[0,1]^3$ for efficiency. All such decisions will change the the projection matrix slightly.

6.4 Some Properties of the Perspective Transform

An important property of the perspective transform is that it takes lines to lines and planes to planes. In addition, it takes line segments in the view-volume to line segments in the canonical volume. To see this, consider the line segment

$$\mathbf{q} + t(\mathbf{Q} - \mathbf{q}).$$

When transformed by a 4 by 4 matrix $\mathbf{M}$, it is a point with possibly varying homogeneous coordinate:

$$\mathbf{Mq} + t(\mathbf{MQ} - \mathbf{Mq}) \equiv \mathbf{r} + t(\mathbf{R} - \mathbf{r}).$$

The homogenized 3D line segment is:

$$\frac{\mathbf{r} + t(\mathbf{R} - \mathbf{r})}{h_r + t(h_R - h_r)} \tag{6.7}$$

If Equation 6.7 can be rewritten in a form

$$\frac{\mathbf{r}}{h_r} + f(t)\left(\frac{\mathbf{R}}{h_R} - \frac{\mathbf{r}}{h_r}\right) \tag{6.8}$$

then all the homogenized points lie on a 3D line. Brute force manipulation of Equation 6.7 yields such a form with

$$f(t) = \frac{h_R t}{h_r + t(h_R - h_r)}. \tag{6.9}$$

It also turns out that the line segments do map to line segments preserving the ordering of the points (Exercise 8), i.e., they do not get reordered or "torn".

A by-product of the transform taking line segments to line segments is that it takes the edges and vertices of a triangle to the edges and vertices of another triangle. Thus it takes triangles to triangles and planes to planes.

6.5 Field-of-View

While we can specify any window using the (l, r, b, t) and n values, sometimes we would like to have a simpler system where we look through the center of the window. This implies the constraint that:

$$\begin{aligned} l &= -r \\ b &= -t \end{aligned}$$

If we also add the constraint that the pixels are square, i.e., there is no distortion of shape in the image, then the ratio of r to t must be the same as the ratio of the number of horizontal pixels to the number of vertical pixels:

$$\frac{n_x}{n_y} = \frac{r}{t}$$

Once n_x and n_y are specified, this leaves only one degree of freedom. That is often set using the *field-of-view* shown as θ in Figure 6.14. This is sometimes called the vertical field-of-view to distinguish it from the angle between left and right sides or from the angle between diagonal corners. From the figure we can see that:

$$\tan\frac{\theta}{2} = \frac{t}{|n|}$$

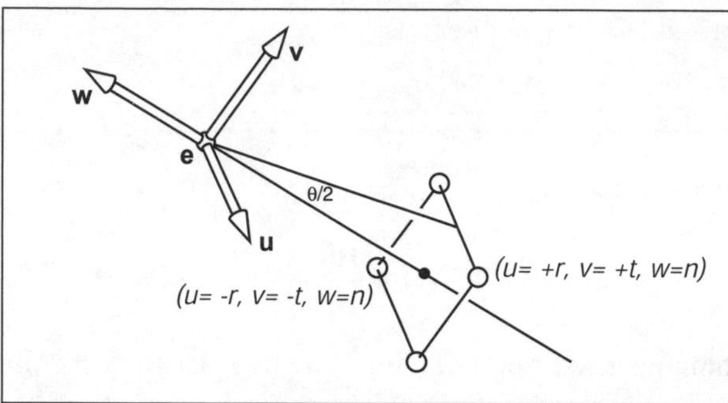

Figure 6.14. The field-of-view θ is the angle from the bottom of the screen to the top of the screen as measured from the eye.

If n and θ are specified, then we can derive t and use code for the more general viewing system. In some systems, the value of n is hard-coded to some reasonable value and thus we have one fewer degree of freedom.

Frequently Asked Questions

• **Is orthographic projection ever useful in practice?**

It is useful in applications where relative length judgements are important. It can also yield simplifications where perspective would be too expensive as occurs in some medical visualization applications.

• **The tessellated spheres I draw in perspective look like ovals. Is this a bug?**

No. It is correct behavior. If you place your eye in the same relative position to the screen as the virtual viewer has with respect to the viewport, then these ovals will look like circles because they themselves are viewed at an angle.

• **Does the perspective matrix take negative z values to positive z-values with a reversed ordering? Doesn't that cause trouble?**

Yes. The equation for transformed z is:

$$z' = n + f - \frac{fn}{z}.$$

So $z = +\epsilon$ is transformed to $z' = -\infty$ and $z = -\epsilon$ is transformed to $z = \infty$. So any line segments that span $z = 0$ will be "torn" although all points will be projected to an appropriate screen location. This tearing is not relevant when all objects are contained in the viewing volume. This is usually assured by *clipping* to the view volume. However, clipping itself is made more complicated by the tearing phenomenon as is discussed in Chapter 11.

Notes

Most of the discussion of transformation matrices is based on information in *Real-Time Rendering* (Möller and Haines, A K Peters, 1999), the *OpenGL Programming Guide* by Neider, Davis, and Woo (Addison-Wesley, 1993), and *Computer Graphics, C Version* by Hearn and Baker (Prentice Hall, 1996). There is a nice discussion of homogeneous coordinates in *Game Engine Design* (Eberly, Morgan-Kaufmann, 2000).

Exercises

1. Show algebraically that the perspective matrix preserves order of z values within the view volume.

2. For a four by matrix whose top three rows are arbitrary and whose bottom row is $(0, 0, 0, 1)$, show that the points $(x, y, z, 1)$ and (hx, hy, hz, h) transform to the same point after homogenization.

3. Verify that the form of $\mathbf{M}_p^{-1}$ given in the text is correct.

4. Verify that the full perspective to canonical matrix $\mathbf{M}_{\text{projection}}$ takes (r, t, n) to $(1, 1, 1)$.

5. Write down a perspective matrix for $n = 1$, $f = 2$.

6. For the point $\mathbf{p} = (x, y, z, 1)$, what are the homogenized and unhomogenized result for that point transformed by the perspective matrix in Problem 3?

7. For the eye position $\mathbf{e} = (0, 1, 0)$, a gaze vector $\mathbf{g} = (0, -1, 0)$, and a view-up-vector $\mathbf{t} = (1, 1, 0)$, what is the resulting orthonormal $\mathbf{uvw}$ basis used for coordinate rotations?

8. Show, that for a perspective transform, line segments that start in the view volume do map to line segments in the canonical volume after homogenization. Further, show that the relative ordering of

points on the two segments is the same. Hint: show that the $f(t)$ in Equation 6.9 has the properties $f(0) = 0$, $f(1) = 1$, the derivative of f is positive for all $t \in [0, 1]$, and the homogeneous coordinate does not change sign.

Hidden Surface Elimination

While we know how to get a single triangle onto the screen by projecting its vertices from 3D to the canonical view volume, we will achieve more realism if we also do *hidden surface elimination*, where only the closest surface is visible to the viewer. This can be achieved through numerous methods; we only cover the two most commonly used ones here: BSP tress and z-buffering. Ray tracing can also be thought of as a hidden surface algorithm, but it will be discussed in its own chapter since it does not integrate well into the standard project-and-rasterize process.

7.1 BSP Tree

If we are making many images of the same geometry from different viewpoints, as is often the case for applications such as games, we can use a *binary space partitioning* (BSP) tree algorithm to order the surfaces from front to back. The key aspect of the BSP tree is that it uses a preprocess to create a data structure that is useful for any viewpoint. So, as the viewpoint changes, the same data structure is used without change.

7.1.1 Overview of BSP Tree Algorithm

The BSP tree algorithm is an example of a *painter's algorithm*. A painter's algorithm draws every object from back-to-front, with each new polygon

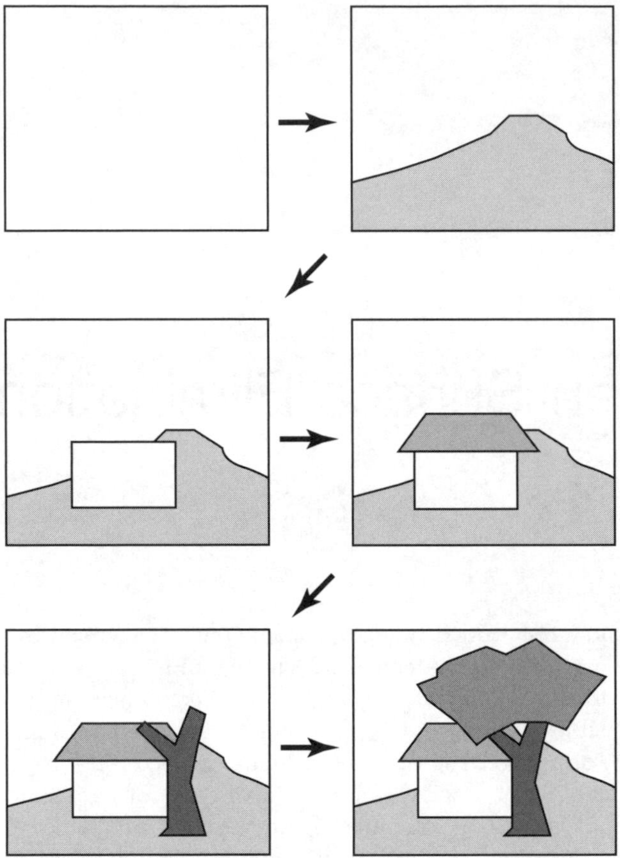

Figure 7.1. A painter's algorithm starts with a blank image and then draws the scene one object at a time from back-to-front, overdrawing whatever is already there. This automatically eliminates hidden surfaces.

potentially overdrawing previous polygons, as is shown in Figure 7.1. It can be implemented as follows:

sort objects back to front relative to viewpoint
for *each object* ***do***
  draw object on screen

The problem with the first step (the sort) is that the relative order of multiple objects is not always well defined, even if the order of every pair of objects is. This problem is illustrated in Figure 7.2 where the three triangles form a *cycle.*

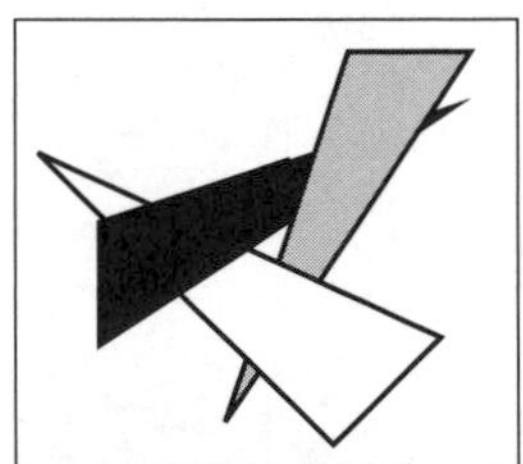

Figure 7.2. A cycle occurs if a global back-to-front ordering is not possible for a particular eye position.

The BSP tree algorithm works on any scene composed of polygons where no polygon crosses the plane defined by any other polygon. This restriction is then relaxed by a preprocessing step. For the rest of this discussion,

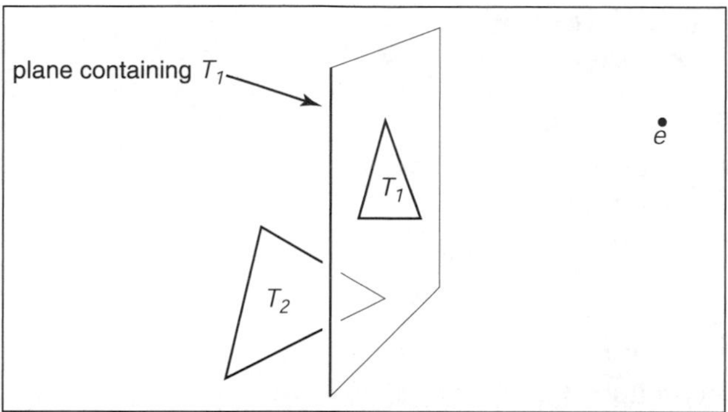

Figure 7.3. When **e** and T_2 are on opposite sides of the plane containing T_1, then it is safe to draw T_2 first and T_1 second. If **e** and T_2 are on the same side of the plane, then T_1 should be drawn before T_2. This is the core idea of the BSP tree algorithm.

triangles are assumed to be the only primitive, but the ideas extend to arbitrary polygons.

The basic idea of the BSP tree can be illustrated with two triangles, T_1 and T_2. We first recall (see Section 2.7) the implicit plane equation of the plane containing T_1: $f_1(\mathbf{p}) = 0$. The key property of implicit planes that we wish to take advantage of is that for all points $\mathbf{p}^+$ on one side of the plane, $f_1(\mathbf{p}^+) > 0$; and for all points $\mathbf{p}^-$ on the other side of the plane, $f_1(\mathbf{p}^-) < 0$. Using this property, we can find out on which side of the plane T_2 lies. Again, this assumes all three vertices of T_2 are on the same side of the plane. For discussion, assume that T_2 is on the $f_1(\mathbf{p} < 0)$ side of the plane. Then, we can draw T_1 and T_2 in the right order for any eyepoint $\mathbf{e}$:

if *(*$f_1(\mathbf{e}) < 0$*)* ***then***
  draw T_1
  draw T_2
else
  draw T_2
  draw T_1

The reason this works is that if T_2 and $\mathbf{e}$ are on the same side of the plane containing T_1, there is no way for T_2 to be fully or partially blocked by T_1 as seen from $\mathbf{e}$, so it is safe to draw T_1 first. If $\mathbf{e}$ and T_2 are on opposite sides of the plane containing T_1, then T_2 cannot fully or partially block T_1, and the opposite drawing order is safe (Figure 7.3).

This observation can be generalized to many objects provided none of them span the plane defined by T_1. If we use a binary tree data structure with T_1 as root, the *negative* branch of the tree contains all the triangles whose vertices have $f_i(\mathbf{p}) < 0$, and the *positive* branch of the tree contains all the triangles whose vertices have $f_i(\mathbf{p}) > 0$. We can draw in proper order as follows:

```
function draw(bsptree tree, point e)
if (tree.empty) then
    return
if (f_tree.root(e) < 0) then
    draw(tree.plus, e)
    rasterize tree.triangle
    draw(tree.minus, e)
else
    draw(tree.plus, e)
    rasterize tree.triangle
    draw(tree.minus, e)
```

The nice thing about that code is that it will work for any viewpoint **e**, so the tree can be precomputed. Note that, if each subtree is itself a tree where the root triangle divides the other triangles into two groups relative to the plane containing it, the code will work as is. It can be made slightly more efficient by terminating the recursive calls one level higher, but the code will still be simple. A tree illustrating this code is shown in Figure 7.4. As discussed in Section 2.7.2, the implicit equation for a point **p** on a plane containing three non-colinear points **a**, **b**, and **c** is:

$$f(\mathbf{p}) = ((\mathbf{b} - \mathbf{a}) \times (\mathbf{c} - \mathbf{a})) \cdot (\mathbf{p} - \mathbf{a}) = 0. \tag{7.1}$$

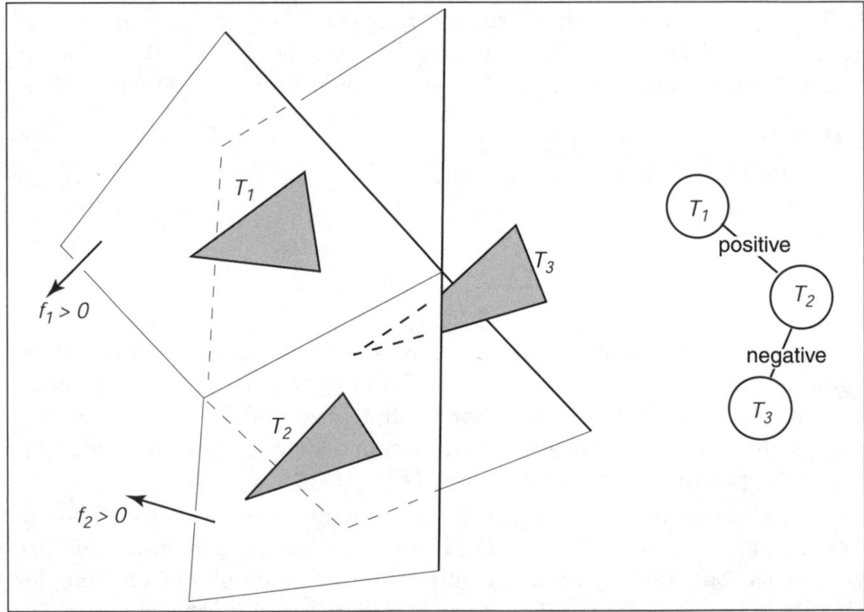

Figure 7.4. Three triangles and a BSP tree that is valid for them. The "positive" and "negative" are encoded by right and left subtree position respectively.

It can be faster to store the (A, B, C, D) of the implicit equation of the form:

$$f(x, y, z) = Ax + By + Cz + D = 0. \tag{7.2}$$

Equations 7.1 and 7.2 are equivalent, as is clear when you recall that the gradient of the implicit equation is the normal to the triangle. The gradient of Equation 7.2 is $\mathbf{n} = (A, B, C)$ which is just the normal vector

$$\mathbf{n} = (\mathbf{b} - \mathbf{a}) \times (\mathbf{c} - \mathbf{a}).$$

We can solve for D by plugging in any point on the plane, e.g., $\mathbf{a}$:

$$\begin{aligned} D &= -Ax_a - By_a - Cz_a \\ &= -\mathbf{n} \cdot \mathbf{a} \end{aligned}$$

This suggests the form:

$$\begin{aligned} f(\mathbf{p}) &= \mathbf{n} \cdot \mathbf{p} - \mathbf{n} \cdot \mathbf{a} \\ &= \mathbf{n} \cdot (\mathbf{p} - \mathbf{a}) \\ &= 0, \end{aligned}$$

which is the same as Equation 7.1 once you recall that $\mathbf{n}$ is computed using the cross product. Which form of the plane equation you use and whether you store only the vertices, $\mathbf{n}$ and the vertices, or $\mathbf{n}$, D, and the vertices, is probably a matter of taste—a classic time-storage tradeoff that will be settled best by profiling. For debugging, using Equation 7.1 is probably the best.

The only issue that prevents the code above from working in general is that one cannot guarantee that a triangle can be uniquely classified on one side of a plane or the other. It can have two vertices on on side of the plane and the third on the other. Or it can have vertices on the plane. This is handled by splitting the triangle into smaller triangles using the plane to "cut" them.

7.1.2 Building the Tree

If none of the triangles in the dataset cross each other's planes, so that all triangles are on one side of all other triangles, a BSP tree that can be traversed using the code above can be built using the following algorithm:

tree-root = *node*(T_1)
for $i \in \{2, \ldots, N\}$ ***do***
  tree-root.add(T_i)

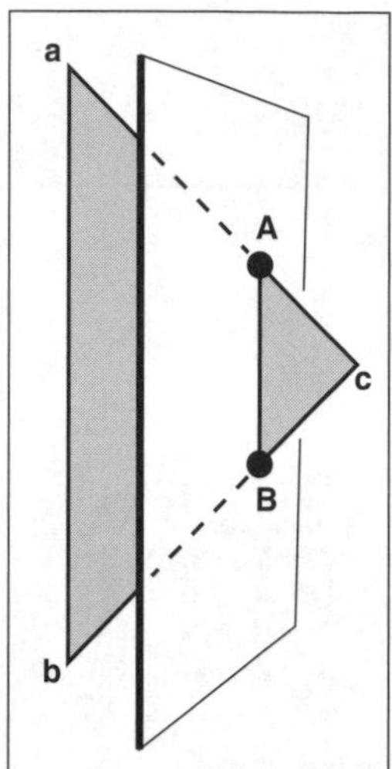

Figure 7.5. When a triangle spans a plane, there will be one vertex on one side, and two on the other.

function *add* (*triangle* T)
if $(f(\mathbf{a}) < 0$ *and* $f(\mathbf{b}) < 0$ *and* $f(\mathbf{c}) < 0)$ ***then***
  if (*negative subtree is empty*) ***then***
    negative-subtree = *node*(T)
  else
    negative-subtree.add (T)
else if $(f(\mathbf{a}) > 0$ *and* $f(\mathbf{b}) > 0$ *and* $f(\mathbf{c}) > 0)$ ***then***
  if *positive subtree is empty* ***then***
    positive-subtree = *node*(T)
  else
    positive-subtree.add (T)
else
  we have assumed this case is impossible

The only thing we need to fix is the case where the triangle crosses the dividing plane, as shown in the Figure 7.5. Assume, for simplicity, that the triangle has vertices **a** and **b** on one side of the plane, and vertex **c** is on the other side. In this case, we can find the intersection points **A** and **B**, and cut the triangle into three new triangles with vertices:

$$T_1 = (\mathbf{a}, \mathbf{b}, \mathbf{A}),$$
$$T_2 = (\mathbf{b}, \mathbf{B}, \mathbf{A}),$$
$$T_3 = (\mathbf{A}, \mathbf{B}, \mathbf{c}),$$

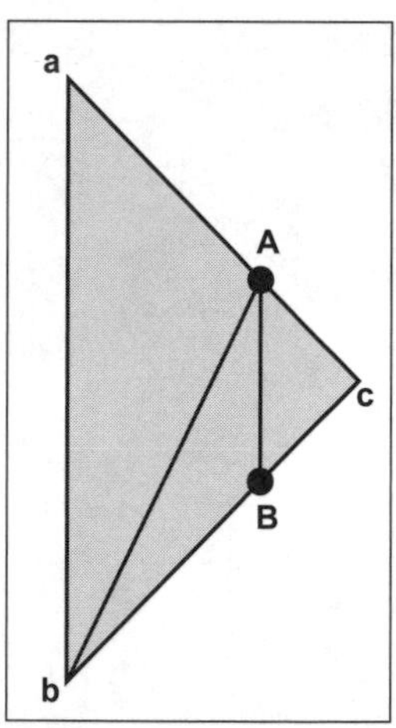

Figure 7.6. When a triangle is cut, we break it into three triangles, none of which span the cutting plane.

as shown in Figure 7.6. This order of vertices is important so that the direction of the normal remains the same as for the original triangle. If we assume that $f(\mathbf{c}) < 0$, the following code could add these three triangles to the tree assuming the positive and negative subtrees are not empty:

positive-subtree = *node* (T_1)
positive-subtree = *node* (T_2)
negative-subtree = *node* (T_3)

A precision problem that will plague a naive implementation occurs when a vertex is very near the splitting plane. For example, if we have two vertices on one side of the splitting plane and the other vertex is only an extremely small distance on the other side, we will create a new triangle almost the same as the old one, a triangle that is a sliver, and a triangle of almost zero size. It would be better to detect this as a special case and not split into three new triangles. One might expect this case to be rare, but because many models have tessellated planes and triangles with shared vertices, it occurs frequently, and thus must be handled carefully. Some simple manipulations that accomplish this are:

function *add*(*triangle* T)
fa = $f(\mathbf{a})$
fb = $f(\mathbf{b})$

```
fc = f(c)
if (abs(fa) < ε) then
  fa = 0
if (abs(fb) < ε) then
  fb = 0
if (abs(fc) < ε) then
  fc = 0
if (fa ≤ 0 and fb ≤ 0 and fc ≤ 0) then
  if (negative subtree is empty) then
    negative-subtree = node(T)
  else
    negative-subtree.add(T)
else if (fa ≥ 0 and fb ≥ 0 and fc ≥ 0) then
  if (positive subtree is empty) then
    positive-subtree = node(T)
  else
    positive-subtree.add(T)
else
  cut triangle into three triangles and add to each side
```

This takes any vertex whose f value is within ϵ of the plane and counts it as positive or negative. The constant ϵ is a small positive real chosen by the user. The technique above is a rare instance where testing for floating point equality is useful, and works because the zero value is set rather than being computed. Comparing for equality with a computed floating point value is almost never advisable, but we are not doing that.

7.1.3 Cutting Triangles

Filling out the details of the last case "cut triangle into three triangles and add to each side" is straightforward, but tedious. We should take advantage of the BSP tree construction as a preprocess where highest efficiency is not key. Instead, we should attempt to have a clean compact code. A nice trick is to force many of the cases into one by ensuring that **c** is on one side of the plane and the other two vertices are on the other. This is easily done with swaps. Filling out the details in the final else statement (assuming the subtrees are non-empty for simplicity) gives:

```
if (fa * fc ≥ 0) then
  swap(fa, fc)
  swap(a, c)
  swap(fa, fb)
  swap(a, b)
```

```
else if (fb * fc ≥ 0) then
    swap(fb, fc)
    swap(b, c)
    swap(fa, fb)
    swap(a, b)
compute A
compute B
T1 = (a, b, A)
T2 = (b, B, A)
T3 = (A, B, c)
if (fc ≥ 0) then
    negative-subtree.add(T1)
    negative-subtree.add(T2)
    positive-subtree.add(T3)
else
    positive-subtree.add(T1)
    positive-subtree.add(T2)
    negative-subtree.add(T3)
```

This code takes advantage of the fact that the product of a and b are positive if they have the same sign—thus, the first if statement. If vertices are swapped, we must do two swaps to keep the vertices ordered counterclockwise. Note that exactly one of the vertices may lie exactly on the plane, in which case the code above will work, but one of the generated triangles will have zero area. This can be handled by ignoring the possibility, which is not that risky because the rasterization code must handle zero area triangles in screen space (i.e., edge-on triangles). You can also add a check that does not add zero-area triangles to the tree. Finally, you can put in a special case for when exactly one of fa, fb, and fc is zero which cuts the triangle into two triangles.

To compute $\mathbf{A}$ and $\mathbf{B}$, a line-segment and implicit plane intersection is needed. For example, the parametric line connecting $\mathbf{a}$ and $\mathbf{c}$ is:

$$\mathbf{p}(t) = \mathbf{a} + t(\mathbf{c} - \mathbf{a}).$$

The point of intersection with the plane $\mathbf{n} \cdot \mathbf{p} + D = 0$ is found by plugging $\mathbf{p}(t)$ into the plane equation:

$$\mathbf{n} \cdot (\mathbf{a} + t(\mathbf{c} - \mathbf{a})) + D = 0,$$

and solving for t:

$$t = -\frac{\mathbf{n} \cdot \mathbf{a} + D}{\mathbf{n} \cdot (\mathbf{c} - \mathbf{a})}.$$

Calling this solution t_A, we can write the expression for $\mathbf{A}$:

$$\mathbf{A} = \mathbf{a} + t_A(\mathbf{c} - \mathbf{a}).$$

A similar computation will give $\mathbf{B}$.

7.1.4 Optimizing the Tree

The efficiency of tree creation is much less of a concern than tree traversal because it is a preprocess. The traversal of the BSP tree takes time proportional to the number of nodes in the tree. (How well balanced the tree is does not matter.) There will be one node for each triangle, including the triangles that are created as a result of splitting. This number can depend on the order triangles are added to the tree. For example, in Figure 7.7, if T_1 is the root, there will be two nodes in the tree, but if T_2 is the root, there will be more nodes because T_1 will be split.

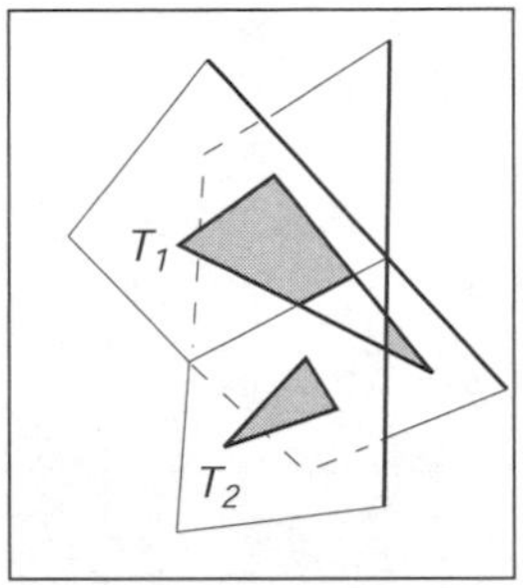

It difficult to find the "best" order of triangles to add to the tree. For N triangles there are $N!$ orderings that are possible. So trying all orderings is not usually feasible. Alternatively, some predetermined number of orderings can be tried from a random collection of permutations, and the best one can be kept for the final tree.

The splitting algorithm described above splits one triangle into three triangles. It could be more efficient to split a triangle into a triangle and a convex quadrilateral. This is probably not worth it if all input models have only triangles, but would be easy to support for implementations that accommodate arbitrary polygons.

Figure 7.7. Using T_1 as the root of a BSP tree will result in a tree with two nodes. Using T_2 as the root will require a cut and thus make a larger tree.

7.2 Z-Buffer

The z-buffer algorithm can be found in hardware on almost every video game and graphics PC. However, it is also a useful software algorithm. The z-buffer takes advantage of the fact that our real problem is to find the closest polygon to the center of each pixel; this can be an easier problem than finding a true depth order in continuous screen space.

7.2.1 Z-Buffer Algorithm

The z-buffer algorithm is remarkably simple. At each pixel, we store a real z value that is the distance to the closest triangle rasterized so far. When we rasterize a triangle, as discussed in Section 3.6, we can use the barycentric coordinates to interpolate the depth values of the vertices to each pixel. We only write the rgb and z values into the raster if the z value is closer to the viewer than what is already in that pixel. The z-buffer is first initialized to hold the farthest value that can be represented. For this discussion, we will assume z is positive. If your implementation uses negative z, as in the last chapter, then you should change the less-than test below to a greater than test. We use the following operation in place of a straight write of the rgb value:

```
function setpixel(int i, int j, rgb c, real z )
if (z < z-buffer(i, j)) then
  z-buffer(i, j) = z
  screen(i, j) = c
```

The simplcity of the algorithm suggests why the z-buffer is well suited to hardware implementation. The computation is straightforward, provided we have fast memory to use for the "z-buffer".

The final result of the z-buffer does not depend on triangle rasterization order, as is shown in Figure 7.8. An exceptional case, however, is when two triangles tie in z-depth for a given pixel. In that case, any of a number of conventions can hold, the most common of which is to assume the last triangle drawn has priority. It can be a better idea to leave the resolution of ties undefined so that optimization can reorder rasterization.

7.2.2 Integer Z-Buffer

In practice, the z values stored in the buffer are non-negative integers. This is preferable to true floats because the fast memory needed for the z-buffer is somewhat expensive, and is worth keeping to a minimum.

The use of integers can cause some precision problems. If we use an integer range having B values $\{0, 1, \ldots, B-1\}$, we can map 0 to the near clipping plane $z = n$ and $B - 1$ to the far clipping plane $z = f$. Note, that for this discussion, we assume z, n, and f are positive. This will result in the same results as the negative case, but the details of the argument are easier to follow. We send each z value to a "bucket" with depth $\Delta z = (f - n)/B$. We would not use the integer z-buffer if memory was not a premium, so it is useful to make B as small as possible.

If we allocate b bits to store the z-value, then $B = 2^b$. We need enough bits to make sure any triangle in front of another triangle will have its depth mapped to distinct depth bins.

For example, if you are rendering a scene where triangles have a separation of at least one meter, then $\Delta z < 1$ should yield images without artifacts. There are two ways to make Δz smaller: move n and f closer together or increase b. If b is fixed, as it may be in APIs or on particular hardware platforms, adjusting n and f is the only option.

The precision of z-buffers must be handled with great care when perspective images are created. The value Δz above is used *after* the perspective divide. Recall from Section 6.3 that the result of the perspective divide is:

$$z = n + f - \frac{fn}{z_w}$$

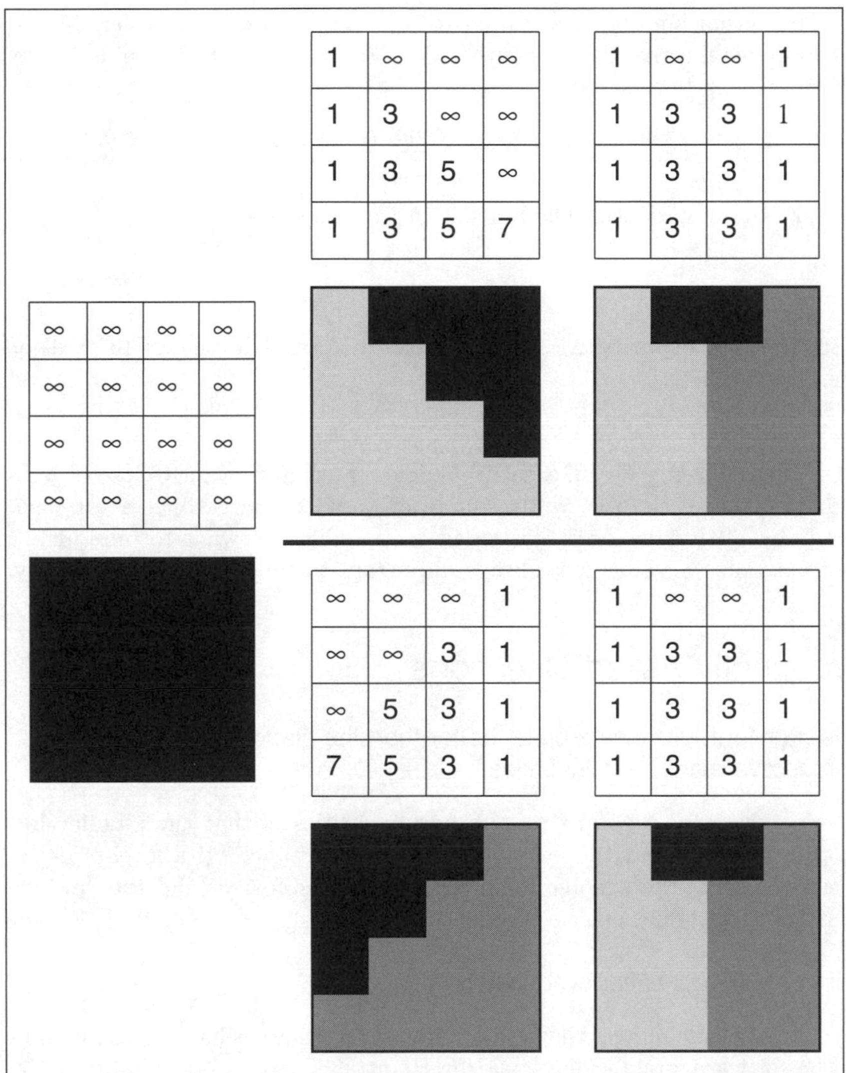

Figure 7.8. A z-buffer rasterizing two triangles in each of two possible orders. The first triangle is fully rasterized. The second triangle has every pixel computed, but for three of the pixels the depth-contest is lost and those pixels are not drawn. The final image is the same regardless.

The actual bin depth is related to z_w, the world depth, rather than z, the post-perspective divide depth. We can approximate the bin size by differentiating both sides:

$$\Delta z \approx \frac{fn\Delta z_w}{z_w^2}.$$

Bin sizes vary in depth. The bin size in world space is:

$$\Delta z_w \approx \frac{z_w^2 \Delta z}{fn}.$$

Note that the quantity Δz is as discussed before. The biggest bin will be for $z' = f$, where:

$$\Delta z_w^{\max} \approx \frac{f\Delta z}{n}.$$

Note that choosing $n = 0$, a natural choice if we don't want to lose objects right in front of the eye, will result in an infinitely large bin—a very bad condition. To make $\Delta z_w^{\max}$ as small as possible, we want to minimize f and maximize n. Thus it is always important to choose n and f carefully.

Frequently Asked Questions

• **Is a uniform distance z-buffer better than the standard one that includes perspective matrix non-linearities?**

It depends. One "feature" of the non-linearities is that the z-buffer has more resolution near the eye and less in the distance. If a level-of-detail system is used, then geometry in the distance is coarser and the "unfairness" of the z-buffer can be a good thing.

• **Is a software z-buffer ever useful?**

Yes. Most of the movies that use 3D computer graphics have used a variant of the software z-buffer developed by Pixar.

Notes

A summary of exact hidden-surface algorithms is given in *A Characterization of Ten Hidden-Surface Algorithms* (Sutherland, Sproull and Schumacker, Computer Surveys, January 1974). The BSP-tree was introduced to graphics in *On Visible Surface Generation by A Priori Tree Structures* (Fuchs, SIGGRAPH, 1980). The z-buffer algorithm was introduced in *A Hidden Surface Algorithm with Antialiasing* (Catmull, SIGGRAPH, 1978).

Exercises

1. Given N triangles, what is the minimum number of triangles that could be added to a resulting BSP tree? What is the maximum number?

2. Suppose you are designing an integer z-buffer for flight simulation where all of the objects are at least one meter thick, are never closer to the viewer than 4 meters, and may be as far away as 100 km. How many bits are needed in the z-buffer to ensure there are no visibility errors? Suppose that visibility errors only matter near the viewer, i.e., for distances less than 100 m. How many bits are needed in that case?

Surface Shading

To make objects appear to have more volume, it can help to use *shading*, i.e., the surface is "painted" with light. This chapter presents the most common heuristic shading methods. The first two, Diffuse and Phong shading, where developed in the 1970s and are available in most graphics libraries. The last, artistic shading, uses artistic conventions to assign color to objects. This creates images reminiscent of technical drawings which is desirable in many applications.

8.1 Diffuse Shading

Many objects in the world have a surface appearance loosely described as "matte," indicating that the object is not at all shiny. Examples include paper, unfinished wood, and dry unpolished stones. To a large degree, such objects do not have a color change with a change in viewpoint. For example, if you stare at a particular point on a piece of paper and move while keeping your gaze fixed on that point, the color at that point will stay relatively constant. Such matte objects can be considered as behaving as *Lambertian* objects. This section discusses how to implement the shading of such objects.

8.1.1 Lambertian Shading Model

A Lambertian object obeys *Lambert's Law*, which states that the color c of a surface is proportional to the cosine of the angle between the surface

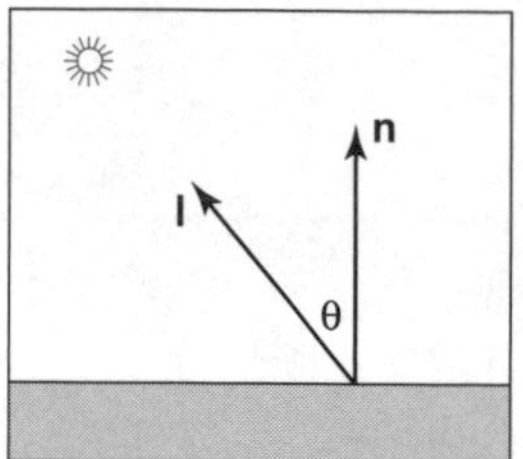

Figure 8.1. The geometry for Lambert's Law. Both **n** and **l** are unit vectors.

normal and the direction to the light source:

$$c \propto \cos\theta,$$

or in vector form:

$$c \propto \mathbf{n} \cdot \mathbf{l},$$

where $\mathbf{n}$ and $\mathbf{l}$ are shown in Figure 8.1. Thus, the color on the surface will vary according to the cosine of the angle between the surface normal and the light direction. Note that the vector $\mathbf{l}$ is typically assumed not to depend on the location of the object. That assumption is equivalent to assuming the light is "distant" relative to object size. Such a "distant" light is often called a *directional light*, because its position is specified only by a direction.

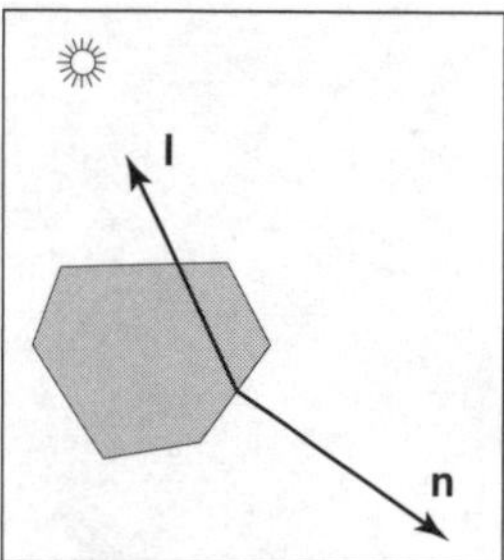

Figure 8.2. When a surface points away from the light, it should receive no light. This case can be verified by checking whether the dot product of **l** and **n** is negative.

A surface can be made lighter or darker by changing the intensity of the light source or the reflectance of the surface. The diffuse reflectance c_r is the fraction of light reflected by the surface. This fraction will be different for different color components. For example, a surface is red if it reflects a higher fraction of red incident light than blue incident light. If we assume surface color is proportional to the light reflected from a surface, then the diffuse reflectance c_r—an RGB color—must also be included:

$$c \propto c_r \mathbf{n} \cdot \mathbf{l}. \tag{8.1}$$

The right-hand side of Equation 8.1 is an RGB color with all RGB components in the range $[0, 1]$. We would like to add the effects of light intensity while keeping the RGB components in the range $[0, 1]$. This suggests adding an RGB intensity term c_l which itself has components in the range $[0, 1]$:

$$c = c_r c_l \mathbf{n} \cdot \mathbf{l}. \tag{8.2}$$

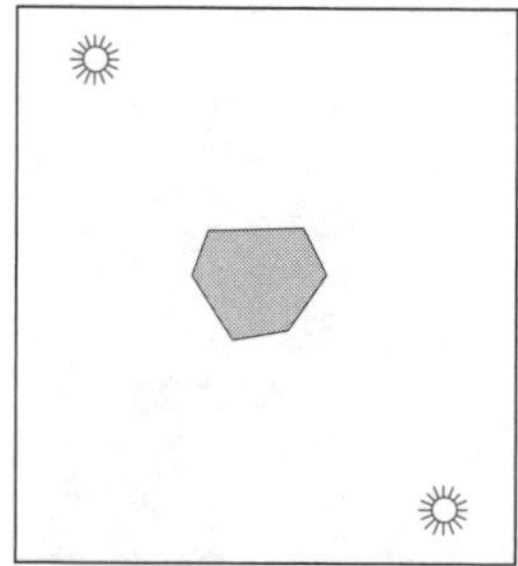

Figure 8.3. Using Equation 8.4, the two-sided lighting formula, is equivalent to assuming two opposing light sources of the same color.

This is a very convenient form, but it can produce RGB components for c that are outside the range $[0, 1]$, because the dot product can be negative. The dot product is negative when the surface is pointing away from the light as shown in Figure 8.2.

The "max" function can be added to Equation 8.2 to test for that case:

$$c = c_r c_l \max(0, \mathbf{n} \cdot \mathbf{l}). \tag{8.3}$$

Another way to deal with the "negative" light is to use an absolute value:

$$c = c_r c_l |\mathbf{n} \cdot \mathbf{l}|. \tag{8.4}$$

While Equation 8.4 may seem physically implausible, it actually corresponds to Equation 8.3 with two lights in opposite directions. For this reason it is often called *two-sided* lighting (Figure 8.3).

8.1.2 Ambient Shading

One problem with the diffuse shading of Equation 8.3 is that any point whose normal faces away from the light will be black. In real life, light is reflected all over, and some light is incident from every direction. In addition, there is often skylight giving "ambient" lighting. One way to handle this is to use several light sources. A common trick is to always put a dim source at the eye so that all visible points will receive some light. Another is to use two-sided lighting as described by Equation 8.4. A more common approach is to add an ambient term. This is just a constant color term added to Equation 8.3:

$$c = c_r \left(c_a + c_l \max\left(0, \mathbf{n} \cdot \mathbf{l}\right)\right).$$

Intuitively, you can think of the ambient color c_a as the average color of all surfaces in the scene. If you want to ensure that the computed RGB color stays in the range $[0, 1]^3$, then $c_a + c_l \leq (1, 1, 1)$. Otherwise your code should "clamp" RGB values above one to have the value one.

8.1.3 Vertex-Based Diffuse Shading

If we apply Equation 8.1 to an object made of triangles, it will typically have a faceted appearance. Often, the triangles are an approximation to a smooth surface. To avoid the faceted appearance, we can place surface

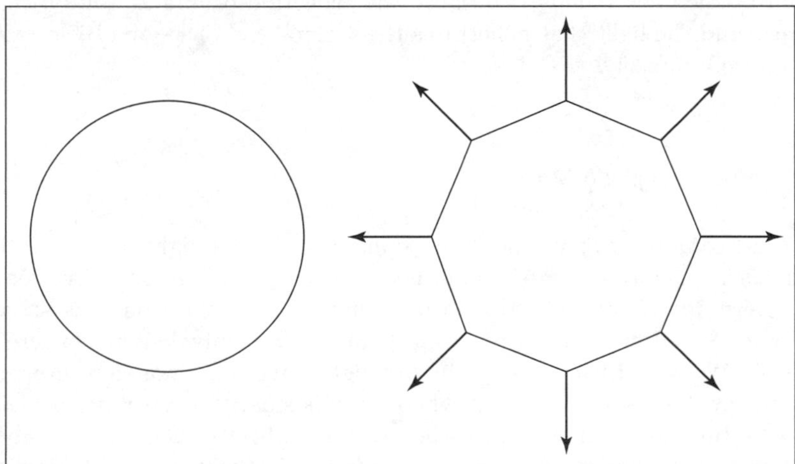

Figure 8.4. A circle (left) is approximated by an octagon (right). Vertex normals record the surface normal of the original curve.

normal vectors at the vertices of the triangles, apply Equation 8.3 at each of the vertices using the normal vectors at the vertices (see Figure 8.4). This will give a color at each triangle vertex, and this color can be interpolated using the barycentric interpolation described in Section 3.6.

One problem with shading at triangle vertices is that we need to get the normals from somewhere. Many models will come with normals supplied. If you tessellate your own smooth model, you can create normals when you create the triangles. If you are presented with a polygonal model that does not have normals at vertices and you want to shade it smoothly, you can compute normals by a variety of heuristic methods. The simplest is to just average the normals of the triangles that share each vertex and use this average normal at the vertex. This average normal will not automatically be of unit length, so you should convert it to a unit vector before using it for shading.

8.2 Phong Shading

Some surfaces are essentially like matte surfaces, but they have *highlights*. Examples of such surfaces include polished tile floors, gloss paint, and whiteboards. Highlights move across a surface as the viewpoint moves. This means that we must add a unit vector $\mathbf{e}$ toward the eye into our equations. If you look carefully at highlights, you will see that they are really reflections of the light; sometimes these reflections are blurred. The color of these highlights is the color of the light—the surface color seems to have little effect. This is because the reflection occurs at the object's surface, and the light that penetrates the surface and picks up object color is scattered diffusely.

8.2.1 Phong Lighting Model

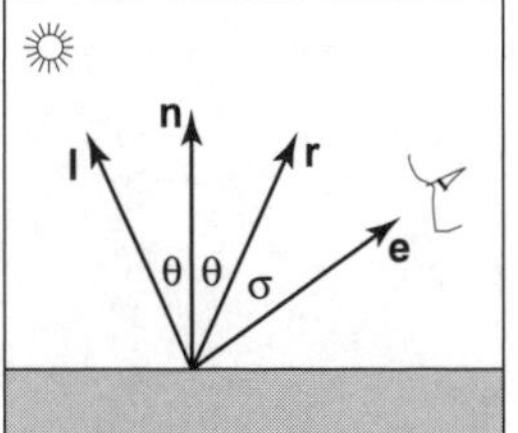

Figure 8.5. The geometry for the Phong illumination model. The eye should see a highlight if σ is small.

We want to add a fuzzy "spot" the same color as the light source in the right place. The center of the dot should be drawn where the direction $\mathbf{e}$ to the eye "lines" up with the natural direction of reflection $\mathbf{r}$ as shown in Figure 8.5. Here "lines up" is mathematically equivalent to "where σ is zero". We would like to have the highlight have some non-zero area, so that the eye sees some highlight wherever σ is small. Given $\mathbf{r}$, we'd like a heuristic function that is bright when $\mathbf{e} = \mathbf{r}$ and falls off gradually when $\mathbf{e}$ moves away from $\mathbf{r}$. An obvious candidate is the cosine of the angle between them:

$$c = c_l(\mathbf{e} \cdot \mathbf{r}),$$

There are two problems with using this equation. The first is that the dot product can be negative. This can be solved computationally with an "if" statement that sets the color to zero when the dot product is negative. The more serious problem is that the highlight produced by this equation is much wider than that seen in real life. The maximum is in the right place and it is the right color, but it is just too big. We can narrow it without reducing its maximum color by raising to a power:

$$c = c_l \max(0, \mathbf{e} \cdot \mathbf{r})^p. \tag{8.5}$$

Here p is called the *Phong exponent*; it is a positive real number. The effect that changing the Phong exponent has on the highlight can be seen in Figure 8.6.

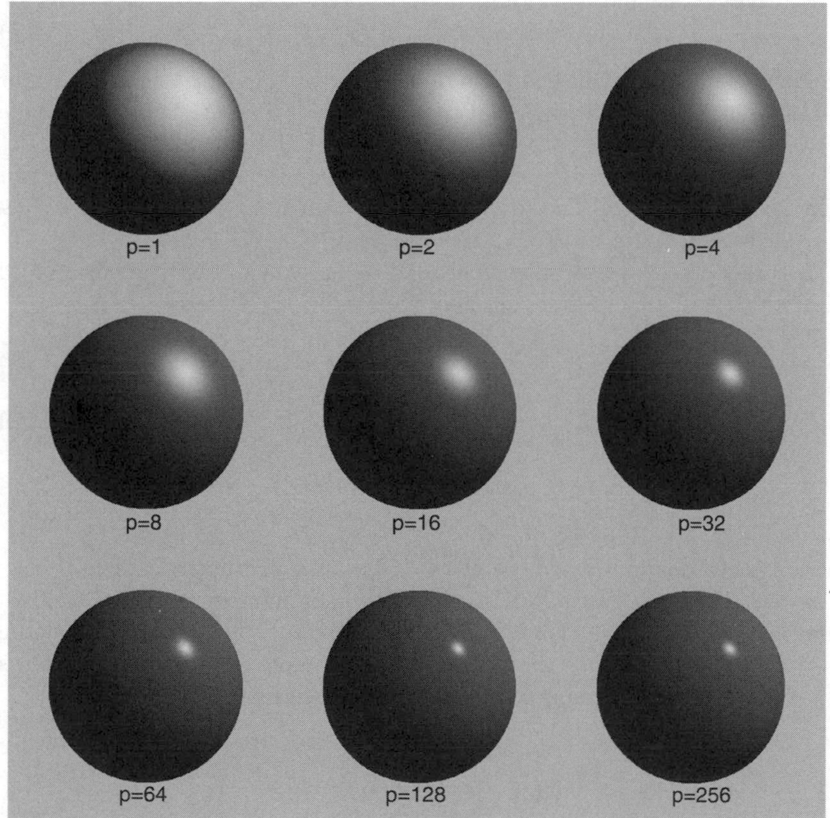

Figure 8.6. The effect of the Phong exponent on highlight characteristics. This uses Equation 8.5 for the highlight. There is also a diffuse component, giving the objects a shiny but non-metallic appearance. Image courtesy of Nate Robins. (See also Plate XII.)

To implement Equation 8.5 we first need to compute the unit vector $\mathbf{r}$. Given unit vectors $\mathbf{l}$ and $\mathbf{n}$, $\mathbf{r}$ is the vector $\mathbf{l}$ reflected about $\mathbf{n}$. Figure 8.7 shows that this vector can be computed as:

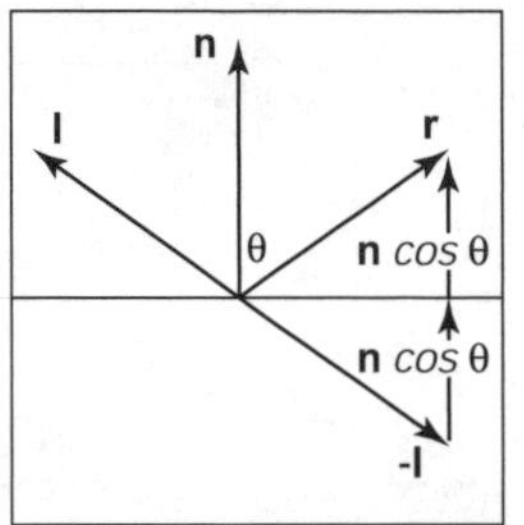

Figure 8.7. The geometry for calculating the vector **r**.

$$\mathbf{r} = -\mathbf{l} + 2(\mathbf{l} \cdot \mathbf{n})\mathbf{n}, \tag{8.6}$$

where the dot product is used to compute $\cos\theta$.

An alternative heuristic model based on Equation 8.5 eliminates the need to check for negative values of the number used as a base for exponentiation. Instead of $\mathbf{r}$, we compute $\mathbf{h}$, the unit vector halfway between $\mathbf{l}$ and $\mathbf{e}$ (Figure 8.8):

$$\mathbf{h} = \frac{\mathbf{e} + \mathbf{l}}{\|\mathbf{e} + \mathbf{l}\|}$$

The highlight occurs when $\mathbf{h}$ is near $\mathbf{n}$, i.e., when $\cos\omega = \mathbf{h} \cdot \mathbf{n}$ is near 1. This suggests the rule:

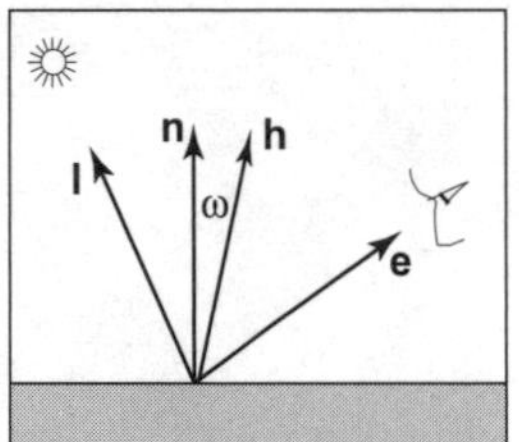

Figure 8.8. The unit vector **h** is halfway between **l** and **e**.

$$c = c_l(\mathbf{h} \cdot \mathbf{n})^p. \tag{8.7}$$

The exponent p here will have analogous control behavior to the exponent in Equation 8.5, but the angle between $\mathbf{h}$ and $\mathbf{n}$ is half the size of the angle between $\mathbf{e}$ and $\mathbf{r}$, so the details will be slightly different. The advantage of using the cosine between $\mathbf{n}$ and $\mathbf{h}$ is that it is always positive for eye and light above the plane. The disadvantage is that a square root and divide is needed to compute $\mathbf{h}$.

In practice, we want most materials to have a diffuse appearance in addition to a highlight. We can combine Equations 8.3 and 8.7 to get:

$$c = c_r\,(c_a + c_l \max(0, \mathbf{n} \cdot \mathbf{l})) + c_l(\mathbf{h} \cdot \mathbf{n})^p. \tag{8.8}$$

If we want to allow the user to dim the highlight, we can add a control term c_p:

$$c = c_r\,(c_a + c_l \max(0, \mathbf{n} \cdot \mathbf{l})) + c_l c_p(\mathbf{h} \cdot \mathbf{n})^p. \tag{8.9}$$

The term c_p is a RGB color, which allows us to change highlight colors. This is useful for metals where $c_h = c_r$ because highlights on metal take on a metallic color. In addition, it is often useful to make c_p a neutral value less than one, so that colors stay below one. For example, setting $c_p = 1 - M$ where M is the maximum component of c_r will keep colors below one for one light source and no ambient term.

8.2.2 Surface Normal Vector Interpolation

Smooth surfaces with highlights tend to change color quickly compared to Lambertian surfaces with the same geometry. Thus, shading at the normal vectors can generate disturbing artifacts.

Plate I. Ray-traced and photon-mapped image of an interior. Most of the lighting is indirect. Image courtesy Henrik Jensen.

Plate II. The brightly colored pattern in the shadow is a "caustic" and is a product of light focused through the glass. It was computed using photon tracing. Image courtesy Henrik Jensen.

Plate III. Top: a diffuse shading model is used. Bottom: subsurface scattering is allowed using a technique from "A Practical Model for Sub-surface Light Transport" Jensen et. al, Proceedings of SIGGRAPH 2001. Images courtesy Henrik Jensen.

Plate IV. Distribution ray-traced images with 1 sample per pixel, 16 samples per pixel, and 256 samples per pixel. Images courtesy Jason Waltman.

Plate V. The colored line switching from red to green. The middle pixel is half red and half green which is a "dark yellow". (See also Figure 3.9)

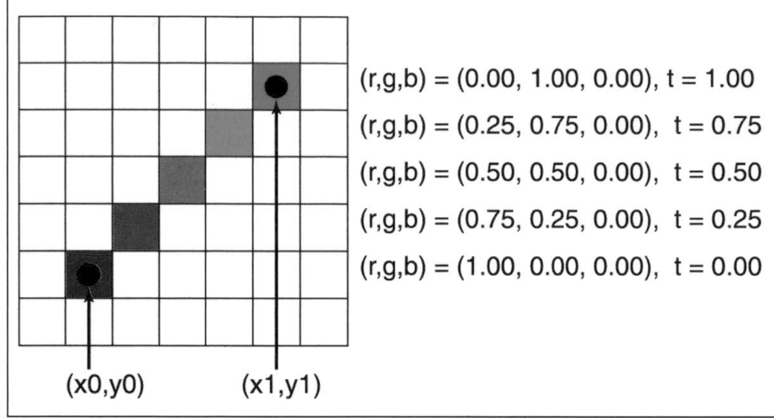

Plate VI. A colored triangle with barycentric interpolation. Note that the changes in color components are linear in each row and column as well as along each edge. In fact it is constant along every line, such as the diagonals, as well. (See also Figure 3.10)

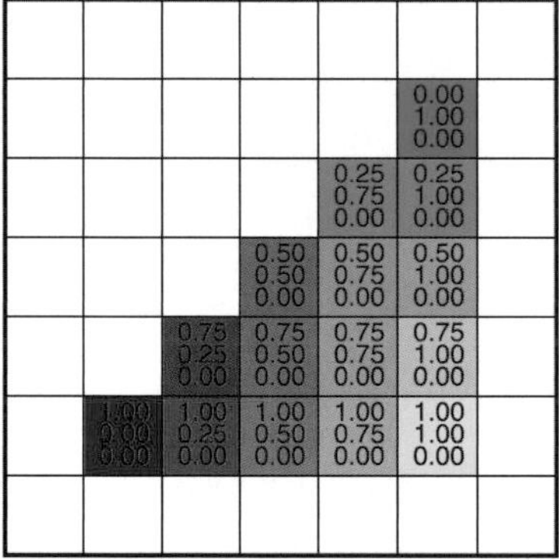

Plate VII. The RGB color cube in 3D and its faces unfolded. Any RGB color is a point in the cube. (See also Figure 3.4)

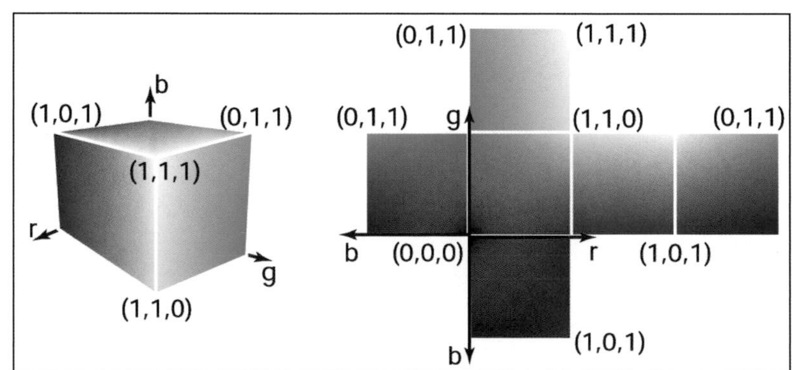

Plate VIII. Ray-traced image of blocks defined as displacement maps. This uses a form of ray tracing described in "Rendering Complex Scenes with Memory-Coherent Ray Tracing", Pharr et al., Proceedings of SIGGRAPH 1997. Image courtesy Matt Pharr.

Plate IX. An example of depth of field. The caustic in the shadow of the wine glass is computed using particle tracing (Chapter 19). (See also Figure 9.35)

Plate X. A comparison between a rendering and a photo. Figure courtesy Sumant Pattanaik and the Cornell Program of Computer Graphics (See also Figure 19.5)

Plate XI. The color of the glass is affected by total internal reflection and Beer's Law. The amount of light transmitted and reflected is determined by the Fresnel Equations. The complex lighting on the ground plane was computed using particle tracing as described in Chapter 19. (See also Figure 9.11)

Plate XII. The effect of the Phong exponent on highlight characteristics. This uses Equation 8.5 for the highlight. There is also a diffuse component, giving the objects a shiny but non-metallic appearence. Image courtesy of Nate Robins. (See also Figure 8.6)

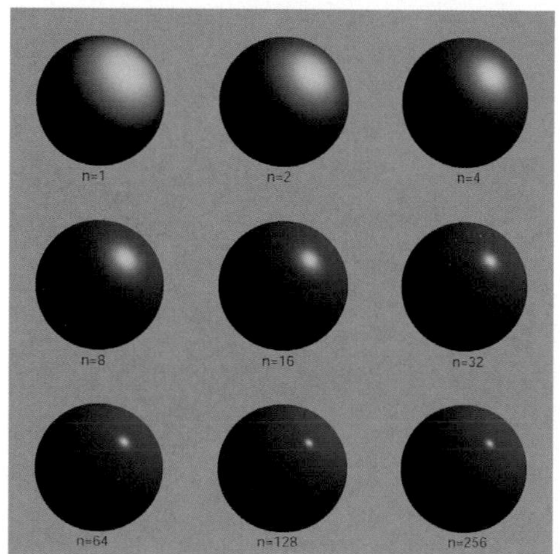

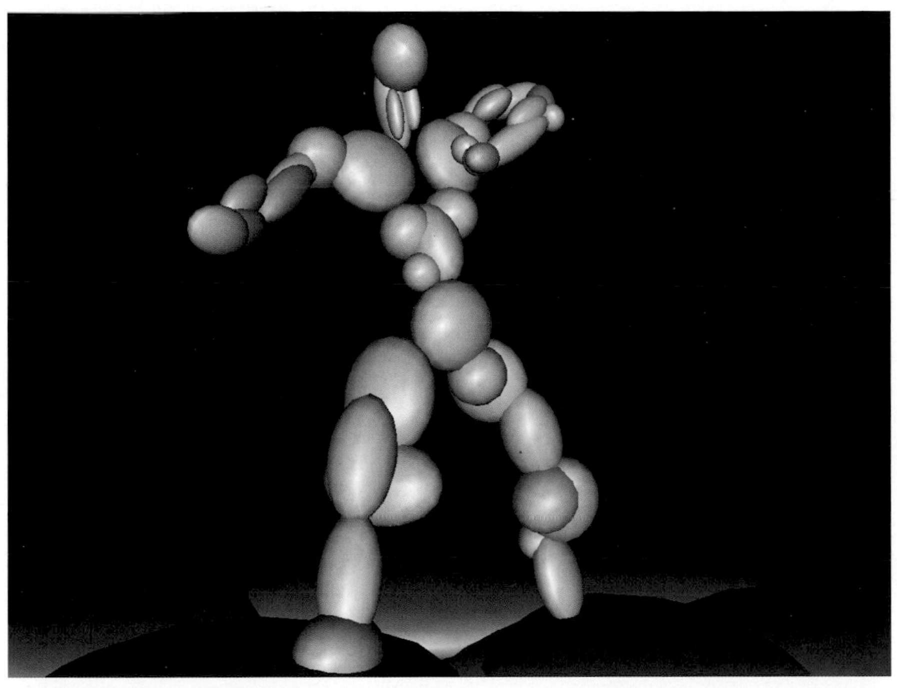

Plate XIII. Top: a set of ellipsoids approximates the model. Bottom: the ellipsoids are used to create a garvity-like implicit function, which is then displaced. Image courtesy Eric Levin.

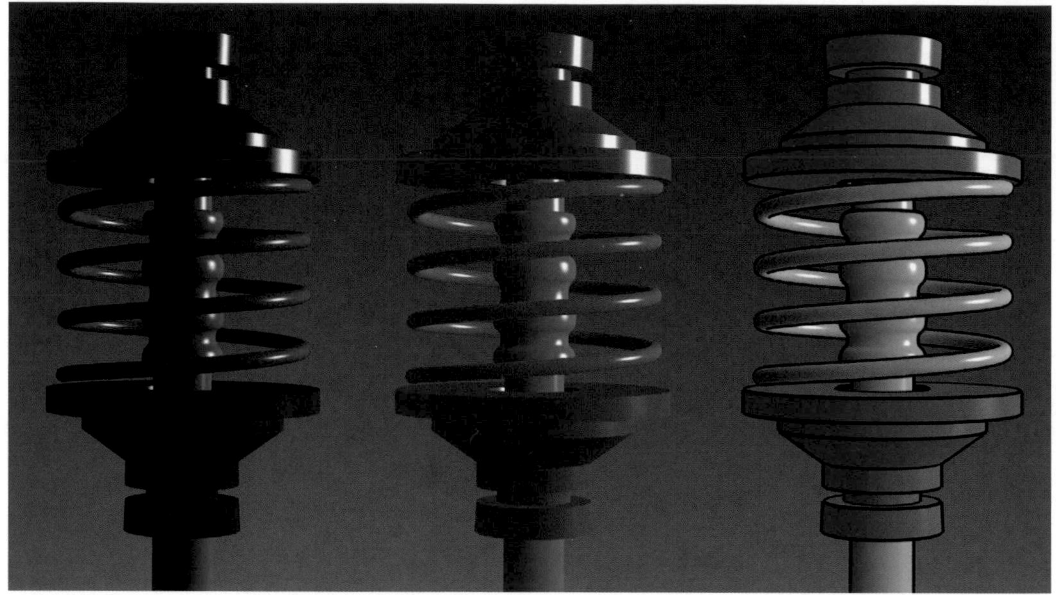

Plate XIV. Left: a Phong-illuminated image. Middle: cool-to-warm shading is not useful without silhouettes. Right: cool-to-warm shading plus silhouettes. Image courtesy Amy Gooch. (See also Figure 8.9)

Plate XV. This image shows extreme motion blur effects. The shadows use distribution ray tracing because they are moving during the image. Model by Joseph Hamdorf and Young Song. Rendering by Eric Levin.

These problems can be reduced by interpolating the normal vectors across the polygon and then applying Phong shading at each pixel. This allows you to get good images without making the size of the triangles extremely small. Recall from Chapter 3 that when rasterizing a triangle we compute barycentric coordinates (α, β, γ) to interpolate the vertex colors c_0, c_1, c_2:

$$c = \alpha c_0 + \beta c_1 + \gamma c_2. \tag{8.10}$$

We can use the same equation to interpolate surface normals $\mathbf{n}_0$, $\mathbf{n}_1$, and $\mathbf{n}_2$:

$$\mathbf{n} = \alpha \mathbf{n}_0 + \beta \mathbf{n}_1 + \gamma \mathbf{n}_2. \tag{8.11}$$

And Equation 8.9 can then be evaluated for the $\mathbf{n}$ computed at each pixel. Note that the $\mathbf{n}$ resulting from Equation 8.11 is usually not a unit normal. Better visual results will be achieved if it is converted to a unit vector before it is used in shading computations. This type of normal interpolation is often called *Phong normal interpolation.*

8.3 Artistic Shading

The Lambertian and Phong shading methods are based on heuristics designed to imitate the appearance of objects in the real world. Artistic shading is designed to mimic drawings made by human artists. Such shading seems to have advantages in many applications. For example, auto manufacturers hire artists to draw diagrams for car owners' manuals. This is more expensive than using much more "realistic" photographs, so there is probably some intrinsic advantage to the techniques of artists when certain types of communication are needed. In this section, we show how to make subtly shaded line drawings reminiscent of human drawn images. Creating such images is often called *non-photorealistic rendering*, , but we will avoid that term because many non-photorealistic techniques are used for efficiency that are not related to any artistic practice.

8.3.1 Line Drawing

The most obvious thing we see in human drawings that we don't see in real life is *silhouettes*. When we have a set of triangles with shared edges, we should draw an edge as a silhouette when one of the two triangles sharing an edge faces toward the viewer, and the other triangle faces away from the viewer. This condition can be tested for two normals $\mathbf{n}_0$ and $\mathbf{n}_1$ by:

$$\text{draw silhouette if } (\mathbf{e} \cdot \mathbf{n}_0)(\mathbf{e} \cdot \mathbf{n}_1) \leq 0.$$

Here $\mathbf{e}$ is a vector from the edge to the eye. This can be any point on the edge or either of the triangles. Alternatively, if $f_i(\mathbf{p}) = 0$ are the implicit plane equations for the two triangles, the test can be written:

$$\text{draw silhouette if } f_0(\mathbf{e}) f_1(\mathbf{e}) \leq 0.$$

We would also like to draw visible edges of a polygonal model. To do this, we can use either of the hidden surface methods of Chapter 7 for drawing in the background color, and then draw the outlines of each triangle in black. This, in fact, will also capture the silhouettes. Unfortunately, if the polygons represent a smooth surface, we really don't want to draw most of those edges. However, we might want to draw all *creases* where there really is a corner in the geometry. We can test for creases by using a heuristic threshold:

$$\text{draw crease if } (\mathbf{n}_0 \cdot \mathbf{n}_1) \leq \text{threshold}.$$

This combined with the silhouette test will give nice-looking line drawings.

8.3.2 Cool-to-Warm Shading

When artists shade line drawings, they often use low intensity shading to give some impression of curve to the surface, and to give colors to objects. Surfaces facing in one direction are shaded with a cool color, such as a blue, and surfaces facing in the opposite direction are shaded with a warm color, such as orange. Typically these colors are not very saturated and are also not dark. That way black silhouettes show up nicely. Overall this gives a cartoon-like effect. This can be achieved by setting up a direction to a "warm" light $\mathbf{l}$ and using the cosine to modulate color, where the warmth constant k_w is defined on $[0, 1]$:

$$k_w = \frac{1 + \mathbf{n} \cdot \mathbf{l}}{2}.$$

The color c is then just a linear blend of the cool color c_c and the warm color c_w:

$$c = k_w c_w + (1 - k_w) c_c.$$

There are many possible c_w and c_b that will produce reasonable looking results. A good starting place for a guess is:

$$\begin{aligned} c_c &= (0.4, 0.4, 0.7), \\ c_c &= (0.8, 0.6, 0.6). \end{aligned}$$

Figure 8.9 shows a comparison between traditional Phong lighting and this type of artistic shading.

Figure 8.9. Left: a Phong-illuminated image. Middle: cool-to-warm shading is not useful without silhouettes. Right: cool-to-warm shading plus silhouettes. Image courtesy Amy Gooch. (See also Plate XIV.)

Frequently Asked Questions

• **All of the shading in this chapter seems like enormous hacks. Is that true?**

Yes. However, they are carefully designed hacks that have proven useful in practice. In the long-run, we will probably have better-motivated algorithms that include physics, psychology, and tone-mapping. However, the improvements in image quality will probably be incremental.

• **I hate calling pow(). Is there a way to avoid it when doing Phong lighting?**

A simple way is to only have exponents that are themselves a power of two, i.e, 2, 4, 8, 16, ... In practice, this is not a problematic restriction for most applications. A look-up table is also possible, but will often not give a large speed-up.

Notes

Diffuse shading was introduced to graphics in *Continuous Shading of Curved Surfaces* (Gouraud, Communications of the ACM, June, 1971). Phong illumination and normal interpolation were introduced in *Illumination for Computer-Generated Images* (Phong, Communications of the ACM, June, 1975). The alternate half-angle form is from *Lighting Controls for Syn-*

thetic Images (Warn, SIGGRAPH, 1983). The book *Non-Photorealistic Rendering* (Gooch and Gooch, A K Peters, 2001) discusses the work called "artistic shading" in this chapter, as well as other art-inspired methods of rendering.

Exercises

1. The moon is poorly approximated by Diffuse or Phong shading. What observations tell you that this is true?

2. Velvet is poorly approximated by Diffuse or Phong shading. What observations tell you that this is true?

3. Why do most highlights on plastic objects look white, while those on gold metal look gold?

Ray Tracing

Ray tracing is a method to produce realistic images; it determines visible surfaces in an image at the pixel level. Unlike the z-buffer and BSP tree, ray tracing operates pixel-by-pixel rather than primitive-by-primitive. This tends to make ray tracing relatively slow for scenes with large objects in screen space. However, it has a variety of nice features which often make it the right choice for batch rendering and even for some interactive applications.

Ray tracing's primary benefit is that it is relatively straightforward to compute shadows and reflections. In addition, ray tracing is well suited to "walkthroughs" of extremely large models due to advanced ray tracing's low asymptotic time complexity which makes up for the required preprocessing of the model.

In an interactive 3D program implemented in a conventional z-buffer environment, it is often useful to be able to select an object using a mouse. The mouse is clicked in pixel (i, j) and the "picked" object is whatever object is "seen" through that pixel. If the rasterization process includes an object identification buffer, this is just a matter of looking up the value in pixel (i, j) of that buffer. However, if that buffer is not available, we can solve the problem of what object is visible via brute force geometrical computation using a "ray intersection test." In this way, ray tracing is useful also to programmers who use only standard graphics APIs.

This chapter also discusses *distribution ray tracing*, where multiple random rays are sent through each pixel in an image to simultaneously solve the antialiasing, soft shadow, fuzzy reflection, and depth-of-field problems.

9.1 The Basic Ray Tracing Algorithm

The simplest use of ray tracing is to produce images similar to those produced by the z-buffer and BSP-tree algorithms. Fundamentally, those methods make sure the appropriate object is "seen" through each pixel, and that the pixel color is shaded based on that object's material properties, the surface normal seen through that pixel, and the light geometry.

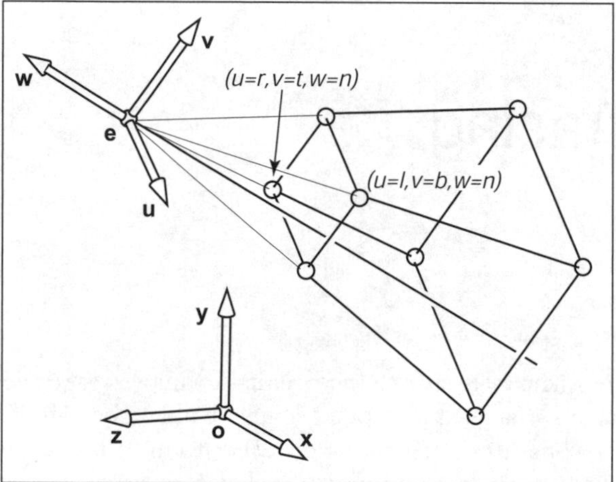

Figure 9.1. The 3D window we look through is the same as in Chapter 6. The borders of the window have simple coordinates in the *uvw* coordinate system with respect to origin **e**.

Figure 9.1 shows the basic viewing geometry for ray tracing, which is the same as we saw earlier in Chapter 6. The geometry is aligned to a uvw coordinate system with the origin at the eye location $\mathbf{e}$. The key idea in ray tracing is to identify locations on the view-plane at $w = n$ that correspond to pixel centers, as shown in Figure 9.2. A "ray," really just a

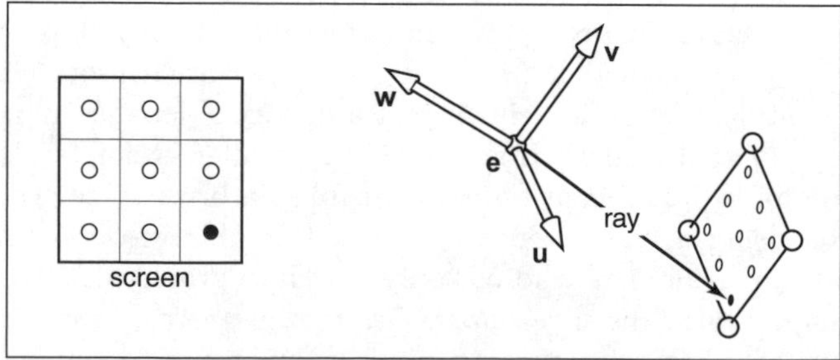

Figure 9.2. The sample points on the screen are mapped to a similar array on the 3D window. A viewing ray is sent to each of these locations.

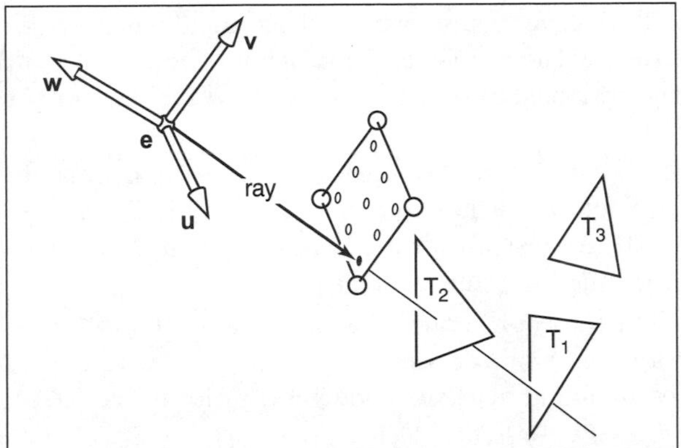

Figure 9.3. The ray is "traced" into the scene and the first object hit is the one seen through the pixel. In this case the triangle T_2 is returned.

directed 3D line, is then sent from **e** to that point. We then "gaze" in the direction of the ray to see the first object seen in that direction. This is shown in Figure 9.3, where the ray intersects two triangles, but only the first triangle hit, T_2, is returned. The structure of the basic ray tracing program is:

Compute **u**, **v**, **w** *basis vectors*
for *each pixel* **do**
  compute viewing ray
  find first object hit by ray and its surface normal **n**
  set pixel color to value based on material, light, and **n**

The pixel color can be computed using the shading equations of the last chapter.

9.2 Computing Viewing Rays

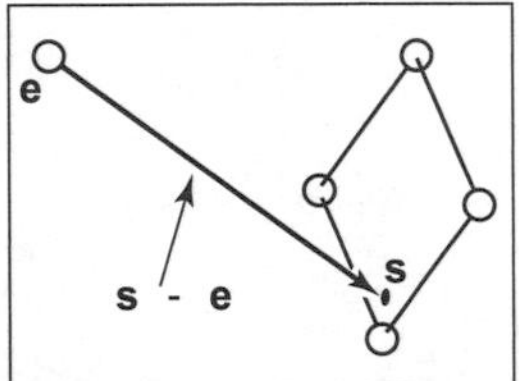

Figure 9.4. The ray from the eye to a point on the screen.

First we need to determine a mathematical representation for a ray. A ray is really just an origin point and a propagation direction; a 3D parametric line is ideal for this. As discussed in Section 2.8.1, the 3D parametric line from the eye **e** to a point **s** on the screen (see Figure 9.4) is given by:

$$\mathbf{p}(t) = \mathbf{e} + t(\mathbf{s} - \mathbf{e}).$$

This should be interpreted as, "we advance from **e** along the vector $(\mathbf{s} - \mathbf{e})$ a fractional distance t to find the point **p**." So given t, we can determine a point **p**. Note that $\mathbf{p}(0) = \mathbf{e}$, and $\mathbf{p}(1) = \mathbf{s}$. Also note that for positive t, if $t_1 < t_2$, then $\mathbf{p}(t_1)$ is closer to the eye than $\mathbf{p}(t_2)$. Also, if $t < 0$, then

$\mathbf{p}(t)$ is "behind" the eye. These facts will be useful when we search for the closest object hit by the ray that is not behind the eye. Note that we are overloading the variable t here which is also used for the top of the screen's v coordinate.

To compute a viewing ray, we need to know $\mathbf{e}$ (which is given), and $\mathbf{s}$. Finding $\mathbf{s}$ may look somewhat difficult. In fact, it is relatively straightforward using the same transform machinery we used for viewing in the context of projecting lines and triangles.

First, we find the coordinates of $\mathbf{s}$ in the uvw coordinate system with origin $\mathbf{e}$. For all points on the screen, $w_s = n$ as shown in Figure 9.2. The uv coordinates are found by the windowing transform that takes $[-0.5, n_x - 0.5] \times [-0.5, n_y - 0.5]$ to $[l, r] \times [b, t]$:

$$u_s = l + (r - l)\frac{i + 0.5}{n_x}$$
$$v_s = b + (t - b)\frac{j + 0.5}{n_y}$$

where (i, j) are the pixel indices. This gives us $\mathbf{s}$ in uvw coordinates. By definition, we can convert to canonical coordinates:

$$\mathbf{s} = \mathbf{e} + u_s\mathbf{u} + v_s\mathbf{v} + w_s\mathbf{w}. \tag{9.1}$$

Alternatively, we could use the matrix form (Equation 5.8):

$$\begin{bmatrix} x_s \\ y_s \\ z_s \\ 1 \end{bmatrix} = \begin{bmatrix} 1 & 0 & 0 & x_e \\ 0 & 1 & 0 & y_e \\ 0 & 0 & 1 & z_e \\ 0 & 0 & 0 & 1 \end{bmatrix} \begin{bmatrix} x_u & x_v & x_w & 0 \\ y_u & y_v & y_w & 0 \\ z_u & z_v & z_w & 0 \\ 0 & 0 & 0 & 1 \end{bmatrix} \begin{bmatrix} u_s \\ v_s \\ w_s \\ 1 \end{bmatrix} \tag{9.2}$$

which is just the matrix form of Equation 9.1. We can compose this with the windowing transform in matrix form if we wished, but this is probably not worth doing unless you like the matrix form of equations better.

9.3 Ray-Object Intersection

Given a ray $\mathbf{e} + t\mathbf{d}$, we want to find the first intersection with any object where $t > 0$. It will later prove useful to solve a slightly more general problem of finding the first intersection in the interval $[t_0, t_1]$, and using $[0, \infty)$ for viewing rays. We solve this for both spheres and triangles in this section. In the next section, multiple objects are discussed.

9.3.1 Ray-Sphere Intersection

Given a ray $\mathbf{p}(t) = \mathbf{o} + t\mathbf{d}$ and an implicit surface $f(\mathbf{p}) = 0$, we'd like to know where they intersect. The intersection points occur when points on the ray satisfy the implicit equation

$$f(\mathbf{p}(t)) = 0.$$

This is just

$$f(\mathbf{e} + t\mathbf{d}) = 0.$$

A sphere with center $\mathbf{c} = (c_x, c_y, c_z)$ and radius R can be represented by the implicit equation

$$(x - c_x)^2 + (y - c_y)^2 + (z - c_z)^2 - R^2 = 0.$$

We can write this same equation in vector form:

$$(\mathbf{p} - \mathbf{c}) \cdot (\mathbf{p} - \mathbf{c}) - R^2 = 0.$$

Any point $\mathbf{p}$ that satisfies this equation is on the sphere. If we plug points on the ray $\mathbf{p}(t) = \mathbf{e} + t\mathbf{d}$ into this equation, we can solve for the values of t on the ray that yield points on the sphere:

$$(\mathbf{e} + t\mathbf{d} - \mathbf{c}) \cdot (\mathbf{e} + t\mathbf{d} - \mathbf{c}) - R^2 = 0.$$

Rearranging terms yields

$$(\mathbf{d} \cdot \mathbf{d})t^2 + 2\mathbf{d} \cdot (\mathbf{o} - \mathbf{e})t + (\mathbf{e} - \mathbf{c}) \cdot (\mathbf{e} - \mathbf{c}) - R^2 = 0.$$

Here, everything is known except the parameter t, so this is a classic quadratic equation in t, meaning it has the form

$$At^2 + Bt + C = 0.$$

The solution to this equation is discussed in Section 2.2. The term under the square root sign in the quadratic solution, $B^2 - 4AC$, is called the *discriminant* and tells us how many real solutions there are. If the discriminant is negative, its square root is imaginary and there are no intersections between the sphere and the line. If the discriminant is positive, there are two solutions; one solution where the ray enters the sphere, and one where it leaves. If the discriminant is zero, the ray grazes the sphere touching it at exactly one point. Plugging in the actual terms for the sphere and eliminating the common factors of two, we get:

$$t = \frac{-\mathbf{d} \cdot (\mathbf{e} - \mathbf{c}) \pm \sqrt{(\mathbf{d} \cdot (\mathbf{e} - \mathbf{c}))^2 - (\mathbf{d} \cdot \mathbf{d}) \left((\mathbf{e} - \mathbf{c}) \cdot (\mathbf{e} - \mathbf{c}) - R^2\right)}}{(\mathbf{d} \cdot \mathbf{d})}.$$

In an actual implementation, you should first check the value of the discriminant before computing other terms. If the sphere is used only as a bounding object for more complex objects, then we need only determine whether we hit it; checking the discriminant suffices.

As discussed in Section 2.7.1, the normal vector at point $\mathbf{p}$ is given by the gradient $\mathbf{n} = 2(\mathbf{p} - \mathbf{c})$. The unit normal is $(\mathbf{p} - \mathbf{c})/R$.

9.3.2 Ray-Triangle Intersection

There are many algorithms for computing ray-triangle intersections. We will use the form that uses barycentric coordinates for the parametric plane containing the triangle, because it requires no long-term storage other than the vertices of the triangle.

To intersect a ray with a parametric surface, we set up a system of equations where the Cartesian coordinates all match:

$$\begin{aligned} x_e + tx_d &= f(u, v), \\ y_e + ty_d &= g(u, v), \\ z_e + tz_d &= h(u, v). \end{aligned}$$

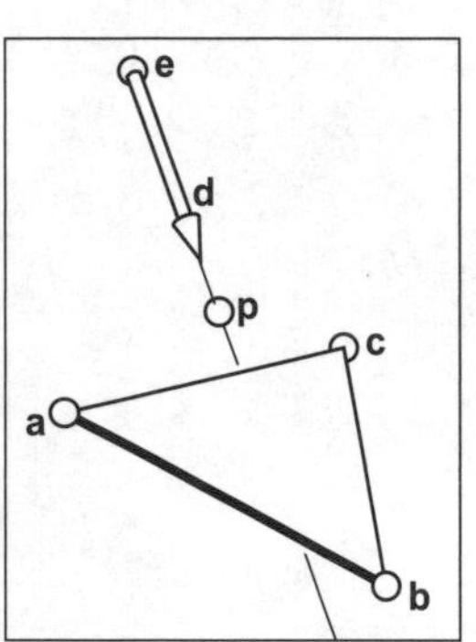

Figure 9.5. The ray hits the plane containing the triangle at point **p**.

Here, we have three equations and three unknowns (t, u, and v), so we can solve numerically for the unknowns. If we are lucky, we can solve for them analytically.

In the case where the parametric surface is a parametric plane, the parametric equation can be written in vector form as discussed in Section 2.11.2. If the vertices of the triangle are $\mathbf{a}$, $\mathbf{b}$ and $\mathbf{c}$, then the intersection will occur when:

$$\mathbf{e} + t\mathbf{d} = \mathbf{a} + \beta(\mathbf{b} - \mathbf{a}) + \gamma(\mathbf{c} - \mathbf{a}). \tag{9.3}$$

The hitpoint $\mathbf{p}$ will be at $\mathbf{e} + t\mathbf{d}$ as shown in Figure 9.5. Again, from Section 2.11.2, we know the hitpoint is in the triangle if and only if $\beta > 0$, $\gamma > 0$, and $\beta + \gamma < 1$. Otherwise, it hits the plane outside the triangle. If there are no solutions, either the triangle is degenerate, or the ray is parallel to the plane containing the triangle.

To solve for t, β, and γ in Equation 9.3, we expand it from its vector form into the three equations for the three coordinates:

$$\begin{aligned} x_e + tx_d &= x_a + \beta(x_b - x_a) + \gamma(x_c - x_a), \\ y_e + ty_d &= y_a + \beta(y_b - y_a) + \gamma(y_c - y_a), \\ z_e + tz_d &= z_a + \beta(z_b - z_a) + \gamma(z_c - z_a). \end{aligned}$$

This can be rewritten as a standard linear equation:

$$\begin{bmatrix} x_a - x_b & x_a - x_c & x_d \\ y_a - y_b & y_a - y_c & y_d \\ z_a - z_b & z_a - z_c & z_d \end{bmatrix} \begin{bmatrix} \beta \\ \gamma \\ t \end{bmatrix} = \begin{bmatrix} x_a - x_e \\ y_a - y_e \\ z_a - z_e \end{bmatrix}.$$

The fastest classic method to solve this 3×3 linear system is *Cramer's Rule*. This gives us the solutions:

$$\beta = \frac{\begin{vmatrix} x_a - x_e & x_a - x_c & x_d \\ y_a - y_e & y_a - y_c & y_d \\ z_a - z_e & z_a - z_c & z_d \end{vmatrix}}{|\mathbf{A}|},$$

$$\gamma = \frac{\begin{vmatrix} x_a - x_b & x_a - x_e & x_d \\ y_a - y_b & y_a - y_e & y_d \\ z_a - z_b & z_a - z_e & z_d \end{vmatrix}}{|\mathbf{A}|},$$

$$t = \frac{\begin{vmatrix} x_a - x_b & x_a - c_x & x_a - x_e \\ y_a - y_b & y_a - c_y & y_a - y_e \\ z_a - z_b & z_a - c_z & z_a - z_e \end{vmatrix}}{|\mathbf{A}|},$$

where the matrix $\mathbf{A}$ is

$$\mathbf{A} = \begin{bmatrix} x_a - b_x & x_a - c_x & d_x \\ a_y - b_y & a_y - c_y & d_y \\ a_z - b_z & a_z - c_z & d_z \end{bmatrix}$$

and $|\mathbf{A}|$ denotes the determinant of $\mathbf{A}$. The 3×3 determinants have common subterms that can be exploited. Looking at the linear systems with dummy variables

$$\begin{bmatrix} a & d & g \\ b & e & h \\ c & f & i \end{bmatrix} \begin{bmatrix} \beta \\ \gamma \\ t \end{bmatrix} = \begin{bmatrix} j \\ k \\ l \end{bmatrix}$$

Cramer's rule gives us

$$\beta = \frac{j(ei - hf) + k(gf - di) + l(dh - eg)}{M},$$

$$\gamma = \frac{i(ak - jb) + h(jc - al) + g(bl - kc)}{M},$$

$$t = -\frac{f(ak - jb) + e(jc - al) + d(bl - kc)}{M},$$

where

$$M = a(ei - hf) + b(gf - di) + c(dh - eg).$$

We can reduce the number of operations by reusing numbers such as "*ei-minus-hf*."

The algorithm for the ray-triangle intersection for which we need the linear solution can have some conditions for early termination. Thus, the function should look something like:

boolean raytri (*ray* $\mathbf{r}$, *vector3* $\mathbf{a}$, *vector3* $\mathbf{b}$, *vector3* $\mathbf{c}$, *interval* $[t_0, t_1]$)
compute t
if $(t < t_0)$ *or* $(t > t_1)$ ***then***
  return false
compute γ
if $(\gamma < 0)$ *or* $(\gamma > 1)$ ***then***
  return false
compute β
if $(\beta < 0)$ *or* $(\beta > 1 - \gamma)$ ***then***
  return false
return true

9.3.3 Ray-Polygon Intersection

Given a polygon with m vertices $\mathbf{p}_1$ through $\mathbf{p}_m$ and surface normal $\mathbf{n}$, we first compute the intersection points between the ray $\mathbf{e} + t\mathbf{d}$ and the plane containing the polygon with implicit equation

$$(\mathbf{p} - \mathbf{p}_1) \cdot \mathbf{n} = 0.$$

We do this by setting $\mathbf{p} = \mathbf{e} + t\mathbf{d}$ and solving for t to get:

$$t = \frac{(\mathbf{p}_1 - \mathbf{e}) \cdot \mathbf{n}}{\mathbf{d} \cdot \mathbf{n}}.$$

This allows us to compute $\mathbf{p}$. If $\mathbf{p}$ is inside the polygon, then the ray hits it, and otherwise it does not.

We can answer the question of whether $\mathbf{p}$ is inside the polygon by projecting the point and polygon vertices to the xy plane and answering it there. The easiest way to do this is to send any 2D ray out from $\mathbf{p}$ and to count the number of intersections between that ray and the boundary of the polygon. If the number of intersections is odd, then the point is inside the polygon, and otherwise it is not. This is true, because a ray that goes in must go out, thus creating a pair of intersections. Only a ray that starts inside will not create such a pair. To make computation simple, the 2D ray may as well propagate along the x axis:

$$\begin{bmatrix} x \\ y \end{bmatrix} = \begin{bmatrix} x_p \\ y_p \end{bmatrix} + s \begin{bmatrix} 1 \\ 0 \end{bmatrix}$$

It is straightforward to compute the intersection of that ray with the edges such as (x_1, y_1, x_2, y_2) for $s \in (0, \infty)$.

A problem arises, however, for polygons whose projection into the xy plane is a line. To get around this, we can choose among the xy, yz or zx planes for whichever is best. If we implement our points to allow an indexing operation, e.g., $\mathbf{p}(0) = x_p$ then this can be accomplished as follows:

if *(abs(z_n) > abs(x_n)) and (abs(z_n) > abs(x_n))* ***then***
  index0 = 0
  index1 = 1
else if *(abs(y_n) > abs (x_n))* ***then***
  index0 = 0
  index1 = 2
else
  index0 = 1
  index1 = 2

Now, all computations can use $\mathbf{p}$(index0) rather than x_p, and so on.

9.4 A Ray Tracing Program

We now know how to generate a viewing ray for a given pixel, and how to find the intersection with one object. This can be easily extended to a program that produces images similar to the z-buffer of BSP-tree codes of earlier chapters:

for *each pixel* ***do***
  compute viewing ray
  if *(ray hits an object with $t \in [0, \infty)$)* ***then***
    Compute $\mathbf{n}$
    Evaluate lighting equation and set pixel to that color
  else
    set pixel color to background color

Here the statement "if ray hits an object..." can be implemented as a function that tests for hits in the interval $t \in [t_0, t_1]$:

hit = false
for *each object* $\mathbf{o}$ ***do***
  if *(object is hit at ray parameter t and $t \in [t_0, t_1]$)* ***then***
    hit = true
    hitobject = $\mathbf{o}$
    $t_1 = t$
return hit

In an actual implementation, you will need to somehow return either a reference to the object that is hit, or at least its normal vector and material properties. This is often done by passing a record/structure with such information. In an object-oriented implementation, it is a good idea to have a class called something like *surface* with derived classes triangle, sphere, surface-list, etc. Anything that a ray can interesect would be under that class. The ray tracing program would then have one reference to a "surface" for the whole model, and new types of objects and efficiency structures can be added transparently.

9.4.1 Object-Oriented Design for a Ray Tracing Program

As mentioned earlier, the key class hierarchy in a ray tracer are the geometric objects that make up the model. These should be subclasses of some geometric object class, and they should support a *hit* function. To avoid confusion from use of the word "object," *surface* is the class name often used. With such a class, you can create a ray tracer that has a general interface that assumes little about modeling primitives, and debug it using only spheres. An important point is that anything that can be "hit" by a ray should be part of this class hierarchy, e.g., even a collection of surfaces should be considered a subclass of the surface class. This includes efficiency structures, such as bounding volume hierarchies; they can be hit by a ray, so they are in the class.

For example, the "abstract" or "base" class would specify the hit function, as well as a bounding box function which will prove useful later:

class surface
virtual bool hit(*ray* $\mathbf{e} + t\mathbf{d}$, *real* t_0, *real* t_1, *hit-record rec*)
virtual box bounding-box()

Here (t_0, t_1) is the interval on the ray where hits will be returned, and *rec* is a record that is passed by reference; it contains data such as the t at intersection when *hit* returns true. The type *box* is a 3D "bounding box", that is two points that define an axis-aligned box that encloses the surface. For example, for a sphere, the function would be implemented by:

box sphere::bounding-box()
vector3 min = *center* - *vector3*(*radius,radius,radius*)
vector3 max = *center* + *vector3*(*radius,radius,radius*)
return box(*min, max*)

Another class that is useful is *material.* This allows you to abstract the material behavior and later add materials transparently. A simple way to link objects and materials is to add a pointer to a material in the surface class, although more programmable behavior might be desirable. A big question is what to do with textures; are they part of the material class or do they live outside of the material class? This will be discussed more in Chapter 10.

9.5 Shadows

Once you have a basic ray tracing program, shadows can be added very easily. Recall from Chapter 8 that light comes from some direction $\mathbf{l}$. If we imagine ourselves at a point $\mathbf{p}$ on a surface being shaded, the point is in shadow if we "look" in direction $\mathbf{l}$ and see an object. If there are no objects, then the light is not blocked.

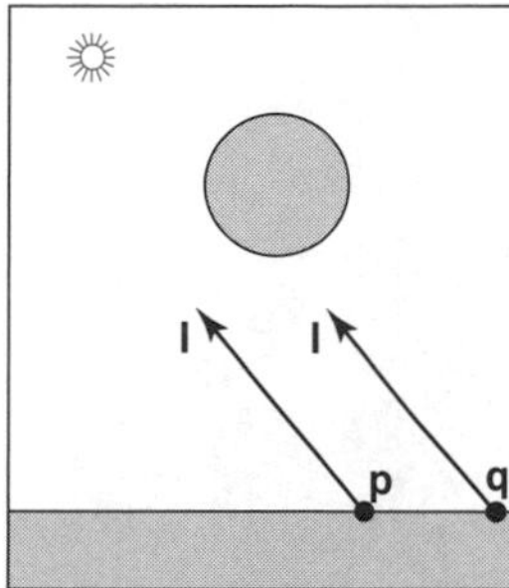

Figure 9.6. The point $\mathbf{p}$ is not in shadow while the point $\mathbf{q}$ is in shadow.

This is shown in Figure 9.6, where the ray $\mathbf{p}+t\mathbf{l}$ does not hit any objects and is thus not in shadow. The point $\mathbf{q}$ is in shadow because the ray $\mathbf{q}+t\mathbf{l}$ does hit an object. The vector $\mathbf{l}$ is the same for both points because the light is "far" away. This assumption will later be relaxed. The rays that determine in or out of shadow are called *shadow rays* to distinguish them from viewing rays.

To get the algorithm for shading, we add an if statement to determine whether the point is in shadow. In a naive implementation, the shadow ray will check for $t \in [0, \infty)$, but because of numerical imprecision, this can result in an intersection with the surface on which $\mathbf{p}$ lies. Instead, the usual adjustment to avoid that problem is to test for $t \in [\epsilon, \infty)$ where ϵ is some small positive constant (Figure 9.7).

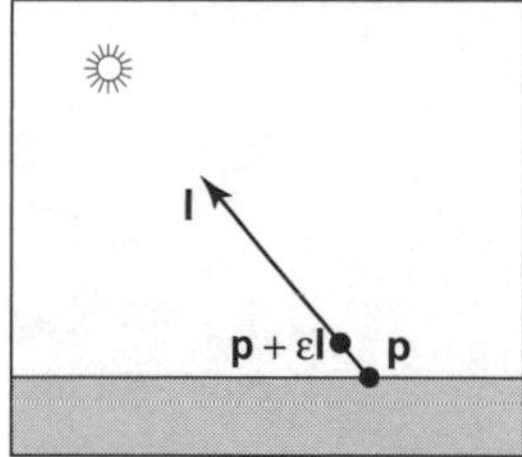

Figure 9.7. By testing in the interval starting at ϵ, we avoid numerical imprecision causing the ray to hit the surface $\mathbf{p}$ is on.

If we implement shadow rays for Phong lighting with Equation 8.9 then we have:

function raycolor(*ray* $\mathbf{e} + t\mathbf{d}$, *real* t_0, *real* t_1)
hit-record rec, srec
if (*scene*→*hit*($\mathbf{e} + t\mathbf{d}$, t_0, t_1, *rec*)) ***then***
  $\mathbf{p} = \mathbf{e} + rec.t\mathbf{d}$
  color $c = rec.c_r \; rec.c_l$
  if (*not scene*→*hit*($\mathbf{p} + s\mathbf{l}$, ϵ, ∞, *srec*)) ***then***
    vector3 $\mathbf{h} = normalized(normalized(\mathbf{l}) + normalized(-\mathbf{d}))$
    $c = c + rec.c_r \, c_l max(0, rec.\mathbf{n} \cdot \mathbf{l}) + c_l rec.c_p (\mathbf{h} \cdot rec.\mathbf{n})^{rec.p}$
  return c
else
  return background-color

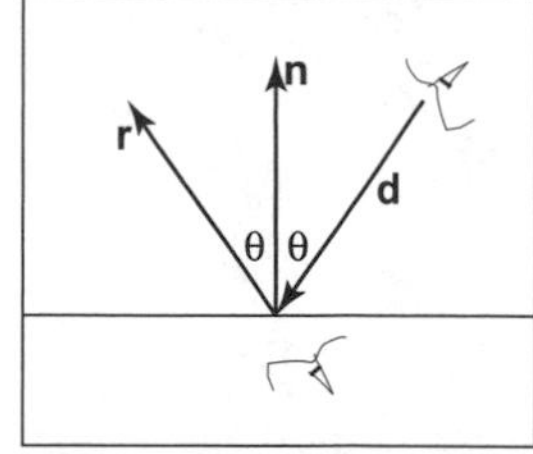

Figure 9.8. When looking into a perfect mirror, the viewer looking in direction $\mathbf{d}$ will see whatever the viewer "below" the surface would see in direction $\mathbf{r}$.

Note that the ambient color is added in either case. If there are multiple light sources, we can send a shadow ray and evaluate the diffuse/phong terms for each light. The code above assumes that $\mathbf{d}$ and $\mathbf{l}$ are not necessarily unit vectors. This is crucial for $\mathbf{d}$, in particular, if we wish to cleanly add *instancing* later.

9.6 Specular Reflection

It is straightforward to add *specular* reflection to a ray tracing program. The key observation is shown in Figure 9.8 where a viewer looking from direction $\mathbf{e}$ sees what is in direction $\mathbf{r}$ as seen from the surface. The vector

$\mathbf{r}$ is found using a variant of the Phong lighting reflection Equation 8.6. There are sign changes because the vector $\mathbf{d}$ points toward the surface in this case, so:

$$\mathbf{r} = \mathbf{d} - 2(\mathbf{d} \cdot \mathbf{n})\mathbf{n}, \tag{9.4}$$

In the real world, some energy is lost when the light reflects from the surface, and this loss can be different for different colors. For example, gold reflects yellow more efficiently than blue, so it shifts the colors of the objects it reflects. This can be implemented by adding a recursive call in raycolor:

$$\textit{color } c = c + c_s \textit{raycolor}(\mathbf{p} + s\mathbf{r},\ \epsilon,\ \infty)$$

where c_s is the specular RGB color. We need to make sure we test for $s \in [\epsilon, \infty)$ for the same reason as we did with shadow rays; we don't want the reflection ray to hit the object that generates it.

The problem with the recursive call above is that it may never terminate. For example, if a ray starts inside a room, it will bounce forever. This can be fixed by adding a maximum recursion depth. The code will be more efficient if a reflection ray is generated only if c_s is not zero (black).

9.7 Refraction

Another type of specular object is a *dielectric*—a transparent material that refracts light. Diamonds, glass, water, and air are dielectrics. Dielectrics also filter light; some glass filters out more red and blue light than green light, so the glass takes on a green tint. When a ray travels from a medium with refractive index n into one with a refractive index n_t, some of the light is transmitted, and it bends. This is shown for $n_t > n$ in Figure 9.9. Snell's law tells us that:

$$n \sin\theta = n_t \sin\phi.$$

Computing the sine of an angle between two vectors is usually not as convenient as computing the cosine which is a simple dot product for the unit vectors such as we have here. Using the trigonometric identity $\sin^2\theta + \cos^2\theta = 1$, we can derive a refraction relationship for cosines:

$$\cos^2\phi = 1 - \frac{n^2\left(1 - \cos^2\theta\right)}{n_t^2}.$$

Note that if n and n_t are reversed, then so are θ and ϕ as shown on the right of Figure 9.9.

To convert $\sin\phi$ and $\cos\phi$ into a 3D vector, we can set up a 2D orthonormal basis in the plane of $\mathbf{n}$ and $\mathbf{d}$.

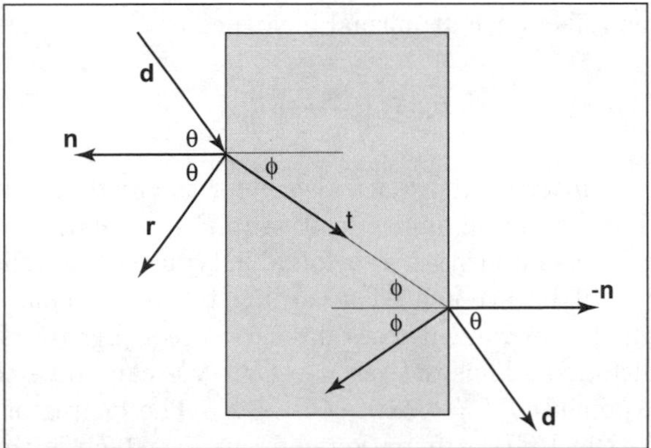

Figure 9.9. Snells' Law describes how the angle ϕ depends on the angle θ and the refractive indices of the object and the surrounding medium.

From Figure 9.10, we can see that $\mathbf{n}$ and $\mathbf{b}$ form an orthonormal basis for the plane of refraction. By definition, we can describe $\mathbf{t}$ in terms of this basis:

$$\mathbf{t} = \sin\phi\mathbf{b} - \cos\phi\mathbf{n}.$$

Since we can describe $\mathbf{d}$ in the same basis, and $\mathbf{d}$ is known, we can solve for $\mathbf{b}$:

$$\mathbf{d} = \sin\theta\mathbf{b} - \cos\theta\mathbf{n},$$
$$\mathbf{b} = \frac{\mathbf{d} + \mathbf{n}\cos\theta}{\sin\theta}.$$

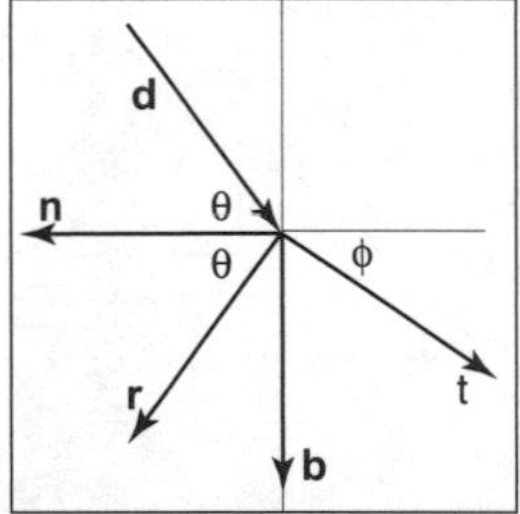

Figure 9.10. The vectors **n** and **b** form a 2D orthonormal basis that is parallel to the transmission vector **t**.

This means that we can solve for $\mathbf{t}$ with known variables:

$$\begin{aligned}\mathbf{t} &= \frac{n\left(\mathbf{d} + \mathbf{n}\cos\theta\right)}{n_t} - \mathbf{n}\cos\theta \\ &= \frac{n\left(\mathbf{d} - \mathbf{n}(\mathbf{d}\cdot\mathbf{n})\right)}{n_t} - \mathbf{n}\sqrt{1 - \frac{n^2\left(1 - (\mathbf{d}\cdot\mathbf{n})^2\right)}{n_t^2}}.\end{aligned}$$

Note that this equation works regardless of which of n and n_t is larger. An immediate question is, "What should you do if the number under the square root is negative?" In this case, there is no refracted ray and all of the energy is reflected. This is known as *total internal reflection* and it is responsible for much of the rich appearance of glass objects.

The reflectivity of a dielectric varies with the incident angle according to the *Fresnel Equations.* An nice way to implement something close to the Fresnel Equations is to use the *Schlick approximation*:

$$R(\theta) = R_0 + (1 - R_0)\left(1 - \cos\theta\right)^5,$$

where R_0 is the reflectance at normal incidence:

$$R_0 = \left(\frac{n_t - 1}{n_t + 1}\right)^2.$$

Note that the $\cos\theta$ terms above are always for the angle in air (the larger of the internal and external angles relative to the normal).

For homogeneous impurities, as is found in typical glass, a light-carrying ray's intensity will be attenuated according to *Beer's Law.* As the ray travels through the medium it loses intensity according to $dI = -CI\,dx$, where dx is distance. Thus, $dI/dx = -CI$. We can solve this equation and get the exponential $I = k\exp(-Cx) + k'$. The degree of attenuation is described by the RGB attenuation constant a, which is the amount of attenuation after one unit of distance. Putting in boundary conditions, we know that $I(0) = I_0$, and $I(1) = aI(0)$. The former implies $I(x) = I_0 \exp(-Cx)$. The latter implies $I_0 a = I_0 \exp(-C)$, so $-C = \ln(a)$. Thus, the final formula is:

$$I(s) = I(0)e^{-\ln(a)s},$$

where $I(s)$ is the intensity of the beam at distance s from the interface. In practice, we reverse-engineer a by eye, because such data is rarely easy to find. The effect of Beer's Law can be seen in Color Plate 9.11, where the glass takes on a green tint.

To add transparent materials to our code, we need a way to determine when a ray is going "into" an object. The simplest way to do this is to assume that all objects are embedded in air with refractive index very close to 1.0, and that surface normals point "out" (toward the air). The code segment for rays and dielectrics with these assumptions is:

```
if (p is on a dielectric) then
  r = reflect(d, n )
  if (d · n < 0) then
    refract(d, n,n, t )
    c = −d · n
    k_r = k_g = k_b = 1
  else
    k_r = exp(−a_r t)
    k_g = exp(−a_g t)
    k_b = exp(−a_b t)
    if refract(d, -n,1/n, t ) then
      c = t · n
    else
      return k∗color(p + tr)
  R_0 = (n − 1)^2/(n + 1)^2
  R = R_0 + (1 − R_0)(1 − c)^5
  return k(R color(p + tr) + (1 − R) color(p + tt))
```

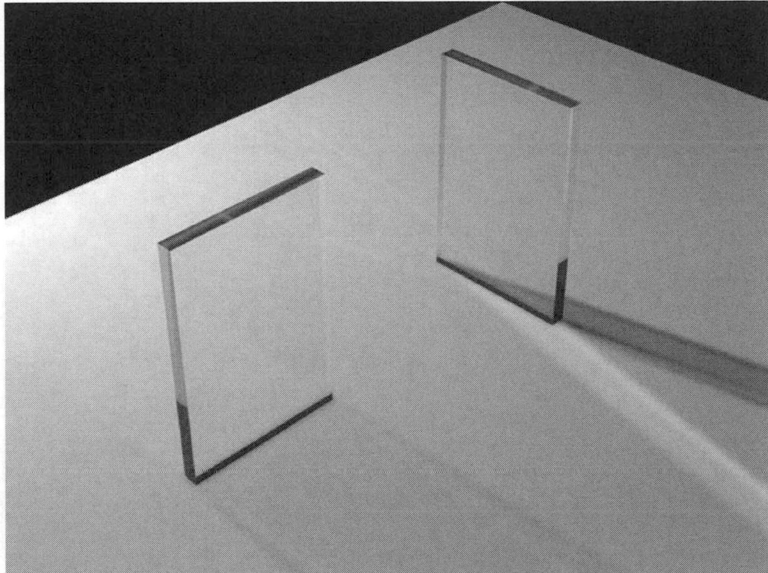

Figure 9.11. The color of the glass is affected by total internal reflection and Beer's Law. The amount of light transmitted and reflected is determined by the Fresnel Equations. The complex lighting on the ground plane was computed using particle tracing as described in Chapter 19. (See also Plate XI.)

The code above assumes that the natural log has been folded into the constants (a_r, a_g, a_b). The *refract* function returns false if there is total internal reflection, and otherwise it fills in the last argument of the argument list.

9.8 Instancing

An elegant property of ray tracing is that it allows very natural *instancing*. The basic idea of instancing is to distort all points on an object by a transformation matrix before the object is displayed. For example, if we transform the unit circle (in 2D) by a scale factor $(2, 1)$ in x and y respectively, then rotate it by 45°, and move one unit in the x direction, the result is an ellipse with an eccentricity of 2 and a long axis along the $x = -y$ direction centered at $(0, 1)$ (Figure 9.12). The key thing that makes that entity an "instance" is that we store the circle and the composite transform matrix. Thus, the explicit construction of the ellipse is left as a future procedure operation at render time.

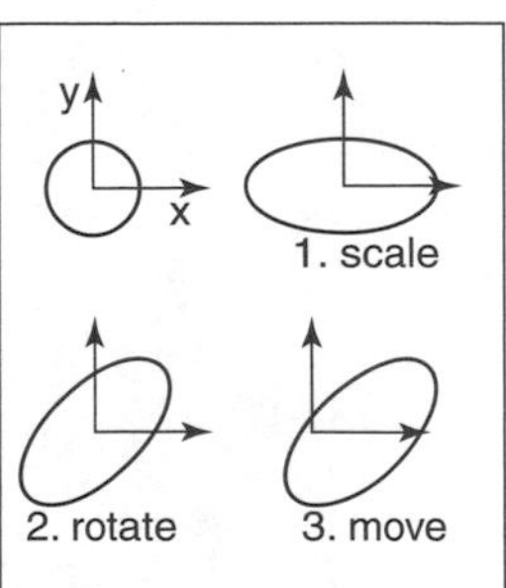

Figure 9.12. An instance of a circle with a series of three transforms is an ellipse.

The advantage of instancing in ray tracing is that we can choose the space in which to do intersection. If the base object is composed of a set of points, one of which is $\mathbf{p}$, then the transformed object is composed of

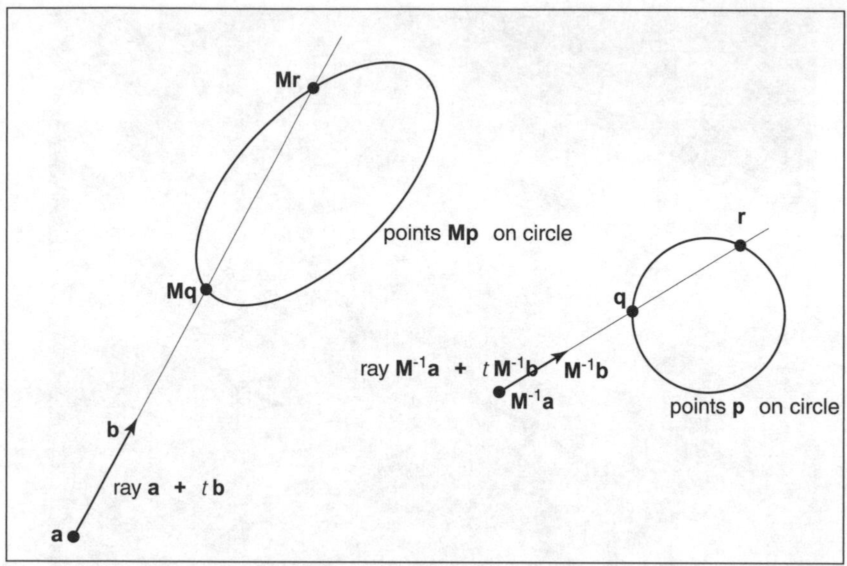

Figure 9.13. The ray intersection problem in the two spaces are just simple transforms of each other. The object is specified as a sphere plus matrix **M**. The ray is specified in the transformed (world) space by location **a** and direction **b**.

that set of points transformed by matrix $\mathbf{M}$, where the example point is transformed to $\mathbf{Mp}$. If we have a ray $\mathbf{a}+t\mathbf{b}$ which we want to intersect with the transformed object, we can instead intersect an *inverse-transformed ray* with the untransformed object (Figure 9.13). There are two potential advantages to computing in the untransformed space (i.e., the right-hand side of Figure 9.13):

1. the untransformed object may have a simpler intersection routine, e.g., a sphere versus an ellipsoid;

2. many transformed objects can share the same untransformed object thus reducing storage, e.g., a traffic jam of cars, where individual cars are just transforms of a few base (untransformed) models.

As discussed in Section 5.2.2, surface normal vectors transform differently. With this in mind and using the concepts illustrated in Figure 9.13, we can determine the intersection of a ray and an object transformed by matrix $\mathbf{M}$. If we create an instance class of type *surface* we need to create a *hit* function:

instance::hit(*ray* $\mathbf{a} + t\mathbf{b}$, *real* t_0, *real* t_1, *hit-record rec*)
ray $\mathbf{r}' = \mathbf{M}^{-1}\mathbf{a} + t\mathbf{M}^{-1}\mathbf{b}$
if (*base-object*→*hit*($\mathbf{r}'$, t_0, t_1, *rec*)) ***then***
  rec.$\mathbf{n} = (\mathbf{M}^{-1})^T$ *rec*.$\mathbf{n}$

return true
else
return false

An elegant thing about this function is that the parameter rec.t does not need to be changed, because it is the same in either space. Also note that we need not compute or store the matrix M.

This brings up a very important point: the ray direction $\mathbf{b}$ must *not* be restricted to a unit-length vector, or none of the infrastructure above works. For this reason, it is useful not to restrict ray directions to unit vectors.

For the purpose of solid texturing, you may want to record the local coordinates of the hitpoint and return this in the hit-record. This is just ray $\mathbf{r}'$ advanced by parameter rec.t.

To implement the bounding-box function of class instance, we can just take the eight corners of the bounding-box of the base-object and transform all of them by $\mathbf{M}$, and then take the bounding box of those eight points. That will not necessarily yield the tightest bounding box, but it is general and straightforward to implement.

9.9 Sub-Linear Ray-Object Intersection

In the earlier ray-object intersection pseudocode, all objects are looped over checking for intersections. For N objects this is an $O(N)$ linear search and is thus slow for large values of N. Like most search problems, the ray-object intersection can be computed in sub-linear time using "divide and conquer" techniques, provided we can create an ordered data structure as a preprocess. There are a plethora of techniques to do this.

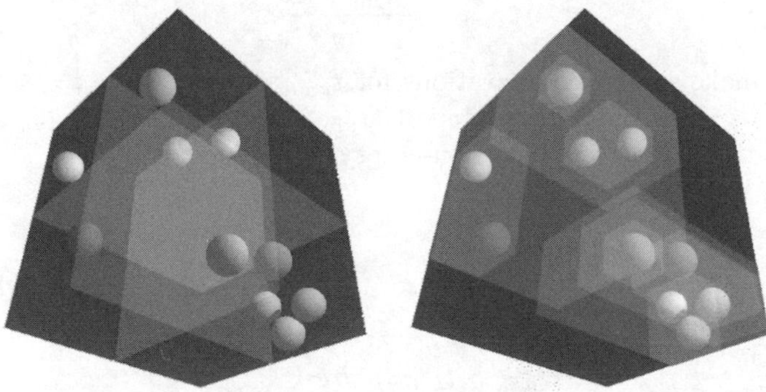

Figure 9.14. Left: a uniform partitioning of space. Right: adaptive bounding box hierarchy. Image courtesy David DeMarle.

This section discusses three of these techniques in detail: bounding volume hierarchies, uniform spatial subdivision, and binary-space partitioning. An example of the first two strategies is shown in Figure 9.14. References for other popular strategies are given in the notes at the end of the chapter.

9.9.1 Bounding Boxes

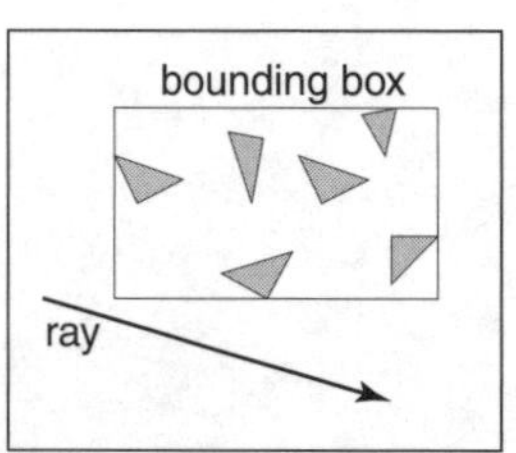

Figure 9.15. The ray is only tested for intersection with the surfaces if it hits the bounding box.

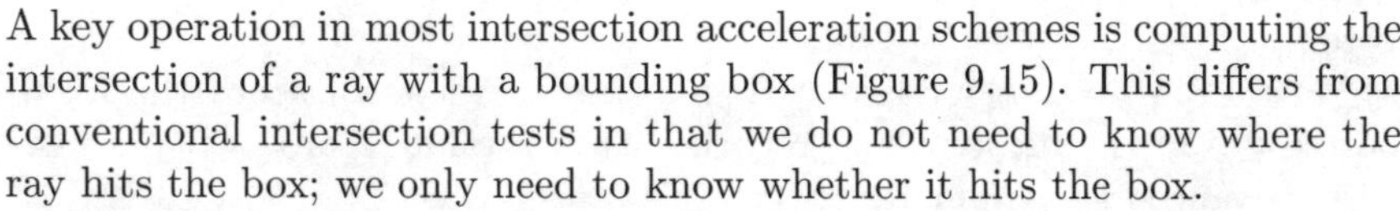

A key operation in most intersection acceleration schemes is computing the intersection of a ray with a bounding box (Figure 9.15). This differs from conventional intersection tests in that we do not need to know where the ray hits the box; we only need to know whether it hits the box.

To build an algorithm for ray-box intersection, we begin by considering a 2D ray whose direction vector has positive x and y components. We can generalize this to arbitrary 3D rays later. The 2D bounding box is defined by two horizontal and two vertical lines:

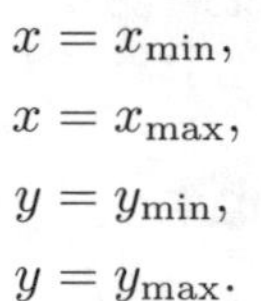

$$x = x_{\text{min}},$$
$$x = x_{\text{max}},$$
$$y = y_{\text{min}},$$
$$y = y_{\text{max}}.$$

The points bounded by these lines can be described in interval notation:

$$(x, y) \in [x_{\text{min}}, x_{\text{max}}] \times [y_{\text{min}}, y_{\text{max}}].$$

As shown in Figure 9.16, the intersection test can be phrased in terms of these intervals. First, we compute the ray parameter where the ray hits the line $x = x_{\text{min}}$:

$$t_{\text{xmin}} = \frac{x_{\text{min}} - x_e}{x_d}.$$

We then make similar computations for t_{xmax}, t_{ymin}, and t_{ymax}. The ray hits the box if and only if the intervals $[t_{\text{xmin}}, t_{\text{xmax}}]$ and $[t_{\text{ymin}}, t_{\text{ymax}}]$ overlap, i.e., their intersection is non-empty. In pseudocode this algorithm is:

$t_{xmin} = (x_{min} - x_e)/x_d$
$t_{xmax} = (x_{max} - x_e)/x_d$
$t_{ymin} = (y_{min} - y_e)/x_d$
$t_{ymax} = (y_{max} - y_e)/x_d$
if $(t_{xmin} > t_{ymax})$ *or* $(t_{ymin} > t_{xmax})$ ***then***
  return false
else
  return true

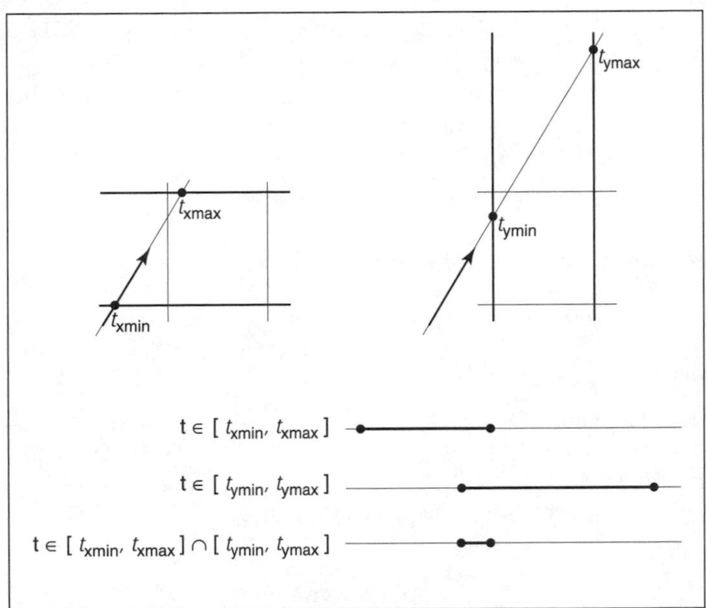

Figure 9.16. The ray will be inside the interval $x \in [x_{\min}, x_{\max}]$ for some interval in its parameter space $t \in [t_{\text{xmin}}, t_{\text{xmax}}]$. A similar interval exists for the y interval. The ray intersects the box if it is in both the x interval and y interval at the same time, i.e., the intersection of the two one-dimensional intervals is not empty.

The if statement may seem non-obvious. To see the logic of it, note that there is no overlap if the first interval is either entirely to the right or entirely to the left of the second interval.

The first thing we must address is the case when x_d or y_d is negative. If x_d is negative, then the ray will hit $x_{\max}$ before it hits $x_{\min}$. Thus the code for computing t_{xmin} and t_{xmax} expands to:

```
if (x_d ≥ 0) then
    t_xmin = (x_min − x_e)/x_d
    t_xmax = (x_max − x_e)/x_d
else
    t_xmin = (x_max − x_e)/x_d
    t_xmax = (x_min − x_e)/x_d
```

A similar code expansion must be made for the y cases. A major concern is that horizontal and vertical rays have a zero value for y_d and x_d, respectively. This will cause divide by zero which may be a problem. However, before addressing this directly, we check whether IEEE floating point computation handles these cases gracefully for us. Recall from Section 1.6 the rules for divide by zero: for any positive real number a:

$$+a/0 = +\infty;$$
$$-a/0 = -\infty.$$

Consider the case of a vertical ray where $x_d = 0$ and $y_d > 0$. We can then calculate

$$t_{\text{xmin}} = \frac{x_{\text{min}} - x_e}{0};$$

$$t_{\text{xmax}} = \frac{x_{\text{max}} - x_e}{0}.$$

There are three possibilities of interest:

1. $x_e \leq t_{\text{xmin}}$ (no hit)
2. $t_{\text{xmin}} < x_e < t_{\text{xmax}}$ (hit)
3. $t_{\text{xmax}} \leq x_e$ (no hit)

For the first case we have:

$$t_{\text{xmin}} = \frac{\text{positive number}}{0};$$

$$t_{\text{xmax}} = \frac{\text{positive number}}{0}.$$

This yields the interval $(t_{\text{xmin}}, t_{\text{xmin}}) = (\infty, \infty)$. That interval will not overlap with any interval, so there will be no hit, as desired. For the second case, we have:

$$t_{\text{xmin}} = \frac{\text{negative number}}{0};$$

$$t_{\text{xmax}} = \frac{\text{positive number}}{0}.$$

This yields the interval $(t_{\text{xmin}}, t_{\text{xmin}}) = (-\infty, \infty)$ which will overlap with all intervals and thus will yield a hit as desired. The third case results in the interval $(-\infty, -\infty)$ which yields no hit, as desired. Because these cases work as desired, we need no special checks for them. As is often the case, IEEE floating point conventions are our ally.

In the full 3D case, the procedure for determining whether ray $\mathbf{e} + t\mathbf{d}$ hits a 3D box within the interval (t_0, t_1) can be determined by:

bool box::hitbox(ray $(\mathbf{e} + t\mathbf{d})$, *real* t_0, *real* t_1)
if $(x_d \geq 0)$ ***then***
  $t_{min} = (x_{min} - x_e)/x_d$
  $t_{max} = (x_{max} - x_e)/x_d$
else
  $t_{min} = (x_{max} - x_e)/x_d$
  $t_{max} = (x_{min} - x_e)/x_d$

if $(y_d \geq 0)$ ***then***
  $t_{ymin} = (y_{min} - y_e)/y_d$
  $t_{ymax} = (y_{max} - x_e)/y_d$
else
  $t_{ymin} = (y_{max} - y_e)/y_d$
  $t_{ymax} = (y_{min} - y_e)/y_d$
if $(t_{min} > t_{ymax})$ *or* $(t_{ymin} > t_{max})$ ***then***
  return false
if $(t_{ymin} > t_{min})$ ***then***
  $t_{min} = t_{ymin}$
if $(t_{ymax} < t_{max})$ ***then***
  $t_{max} = t_{ymax}$
if $(z_d \geq 0)$ ***then***
  $t_{zmin} = (z_{min} - z_e)/z_d$
  $t_{zmax} = (z_{max} - z_e)/z_d$
else
  $t_{zmin} = (z_{max} - z_e)/z_d$
  $t_{zmax} = (z_{min} - z_e)/z_d$
if $(t_{min} > t_{zmax})$ *or* $(t_{zmin} > t_{max})$ ***then***
  return false
if $(t_{zmin} > t_{min})$ ***then***
  $t_{min} = t_{zmin}$
if $(t_{zmax} < t_{max})$ ***then***
  $t_{max} = t_{zmax}$
return $t_{min} < t_1$ *and* $t_{max} > t_0$

This code often ends up being the bottleneck, so it is important to write it very tightly as above. Note that *hitbox* is a member of *box*. The *box* class is *not* a subclass of *surface*. Its only job is to bound objects and return intersections. It does not have material properties so it is never rendered directly. However, you may find it useful to also implement a *box-surface* as a distinct class that is renderable and implements *surface::hit*.

9.9.2 Hierarchical Bounding Boxes

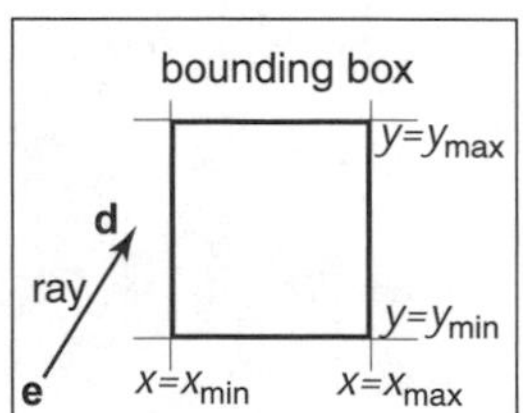

Figure 9.17. A 2D ray **e** + *t***d** is tested against a 2D bounding box.

The basic idea of hierarchical bounding boxes can be seen by the common tactic of placing an axis-aligned 3D bounding box around all the objects as shown in Figure 9.17. Rays that hit the bounding box will actually be more expensive to compute than in a brute force search, because testing for intersection with the box is not free. However, rays that miss the box are cheaper than the brute force search. Such bounding boxes can be made hierarchical by partitioning the set of objects in a box and placing a box around each partition as shown in Figure 9.18. The data structure for the hierarchy shown in Figure 9.19 might be a tree with the large bounding box at the root and the two smaller bounding boxes as left and right subtrees. These would in turn each point to a list of three triangles. The intersection of a ray with this particular hard-coded tree would be:

```
if (ray hits root box) then
   if (ray hits left subtree box) then
      check three triangles for intersection
   if (ray intersects right subtree box) then
      check other three triangles for intersection
   if (an intersections returned from each subtree) then
      return the closest of the two hits
   else if (a intersection is returned from exactly one subtree) then
      return that intersection
   else
      return false
else
   return false
```

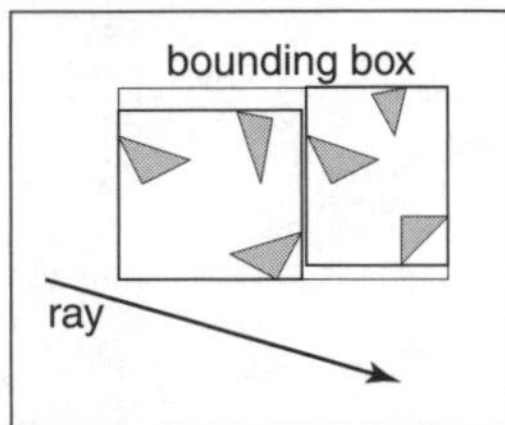

Figure 9.18. The bounding boxes can be nested by creating boxes around subsets of the model.

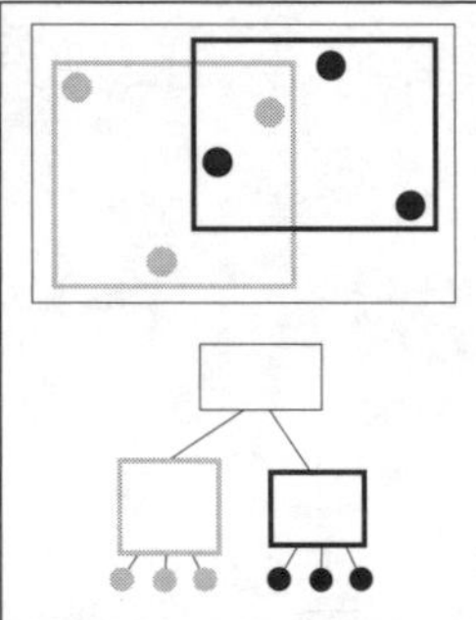

Figure 9.19. The grey box is a tree node that points to the three grey spheres, and the thick black box points to the three black spheres. Note that not all spheres enclosed by the box are guaranteed to be pointed to by the corresponding tree node.

Some observations related to this algorithm are that there is no geometric ordering between the two subtrees, and there is no reason a ray might not hit both subtrees. Indeed, there is no reason that the two subtrees might not overlap.

A key point of such data hierarchies is that a box is guaranteed to bound all objects that are below it in the hierarchy, but they are *not* guaranteed to contain all objects that overlap it spatially, as shown in Figure 9.19. This makes this geometric search somewhat more complicated than a traditional binary search on strictly ordered one-dimensional data. The reader may note that several possible optimizations present themselves. We defer optimizations until we have a full hierarchical algorithm.

If we restrict the tree to be binary, and require that each node in the tree have a bounding box, then this traversal code extends naturally. Further, assume that all nodes are either leaves in the tree and contain a primitive, or that they contain one or two subtrees.

The *bvh-node* class should be of type surface, so it should implement *surface::hit.* The data it contains should be simple:

class bvh-node subclass of surface
virtual bool hit(ray $\mathbf{e} + t\mathbf{d}$, *real* t_0, *real* t_1, *hit-record rec)*
virtual box bounding-box()
surface-pointer left
surface-pointer right
box bbox

The traversal code can then be called recursively in an object-oriented style:

bool bvh-node::hit(ray $\mathbf{a} + t\mathbf{b}$, *real* t_0, *real* t_1, *hit-record rec)*

```
if (bbox.hitbox(a + tb, t0, t1)) then
   hit-record lrec, rrec
   left-hit = (left ≠ NULL) and (left → hit(a + tb, t0, t1, lrec))
   right-hit = (right ≠ NULL) and (right → hit(a + tb, t0, t1, rrec))
   if (left-hit and right-hit) then
      if (lrec.t < rrec.t) then
         rec = lrec
      else
         rec = rrec
      return true
   else if (left-hit) then
      rec = lrec
      return true
   else if (right-hit) then
      rec = rrec
      return true
   else
      return false
else
   return false
```

Note that because *left* and *right* point to surfaces rather than bvh-nodes specifically, we can let the virtual functions take care of distinguishing between internal and leaf nodes; the appropriate *hit* function will be called. Note, that if the tree is built properly, we can eliminate the check for *left* being *NULL*. If we want to eliminate the check for *right* being *NULL*, we can replace NULL right pointers with a redundant pointer to left. This will end up checking left twice, but will eliminate the check throughout the tree. Whether that is worth it will depend on the details of tree construction.

There are many ways to build a tree for a bounding volume hierarchy. It is convenient to make the tree binary, roughly balanced, and to have the boxes of sibling subtrees not overlap too much. A heuristic to accomplish this is to sort the surfaces along an axis before dividing them into two sublists. If the axes are defined by an integer with $x = 0$, $y = 1$, and $z = 2$ we have:

```
bvh-node::bvh-node(object-array A, int AXIS)
N = A.length
if (N = 1) then
   left = A[0]
   right = NULL
   bbox = bounding-box(A[0])
else if (N = 2) then
   left-node = A[0]
   right-node = A[1]
```

```
    bbox = combine(bounding-box(A[0]), bounding-box(A[1]))
  else
    sort A by the object center along AXIS
    left= new bvh-node(A[0..N/2-1], (AXIS +1)  mod 3)
    right = new bvh-node(A[N/2..N-1], (AXIS +1)  mod 3)
    bbox = combine(left-node → bbox, right-node → bbox)
```

The quality of the tree can be improved by carefully choosing *AXIS* each time. One way to do this is to choose the axis such that the sum of the volumes of the bounding boxes of the two subtrees is minimized. This change compared to rotating through the axes will make little difference for scenes composed of isotopically distributed small objects, but it may help significantly in less well-behaved scenes. This code can also be made more efficient by doing just a partition rather than a full sort.

Another, and probably better, way to build the tree is to have the subtrees contain about the same amount of space rather than the same number of objects. To do this we partition the list based on space:

```
bvh-node::bvh-node(object-array A, int AXIS)
N = A.length
if (N = 1) then
  left = A[0]
  right = NULL
  bbox = bounding-box(A[0])
else if (N = 2) then
  left = A[0]
  right = A[1]
  bbox = combine(bounding-box(A[0]), bounding-box(A[1]))
else
  find the midpoint m of the bounding box of A along AXIS
  partition A into lists with lengths k and (N-k) surrounding m
  left = new node(A[0..k], (AXIS +1)  mod 3)
  right = new node(A[k+1..N-1], (AXIS +1)  mod 3)
  bbox = combine(left-node → bbox, right-node → bbox)
```

Although this results in an unbalanced tree, it allows for easy traversal of empty space and is cheaper to build because partitioning is cheaper than sorting.

9.9.3 Uniform Spatial Subdivision

Another strategy to reduce intersection tests is to divide space. This is fundamentally different from dividing objects as was done with hierarchical bounding volumes:

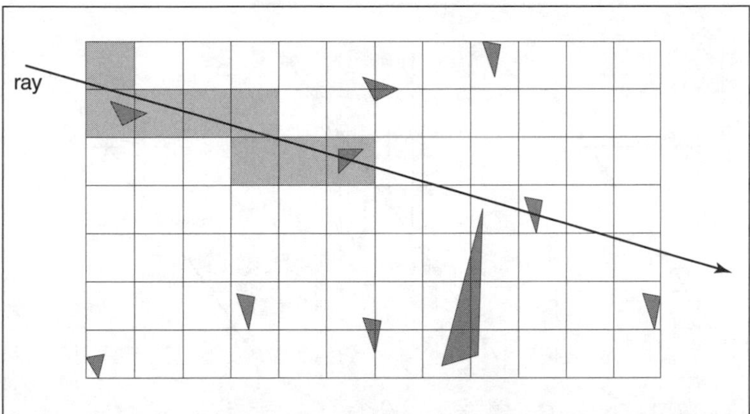

Figure 9.20. In uniform spatial subdivision, the ray is tracked forward through cells until an object in one of those cells is hit. In this example, only objects in the shaded cells are checked.

- In hierarchical bounding volumes, each object belongs to one of two sibling nodes, whereas a point in space may be inside both sibling nodes.
- In spatial subdivision, each point in space belongs to exactly one node, whereas objects may belong to many nodes.

The scene is partitioned into axis-aligned boxes. These boxes are all the same size, although they are not necessarily cubes. The ray traverses these boxes as shown in Figure 9.20. When an object is hit, the traversal ends.

The grid itself should be a subclass of surface, and should be implemented as a 3D array of pointers to surface. For empty cells these pointers are NULL. For cells with one object the pointer points to that object. For cells with more than one object, the pointer can point to a list, another grid, or another data structure such as a bounding volume hierarchy.

This traversal is done in an incremental fashion. The regularity comes from the way that a ray hits each set of parallel planes, as shown in Figure 9.21. To see how this traversal works, first consider the 2D case where the ray direction has positive x and y components and starts outside the grid. Assume the grid is bounded by points $(x_{\min}, y_{\min})$ and $(x_{\max}, y_{\max})$. The grid has n_x by n_y cells.

Our first order of business is to find the index (i, j) of the first cell hit by the ray $\mathbf{e} + t\mathbf{d}$. Then, we need to traverse the cells in an appropriate order. This can be accomplished by:

$$t_{xmin} = (x_{min} - x_e)/x_d$$
$$t_{xmax} = (x_{max} - x_e)/x_d$$

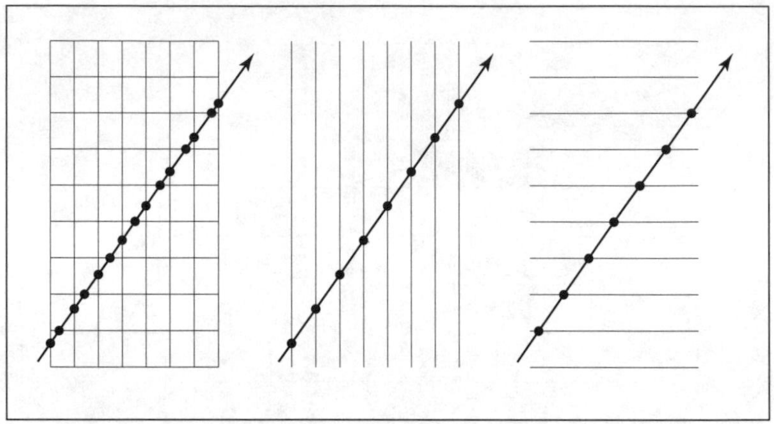

Figure 9.21. Although the pattern of cell hits seems irregular (left), the hits on sets of parallel planes are very even.

$t_{ymin} = (y_{min} - y_e)/y_d$
$t_{ymax} = (y_{max} - y_e)/y_d$
if $(t_{xmin} > t_{ymax})$ *or* $(t_{ymin} > t_{xmax})$ ***then***
  return false
$dt_x = (t_{xmax} - t_{xmin})/n_x$
$dt_y = (t_{ymax} - t_{ymin})/n_y$
if $(t_{xmin} > t_{ymin})$ ***then***
  $i = 0$
  $y = y_e + t_{xmin} y_d$
  $j = \mathit{floor}(n_y(y - y_{min})/(y_{max} - y_{min}))$
  $t_{xnext} = t_{xmin} + dt_x$
  $t_{ynext} = t_{ymin} + (j+1)dt_y$
  $t_{last} = t_{xmin}$
else
  $j = 0$
  $x = x_e + t_{ymin} x_d$
  $i = \mathit{floor}(n_x(x - x_{min})/(x_{max} - x_{min}))$
  $t_{ynext} = t_{ymin} + dt_y$
  $t_{xnext} = t_{xmin} + (i+1)dt_x$
  $t_{last} = t_{ymin}$
while *(true)* ***do***
  if $(t_{xnext} < t_{ynext})$ ***then***
    if $(\mathit{cell} \neq \mathit{NULL})$ *and* $(\mathit{cell}(i,j) \rightarrow \mathit{hit}(\mathbf{e}, \mathbf{d}, t_{last}, t_{xnext}, \mathit{rec}))$ ***then***
      return true
    $t_{last} = t_{xnext}$
    $t_{xnext} = t_{xnext} + dt_x$

$i = i + 1$
if $(i == n_x)$ ***then***
return false
else
if $(cell \neq NULL)$ *and* $(cell(i,j) \rightarrow hit(\mathbf{e}, \mathbf{d}, t_{last}, t_{ynext}, rec))$ ***then***
return true
$t_{last} = t_{ynext}$
$t_{ynext} = t_{ynext} + dt_y$
$j = j + 1$
if $(j == n_y)$ ***then***
return false

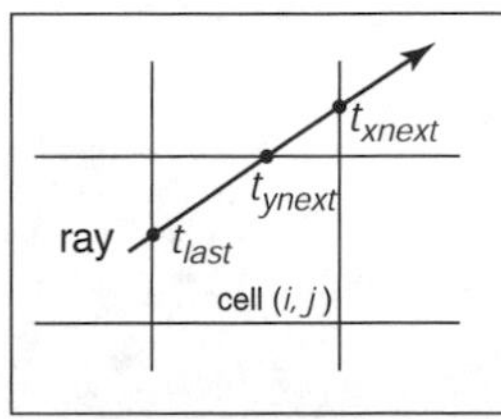

Figure 9.22. To decide whether we advance right or upwards, we keep track of the intersections with the next vertical and horizontal boundary of the cell.

The key parts to this algorithm are finding the initial cell (i, j) and deciding whether to increment i or j (Figure 9.22). Note that when we check for an intersection with objects in a cell, we restrict the range of t to be within the cell (Figure 9.23).

There are several extensions we need to make to the code above for the general case:

- adding the z axis,
- allowing for negative components in $\mathbf{d}$,
- allowing for floating point error to make the array indices out of range,
- allowing the ray to start in the grid.
- making sure hits with rec.$t > t_1$ are not returned.

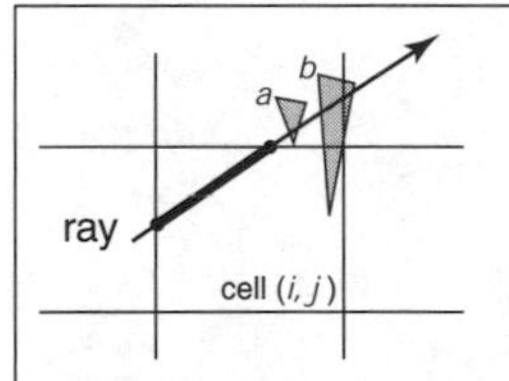

Figure 9.23. Only hits within the cell should be reported. Otherwise the case above would cause us to report hitting object *b* rather than object *a*.

The code now looks like:

bool grid::hit(ray $\mathbf{e} + t\mathbf{d}$*, real* t_0*, real* t_1*, hit-record rec)*
if $(x_d > 0)$ ***then***
$t_{xmin} = (x_{min} - x_e)/x_d$
$t_{xmax} = (x_{max} - x_e)/x_d$
$i_{inc} = +1$
$i_{stop} = n_x$
else
$t_{xmin} = (x_{max} - x_e)/x_d$
$t_{xmax} = (x_{min} - x_e)/x_d$
$i_{inc} = -1$
$i_{stop} = -1$
if $(y_d > 0)$ ***then***
$t_{ymin} = (y_{min} - y_e)/y_d$
$t_{ymax} = (y_{max} - y_e)/y_d$
$j_{inc} = +1$
$j_{stop} = n_y$

```
else
  t_ymin = (y_max − y_e)/y_d
  t_ymax = (y_min − y_e)/y_d
  j_inc = −1
  j_stop = −1
if (t_xmin > t_ymax) or (t_ymin > t_xmax) then
  return false
if (z_d > 0) then
  t_zmin = (z_min − z_e)/z_d
  t_zmax = (z_max − z_e)/z_d
  k_inc = +1
  k_stop = n_z
else
  t_zmin = (z_max − z_e)/z_d
  t_zmax = (z_min − z_e)/z_d
  k_inc = −1
  k_stop = −1
if (t_zmin > t_xmax) or (t_xmin > t_zmax) then
  return false
if (t_zmin > t_ymax) or (t_ymin > t_zmax) then
  return false
dt_x = (t_xmax − t_xmin)/n_x
dt_y = (t_ymax − t_ymin)/n_y
dt_z = (t_zmax − t_zmin)/n_z
if ((p = e + t_0 d) is inside grid) then
  x = x_p
  i = floor(n_x(x − x_min)/(x_max − x_min))
  if (i < 0) then
    i = 0
  if (i > n_x − 1) then
    i = n_x − 1
  y = y_p
  j = floor(n_y(y − y_min)/(y_max − y_min))
  if (j < 0) then
    j = 0
  if (j > n_y − 1) then
    j = n_y − 1
  z = z_p
  k = floor(n_z(z − z_min)/(z_max − z_min))
  if (k < 0) then
    k = 0
  if (k > n_z − 1) then
    k = n_z − 1
  t_xnext = t_xmin + (i + (i_inc + 1)/2)dt_x
```

  $t_{ynext} = t_{ymin} + (j + (j_{inc} + 1)/2)dt_y$
  $t_{znext} = t_{zmin} + (k + (k_{inc} + 1)/2)dt_z$
  $t_{last} = t_0$
else if $(t_{xmin} > t_{ymin})$ *and* $(t_{xmin} > t_{zmin})$ **then**
  $i = i_{stop} - i_{inc}$
  $y = y_e + t_{xmin}y_d$
  $j = floor(n_y(y - y_{min})/(y_{max} - y_{min}))$
  if $(j < 0)$ **then**
    $j = 0$
  if $(j > n_y - 1)$ **then**
    $j = n_y - 1$
  $z = z_e + t_{xmin}z_d$
  $k = floor(n_z(z - z_{min})/(z_{max} - z_{min}))$
  if $(k < 0)$ **then**
    $k = 0$
  if $(k > n_z - 1)$ **then**
    $k = n_z - 1$
  $t_{xnext} = t_{xmin} + dt_x$
  $t_{ynext} = t_{ymin} + (j + (j_{inc} + 1)/2)dt_y$
  $t_{znext} = t_{zmin} + (k + (k_{inc} + 1)/2)dt_z$
  $t_{last} = t_{xmin}$
else if $(t_{ymin} > t_{zmin})$ **then**
  $j = j_{stop} - j_{inc}$
  $x = x_e + t_{ymin}x_d$
  $i = floor(n_x(x - x_{min})/(x_{max} - x_{min}))$
  if $(i < 0)$ **then**
    $i = 0$
  if $(i > n_x - 1)$ **then**
    $i = n_x - 1$
  $z = z_e + t_{ymin}z_d$
  $k = floor(n_z(z - z_{min})/(z_{max} - z_{min}))$
  if $(k < 0)$ **then**
    $k = 0$
  if $(k > n_z - 1)$ **then**
    $k = n_z - 1$
  $t_{ynext} = t_{ymin} + dt_y$
  $t_{xnext} = t_{xmin} + (i + (i_{inc} + 1)/2)dt_x$
  $t_{znext} = t_{zmin} + (k + (k_{inc} + 1)/2)dt_z$
  $t_{last} = t_{ymin}$
else
  $k = k_{stop} - k_{inc}$
  $x = x_e + t_{zmin}x_d$
  $i = floor(n_x(x - x_{min})/(x_{max} - x_{min}))$
  if $(i < 0)$ **then**

```
        i = 0
    if (i > n_x − 1) then
        i = n_x − 1
    y = y_e + t_zmin y_d
    j = floor(n_y(y − y_min)/(y_max − y_min))
    if (j < 0) then
        j = 0
    if (j > n_y − 1) then
        j = n_y − 1
    t_znext = t_zmin + dt_z
    t_xnext = t_xmin + (i + (i_inc + 1)/2))dt_x
    t_ynext = t_ymin + (j + (j_inc + 1)/2))dt_y
    t_last = t_zmin
if (t_last > t_1) then
    return false
while (true) do
    if (t_xnext < t_ynext) and (t_xnext < t_znext) then
        if (cell(i, j)→hit(e, d, t_last, t_xnext, rec)) and (rec.t ≤ t_1) then
            return true
        t_last = t_xnext
        t_xnext = t_xnext + dt_x
        i = i + i_inc
        if (i == i_stop) then
            return false
    else if (t_ynext < t_znext) then
        if (cell(i, j)→hit(e, d, t_last, t_ynext, rec)) and (rec.t ≤ t_1) then
            return true
        t_last = t_ynext
        t_ynext = t_ynext + dt_y
        j = j + j_inc
        if (j == j_stop) then
            return false
    else
        if (cell(i, j)→hit(e, d, t_last, t_znext, rec)) and (rec.t ≤ t_1) then
            return true
        t_last = t_znext
        t_znext = t_znext + dt_z
        k = k + k_inc
        if (k == k_stop) then
            return false
```

Most implementations make the 3D array of type "pointer to surface." To improve the locality of the traversal, the array can be tiled as discussed in Section 12.4.

9.9.4 Binary-Space Partitioning

We can also partition space in a hierarchical data structure such as a binary-space-partioning tree (BSP tree). This is similar to the BSP tree used for a painter's algorithm in Chapter 7, but it usually uses axis-aligned cutting planes for easier ray intersection. A node in this structure might contain a single cutting plane and a left and right subtree. These subtrees would contain all objects on either side of the cutting plane. Objects that pass through the plane would be in each subtree. If we assume the cutting plane is parallel to the yz plane at $x = D$, then the node class is:

```
class bsp-node subclass of surface
virtual bool hit(ray e + td, real t0, real t1, hit-record rec)
virtual box bounding-box()
surface-pointer left
surface-pointer right
real D
```

We generalize this to y and z cutting planes later. The intersection code can then be called recursively in an object-oriented style. The code considers the four cases shown in Figure 9.24. For our purposes, the origin of these rays is a point at parameter t_0:

$$\mathbf{p} = \mathbf{a} + t_0\mathbf{b}.$$

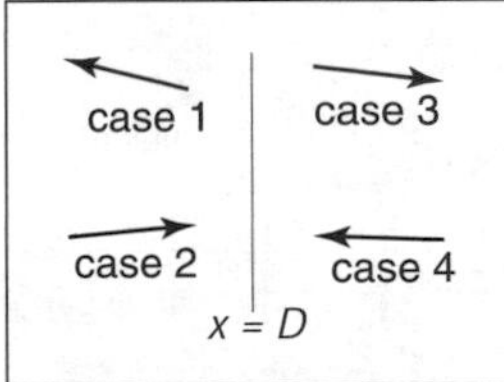

Figure 9.24. The four cases of how a ray relates to the BSP cutting plane $x = D$.

The four cases are:

1. The ray only interacts with the left subtree, and we need not test it for intersection with the cutting plane. It occurs for $x_p < D$ and $x_b < 0$.

2. The ray is tested against the left subtree, and if there are no hits, it is then tested against the right subtree. We need to find the ray parameter at $x = D$ so we can make sure we only test for intersections within the subtree. This case occurs for $x_p < D$ and $x_b > 0$.

3. This case is analogous to case 1 and occurs for $x_p > D$ and $x_b > 0$.

4. This case is analogous to case 2 and occurs for $x_p > D$ and $x_b < 0$.

The resulting traversal code handling these cases in order is:

```
bool bsp-node::hit( ray a + tb, real t0, real t1, hit-record rec)
x_p = x_a + t0 x_b
if (x_p < D) then
  if (x_b < 0) then
    return (left ≠ NULL) and (left→hit(a + tb, t0, t1, rec))
  t = (x_p − x_a)/x_b
  if (t > t1) then
```

```
      return (left ≠ NULL) and (left→hit(a + tb, t0, t1, rec))
    if (left ≠ NULL) and (left→hit(a + tb, t0, t, rec)) then
      return true
    return (right ≠ NULL) and (right→hit(a + tb, t, t1, rec))
  else
    analogous code for cases 3 and 4
```

This is very clean code. However, to get it started, we need to hit some root object that includes a bounding box so we can initialize the traversal, t_0 and t_1. An issue we have to address is that the cutting plane may be along any axis. We can add an interger index *axis* to the bsp-node class. If we allow an indexing operator for points, this will result in some simple modifications to the code above, for example,

$x_p = x_a + t_0 x_b$

would become

$u_p = a[axis] + t_0 b[axis]$

which will result in some additional array indexing, but will not generate more branches.

While the processing of a single bsp-node is faster than processing a bvh-node, the fact that a single surface may exist in more than one subtree means there are more nodes and, potentially, a higher memory use. How "well" the trees are built determines which is faster. Building the tree is similar to building the BVH tree. We can pick axes to split in a cycle, and we can split in half each time, or we can try to be more sophisticated in how we divide.

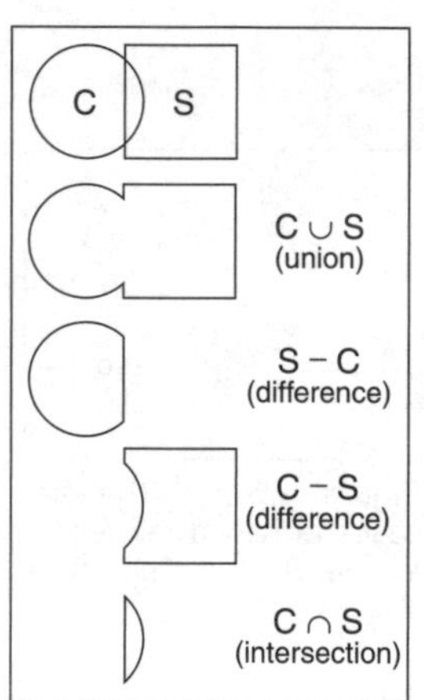

Figure 9.25. The basic CSG operations on a 2D circle and square.

9.10 Constructive Solid Geometry

One nice thing about ray tracing is that any geometric primitive whose intersection with a 3D line can be computed can be seamlessly added to a ray tracer. It turns out to also be straightforward to add *constructive solid geometry* (CSG) to a ray tracer. The basic idea of CSG is to use set operations to combine solid shapes. These basic operations are shown in Figure 9.25. The operations can be viewed as *set* operations. For example, we can consider C the set of all points in the circle, and S the set of all points in the square. The intersection operation $C \cap S$ is the set of all points that are both members of C and S. The other operations are analogous.

Although one can do CSG directly on the model, if all that is desired is an image, we do not need to explicitly change the model. Instead, we perform the set operations directly on the rays as they interact with a model. To make this natural, we find all the intersections of a ray with a model rather than just the closest. For example, a ray $\mathbf{a} + t\mathbf{b}$ might hit a sphere at $t = 1$ and $t = 2$. In the context of CSG, we think of this as the ray being inside the sphere for $t \in [1, 2]$. We can compute these "inside intervals" for all of the surfaces and do set operations on those intervals (recall Section 2.1.2). This is illustrated in Figure 9.26, where the hit intervals are processed to indicate that there are two intervals inside the difference object. The first hit for $t > 0$ is what the ray actually intersects.

In practice, the CSG intersection routine must maintain a list of intervals. When the first hitpoint is determined, the material property and surface normal is that associated with the hitpoint. In addition, you must pay attention to precision issues because there is nothing to prevent the user from taking two objects that abut and taking an intersection. This can be made robust by eliminating any interval whose thickness is below a certain tolerance.

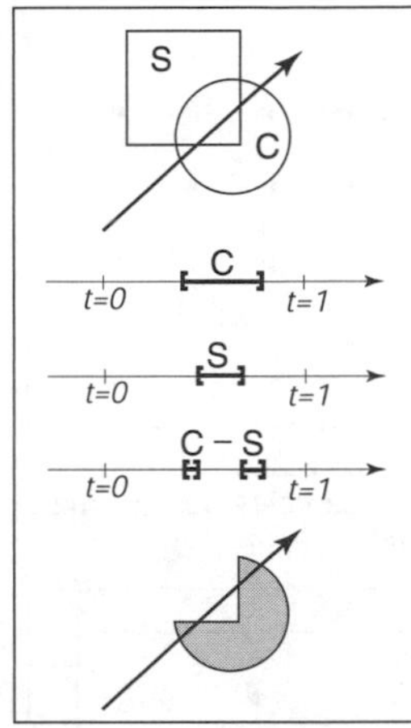

Figure 9.26. Intervals are processed to indicate how the ray hits the composite object.

9.11 Distribution Ray Tracing

For some applications, ray-traced images are just too "clean." This effect can be mitigated using *distribution ray tracing* . The conventionally ray-traced images look clean, because everything is crisp; the shadows are perfectly sharp, the reflections have no fuzziness, and everything is in perfect focus. Sometimes we would like to have the shadows be soft (as they are in real life), the reflections be fuzzy as with brushed metal, and the image have variable degrees of focus as in a photograph with a large aperture. While accomplishing these things from first principles is somewhat involved (as is developed in Chapter 19), we can get most of the visual impact with some fairly simple changes to the basic ray tracing algorithm. In addition, the framework gives us a relatively simple way to antialias (recall Section 3.7) the image.

9.11.1 Antialiasing

Recall that a simple way to antialias an image is to compute the average color for the area of the pixel rather than the color at the center point (Chapter 15 will have a more sophisticated discussion of this issue). In ray tracing, our computational primitive is to compute the color at a point on the screen. If we average many of these points across the pixel, we are approximating the true average. If the screen coordinates bounding the pixel are $[i, i+1] \times [j, j+1]$ then we can replace the loop:

for** each pixel* (i, j) ***do
  $c_{ij} = \textit{ray-color}(i + 0.5, j + 0.5)$

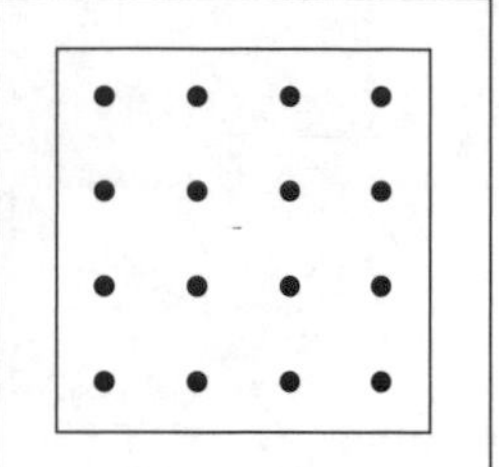

Figure 9.27. Sixteen regular samples for a single pixel.

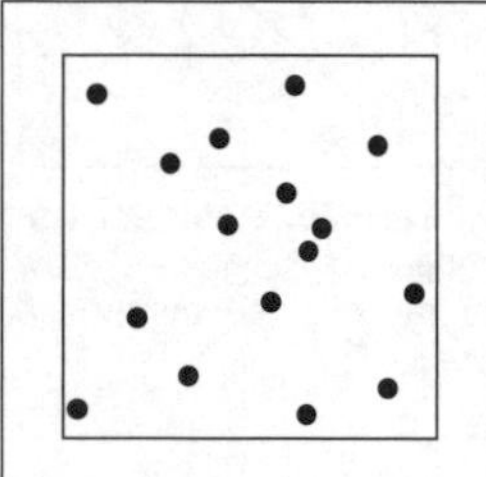

Figure 9.28. Sixteen random samples for a single pixel.

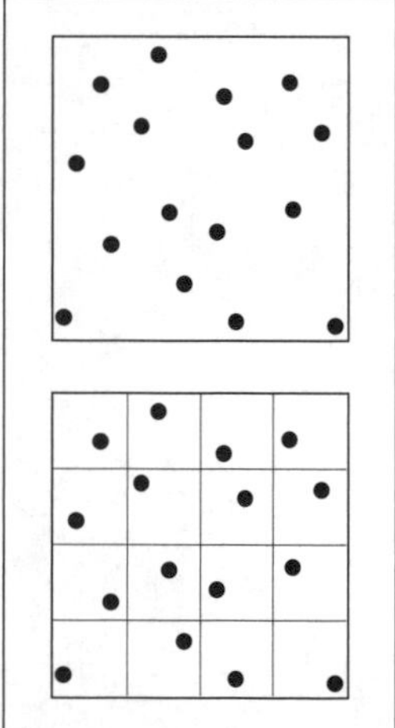

Figure 9.29. Sixteen stratified (jittered) samples for a single pixel shown with and without the bins highlighted. There is exactly one random sample taken within each bin.

with code that samples on a regular $n \times n$ grid of samples within each pixel:

```
for each pixel (i, j) do
  c = 0
  for p = 0 to n − 1 do
    for q = 0 to n − 1 do
      c = c+ ray-color(i + (p + 0.5)/n, j + (q + 0.5)/n)
  c_ij = c/n^2
```

This is usually called *regular sampling* The 16 sample locations in a pixel for $n = 4$ are shown in Figure 9.27. Note that this produces the same answer as rendering a traditional ray-traced image with one sample per pixel at $n_x n$ by $n_y n$ resolution and then averaging blocks of n by n pixels to get a n_x by n_y image.

One potential problem with taking samples in a regular pattern within a pixel is that regular artifacts such as Moire patterns can arise. These artifacts can be turned into noise by taking samples in a random pattern within each pixel as shown in Figure 9.28. This is usually called *random sampling* and involves just a small change to the code:

```
for each pixel (i, j) do
  c = 0
  for p = 1 to n^2 do
    c = c+ ray-color(i + ξ, j + ξ)
  c_ij = c/n^2
```

Here ξ is a call that returns a uniform random number in the range $[0, 1)$. Unfortunately, the noise can be quite objectionable unless many samples are taken. A compromise is to make a hybrid strategy that randomly perturbs a regular grid:

```
for each pixel (i, j) do
  c = 0
  for p = 0 to n − 1 do
    for q = 0 to n − 1 do
      c = c+ ray-color(i + (p + ξ)/n, j + (q + ξ)/n)
  c_ij = c/n^2
```

That method is usually called *jittering* or *stratified sampling* (Figure 9.29).

9.11.2 Soft Shadows

The reason shadows are hard to handle in standard ray tracing is that lights are infinitesimal points or directions and are thus either visible or invisible. In real life, lights have non-zero area and can thus be partially visible. This idea is shown in 2D in Figure 9.30. The region where the light is entirely visible is called the *umbra*. The partially visible region is called the *penumbra*. There is not a commonly-used term for the region not in shadow, but it is sometimes called the *anti-umbra*.

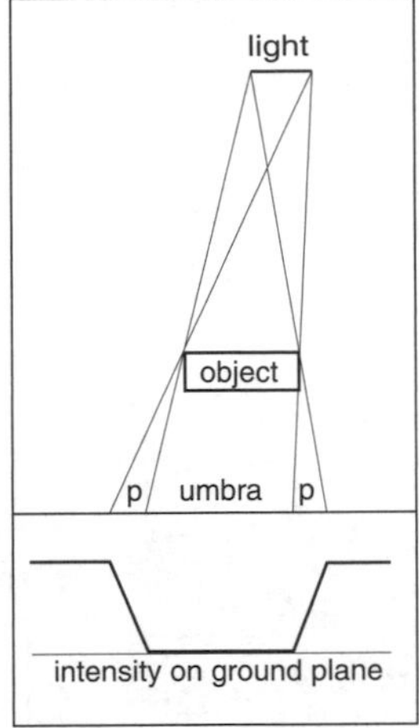

Figure 9.30. A soft shadow has a gradual transition from the unshadowed to shadowed region. The transition zone is the "penumbra" denoted by p in the figure.

The key to implementing soft shadows is to somehow account for the light being an area rather than a point. An easy way to do this is to approximate the light with a distributed set of N point lights each with one Nth of the intensity of the base light. This concept is illustrated at the left of Figure 9.31 where nine lights are used. You can do this in a standard ray tracer, and it is a common trick to get soft shadows in an off-the-shelf renderer. There are two potential problems with this technique. First typically dozens of point lights are needed to achieve visually smooth results, which slows down the program a great deal. The second problem is that the shadows have sharp transitions inside the penumbra.

Distribution ray tracing introduces a small change in the shadowing code. Instead of representing the area light at a discrete number of point sources, we represent it as an infinite number and choose one at random for each viewing ray. This amounts to choosing a random point on the light for any surface point being lit as is shown at the right of Figure 9.31.

If the light is a parallelogram specified by a corner point $\mathbf{c}$ and two edge vectors $\mathbf{a}$ and $\mathbf{b}$ (Figure 9.32), then choosing a random point $\mathbf{r}$ is straightforward:

$$\mathbf{r} = \mathbf{c} + \xi_1 \mathbf{a} + \xi_2 \mathbf{b},$$

where ξ_1 and ξ_2 are uniform random numbers in the range $[0, 1)$.

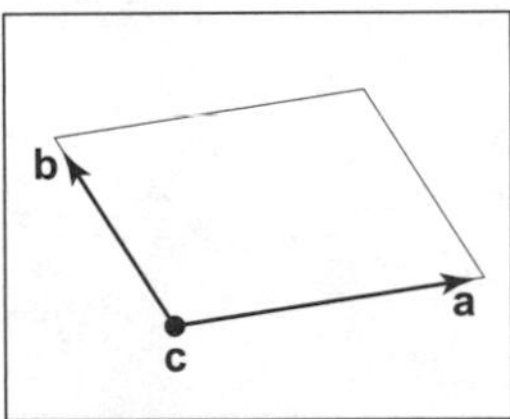

Figure 9.32. The geometry of a parallelogram light specified by a corner point and two edge vectors.

We then send a shadow ray to this point as shown at the right in Figure 9.31. Note that the direction of this ray is not unit length, which may require some modification to your basic ray tracer depending upon its assumptions.

We would really like to jitter points on the light. However, it can be dangerous to implement this without some thought. We would not want

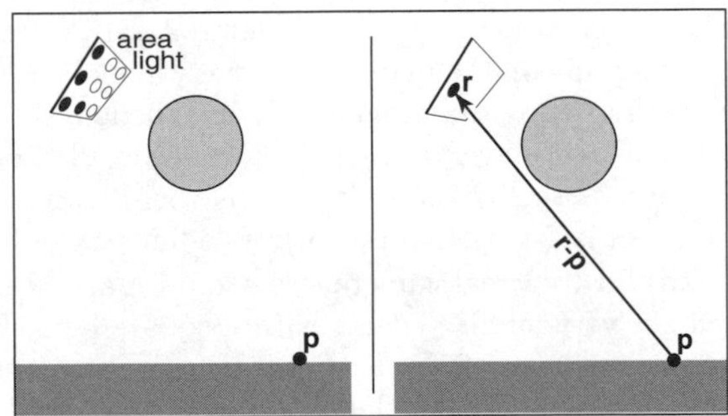

Figure 9.31. Left: an area light can be approximated by some number of point lights; four of the nine points are visible to $\mathbf{p}$ so it is in the penumbra. Right: a random point on the light is chosen for the shadow ray, and it has some chance of hitting the light or not.

to always have the ray in the upper-left hand corner of the pixel generate a shadow ray to the upper-left hand corner of the light. Instead we would like to scramble the samples, such that the pixel samples and the light samples are each themselves jittered, but so that there is no correlation between pixel samples and light samples. A good way to accomplish this is to generate two distinct sets of n^2 jittered samples, and pass samples into the light source routine:

```
for each pixel (i, j) do
    c = 0
    generate N = n^2 jittered 2D points and store in array r[]
    generate N = n^2 jittered 2D points and store in array s[]
    shuffle the points in array s[]
    for p = 0 to N − 1 do
        c = c+ ray-color(i + r[p].x(), j +r[p].y(), s[p])
    c_ij = c/N
```

This shuffle routine eliminates any coherence between arrays r and s. The shadow routine will just use the 2D random point stored in *s[p]* rather than calling the random number generator. A shuffle routine for an array indexed from 0 to $n-1$ is:

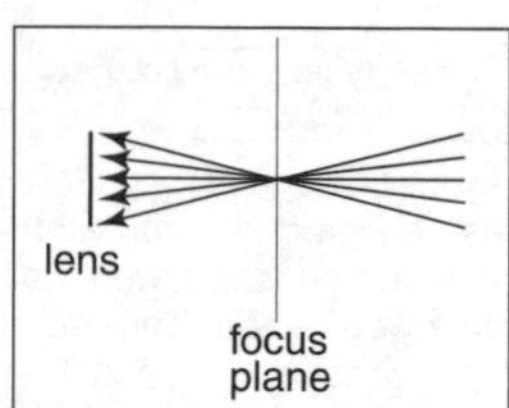

Figure 9.33. The lens averages over a cone of directions that hit the pixel location being sampled.

```
for i = N − 1 downto 1 do
    choose random integer j between 0 and i inclusive
    swap array elements i and j
```

9.11.3 Depth of Field

The soft focus effects seen in most photos can be simulated by collecting light at a non-zero size "lens" rather than at a point. This is called *depth of field.* The lens collects light from a cone of directions that has its apex at a distance where everything is in focus (Figure 9.33). We can place the "window" we are sampling on the plane where everything is in focus (rather than at the $z = n$ plane as we did previously), and the lens at the eye. The distance to the plane where everything is in focus we call the *focus plane*, and the distance to it is set by the user, just as the distance to the focus plane in a real camera is set by the user or range finder.

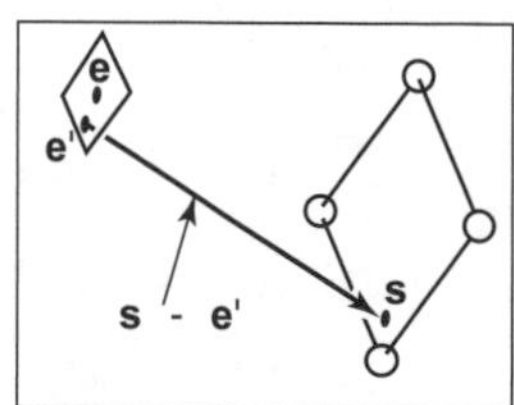

Figure 9.34. To create depth of field effects, the eye is randomly selected from a square region.

To be most faithful to a real camera, we should make the lens a disk. However, we will get very similar effects with a square lens (Figure 9.34). So we choose the side-length of the lens and take random samples on it. The origin of the view rays will be these perturbed positions rather than the eye position. Again, a shuffling routine is used to prevent correlation with the pixel sample positions. An example using 25 samples per pixel and a large disk lens is shown in Figure 9.35.

Figure 9.35. An example of depth of field. The caustic in the shadow of the wine glass is computed using particle tracing (Chapter 19). (See also Plate IX.)

9.11.4 Glossy Reflection

Some surfaces, such as brushed metal, are somewhere between an ideal mirror and a diffuse surface. Some discernible image is visible in the reflection but it is blurred. We can simulate this by randomly perturbing ideal specular reflection rays as shown in Figure 9.36.

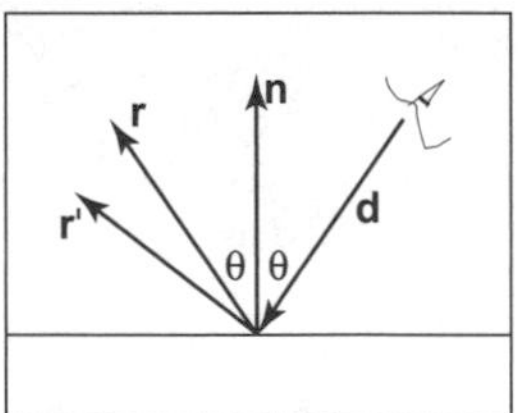

Figure 9.36. The reflection ray is perturbed to a random vector **r**'.

Only two details need to be worked out: how to choose the vector $\mathbf{r}'$, and what to do when the resulting perturbed ray is below the surface the ray is reflected from. The latter detail is usually settled by returning a zero color when the ray is below the surface.

To choose $\mathbf{r}'$, we again sample a random square. This square is perpendicular to $\mathbf{r}$ and has width a which controls the degree of blur. We can set up the square's orientation by creating an orthonormal basis with $\mathbf{w} = \mathbf{r}$ using the techniques in Section 2.4.6. Then, we create a random point in the 2D square with side length a centered at the origin. If we have 2D sample points $(\xi, \xi') \in [0, 1]^2$, then the analogous point on the desired square is

$$u = -\frac{a}{2} + \xi a,$$

$$v = -\frac{a}{2} + \xi' a.$$

Because the square over which we will perturb is parallel to both the **u** and **v** vectors, the ray $\mathbf{r}'$ is just:

$$\mathbf{r}' = \mathbf{r} + u\mathbf{u} + v\mathbf{v}.$$

Note that $\mathbf{r}'$ is not necessarily a unit vector and should be normalized if your code requires that for ray directions.

9.11.5 Motion Blur

We can add a blurred appearance to objects as shown in Figure 9.37. This is called *motion blur* and is the result of the image being formed over a non-zero span of time. In a real camera, the aperture is open for some time interval during which objects move. We can simulate the open aperture by setting a time variable ranging from T_0 to T_1. For each viewing ray we

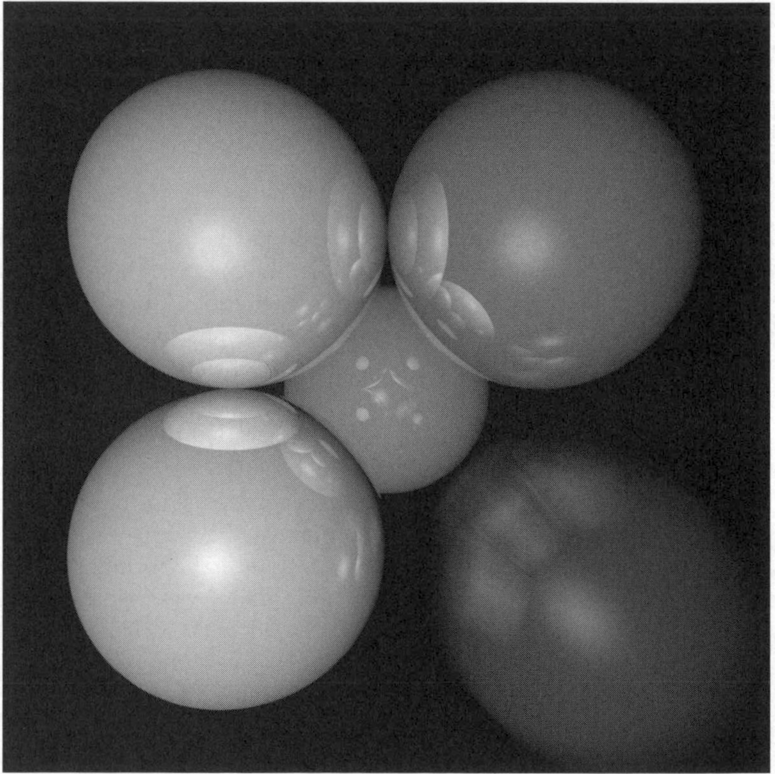

Figure 9.37. The bottom right sphere is in motion and a blurred appearance results. Image courtesy Chad Barb.

choose a random time:

$$T = T_0 + \xi(T_1 - T_0).$$

We may also need to create some objects to move with time. For example, we might have a moving sphere whose center travels from $\mathbf{c}_0$ to $\mathbf{c}_1$ during the interval. Given T, we could compute the actual center and do a ray–intersection with that sphere. Because each ray is sent at a different time, each will encounter the sphere at a different position and the final appearance will be blurred. Note that the bounding box for the moving sphere should bound its entire path so an efficiency structure can be built for the whole time interval.

Frequently Asked Questions

- **Why is there no perspective matrix in ray tracing?**

The perspective matrix in a z-buffer exists so that we can turn the perspective projection into a parallel projection. This is not needed in ray tracing, because it is easy to do the perspective projection implicitly by fanning the rays out from the eye.

- **What is the best ray-intersection efficiency structure?**

The most popular structures are binary-space partitioning trees (BSP trees), uniform subdivision grids, and bounding volume hierarchies. There is no clear-cut answer for which is best, but all are much, much better than brute-force search in practice. If I were to implement only one, it would be the bounding-volume hierarchy because of its simplicity and robustness.

- **Why do people use bounding boxes rather than spheres or ellipsoids?**

Sometimes spheres or ellipsoids are better. However, many models have polygonal elements that are tightly bounded by boxes, but they would be difficult to tightly bind with an ellipsoid.

- **Can ray tracing be made interactive?**

For sufficiently small models and images, any modern PC is sufficiently powerful for ray tracing to be interactive. In practice, multiple CPUs with a shared frame-buffer are required for a full-screen implementation. Computer power is increasing much faster than screen resolution, and it is just a matter of time before conventional PCs can ray trace complex scenes at screen resolution.

- Is ray tracing useful in a hardware graphics program?

Ray tracing is frequently used for *picking*. When the user clicks the mouse on a pixel in a 3D graphics program, the program needs to determine which object is visible within that pixel. Ray tracing is an ideal way to determine that.

Notes

Modern ray tracing was introduced in *An Improved Illumination Model for Shaded Display* (Whitted, Communications of the ACM, June 1980). CSG via ray tracing was introduced in *Ray Casting for Modelling Solids* (Computer Graphics and Image Processing, February, 1982). A description of picking using ray tracing can be found in *Real-Time Rendering* (Möller and Haines, A K Peters, 1999). A survey of efficiency structures for ray tracing is in the classic *A Survey of Ray Tracing Acceleration Techniques* (Arvo and Kirk in *An Introduction to Ray Tracing*, Academic Press, 1989). A general discussion of efficiency issues for ray tracing, especially involving hierarchical bounding volumes, can be found in *Efficiency Issues for Ray Tracing* (Smits, journal of graphics tools, 3(2), 1998).

Exercises

1. What are the ray parameters of the intersection points between ray $(1, 1, 1) + t(-1, -1, -1)$ and the sphere centered at the origin with radius 1? Note: this is a good debugging case.

2. What are the barycentric coordinates and ray parameter where the ray $(1, 1, 1) + t(-1, -1, -1)$ hits the triangle with vertices $(1, 0, 0)$, $(0, 1, 0)$, and $(0, 0, 1)$? Note: this is a good debugging case.

3. Do a back of the envelope computation of the approximate time complexity of ray tracing on "nice" (non-adversarial) models. Split your analysis into the cases of preprocessing and computing the image, so that you can predict the behavior of ray tracing multiple frames for a static model.

Texture Mapping

The shading models presented in Chapter 8 assume that a diffuse surface has uniform reflectance c_r. This is fine for surfaces such as blank paper or painted walls, but it is inefficient for objects such as a printed sheet of paper. Such objects have an appearance whose complexity arises from variation in reflectance properties. While we could use such small triangles that the variation is captured by varying the reflectance properties of the triangles, this would be inefficient.

The common technique to handle variations of reflectance is to store the reflectance as a function or a a pixel-based image and "map" it onto a surface. The function or image is called a *texture map* and the process of controlling reflectance properties is called *texture mapping*. This is not hard to implement once you understand the coordinate systems involved. Texture mapping can be classified by several different properties:

1. the dimensionality of the texture function,
2. the correspondences defined between points on the surface and points in the texture function, and
3. whether the texture function is primarily procedural or primarily a table look-up.

These items are usually closely related, so we will somewhat arbitrarily classify textures by their dimension. We first cover 3D textures, often called *solid* textures or *volume* textures. We will then cover 2D textures, sometimes called *image* textures. When graphics programmers talk about textures without specifying dimension, they usually mean 2D textures. However, we begin with 3D textures because, in many ways, they are easier to understand and implement. At the end of the chapter we discuss bump mapping and displacement mapping which use textures to change surface normals and position, respectively. Although those methods modify properties other than reflectance, the images/functions they use are still called textured. This is consistent with common usage where any image used to modify object appearance is called a texture.

10.1 3D Texture Mapping

In previous chapters we used c_r as the diffuse reflectance at a point on an object. For an object that does not have a solid color, we can replace this with a function $c_r(\mathbf{p})$ which maps 3D points to RGB colors. This function might just return the reflectance of the object that contains $\mathbf{p}$. But for objects with *texture*, we should expect $c_r(\mathbf{p})$ to vary as $\mathbf{p}$ moves across a surface. One way to do this is to create a 3D texture that defines an RGB value at every point in 3D space. We will only call it for points $\mathbf{p}$ on the surface, but it is usually easier to define it for all 3D points than a potentially strange 2D subset of points that are on an arbitrary surface. Such a strategy is clearly suitable for surfaces that are "carved" from a solid medium, such as a marble sculpture.

Note that in a ray tracing program, we have immediate access to the point $\mathbf{p}$ seen through a pixel. However, for a z-buffer or BSP-tree program, we only know the point after projection into device coordinates. We will show how to resolve this problem in Section 10.4.1.

Figure 10.1. Various stripe textures result from drawing an regular array of *xy* points while keeping *z* constant.

10.1.1 3D Stripe Textures

There are a surprising number of ways to make a striped texture. Let's assume we have two colors c_0 and c_1 that we want to use to make the stripe color. We need some oscillating function to switch between the two colors. An easy one is a cosine:

```
RGB stripe( point p )
if (sin(x_p) > 0) then
    return c_0
else
    return c_1
```

We can also make the stripe's width w controllable:

```
RGB stripe( point p, real w)
if (sin(πx_p/w) > 0) then
```

return c_0
else
return c_1

If we want to interpolate smoothly between the stripe colors, we can use a parameter t to vary the color linearly:

RGB stripe(point $\mathbf{p}$, *real* w *)*
$t = (1 + \sin(\pi p_x / w))/2$
return $(1-t)c_0 + tc_1$

These three possibilities are shown in Figure 10.1.

10.1.2 Texture Arrays

Another way we can specify texture in space is to store a 3D array of color values, and to associate a spatial position to each of these values. We first discuss this for 2D arrays in 2D space. Such textures can be applied in 3D by using two of the dimensions, e.g. x and y, to determine what texture values are used. We then extend those 2D results to 3D.

We will assume the two dimensions to be mapped are called u and v. We also assume we have an n_x by n_y image that we use as the texture. Somehow we need every (u, v) to have an associated color found from the

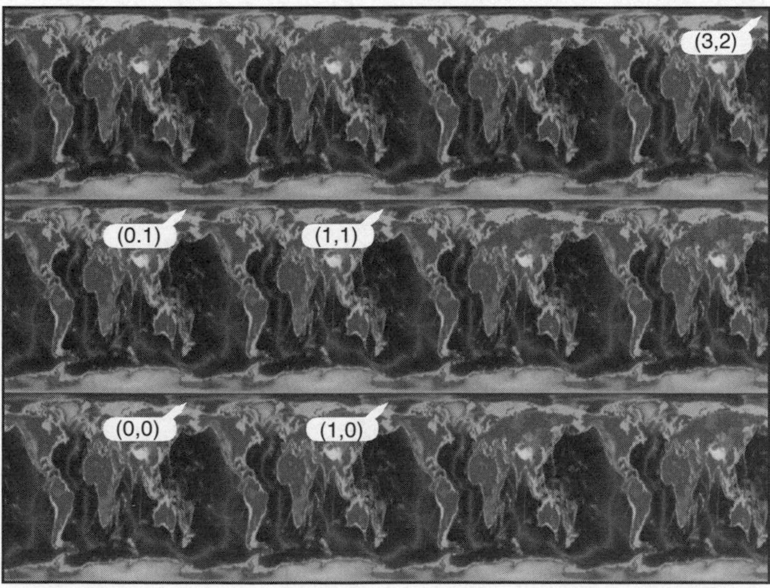

Figure 10.2. The tiling of an image onto the (u,v) plane. Note that the input image is rectangular, and that this rectangle is mapped to a unit square on the (u,v) plane.

image. A fairly standard way to make texturing work for (u, v) is to first remove the integer portion of (u, v) so that it lies in the unit square. This has the effect of "tiling" the entire uv plane with copies of the now-square texture (Figure 10.2). We then use one of three interpolation strategies to compute the image color for that coordinate. The simplest strategy is to treat each image pixel as a constant colored rectangular tile (Figure 10.3 (a). To compute the colors, we apply $c(u, v) = c_{ij}$, where $c(u, v)$ is the texture color at (u, v) and c_{ij} is the pixel color for pixel indices:

$$\begin{aligned} i &= \lfloor u n_x \rfloor, \\ j &= \lfloor v n_y \rfloor; \end{aligned} \tag{10.1}$$

$\lfloor x \rfloor$ is the floor of x, (n_x, n_y) is the size of the image being textured, and the indices start at $(i, j) = (0, 0)$. This method for a simple image is shown in Figure 10.3 (b).

For a smoother texture, a bilinear interpolation can be used as shown in Figure 10.3 (c). Here we use the formula:

$$\begin{aligned} c(u, v) = (1 - u')(1 - v')c_{ij} \\ + u'(1 - v')c_{(i+1)j} \\ + (1 - u')v'c_{i(j+1)} \\ + u'v'c_{(i+1)(j+1)} \end{aligned}$$

where

$$\begin{aligned} u' &= nu - \lfloor nu \rfloor, \\ v' &= nv - \lfloor nv \rfloor. \end{aligned}$$

The discontinuities in the derivative in intensity can cause visible mach bands, so hermite smoothing can be used:

$$\begin{aligned} c(u, v) = (1 - u'')(1 - v'')c_{ij} + \\ + u''(1 - v'')c_{(i+1)j} \\ + (1 - u'')v''c_{i(j+1)} \\ + u''v''c_{(i+1)(j+1)}, \end{aligned}$$

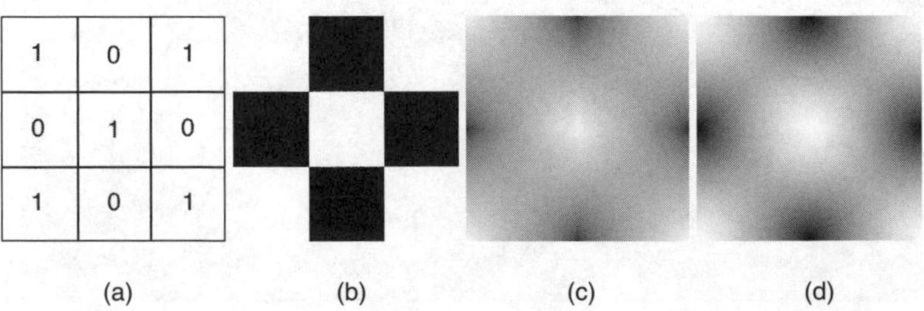

Figure 10.3. (a) The image on the left has nine pixels that are all either black or white. The three interpolation strategies are (b) nearest-neighbor, (c) bilinear, and (d) hermite.

where

$$u'' = 3(u')^2 - 2(u')^3,$$
$$v'' = 3(v')^2 - 2(v')^3$$

which results in Figure 10.3 (d).

In 3D, we have a 3D array of values. All of the ideas from 2D extend naturally. As an example, let's assume that we will do *trilinear* interpolation between values. First, we compute the texture coordinates (u', v', w') and the lower indices (i, j, k) of the array element to be interpolated:

$$\begin{aligned} c(u,v,w) = {} & (1-u')(1-v')(1-w')c_{ijk} \\ & + u'(1-v')(1-w')c_{(i+1)jk} \\ & + (1-u')v'(1-w')c_{i(j+1)k} \\ & + (1-u')(1-v')w'c_{ij(k+1)} \\ & + u'v'(1-w')c_{(i+1)(j+1)k} \\ & + u'(1-v')w'c_{(i+1)j(k+1)} \\ & + (1-u')v'w'c_{i(j+1)(k+1)} \\ & + u'v'w'c_{(i+1)(j+1)(k+1)} \end{aligned} \tag{10.2}$$

where

$$\begin{aligned} u' &= nu - \lfloor nu \rfloor, \\ v' &= nv - \lfloor nv \rfloor, \\ w' &= nw - \lfloor nw \rfloor. \end{aligned} \tag{10.3}$$

10.1.3 Solid Noise

Although regular textures such as stripes are often useful, we would like to be able to make "mottled" textures such as we see on birds' eggs. This is usually done by using a sort of "solid noise," usually called *Perlin noise* after its inventor who received a technical Academy Award for its impact in the film industry.

Getting a noisy appearance by calling a random number for every point wouldn't be appropriate, because it would just be like "white noise" in TV static. We would like to make it smoother without losing the random quality. One possibility is to blur white noise, but there is no practical implementation of this. Another possibility is to make a large lattice with a random number at every lattice point, and then interpolate these random points for new points between lattice nodes; this is just a 3D texture array as described in the last section with random numbers in the array. This technique makes the lattice too obvious. Perlin used a variety of tricks to improve this basic lattice technique so the lattice was not so obvious. This results in a rather baroque-looking set of steps, but essentially there are just three changes from linearly interpolating a 3D array of random values. The first change is to use Hermite interpolation to avoid mach bands, just as can be done with regular textures. The second change is the use of random vectors rather than values, with a dot product to derive a random number; this makes the underlying grid structure less visually obvious by moving the local minima and maxima off the grid vertices. The third change is to use a 1D array and hashing to create a virtual 3D array of random vectors. This adds computation to lower memory use. Here is his basic method:

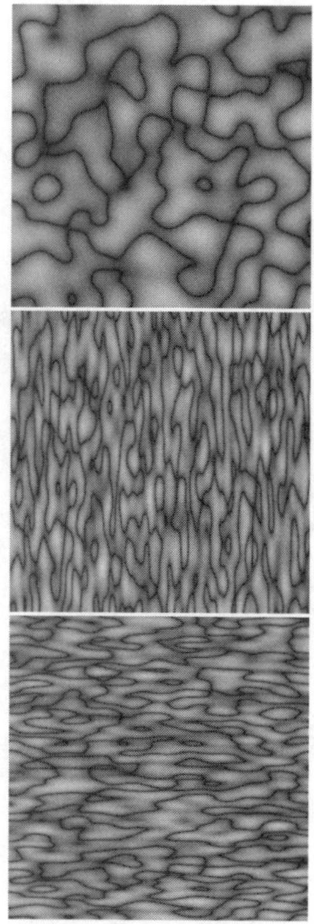

Figure 10.4. Absolute value of solid noise, and noise for scaled *x* and *y* values.

$$n(x, y, z) = \sum_{i=\lfloor x \rfloor}^{\lfloor x \rfloor+1} \sum_{j=\lfloor y \rfloor}^{\lfloor y \rfloor+1} \sum_{k=\lfloor z \rfloor}^{\lfloor z \rfloor+1} \Omega_{ijk}(x - i, y - j, z - k),$$

where (x, y, z) are the Cartesian coordinates of $\mathbf{x}$, and

$$\Omega_{ijk}(u, v, w) = \omega(u)\omega(v)\omega(w) \left(\Gamma_{ijk} \cdot (u, v, w)\right),$$

and $\omega(t)$ is the cubic weighting function:

$$\omega(t) = \begin{cases} 2|t|^3 - 3|t|^2 + 1 & \text{if } |t| < 1, \\ 0 & \text{otherwise.} \end{cases}$$

The final piece is that Γ_{ijk} is a random unit vector for the lattice point $(x, y, z) = (i, j, k)$. Since we want any potential ijk, we use a pseudorandom table:

$$\Gamma_{ijk} = \mathbf{G}\left(\phi(i + \phi(j + \phi(k)))\right),$$

where $\mathbf{G}$ is a precomputed array of n random unit vectors, and $\phi(i) = P[i \mod n]$ where P is an array of length n containing a permutation of the integers 0 through $n - 1$. In practice, Perlin reports $n = 256$ works well. To choose a random unit vector (v_x, v_y, v_z) first set:

$$\begin{aligned} v_x &= 2\xi \quad - 1, \\ v_y &= 2\xi' \; - 1, \\ v_z &= 2\xi'' - 1, \end{aligned}$$

where ξ, ξ', ξ'' are canonical random numbers (uniform in the interval $[0, 1)$). Then, if $(v_x^2 + v_y^2 + v_z^2) < 1$, make the vector a unit vector. Otherwise keep setting it randomly until its length is less than one, and then make it a unit vector. This is an example of a *rejection method*, which will be discussed more in Chapter 14. Essentially, the "less than" test gets a random point in the unit sphere, and the vector for the origin to that point is uniformly random. That would not be true of random points in the cube, so we "get rid" of the corners with the test.

Because solid noise can be positive or negative, it must be transformed before being converted to a color. The absolute value of noise over a ten by ten square is shown in Figure 10.4, along with stretched versions. There versions are stretched by scaling the points input to the noise function.

The dark curves are where the original noise function changed from positive to negative. Since noise varies from -1 to 1, a smoother image can be achieved by using (noise + 1)/2 for color. However, since noise values close to 1 or -1 are rare, this will be a fairly smooth image. Larger scaling can increase the contrast (Figure 10.5).

Figure 10.5. Using 0.5(noise+1) (top) and 0.8(noise+1) (bottom) for intensity.

10.1.4 Turbulence

Many natural textures contain a variety of feature sizes in the same texture. Perlin uses a pseudofractal "turbulence" function:

$$n_t(\mathbf{x}) = \sum_i \frac{|n(2^i \mathbf{x})|}{2^i}$$

This effectively repeatedly adds scaled copies of the noise function on top of itself as shown in Figure 10.6.

The turbulence can be used to distort the stripe function:

RGB turbstripe(point $\mathbf{p}$, *double* w *)*
double $t = (1 + \sin(k_1 z_p + turbulence(k_2 \mathbf{p})))/w)/2$
return $t * s0 + (1 - t) * s1$

Various values for k_1 and k_2 were used to generate Figure 10.7.

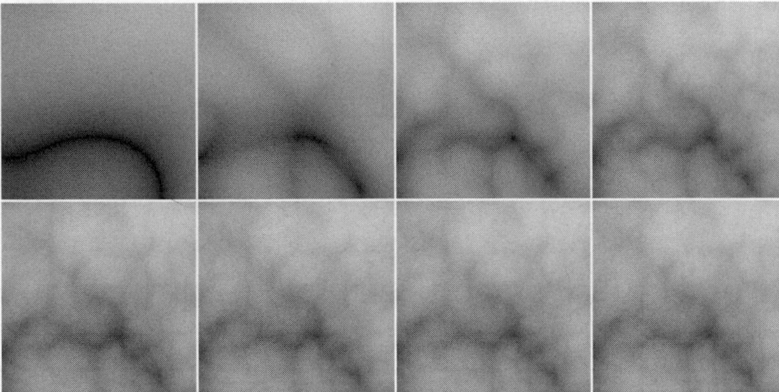

Figure 10.6. Turbulence function with (from top left to bottom right) one through eight terms in the summation.

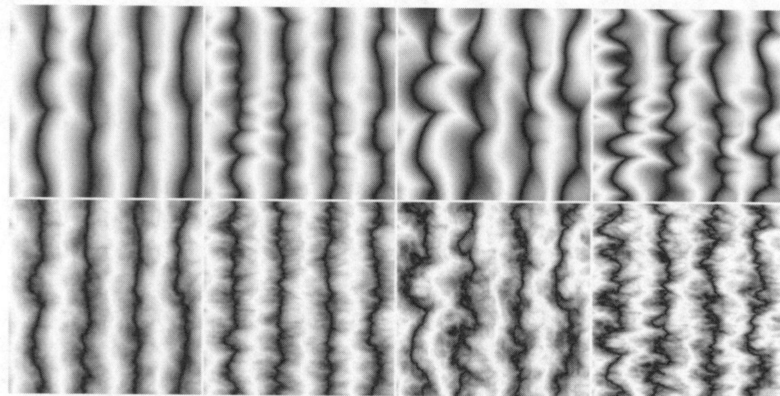

Figure 10.7. Various turbulent stripe textures with different k_1, k_2. The top row has only the first term of the turbulence series.

10.2 2D Texture Mapping

For 2D texture mapping, we use a 2D coordinate, often called uv, which is used to create a reflectance $R(u, v)$. The key is to take an image and associate a (u, v) coordinate system on it so that it can, in turn, be associated with points on a 3D surface. For example, if the latitudes and longitudes on the world map are associated with a polar coordinate system on the sphere, we get a globe (Figure 10.8).

As should be clear from Figure 10.8, it is crucial that the coordinates on the image and the object match in "just the right way." As a convention, the coordinate system on the image is set to be the unit square $(u, v) \in [0, 1]^2$. For (u, v) outside of this square, only the fractional parts of the coordinates are used resulting in a tiling of the plane (Figure 10.2). Note that the image has a different number of pixels horizontally and vertically, so the image pixels have a non-uniform aspect ratio in (u, v) space.

Figure 10.8. A Mercator projection map world map and its placement on the sphere. The distortions in the texture map (i.e., Greenland being so large) exactly correspond to the shrinking that occurs when the map is applied to the sphere.

To map this $(u, v) \in [0, 1]^2$ image onto a sphere, we first compute the polar coordinates. Recall the spherical coordinate system described by Equation 2.25. For a sphere of radius R with center (c_x, c_y, c_z), the parametric equation of the sphere is:

$$\begin{aligned} x &= x_c + R\cos\phi\sin\theta, \\ y &= y_c + R\sin\phi\sin\theta, \\ z &= z_c + R\cos\theta. \end{aligned}$$

We can find (θ, ϕ):

$$\begin{aligned} \theta &= \arccos\left(\frac{z - z_c}{R}\right), \\ \phi &= \arctan2(y - y_c, x - x_c), \end{aligned}$$

where $\arctan2(a, b)$ is the the *atan2* of most math libraries which returns the arctangent of a/b. Because $(\theta, \phi) \in [0, \pi] \times [-\pi, \pi]$, we convert to (u, v) as follows, after first adding 2π to ϕ if it is negative:

$$\begin{aligned} u &= \frac{\phi}{2\pi}, \\ v &= \frac{\pi - \theta}{\pi}. \end{aligned}$$

This mapping is shown in Figure 10.8. There is a similar, although likely more complicated way, to generate coordinates for most 3D shapes.

10.3 Tessellated Models

Most real-world models are composed of complexes of triangles with shared vertices. These are usually known as *triangular meshes* or *triangular irregular networks* (TINs). Most graphics programs need to make these models without using too much storage, and able to handle texture-maps.

A simple triangular mesh is shown in Figure 10.9. You could store these three triangles as independent entities, and thus store point $\mathbf{p}_1$ three times, and the other vertices twice each for a total of nine stored points (three vertices for each of three triangles), or you could try to somehow share the common vertices and store only four. So instead of

class triangle
material m
vector3 $\mathbf{p}_0$, $\mathbf{p}_1$, $\mathbf{p}_2$

you would have two classes:

class mesh
material m
array of vector3 vertices

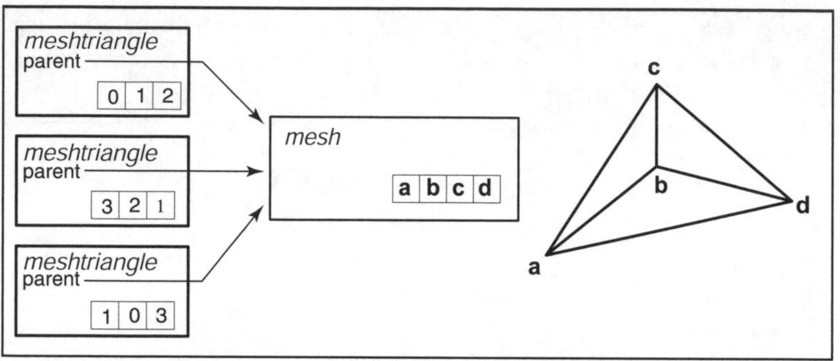

Figure 10.9. A three triangle mesh with four vertices.

and

class meshtriangle
pointer to mesh meshptr
int i_0, i_1, i_2

where i_0, i_1, and i_2 are indices into the *vertices* array. Either the triangle class or the mesh class will work. Is there a space advantage for the mesh class? Typically, a large mesh has each vertex being stored by about six triangles, although there can be any number for extreme cases. This means about two triangles for each shared vertex. If you have n triangles, then there are about $n/2$ vertices in the shared case and $3n$ in the unshared case. But, when you share, you need an additional $3n$ integers and n pointers. Since you don't have to store the material in each mesh triangle, that saves n pointers, which cancels out the storage for *meshptr*. If we assume that the data for floats, pointers, and ints all require the same storage (a dubious assumption), the triangles will take $10n$ storage units and the mesh will take $5.5n$ storage units. So the mesh reduces the storage by about a factor of two; this seems to hold for most implementations. Is this factor of two worth the complication? I think the answer is yes as soon as you start adding "properties" to the vertices.

Each vertex can have material parameters, texture coordinates, irradiances, and essentially any parameter that a renderer might use. In practice, these parameters are bilinearly interpolated across the triangle. So, if a triangle is intersected at barycentric coordinates (β, γ), you interpolate the (u, v) coordinates the same way you interpolate points. Recall that the point at barycentric coordinate (β, γ) is:

$$\mathbf{p}(\beta, \gamma) = \mathbf{a} + \beta(\mathbf{b} - \mathbf{a}) + \gamma(\mathbf{c} - \mathbf{a}).$$

A similar equation applies for (u, v):

$$u(\beta, \gamma) = u_a + \beta(u_b - u_a) + \gamma(u_c - u_a),$$
$$v(\beta, \gamma) = v_a + \beta(v_b - v_a) + \gamma(v_c - v_a.$$

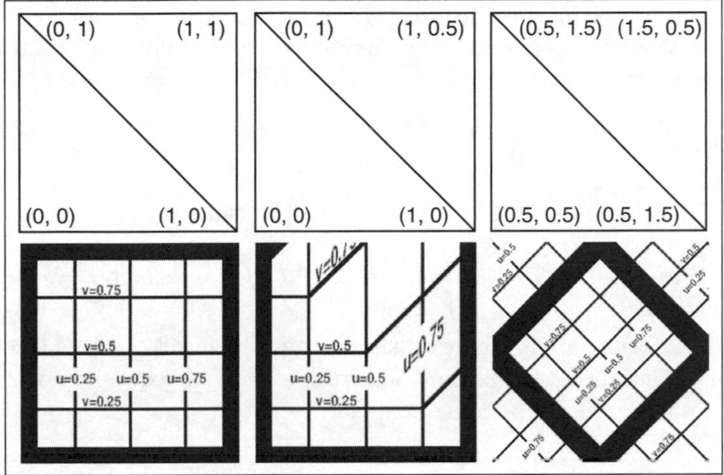

Figure 10.10. Various mesh textures obtained by changing (*u*,*v*) coordinates stored at vertices.

Several ways a texture can be applied by changing the (u, v) at triangle vertices are shown in Figure 10.10. This sort of calibration texture map makes it easier to understand the texture coordinates of your objects during debugging (Figure 10.11).

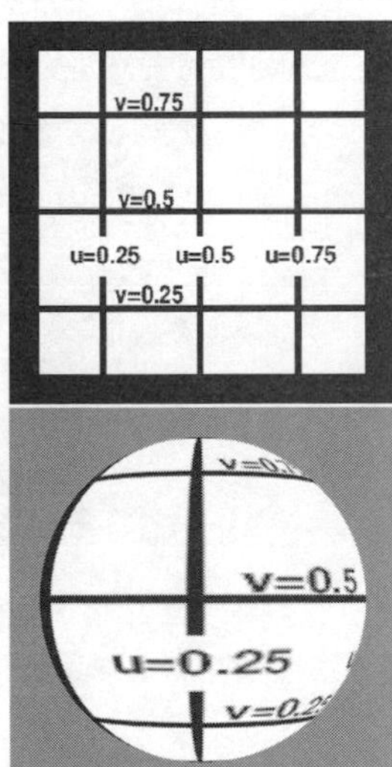

Figure 10.11. Top: a calibration texture map. Bottom: the sphere viewed along the *y* axis.

10.4 Texture Mapping for Rasterized Triangles

We would like to get the same texture images whether we use a ray tracing program or a rasterization method, such as a z-buffer. There are some subtleties in achieving this with correct-looking perspective, but we can address this at the rasterization stage. The reason things are not straightforward is that just interpolating texture coordinates in screen space results in incorrect images, as shown for the grid texture shown in Figure 10.12. Because things in perspective get smaller as the distance to the viewer increases, the lines that are evenly spaced in 3D should compress in 2D image space. More careful interpolation of texture coordinates is needed to accomplish this.

10.4.1 Perspective Correct Textures

We can implement texture mapping on triangles by interpolating the (u, v) coordinates, modifying the rasterization method of Section 3.6, but this results in the problem shown at the right of Figure 10.12. A similar problem occurs for triangles if screen-space barycentric coordinates are used as in the following rasterization code:

for *all* x **do**
  for *all* y **do**
    compute (α, β, γ) *for* (x, y)
    if $\alpha \in (0,1)$ *and* $\beta \in (0,1)$ *and* $\gamma \in (0,1)$ **then**
      $\mathbf{t} = \alpha\mathbf{t}_0 + \beta\mathbf{t}_1 + \gamma\mathbf{t}_2$
      drawpixel (x, y) *with color texture*$(\mathbf{t})$ *for a solid texture or with texture*(β, γ) *for a 2D texture.*

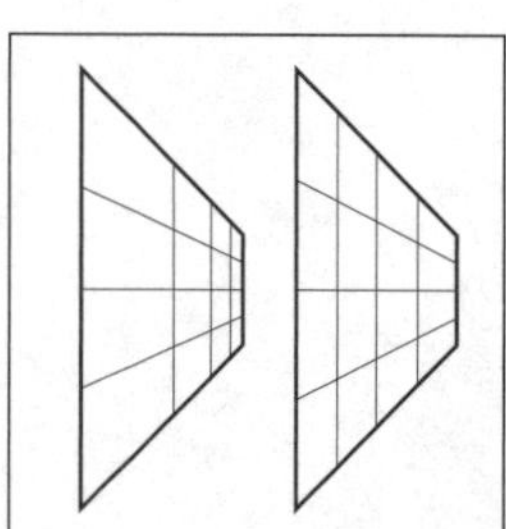

Figure 10.12. Left: correct perspective. Right: interpolation in screen space.

This code will generate images, but there is a problem. To unravel the basic problem, let's consider the progression from world-space $\mathbf{q}$ to homogeneous point $\mathbf{r}$ to homogenized point $\mathbf{s}$:

$$\begin{bmatrix} x_q \\ y_q \\ z_q \\ 1 \end{bmatrix} \xrightarrow{\text{transform}} \begin{bmatrix} x_r \\ y_r \\ z_r \\ h_r \end{bmatrix} \xrightarrow{\text{homogenize}} \begin{bmatrix} x_r/h_r \\ y_r/h_r \\ z_r/h_r \\ 1 \end{bmatrix} \equiv \begin{bmatrix} x_s \\ y_s \\ z_s \\ 1 \end{bmatrix}$$

If we use screen space, we are interpolating in $\mathbf{s}$. However, we would like to be interpolating in space $\mathbf{q}$ or $\mathbf{r}$, where the homogeneous division has not yet non-linearly distorted the barycentric coordinates of the triangle.

The key observation is that $1/h_r$ is interpolated with no distortion. Likewise, so is u/h_r and v/h_r. In fact, so is k/h_r, where k is any quantity that varies linearly across the triangle. Recall from Section 6.4 that if we transform all points along the line segment between points $\mathbf{q}$ and $\mathbf{Q}$ and homogenize, we have:

$$\mathbf{s} + \frac{h_R t}{h_r + t(h_R - h_r)}(\mathbf{S} - \mathbf{s}),$$

but if we linearly interpolate in the homogenized space we have:

$$\mathbf{s} + a(\mathbf{S} - \mathbf{s}).$$

Although those lines sweep out the same points, typically $a \neq t$ for the same points on the line segment. However, if we interpolate $1/h$, we *do* get the same answer regardless of which space we interpolate in. To see this is true, confirm that (Exercise 2):

$$\frac{1}{h_r} + \frac{h_R t}{h_r + t(h_R - h_r)}\left(\frac{1}{h_R} - \frac{1}{h_r}\right) = \frac{1}{h_r} + t\left(\frac{1}{h_R} - \frac{1}{h_r}\right) \qquad (10.4)$$

This ability to interpolate $1/h$ linearly with no error in the transformed space allows us to correctly texture triangles. Perhaps the least confusing way to deal with this distortion is to compute the world space barycentric coordinates of the triangle (β_w, γ_w) in terms of screen space coordinates (β, γ). We note that β_s/h and γ_s/h can be interpolated linearly in screen space. For example, at the screen space position associated with screen space barycentric coordinates (β, γ), we can interpolate β_w/h without distortion. Because $\beta_w = 0$ at vertex 0 and vertex 2, and $\beta_w = 1$ at vertex 1, we have:

$$\frac{\beta_s}{h} = \frac{0}{h_0} + \beta\left(\frac{1}{h_1} - \frac{0}{h_0}\right) + \gamma\left(\frac{0}{h_2} - \frac{0}{h_0}\right). \tag{10.5}$$

Because of all the zero terms, Equation 10.5 is fairly simple. However, to get β_w from it, we must know h. Because we know $1/h$ is linear in screen space, we have:

$$\frac{1}{h} = \frac{1}{h_0} + \beta\left(\frac{1}{h_1} - \frac{1}{h_0}\right) + \gamma\left(\frac{1}{h_2} - \frac{1}{h_0}\right). \tag{10.6}$$

Dividing Equation 10.5 by Equation 10.6 gives:

$$\beta_w = \frac{\frac{\beta}{h_1}}{\frac{1}{h_0} + \beta\left(\frac{1}{h_1} - \frac{1}{h_0}\right) + \gamma\left(\frac{1}{h_2} - \frac{1}{h_0}\right)}.$$

Multiplying numerator and denominator by $h_0 h_1 h_2$ and doing a similar set of manipulations for the analogous equations in γ_w gives:

$$\begin{aligned}\beta_w &= \frac{h_0 h_2 \beta}{h_1 h_2 + h_2\beta(h_0 - h_1) + h_1\gamma(h_0 - h_2)}\\ \gamma_w &= \frac{h_0 h_1 \gamma}{h_1 h_2 + h_2\beta(h_0 - h_1) + h_1\gamma(h_0 - h_2)}\end{aligned} \tag{10.7}$$

Note that the two denominators are the same.

For triangles that use the perspective matrix from Chapter 6, recall that $w = z/n$ where z is the distance from the viewer perpendicular to the screen. Thus, for that matrix $1/z$ also varies linearly. We can use this fact to modify our scan-conversion code for three points $\mathbf{t}_i = (x_i, y_i, z_i, h_i)$ that have been passed through the viewing matrices, but have not been homogenized:

```
Compute bounds for x = x_i/h_i and y = y_i/h_i
for all x do
  for all y do
    compute (α, β, γ) for (x, y)
    if (α ∈ [0, 1] and β ∈ [0, 1] and γ ∈ [0, 1]) then
      d = h_1 h_2 + h_2 β(h_0 − h_1) + h_1 γ(h_0 − h_2)
      β_w = h_0 h_2 β/d
```

$\gamma_w = h_0 h_1 \gamma / d$
$\alpha_w = 1 - \beta_w - \gamma_w$
$u = \alpha_w u_0 + \beta_w u_1 + \gamma_w u_2$
$v = \alpha_w v_0 + \beta_w v_1 + \gamma_w v_2$
drawpixel (x, y) *with color texture*(u, v)

For solid textures, just recall that by the definition of barycentric coordinates:

$$\mathbf{p} = (1 - \beta_w - \gamma_w)\mathbf{p}_0 + \beta_w \mathbf{p}_1 + \gamma_w \mathbf{p}_2,$$

where $\mathbf{p}_i$ are the world space vertices. Then, just call a solid texture routine for point $\mathbf{p}$.

10.5 Bump Textures

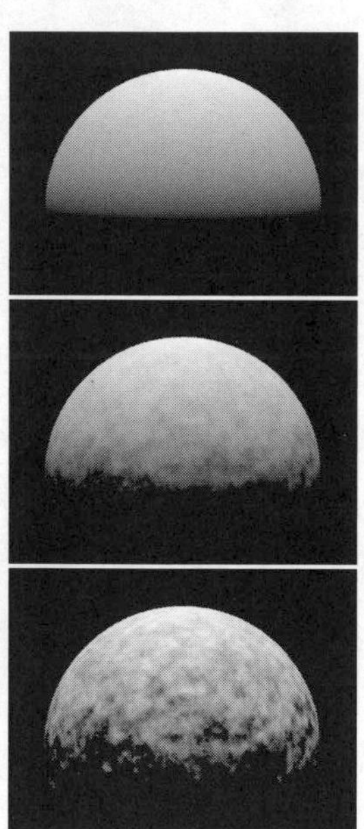

Figure 10.13. Vector turbulence on a sphere of radius 1.6. Lighting directly from above. Top: $k_1 = 0$. Middle: $k_1 = 0.08$, $k_2 = 8$. Bottom: $k_1 = 0.24$, k_2=8.

Although, so far, we have only discussed changing reflectance using texture, you can also change the surface normal to give an illusion of fine-scale geometry on the surface. We can apply a *bump map* which perturbs the surface normal. One way to do this is:

vector3 $n =$ *surfaceNormal*(x)
$n+ = k_1 * vectorTurbulence(k_2 * x)))/w)/2$
return $t * s0 + (1 - t) * s1$

This is shown in Figure 10.13.

To implement *vectorTurbulence*, we first need *vectorNoise* which produces a simple spatially-varying 3D vector:

$$n_v(x, y, z) = \sum_{i=\lfloor x \rfloor}^{\lfloor x \rfloor + 1} \sum_{j=\lfloor y \rfloor}^{\lfloor y \rfloor + 1} \sum_{k=\lfloor z \rfloor}^{\lfloor z \rfloor + 1} \Gamma_{ijk} \omega(x) \omega(y) \omega(z)$$

Then, *vectorTurbulence* is a direct analog of *turbulence*: sum a series of scaled versions of *vectorNoise*.

10.6 Displacement Mapping

One problem with Figure 10.13 is that the bumps neither cast shadows nor affect the silhouette of the object. These limitations occur, because we are not really changing any geometry. If we want more realism, we can apply a *displacement map*. A displacement map actually changes the geometry using a texture. A common simplification is that the displacement will be in the direction of the surface normal.

If we take all points $\mathbf{p}$ on a surface, with associated surface normal vectors $\mathbf{n}$, then we can make a new surface using a 3D texture $d(\mathbf{p})$:

$$\mathbf{p}' = \mathbf{p} + f(\mathbf{p})\mathbf{n}.$$

This concept is shown in Figure 10.14.

Displacement mapping is straightforward to implement in a z-buffer code by storing the surface to be displaced as a fine mesh of many triangles. Each vertex in the mesh can then be displaced along the normal vector direction. This results in large models, but it is quite robust.

10.7 Environment Maps

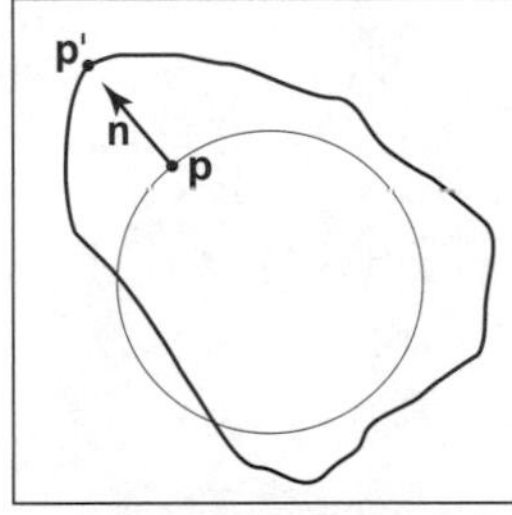

Figure 10.14. The points $\mathbf{p}$ on the circle are each displaced in the direction of $\mathbf{n}$ by the function $f(\mathbf{p})$. If f is continuous, then the resulting points $\mathbf{p}'$ form a continuous surface.

Often we would like to have a texture-mapped background and for objects to have specular reflections of that background. This can be accomplished using *environment maps* An environment map can be implemented as a background function that takes in a viewing direction $\mathbf{b}$ and returns an RGB color from a texture map. There are many ways to store environment maps. For example, we can use a spherical table indexed by spherical coordinates. In this section, we will instead describe a cube-based table with six square texture maps often called a *cube map.*

The basic idea of a cube map is that we have an infinitely large cube with a texture on each face. Because the cube is large, the origin of a ray does not change what the ray "sees." This is equivalent to an arbitrarily-sized cube that is queried by a ray whose origin is at the Cartesian origin. As an example of how a given direction $\mathbf{b}$ is converted to (u, v) coordinates, consider the right face of Figure 10.15. Here we have x_b as the maximum magnitude component. In that case, we can compute (u, v) for that texture to be:

$$u = \frac{y + x}{2x}$$
$$v = \frac{z + x}{2x}$$

There are analogous formulas for the other five faces.

So for any reflection ray $\mathbf{a} + t\mathbf{b}$ we return $cubemmap(\mathbf{b})$ for the background color. In a z-buffer implementation, we need to perform this calculation on a pixel-by-pixel basis. If at a given pixel we know the viewing direction $\mathbf{c}$ and the surface normal vector $\mathbf{n}$, we can compute the reflected direction $\mathbf{b}$ (Figure 10.16). We can do this by modifying Equation 8.6 to get:

$$\mathbf{b} = -\mathbf{c} + \frac{2(\mathbf{c} \cdot \mathbf{n})\mathbf{n}}{\|\mathbf{c}\|^2}, \tag{10.8}$$

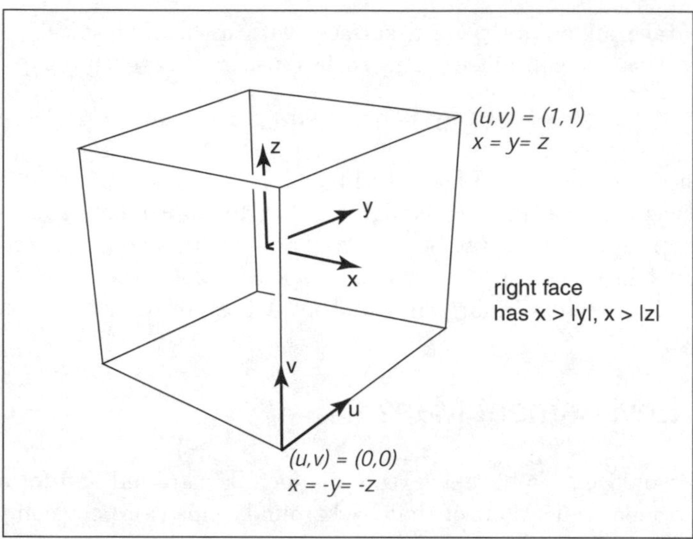

Figure 10.15. The cubemap has six axis-aligned textures that store the background. The right face contains a single texture.

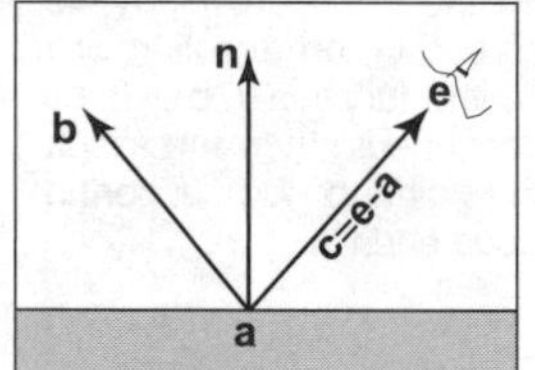

Figure 10.16. The vector **b** is the reflection of vector **c** with respect to the surface normal **n**.

Here the denomonator of the fraction accounts for the fact that **c** may not be a unit vector. Because we need to know **b** at each pixel, we can either compute **b** at each triangle vertex and interpolate **b** in a perspective correct manner, or we can interpolate **n** and compute **b** for each pixel. This will allow us to call *cubemmap*(**b**) at each pixel.

10.8 Shadow Maps

The basic observation to be made about a shadow map is that if we rendered the scene using the location of a light source as the eye, the visible surfaces would all be lit, and the hidden surfaces would all be in shadow. This can be used to determine whether a point being rasterized is in shadow. First, we rasterize the scene from the point of view of the light source using matrix $\mathbf{M}_s$. This matrix is just the same as the full transform matrix $\mathbf{M}$ used for viewing in Section 6.3, but it uses the light position for the eye, and the light's main direction for the view-plane-normal.

Recall that the matrix $\mathbf{M}$ takes an (x, y, z) in world coordinates and converts it to an (x', y', z') in relation to the screen. While rasterizing in a perspectively correct manner, we can get the (x, y, z) that is seen through the center of each pixel. If we also rasterize that point using $\mathbf{M}_s$ and round the resulting x and y coordinates, we will get:

$$(i, j, \text{depth})$$

We can compare this depth with the z value in the shadow depth map at pixel (i, j). If it is the same, then the point is lit, and otherwise it is in shadow. Because of computational innacuracies, we should actually test whether the points are the same to within a small constant.

Because we typically don't want the light to only be within a square window, often a *spot light* is used. This attenuates the value of the light source based on closeness to the sides of the shadow buffer. For example, if the shadow buffer is n by n pixels, then for pixel (i, j) in the shadow buffer, we can apply the attenuation coefficient based on the fractional radius r:

$$r = \sqrt{\left(\frac{2i - n}{n}\right)^2 + \left(\frac{2j - n}{n}\right)^2}$$

Any radially decreasing function will then give a spot-like look.

Frequently Asked Questions

• How do I implement displacement mapping in ray tracing?

There is no ideal way to do it. Generating all the triangles is probably the best method, and caching the geometry when necessary will prevent memory overload.

• Why don't my images with textures look realistic?

Humans are good at seeing small imperfections in surfaces. Geometric imperfections are typically absent in computer-generated images that use texture maps for details, so they look "too smooth."

• My textured animations look bad when there are many texels visible inside a pixel. What should I do?

The problem is that the texture resolution is too high for that image. We would like a smaller down-sampled version of the texture. However, if we move closer, such a down-sampled texture would look too blurry. What we really need is to be able to dynamically choose the texture resolution based on viewing conditions so that about one texel is visible through each pixel. A common way to do that is to use *MIP-mapping.* That technique establishes a multi-resolution set of textures and chooses one of the textures for each polygon or pixel. Typically the resolutions vary by a factor of two, e.g., 512^2, 256^2, 128^2, etc.

Notes

Solid texture with noise was introduced in separate papers by Perlin and Lewis at SIGGRAPH 85. The paper *Hypertexture* (Perlin, SIGGRAPH, 1989) was used for the noise algorithm in this chapter. Perlin won a technical Academy Award for his work on solid procedural textures. Texture mapping was introduced in *Texture and Reflection in Computer Generated Images* (Blinn and Newell, Communications of the ACM, October, 1976). The discussion of perpective-correct textures is based on *Fast Shadows and Lighting Effects Using Texture Mapping* (Segal, Korobkin and van Widenfelt, SIGGRAPH, 1992) and on *3D Game Engine Design* (Eberly, Morgan-Kaufmann, 2000).

Exercises

1. Find several ways to implement an infinite 2D checkerboard using surface and solid techniques. Which is best?
2. Verify that Equation 10.4 is a valid equality using brute-force algebra.
3. How could you implement solid texturing by using the z-buffer depth and a matrix transform?

11

A Full Graphics Pipeline

So far we have covered how to rasterize triangles and how to use transformation matrices and z-buffers/BSP-trees to create perspective views of 3D triangles. Although this is the core of most modern graphics systems, there are a number of details that must be addressed before our system is complete. We have not yet addressed the case where some or all of a triangle is outside the view-volume; this is handled by a process called "clipping;" parts of triangles outside the view-volume are cut away (clipped). The other important details in this chapter are related to improving efficiency and appearance in a graphics pipeline.

11.1 Clipping

A common operation in graphics is *clipping*, where one geometric entity "cuts" another. For example, if you clip a triangle against the plane $x = 0$, the plane cuts the triangle. In most application of clipping, the portion of the triangle on the "wrong" side of the plane is discarded. Here the wrong side is whichever side is specified by the details of the application. This operation for a single plane is shown in Figure 11.1. This section discusses the basic implementation of a clipping module. Those interested in implementing an industrial-speed clipper should see the book by Blinn mentioned in the notes at the end of this chapter.

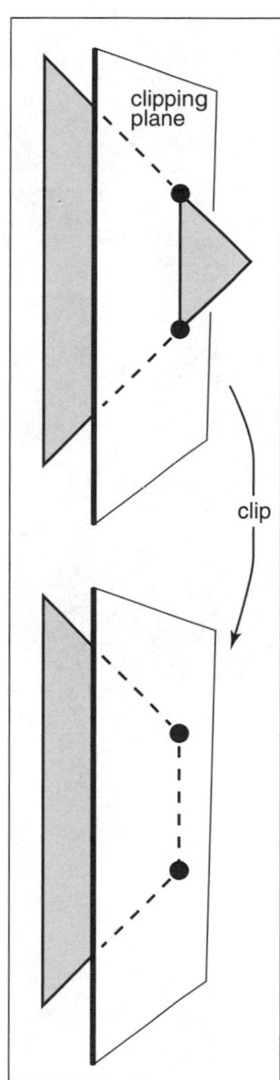

Figure 11.1. A polygon is clipped against a clipping plane. The portion"inside" the plane is retained.

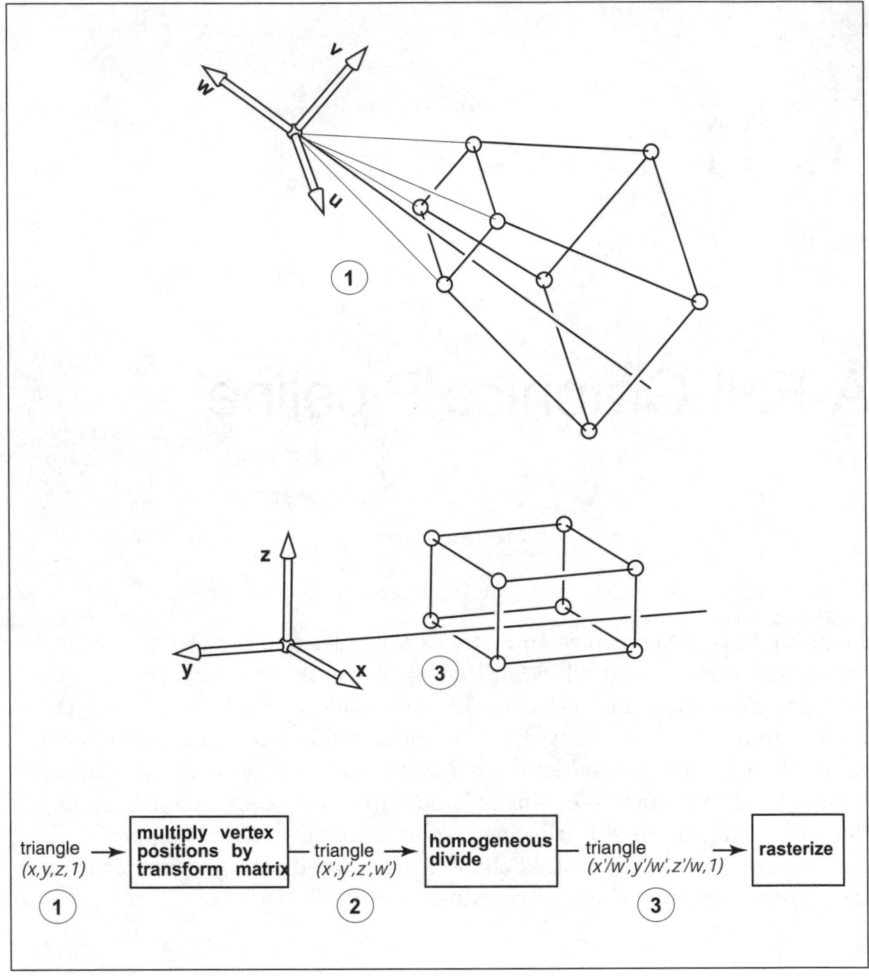

Figure 11.2. A bare-bones graphics pipeline with three possibilities for where to do clipping. The geometry associated with Options 1 and 3 are illustrated above the pipeline. The geometry associated with Option 2 is four-dimensional and thus too hard to depict.

11.2 Location of Clipping Segment of the Pipeline

The basic graphics pipeline takes triangles with vertices in world coordinates and:

- multiplies each vertex by a transformation matrix,
- divides each component of the vertex by its homogeneous coordinate,
- rasterizes the triangle.

The big question for clipping is where in the pipeline to do it. The possible locations are shown in Figure 11.2, they are:

1. in world coordinates using the six planes that bound the truncated viewing pyramid,
2. in the 4D transformed space before the homogeneous divide,
3. in the transformed 3D space with respect to the six axis-aligned planes.

Any of the possibilities can be effectively implemented as discussed by Blinn (see the chapter notes). For all of them, the triangle-based implementation for a single triangle is:

for *each of six planes* ***do***
  if *(triangle entirely outside of plane)* ***then***
    break (triangle is not visible)
  else if *triangle spans plane* ***then***
    clip triangle
    if *(quadrilateral is left)* ***then***
      break into two triangle

The only question is which six planes to use at what stage of the pipeline.

11.2.1 Clipping After the Perspective Divide (Option 3)

At first glance, it seems that Option 3 is the easiest to implement and the most efficient. The six plane equations are simple and efficient to evaluate:

$$
\begin{aligned}
-x + l &= 0 \\
x - r &= 0 \\
-y + b &= 0 \\
y - t &= 0 \\
-z + n &= 0 \\
z - f &= 0
\end{aligned}
$$

These plane equations are set up to be positive for any point outside the view volume. However, Option 3 is in fact the most problematic for a subtle reason (see Figure 11.3). Although the perspective transform does preserve depth-order for depths greater than zero, it has a discontinuity at zero depth. Recall the actual transform after the homogeneous divide:

$$z' = n + f - \frac{fn}{z}.$$

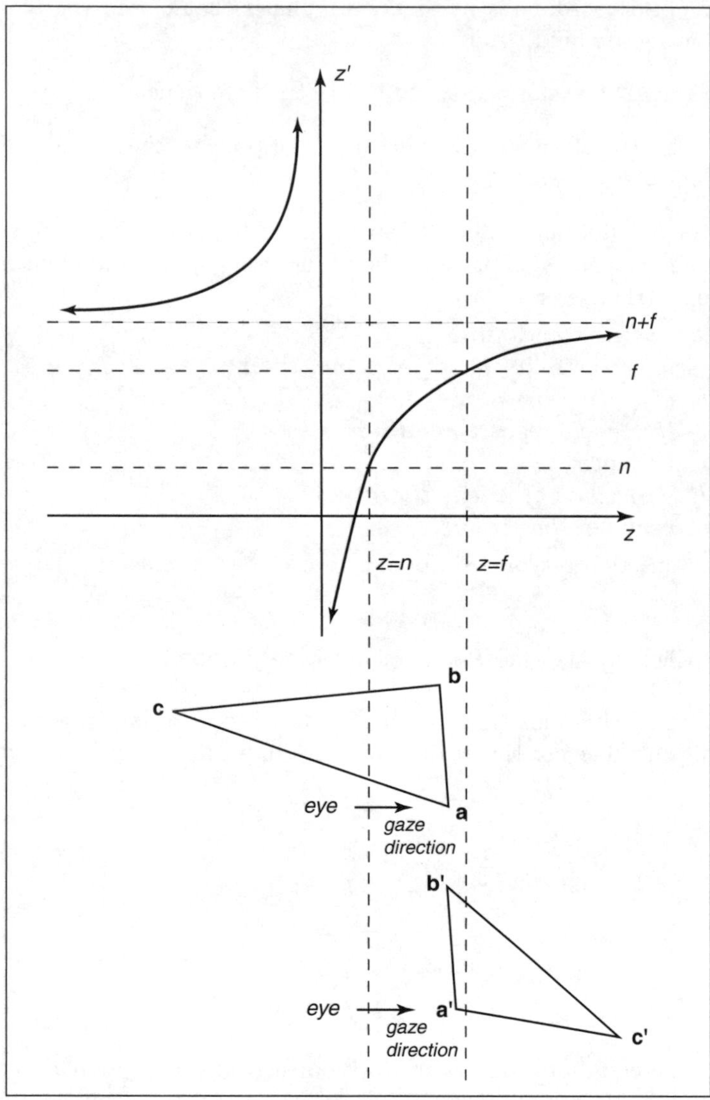

Figure 11.3. The depth z is transformed to the depth z' by the perspective transform. Note that when z moves from positive to negative, z' switches from negative to positive. Thus vertices behind the eye are moved in front of the eye beyond $z' = n + f$. This can make clipping complicated, for example, for the triangle shown.

11.2.2 Clipping Before the Transform (Option 1)

Option 1 has a straightforward implementation. The only question is, "What are the six plane equations?" Because these equations are the same for all triangles rendered in the single image, we do not need to compute them very efficiently. For this reason, we can just invert the transform shown in Figure 5.11 and apply it to the eight vertices of the transformed view volume:

$$
\begin{aligned}
(x, y, z) = &(l, b, n)\\
&(r, b, n)\\
&(l, t, n)\\
&(r, t, n)\\
&(l, b, f)\\
&(r, b, f)\\
&(l, t, f)\\
&(r, t, f)
\end{aligned}
$$

The plane equations can be inferred from here. Alternatively, we can use vector geometry to get the planes directly from the viewing parameters.

11.2.3 Clipping in Homogeneous Coordinates (Option 2)

Surprisingly, the option usually implemented is that of clipping in homogeneous coordinates before the divide. Here the view volume is 4D and it is bounded by 3D volumes (hyperplanes). These are:

$$
\begin{aligned}
-x + lw &= 0\\
x - rw &= 0\\
-y + bw &= 0\\
y - tw &= 0\\
-z + nw &= 0\\
z - fw &= 0
\end{aligned}
$$

These planes are quite simple, so the efficiency is better than for Option 1. They still can be improved by transforming the view-volume $[l, r] \times [b, t] \times [n, f]$ to $[0, 1]^3$. It turns out that the clipping of the triangles is not much more complicated than in 3D.

11.2.4 Clipping Against a Plane

No matter which option we choose, we must clip against a plane. Recall from Section 2.7.2 that the implicit equation for a plane through point $\mathbf{q}$ with normal $\mathbf{n}$ is:

$$f(\mathbf{p}) = \mathbf{n} \cdot (\mathbf{p} - \mathbf{q}) = 0.$$

This is often written

$$f(\mathbf{p}) = \mathbf{n} \cdot \mathbf{p} + D = 0. \tag{11.1}$$

Interestingly, this equation not only describes a 3D plane, but it also describes a line in 2D and the volume analog of a plane in 4D. All of these entities are usually called planes in their appropriate dimension.

If we have a line segment between points $\mathbf{a}$ and $\mathbf{b}$, we can "clip" it against a plane using the techniques for cutting the edges of 3D triangles in BSP tree programs described in Section 7.1.3. Here, the points $\mathbf{a}$ and $\mathbf{b}$ are tested to determine whether they are on opposite sides of the plane $f(\mathbf{p}) = 0$ by checking whether $f(\mathbf{a})$ and $f(\mathbf{b})$ have different signs. Typically $f(\mathbf{p}) < 0$ is defined to be "inside" the plane, and $f(\mathbf{p}) < 0$ is "outside" the plane. If the plane does split the line, then we can solve for the intersection point by substituting the equation for the parametric line:

$$\mathbf{p} = \mathbf{a} + t(\mathbf{b} - \mathbf{a}),$$

into the $f(\mathbf{p}) = 0$ plane of Equation 11.1. This yields:

$$\mathbf{n} \cdot (\mathbf{a} + t(\mathbf{b} - \mathbf{a})) + D = 0.$$

Solving for t gives:

$$t = \frac{\mathbf{n} \cdot \mathbf{a} + D}{\mathbf{n} \cdot (\mathbf{a} - \mathbf{b})}.$$

We can then find the intersection point and "shorten" the line.

To clip a triangle, we again can follow Section 7.1.3 to produce one or two triangles .

11.3 An Expanded Graphics Pipeline

A full graphics pipeline typically adds shading and some efficiency modes to make a full system. These pipelines are usually optimized to render large numbers of small triangles. This section discusses several issues which must be handled in the pipeline.

11.3.1 Culling

When the entire triangle lies outside the view volume, it can be *culled*, i.e., eliminated from the pipeline. In practice, perfect culling is more expensive than letting the clipping module eliminate the object. Culling is especially helpful when many triangles are grouped into an object with an associated bounding volume. If the bounding volume lies outside the view volume, then so do all the triangles that make up the object. For example, if we have 1000 triangles bounded by a single sphere with center $\mathbf{c}$ and radius r, we can check whether the sphere lies outside the clipping plane

$$(\mathbf{p} - \mathbf{a}) \cdot \mathbf{n} = 0,$$

where $\mathbf{a}$ is a point on the plane, and $\mathbf{p}$ is a variable. This is equivalent to checking whether the signed distance from the center of the sphere $\mathbf{c}$ to the plane is greater than $+r$. This amounts to the check:

$$\frac{(\mathbf{c} - \mathbf{a}) \cdot \mathbf{n}}{\|\mathbf{n}\|} > r.$$

Note that the sphere may overlap the plane even in a case where all the triangles do lie outside the plane. Thus, this is a conservative test. How conservative the test is depends on how well the sphere bounds the object.

11.3.2 Lighting and Shading

Lighting and shading must be placed somewhere in the pipeline. Traditionally, lighting has been done at vertices early in the pipeline, and pixels between the vertices have their colors set using barycentric interpolation at the rasterization stage. However, if normal interpolation is used at the rasterization stage, then it makes more sense to defer lighting until the rasterization stage. This is the trend in most modern pipelines.

11.4 Backface Elimination

When polygonal models are closed, i.e., they bound a closed space with no holes, then they are often assumed to have outward facing normal vectors as discussed in Chapter 8. For such models, the polygons that face away from the eye are certain to be overdrawn by polygons that face the eye. Thus, those polygons can be culled before the pipeline even starts. The test for this condition is the same one used for silhouette drawing given in Section 8.3.1.

11.5 Triangle Strips and Fans

Two fundamental primitives associated with most modern graphics pipelines are *triangle strips* and *triangle fans.*

A triangle fan is shown in Figure 11.4. In a simple triangle-drawing pipeline, the needed calls would be

draw $(\mathbf{p}_0, \mathbf{p}_1, \mathbf{p}_2)$
draw $(\mathbf{p}_0, \mathbf{p}_2, \mathbf{p}_3)$
draw $(\mathbf{p}_0, \mathbf{p}_3, \mathbf{p}_4)$
draw $(\mathbf{p}_0, \mathbf{p}_4, \mathbf{p}_5)$

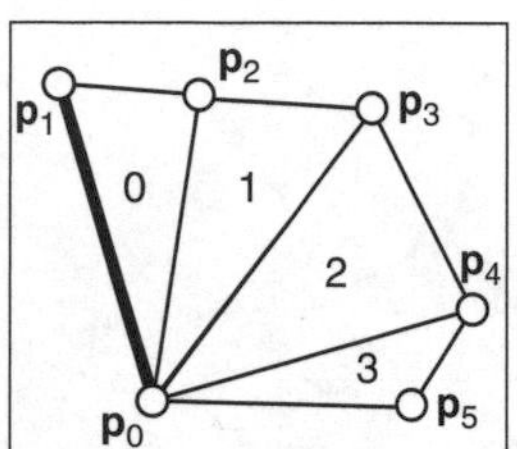

Figure 11.4. A triangle fan.

Note that this requires twelve vertices to pass through the pipeline, although there are only six distinct vertices. The triangle fan assumes an axis vertex and a series of other vertices being swept out like the ends of a collapsible fan. This function call is something like:

triangle-fan $(\mathbf{p}_0, \mathbf{p}_1, \mathbf{p}_2, \mathbf{p}_3, \mathbf{p}_4, \mathbf{p}_5)$

The first vertex is assumed to be the axis. Often the API will have a function call for each vertex so that a variable number of arguments in not required in the call.

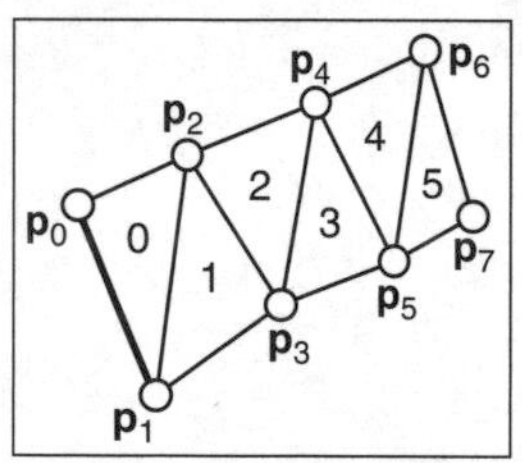

Figure 11.5. A triangle strip.

The triangle strip is a similar concept, but it is designed for more traditional meshes. Here, vertices are added alternating top and bottom in a linear strip as shown in Figure 11.5. Long triangle strips will save approximately a factor of three if the program is vertex-bound.

It might seem that triangle strips are only useful if the strips are long. However, that is not the case. If the runtime is proportional to the number of vertices transferred the savings are as follows:

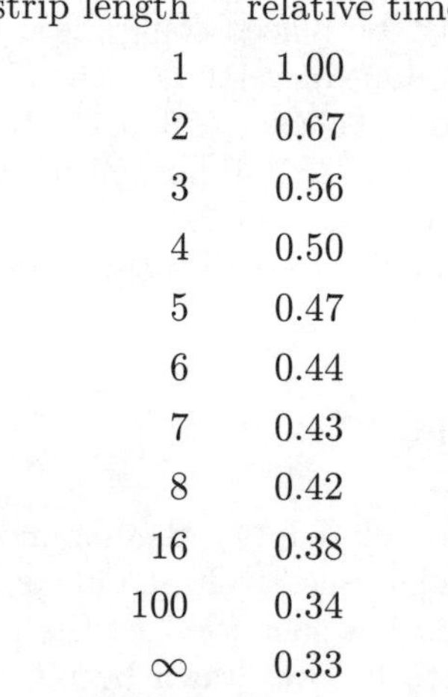

strip length	relative time
1	1.00
2	0.67
3	0.56
4	0.50
5	0.47
6	0.44
7	0.43
8	0.42
16	0.38
100	0.34
∞	0.33

So, in fact, there is a rather rapid diminishing return as the strips grow longer. Thus, even for an unstructured mesh, it is worthwhile to use some greedy algorithm to gather them into short strips.

11.6 Preserved State

When processing vertices for scan conversion and lighting, it is necessary to know the shading mode, e.g., is lighting on or off. In addition, it is necessary to know the color and/or material properties of each vertex. Many APIs support the ability to share such state information across triangles. For example, a simple implementation that does not share state information might have the calls:

set-triangle-attributes T_1
draw-triangle T_1
set-triangle-attributes T_2
draw-triangle T_2

Here both T_1 and T_2 are processed through the graphics pipeline each with its own set of attributes, such as vertex color. Instead, in APIs/hardware that support the sharing feature, we can set the state for all triangles going through the pipeline:

set-state-triangle-attributes
draw-triangle T_1
draw-triangle T_2

Here both triangles are drawn with the same attributes. This can result in a considerable efficiency increase on some hardware.

Another state that can be saved is the geometry itself. This is useful in applications where a significant fraction of the geometry does not change from frame to frame. The geometry is saved in a *display list.* This can result in increased efficiency for two reasons. First, if the hardware allows, the display list can live on the graphics board and does not need to be transferred across the bus from main memory to the graphics board each frame. Second, the list can be optimized to improve performance. For example, triangles that share the same vertex/shading properties can be grouped so that they can live within the same set of calls with shared attributes.

11.7 A Full Graphics Pipeline

As mentioned in the clipping section, the pipeline can be arranged in a number of ways. The modern trend seems to be to move shading to the rasterization stage because better visual quality results. Such a pipeline is shown in Figure 11.6.

A number of other issues must be addressed in a full pipeline that the programmer should be somewhat aware of when efficiency lapses. Otherwise they are principally in the domain of hardware designers. These include:

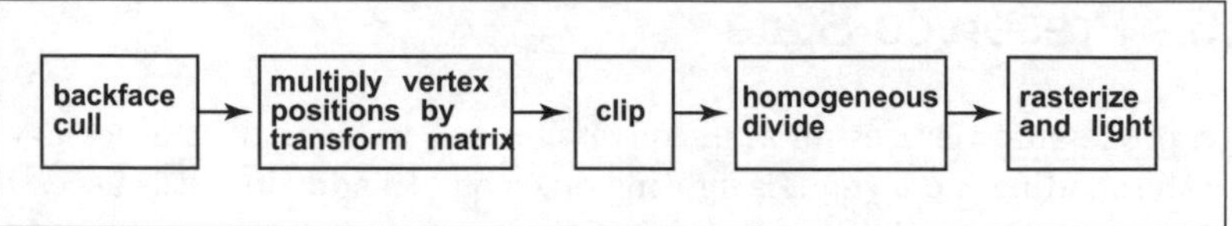

Figure 11.6. A full graphics pipeline. Polygons enter at the left and pass one by one through each stage of the pipeline.

- Are polygons rasterized directly in the pipeline or are they triangulated at the beginning of the pipeline?

- How are textures handled? Are they stored at multiple levels of detail (e.g., MIP-maps)? Is there a fixed-size texture memory?

Frequently Asked Questions

• I've often seen clipping discussed at length and it is a much more involved process than that described in this chapter. What is going on here?

The clipping described in this chapter works, but lacks optimizations that an industrial-strength clipper would have. These optimizations are discussed in detail in Blinn's definitive work listed in the chapter notes.

• The documentation for my API talks about "scene graphs" and "matrix stacks." Are these part of the graphics pipeline?

The graphics pipeline is certainly designed with these in mind, and whether we define them as part of the pipeline is a matter of taste. This book delays their discussion until the next chapter.

Notes

A wonderful book about designing a graphics pipeline is *Jim Blinn's Corner: A Trip Down the Graphics Pipeline* (Blinn, Morgan-Kaufmann, 1996). Many nice details of the pipeline and culling are in *3D Game Engine Design* (Eberly, Morgan-Kaufmann, 2000) and *Real-Time Rendering* (Möller and Haines, A K Peters, 1999).

Exercises

1. Suppose that in the perspective transform we have $n = 1$ and $f = 2$. Under what circumstances will we have a "reversal" where a vertex before and after the perspective transform flips from in front of to behind the eye or vice-versa?

2. Is there any reason not to clip in x and y after the perspective divide (see Figure 11.2, stage 3)?

Data Structures for Graphics

There are a variety of data structures that seem to pop up repeatedly in graphics applications. This chapter talks about three basic and unrelated data structures that are among the most common and useful. There are many variants of these data structures, but the basic ideas behind them can be conveyed using an example of each.

First the winged-edge data structure for storing tessellated geometric models is discussed. The winged-edge data structure is useful for managing models where the tessellation changes, such as in subdivision or simplification routines.

Next, the scene-graph data structure is presented. These are rapidly becoming well supported features of all new graphics APIs because they are so useful in managing objects and transformations.

Finally, the tiled multidimensional array is presented. Originally developed to help paging performance, such structures are now crucial for memory locality on machines regardless of whether the array fits in main memory.

12.1 Triangle Meshes

One of the most common model representations is a polygonal mesh as discussed in Section 10.3. When such meshes are unchanging in the program, the simple structure described in that section is usually sufficient. However, when the meshes are to be modified, more complicated data representations are needed to efficiently answer queries such as:

- given a triangle, what are the three adjacent triangles?
- given an edge, which two triangles share it?
- given a vertex, which faces share it?
- given a vertex, which edges share it?

There are many data structures for triangle meshes, polygonal meshes, and polygonal meshes with holes (see the notes at the end of the chapter for references). In many applications the meshes are very large, so an efficient representation can be crucial.

The most straightforward, though bloated, implementation is to have three types: *vertex*, *edge*, and *triangle*. There are a variety of ways to divide the data among these types. While one might be tempted to just store all the relationships, this makes for variable-length data structures that really are not needed. For example, a vertex can have an arbitrarily large number of edges incident to it.

It is best, therefore, to hide the implementation behind a class interface.

12.2 Winged-Edge Data Structure

We can use the class *winged-edge* data structure. This data structure makes edges the first-class citizen of the data structure. This data structure, a more efficient implementation, is illustrated in Figures 12.1 and 12.2.

Note that the winged-edge data structure makes the desired queries in constant time. For example, a face can access one of its edges and follow the

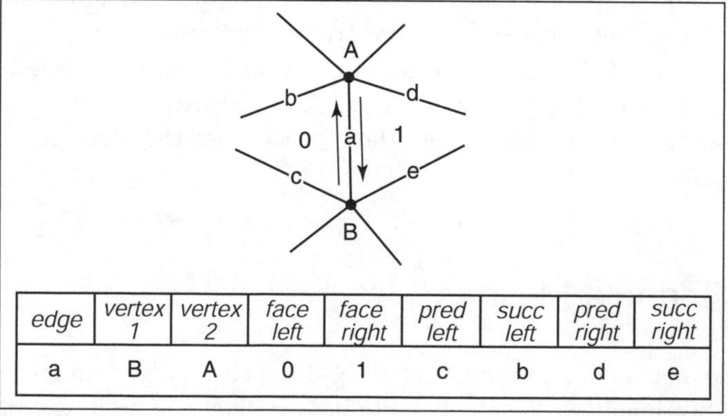

edge	vertex 1	vertex 2	face left	face right	pred left	succ left	pred right	succ right
a	B	A	0	1	c	b	d	e

Figure 12.1. An edge in a winged-edge data structure. Stored with each edge are the face (polygon) to the left of the edge, the face to the right of the edge, and the previous and successor edges in the traversal of each of those faces.

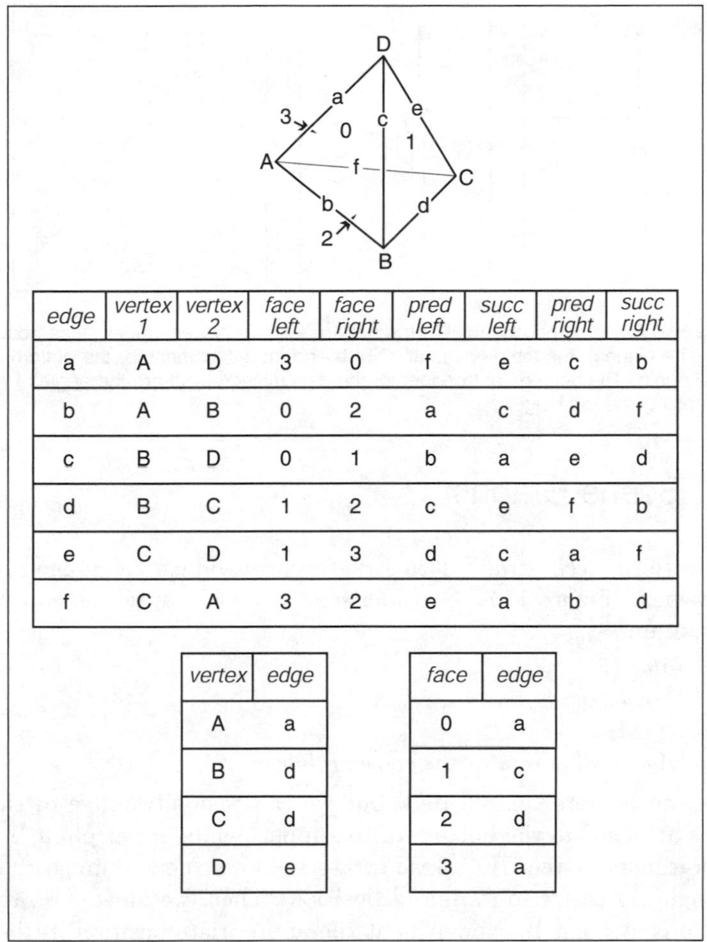

edge	vertex 1	vertex 2	face left	face right	pred left	succ left	pred right	succ right
a	A	D	3	0	f	e	c	b
b	A	B	0	2	a	c	d	f
c	B	D	0	1	b	a	e	d
d	B	C	1	2	c	e	f	b
e	C	D	1	3	d	c	a	f
f	C	A	3	2	e	a	b	d

vertex	edge
A	a
B	d
C	d
D	e

face	edge
0	a
1	c
2	d
3	a

Figure 12.2. A tetrahedron and the associated elements for a winged-edge data structure. The two small tables are not unique; each vertex and face stores any one of the edges with which it is associated.

traversal pointers to find all of its edges. Those edges store the adjoining face.

As with any data structure, the winged-edge data structure makes a variety of time/space trade-offs. For example, we could eliminate the *prev* references. When we need to know the previous edge, we could follow the successor edges in a circle until we get back to the original edge. This would save space, but it would make the computation of the previous edge take longer. This type of issue has led to a proliferation of mesh data structures (see the chapter notes for more information on those structures).

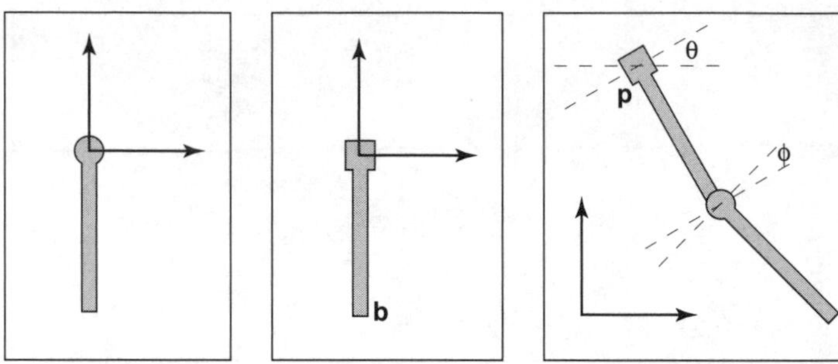

Figure 12.3. A hinged pendulum. On the left are the two pieces in their "local" coordinate systems. The hinge of the top piece is at point **b** and the attachment for the bottom piece is at its local origin. The degrees of freedom for the assembled object are the angles (θ,ϕ) and the location **p** of the top hinge.

12.3 Scene Graphs

To motivate the scene-graph data structure, we will use the hinged pendulum shown in Figure 12.3. Consider how we would draw the top part of the pendulum:

$\mathbf{M}_1 = \mathit{rotate}(\theta)$
$\mathbf{M}_2 = \mathit{translate}(\mathbf{p})$
$\mathbf{M}_3 = \mathbf{M}_2\mathbf{M}_1$
Apply $\mathbf{M}_3$ *to all points in upper pendulum*

The bottom is more complicated, but we can take advantage of the fact that it is attached to the bottom of the upper pendulum at point **b** in the local coordinate system. First, we rotate the lower pendulum so that it is at an angle ϕ relative to its initial position. Then, we move it so that its top hinge is at point **b**. Now it is at the appropriate position in the local coordinates of the upper pendulum, and it can then be moved along with that coordinate system. The composite transform for the lower pendulum is:

$\mathbf{M}_a = \mathit{rotate}(\phi)$
$\mathbf{M}_b = \mathit{translate}(\mathbf{b})$
$\mathbf{M}_c = \mathbf{M}_b\mathbf{M}_a$
$\mathbf{M}_d = \mathbf{M}_3\mathbf{M}_c$
Apply $\mathbf{M}_d$ *to all points in lower pendulum*

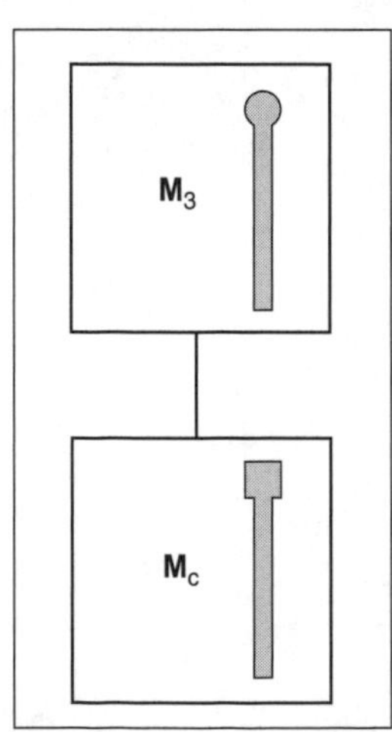

Figure 12.4. The scene-graph for the hinged pendulum of Figure 12.3.

Thus, we see that the lower pendulum not only lives in its own local coordinate system, but also that coordinate system itself is moved along with that of the upper pendulum.

We can encode the pendulum in a data structure that makes management of these coordinate system issues easier, as shown in Figure 12.4. The appropriate matrix to apply to an object is just the product of all the matrices in the chain from the object to the root of the data structure. For example, consider the model of a ferry that has a car that can move freely on the deck of the ferry, and wheels that each move relative to the car as shown in Figure 12.5.

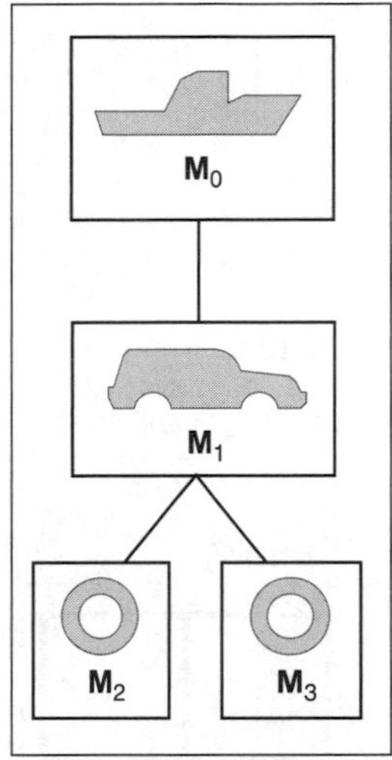

Figure 12.5. A ferry carries a car which has wheels attached (only two shown) are stored in a scene-graph.

As with the pendulum, each object should be transformed by the product of the matrices in the path from the root to the object:

ferry transform using M_0

car body transform using M_0M_1

left wheel transform using $M_0M_1M_2$

left wheel transform using $M_0M_1M_3$

An efficient implementation can be achieved using a *matrix stack*, a data structure supported by many APIs. A matrix stack is manipulated using *push* and *pop* operations that add and delete matrices from the right-hand side of a matrix product. For example, calling:

push($\mathbf{M}_0$)
push($\mathbf{M}_1$)
push($\mathbf{M}_2$)

creates the active matrix $\mathbf{M} = \mathbf{M}_0\mathbf{M}_1\mathbf{M}_2$. A subsequent call to *pop()* strips the last matrix added so that the active matrix becomes: $\mathbf{M} = \mathbf{M}_0\mathbf{M}_1$. Combining the matrix stack with a recursive traversal of a scene graph gives us:

function *traverse*(*node*)
push($\mathbf{M}_{local}$)
draw object using composite matrix from stack
traverse(*left child*)
traverse(*right child*)
push()

There are many variations on scene graphs but all follow the basic idea above.

12.4 Tiling Multidimensional Arrays

Effectively utilizing the cache hierarchy is a crucial task in designing algorithms for modern architectures. Making sure that multidimensional arrays have data in a "nice" arrangement is accomplished by *tiling*, sometimes also called *bricking*. A traditional 2D array is stored as a 1D array together with an indexing mechanism; for example, an N_x by N_y array is stored in a 1D array of length N_xN_y and the 2D index (x, y) (which runs from $(0, 0)$ to

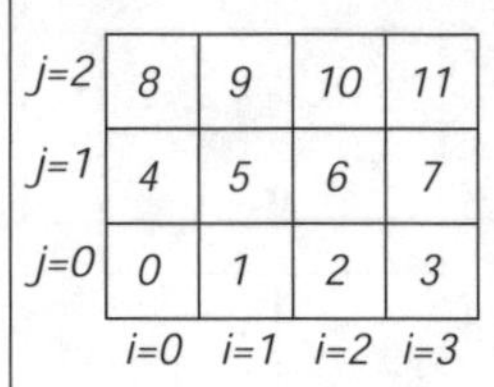

Figure 12.6. The memory layout for an untiled 2D array with $N_x = 4$ and $N_y = 3$.

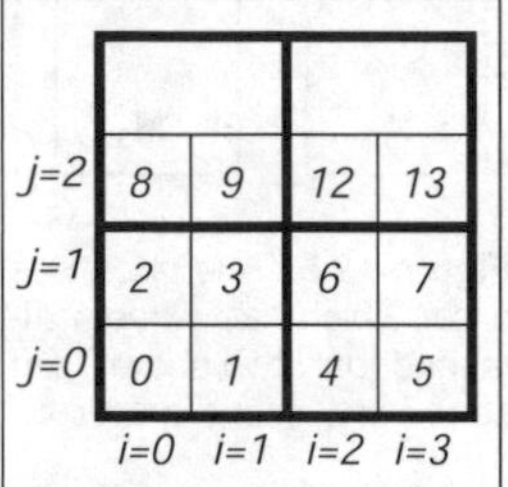

Figure 12.7. The memory layout for a tiled 2D array with $N_x = 4$ and $N_y = 3$ and two by two tiles. Note that padding on the top of the array is needed because N_y is not a multiple of the tile size two.

$(N_x - 1, N_y - 1))$ and maps it to the 1D index (running from 0 to $N_xN_y - 1$ using the formula:

$$\text{index} = x + N_x y.$$

An example of how that memory lays out is shown in Figure 12.6. A problem with this layout is that although two adjacent array elements that are in the same row are next to each other in memory, two adjacent elements in the same column will be separated by N_x elements in memory. This can cause poor memory locality for large N_x. The standard solution to this is to use *tiles* to make memory locality for rows and columns more equal. An example is shown in Figure 12.7 where two by two tiles are used. The details of indexing such an array are discussed in the next section. A more complicated example with two levels of tiling on a 3D array are covered after that.

A key question is what size to make the tiles. In practice, they should be similar to the memory-unit size on the machine. For example, on a machine with 128-byte cache lines, and using 16-bit data values, n is exactly 8. However, using float (32-bit) datasets, n is closer to 5. Because there are also coarser-sized memory units such as pages, hierarchical tiling with similar logic can be useful.

12.4.1 One-Level Tiling for 2D Arrays

If we assume an N_x by N_y array decomposed into square n by n tiles (Figure 12.8), then the number of tiles required is:

$$B_x = N_x/n,$$
$$B_y = N_y/n.$$

Here, we assume that n divides N_x and N_y exactly. When this is not true, the array should be *padded*. For example, if $N_x = 15$ and $n = 4$, then N_x should be changed to 16. To work out a formula for indexing such an array, we first find the tile indices (b_x, b_y) which give the row/column for the tiles (the tiles themselves form a 2D array):

$$b_x = x \div n,$$
$$b_y = y \div n,$$

where $\div$ is integer division, e.g., $12 \div 5 = 2$. If we order the tiles along rows as shown in Figure 12.6, then the index of the first element of the tile (b_x, b_y) is:

$$\text{index} = n^2(B_x b_y + b_x).$$

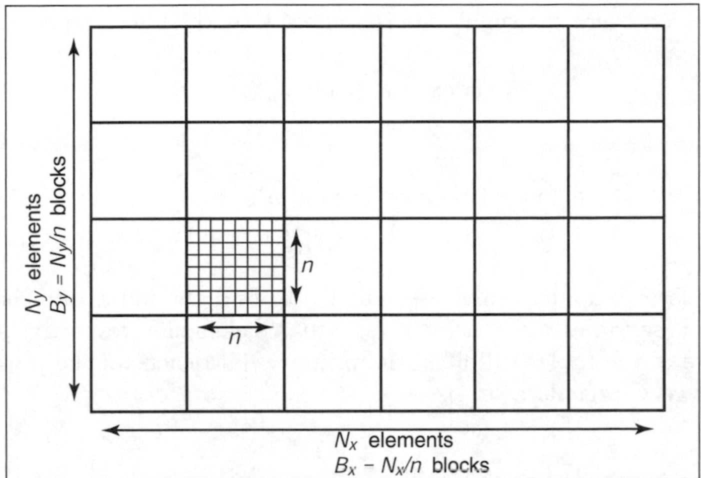

Figure 12.8. A tiled 2D array composed of B_x by B_y tiles each of size n by n.

The memory in that tile is arranged like a traditional 2D array as shown in Figure 12.7. The partial offsets (x', y') inside the tile are:

$$\begin{aligned} x' &= x \bmod n, \\ y' &= y \bmod n, \end{aligned}$$

where mod is the remainder operator, e.g., 12 mod 5 = 2. Therefore, the offset inside the tile is

$$\text{offset} = y'n + x'.$$

Thus the full formula for finding the 1D index element (x, y) in an N_x by N_y array with n by n tiles is:

$$\begin{aligned} \text{index} &= n^2(B_x b_y + b_x) + y'n + x', \\ &= n^2((N_x \div n)(y \div n) + x \div n) + (y \bmod n)n + (x \bmod n). \end{aligned}$$

This expression contains many integer multiplication, divide and modulus operations. On modern processors, these operations are extremely costly. For n which are powers of two, these operations can be converted to bitshifts and bitwise logical operations. However, as noted above, the ideal size is not always a power of two. Some of the multiplications can be converted to shift/add operations, but the divide and modulus operations are more problematic. The indices could be computed incrementally, but this would require tracking counters, with numerous comparisons and poor branch prediction performance.

However, there is a simple solution; note that the index expression can be written as:

$$\text{index} = F_x(x) + F_y(y)$$

where

$$F_x(x) = (x \div n) + (x \bmod n),$$
$$F_y(y) = (N_x \div n)(y \div n) + (y \bmod n)n.$$

We tabulate F_x and F_y, and use x and y to find the index into the data array. These tables will consist of N_x and N_y elements, respectively. The total size of the tables will fit in the primary data cache of the processor, even for very large data set sizes.

12.4.2 Example: Two-Level Tiling for 3D Arrays

Effective TLB utilization is also becoming a crucial factor in algorithm performance. The same technique can be used to improve TLB hit rates in a 3D array by creating $m \times m \times m$ bricks of $n \times n \times n$ cells. For example, a $40 \times 20 \times 19$ volume could be decomposed into $4 \times 2 \times 2$ macrobricks of $2 \times 2 \times 2$ bricks of $5 \times 5 \times 5$ cells. This corresponds to $m = 2$ and $n = 5$. Because 19 cannot be factored by $mn = 10$, one level of padding is needed. Empirically useful sizes are $m = 5$ for 16 bit datasets, and $m = 6$ for float datasets.

The resulting index into the data array can be computed for any (x, y, z) triple with the expression:

$$\begin{aligned}
\text{index} \quad = \quad & ((x \div n) \div m)n^3m^3((N_z \div n) \div m)((N_y \div n) \div m) \\
& +((y \div n) \div m)n^3m^3((N_z \div n) \div m) \\
& +((z \div n) \div m)n^3m^3 \\
& +((x \div n) \bmod m)n^3m^2 \\
& +((y \div n) \bmod m)n^3m \\
& +((z \div n) \bmod m)n^3 \\
& +(x \bmod (n^2))n^2 \\
& +(y \bmod n)n \\
& +(z \bmod n)
\end{aligned}$$

where N_x, N_y and N_z are the respective sizes of the dataset.

Note that, as in the simpler 2D one-level case, this expression can be written as:

$$\text{index} = F_x(x) + F_y(y) + F_z(z),$$

where

$$
\begin{aligned}
F_x(x) &= ((x \div n) \div m)n^3m^3((N_z \div n) \div m)((N_y \div n) \div m) \\
&\quad +((x \div n) \bmod m)n^3m^2 \\
&\quad +(x \bmod (n^2))n^2 \\
F_y(y) &= ((y \div n) \div m)n^3m^3((N_z \div n) \div m) \\
&\quad +((y \div n) \bmod m)n^3m + \\
&\quad +(y \bmod n)n \\
F_z(z) &= ((z \div n) \div m)n^3m^3 \\
&\quad +((z \div n) \bmod m)n^3 \\
&\quad +(z \bmod n)
\end{aligned}
$$

Frequently Asked Questions

- **Does tiling really make that much difference in performance?**

On some volume rendering applications, a two-level tiling strategy made as much as a factor-of-ten performance difference. When the array does not fit in main memory, it can effectively prevent thrashing in some applications such as image editing.

- **How do I store the lists in a winged-edge structure?**

For most applications it is feasible to use arrays and indices for the references. However, if many delete operations are to be performed, then it is wise to use linked lists and pointers.

Notes

The discussion of the winged-edge data structure is based on the course notes of *Ching-Kuang Shene*. There are smaller mesh data structures than winged-edge. The trade-offs in using such structures is discussed in *Directed Edges— A Scalable Representation for Triangle Meshes* (Campagna, Kobbelt and Seidel, journal of graphics tools, 3(4), 1998). The tiled-array discussion is based on *A Ray Tracing Method for Isosurface Rendering* (Parker et al., IEEE Visualization Conference, 1998).

Exercises

1. What is the memory difference for a simple tetrahedron stored as four independent triangles and one stored in a winged-edge data structure?
2. Diagram a scene graph for a bicycle.
3. How many look-up tables are needed for a single-level tiling of an n-dimensional array?

Curves and Surfaces

Often we need *smooth* curves and surfaces for graphics models, e.g., the fender on a car. This chapter covers the most common smooth curves and surfaces—various *spline* and *subdivision* primitives. After introducing bilinear patches, we will begin with the quadratic Bézier curve to establish concepts and terminology, and we will then treat other common forms in that context.

13.1 Bilinear Patches

We have considered the line segment between points $\mathbf{p}_0$ and $\mathbf{p}_1$ as a finite linear primitive:

$$\mathbf{p}(t) = (1-t)\mathbf{p}_0 + t\mathbf{p}_1,\ t \in [0,1].$$

We might ask, "What surfaces are similarly simple?" We have treated the triangle as a weighted average of three points where the weights are all at most one. However, there is another useful primitive that is a combination of *four* vertices—the *bilinear patch*:

$$\begin{aligned}\mathbf{p}(u,v) = &(1-u)\,(1-v)\mathbf{p}_{00}\\ &+(u)\,(1-v)\mathbf{p}_{10}\\ &+(1-u)\,(v)\mathbf{p}_{01}\\ &+(u)\,(v)\mathbf{p}_{11}\end{aligned}$$

with the domain $(u,v) \in [0,1]^2$. This is similar in form and concept to bilinear texture interpolation. The bilinear patch is the simplest smooth surface that interpolates four potentially non-coplanar 3D points (Figure 13.1).

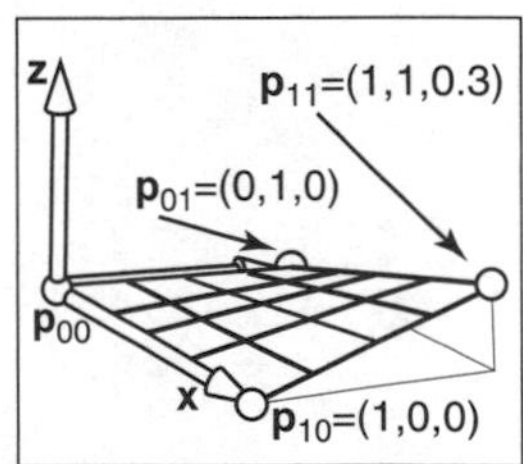

Figure 13.1. A bilinear patch with four non-coplanar vertices.

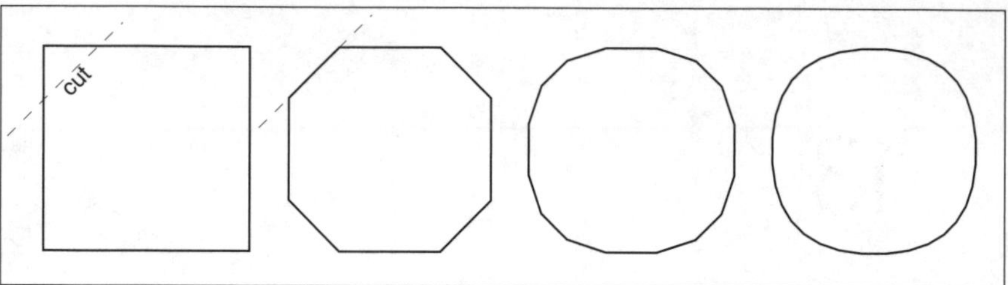

Figure 13.2. By repeatedly cutting the corners off a polygon, we approach a smooth curve.

13.2 Quadratic Bézier Curves

In 2D, we would like to be able to draw smooth curves that approximate line segments, e.g., to smooth a polygonal boundary drawn by a user in a drawing package. We can accomplish this by *subdivison*. One form of subdivision is *corner-cutting*: we repeatedly take a polygon and "chop off" its corners as shown in Figure 13.2. This procedure is called subdivision, because the series of line segments is being "subdivided" into more line segments. The final smooth curve is called the *limit curve* because it results from the limit of infinitely many subdivisions.

We can make a subdivision procedure a simple set of recursive modifications to the line segments:

function subdivide$(\mathbf{p}_0, \mathbf{p}_1, \mathbf{p}_2)$
$\mathbf{p}_{01} = (\mathbf{p}_0 + \mathbf{p}_1)/2$
$\mathbf{p}_{12} = (\mathbf{p}_2 + \mathbf{p}_2)/2$
$\mathbf{p}_m = (\mathbf{p}_{01} + \mathbf{p}_{02})/2$
subdivide$(\mathbf{p}_0, \mathbf{p}_{01}, \mathbf{p}_m)$
subdivide$(\mathbf{p}_m, \mathbf{p}_{12}, \mathbf{p}_2)$

At some depth, we can replace the recursive calls with calls to draw two line segments between the three points. This will generate a drawing of a smooth curve. This process is illustrates in Figure 13.3. It turns out that four of the curves in Figure 13.3 match the closed curve in Figures 13.2.

An interesting property of the subdivision process here is that each of the new "midpoints" created (the black points in Figure 13.3) is on the final curve; they are never moved. The first point has the form:

$$\mathbf{p} = \frac{1}{2}\left(\frac{1}{2}\mathbf{p}_0 + \frac{1}{2}\mathbf{p}_1\right) + \frac{1}{2}\left(\frac{1}{2}\mathbf{p}_1 + \frac{1}{2}\mathbf{p}_2\right).$$

The next two points in depth in the recursion have similar forms:

$$\mathbf{p} = \frac{1}{4}\left(\frac{1}{4}\mathbf{p}_0 + \frac{3}{4}\mathbf{p}_1\right) + \frac{3}{4}\left(\frac{1}{4}\mathbf{p}_1 + \frac{3}{4}\mathbf{p}_2\right),$$

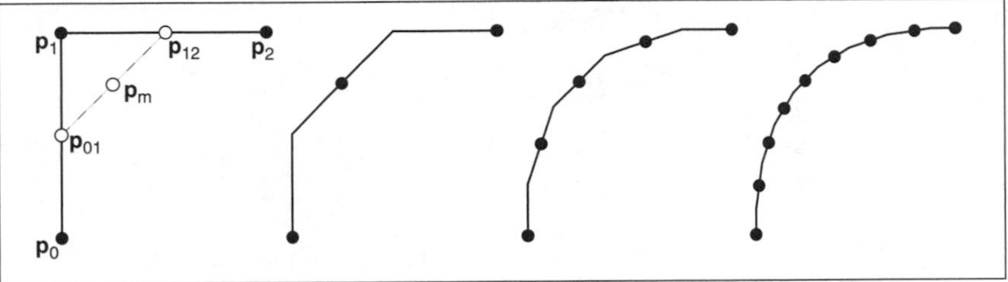

Figure 13.3. The two-segment unit on the left is subdivided into two two-segment units. This process is repeated, doubling the number of segments in each iteration.

and

$$\mathbf{p} = \frac{3}{4}\left(\frac{3}{4}\mathbf{p}_0 + \frac{1}{4}\mathbf{p}_1\right) + \frac{1}{4}\left(\frac{3}{4}\mathbf{p}_1 + \frac{1}{4}\mathbf{p}_2\right).$$

The geometry of these expressions is shown in Figure 13.4.

Figure 13.4 makes one wonder whether the point shown in Figure 13.5 is also on the limit curve, namely:

$$\mathbf{p} = \frac{2}{3}\left(\frac{2}{3}\mathbf{p}_0 + \frac{1}{3}\mathbf{p}_1\right) + \frac{1}{3}\left(\frac{2}{3}\mathbf{p}_1 + \frac{1}{3}\mathbf{p}_2\right),$$

and more generally, for any $t \in [0, 1]$:

$$\mathbf{p} = (1-t)\left((1-t)\mathbf{p}_0 + t\mathbf{p}_1\right) + t\left((1-t)\mathbf{p}_1 + t\mathbf{p}_2\right). \tag{13.1}$$

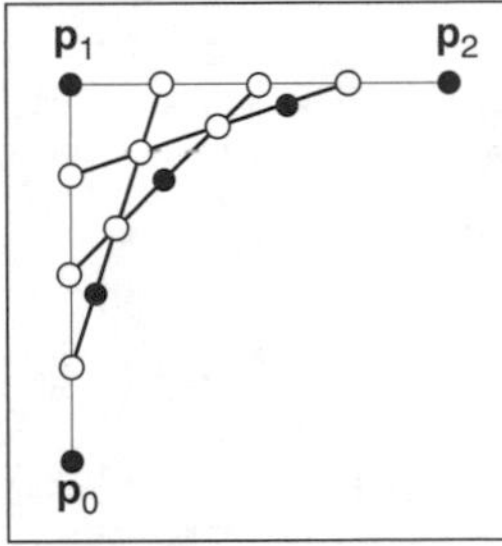

Figure 13.4. The first three subdivision points all divide the line segments shown into four equal parts.

In fact, it can be shown that this point is on the limit curve; it is not surprising once you realize that Figure 13.4 can be generalized iteratively to include fractions $i/8, i/16, i/32, \ldots$.

The observation shown by example in Figure 13.5 allows us to write down an algebraic form of the curve. Grouping terms in Equation 13.1, we have the parametric equation:

$$\mathbf{p}(t) = (1-t)^2\mathbf{p}_0 + 2(1-t)t\mathbf{p}_1 + t^2\mathbf{p}_2.$$

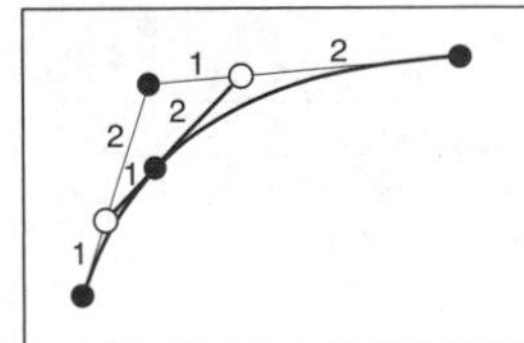

Figure 13.5. Figure 13.4 raises the question of whether one third of the way up the segment connecting one third of the way along each of the initial sides is on the curve.

This is the standard form of the *quadratic Bézier curve*, also called the Bézier curve of degree two. An important property of the weights in the above equation is that they are both positive and they sum to one. This means that $\mathbf{p}(t)$ is a weighted average of the *control points* $\mathbf{p}_i$. This gives rise to the terminology that the control points are *blended* together using *blending functions*:

$$\mathbf{p}(t) = \sum_{i=0}^{N-1} w_i(t)\mathbf{p}_i.$$

For quadratic Bézier curves, $N = 2$ and

$$w_0(t) = (1-t)^2,$$
$$w_1(t) = 2(1-t)t,$$
$$w_2(t) = t^2.$$

Figure 13.6. The three quadratic Bézier blending functions.

These functions are quadratic in t, and thus the name *quadratic* Bézier curves. We will see higher-order Bézier curves in the next section.

It is informative to look at graphs of the blending functions themselves; Figure 13.6 shows the three functions. Note that at $t = 0$, the function w_0 is one and the other two functions are zero. This means that the curve starts at point $\mathbf{p}_0$. Similarly, at $t = 1$, only the last basis function is non-zero and thus the curve ends at $\mathbf{p}_2$.

As t increases toward one half, the influence of $\mathbf{p}_0$ falls off rapidly, and the middle control point becomes more influential. At $t = 0.5$, the influence of $\mathbf{p}_1$ reaches its maximum, and we expect the curve to be pulled toward it.

13.3 Higher-Order Bézier Curves

We might ask what we should do to approximate four points in series since the quadratic Bézier curve is tailored to exactly three points. We can take the geometric procedure shown in Figure 13.5 and try to generalize it as shown in Figure 13.7. Algebraically, this is equivalent to:

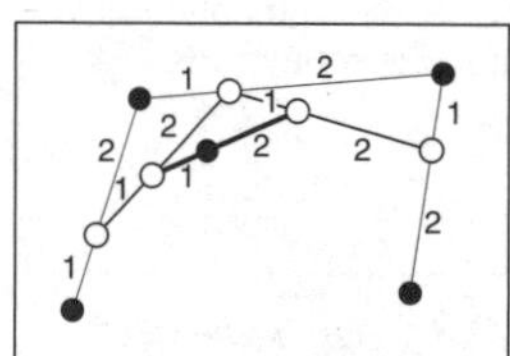
Figure 13.7. A generalization of Figure 13.5 to four control points.

$$\mathbf{p}(t) = (1-t)^3\mathbf{p}_0 + 3(1-t)^2 t\mathbf{p}_1 + 3(1-t)^2 t\mathbf{p}_2 + t^3\mathbf{p}_3.$$

This is called the *cubic* Bézier curve. Its blending functions are:

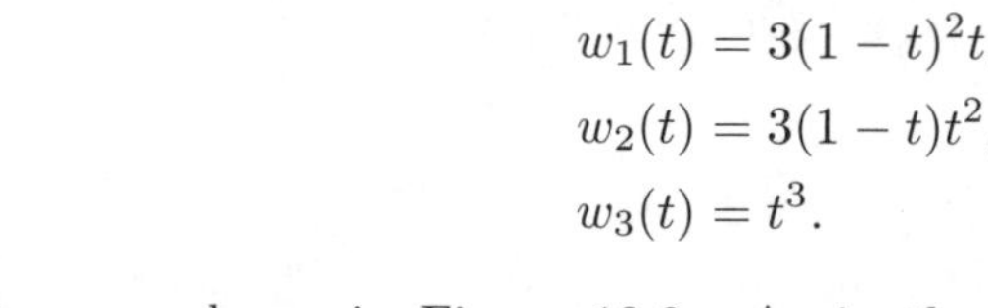

$$w_0(t) = (1-t)^3,$$
$$w_1(t) = 3(1-t)^2 t,$$
$$w_2(t) = 3(1-t)t^2,$$
$$w_3(t) = t^3.$$

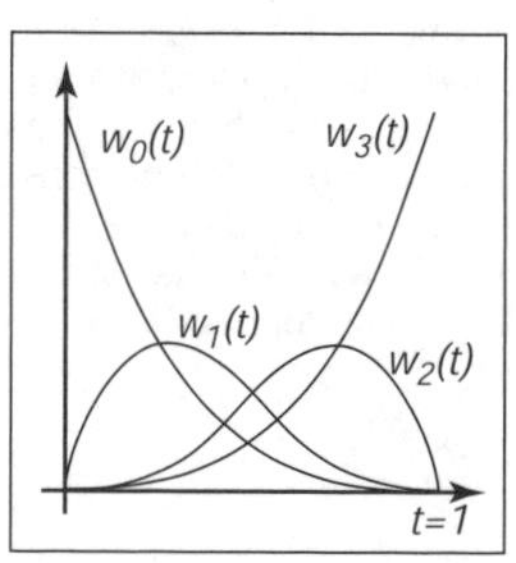

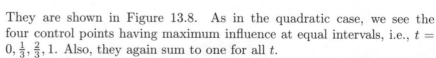

Figure 13.8. The three quadratic Bézier blending functions.

They are shown in Figure 13.8. As in the quadratic case, we see the four control points having maximum influence at equal intervals, i.e., $t = 0, \frac{1}{3}, \frac{2}{3}, 1$. Also, they again sum to one for all t.

The subdivision idea can be generalized to any number of N vertices, and the degree of the blending functions will be $N-1$. The coefficients all have the same pattern of binomial coefficients times $(1-t)^{N-i-1}t^i$:

$$w_i^N(t) = \frac{N!}{i!(N-i)!}(1-t)^{N-i-1}t^i,$$

where $0! = 1$. For example, with $N = 6$ control points, the curve is

$$\mathbf{p}(t) = \sum_{i=0}^{5} w_i(t)\mathbf{p}_i,$$

and

$$\begin{aligned} w_0^6(t) &= (1-t)^5, \\ w_1^6(t) &= 5(1-t)^4 t, \\ w_2^6(t) &= 10(1-t)^3 t^2, \\ w_3^6(t) &= 10(1-t)^2 t^3, \\ w_4^6(t) &= 5(1-t) t^4, \\ w_5^6(t) &= t^5. \end{aligned}$$

This is a fifth-degree Bézier curve.

A recursive form of the Bézier blending functions make them easy to implement, if somewhat inefficiently:

$$w_i^N = (1-t)w_i^{N-1} + t w_{i-1}^{N-1}$$

where $w_0^0 = 1$ and $w_i^N = 0$, if i is out of range. Note that this is an iterative linear expression, and it is thus the algebraic analog of the repeated linear subdivision procedure.

13.4 Properties of Bézier Curves

Now that we have the basic idea of a Bézier curve, we introduce some terms and observations:

- The set of points $\mathbf{p}_i$ are called the *control points* of the curve.
- The Bézier curve is a *spline curve*, and it is thus sometimes called a Bézier spline. Spline curves are a family of functions that create smooth curves from control points.
- The degree of the Bézier curve is one less than the number of control points.
- All of the blending functions are positive for $0 < t < 1$. This means all control points affect all parts of the curve except the endpoints.
- The set of ordered line segments connecting adjacent pairs of control points define the *control polygon* (Figure 13.9).
- Because the curve is a weighted average of the control points, it is restricted to their *convex hull* (Figure 13.10).

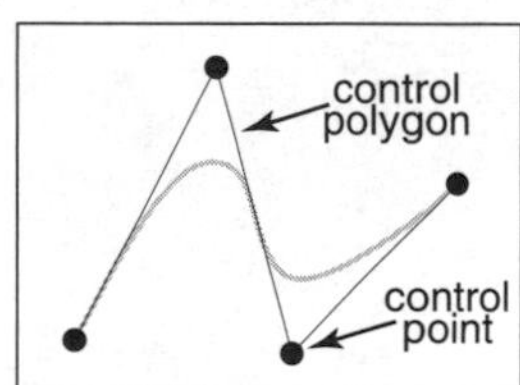

Figure 13.9. The control polygon and points of a spline curve.

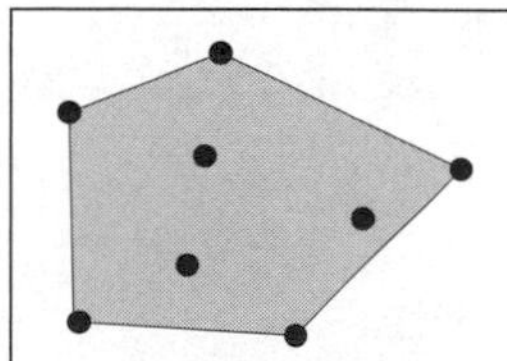

Figure 13.10. The convex hull of a set of points is the smallest convex polygon that includes them all.

- The control points can be 3D, in which case the curve is a *space curve.*
- The beginning and end of the curve are tangent to the control polygon.

13.5 Bézier Surfaces

It is straightforward to generalize spline curves to surfaces defined for lattices of 3D control points. The key observation we need is that the 1D blending functions for curves can be multiplied to form 2D blending functions for surfaces. Note, that in a spline curve with N control points, the blending functions $w_i(t)$ have the following two properties:

- $w_i(t)$ is maximum at $t = i/(N-1)$,
- the sum of the $w_i(t)$ is one for all t.

Given an M by N grid of MN control points $\mathbf{p}_{ij}$, we can create a smooth surface by taking a weighted average of the control points with MN weighting functions $w_{ij}(u, v)$:

$$\mathbf{p}(u, v) = \sum_{i=0}^{M-1} \sum_{j=0}^{N-1} w_{ij}(u, v)\mathbf{p}_{ij}.$$

These 2D blending functions will work well if they are continuous and have the properties analogous to the 1D case:

- $w_{ij}(u, v)$ is maximum at $(u, v) = (i/(M-1), j/(N-1)$,
- the sum of the $w_{ij}(u, v)$ is one for all (u, v).

It is straightforward to verify that the product of two 1D blending functions has this property. First, from elementary calculus we know that the maximum occurs at $w_i(i/(N-1))$ if and only if:

$$\frac{d}{dt} w_i \left(\frac{i}{N-1} \right) = 0$$

For the 2D blending function $w_{ij}(u, v)$, the analogous property is:

$$\frac{\partial}{\partial u} w_{ij} \left(\frac{i}{M-1}, \frac{j}{N-1} \right) = \frac{\partial}{\partial v} w_{ij} \left(\frac{i}{M-1}, \frac{j}{N-1} \right) = 0. \qquad (13.2)$$

The chain rule tells us that if:

$$w_{ij}(u, v) = w_i(u) w_j(v)$$

then the partial derivatives are:

$$\frac{\partial}{\partial u} w_{ij}(u, v) = w_j(v) \frac{d}{du} w_i(u),$$
$$\frac{\partial}{\partial u} w_{ij}(u, v) = w_i(v) \frac{d}{du} w_j(v).$$

Thus, the property of Equation 13.2 is achieved. The normalization property is also achieved:

$$\sum_{i=0}^{M-1} \sum_{j=0}^{N-1} w_i(u) w_j(v) = \sum_{i=0}^{M-1} w_i(u) \left(\sum_{j=0}^{N-1} w_j(v) \right) = \sum_{i=0}^{M-1} w_i(u) = 1.$$

So a Bézier surface is just a *tensor product* surface that uses the 1D blending function:

$$\mathbf{p}(u, v) = \sum_{i=0}^{M-1} \sum_{j=0}^{N-1} w_i(u) w_j(v) \mathbf{p}_{ij}.$$

For example, if we have a Bézier surface with four $\times$ three control points, the blending function w_{12} is:

$$w_{12}(u, v) = 3(1 - u)^2 uv^2.$$

Because the number of control points in each dimension is different, so is the degree of the polynomials u and v.

13.5.1 Subdivision and Trimming for Bézier Surfaces

Just as in the 1D case, there are subdivision rules on the initial control points that converge to the Bézier surface. These subdivision rules actually

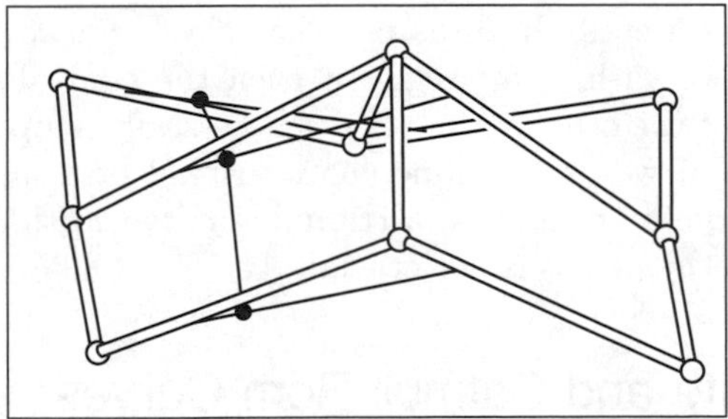

Figure 13.11. To evaluate **p** (0.2, *v*), we first subdivide each of the three rows as 1D Bezier curves to find three control points we can use to evaluate *v* as a normal 1D spline. This can be done either first in *u* or first in *v*.

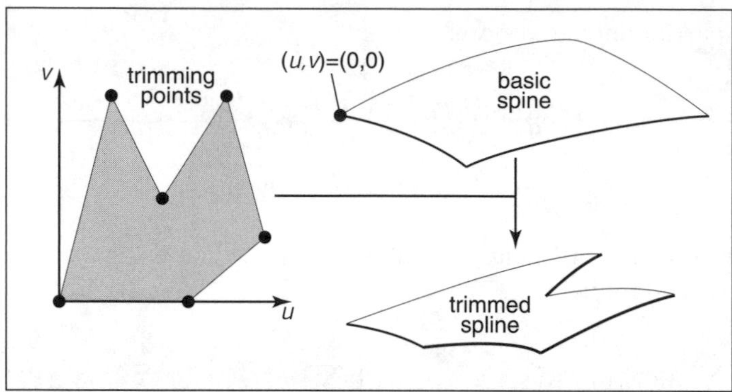

Figure 13.12. A trimming curve specifies which parts of a spline curve are "on." Once can think of the boundary of the trimming curve as a path along which scissors run in parameter space.

amount to just applying subdivision separately in each dimension. First, we can subdivide in u along each strip of M control points, generating N Bézier curves. Holding a particular u constant, we can take the N points on our N Bézier curves and subdivide in v along each of the curves. This idea is illustrated in Figure 13.11.

Bézier surfaces work fine provided there is a natural way to apply a rectangular domain to the surface; sometimes this is not the case. An example is the roughly triangular side window in a car. In that case, we should either use another type of surface, or we can use a *trimming curve*. The basic idea of a trimming curve is to create a pseudo-polygon in (u, v) space that bounds the part of the spline surface we want to "count." This idea is shown in Figure 13.12.

A subtlety of trimming curves is that they are only defined as a series of points; exactly how those points are connected is left up to the application. A common application for trimming curves is to allow two spline surfaces to intersect and trim away the overshoot so there is a smooth "corner" between the two surfaces. It turns out that if we connect two points on the trimming curve with a line segment then the equivalent path in the parameter space of the other surface is not necessarily simple algebraically. The same is true if we use a spline curve instead of a line segment. In practice, many points are used in a trimming curve so that exactly what happens between the points is not crucial.

13.6 Hermite and Catmull-Rom Curves

Sometimes we want to smoothly *interpolate* a series of points, i.e., we want the curve to go through the points. The *Hermite curve* is a curve that can accomplish this. A special case of a Hermite curve is the Catmull-Rom spline that easily interpolate series of points. If we make the observation that cubic Bézier curves interpolate their endpoints, we then can add intermediate points to ensure interpolation as illustrated in Figure 13.12.

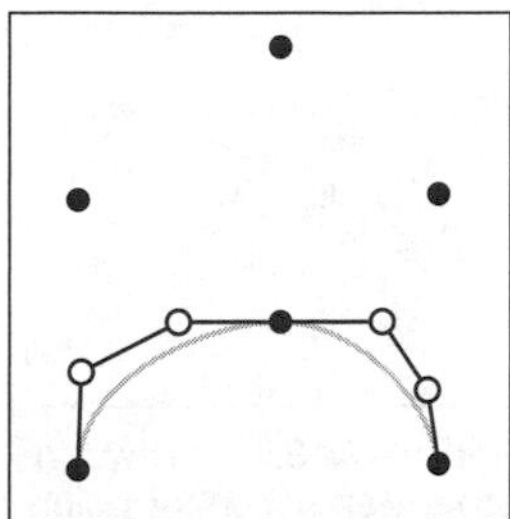

Figure 13.12. The Catmull-Rom curve adds four control points and uses cubic Bézier curves to smoothly interpolate the three data points shown.

The more general Hermite curve applies specifically to two 3D points and their parametric tangent vectors. Given a curve $\mathbf{p}(t)$, the tangent vector $\mathbf{d}(t)$ is given by the parametric derivative:

$$\mathbf{d}(t) = \frac{d}{dt}(\mathbf{p}(t)).$$

The vector $\mathbf{d}$ is tangent to the curve, and its length indicates the "velocity" of the curve, i.e., the differential distance the curve moves in space for a differential change in t (Figure 13.13). If we view t as time, the magnitude of the tangent vector is the literal velocity of the point $\mathbf{p}(t)$.

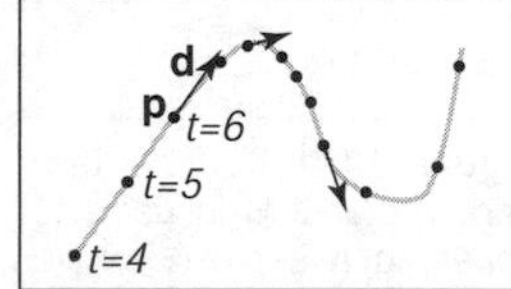

Figure 13.13. The tangent vector $\mathbf{d}(t)$ has the approximate length of the distance between $\mathbf{p}(t)$ and $\mathbf{p}(t+1)$.

Given two points $\mathbf{q}_0$ and $\mathbf{q}_1$ and their two associated tangent vectors $\mathbf{d}_0$ and $\mathbf{d}_1$ (Figure 13.14); we assume a cubic parametric curve:

$$\mathbf{p}(t) = t^3\mathbf{a}_3 + t^2\mathbf{a}_2 + t\mathbf{a}_1 + \mathbf{a}_0.$$

Here the four constants $\mathbf{a}_i$ are 3D vectors. The tangent vector to the curve is:

$$\mathbf{p}(t) = 3t^2\mathbf{a}_3 + 2t\mathbf{a}_2 + \mathbf{a}_1.$$

For this curve to fit our points and tangent vectors, we must satisfy the conditions:

$$\begin{aligned}
\mathbf{q}_0 &= \mathbf{p}(0) = \mathbf{a}_0,\\
\mathbf{q}_1 &= \mathbf{p}(1) = \mathbf{a}_3 + \mathbf{a}_2 + \mathbf{a}_1 + \mathbf{a}_0,\\
\mathbf{d}_0 &= \mathbf{d}(0) = \mathbf{a}_1,\\
\mathbf{d}_1 &= \mathbf{d}(1) = 3\mathbf{a}_3 + 2\mathbf{a}_2 + \mathbf{a}_1.
\end{aligned}$$

These equations can be solved easily to yield:

$$\begin{aligned}
\mathbf{a}_3 &= 2\mathbf{q}_0 - 2\mathbf{q}_1 + \mathbf{d}_0 + \mathbf{d}_1,\\
\mathbf{a}_2 &= -3\mathbf{q}_0 + 3\mathbf{q}_1 - 2\mathbf{d}_0 - \mathbf{d}_1\\
\mathbf{a}_1 &= \mathbf{d}_0,\\
\mathbf{a}_0 &= \mathbf{q}_0.
\end{aligned}$$

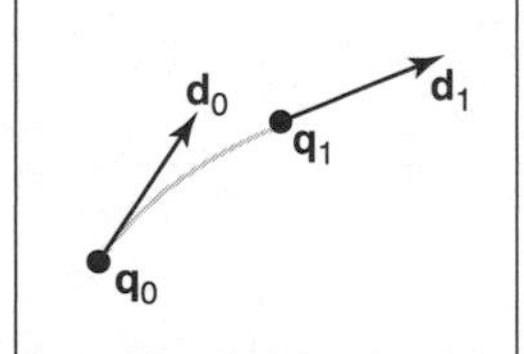

Figure 13.14. A Hermite curve has the endpoints and parametric tangent vectors specified.

We can rearrange the equations, substituting in the equation for the tangent vector to get:

$$\mathbf{p}(t) = (2u^3 - 3u^2 + 1)\mathbf{q}_0 + (-2u^3 + 3u^2)\mathbf{q}_1 + (u^3 - 2u^2 + u)\mathbf{d}_0 + (u^3 - u^2)\mathbf{d}_1.$$

To see that this is a Bézier curve, we rearrange terms:

$$\mathbf{p}(t) = (1-u)^3\mathbf{q}_0 + 3(1-u)^2u(\mathbf{q}_0 + \frac{1}{3}\mathbf{d}_0) + 3(1-u)u^2(\mathbf{q}_1 - \frac{1}{3}\mathbf{d}_1) + u^3\mathbf{q}_1,$$

which is just a Bézier curve with control points (Figure 13.15):

$$\mathbf{p}_0 = \mathbf{q}_0,$$
$$\mathbf{p}_1 = \mathbf{q}_0 + \frac{1}{3}\mathbf{d}_0,$$
$$\mathbf{p}_2 = \mathbf{q}_1 - \frac{1}{3}\mathbf{d}_1,$$
$$\mathbf{p}_3 = \mathbf{q}_1,$$

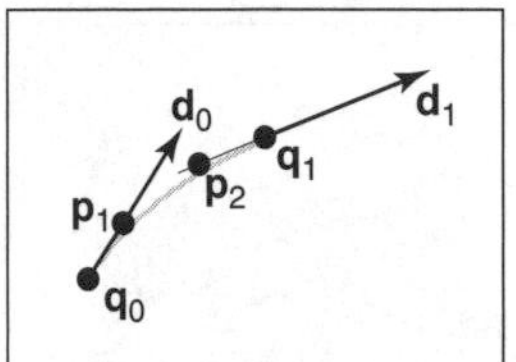

Figure 13.15. The two internal Bézier control points are one third of the way along the positive/negative tangent vectors of a Hermite curve.

Coming back to our original problem of interpolating a series of points, we need to pick sensible tangent vectors. The tangent vectors should get the curve to bend toward the adjacent control points, and they should be approximately the length of the distance between control points. This suggests the choice that defines the Catmull-Rom spline (Figure 13.16):

$$\mathbf{d}_i = \frac{\mathbf{q}_{i+1} - \mathbf{q}_{i-1}}{2}.$$

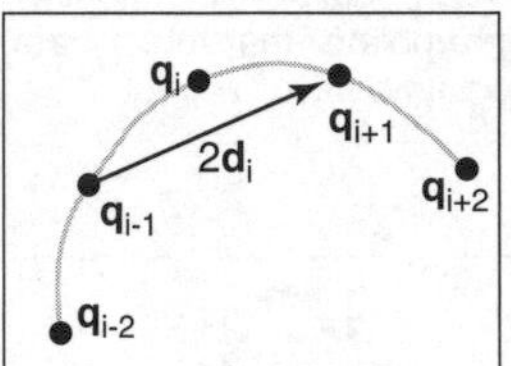

Figure 13.16. The tangent vector that is used to constrain a set of Hermite segments to an interpolating Catmull-Rom Spline.

This direction is "fair" for both adjacent points and will tend to approximate the curve length for a unit change in parameter. That vector can be scaled up or down to create an extra degree of freedom in curve shape, which is then called a *cardinal spline.*

13.7 B-Splines

One problem with Bézier curves is that, if there are many control points we have a very high-degree polynomial, which is not usually desirable from a computational standpoint. In addition, every control point contributes to every part of the curve, which seems unnecessary. For example, when designing a ship hull one hundred meters long, a change in a control point near the bow requires recomputation of the entire hull shape. Recall that the reason Bézier curves work well is that their blending functions sum to one, and each is a "lump" with its mass near a part of parameter space we associate with the respective control point. It would seem we could set most of the blending function to zero away from the lump and Bézier curves would work almost as well. However, their normalization property would be gone. This gives rise to the following question:

> Can we create a low-degree polynomial that has an appropriate "lump" shape to use as a blending function, but is limited to a small region of parameter space?

The answer, it turns out, is almost; we can create such a blending function made up of pieces of polynomials, and this new function is called the B-

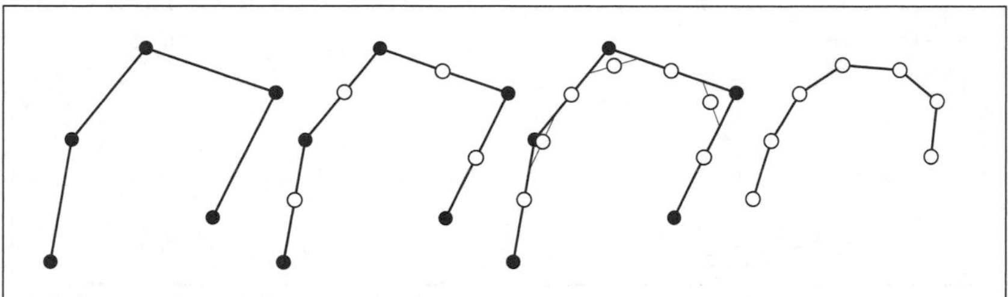

Figure 13.17. One step in the cubic B-spline subdivision procedure. First the midpoints of each segment of the control polygons are chosen. Then the midpoints of these and the original control points are connected, and the midpoints of these corner segments are also used.

spline blending function. We restrict most of our discussion to the uniform cubic B-spline; a summary of other spline forms can be found at the end of this section.

As with Bézier curves, there is a recursive subdivision procedure that converges to a cubic B-spline curve. One step of this procedure is illustrated in Figure 13.17. This results in the endpoints of the curve contracting approximately the length of the first and last legs of the control polygon, as illustrated in Figure 13.18.

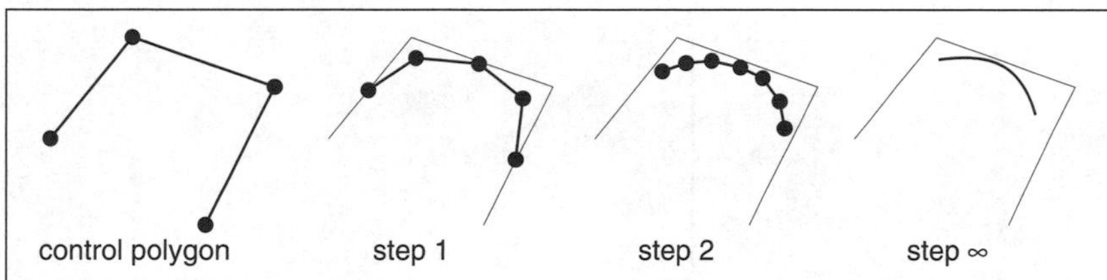

Figure 13.18. The cubic B-spline subdivision for two steps and the limit curve illustrates that the contraction of the endpoints is only about the size of one segment of the control polygon.

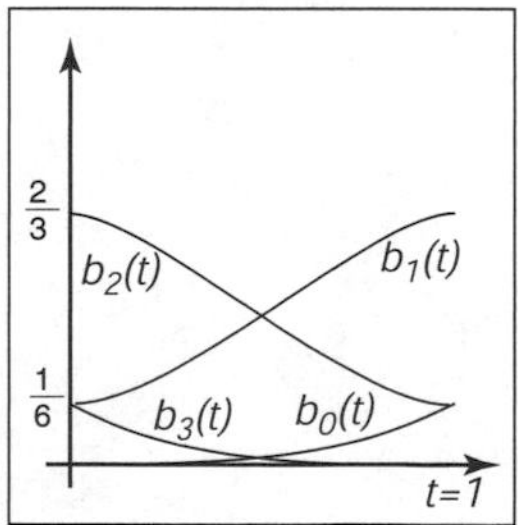

Figure 13.19. The four segments of the cubic B-spline blending function.

An interesting implication of this is that all stages of the subdivision are control polygons of the same underlying limit curve. This allows the common technique of adding control points to a curve without changing the underlying curve for the purposes of future curve modification.

This subdivision procedure can be shown to have the the underlying blending function of four cubic "segments" stitched together in series. The pieces of the cubic B-spline basis function are given by the following cubic polynomials on $t \in [0, 1]$ (Figure 13.19):

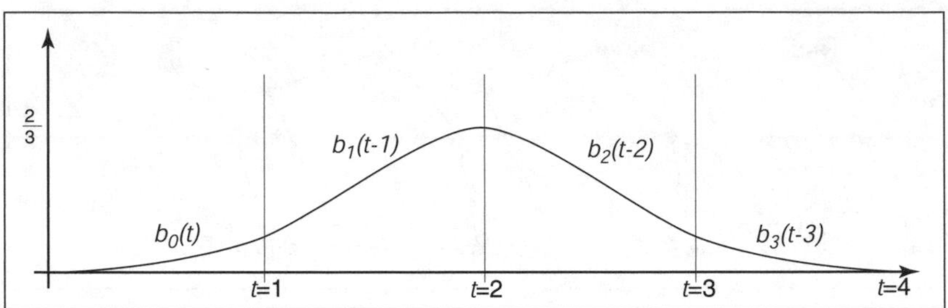

Figure 13.20. The B-spline blending function on the interval [0,4] is composed of four unit-width segments.

$$
\begin{aligned}
b_0(t) &= \frac{1}{6}s^3 \\
b_1(t) &= \frac{1}{6}\left(-3t^3 + 3t^2 + 3t + 1\right) \\
b_2(t) &= \frac{1}{6}\left(3t^3 - 6t^2 + 4\right) \\
b_3(t) &= \frac{1}{6}\left(-s^3 + 3s^2 - 3s + 1\right)
\end{aligned}
$$

These segments can be "spliced" together to form a "lumpy" blending function that is non-zero on $(0,1)$ (Figure 13.20):

$$
w(t) = \begin{cases} b_0(t) & \text{if } 0 < t \leq 1, \\ b_1(t-1) & \text{if } 1 < t \leq 2, \\ b_2(t-2) & \text{if } 2 < t \leq 3, \\ b_3(t-3) & \text{if } 3 < t \leq 4, \\ 0 & \text{otherwise.} \end{cases}
$$

To create a spline curve using this function, we need to create a blending function for every control point, with the maxima being at intervals in t. We can accomplish this by shifting $w(t)$ to a new location for each control point. If we want $t = 2$ to be where $\mathbf{p}_0$ has maximum influence, then the following is a valid B-spline curve (Figure 13.21):

$$
\mathbf{p}(t) = \sum_{i=0}^{N-1} w(t-i)\mathbf{p}_i.
$$

Note that now the valid parameter range is $[3, N]$ rather than $[0, 1]$. The ends of parameter space $[2, 3)$ and $(N, N+1]$ are left off because there are not enough points for the blending functions to sum to one in those

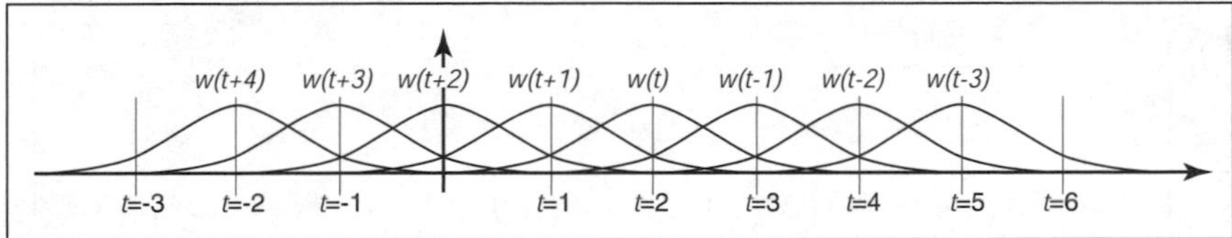

Figure 13.21. The B-spline blending functions are created by shifts.

regions. This is the algebraic representation of the contraction shown in Figure 13.18.

Note that if we want the endpoints of the curve to hit control points, we can duplicate the first and last control points three times each, and at $t = 2$ and $t = N$, we will be taking a weighted average of a single point with itself, which results in that point.

As with Bézier curves, a simple product form allows B-spline surfaces. There are two very important advantages of cubic B-spline curves and surfaces over Bézier forms. First, the degree of the blending function does not increase with the number of control points, improving numerical stability and efficiency. Second, B-splines exhibit *local control*, meaning that when a control point is moved, only points on the curve near the control point change. This is an efficiency and usability advantage when dealing with interactive modification of control points in a modeling system.

13.7.1 Non-Cubic B-splines

The cubic B-spline is just one of a family of blending functions. For every degree n, there is a blending function defined on $[0, n+1]$ composed of $n+1$ segments of polynomial degree n. The 0th order B-spline blending function is a constant on $[0, 1]$:

$$w^0(t) = \begin{cases} 1 & \text{if } 0 < t \leq 1, \\ 0 & \text{otherwise.} \end{cases}$$

The second-order blending function is just w^1 convolved with itself (each point $w^2(t_0)$ is a weighted average of $w^1(t)$ in the interval $t \in [t_0, t_0+1]$). This progression continues with $w^a(t)$ equal to w^0 convolved with itself a times. The first four such blending functions are shown in Figure 13.22. The function w_1 will give a linear interpolation of the control points so it just returns the control polygon. The function w_2 does not give continuous derivatives, so it is rarely used. Functions with degree higher than 3 give more smoothness, but they are usually used only when such smoothness is crucial.

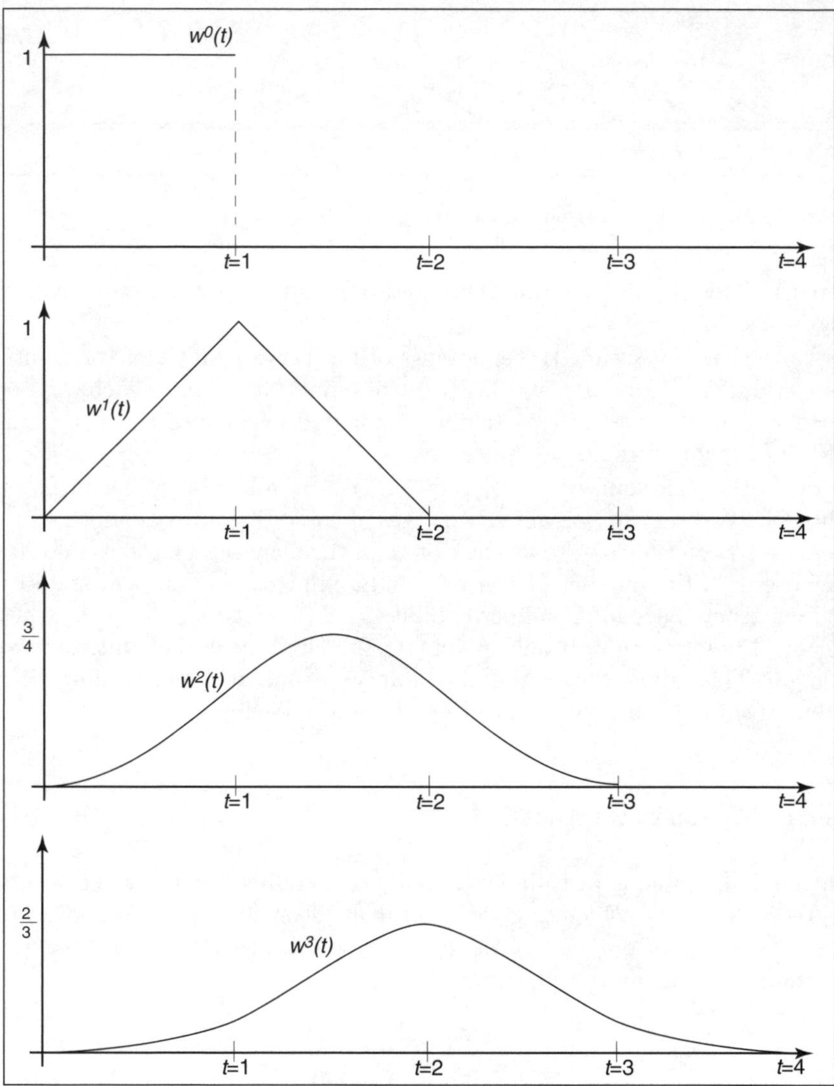

Figure 13.22. The unshifted B-spline blending functions of degree zero, one, two, and three.

As with Bézier blending functions, the B-spline blending functions have a recursive form that is easy to implement, if somewhat inefficiently:

$$w^k(t) = \frac{t}{k-1} w^{k-1}(t) + \frac{k-t}{k-1} w^{k-1}(t+1),$$

with $w^0(t) = 1$ for $t \in [0, 1)$ and zero otherwise. This is the algebraic form of the linear subdivision rule for the curves of varying degrees.

13.7.2 NURBS

In practice, a more complicated form of B-spline than the uniform cubic B-spline is used—the *nonuniform rational B-spline* curve, called the *NURBS* curve for short. This section summarizes the properties of such curves so that the reader will be aware of when they might be useful. The notes list a number of books specifically on NURBS.

The *rational* in NURBS refers to the use of a blending function that is the *ratio* of two polynomials—that is, by definition, a *rational* function. The use of such rational blending functions determines a *rational B-spline.* The important advantage of rational B-splines over "normal" (polynomial) B-splines is that they can represent conics exactly. So, in a design application that uses cylinders and spheres, rational blending functions are preferred.

Thc *nonuniform* in NURBS implies a curve parameterization that does not have the blending functions centered at integer parameter values. Note that our B-spline formulation could have used a spacing of $t = 2$ between the maximum influences of adjacent control points. We used $t = 1$ merely as an algebraic convenience. In nonuniform B-splines, we have arbitrary user-specified gaps between blending function peaks. These peaks occur at *knot values* $(t_0, t_1, \ldots, t_{N-1})$. For a "normal" (uniform) B-spline, the knot values are $(0, 1, 2, \ldots, N - 1)$. There is an advantage to using nonuniform B-splines when we add or delete control points to a curve or surface. While adding a control point in the middle of a control point sequence can be done in a way that does not change the geometry of a uniform B-spline, it will change the equation for the B-spline because the parameter values all are shifted by one in parameter space. Using nonuniform B-splines, we can make the knot value lie in between the integers so that, for example, a curve with knots $(0, 1, 2, 3, 4, 5, 6)$ can have a control point added between control points 1 and 2 so that the new knot values are $(0, 1, 1.5, 2, 3, 4, 5, 6)$. Thus, the parametric equation of the curve only changes locally; thus local control becomes an algebraic as well as a geometric concept.

13.8 Loop Subdivision Surfaces

The spline subdivision technology just discussed works best on meshes with a natural rectangular coordinate system. We often want to do similar subdivision on meshes of triangles to improve their smoothness. These meshes typically have arbitrary connectivity that makes it problematic to find even local rectangular coordinate systems. The classic method to subdivide such meshes is *Loop subdivision.* The basic idea of Loop subdivision is to divide all triangles simultaneously into four triangles, and to modify their vertices to create a smoother-looking surface.

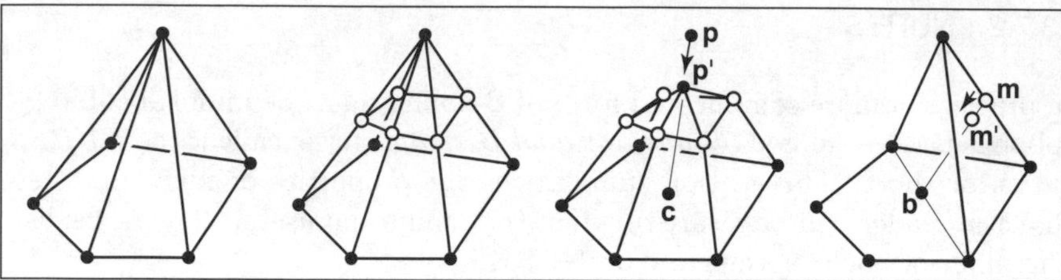

Figure 13.23. The moves near one vertex in a Loop subdivision.

To gain some intuition on how Loop subdivision works, consider trying to "round" the top of the pyramid shown in Figure 13.23. We want to move the top vertex down, and then add a vertex to the midpoint of each edge to allow this change to be a bend rather than just a lowering. If we move the vertex $\mathbf{p}$ toward the centroid $\mathbf{c}$ of the base polygon by a fraction s, we get:

$$\mathbf{p}' = (1-s)\mathbf{p} + s\mathbf{c}.$$

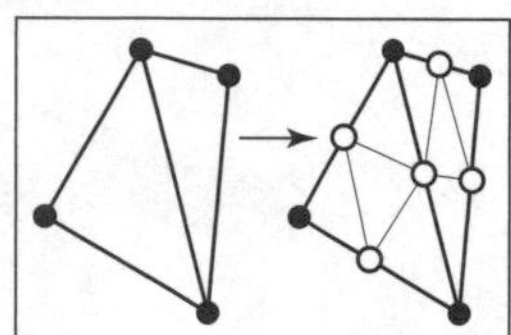

Figure 13.24. In Loop subdivision, each iteration turns a triangle into four triangles.

That operation tends to shorten the edges from the new midpoint vertices to the apex vertex. We can adjust these new vertices in and down to modify that shortening, and we can create a parameter to control the degree of rounding by moving each midpoint vertex $\mathbf{m}$ toward the midpoint $\mathbf{b}$ of the base vertices that surround it:

$$\mathbf{m}' = (1-t)\mathbf{m} + t\mathbf{b}.$$

The parameters that control how the subdivision will converge are (s, t). This basic idea can be generalized to apply to an arbitrary mesh of triangles. Every vertex is like the apex of the pyramid in the example, and every triangular face is divided into four triangular faces as shown for the two triangles in Figure 13.24.

For a given vertex $\mathbf{p}$ in the mesh before subdivision (Figure 13.25), there are n vertices (also called its *valence*) connected to it by edges. We create n midpoint vertices:

$$\mathbf{m}_i = \frac{\mathbf{p} + \mathbf{p}_i}{2}.$$

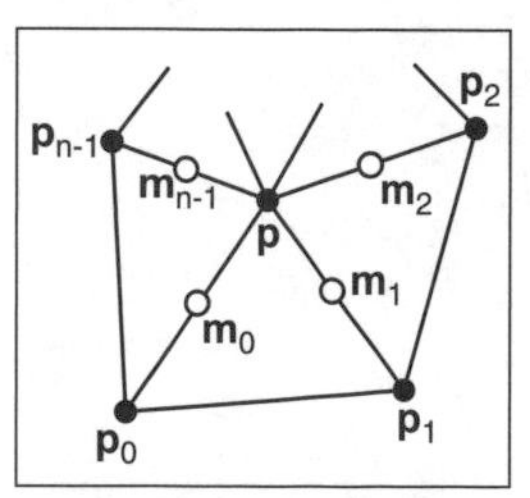

Figure 13.25. The vertices just before Loop subdivision.

The centroid $\mathbf{c}$ of the surrounding vertices is:

$$\mathbf{c} = \frac{1}{n}\sum_{i=0}^{n-1} \mathbf{p}_i.$$

Now, we displace $\mathbf{p}$ toward $\mathbf{c}$:

$$\mathbf{p}' = (1-s)\mathbf{p} + s\mathbf{c},$$

and each midpoint toward the center of the two $\mathbf{p}_i$ that "surround" it:

$$\mathbf{m}'_i = (1-t)\mathbf{m}_i + t\left(\frac{\mathbf{p}_{i-1}+\mathbf{p}_{i+1}}{2}\right).$$

Here the subscripts are modulo n, so that if $i = 0$, then $i - 1 = n - 1$ and if $i = n - 1$, then $i + 1 = 0$. Now, we just need to find good values for s and t. Loop showed that the surfaces may not be smooth if these values are chosen poorly. He proved that the following values always work to produce smooth surfaces:

$$s = \frac{5}{8} - \frac{\left[3 + 2\cos\left(\frac{2\pi}{n}\right)\right]^2}{64},$$
$$t = 0.25.$$

Rewriting this in terms of the original vertices only, we have:

$$\mathbf{m}'_i = \frac{3\mathbf{p} + 3\mathbf{p}_i + \mathbf{p}_{i-1} + \mathbf{p}_{i+1}}{8},$$

and

$$\mathbf{p}' = \frac{\alpha_n \mathbf{p} + \mathbf{p}_0 + \cdots \mathbf{p}_{n-1}}{\alpha_n + n},$$

where

$$\alpha_n = \frac{64n}{40 - \left[3 + 2\cos\left(\frac{2\pi}{n}\right)\right]^2} - 1.$$

Frequently Asked Questions

• Wouldn't B-splines be more elegant if the unshifted blending functions were centered at the origin?

Perhaps, but the literature is fairly standard in the convention that they start at zero so it is unwise to reformulate them.

• How do I implement Loop subdivision?

Perhaps the most straightforward implementation is to use a data structure that stores the vertices of the mesh in an array. Given a mesh of size M, we first create an array of size M to store the new vertices $\mathbf{p}'$. Then, we create the new vertices $\mathbf{m}$ and update the connectivity. Now we move the $\mathbf{m}$ to be $\mathbf{m}'$. Finally, we copy the $\mathbf{p}'$ over the original $\mathbf{p}$.

Notes

A popular subdivision method that works on general polygonal meshes (not only triangles) is *Catmull-Clark* subdivision; it is described in *Recursively-Generated B-spline Surfaces on Arbitrary Topological Meshes* (Catmull and Clark, Computer-Aided Design, September 1978). Several books describe NURBS technology in detail. These include *NURBS: from Projective Geometry to Practical Use* (Farin, A K Peters, 1999), *Interactive Curves and Surfaces* (Rockwood and Chambers, Morgan-Kaufmann, 1996), *NURBS: an Historical Perspective* (Rogers, Morgan-Kaufmann, 2000), and *Geometric Modeling with Splines* (Cohen, Riesenfeld and Elber, A K Peters, 2001). An excellent review of spline basics can be found in Kenneth Joy's online course notes at the University of California at Davis. These notes influenced much of the presentation in this chapter. Loop subdivision was introduced in *Smooth Subdivision Surfaces Based on Triangles* (Loop, University of Utah MS Thesis, 1987). A subdivision scheme similar to Loop's that generates fewer new triangles is described in *$\sqrt{3}$-Subdivision* (Kobbelt, SIGGRAPH 00).

Exercises

1. What are the control points of a cubic Bézier curve that corresponds to a cubic B-spline with four control points $\mathbf{p}_i$?
2. What is the correspondence between distance along a B-spline and the parameter of the curve?
3. What is a regular tetrahedron tranformed to after one iteration of Loop subdivision?
4. In the limit, does Loop subdivision of a tetrahedron produce a sphere?

Measure and Sampling

Many applications in graphics require "fair" sampling of unusual spaces, such as the space of all possible lines. For example, we might need to generate random edges within a pixel, or random sample points on a pixel that vary in density according to some density function. This chapter provides the machinery for such operations: basic measure theory and probability theory. These two areas are closely related, and some would argue they are really one area, so the discussion will not be tightly segregated. These techniques will also prove useful for numerically evaluating complicated integrals using *Monte Carlo integration*, also covered in this chapter.

14.1 Integrals and Measure

Although the words "integral" and "measure" often seem intimidating, they relate to some of the most intuitive concepts found in mathematics, and they should not be feared. For our very non-rigorous purposes, a *measure* is just a function that maps subsets to $\mathbb{R}^+$ in a manner consistent with our intuitive notions of length, area, and volume. For example, on the 2D real plane $\mathbb{R}^2$, we have the area measure A which assigns a value to a set of points in the plane. Note that A is just a function that takes pieces of the plane and returns area. This means the domain of A is all possible subsets of $\mathbb{R}^2$, which we denote as the *power set* $\mathcal{P}(\mathbb{R}^2)$. Thus, we can characterize A in arrow notation:

$$A : \mathcal{P}(\mathbb{R}^2) \to \mathbb{R}^+.$$

An example of applying the area measure shows that the area of the square with side length one is one:

$$A([a, a+1] \times [b, b+1]) = 1,$$

where (a, b) is just the lower lefthand corner of the square. Note that a single point such as $(3, 7)$ is a valid subset of $\mathbb{R}^2$ and has zero area: $A((3, 7)) = 0$. The same is true of the set of points S on the x-axis, $S = (x, y)$ such that $(x, y) \in \mathbb{R}^2$ and $y = 0$, i.e., $A(S) = 0$. Such sets are called *zero measure sets* .

To be considered a measure, a function has to obey certain area-like properties. For example, we have a function $\mu : \mathcal{P}(\mathbb{S}) \to \mathbb{R}^+$. For μ to be a measure, the following conditions must be true:

1. The measure of the empty set is zero: $\mu(\emptyset) = 0$,
2. The measure of two distinct sets together is the sum of their measure alone. This rule with possible intersections is: $\mu(A \cup B) = \mu(A) + \mu(B) - \mu(A \cap B)$, where $\cup$ is the set union operator and $\cap$ is the set intersection operator.

When we actually compute measures we usually use *integration*. We can think of integration as really just notation:

$$A(S) \equiv \int_{x \in S} dA(\mathbf{x}).$$

You can informally read the right hand side as "take all points $\mathbf{x}$ in the region S, and sum their associated differential areas". The integral is often written other ways including:

$$\int_S dA, \qquad \int_{\mathbf{x} \in S} d\mathbf{x}, \qquad \int_{\mathbf{x} \in S} dA_{\mathbf{x}}, \qquad \int_{\mathbf{x}} d\mathbf{x}.$$

All of the above formulas represent "the area of region S." We will stick with the first one we used, because it is so verbose it avoids ambiguity. To evaluate such integrals analytically, we usually need to lay down some coordinate system and use our bag of calculus tricks to solve the equations. But have no fear if those skills have faded, as we usually have to numerically approximate integrals, and that requires only a few simple techniques which are covered later in this chapter.

Given a measure on a set $\mathbb{S}$, we can always create a new measure by weighting with a non-negative function $w : \mathbb{S} \to \mathbb{R}^+$. This is best expressed in integral notation. For example, we can start with the example of the simple area measure on $[0, 1]^2$:

$$\int_{\mathbf{x} \in [0,1]^2} dA(\mathbf{x}),$$

and we can use a "radially weighted" measure by inserting a weighting function of radius squared:

$$\int_{\mathbf{x}\in[0,1]^2} \|\mathbf{x}\|^2 dA(\mathbf{x}).$$

To evaluate this analytically, we can expand using a Cartesian coordinate system with $dA \equiv dx\, dy$:

$$\int_{\mathbf{x}\in[0,1]^2} \|\mathbf{x}\|^2 dA(\mathbf{x}) = \int_{x=0}^{1} \int_{y=0}^{1} (x^2 + y^2)\ dx\, dy.$$

The key thing here is that if you think of the $\|\mathbf{x}\|^2$ term as married to the dA term, and that these together form a new measure, we can call that measure ν. This would allow us to write $\nu(S)$ instead of the whole integral. If this strikes you as just a bunch of notation and bookkeeping, you are right. But it does allow us to write down equations that are either compact or expanded depending on our preference.

14.1.1 Measures and Averages

Measures really start paying off when taking averages of a function. You can only take an average with respect to a particular measure, and you would like to select a measure that is "natural" for the application or domain. Once a measure is chosen, the average of a function f over a region S with respect to measure μ is:

$$\text{average}(f) \equiv \frac{\int_{x\in S} f(\mathbf{x})\ d\mu(\mathbf{x})}{\int_{x\in S} d\mu(\mathbf{x})}.$$

For example, the average of the function $f(x, y) = x^2$ over $[0, 2]^2$ with respect to the area measure is

$$\text{average}(f) \equiv \frac{\int_{x=0}^{2} \int_{y=0}^{2} x^2\ dx\, dy}{\int_{x=0}^{2} \int_{y=0}^{2}\ dx\, dy} = \frac{4}{3}.$$

This machinery helps solve seemingly hard problems where choosing the measure is the tricky part. Such problems often arise in *integral geometry*, a field that studies measures on geometric entities, such as lines and planes. For example, one might want to know the average length of a line through $[0, 1]^2$. That is, by definition,

$$\text{average(length)} = \frac{\int_{\text{lines } L \text{ through } [0,1]^2} \text{length}(L) d\mu(L)}{\int_{\text{lines } L \text{ through } [0,1]^2} d\mu(L)}.$$

All that is left, once we know that, is choosing the appropriate μ for the application. This is dealt with for lines in the next section.

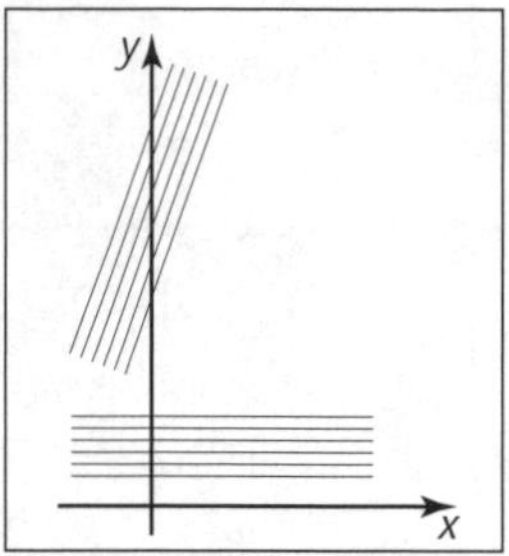

Figure 14.1. These two bundles of lines should have the same measure. They have different intersection lengths with the *y* axis so using *db* would be a poor choice for a differential measure.

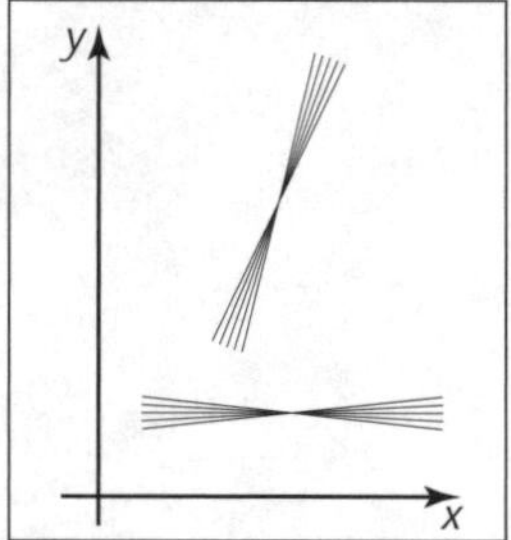

Figure 14.2. These two bundles of lines should have the same measure. Since they have different values for change in slope, using *dm* would be a poor choice for a differential measure.

14.1.2 Example: Measures on the Lines in the 2D Plane

What measure μ is "natural"? If you parameterize the lines as $y = mx + b$, you might think of a given line as a point (m, b) in "slope-intercept" space. An easy measure to use would be $dm\, db$, but this would not be a "good" measure in that not all equal size "bundles" of lines would have the same measure. More precisely, the measure would not be invariant with respect to change of coordinate system. For example, if you took all lines through the square $[0, 1]^2$, the measure of lines through it would not be the same as the measure through a unit square rotated forty-five degrees. What we would really like is a "fair" measure that does not change with rotation or translation of a set of lines. This idea is illustrated in Figures 14.1 and 14.2.

To develop a natural measure on the lines, we should first start thinking of them as points in a dual space. This is a simple concept: the line $y = mx + b$ can be specified as the point (m, b) in a slope-intercept space. This concept is illustrated in Figure 14.3. It is more straightforward to develop a measure in (ϕ, b) space. In that space b is the y-intercept, while ϕ is the angle the line makes with the x-axis, as shown in Figure 14.4. Here, the differential measure $d\phi\, db$ almost works, but it would not be fair due to the effect shown in Figure 14.1. To account for the larger span b that a constant width bundle of lines makes, we must add a cosine factor:

$$d\mu = \cos\phi \; d\phi \; db.$$

It can be shown that this measure, up to a constant, is the only one that is invariant with respect to rotation and translation.

This measure can be converted into an appropriate measure for other parameterizations of the line. For example, the appropriate measure for (y, b) space is:

$$d\mu = \frac{dm\ db}{(1 + m^2)^{\frac{3}{2}}}.$$

For the space of lines parameterized in (u, v) space:

$$ux + vy + 1 = 0,$$

the appropriate measure is:

$$d\mu = \frac{du\ dv}{(u^2 + v^2)^{\frac{3}{2}}}.$$

For lines parameterized in terms of (a, b), the x-intercept and y-intercept, the measure is:

$$d\mu = \frac{ab\ da\ db}{(a^2 + b^2)^{\frac{3}{2}}}.$$

Note that any of those spaces are equally valid ways to specify lines, and which is best depends upon the circumstances. However, one might wonder whether there exists a coordinate system where the measure of a set of lines is just an area in the dual space. In fact, there is such a coordinate system, and it is delightfully simple; it is the *normal coordinates* which specify a line in terms of the normal distance from the origin to the line, and the angle the normal of the line makes with respect to the x-axis (Figure 14.5). The implicit equation for such lines is:

$$x \cos\theta + y \sin\theta - p = 0.$$

And, indeed, the measure in that space is:

$$d\mu = dp\, d\theta.$$

We shall use these measures to choose fair random lines in a later section.

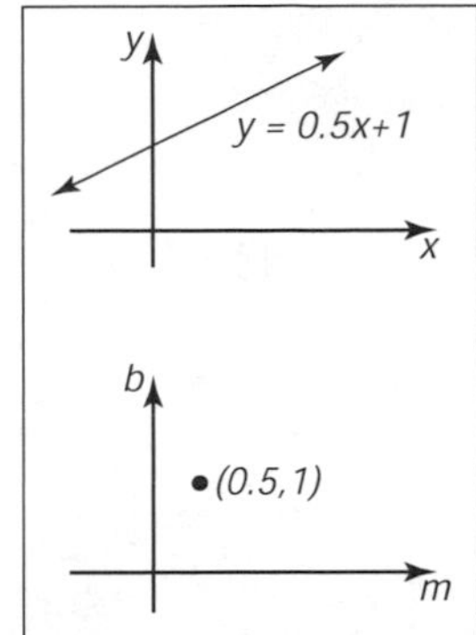

Figure 14.3. The set of points on the line $y=mx+b$ in (x, y) space can also be represented by a single point in (m, b) space so the top line and the bottom point represent the same geometric entity: a 2D line.

14.1.3 Example: Measure of Lines in 3D

In 3D there are many ways to parameterize lines. Perhaps, the simplest way is to use their intersection with a particular plane along with some specification of their orientation. For example, we could chart the intersection with the xy plane along with the spherical coordinates of its orientation. Thus, each line would be specified as a (x, y, θ, ϕ) quadruple. This shows that lines in 3D are 4D entities, i.e., they can be described as points in a 4D space.

The differential measure of a line should not vary with (x, y), but bundles of lines with equal cross-section should have equal measure. Thus, a fair differential measure is:

$$d\mu = dx\, dy\, \sin\theta\, d\theta\, d\phi.$$

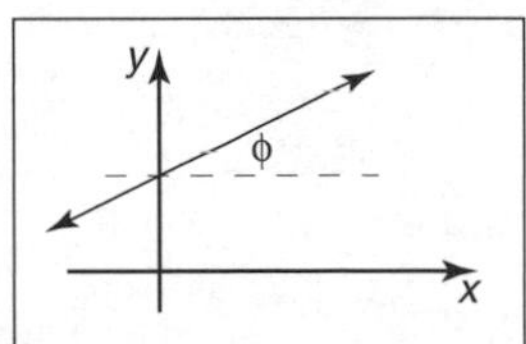

Figure 14.4. In angle-intercept space we parameterize the line by angle $\phi \in [-\pi/2, \pi/2)$ rather than slope.

Another way to parameterize lines is to chart the intersection with two parallel planes. For example, if the line intersects the plane $z = 0$ at $(x = u, y = v)$ and the plane $z = 1$ at $(x = s, y = t)$, then the line can be described by the quadruple (u, v, s, t). Note, that like the previous parameterization, this one is degenerate for lines parallel to the xy plane. The differential measure is more complicated for this parameterization although it can be approximated as:

$$d\mu \approx du\, dv\, a\, ds\, dt,$$

for bundles of lines nearly parallel to the z axis. This is the measure often implicitly used in image-based rendering (Chapter 22).

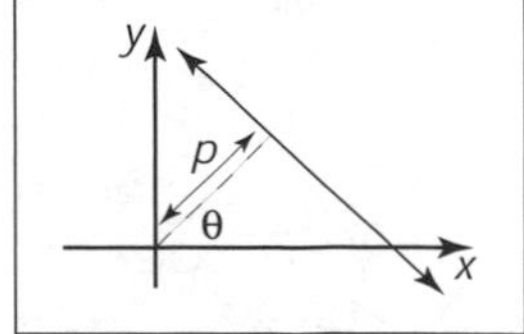

Figure 14.5. The normal coordinates of a line use the normal distance to the origin and an angle to specify a line.

For sets of lines that intersect a sphere, we can use the parameterization of the two points where the line intersects the sphere. If these are in spherical coordinates, then the point can be described by the quadruple $(\theta_1, \phi_1, \theta_2, \phi_2)$ and the measure is just the differential area associated with each point:

$$d\mu = \sin\theta_1 \, d\theta_1 \, d\phi_1 \, \sin\theta_2 \, d\theta_2 \, d\phi_2.$$

This implies that picking two uniform random endpoints on the sphere results in a line with uniform density. This observation was used to compute form-factors by Mateu Sbert in his dissertation.

Note that sometimes we want to parameterize directed lines, and sometimes we want the order of the endpoints not to matter. This is a bookkeeping detail that is especially important for rendering applications where the amount of light flowing along a line is different in the two directions along the line.

14.2 Continuous Probability

Many graphics algorithms use probability to construct random samples to solve integration and averaging problems. This is the domain of applied continuous probability which has basic connections to measure theory.

14.2.1 One-Dimensional Continuous Probability Density Functions

Loosely speaking, a *continuous random variable* x is a scalar or vector quantity that "randomly" takes on some value from the real line $\mathbb{R} = (-\infty, +\infty)$. The behavior of x is entirely described by the distribution of values it takes. This distribution of values can be quantitatively described by the *probability density function (pdf)*, p, associated with x (the relationship is denoted $x \sim p$). The probability that x assumes a particular value in some interval $[a, b]$ is given by the integral:

$$\text{Probability}(x \in [a,b]) = \int_a^b p(x)dx. \tag{14.1}$$

Loosely speaking, the probability density function p describes the relative likelihood of a random variable taking a certain value; if $p(x_1) = 6.0$ and $p(x_2) = 3.0$, then a random variable with density p is twice as likely to have a value "near" x_1 than it it to have a value near x_2. The density p has two characteristics:

$$p(x) \geq 0 \quad \text{(probability is nonnegative)}, \tag{14.2}$$

$$\int_{-\infty}^{+\infty} p(x)dx = 1 \quad (\text{Probability}(x \in \mathbb{R}) = 1). \tag{14.3}$$

As an example, the *canonical* random variable ξ takes on values between zero (inclusive) and one (non-inclusive) with uniform probability (here *uniform* simply means each value for ξ is equally likely). This implies that the probability density function q for ξ is:

$$q(\xi) = \begin{cases} 1 & \text{if } 0 \leq \xi \leq 1 \\ 0 & \text{otherwise} \end{cases}$$

The space over which ξ is defined is simply the interval $[0, 1)$. The probability that ξ takes on a value in a certain interval $[a, b] \in [0, 1)$ is:

$$\text{Probability}(a \leq \xi \leq b) = \int_a^b 1\,dx \;=\; b - a.$$

14.2.2 One-Dimensional Expected Value

The average value that a real function f of a one-dimensional random variable with underlying pdf p will take on is called its *expected value*, $E(f(x))$ (sometimes written $Ef(x)$):

$$E(f(x)) = \int f(x)p(x)dx.$$

The expected value of a one-dimensional random variable can be calculated by setting $f(x) = x$. The expected value has a surprising and useful property: the expected value of the sum of two random variables is the sum of the expected values of those variables:

$$E(x + y) = E(x) + E(y),$$

for random variables x and y. Because functions of random variables are themselves random variables, this linearity of expectation applies to them as well:

$$E(f(x) + g(y)) = E(f(x)) + E(g(y)).$$

An obvious question to ask is whether this property holds if the random variables being summed are correlated (variables that are not correlated are called *independent*). This linearity property in fact does hold *whether or not* the variables are independent! This summation property is vital for most Monte Carlo applications.

14.2.3 Multi-Dimensional Random Variables

The discussion of random variables and their expected values extends naturally to multi-dimensional spaces. Most graphics problems will be in such higher-dimensional spaces. For example, many lighting problems are phrased on the surface of the hemisphere. Fortunately, if we define a measure μ on the space the random variables occupy, everything is very similar to the one-dimensional case. Suppose the space S has associated measure μ; for example S is the surface of a sphere and μ measures area. We can define a pdf $p : S \mapsto \mathbb{R}$, and if x is a random variable with $x \sim p$, then the probability that x will take on a value in some region $S_i \subset S$ is given by the integral:

$$\text{Probability}(x \in S_i) = \int_{S_i} p(x) d\mu$$

Here *Probabilty* (*event*) is the probability that *event* is true, so the integral is the probability that x takes on a value in the region S_i.

In graphics, S is often an area ($d\mu = dA = dxdy$), or a set of directions (points on a unit sphere: $d\mu = d\omega = \sin\theta \, d\theta \, d\phi$). As an example, a two-dimensional random variable α is a uniformly distributed random variable on a disk of radius R. Here *uniformly* means uniform with respect to area, e.g., the way a bad dart player's hits would be distributed on a dart board. Since it is uniform, we know that $p(\alpha)$ is some constant. From the fact that the area of the disk is πr^2 and that the total probability is one, we can deduce that:

$$p(\alpha) = \frac{1}{\pi R^2}.$$

This means that the probability that α is in a certain subset S_1 of the disk is just:

$$\text{Probability}(\alpha \in S_1) = \int_{S_1} \frac{1}{\pi R^2} dA.$$

This is all very abstract. To actually use this information, we need the integral in a form we can evaluate. Suppose S_i is the portion of the disk closer to the center than the perimeter. If we convert to polar coordinates, then α is represented as a (r, ϕ) pair, and S_1 is the region where $r < R/2$. Note, that just because α is uniform, it does not imply that ϕ or r are necessarily uniform (in fact, ϕ is uniform, and r is not uniform). The differential area dA is jsut $r \, dr \, d\phi$. Thus,

$$\text{Probability}\left(r < \frac{R}{2}\right) = \int_0^{2\pi} \int_0^{\frac{R}{2}} \frac{1}{\pi R^2} r \, dr \, d\phi = 0.25.$$

The formula for expected value of a real function applies to the multi-dimensional case:

$$E(f(x)) = \int_S f(x) p(x) d\mu,$$

where $x \in S$ and $f : S \mapsto \mathbb{R}$, and $p : S \mapsto \mathbb{R}$. For example, on the unit square $S = [0,1] \times [0,1]$ and $p(x,y) = 4xy$, the expected value of the x coordinate for $(x,y) \sim p$ is:

$$\begin{aligned} E(x) &= \int_S f(x,y)p(x,y)dA \\ &= \int_0^1 \int_0^1 4x^2y \, dx \, dy \\ &= \frac{2}{3} \end{aligned}$$

Note that here $f(x,y) = x$.

14.2.4 Variance

The *variance*, $V(x)$, of a one-dimensional random variable is, by definition, the expected value of the square of the difference between x and $E(x)$:

$$V(x) \equiv E([x - E(x)]^2).$$

Some algebraic manipulation gives the non-obvious expression:

$$V(x) = E(x^2) - [E(x)]^2 .$$

The expression $E([x - E(x)]^2)$ is more useful for thinking intuitively about variance, while the algebraically equivalent expression $E(x^2) - [E(x)]^2$ is usually convenient for calculations. The variance of a sum of random variables is the sum of the variances *if the variables are independent.* This summation property of variance is one of the reasons it is frequently used in analysis of probabilistic models. The square root of the variance is called the *standard deviation*, σ, which gives some indication of expected absolute deviation from the expected value.

14.2.5 Estimated Means

Many problems involve sums of independent random variables x_i, where the variables share a common density p. Such variables are said to be *independent identically distributed* (iid) random variables. When the sum is divided by the number of variables, we get an estimate of $E(x)$:

$$E(x) \approx \frac{1}{N} \sum_{i=1}^{N} x_i.$$

As N increases, the variance of this estimate decreases. We want N to be large enough so that we have confidence that the estimate is "close enough." However, there are no sure things in Monte Carlo; we just gain statistical confidence that our estimate is good. To be sure, we would have to have $N = \infty$. This confidence is expressed by the *Law of Large Numbers*:

$$\text{Probability}\left[E(x) = \lim_{N\to\infty} \frac{1}{N}\sum_{i=1}^{N} x_i\right] = 1.$$

14.3 Monte Carlo Integration

In this section the basic Monte Carlo solution methods for definite integrals are outlined. These techniques are then straightforwardly applied to certain integral problems. All of the basic material of this section is also covered in several of the classic Monte Carlo texts. (See the Notes section at the end of this chapter.)

As discussed earlier, given a function $f : S \mapsto \mathbb{R}$ and a random variable $x \sim p$, we can approximate the expected value of $f(x)$ by a sum:

$$E(f(x)) = \int_{x\in S} f(x)p(x)d\mu \approx \frac{1}{N}\sum_{i=1}^{N} f(x_i). \tag{14.4}$$

Because the expected value can be expressed as an integral, the integral is also approximated by the sum. The form of Equation 14.4 is a bit awkward; we would usually like to approximate an integral of a single function g rather than a product fp. We can accomplish this by substituting $g = fp$ as the integrand:

$$\int_{x\in S} g(x)d\mu \approx \frac{1}{N}\sum_{i=1}^{N} \frac{g(x_i)}{p(x_i)}. \tag{14.5}$$

For this formula to be valid, p must be positive when g is nonzero.

So to get a good estimate, we want as many samples as possible, and we want the g/p to have a low variance (g and p should have a similar shape). Choosing p intelligently is called *importance sampling*, because if p is large where g is large, there will be more samples in important regions. Equation 14.4 also shows the fundamental problem with Monte Carlo integration: *diminishing return*. Because the variance of the estimate is proportional to $1/N$, the standard deviation is proportional to $1/\sqrt{N}$. Since the error in the estimate behaves similarly to the standard deviation, we will need to quadruple N to halve the error.

Another way to reduce variance is to partition S, the domain of the integral, into several smaller domains S_i, and evaluate the integral as a sum of integrals over the S_i. This is called *stratified sampling*, the technique that jittering employs in pixel sampling (Chapter 9). Normally only one sample is taken in each S_i (with density p_i), and in this case the variance of the estimate is:

$$var\left(\sum_{i=1}^{N}\frac{g(x_i)}{p_i(x_i)}\right)=\sum_{i=1}^{N}var\left(\frac{g(x_i)}{p_i(x_i)}\right). \tag{14.6}$$

It can be shown that the variance of stratified sampling is never higher than unstratified if all strata have equal measure:

$$\int_{S_i} p(x)d\mu = \frac{1}{N}\int_S p(x)d\mu.$$

The most common example of stratified sampling in graphics is jittering for pixel sampling as discussed in Section 9.11.

As an example of the Monte Carlo solution of an integral I, set $g(x)$ equal to x over the interval (0, 4):

$$I=\int_0^4 x\,dx = 8. \tag{14.7}$$

The impact of the shape of the function p on the variance of the N sample estimates is shown in Table 14.1. Note that the variance is reduced when the shape of p is similar to the shape of g. The variance drops to zero if $p = g/I$, but I is not usually known or we would not have to resort to Monte Carlo. One important principle illustrated in Table 14.1 is that stratified sampling is often *far* superior to importance sampling. Although the variance for this stratification on I is inversely proportional to the cube of the number of samples, there is no general result for the behavior of variance under stratification. There are some functions for which stratification does no good. One example is a white noise function, where the variance is constant for all regions. On the other hand, most functions will benefit from stratified sampling because the variance in each subcell will usually be smaller than the variance of the entire domain.

Method	**Sampling function**	**Variance**	**Samples needed for standard error of 0.008**
importance	$(6-x)/(16)$	$56.8N^{-1}$	887,500
importance	$1/4$	$21.3N^{-1}$	332,812
importance	$(x+2)/16$	$6.3N^{-1}$	98,437
importance	$x/8$	0	1
stratified	$1/4$	$21.3N^{-3}$	70

Table 14.1. Variance for Monte Carlo estimate of $\int_0^4 x\,dx$.

14.3.1 Quasi-Monte Carlo Integration

A popular method for quadrature is to replace the random points in Monte Carlo integration with *quasi-random* points. Such points are deterministic, but are in some sense uniform. For example, on the unit square $[0, 1]^2$, a set of N quasi-random points should have the following property on a region of area A within the square:

$$\text{number of points in the region} \approx AN.$$

For example, a set of regular samples in a lattice has this property.

Quasi-random points can improve performance in many integration applications. Sometimes care must be taken to make sure that they do not introduce aliasing. It is especially nice that, in any application where calls are made to random or stratified points in $[0, 1]^d$, one can substitute d-dimensional quasi-random points with no other changes.

The key intuition motivating quasi-Monte Carlo integration is that when estimating the average value of an integrand, any set of sample points will do provided they are "fair".

14.4 Choosing Random Points

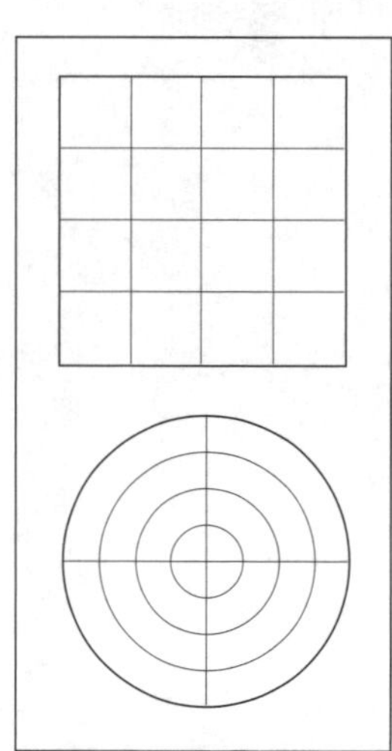

Figure 14.6. The transform that takes the horizontal and vertical dimensions uniformly to (r, ϕ) does not preserve relative area; not all of the resulting areas are the same.

We often want to generate sets of random or pseudo-random points on the unit square for applications such as distribution ray tracing. There are several methods for doing this, e.g., jittering (see Section 9.11). These methods give us a set of N reasonably equidistributed points on the unit square $[0, 1]^2 : (u_1, v_1)$ through (u_N, v_N).

Sometimes, our sampling space may not be square (e.g., a circular lens), or may not be uniform (e.g, a filter function centered on a pixel). It would be nice if we could write a mathematical transformation that would take our equidistributed points (u_i, v_i) as input, and output a set of points in our desired sampling space with our desired density. For example, to sample a camera lens, the transformation would take (u_i, v_i) and output (r_i, ϕ_i) such that the new points are approximately equidistributed on the disk of the lens. While we might be tempted to use the transform:

$$\begin{aligned} \phi_i &= 2\pi u_i, \\ r_i &= v_i R, \end{aligned}$$

it has a serious problem. While the points do cover the lens, they do so non-uniformly (Figure 14.6). What we need in this case is a transformation that takes equal-area regions to equal-area regions—one that takes uniform sampling distributions on the square to uniform distributions on the new domain.

There are several ways to generate such non-uniform points, or uniform points on non-rectangular domains, and the following sections review the three most often used: function inversion, rejection, and Metropolis.

14.4.1 Function Inversion

If the density is a one-dimensional function, $f(x)$, defined over the interval $x \in [x_{min}, x_{max}]$, then we can generate random numbers α_i that have density f from a set of uniform random numbers ξ_i, where $\xi_i \in [0, 1]$. To do this we need the cumulative probability distribution function $P(x)$:

$$\text{Probability}(\alpha < x) = P(x) = \int_{x_{min}}^{x} f(x')d\mu$$

To get α_i, we simply transform ξ_i:

$$\alpha_i = P^{-1}(\xi_i)$$

where P^{-1} is the inverse of P. If P is not analytically invertible, then numerical methods will suffice because an inverse exists for all valid probability distribution functions.

Note that analytically inverting a function is more confusing than it should be due to notation. For example, if we have the function

$$y = x^2,$$

for $x > 0$, then the inverse function is expressed in terms of y as a function of x:

$$x = \sqrt{y}.$$

When the function is analytically invertible, it is almost always that simple. However, things are a little more opaque with the standard notation:

$$f(x) = x^2,$$
$$f^{-1}(x) = \sqrt{x}.$$

Here x is just a dummy variable. You may find it easier to use the less standard notation:

$$y = x^2,$$
$$x = \sqrt{y},$$

while keeping in mind that these are inverse functions of each other.

For example, to choose random points x_i that have density

$$p(x) = \frac{3x^2}{2}$$

on $[-1,1]$, we see that

$$P(x) = \frac{x^3+1}{2},$$

and

$$P^{-1}(x) = \sqrt[3]{2x-1},$$

so we can "warp" a set of canonical random numbers $(\xi_1, \cdots, \xi_N)$ to the properly distributed numbers

$$(x_1, \cdots, x_N) = (\sqrt[3]{2\xi_1 - 1}, \cdots, \sqrt[3]{2\xi_N - 1}).$$

Of course, this same warping function can be used to transform "uniform" jittered samples into nicely distributed samples with the desired density.

If we have a random variable $\alpha = (\alpha_x, \alpha_y)$ with two-dimensional density (x, y) defined on $[x_{min}, x_{max}] \times [y_{min}, y_{max}]$, then we need the two-dimensional distribution function:

$$\text{Probability}(\alpha_x < x \text{ and } \alpha_y < y) = F(x,y) = \int_{y_{min}}^{y} \int_{x_{min}}^{x} f(x', y') d\mu(x', y')$$

We first choose an x_i using the marginal distribution $F(x, y_{max})$, and then choose y_i according to $F(x_i, y)/F(x_i, y_{max})$. If $f(x, y)$ is separable (expressible as $g(x)h(y)$), then the one-dimensional techniques can be used on each dimension.

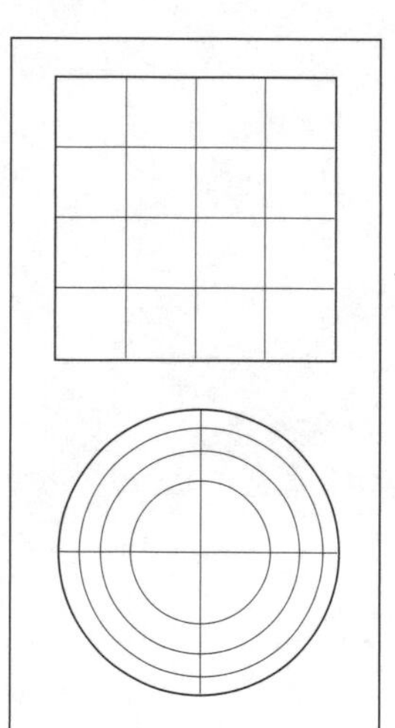

Figure 14.7. A mapping that takes equal area regions in the unit square to equal area regions in the disk.

Returning to our earlier example, suppose we are sampling uniformly from the disk of radius R, so $p(r, \phi) = 1/(\pi R^2)$. The two-dimensional distribution function is:

$$\text{Probability}(r < r_0 \text{ and } \phi < \phi_0) = F(r_0, \phi_0) = \int_0^{\phi_0} \int_0^{r_0} \frac{r dr d\phi}{\pi R^2} = \frac{\phi r^2}{2\pi R^2}$$

This means that a canonical pair (ξ_1, ξ_2) can be transformed to a uniform random point on the disk:

$$\phi = 2\pi\xi_1,$$
$$r = R\sqrt{\xi_2}.$$

This mapping is shown in Figure 14.7.

To choose reflected ray directions for some realistic rendering applications, we choose points on the unit hemisphere according to the density:

$$p(\theta, \phi) = \frac{n+1}{2\pi} \cos^n \theta$$

Where n is a Phong-like exponent, θ is the angle from the surface normal and $\theta \in [0, \pi/2]$ (is on the upper hemisphere) and ϕ is the azimuthal angle ($\phi \in [0, 2\pi]$). The cumulative distribution function is:

$$P(\theta, \phi) = \int_0^{\phi} \int_0^{\theta} p(\theta', \phi') \sin\theta' d\theta' d\phi' \qquad (14.8)$$

The $\cos\theta'$ term arises because, on the sphere, $d\omega = \cos\theta d\theta d\phi$. When the marginal densities are found, p (as expected) is separable, and we find that a (ξ_1, ξ_2) pair of canonical random numbers can be transformed to a direction by:

$$\theta = \arccos\left((1 - r_1)^{\frac{1}{n+1}}\right)$$
$$\phi = 2\pi r_2$$

Again, a nice thing about this is that a set of jittered points on the unit square can be easily transformed to a set of jittered points on the hemisphere with the desired distribution. Note that if n is set to 1, we have a diffuse distribution, as is often needed.

Often we must map the point on the sphere into an appropriate direction with respect to a *uvw* basis. To do this, we can first convert the angles to a unit vector $\vec{a}$:

$$\mathbf{a} = (\cos\phi \sin\theta,\ \sin\phi \sin\theta,\ \cos\theta)$$

As an efficiency improvement, we can avoid taking trigonometric functions of inverse trigonometric functions (e.g., $\cos(\arccos\theta)$). For example, when $n = 1$ (a diffuse distribution), the vector $\mathbf{a}$ simplifies to

$$\mathbf{a} = \left(\cos(2\pi\xi_1)\sqrt{\xi_2}, \sin(2\pi\xi_1)\sqrt{\xi_2}, \sqrt{1-\xi_2}\right)$$

14.4.2 Rejection

A *rejection* method chooses points according to some simple distribution and rejects some of them that are in a more complex distribution. There are several scenarios where rejection is used, and we show some of these by example.

Suppose we want uniform random points within the unit circle. We can first choose uniform random points $(x, y) \in [-1, 1]^2$ and reject those outside the circle. If the function $r()$ returns a canonical random number, then the procedure is:

```
done = false
while (not done) do
   x = -1 + 2r()
   y = -1 + 2r()
   if (x^2 + y^2 < 1) then
      done = true
```

If we want a random number $x \sim p$ and we know that $p : [a, b] \mapsto \mathbb{R}$, and that for all x, $p(x) < m$, then we can generate random points in the rectangle $[a, b] \times [0, m]$ and take those where $y < p(x)$:

```
done = false
while (not done) do
   x = a + r()(b − a)
   y = r()m
   if (y < p(x)) then
      done = true
```

This same idea can be applied to take random points on the surface of a sphere. To pick a random unit vector with uniform directional distribution, we first pick a random point in the unit sphere and then treat that point as a direction vector by taking the unit vector in the same direction:

```
done = false
while (not done) do
   x = −1 + 2r()
   y = −1 + 2r()
   z = −1 + 2r()
   if ((l = sqrt(x² + y² + z²)) < 1) then
      done = true
x = x/l
y = y/l
z = z/l
```

Although the rejection method is usually simple to code, it is rarely compatible with stratification. For this reason, it tends to converge more slowly and should thus be used only for debugging, or in particularly difficult circumstances.

14.4.3 Metropolis

The *Metropolis* method uses random *mutations* to produce a set of samples with a desired density. This concept is used extensively in the *Metropolis Light Transport* algorithm referenced in the chapter notes. Suppose we have a random point x_0 in a domain S. Further, suppose for any point x, we have a way to generate random $y \sim p_x$. We use the marginal notation $p_x(y) \equiv p(x \to y)$ to denote this density function. Now, suppose we let x_1 be a random point in S selected with underlying density $p(x_0 \to x_1)$. We generate x_2 with density $p(x_1 \to x_0)$ and so on. In the limit, where we generate an infinite number of samples, it can be proved that the samples will have some underlying density determined by p regardless of the initial point x_0.

Now, suppose we want to chose p such that the underlying density of samples to which we converge is proportional to a function $f(x)$ where f is a non-negative function with domain S. Further, suppose we can evaluate

f, but we have little or no additional knowledge about its properties (such functions are common in graphics). Also, suppose we have the ability to make "transitions" from x_i to x_{i+1} with underlying density function $t(x_i \rightarrow x_{i+1})$. To add flexibility, further suppose we add the potentially non-zero probability that x_i transitions to itself, i.e., $x_{i+1} = x_i$. We phrase this as generating a potential candidate $y \sim t(x_i \rightarrow y)$ and "accepting" this candidate (i.e., $x_{i+1} = y$) with probability $a(x_i \rightarrow y)$ and rejecting it (i.e., $x_{i+1} = x_i$) with probability $1 - a(x_i \rightarrow y)$. Note that the sequence $x_0, x_1, x_2, \ldots$ will be a random set, but there will be some correlation among samples. They will still be suitable for Monte Carlo integration or density estimation, but analyzing the variance of those estimates is much more challenging.

Now, suppose we are given a transition function $t(x \rightarrow y)$ and a function $f(x)$ of which we want to mimic the distribution, can we use $a(y \rightarrow x)$ such that the points are distributed in the shape of f? Or more precisely:

$$\{x_0, x_1, x_2, \ldots\} \sim \frac{f}{\int_s f}$$

It turns out this can be forced by making sure the x_i are *stationary* in some strong sense. If you visualize a huge collection of sample points x, you want the "flow" between two points to be the same in each direction. If we assume the density of points near x and y are proportional to $f(x)$ and $f(y)$ respectively, then the flow in the two directions should be the same:

$$\begin{aligned} \text{flow}(x \rightarrow y) &= kf(x)t(x \rightarrow y)a(x \rightarrow y) \\ \text{flow}(y \rightarrow x) &= kf(y)t(y \rightarrow x)a(y \rightarrow x) \end{aligned}$$

where k is some positive constant. Setting these two flows constant gives a constraint on a:

$$\frac{a(y \rightarrow x)}{a(x \rightarrow y)} = \frac{f(x)t(x \rightarrow y)}{f(y)t(y \rightarrow x)}.$$

Thus, if either $a(y \rightarrow x)$ or $a(x \rightarrow y)$ is known, so is the other. Making them larger improves the chance of acceptance, so the usual technique is to set the larger of the two to 1.

A difficulty in using the Metropolis sample generation technique is that it is hard to estimate how many points are needed before the set of points is "good." Things are accelerated if the first n points are discarded, although choosing n wisely is non-trivial.

14.4.4 Example: Choosing Random Lines in the Square

As an example of the full process of designing a sampling strategy, consider the problem of finding random lines that intersect the unit square $[0, 1]^2$.

We want this process to be fair, that is, we would like the lines to be uniformly distributed within the square. Intuitively, we can see that there is some subtlety to this problem; there are "more" lines at an oblique angle than in horizontal or vertical directions. This is because the cross-section of the square is not uniform.

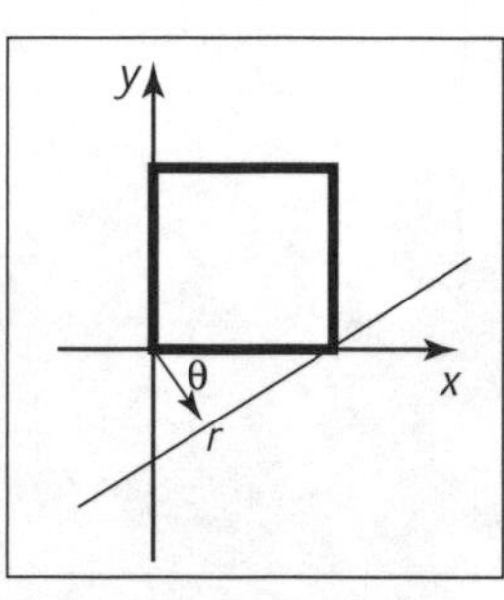

Figure 14.8. The largest distance r corresponds to a line hitting the square for $\theta \in [-\pi/2, 0]$. Because the the square has side-length one, $r = \cos\theta$.

Our first goal is to find a function-inversion method, if one exists, and then to fall back on rejection or Metropolis if that fails. This is because we would like to have stratified samples in line space. We try using normal coordinates first, because the problem of choosing random lines in the square is just the problem of finding uniform random points in whatever part of (r, θ) space corresponds to lines in the square. Consider the region where $-\pi/2 < \theta < 0$. What values of r correspond to lines that hit the square? For those angles, $r < \cos\theta$ are all the lines that hit the square as shown in Figure 14.8. Similar reasoning in the other four quadrants finds the region in (r, θ) space that must be sampled, as shown in Figure 14.9. The equation of the boundary of that region $r_{\text{max}}(\theta)$is:

$$r_{\text{max}}(\theta) = \begin{cases} 0 & \text{if } \theta \in [-\pi, -\frac{\pi}{2}] \\ \cos\theta & \text{if } \theta \in [-\frac{\pi}{2}, 0] \\ \cos\theta + \sin\theta & \text{if } \theta \in [0, \frac{\pi}{2}] \\ \sin\theta & \text{if } \theta \in [\frac{\pi}{2}, \pi] \end{cases}$$

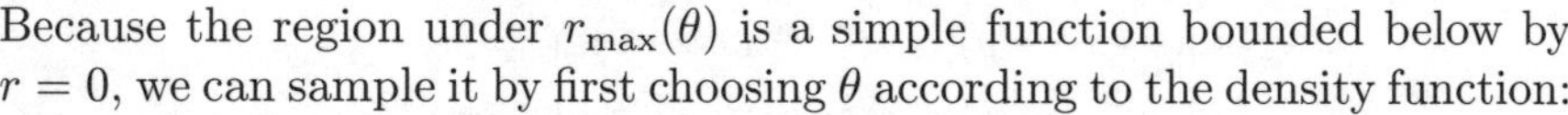

Because the region under $r_{\text{max}}(\theta)$ is a simple function bounded below by $r = 0$, we can sample it by first choosing θ according to the density function:

$$p(\theta) = \frac{r_{\text{max}}(\theta)}{\int_{-\pi}^{\pi} r_{\text{max}}(\theta) d\theta}$$

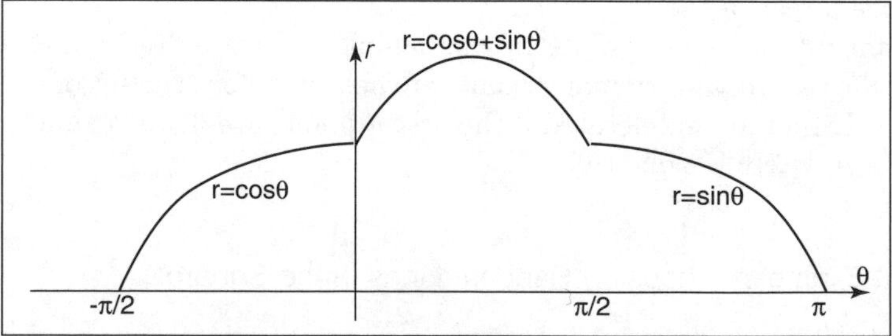

Figure 14.9. The maximum radius for lines hitting the unit square $[0,1]^2$ as a function of θ.

The denominator here is 4. Now, we can compute the cumulative probability distribution function:

$$P(\theta) = \begin{cases} 0 & \text{if } \theta \in [-\pi, -\frac{\pi}{2}] \\ (1+\sin\theta)/4 & \text{if } \theta \in [-\frac{\pi}{2}, 0] \\ (2+\sin\theta - cos\theta)/4 & \text{if } \theta \in [0, \frac{\pi}{2}] \\ (3-\cos\theta)/4 & \text{if } \theta \in [\frac{\pi}{2}, \pi] \end{cases}$$

We can invert this by manipulating $\xi_1 = P(\theta)$ into the form $\theta = g(\xi_1)$. This yields:

$$\theta = \begin{cases} \arcsin(4\xi_1 - 1) & \text{if } \xi_1 < \frac{1}{4} \\ \left(\arcsin\left((4\xi_1 - 2)^2\right)\right)/2 & \text{if } \xi_1 \in [\frac{1}{4}, \frac{3}{4}] \\ \arccos(3 - 4\xi_1) & \text{if } \xi_1 > \frac{3}{4} \end{cases}$$

Once we have θ, then r is simply:

$$r = \xi_2 r_{\max}(\theta).$$

As discussed earlier, there are many parameterizations of the line, and each has an associated "fair" measure. We can generate random lines in any of these spaces as well. For example, in slope-intercept space, the region that hits the square is shown in Figure 14.10. By similar reasoning to the normal space, the density function for the slope is:

$$p(m) = \frac{1+|m|}{4}$$

with respect to the differential measure

$$d\mu = \frac{dm}{(1+m^2)^{\frac{3}{2}}}.$$

This gives rise to the cumulative distribution function:

$$P(m) = \begin{cases} \frac{1}{2} - \frac{m-1}{2\sqrt{1+m^2}} & \text{if } m < 0 \\ 1 + \frac{m-1}{2\sqrt{1+m^2}} & \text{if } m \geq 0 \end{cases}$$

These can be inverted by solving two quadratic equations. Given an m generated using ξ_1, we then have

$$b = \begin{cases} -m + 2(m+1)\xi_2 & \text{if } \xi < \frac{1}{2} \\ (1-m)(2\xi_2 - 1) & \text{otherwise} \end{cases}$$

This is not a better way than using normal coordinates; it is just an alternative way.

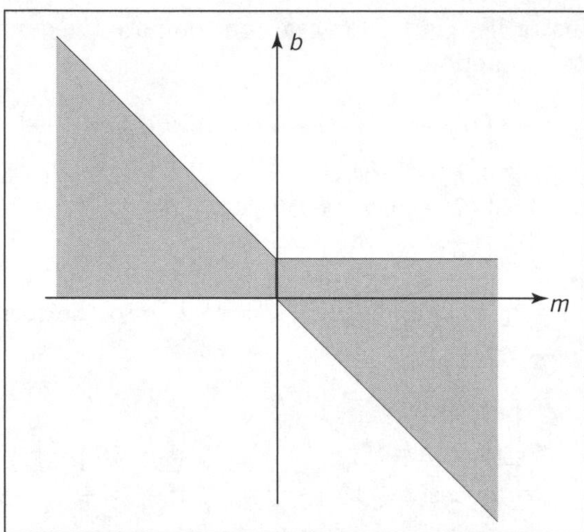

Figure 14.10. The region of (m,b) space that contains lines that intersect the unit square $[0,1]^2$.

Frequently Asked Questions

• This chapter discussed probability but not statistics. What is the distinction?

Probability is the study of how likely an event is. Statistics infers characteristics of large, but finite, populations of random variables. In that sense, statistics could be viewed as a specific type of applied probability.

• Is Metropolis sampling the same as the Metropolis Light Transport Algorithm?

No. The *Metropolis Light Transport* (Veach and Guibas, SIGGRAPH, 1996) algorithm uses Metropolis sampling as part of its procedure, but it is specifically for rendering, and it has other steps as well.

Notes

Monte Carlo methods for graphics are discussed in *Monte Carlo Rendering* (Jensen, SIGGRAPH Course Notes, 2001). The classic reference for geometric probability is *Geometric Probability* (Solomon, SIAM Press, 1978). A method for picking random edges in a square is given in *Random-Edge Discrepancy of Supersampling Patterns* (Dobkin and Mitchell, Graphics Interface Conference, 1993). Some convergence properties of stratified sampling in graphics is given in *Consequences of Stratified Sampling in Graphics* (Mitchell, SIGGRAPH, 1996). More information on Quasi-Monte Carlo methods for graphics can be found in *Efficient Multidimensional Sampling* (Keller and Kollig, Computer Graphics Forum, 2002). Two classic and very readable books on Monte Carlo mathods are *Monte Carlo Methods* (Hammersley and Hanscomb, Chapman & Hall, 1965), and *The Monte Carlo Method* (Sobel, University of Chicago Press, 1975).

Exercises

1. What is the average value of the function xyz in the unit cube $(x, y, z) \in [0, 1]^3$?

2. What is the average value of r on the unit-radius disk: $(r, \phi) \in [0, 1] \times [0, 2\pi)$?

3. Show that the uniform mapping of canonical random points (ξ_1, ξ_2) to the barycentric coordinates of any triangle is: $\beta = 1 - \sqrt{1 - \xi_1}$, and $\gamma = (1 - u)\xi_2$.

4. What is the average length of a line inside the unit square? Verify your answer by generating ten million random lines in the unit square and averaging their lengths.

5. What is the average length of a line inside the unit cube? Verify your answer by generating ten million random lines in the unit cube and averaging their lengths.

6. Show from the definition of variance that $V(x) = E(x^2) - [E(x)]^2$.

Antialiasing

The images we have created so far suffer from jaggies and aliasing. Jaggies are the staircasing that occurs along object edges, and aliasing is the beating patterns that occur in textures. A 1D example of aliasing is given in Figure 15.1. Both artifacts are especially objectionable in an animation, because they attract the eye as they change. An *antialiasing* algorithm attempts to reduce aliasing. This term comes from the field of signal processing, and its discussion is often phased in the mathematical framework of signal processing. Instead, this chapter takes a more operational approach; the human visual issues involved make it problematic to handle it in its entirety using signal processing formalisms.

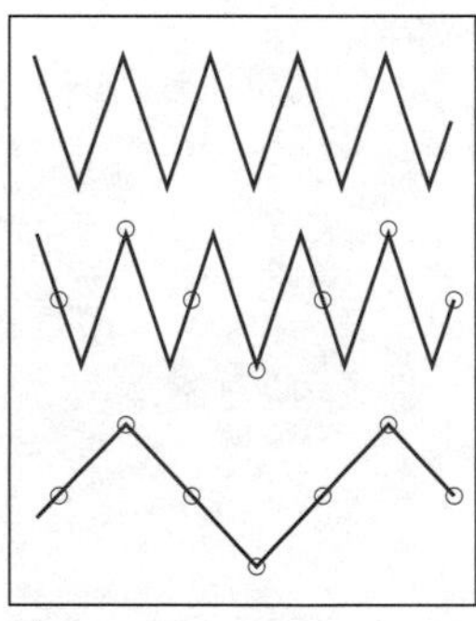

Figure 15.1. An example of aliasing. When the top high frequency function is sampled at regular intervals (like pixel centers) a lower frequency *alias* may be inferred from the insufficient sampling.

As discussed in Chapter 3, aliasing can be reduced by taking the average color "inside" the pixel. More sophisticated antialiasing algorithms still take this basic strategy, but they take weighted averages near the pixel rather than a straight on/off average. This chapter discusses both which weighting function to use, as well as strategies for implementation.

15.1 Filtering

The process of taking a weighted average near a pixel can be easily formalized once we have a coordinate system on the screen. Recall the coordinate system from Chapter 3 shown in Figure 15.2. Assume a potentially high-resolution greyscale function $L(x, y)$ defined for all (x, y). A weighted average near the center of pixel (i, j) gives its resulting color L_{ij}:

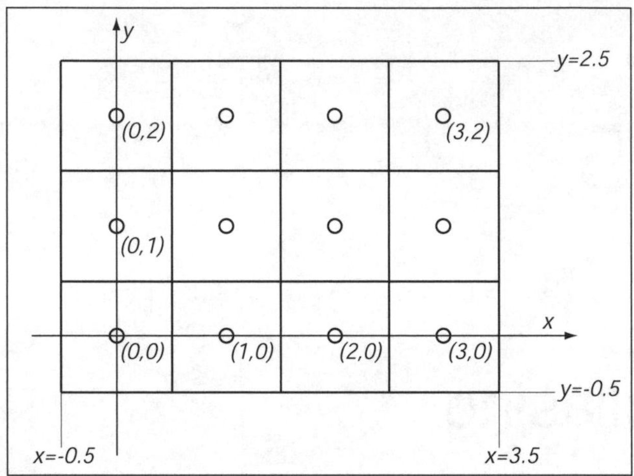

Figure 15.2. Coordinates of a four-pixel by three-pixel screen.

$$L_{ij} = \int_{\text{all } y} \int_{\text{all } x} w(x - i, y - j) L(x, y) \, dx \, dy,$$

where $w(x, y)$ is a unit volume function centered at the origin. For RGB images we just apply that formula in all three color channels.

It has been shown empirically that you can usually get better images if w is a "lumpy" function a few pixels wide with a maximum near the origin. Quite a bit is understood about why this is true, but there are still open questions about the details of what w should be. We will discuss this issue, but first we develop some notation.

We can phrase our earlier antialiasing strategy of uniform averaging inside the pixel by using the filter function:

$$w(x, y) = \begin{cases} 1 & \text{if } (x, y) \in \left[-\frac{1}{2}, \frac{1}{2}\right)^2, \\ 0 & \text{otherwise.} \end{cases}$$

This is a *box filter* of width one.

For the box filer of width W (a generalization of the simple width-one box filter), the weighting function is:

$$w(x, y) = \begin{cases} \frac{1}{W^2} & \text{if } (x, y) \in \left[-\frac{W}{2}, +\frac{W}{2}\right)^2, \\ 0 & \text{otherwise.} \end{cases}$$

Note that we had to decrease the height of this function; for it to be a weighted average we need:

$$\int_{\text{all } y} \int_{\text{all } x} w(x, y) \, dx \, dy = 1.$$

That ensures that we don't change the overall brightness of the image function when we discretize it into pixels.

There are two optional constraints on the weighting function that can help us narrow the possibilities:

1. The weighting function is non-negative.

2. The total contribution of any screen point (x, y) is the same as any other point.

The first constraint does limit us, as negative lobes in the filter can be useful. However, it keeps us from having to avoid negative values for pixel colors. The second constraint ensures that a small moving bright spot contributes the same total intensity to an image as it moves, and can be phrased mathematically as:

$$\text{for all } (x, y)\text{: } \sum_{\text{all } i} \sum_{\text{all } j} w(x - i, y - j) = 1.$$

Interestingly, we have already seen such functions: the B-spline blending functions in Section 13.7. These are shown in Figure 15.3.

The zeroth-order B-spline blending function is just exactly the box filter, except that it needs to be shifted by one-half to be centered at the origin. The first-order B-spline blending function is often called the superable triangle filter with support width two. The term *support* refers to the region where w is non-zero. The term *separable* means the filter is in the form of a product of two 1D functions: $w(x, y) = a(x)(b)$. The separable triangle filter is given by:

$$w(x, y) = \begin{cases} (1 - |x|)(1 - |y|) & \text{if } (x, y) \in [-1, 1]^2, \\ 0 & \text{otherwise.} \end{cases} \tag{15.1}$$

The difference between box and triangle filters is not obvious for most still frames. The differences, however, are more obvious if we use an extreme 2D function used in Chapter 17 to to illustrate human contrast sensitivity:

$$L(x, y) = \frac{1}{2}\left(1 + f \sin(2\pi a e^{5a})\right), \tag{15.2}$$

where $a = x/n_x$, $f = (1 - (y/n_y))^3$.

The box-filtered image is shown in Figure 15.4. The triangle-filtered image is shown in Figure 15.5. Note the "false" stripes are much more obvious in the box-filtered image. For moving images, all of the artifacts are *much* more obvious. For this reason, cubic filters are sometimes used.

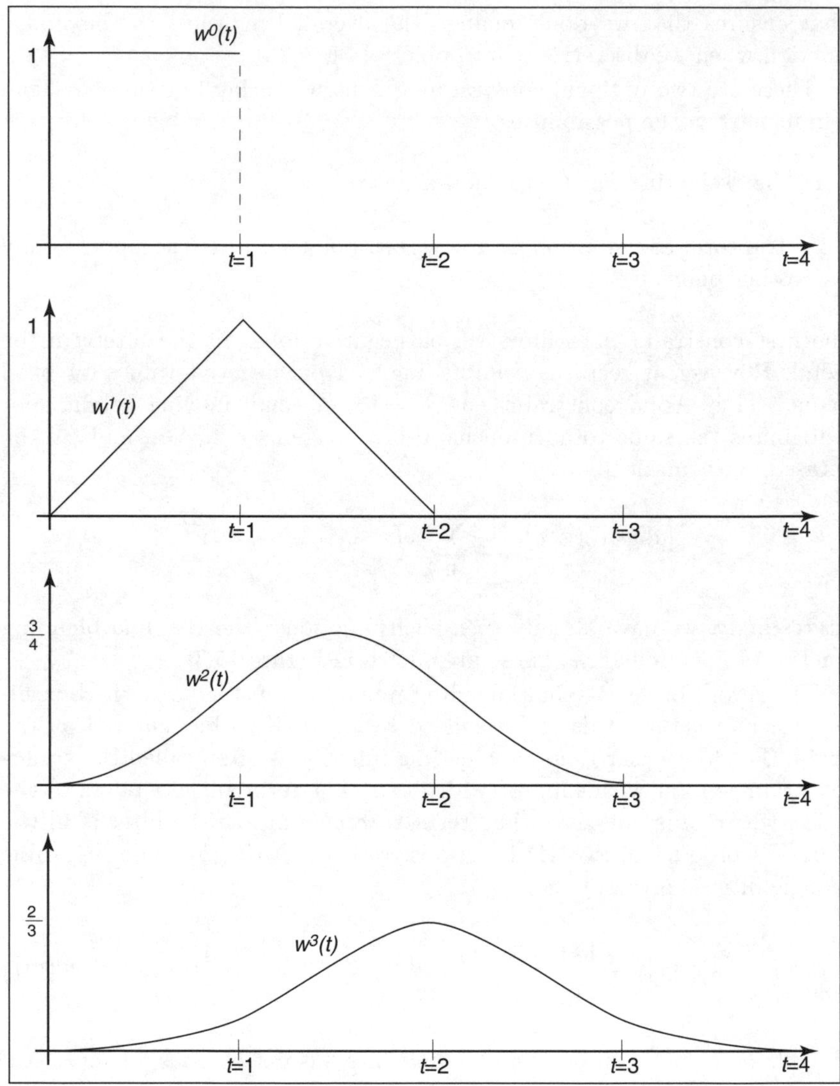

Figure 15.3. The unshifted B-spline blending functions have all the desired characteristics of filters except that they are not centered at the origin. The top function is the box filter and the first-order function is the triangle filter.

Figure 15.4. The function in Equation 15.2 is sampled using a box filter. Notice that the stripes in the right portion of the image are aliases and are thus undesirable.

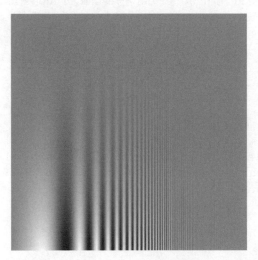

Figure 15.5. The function in Equation 15.2 is sampled using a separable triangle filter. Notice that the stripes in the right portion of the image are less noticeable than with the box filter.

15.2 Implementing Filtering

In most graphics applications we do not have an analytic form for $L(x, y)$. Instead, we can only evaluate $L(x, y)$ at a finite number of points, e.g., where the ray samples are taken in a ray tracer. This reduces L to an integration problem. We can either use uniform sampling or non-uniform sampling to implement filtering.

15.2.1 Uniform Sampling

We can sample the entire screen uniformly using regular, stratified, or some other kind of uniform sampling. Then, within the support of the filter we get:

$$L_{ij} = \frac{A}{N} \sum_{k=0}^{N-1} w(x_k - i, y_k - j) L(x_k, y_k),$$

where A is the area of the support of the filter. For example, for the superable triangle filter, $A = 4$.

When any kind of uniform, but irregular, samples are used, we can optionally add a normalization step to lessen the effects of non-uniform sampling. This gives a discrete weighted average:

$$L_{ij} = \frac{\sum_{k=0}^{N-1} w(x_k - i, y_k - j) L(x_k, y_k)}{\sum_{k=0}^{N-1} w(x_k - i, y_k - j)}.$$

15.2.2 Non-Uniform Sampling

Alternatively, we can use importance sampling (Chapter 14) and not share samples between pixels; each is then a separate integration problem.

For the separable triangle filter, those points that are random (but non-uniform) can be generated by the transform:

$$x_k = \begin{cases} -1 + \sqrt{2\xi_k} & \text{if } \xi_k < 0.5, \\ 1 - \sqrt{2 - 2\xi_k} & \text{otherwise.} \end{cases}$$

An analogous formula transforms ξ'_k into to y_k. The formula for the pixel intensity is then:

$$L(i, j) \approx \frac{1}{N} \sum_{k=0}^{n-1} L(i + x_k, j + y_k).$$

Note that this formula only applies to *non-uniform* points that have been "warped" according to the appropriate function. Also, note that the input

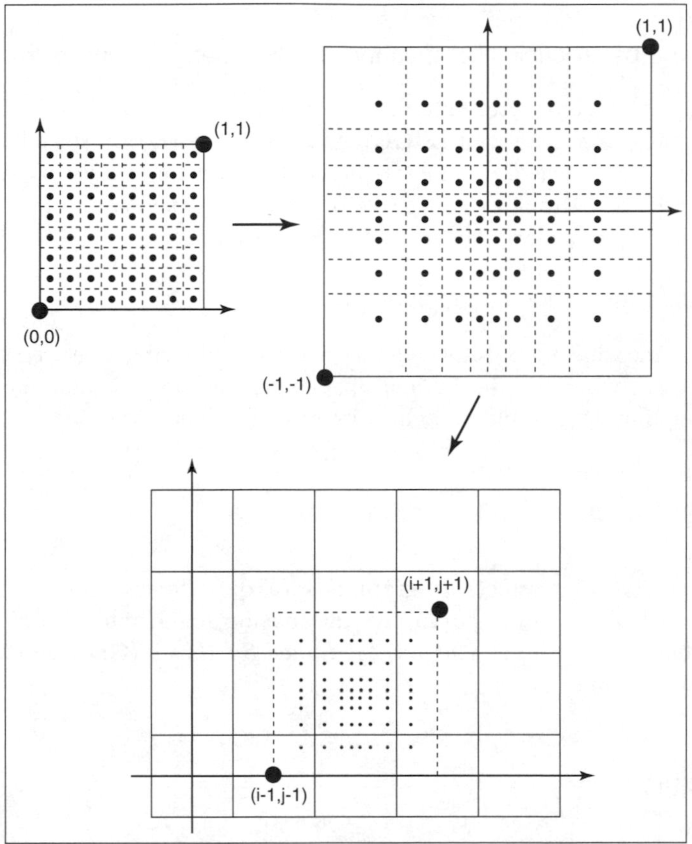

Figure 15.6. In non-uniform sampling the distribution of the samples applies the filter, so they are all weighted the same. The input regular points on the unit square are irregularly shifted. Any set of uniform points can be used, e.g., stratified. This figure shows regular points, but any set of uniform points, such as jittered points, could be used.

points need not be random for this to work; they need only be uniform. The process for sampling a pixel with warped regular sampling is shown in Figure 15.6.

Frequently Asked Questions

• If I had a mathematical model of human visual response, couldn't I optimize the filter choice using signal processing?

Yes. Kajiya examined this question in his dissertation (University of Utah, 1980) and found that the choice of filter depended on the underlying function.

• **Is there a better cubic filter than the B-spline blending function?**

If you allow negative filter values, there is a better cubib filter for at least some applications. Mitchell (SIGGRAPH, 1987) used perceptual tests to "optimize" the choice of parameters in a cubic filter for image up-sampling, and, in practice, the filter can also work well for pixel sampling for some applications, particularly those that need crisp images.

• **Isn't box filtering good enough in practice?**

Bad dynamic aliasing becomes visible when box-filtering textured images, even in cases where the individual images do not show visible aliasing. A cubic B-spline works well enough in practice for such cases.

Notes

Antialiasing was introduced to graphics in Crow's dissertation (University of Utah, 1975). A good survey of antialiasing for graphics applications can be found in *Principles of Digital Image Synthesis* (Glassner, Morgan Kaufmann, 1993).

Exercises

1. Suppose you want to render an image of the stars at night. What filter is best?

2. Modify Equation 15.2 so that it "moves" to the right with time. Make an animation of this using B-spline filters of various degrees. What degree is needed to reduce aliasing to a "reasonable" level?

Light

In this chapter we discuss the practical issues of measuring light, usually called *radiometry*. The terms that arise in radiometry may at first seem strange and have terminology and notation that may be hard to keep straight. However, because radiometry is so fundamental to computer graphics, it is worth studying radiometry until it sinks in. This chapter also covers *photometry*, which takes radiometric quantities and scales them to estimate how much "useful" light is present. For example, a green light may seem twice as bright as a blue light of the same power because the eye is more sensitive to green light. Photometry attempts to quantify such distinctions.

16.1 Radiometry

Although we can define radiometric units in many systems, we use *SI* (International System of Units) units. Familiar SI units include the metric units of meter (m) and gram (g). Light is fundamentally a propagating form of energy, so it is useful to define the *SI* unit of energy which is the Joule (J).

16.1.1 Photons

To aid our intuition, we will describe radiometry in terms of collections of large numbers of *photons*, and this section establishes what is meant by a photon in this context. For the purposes of this chapter, a photon is a quantum of light that has a position, direction of propagation, and a wavelength λ. Somewhat strangely, the SI unit used for wavelength is *nanometer* (nm). This is mainly for historical reasons, and $1nm = 10^{-9}m$. Another unit, the *angstrom* is sometimes used, and one nanometer is ten angstroms. A photon also has a speed c that depends only on the refractive index n of the medium through which it propagates. Sometimes the frequency $f = c/\lambda$ is also used for light. This is convenient because unlike λ and c, f does not change when the photon refracts into a medium with a new refractive index. Another invariant measure is the amount of energy q carried by a photon, which is given by the following relationship:

$$q = hf = \frac{hc}{\lambda}, \tag{16.1}$$

where $h = 6.63 \times 10^{-34} Js^{-1}$ is Plank's Constant. Although these quantities can be measured in many unit systems, we will use *SI* units whenever possible.

16.1.2 Spectral Energy

If we have a large collection of photons, their total energy Q can be computed by summing the energy q_i of each photon. A reasonable question to ask is "How is the energy distributed across wavelengths?" An easy way to answer this is to partition the photons into bins, essentially histogramming them. We then have an energy associated with an interval. For example, we can count all the energy between $\lambda = 500nm$ and $\lambda = 600nm$, and have it turn out to be $10.2J$, and this might be denoted $q[500, 600] = 10.2$. If we divided the wavelength interval into two $50nm$ intervals, we might find that $q[500, 550] = 5.2$ and $q[550, 600] = 5.0$. This tells us there was a little more energy in the short wavelength half of the interval $[500, 600]$. If we divide into $25nm$ bins, we might find $q[500, 525] = 2.5$, and so on. The nice thing about the system is that it is straightforward. The bad thing about it is that the choice of the interval size determines the number.

A more commonly used system is to divide the energy by the size of the interval. So instead of $q[500, 600] = 10.2$ we would have:

$$Q_\lambda[500, 600] = \frac{10.2}{100} = 0.12J(nm)^{-1}$$

This approach is nice, because the size of the interval has much less impact on the overall size of the numbers. An immediate idea would be to drive the interval size $\Delta\lambda$ to zero. This could be awkward, because for a sufficiently small $\Delta\lambda$, Q_λ will either be zero or huge depending on whether there is a single photon or no photon in the interval. There are two schools of thought to solve that dilemma. The first is to assume that $\Delta\lambda$ is small, but not so small that the quantum nature of light comes into play. The second is to assume that the light is a continuum rather than individual photons, so a true derivative $dQ/d\lambda$ is appropriate. Both ways of thinking about it are appropriate and lead to the same computational machinery. In practice, it seems that most people who measure light prefer small, but finite, intervals, because that is what they can measure in the lab. Most people who do theory or computation prefer infinitesimal intervals, because that makes the machinery of calculus available.

The quantity Q_λ is called *spectral energy*, and it is an *intensive* quantity as opposed to an *extensive* quantity such as energy, length, or mass. Intensive quantities can be thought of as density functions that tell the density of an extensive quantity at an infinitesimal point. For example, the energy Q at a specific wavelength is probably zero, but the spectral energy (energy density) Q_λ is a meaningful quantity. A probably more familiar example is that the population of a country may be 25 million, but the population at a point in that country is meaningless. However, the population *density* measured in people per square meter is meaningful, provided it is measured over large enough areas. Much like with photons, population density works best if we pretend that we can view population as a continuum where population density never becomes granular even when the area is small.

We will follow the convention of graphics where spectral energy is almost always used, and energy is rarely used. This results in a proliferation of λ subscripts if "proper" notation is used. Instead, we will drop the subscript and use Q to denote spectral energy. This can result in some confusion when people outside of graphics read graphics papers, so be aware of this standards issue. Your intuition about spectral power might be aided by imagining a measurement device with an energy sensor that measures light energy q. If you place a colored filter in front of the sensor that allows only light in the interval $[\lambda - \Delta\lambda/2, \lambda + \Delta\lambda/2]$, then the spectral power at λ would be $Q = \Delta q/\Delta\lambda$.

16.1.3 Power

It is useful to estimate a rate of energy production for light sources. This rate is called *power*, and it is measured in *Watts*, W, which is another name for *Joules per second.* This is easiest to understand in a *steady state*, but because power is an intensive quantity (a density over time), it is well defined even when energy production is varying over time. The units of power may be more familiar, e.g., a 100 Watt light bulb. Such bulbs draw approximately $100J$ of energy each second. The power of the light produced will actually be less than $100W$ because of heat loss, etc., but we can still use this example to help understand more about photons. For example, we can get a feel for how many photons are produced in a second by a $100W$ light. Suppose the average photon produced has the energy of a $\lambda = 500nm$ photon. The frequency of such a photon is:

$$f = \frac{c}{\lambda} = \frac{3 \times 10^8 ms^{-1}}{500 \times 10^{-9} m} = 6 \times 10^{14} s^{-1}.$$

The energy of that photon is $hf \approx 4 \times 10^{-19} J$. That means a staggering 10^{20} photons are produced each second, even if the bulb is not very efficient. This explains why simulating a camera with a fast shutter speed and directly simulated photons is an inefficient choice for producing images.

As with energy, we are really interested in *spectral power* measured in $W(nm)^{-1}$. Again, although the formal standard symbol for spectral power is Φ_λ, we will use Φ with no subscript for convenience and consistency with most of the graphics literature. One thing to note is that the spectral power for a light source is usually a smaller number than the power. For example, if a light emits a power of $100W$ evenly distributed over wavelengths $400nm$ to $800nm$, then the spectral power will be $100W/400nm = .25W(nm)^{-1}$. This is something to keep in mind if you set the spectral power of light sources by hand for debugging purposes.

The measurement device for spectral energy in the last section could be modified by taking a reading with a shutter that is open for a time interval Δt centered at time t. The spectral power would then be $\Delta Q/(\Delta t \Delta\lambda)$.

16.1.4 Irradiance

The quantity *irradiance* arises naturally if you ask the question "How much light hits this point?". Of course the answer is "none," and again we must use a density function. If the point is on a surface, it is natural to use area to define our density function. We modify the device from the last section to have a finite ΔA area sensor that is smaller than the light field being measured. The spectral irradiance H is just the power per unit area $\Delta\Phi/\Delta A$. Fully expanded this is:

$$\Phi = \frac{\Delta q}{\Delta A \, \Delta t \Delta\lambda} \qquad (16.2)$$

Thus, the full units of irradiance are $Jm^{-2}s^{-1}(nm)^{-1}$. Note that the SI units for radiance include inverse-meter-squared for area and inverse-nanometer for wavelength. This seeming inconsistency (using both nanometer and meter) arises because of the natural units for area and visible light wavelengths.

When the light is leaving a surface, e.g., when it is reflected, the same quantity as irradiance is called *radiant exitance*, E. It is useful to have different words for incident and exitant light, because the same point has potentially different irradiance and radiant exitance.

16.1.5 Radiance

Although irradience tells us how much light is arriving at a point, it tells us little about the direction that light comes from. To measure something analogous to what we see with our eyes, we need to be able to associate "how much light" with a specific direction. We can imagine a simple device to measure such a quantity (Figure 16.1). We use a small irradiance meter and add a conical "baffler" which limits light hitting the counter to a range of angles with solid angle $\Delta\sigma$. The response of the detector is thus:

$$\begin{aligned}\text{response} &= \frac{\Delta H}{\Delta\sigma} \\ &= \frac{\Delta q}{\Delta A\, \Delta\sigma\, \Delta t\, \Delta\lambda}\end{aligned}$$

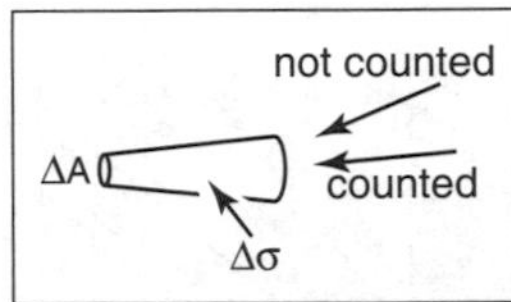

Figure 16.1. By adding a blinder that shows only a small solid angle $\Delta\sigma$ to the irradiance detector, we measure radiance.

This is the spectral *radiance* of light travelling in space. Again, we will drop the "spectral" in our discussion and assume that it is implicit.

Radiance is what we are usually computing in graphics programs. A wonderful property of radiance is that it does not vary along a line in space. To see why this is true, examine the two radiance detectors both looking at a surface as shown in Figure 16.2. Assume the lines the detectors are looking along are close enough together that the surface is emitting/reflecting

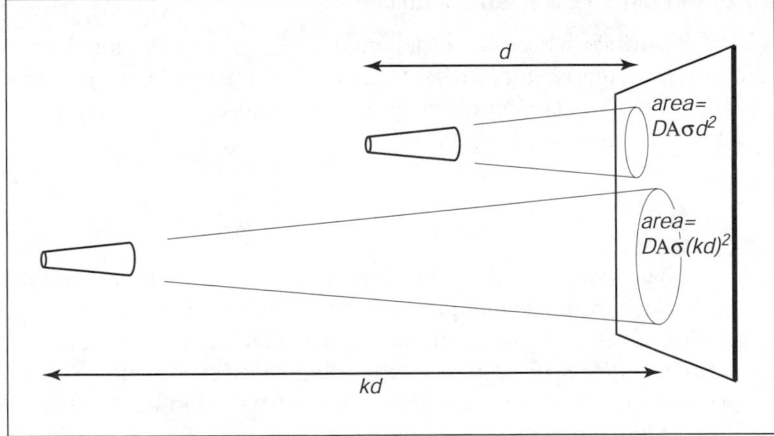

Figure 16.2. The signal a radiance detector receives does not depend on the distance to the surface being measured. This figure assumes the detectors are pointing at areas on the surface that are emitting light in the same way.

light "the same" in both of the areas being measured. Because the area of the surface being sampled is proportional to squared distance, and because the light reaching the detector is *inversely* proportional to squared distance, the two detectors should have the same reading.

It is useful to measure the radiance hitting a surface. We can think of placing the cone baffler from the radiance detector at a point on the surface and measuring the irradiance H on the surface originating from directions within the cone (Figure 16.3). Note that the surface "detector" is not aligned with the cone. For this reason we need to add a cosine correction term to our definition of radiance:

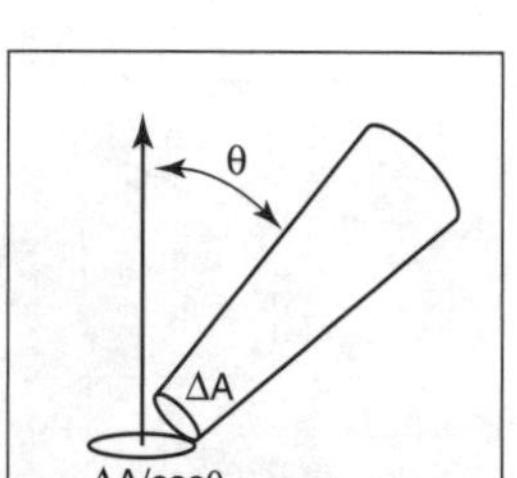

Figure 16.3. The irradiance at the surface as masked by the cone is smaller than that measured at the detector by a cosine factor.

$$\begin{aligned}\text{response} &= \frac{\Delta H}{\Delta\sigma \cos\theta} \\ &= \frac{\Delta q}{\Delta A \cos\theta \; \Delta\sigma \; \Delta t \; \Delta\lambda}\end{aligned}$$

As with irradiance and radiant exitance, it is useful to distinguish between radiance incident at a point on a surface and exitant from that point. Terms for these concepts sometimes used in the graphics literature are *surface radiance* L_s for the radiance of (leaving) a surface, and *field radiance* for the radiance incident at a surface. Both require the cosine term, because they both correspond to the configuration in Figure 16.3:

$$\begin{aligned}L_s &= \frac{\Delta E}{\Delta\sigma \cos\theta} \\ L_f &= \frac{\Delta H}{\Delta\sigma \cos\theta}\end{aligned}$$

Radiance and other radiometric quantities

If we have a surface whose field radiance is L_f, then we can derive all of the other radiometric quantities from it. This is one reason radiance is considered the "fundamental" radiometric quantity. For example, the irradiance can be expressed as:

$$H = \int_{\text{all } \mathbf{k}} L_f(\mathbf{k}) \; \cos\theta \; d\sigma$$

This formula has several notational conventions that are common in graphics that make such formulae opaque to readers not familiar with them (Figure 16.4). First, $\mathbf{k}$ is an incident direction, and can be thought of as a unit vector, a direction, or a (θ, ϕ) pair in spherical coordinates with respect to the surface normal. The direction has a differential solid angle $d\sigma$ associated with it. The field radiance is potentially different for every direction, so we write it as a function $L(\mathbf{k})$.

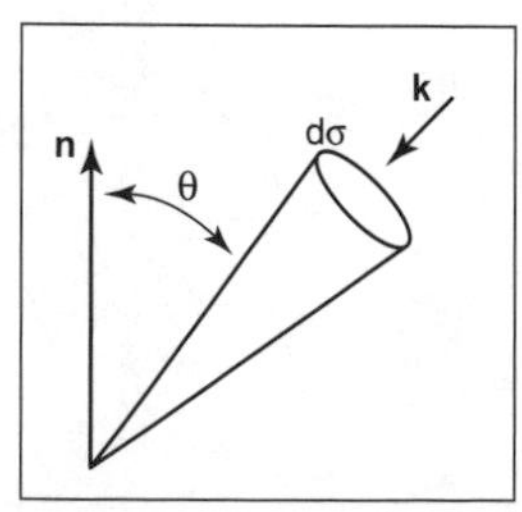

Figure 16.4. The direction **k** has a differential solid angle $d\sigma$ associated with it.

As an example, we can compute the irradiance H at a surface that has constant field radiance L_f in all directions. To integrate, we use a classic spherical coordinate system, and recall that the differential solid angle is

$$d\sigma \equiv \sin\theta \; d\theta \; d\phi$$

so the irradiance is:

$$\begin{aligned} H &= \int_{\phi=0}^{2\pi} \int_{\theta=0}^{\frac{\pi}{2}} L_f \; \sin\theta \; d\theta \; d\phi \\ &= \pi L_f \end{aligned}$$

This relation shows us our first occurrence of a potentially surprising constant π. These factors of π occur frequently in radiometry and are an artifact of how we chose to measure solid angles, i.e., the area of a unit sphere is a multiple of π rather than a multiple of one.

Similarly, we can find the power hitting a surface by integrating the irradiance across the surface area:

$$\Phi = \int_{\text{all } \mathbf{x}} H(\mathbf{x}) dA,$$

where $\mathbf{x}$ is a point on the surface, and dA is the differential area associated with that point. Note that we don't have special terms or symbols for incoming versus outgoing power. That distinction does not seem to come up enough to have encouraged the distinction.

16.1.6 BRDF

Because we are interested in surface appearance, we would like to characterize how a surface reflects light. At an intuitive level, for any incident light coming from direction $\mathbf{k}_i$, there is some fraction scattered in a small solid angle near the outgoing direction $\mathbf{k}_o$. There are many ways we could formalize such a concept, and not surprisingly, the standard way to do so is inspired by building a simple measurement device. Such a device is shown in Figure 16.5, where a small light source is positioned in direction $\mathbf{k}_i$ as seen from a point on a surface, and a detector is placed in direction $\mathbf{k}_o$. For every directional pair $(\mathbf{k}_i, \mathbf{k}_o)$, we take a reading with the detector.

Now we just have to decide how to measure the strength of the light source and make our reflection function independent of this strength. For example, if we replaced the light with a brighter light, we would not want to think of the surface as reflecting light differently. We could place a radiance meter at the point being illuminated to measure the light. However, for this to get an accurate reading that would not depend on the $\Delta\sigma$ of the detector, we would need the light to subtend a solid angle bigger than $\Delta\sigma$. Unfortunately, the measurement taken by our roving radiance detector in

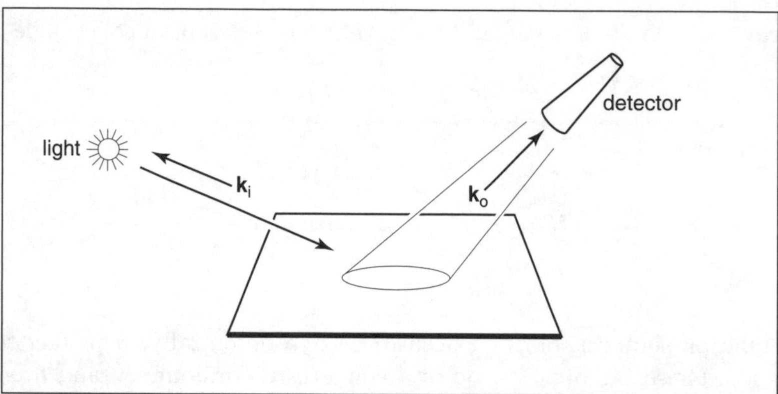

Figure 16.5. A simple measurement device for directional reflectance. The positions of light and detector are moved to each possible pair of directions. Note that both $\mathbf{k}_i$ and $\mathbf{k}_o$ point away from the surface to allow reciprocity.

direction $\mathbf{k}_o$ will also count light that comes from points outside the new detector's cone. So this does not seem like a practical solution.

Alternatively, we can place an irradiance meter at the point on the surface being measured. This will take a reading that does not depend strongly on subtleties of the light source geometry. This suggests characterizing reflectance as a ratio:

$$\rho = \frac{L_s}{H}$$

where this fraction ρ will vary with incident and exitant directions $\mathbf{k}_i$ and $\mathbf{k}_o$, H is the irradiance for light position $\mathbf{k}_i$ and L_s is the surface radiance measured in direction $\mathbf{k}_o$. If we take such a measurement for all direction pairs, we end up with a 4D function $\rho(\mathbf{k}_i, \mathbf{k}_o)$. This function is called the *bidirectional reflectance distribution function* (BRDF). The BRDF is all we need to know to characterize the directional properties of how a surface reflects light.

Directional hemispherical reflectance

Given a BRDF it is straightforward to ask "What fraction of incident light is reflected?" However, the answer is not so easy; the fraction reflected depends on the directional distribution of incoming light. For this reason, we typically only set a fraction reflected for a fixed incident direction $\mathbf{k}_i$. This fraction is called the *directional hemispherical reflectance*. This fraction, $R(\mathbf{k}_i)$ is defined:

$$R(\mathbf{k}_i) = \frac{\text{power in all outgoing directions } \mathbf{k}_o}{\text{power in a beam from direction } \mathbf{k}_i}.$$

Note that this quantity is between zero and one for reasons of energy conservation. If we allow the incident Φ_i power to hit on a small area ΔA, then the irradiance is $\Phi_i/\Delta A$. Also, the ratio of the incoming power is just the ratio of the radiance exitance to irradiance:

$$R(\mathbf{k}_i) = \frac{E}{H}$$

The radiance in a particular direction resulting from this power is by the definition of BRDF:

$$\begin{aligned} L(\mathbf{k}_o) &= H\rho(\mathbf{k}_i, \mathbf{k}_o) \\ &= \frac{\Phi_i}{\Delta A} \end{aligned}$$

And from the definition of radiance, we also have:

$$L(\mathbf{k}_o) = \frac{\Delta E}{\Delta\sigma_o \cos\theta_o}$$

where E is the radiant exitance of the small patch going in direction $\mathbf{k}_o$. Using these two definitions for radiance we get:

$$H\rho(\mathbf{k}_i, \mathbf{k}_o) = \frac{\Delta E}{\Delta\sigma_o \cos\theta_o}$$

Rearranging terms we get:

$$\frac{\Delta E}{H} = \rho(\mathbf{k}_i, \mathbf{k}_o)\Delta\sigma_o \cos\theta_o$$

This is just the small contribution to E/H that is reflected near the particular $\mathbf{k}_o$. To find the total $R(\mathbf{k}_i)$ we sum over all outgoing $\mathbf{k}_o$. In integral form this is:

$$R(\mathbf{k}_i) = \int_{\text{all } \mathbf{k}_o} \rho(\mathbf{k}_i, \mathbf{k}_o) \cos\theta_o \, d\sigma_o$$

Ideal diffuse BRDF

An idealized diffuse surface is called *Lambertian.* Such surfaces are impossible in nature for thermodynamic reasons, but mathematically they do conserve energy. The Lambertian BRDF has ρ equal to a constant for all angles. This means the surface will have the same radiance for all viewing angles, and this radiance will be proportional to the irradiance.

If we compute $R(\mathbf{k}_i)$) for a a Lambertian surface with $\rho = C$ we get:

$$\begin{aligned} R(\omega_i) &= \int_{\text{all } \mathbf{k}_o} C \cos\theta_o \, d\sigma_o \\ &= \int_{\phi_o=0}^{2\pi} \int_{\theta_o=0}^{\pi} k \cos\theta_o \sin\theta_o \, d\theta_o \, d\phi_o \\ &= \pi C \end{aligned}$$

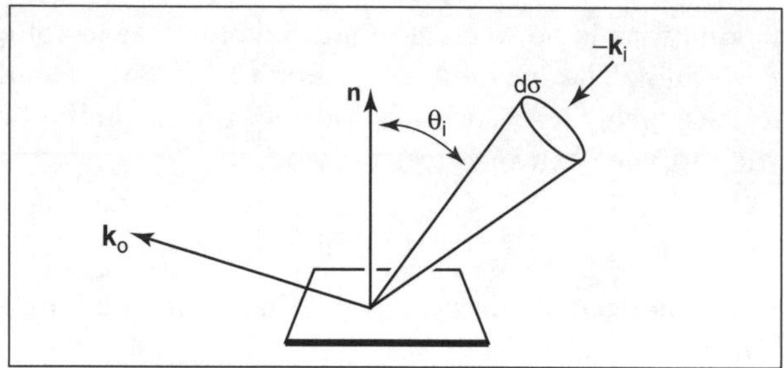

Figure 16.A. The geometry for the transport equation in its directional form.

Thus, for a perfectly reflecting Lambertian surface ($R = 1$), we have $\rho = 1/\pi$, and for a Lambertian surface whose $R(\mathbf{k}_i) = r$, we have:

$$\rho(\mathbf{k}_i, \mathbf{k}_o) = \frac{r}{\pi}$$

This is another example where the use of steradians for solid angle determines the normalizing constant and thus introduces factors of π.

16.2 Transport Equation

With the definition of BRDF, we can describe the radiance of a surface in terms of the incoming radiance from all different directions. Because in computer graphics we can use idealized mathematics that might be impractical to instantiate in the lab, we can also write the BRDF in terms of radiance only. If we take a small part of the light with solid angle $\Delta\sigma_i$ with radiance L_i, and "measure" the refected radiance in direction $\mathbf{k}_o$ due to this small piece of the light, we can compute a BRDF (Figure 16.A). The irradiance due to the small piece of light is $H = L_i \cos\theta_i \Delta\sigma_i$. Thus the BRDF is:

$$\rho = \frac{L_o}{L_i \cos\theta_i \Delta\sigma_i}.$$

That form can be useful in some situations. Rearranging terms we can write down the part of the radiance that is due to light coming from direction $\mathbf{k}_i$:

$$\Delta L_o = \rho(\mathbf{k}_i, \mathbf{k}_o) L_i \cos\theta_i \Delta\sigma_i$$

If there is light coming from many directions $L_i(\mathbf{k}_i)$ we can sum all of them. In integral form, with notation for surface and field radiance, this is:

$$L_s(\mathbf{k}_o) = \int_{\text{all } \mathbf{k}_i} \rho(\mathbf{k}_i, \mathbf{k}_o) L_f(\mathbf{k}_i) \cos\theta_i d\sigma_i$$

This equation is often called the *rendering equation* in computer graphics.

Sometimes it is useful to write the transport equation in terms of surface radiances only. Note, that in a closed environment, the field radiance $L_f(\mathbf{k}_i)$ comes from some surface with surface radiance $L_s(-\mathbf{k}_i) = L_f(\mathbf{k}_i)$ (Figure 16.6). The solid angle subtended by the point $\mathbf{x}'$ in the figure is given by:

$$\Delta\sigma_i = \frac{\Delta A' \cos\theta'}{\|\mathbf{x} - \mathbf{x}'\|^2}$$

where $\Delta A'$ the the area we associate with $\mathbf{x}'$. Substituting for $\Delta\sigma_i$ in terms of $\Delta A'$ suggests the following transport equation:

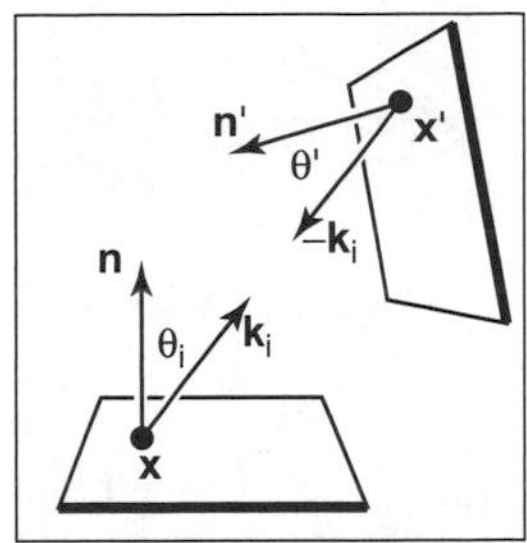

Figure 16.6. The light coming into one point comes from another point.

$$L_s(\mathbf{x}, \mathbf{k}_o) = \int_{\text{all } \mathbf{x}' \text{ visible to } \mathbf{x}} \frac{\rho(\mathbf{k}_i, \mathbf{k}_o) L_s(\mathbf{x}', \mathbf{x} - \mathbf{x}') \cos\theta_i \cos\theta'}{\|\mathbf{x} - \mathbf{x}'\|^2}$$

Note that we are using a non-normalized vector $\mathbf{x} - \mathbf{x}'$ to indicate the direction from $\mathbf{x}'$ to $\mathbf{x}$. Also note that we are writing L_s as a function of position and direction.

The only problem with this new transport equation is that the domain of integration is awkward. If we introduce a visibility function, we can trade off complexity in the domain with complexity in the integrand:

$$L_s(\mathbf{x}, \mathbf{k}_o) = \int_{\text{all } \mathbf{x}'} \frac{\rho(\mathbf{k}_i, \mathbf{k}_o) L_s(\mathbf{x}', \mathbf{x} - \mathbf{x}') v(\mathbf{x}, \mathbf{x}') \cos\theta_i \cos\theta'}{\|\mathbf{x} - \mathbf{x}'\|^2}$$

where

$$v(\mathbf{x}, \mathbf{x}') = \begin{cases} 1 & \text{if } \mathbf{x} \text{ and } \mathbf{x}' \text{ are mutually visible} \\ 0 & \text{otherwise} \end{cases}$$

16.3 Photometry

For every spectral radiometric quantity there is a related *photometric quantity* that measures how much of that quantity is "useful" to a human observer. Given a spectral radiometric quantity $f_r(\lambda)$, the related photometric quantity f_p is:

$$f_p = 683 \frac{lm}{W} \int_{\lambda=380nm}^{800nm} \bar{y}(\lambda) f_r(\lambda)\, d\lambda,$$

where $\bar{y}$ is the *luminous efficiency function* of the human visual system. This function is zero outside the limits of integration above, so the limits could be 0 and ∞ and f_p would not change. The luminous efficiency function will be discussed in more detail in Chapter 18, but we discuss its general properties here. The leading constant is to make the definition consistent with historical absolute photometric quantities.

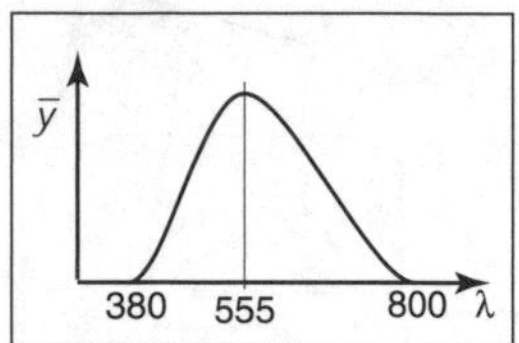

Figure 16.7. The luminous efficiency function versus wavelength (nm).

The luminous efficiency function that quantifies the human visual system is not equally sensitive to all wavelengths (Figure 16.7). For wavelengths below 380nm (the *ultraviolet range*), the light is not visible to humans and thus has a $\bar{y}$ value of zero. From 380nm it gradually increases until $\lambda = 555nm$ where it peaks. This is a pure green light. Then, it gradually decreases until it reaches the boundary of the infrared region at 800nm.

The photometric quantity that is most commonly used in graphics is *luminance*, the photometric analog of radiance:

$$Y = 683\frac{lm}{W}\int_{\lambda=380nm}^{800nm} \bar{y}(\lambda)L(\lambda)\, d\lambda.$$

The symbol Y for luminance comes from colorimetry. Most other fields use the symbol L; we will not follow that convention, because it is to confusing to use L for both luminance and spectral radiance. Luminance gives one a general idea of how "bright" something is independent of the adaptation of the viewer. Note that the black paper under noonday sun is subjectively darker than the lower luminance white paper under moonlight; reading too much into luminance is dangerous, but it is a very useful quantity for getting a quantitative feel for relative perceivable light output. The unit lm stands for lumens. Note that most light bulbs are rated in terms of the power they consume in Watts, and the useful light they produce in lumens. More efficient bulbs produce more of their light where $\bar{y}$ is large and thus produce more lumens per Watt. A "perfect" light would convert all power into $555nm$ light, and would produce 683 lumens per Watt. The units of luminance are thus $(lm/W)(W/(m^2sr)) = lm/(m^2sr)$. The quantity one lumen per steradian is defined to be one *candela* (cd), so luminance is usually described in units cd/m^2.

Frequently Asked Questions

- What is "intensity"?

The term *intensity* is used in a variety of contexts and its use varies with both era and discipline. In practice, it is no longer meaningful as a specific radiometric quantity, but it is useful for intuitive discussion. Most papers that use it do so in place of radiance.

- What is "radiosity"?

The term *radiosity* is used in place of radiant exitance in some fields. It is also sometimes used to describe world-space light transport algorithms.

Notes

A common radiometric quantity not described in the chapter is *radiant intensity* (I), which is the spectral power per steradian emitted from an infinitesimal point source. It should usually be avoided in graphics programs because point sources cause implementational problems. A more rigorous treatment of radiometry can be found in James Arvo's dissertation (Yale University, 1995). The radiometric and photometric terms in this chapter are from the *Illumination Engineering Society's* standard that is increasingly used by all fields of science and engineering.

Exercises

1. For a diffuse surface with outgoing radiance L, what is the radiant exitance?

2. What is the total power exiting a diffuse surface with an area of $4m^2$ and a radiance of L?

3. If a fluorescent light and an incandescent light both emit 20 Watts of power, why is the fluorescent light usually preferred?

Human Vision

Almost all computer graphics images are ultimately intended for viewing by humans. For this reason, it is useful for computer graphics programmers to have a working understanding of the basics of human vision. Human vision is a field of active research, and it is only partially understood. However, enough knowledge has been gathered that engineering can benefit from what is known. This chapter hits some of the high points of that knowledge base, particulary at the low-level. The treatment in this chapter is sparse and should be used only as a survey. Serious students of computer graphics should study the books on computer vision mentioned in the chapter notes.

17.1 Overview of Vision

As more is understood about human function, the distinction between mind and body is increasingly blurred. The distinction between eye and mind is also probably not entirely appropriate. A useful way to look at vision is to consider the brain as a set of processing circuitry that includes the light-sensitive cells in the eye. These cells are on a mobile platform controlled by the eye muscles, and have a lens-system to gather and physically organize light. The light sensitive cells send signals along the optic nerves which engage in some exchange of information on the way to the visual centers in the brain. This exchange is useful for taking advantage of stereo information from the two eyes.

Although we may have the impression that we see the world in realtime and at high resolution, in fact we see only a small part of the world in high resolution at any time, and it is approximately one-third of a second between the time a visual signal hits the eye and when the mind "registers" it. The eyes sweep around the scene passing the small, but high-resolution, sensor over the scene. The visual system integrates this dynamic information to create the familiar impression we have of a full-field high-resolution signal. The visual system discards a tremendous amount of information during this process so that it can concentrate on processing salient features. Graphics programmers can take advantage of this by avoiding the computation of expensive information that the visual system will ignore in any case.

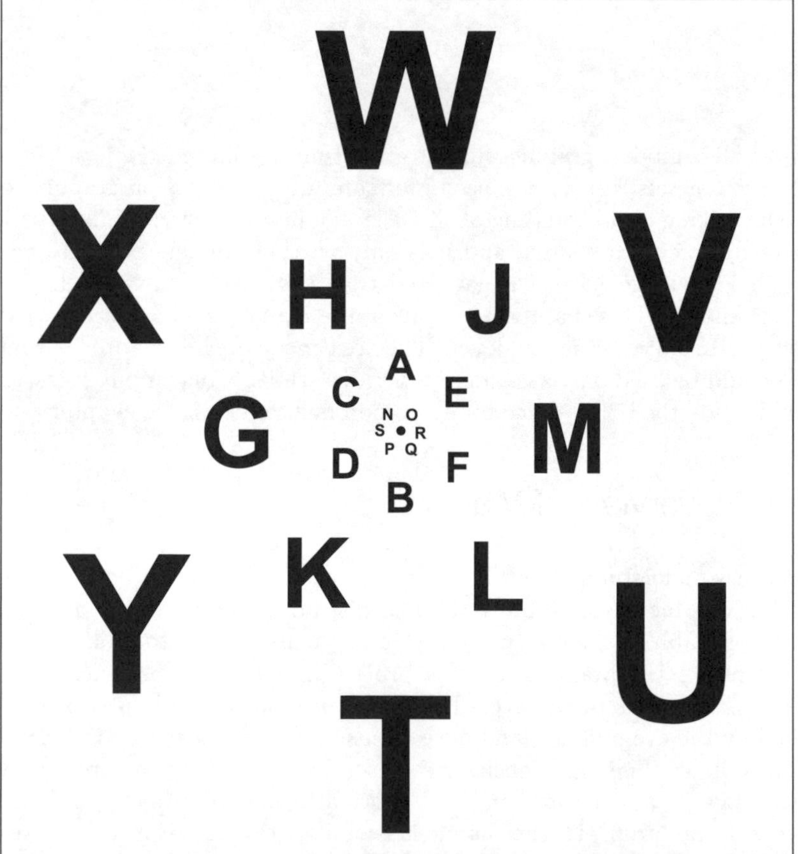

Figure 17.1. Stare fixedly at the center dot, and without moving your eyes you should notice the text is approximately equally detailed because of the density of nonuniform sensors in the eye (after *Vision Science*, Palmer, MIT Press, 1999).

17.2 Makeup of the Eyes

The light-sensitive cells in the eye come in four varieties:

Short (blue) cones: These sense light at mid-to-high levels of illumination and are predominantly sensitive to short (bluish) wavelengths.

Middle (green) cones: These sense light at mid-to-high levels of illumination and are predominantly sensitive to middle (greenish) wavelengths.

Long (red) cones: These sense light at mid-to-high levels of illumination and are predominantly sensitive to long (reddish) wavelengths.

Rods: These sense light at low-to-mid levels of illumination and have peak sensitivity somewhere between the short and middle cones.

These sensors are spread across the back of the *retina* in a very uneven pattern. Near the center of the visual field, the cones have high density in an approximately two-degree region called the *fovea*.. There are no rods in the fovea. The short/middle/long cones have relative counts of approximately 1/40/10 respectively. As you read fine text, the fovea sweeps across the text.

Outside of the fovea, the cones gradually fall off in density and the rods become dominant. However, the rods never have as high a density as the cones in the fovea do. Becausc thc rods cover such a large area, there are millions of rods outside the fovea and only tens of thousands of cones in the fovea. Figure 17.1 gives a feel for this loss of acuity away from the center of visual attention.

All of these sensors are wired together in a variety of specialized circuits for edge-detection, motion-detection, frequency profiling, and many other tasks. The signals from these circuits are collected into a bundle of nerves that go together out the back of the retina into the optic nerve. In that

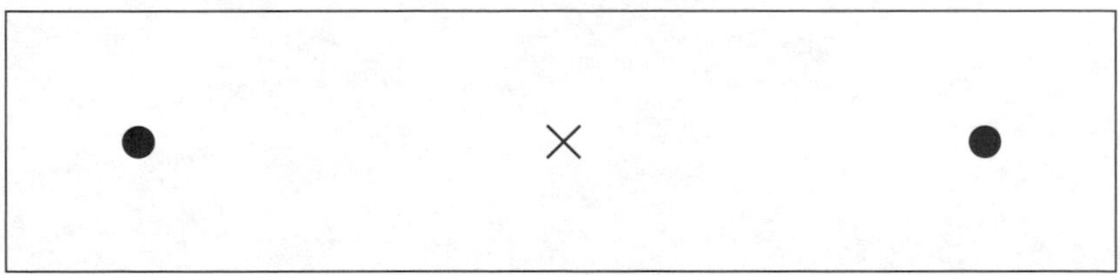

Figure 17.2. Close one eye and stare at the cross in the center. Move you head toward and away from the paper while staring at the cross. When the blind spot moves over one of the dots it will disappear. Because the blind spot is toward your nose from the fovea, the dot on the same side of the dot as the open eye will be the one to disappear (after *Vision Science*, Palmer, MIT Press, 1999).

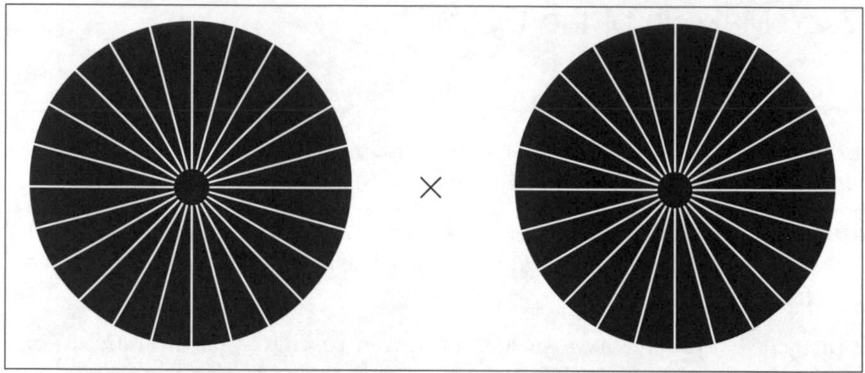

Figure 17.3. Using the same procedure as in Figure 17.2, position your blindspot so that it covers where the lines in one of the circle would intersect. The fill-in mechanism should create an illusion that there are intersecting lines (after *Vision Science*, Palmer, MIT Press, 1999).

region there is no room for sensors, so there is no visual signal from that region. This results in a *blind spot* for each eye (see Figure 17.2).

You might wonder why you don't notice the blind spot in everyday visual experience. One reason is that the two eyes have their signals combined, and their blindspots are on different sides of the visual field. But even in one-eyed viewing we are not aware of the blind spot because of *fill-in*. The fill-in mechanism creates a sort of interpolation into the empty region. For example, if the blind-spot is surrounded by forest, the brain will "see" forest in the blind-spot. This is demonstrated in Figure 17.3.

17.3 Adaptation

The key strategy of the visual system is *adaptation*. Adaptation is used to provide a neutral signal for the average light input and encode visual in-

Figure 17.4. With one eye closed focus on the dot on the left from a few inches away. Over time, the area surrounding the dot should appear to be a uniform color. This effect does not occur on the right because the signal is not effectively constant at the edge (after *Vision Science*, Palmer, MIT Press, 1999).

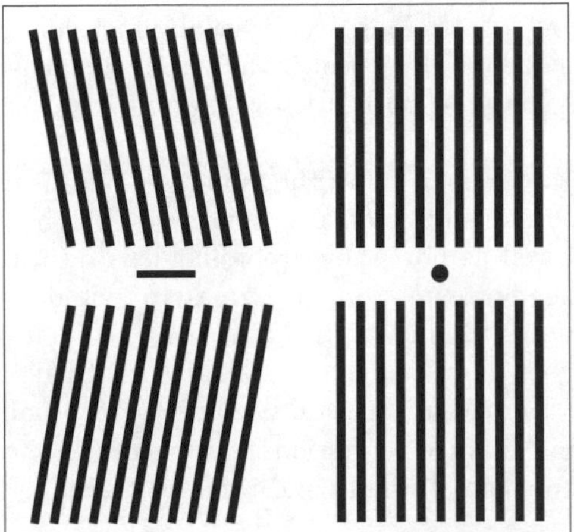

Figure 17.5. To experience orientation adaptation sweep your eyes along the bar on the left between the pattern for at least thirty seconds. Then look at the circle on the right. Your selective deadening of the orientation channels on the left should have an effect (after *Vision Coding and Efficiency*, Blakemore ed., Cambridge Univ. Press, 1990).

formation in terms of differences from that signal. The detectors in the eye settle to a base output for any input they see as constant. A demonstration of this effect is given in Figure 17.4.

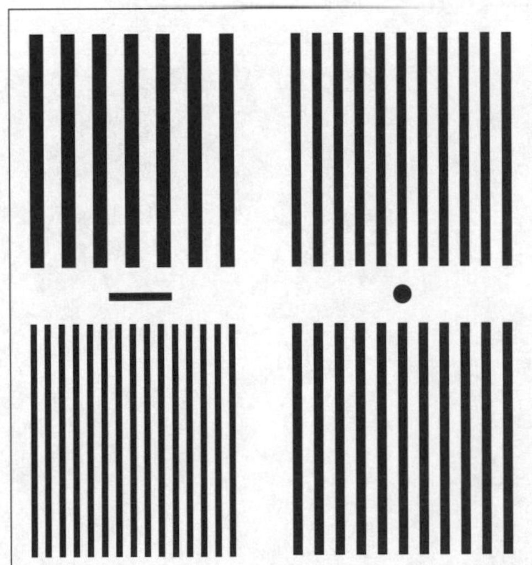

Figure 17.6. To experience frequency adaptation sweep your eyes along the bar on the left between the pattern for at least sixty seconds. Then look at the circle on the right. Your selective deadening of the frequency channels on the left should have an effect (after *Vision Coding and Efficiency*, Blakemore ed., Cambridge Univ. Press, 1990).

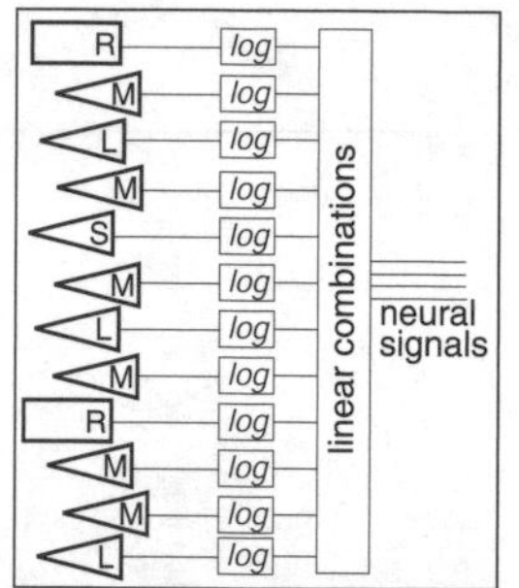

Figure 17.7. A simple model of retinal function (after *Computer Generated Color*, Jackson et al., Wiley, 1994).

Such adaptation occurs along every visual dimension, and is especially evident in the "channels" along which the visual signals are encoded. For example, humans adapt to both orientation and frequency (Figures 17.5 and 17.6).

Adaptation also occurs in color; the dominant color is usually perceived as grey. The dimensions of color are determined by the character of the cone receptors as well as how they are combined to form our perception of color. To a first approximation, the cones are wired together based on a log transformation as indicated in Figure 17.7. When one of the types of receptors receives more stimulation than the others, it becomes less sensitive, and the average stimulation becomes perceptually neutral.

We even become adapted to motion, as we experience when we stare at a waterfall for more than a minute and then look away.

17.4 Dimensions of the Low-Level Visual Experience

Our visual system has several low-level dimensions along which it delivers information. A fundamental one is *contrast.* There are many mathematical definitions of contrast, but here we are just speaking imprecisely. Interestingly, our thresholds for contrast vary with frequency as shown in Figure 17.8.

Two dimensions related to contrast are *lightness* and *brightness.* Lightness is our perception of how reflective something is, while brightness is

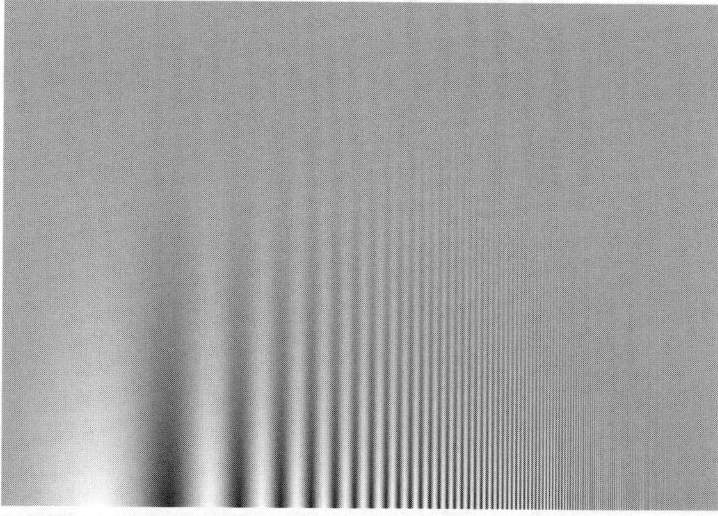

Figure 17.8. The contrast between stripes varies in a constant manner from bottom to top, yet the threshold of visibility varies with frequency.

how intense the light is. This distinction is illustrated in Figure 17.9. To a remarkable extent the visual system is able to achieve *lightness constancy*, where regardless of illumination we can "see" the true reflectance of a surface.

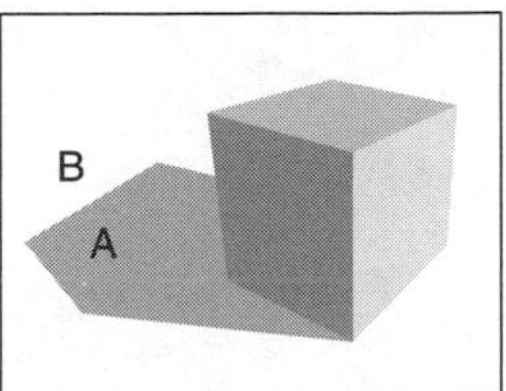

Figure 17.9. The points **A** and **B** have the same lightness because they seem to be the same reflectance. However, they have different brightnesses because of the shadow.

Another basic dimension of the visual experience is color. While there exist many "intuitive" color spaces that create three dimensions within color, perhaps the best motivated are the *opponent color models*. These assume the wiring behind the $r/g/b$ (long/medium/short) is approximately:

$$\begin{aligned} \text{Achromatic} &\propto r + g + b, \\ \text{Yellow-blue} &\propto r + g - b, \\ \text{Red-green} &\propto r - g. \end{aligned} \tag{17.1}$$

Although there is some biological justification for this type of model, it was proposed in the 1800s based on subjective experience. For example, there is an experience of bluish-green, but not yellowish-blue. The implication is that there are different channels for blue and green, but that there is a shared channel that is either yellow or blue but not both.

Some parts of the distance dimension are low-level, particularly those having to do with *accommodation* (the focusing of the lens), and *stereo*. While these mechanisms are linked, they can be used separately to some extent (Figure 17.10).

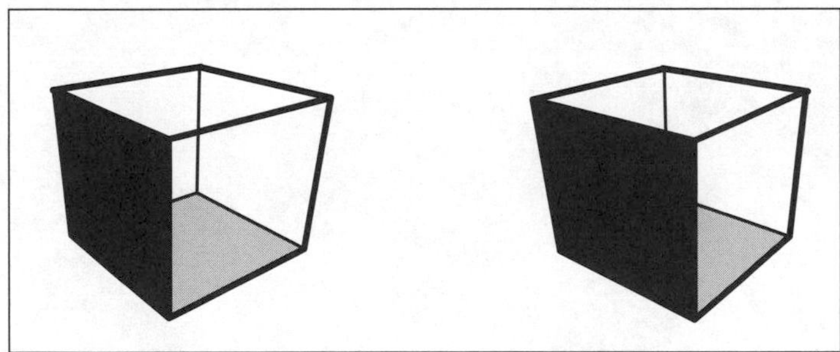

Figure 17.10. Cross your eyes so that three cubes appear. The one in the center should appear three-dimensional due to stereo vision.

Frequently Asked Questions

• If, when I "look at" something, I am using my fovea which is all cones, why am I not blind at night?

Your whole retina sweeps over the scenes and the mind integrates any useful information it finds. However, there is a limited breakdown if you try to stare at something like dim stars. Staring at something centers the fovea on it and if the image is dim, it can disappear. Thus, the practice of looking next to dim stars is common if you want to see them.

• **Why do red and blue text on a screen look like they are at different depths?**

The refracive index of the bodies in your eye vary with wavelength. The lens has to focus at slightly different depths to see red and blue in perfect focus. For achromatic objects, this only happens if they are at different depths, so this is what the brain assumes.

Notes

Two excellent books together make an excellent survey of human vision: *Vision Science* (Palmer, MIT Press, 1999) and *Sensation and Perception* (Goldstein, Wadsworth, 2001).

18 Color

As discussed in the previous chapter, humans have three types of sensors (cones) active at high levels of illumination. The signals to these three sensor types determine the color response of an observer. For this reason, color is naturally a three-dimensional phenomenon. To quantitatively describe color we need to use a well-defined coordinate system on that three-dimensional space. In graphics we usually use "red-green-blue" (RGB) colors to provide such a coordinate system. However, there are infinitely many such coordinate systems we could apply to the space, and none of them is intrinsically superior to any other system. For specific circumstances, some color systems are better than others. This is analogous to having coordinate systems in a city that align with the streets rather than precise north/south/east/west directions. Thus, when we deal with colors, there are a plethora of acronyms such as CMY, XYZ, HSV, and LUV that stand for coordinate systems with three named axes. These are hard to keep straight.

In addition, color is an area that involves the physics of light entering the eye, as well as the psychology of what happens to that light. The distinction between what is physics, what is physiology, and what is cognition also tends to be confusing. Making matters even more complicated is that some color spaces are oriented toward display or print technologies, such as CMYK for ink-based printers with three colored inks plus a black (K) ink. To clarify things as much as possible, this chapter develops color perception from first principles. The discussion may seem a bit too detailed for the humble RGB color spaces that result, but the subject of color is intrinsically complex, and simplification is dangerous for such a central topic in graphics.

We begin with a section on light detectors and then develop basic trichromatic (three color) theory, and this leads naturally to dealing with RGB display systems. We also discuss the LMS, and XYZ systems.

18.1 Light and Light Detectors

When the human eye "sees" something, it is because light enters the eye and hits a light detector on the *retina* at the back of the eye. Similarly, a digital camera records higher readings when more light hits a detector on the digital array at the back of the camera.

The signal that reaches the detector varies with wavelength and can be described by spectral radiance $L(\lambda)$ which represents the intensity of light coming from a particular direction at a particular wavelength. The retina/lens acts much like the radiance detector described in Section 16.1.5, with the lens allowing the eye to collect more light than would be possible with a simple opening.

All light is not created equal; humans are more sensitive to some wavelengths than others, and are not sensitive at all to light outside the range [380nm, 800nm]. Cameras have a similar variable sensitivity. The response of any such detector can be represented as an integral of the product of a weighting function w and the spectral radiance it "sees:"

$$\text{response} = \mathrm{k} \int w(\lambda) L(\lambda) d\lambda,$$

This response equation will thus be fundamental in any color theory. The somewhat arbitrary constant k will vary, as will the response function w which is a characteristic of the sensors underlying the color theory.

18.2 Tristimulus Color Theory

If we assume that human color response is a result of several different types of sensors in the eye, an immediate question is, "With how many types of sensors are we dealing?" We now know that there are three types of sensors, called cones, that describe our day color vision. To see how this was verified in the 1800s, consider an experiment based on the hypothesis of three such sensor types. If we assume the sensors are independent, then the response of the sensors to a specific spectral radiance $A(\lambda)$ is:

$$S = \int s(\lambda)A(\lambda)d\lambda,$$
$$M = \int m(\lambda)A(\lambda)d\lambda,$$
$$L = \int l(\lambda)A(\lambda)d\lambda.$$

If two different radiances $A_1(\lambda)$ and $A_2(\lambda)$ produce the same (S, M, L), then they are indistinguishable as far as the sensor system is concerned. Such matching spectra are seen as the same color and are called *metamers*. This observation is what allows us to verify that there are exactly three sensors.

Suppose we set up three spot lights which, when shined on a screen, have spectral curves $R(\lambda)$, $G(\lambda)$, and $B(\lambda)$, each with a control knob that scales them up and down with fractions (r, g, b). The resulting spectral curve is:

$$A(\lambda) = rR(\lambda) + gG(\lambda) + bB(\lambda).$$

The S response to this mixed light is:

$$\begin{aligned} S_A &= \int s(\lambda)A(\lambda)d\lambda \\ &= \int s(\lambda)\left(rR(\lambda) + gG(\lambda) + bB(\lambda)\right)d\lambda \\ &= r\int s(\lambda)R(\lambda)d\lambda + g\int s(\lambda)G(\lambda)d\lambda + b\int s\lambda)B(\lambda)d\lambda \\ &\equiv rS_R + gS_G + S_B. \end{aligned}$$

The final equivalence is just the result of defining the S response to the full-strength lights to be (S_R, S_G, S_B).

Now suppose we have a fourth light with spectral radiance $C(\lambda)$ that we shine on the screen next to the three overlapping colored lights. The sensor responses to the fourth light are (S_C, M_C, L_C). Here is the key to our experiment: we can adjust the (r, g, b) weightings for the three overlapping lights to make the lights look the same to the sensors, i.e.,

$$\begin{aligned} S_C &= S_A = rS_R + gS_G + bS_B \\ M_C &= M_A = rM_R + gM_G + bM_B \\ L_C &= L_A = rL_R + gL_G + bL_B \end{aligned}$$

Note that this is just a linear system with three equations and three unknowns: (r, g, b). Provided the system is not degenerate, there is a unique (r, g, b) that satisfies it.

This experiment was performed and users were able to make the colors match, and thus it was verified that there are exactly three sensor types. An important detail in the actual performance of the experiments is that there is no guarantee that r, g and b values are non-negative or are bounded above by one, so in these cases matches are impossible. However, if the users are allowed to also mix combinations of the first three lights in with the fourth light, matches can always be made. For example, if the match occurs when $r = -0.2$, then we can mix $0.2R(\lambda)$ in with the fourth light which has the same result as subtracting $0.2R(\lambda)$ from the overlapping lights.

Once we have established that there are three sensors, the next important question is, "What are the response functions $s(\lambda)$, $m(\lambda)$ and $l(\lambda)$?" Unfortunately, it is not possible using non-invasive procedures to infer these functions, and estimates of these response finctions were determined only in the 1980s. However, we do not really need to know the cone response functions to come up with a color matching scheme. We can take any three lights that are linearly independent, and use them to specify a color. For example, for the three lights discussed earlier, we can just use the values (r, g, b) to specify a color. If two spectra are matched by the same (r, g, b), then they are the same "color." Note that it is easily possible to have two different spectra that are matched by the same (r, g, b), and they are then metamers.

What are the best lights to use for matching so that color values can be standardized? This question was addressed in the 1930s and the XYZ color system was developed. It is still the overwhelming choice for specifying tristimulus color. This system is discussed in the next section.

18.3 CIE Tristimulus Values

The CIE, a color standards organization, made the observation that once data was tabulated for a given set of lights, the tristimulus values for a given spectrum could be computed mathematically. They further observed that any set of real lights would result in negative tristimulus values for some test spectra. They decided there was no reason to restrict themselves to physically realizable lights. For example, if data is known for real lights $R(\lambda)$, $G(\lambda)$, $B(\lambda)$, then we can deduce data for linear combinations of those lights such as $-R(\lambda)$, $G(\lambda) - 2B(\lambda)$, $B(\lambda) + R(\lambda)$ even though such lights cannot physically exist. The tristimulus values would then be $(-r, g - 2b, b + r)$.

The CIE decided to use imaginary lights that had two especially nice features:

- one of the lights is "grey" and provides no hue information

- the other two lights have zero luminance and provide only hue information.

The response for these three lights is defined by the triple (X, Y, Z) where Y is the luminance. Because the eye responds only to light in the range 380 to 800 nanometers, these are the limits of integration listed. Since the weighting functions drop to zero outside that range, it is somewhat redundant to have explicit limits. The constant is 683 to conform to standards of luminance. The formula for the CIE *tristimulus* values (X, Y, Z) is:

$$\begin{aligned} X &= 683 \int_{380}^{800} \bar{x}(\lambda) L(\lambda) d\lambda, \\ Y &= 683 \int_{380}^{800} \bar{y}(\lambda) L(\lambda) d\lambda, \\ Z &= 683 \int_{380}^{800} \bar{z}(\lambda) L(\lambda) d\lambda. \end{aligned}$$

Any given spectral radiance will have a corresponding (X, Y, Z).

18.4 Chromaticity

Often, we want to factor out luminance and concentrate on color. The standard way to do this is to use *chromaticity* values (Figure 18.1):

$$(x, y) = \left(\frac{X}{X + Y + Z}, \frac{Y}{X + Y + Z} \right).$$

There is a similar formula for z but it is rarely used because $x + y + z = 1$. Instead of XYZ, people often pass around only xyY. This way we can talk about "color" and "intensity" separately. We can also compute XYZ from xyY:

$$(X, Y, Z) = \left(\frac{xY}{y}, Y, \frac{(1 - x - y)Y}{y} \right). \tag{18.1}$$

In some sense, we can consider (x, y) all of the information we need for *hue*, the chromatic part of color.. Because it is a 2D space, the colors associated with the (x, y) space can all be plotted on a flat page. An apparent oddity is that the (x, y) points that have associated colors form an odd shape, and most points on the real plane have no associated colors. Because all the tristimulus values are non-negative, the values (x, y) are also non-negative. Because each of (x, y) is a non-negative number divided by a non-negative number at least as large, (x, y) is restricted to $[0, 1]^2$. However, the values are even more restricted than that.

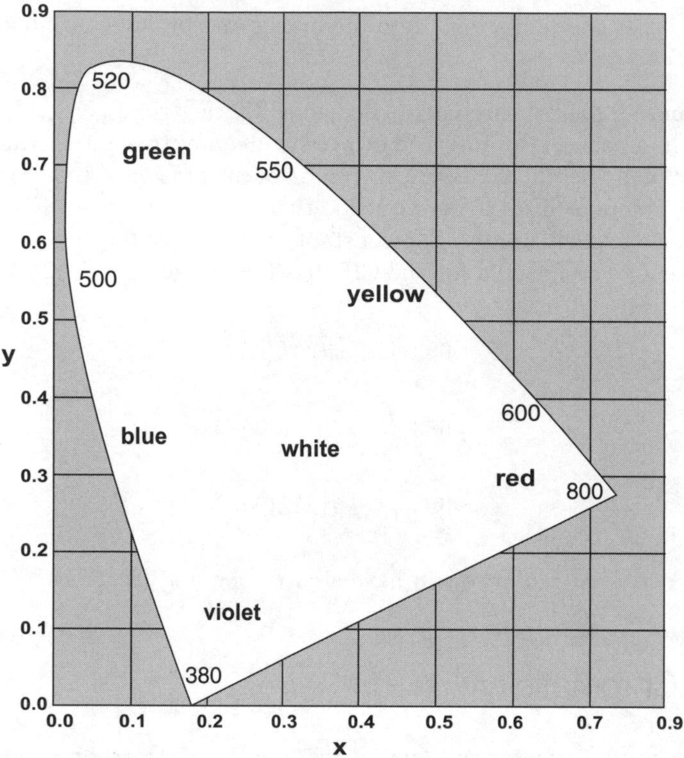

Figure 18.1. The CIE xy space. The pure spectral colors make up the curved boundaries, and the wavelengths (in nanometers) of the pure spectra are shown.

A table with the values for the tristimulus and scoptic sensitity curves is given in Table 18.1 Note that the value of $\bar{y}$ is never more than five times the value of $\bar{x}$. This means that, regardless of the spectral input, Y is never more than five times X, which restricts y to be at most $5/6$. The most extreme cases occur for pure spectral colors. The spectral radiance of a pure spectral color at wavelength λ_0 is a scaled delta function $k\delta(\lambda_0)$. The tristimulus values are:

$$(X, Y, Z) = 683k(\bar{x}(\lambda_0), \bar{y}(\lambda_0), \bar{z}(\lambda_0)).$$

The chromaticity values are thus:

$$(x, y) = \left(\frac{\bar{x}(\lambda_0)}{\bar{x}(\lambda_0) + \bar{y}(\lambda_0) + \bar{z}(\lambda_0)}, \frac{\bar{y}(\lambda_0)}{\bar{x}(\lambda_0) + \bar{y}(\lambda_0) + \bar{z}(\lambda_0)} \right) \tag{18.2}$$

λ (nm)	$\bar{x}$	$\bar{y}$	$\bar{z}$	$\bar{v}'$
380	0.0014	0.0000	0.0065	0.0006
390	0.0042	0.0001	0.0201	0.0022
400	0.0143	0.0004	0.0679	0.0093
410	0.0435	0.0012	0.2074	0.0348
420	0.1344	0.0040	0.6456	0.0966
430	0.2839	0.0116	1.3856	0.1998
440	0.3483	0.0230	1.7471	0.3281
450	0.3362	0.0380	1.7721	0.4550
460	0.2908	0.0600	1.6692	0.5670
470	0.1954	0.0910	1.2876	0.6760
480	0.0956	0.1390	0.8310	0.7930
490	0.0320	0.2080	0.4652	0.9040
500	0.0049	0.3230	0.2720	0.9820
510	0.0093	0.5030	0.1582	0.9970
520	0.0633	0.7100	0.0782	0.8350
530	0.1655	0.8620	0.0422	0.8110
540	0.2904	0.9540	0.0203	0.6500
550	0.4334	0.9950	0.0087	0.4810
560	0.5945	0.9950	0.0039	0.3288
570	0.7621	0.9520	0.0021	0.2076
580	0.9163	0.8700	0.0017	0.1212
590	1.0263	0.7570	0.0011	0.0655
600	1.0622	0.6310	0.0008	0.0332
610	1.0026	0.5030	0.0003	0.0159
620	0.8544	0.3810	0.0002	0.0074
630	0.6424	0.2650	0.0000	0.0033
640	0.4479	0.1750	0.0000	0.0015
650	0.2835	0.1070	0.0000	0.0007
660	0.1649	0.0610	0.0000	0.0003
670	0.0874	0.0320	0.0000	0.0001
680	0.0468	0.0170	0.0000	0.0001
690	0.0227	0.0082	0.0000	0.0000
700	0.0114	0.0041	0.0000	0.0000
710	0.0058	0.0021	0.0000	0.0000
720	0.0029	0.0010	0.0000	0.0000
730	0.0014	0.0005	0.0000	0.0000
740	0.0007	0.0002	0.0000	0.0000
750	0.0003	0.0001	0.0000	0.0000
760	0.0002	0.0001	0.0000	0.0000
770	0.0001	0.0000	0.0000	0.0000

Table 18.1. Values for the tristimulus and scotopic sensitivity curves.

18.5 Scotopic Luminance

For low levels of illumination, such as moonlight, your eyes go into a different perceptual mode, and the spectral sensitivity changes. The values of XYZ become irrelevant, and the *scotopic luminance* determines light and dark:

$$V' = k' \int_{380}^{800} \bar{v}'(\lambda) L(\lambda) d\lambda,$$

where the constant $k' = 1700 \frac{\text{scd}}{\text{W}}$ is chosen so that a monochromic 555nm beam (the peak sensitivity of day vision) will have the same luminance and scotopic luminance.

Often we are presented with trichromatic values (X, Y, Z) for data that is actually in the scotopic range and V would be of more use. Although it is not possible to deduce V from trichromatic values, Ward has shown that in many circumstances the following empirical formula performs reasonably:

$$V = Y \left[1.33 \left(1 + \frac{Y + Z}{X} \right) - 1.68 \right]. \tag{18.3}$$

18.6 RGB Monitors

We sometimes know the tristimulus values for the RGB channels of our CRT. Let's say these are (X_r, Y_r, Z_r) for the red channel, (X_g, Y_g, Z_g) for the green channel, and (X_b, Y_b, Z_b) for the blue channel. If we assume a perfect black point for the monitor (unlikely), then given a gamma-corrected RGB signal of (r, g, b), we can compute the screen tristimulus values (X_s, Y_s, Z_s):

$$\begin{bmatrix} X_s \\ Y_s \\ Z_s \end{bmatrix} = \begin{bmatrix} rX_r + gX_g + bX_b \\ rY_r + gY_g + bY_b \\ rZ_r + gZ_g + bZ_b \end{bmatrix} = \begin{bmatrix} X_r & X_g & X_b \\ Y_r & Y_g & Y_b \\ Z_r & Z_g & Z_b \end{bmatrix} \begin{bmatrix} r \\ g \\ b \end{bmatrix}$$

You can invert the above equation to figure out how to set (r, g, b) given a desired (X, Y, Z). Note that you may get values *much* larger than 1.0, or smaller than 0.0, so you will need to do some manipulation to deal with that problem. However, there is a bigger problem. Monitor manufacturers almost never tell you (X_r, Y_r, Z_r) etc. Instead they provide the chromiticities of the phosphors (x_r, y_r), (x_g, y_g), (x_b, y_b), and the chromiticity of the *white point* (x_w, y_w). In addition, you can usually measure the luminance Y_w of the brightest white screen with a photometer. If you can't measure that, assume it is approximately $Y_w = 100\,\text{cd/m}^2$. The reason manufacturers don't tell you Y_w is that your brightness control changes it. The reason the white point varies is that "white" is usually the average color in the room. Thus, what looks white in a fluorescent-lit room will have dominant short wavelengths, and what looks white in an incandescent-lit room will have dominant long wavelengths. So, if you move a monitor with a white-looking image from a fluorescent-lighted room to a incandescent-lit room that same display will look blue. This same issue causes photographers to buy "daylight" or "tungsten" film.

To convert the information the manufacturers provide (tristimulus values), we need to do some algebra. First, let's write a straightforward equality:

$$\begin{bmatrix} \frac{X_r}{Y_r} & \frac{X_g}{Y_g} & \frac{X_b}{Y_b} \\ 1 & 1 & 1 \\ \frac{Z_r}{Y_r} & \frac{Z_g}{Y_g} & \frac{Z_b}{Y_b} \end{bmatrix} \begin{bmatrix} Y_r \\ Y_g \\ Y_b \end{bmatrix} = \begin{bmatrix} X_w \\ Y_w \\ Z_w \end{bmatrix}.$$

Now, after some substitutions, we have only (Y_r, Y_g, Y_b) as unknowns:

$$\begin{bmatrix} \frac{x_r}{y_r} & \frac{x_g}{y_g} & \frac{x_b}{y_b} \\ 1 & 1 & 1 \\ \frac{1-x_r-y_r}{y_r} & \frac{1-x_g-y_g}{y_g} & \frac{1-x_b-y_b}{y_b} \end{bmatrix} \begin{bmatrix} Y_r \\ Y_g \\ Y_b \end{bmatrix} = \begin{bmatrix} \frac{x_w Y_w}{y_w} \\ Y_w \\ \frac{(1-x_w-y_w)Y_w}{y_w} \end{bmatrix}.$$

We can use numerical methods, or (algebraically) Cramer's rule, to solve for (Y_r, Y_g, Y_b): Once we have that, we can get (X_r, X_g, X_b), (Y_r, Y_g, Y_b), (Z_r, Z_g, Z_b) using Equation 18.1.

18.7 Approximate Color Manipulation

Although the techniques of the previous section are useful for highly controlled settings, in practice we rarely know enough data to use them. Often we make images that are to be displayed on many unknown monitors, e.g., an image for a web page. It's convenient to use a "normalized" space where $(R, G, B) = (1, 1, 1)$ transforms to $(X, Y, Z) = (1, 1, 1)$ and the RGB space is "reasonable" for most real monitors. Such a space is:

$$\begin{bmatrix} X \\ Y \\ Z \end{bmatrix} = \begin{bmatrix} 0.5149 & 0.3244 & 0.1607 \\ 0.2654 & 0.6704 & 0.0642 \\ 0.0248 & 0.1248 & 0.8504 \end{bmatrix} \begin{bmatrix} R \\ G \\ B \end{bmatrix} \tag{18.4}$$

$$\begin{bmatrix} R \\ G \\ B \end{bmatrix} = \begin{bmatrix} 2.5623 & -1.1661 & -0.3962 \\ -1.0215 & 1.9778 & 0.0437 \\ 0.0752 & -0.2562 & 1.1810 \end{bmatrix} \begin{bmatrix} X \\ Y \\ Z \end{bmatrix} \tag{18.5}$$

$$\begin{bmatrix} L \\ M \\ S \end{bmatrix} = \begin{bmatrix} 0.3897 & 0.6890 & -0.0787 \\ -0.2298 & 1.1834 & 0.0464 \\ 0.0000 & 0.0000 & 1.0000 \end{bmatrix} \begin{bmatrix} X \\ Y \\ Z \end{bmatrix} \tag{18.6}$$

$$\begin{bmatrix} X \\ Y \\ Z \end{bmatrix} = \begin{bmatrix} 1.9102 & -1.11218 & 0.2019 \\ 0.3709 & 0.6291 & 0.0000 \\ 0.0000 & 0.0000 & 1.0000 \end{bmatrix} \begin{bmatrix} L \\ M \\ S \end{bmatrix} \tag{18.7}$$

This gives the following transformation between RGB and LMS cone space:

$$\begin{bmatrix} L \\ M \\ S \end{bmatrix} = \begin{bmatrix} 0.3816 & 0.5785 & 0.0399 \\ 0.1969 & 0.7246 & 0.0785 \\ 0.0248 & 0.1248 & 0.8504 \end{bmatrix} \begin{bmatrix} R \\ G \\ B \end{bmatrix} \tag{18.8}$$

$$\begin{bmatrix} R \\ G \\ B \end{bmatrix} = \begin{bmatrix} 4.4620 & -3.5832 & 0.1213 \\ -1.2178 & 2.3803 & -0.1626 \\ 0.0486 & -0.2448 & 1.1962 \end{bmatrix} \begin{bmatrix} L \\ M \\ S \end{bmatrix} \tag{18.9}$$

18.8 Opponent Color Spaces

To make the response of the cones more like their actual signals, we can convert to a log space:

$$\begin{aligned} \mathcal{L} &= \log L \\ \mathcal{M} &= \log M \\ \mathcal{S} &= \log S \end{aligned} \tag{18.10}$$

These can be represented in an *opponent color space*

$$\begin{bmatrix} l \\ \alpha \\ \beta \end{bmatrix} = \begin{bmatrix} \frac{1}{\sqrt{3}} & 0 & 0 \\ 0 & \frac{1}{\sqrt{6}} & 0 \\ 0 & 0 & \frac{1}{\sqrt{2}} \end{bmatrix} \begin{bmatrix} 1 & 1 & 1 \\ 1 & 1 & -2 \\ 1 & -1 & 0 \end{bmatrix} \begin{bmatrix} \mathcal{L} \\ \mathcal{M} \\ \mathcal{S} \end{bmatrix} \tag{18.11}$$

If we think of the the $\mathcal{L}$ channel as "red," the $\mathcal{M}$ channel as "green," and the $\mathcal{S}$ channel as "blue," we can see that this is a variant of the classic opponent-color model:

$$\begin{aligned} \text{Achromatic} &\propto r + g + b, \\ \text{Yellow-blue} &\propto r + g - b, \\ \text{Red-green} &\propto r - g, \end{aligned}$$

Thus the l axis represents an achromatic channel, while the α and β channels are chromatic blue-yellow and red-green opponent channels.

After color processing, the result needs to be transferred back to RGB so that it can be displayed. For convenience, the inverse operations are given here. The conversion from $l\alpha\beta$ to LMS is accomplished using the following matrix multiplication:

$$\begin{bmatrix} \mathcal{L} \\ \mathcal{M} \\ \mathcal{S} \end{bmatrix} = \begin{bmatrix} 1 & 1 & 1 \\ 1 & 1 & -1 \\ 1 & -2 & 0 \end{bmatrix} \begin{bmatrix} \frac{\sqrt{3}}{3} & 0 & 0 \\ 0 & \frac{\sqrt{6}}{6} & 0 \\ 0 & 0 & \frac{\sqrt{2}}{2} \end{bmatrix} \begin{bmatrix} l \\ \alpha \\ \beta \end{bmatrix} \tag{18.12}$$

Then, after raising the pixel values to the power ten to go back to linear space, the data can be converted from LMS to RGB using Equation 18.9.

18.9 Tone Mapping

A physically-based renderer can produce arbitrarily large RGB values to be displayed on a monitor or printed page. *Tone mapping* is used to scale these quantities to a "reasonable" level so that can thay can be seen on the display. This is analogous to what photographers do to make sure their pictures are viewable. For example, a photo of a night scene is really much brighter than the actual night scene.

18.9.1 Visibility Matching

This section will provide just one simple way to tone-map rendered images. It implements the work of Ward.

Given an (X, Y, Z, V), the mapping to a scaled space where $Y \in [0, 1]$ so that Equation 18.5 can be applied is:

$$\begin{aligned} s &= \begin{cases} 0 & \text{if } \log_{10} Y < -2, \\ 3\left(\frac{\log_{10} Y+2}{2.6}\right)^2 - 2\left(\frac{\log_{10} Y+2}{2.6}\right)^3 & \text{if } -2 < \log_{10} Y < 0.6, \\ 1 & \text{otherwise.} \end{cases} \\ W &= X + Y + Z \\ x &= X/W \\ y &= Y/W \\ x &= (1-s)x_w + s(x + x_w - 0.33) \\ y &= (1-s)y_w + s(y + y_w - 0.33) \\ Y &= 0.4468(1-s)V + sY \end{aligned}$$

Here, V is the scotopic luminance. After this process, the scotopic pixels will be desaturated, and the mesopic (the transition state between photopic and scotopic vision) pixels will be partially desaturated. Also, the Y channel will store scaled scotopic luminance for scotopic pixels, photopic luminance for photopic channels, and a combination for mesopic pixels. The scaling factor 0.4468 is the ratio of Y to V for a uniform white field.

To scale the resulting luminance Y we now apply

$$Y = \frac{Y}{Y_w} \left(\frac{1.219 + (Y_w/2)^{0.4}}{1.219 + Y_i^{0.4}} \right)^{2.5}$$

where Y_i is the log-average of luminances in the computed image. Finally, the XZ for the final display is

$$\begin{aligned} X &= \frac{xY}{y}, \\ Z &= \frac{(1-x-y)Y}{y}. \end{aligned}$$

When the final XYZ are converted to RGB, the RGB may be negative or above one. They should be clamped to $[0, 1]$ if that is the case.

18.9.2 Photographic Tone Mapping

The tone reproduction problem was first identified by photographers. Often their goal is to produce realistic "renderings" of captured scenes, while facing the limitations presented by slides or prints on photographic paper. The challenges faced in tone reproduction for rendered or captured digital images are largely the same as those faced in conventional photography. The main difference is that digital images are in a sense "perfect" negatives, so no luminance information has been lost due to the limitations of the film process. This is a blessing in that detail is available in all luminance regions. We can apply a scaling that is analogous to setting exposure in a camera.

We first show how to set the tonal range of the output image based on the scene's key value. Like many tone reproduction methods, we view the log-average luminance as a useful approximation to the key of the scene. This quantity $\bar{L}_w$ is computed by:

$$\bar{L}_w = \frac{1}{N} \exp\left(\sum_{x,y} \log\left(\delta + L_w(x, y)\right) \right) \tag{18.13}$$

where $L_w(x, y)$ is the "world" luminance for pixel (x, y), N is the total number of pixels in the image and δ is a small value to avoid the singularity that occurs if black pixels are present in the image. If the scene has normal-key images, we would like to map this to middle-grey of the displayed image, or 0.18 on a scale from zero to one. This suggests the equation:

$$L(x, y) = \frac{a}{\bar{L}_w} L_w(x, y) \tag{18.14}$$

where $L(x, y)$ is a scaled luminance and $a = 0.18$. For low-key or high-key images, a might vary from 0.18 up to 0.36 and 0.72 and down to 0.09, and 0.045. The value of parameter a is the "key value," because it relates to the key of the image after applying the above scaling.

The main problem with Equation 18.14 is that many scenes have predominantly a normal dynamic range, with a few high luminance regions near highlights or in the sky. In traditional photography, this issue is dealt with by compression of both high and low luminances. However, modern photography has abandoned these "s"-shaped transfer curves in favor of curves that compress mainly the high luminances. A simple tone mapping operator with these characteristics is given by:

$$L_d(x, y) = \frac{L(x, y)}{1 + L(x, y)}. \tag{18.15}$$

Note that high luminances are scaled by approximately $1/L$, while low luminances are scaled by 1. The denominator creates a graceful blend between these two scalings. This formulation is guaranteed to capture all luminances with a displayable range. However, as mentioned in the previous section, this is not always desirable. Equation 18.15 can be extended to allow high luminances to burn out in a controllable fashion:

$$L_d(x, y) = \frac{L(x, y)\left(1 + \frac{L(x,y)}{L^2_{\text{white}}}\right)}{1 + L(x, y)} \tag{18.16}$$

where L_{white} is the smallest luminance that will be mapped to pure white. This function is a blend between Equation 18.15 and a linear mapping. It is shown for various values of L_{white} in Figure 18.2. If the L_{white} value is set to the maximum luminance in the scene, $L_{\max}$ or higher, no burn-out will occur. If it is set to infinity, then the function reverts to Equation 18.15. By default we set L_{white} to the maximum luminance in the scene. If this default is applied to scenes that have a low dynamic range (i.e., $L_{\max} < 1$), the effect is a subtle contrast enhancement.

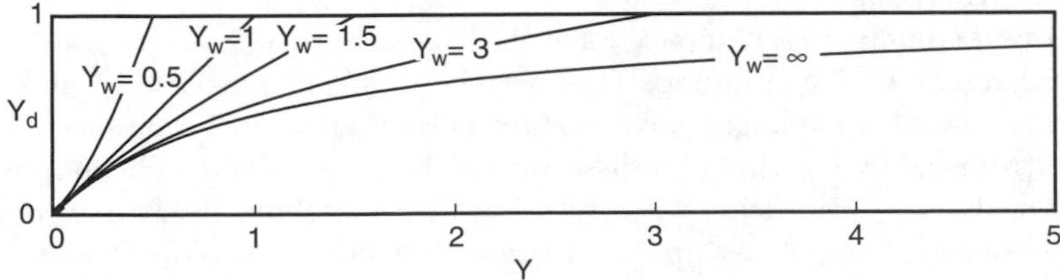

Figure 18.2. Display luminance as function of world luminance for a family of values for Y_w.

Frequently Asked Questions

- What is "Hue"?

Hue is the dominant color name of the "non-white" component of the color. For example, the hue of pink is red. Many color systems encode hue as an angle from $0°$ to $360°$, with red at $0°$, green at $120°$ and blue at $240°$.

- What is "Lightness"?

Lightness is the overall intensity of the reflectance of a surface. This is minimal for black, and maximum for white. Two colors with different hues can have the same lightness. Lightness is often encoded as a zero to one scale.

- What is "Saturation"?

Saturation is the purity of a color. For example, red is more saturated than pink, and grey is not saturated at all.

- What is "Value"?

Value is another word for lightness, but often it is expressed as a numeric scale that is approximate. For example, in some systems value is the average of the RGB values. Thus two colors with the same value might have different subjective lightnesses because the RGB channels are perceived differently.

Notes

The opponent color space used in this chapter is discussed in *Color transfer between images* (Reinhard et al., IEEE Computer Graphics & Applications, 21 (5), 2001). A good survey of color for computer graphics users is *Computer Generated Color* (Jackson et al. Wiley, 1994). Books written from the color science perspective are *The Reproduction of Colour* (Hunt, 6th ed. Fountain Press, 2002) and *Color Appearance Models* (Fairchild, Prentice Hall, 1997).

Tone mapping is a complex issue with hundreds of papers related to it, and research is continuing. The psychophysical approach of making displayed synthetic images have certain correct objective characteristics was introduced by Upstill in his dissertation (Berkeley, 1985). The mapping of intensity has been dealt with by brightness matching in *Two methods for display of high contrast images* (Tumblin et al. ACM Transactions on Graphics, 18 (1), 1999). The contrast threshold model was introduced in *A Contrast-Based Scalefactor for Luminance Display* (Ward, Graphics Gems

IV, Academic Press, 1994). The photographic tone mapping discussed in this chapter was introduced in *Photographic Tone Reproduction for Digital Images* (Reinhard et al. SIGGRAPH 2002).

The visibility-matching tone reproduction operator was introduced in *A Contrast-Based Scalefactor for Luminance Display* (Ward, Graphics Gems IV, Academic Press, 1994). The heuristic function for converting tristimulous values to scotopic luminance is from *A Visibility Matching Tone Reproduction Operator for High Dynamic Range Scenes* (Ward et al. IEEE Transactions on Visualization and Computer Graphics, 3 (4), 1997).

Exercises

1. Plot the outline of the CIE chromaticity diagram using Equation 18.2.

2. What is the one physically possible CIE (x, y) value that can be zero?

3. Write a program to scale the individual color channels separately in RGB and opponent space. Which produces worse artifacts?

Global Illumination

Many surfaces in the real world receive most or all of their incident light from other reflective surfaces. This is often called *indirect lighting* or *mutual illumination.* For example, the ceilings of most rooms receive little or no illumination directly from luminaires (light emitting objects). The direct and indirect components of illumination are shown is Figure 19.1.

Although accounting for the interreflection of light between surfaces is straightforward, it is potentially costly because all surfaces may reflect any given surface, resulting in as many as $O(N^2)$ interactions for N surfaces. Because the entire global database of objects may illuminate any given object, accounting for indirect illumination is often called the *global illumination* problem.

There is a rich and complex literature on solving the global illumination problem as discussed in the chapter notes. In this chapter we discuss two algorithms as examples: particle tracing and path tracing. The first is useful for walkthrough applications such as maze games, and as a component of batch rendering. The second is useful for realistic batch rendering.

19.1 Particle Tracing for Lambertian Scenes

Recall the transport equation from Section 16.2:

$$L_s(\mathbf{k}_o) = \int_{\text{all } \mathbf{k}_i} \rho(\mathbf{k}_i, \mathbf{k}_o) L_f(\mathbf{k}_i) \cos\theta_i d\sigma_i.$$

Figure 19.1. In the left and middle images, the indirect and direct lighting, respectively, are seperated out. On the right, the sum of both components is shown. Global illumination algorithms account for both the direct and the indirect lighting.

The geometry for this equation is shown Figure 19.2. When the illuminated point is Lambertian, this equation reduces to:

$$L_s = \frac{R}{\pi} \int_{\text{all } \mathbf{k}_i} L_f(\mathbf{k}_i) \cos\theta_i d\sigma_i,$$

where R is the diffuse reflectance. One way to approximate the solution to this equation is to use finite element methods. First, we break the scene into N surfaces each with unkown surface radiance L_i, reflectance R_i, and emitted radiance E_i. This results in the set of N simultaneous linear equations:

$$L_i = E_i + \frac{R_i}{\pi} \sum_{j=1}^{N} k_{ij} L_j$$

where k_{ij} is a constant related to the original integral representation. We then solve this set of linear equations, and we can render N constant-colored polygons. This finite element approach is often called *radiosity*.

An alternative method to radiosity is to use a statistical simulation approach by randomly following light "particles" from the luminaire though

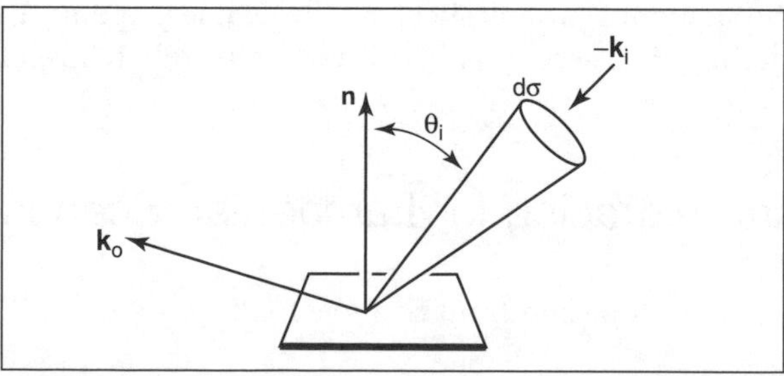

Figure 19.2. The geometry for the transport equation in its directional form.

the environment. This is a type of *particle tracing*. There are many algorithms that use some form of particle tracing; we will discuss a form of particle tracing that deposits light in the textures on triangles. First, we review some basic radiometric relations. For Lambertian surfaces, the radiance L of a Lambertian surface with area A is directly proportional to the incident power per unit area:

$$L = \frac{\Phi}{\pi A}, \tag{19.1}$$

where Φ is the outgoing power from the surface. Note that in this discussion, all radiometric quantities are either spectral or RGB depending on the implementation. If the surface has emitted power Φ_e, incident power Φ_i, and reflectance R, then this equation becomes:

$$L = \frac{\Phi_e + R\Phi_i}{\pi A},$$

If we are given a model with Φ_e and R specified for each triangle, we can proceed luminaire by luminaire, firing power in the form of particles from each luminaire. We associate a texture map with each triangle to store accumulated radiance, with all texels initialized to:

$$L = \frac{\Phi_e}{\pi A},$$

If a given triangle has area A and n_t texels, and it is hit by a particle carrying power ϕ, then the radiance of that texel is incremented by:

$$\Delta L = \frac{n_t \phi}{\pi A}.$$

Once a particle hits a surface, we increment the radiance of the texel it hits, probabilistically decide whether to reflect the particle, and if we reflect it we choose a direction and adjust its power.

Note that we want the particle to be absorbed at some point. For each surface we can assign a reflection probability p to each surface interaction. The power ϕ' for reflected particles should be adjusted to account for the lost power of the absorbed particles:

$$\phi' = \frac{R\phi}{p}$$

Note that p can be set to any positive constant less than one, and that this constant can be different for each interaction. For the remainder of this discussion we set $p = 0.5$. The path of a single particle in such a system is shown in Figure 19.3.

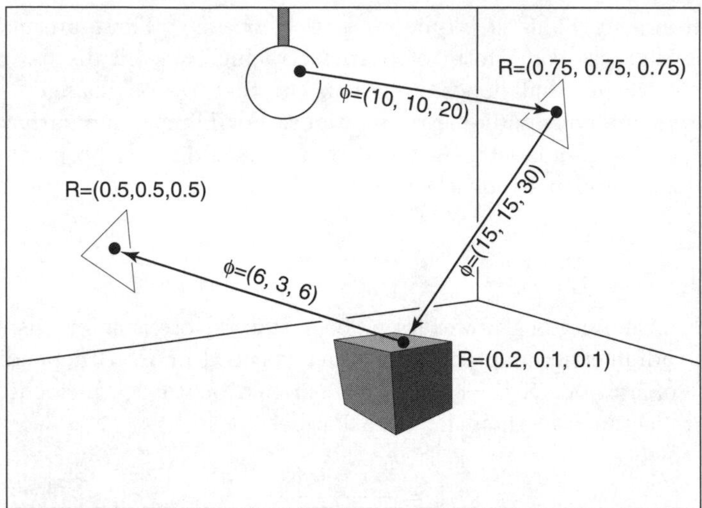

Figure 19.3. The path of a particle that survives with probility 0.5 and is absorbed at the last intersection. The RGB power is shown for each path segment.

A key part to this algorithm is that we scatter the light with an appropriate distribution for Lambertian surfaces. As discussed in Section 14.4.1, we can find a vector with a cosine (Lambertian) distribution by transforming two canonical random numbers (ξ_1, ξ_2) as follows:

$$\mathbf{a} = (\cos(2\pi\xi_1)\sqrt{\xi_2}, \sin(2\pi\xi_1)\sqrt{\xi_2}, \sqrt{1-\xi_2}) \tag{19.2}$$

Note that this assumes the normal vector is parallel to the z axis. For a triangle we must establish an orthonormal basis with $\mathbf{w}$ parallel to the normal vector. We can accomplish this as follows:

$$\mathbf{w} = \frac{\mathbf{n}}{\|\mathbf{n}\|}$$

$$\mathbf{u} = \frac{\mathbf{p}_1 - \mathbf{p}_0}{\|\mathbf{p}_1 - \mathbf{p}_0\|}$$

$$\mathbf{v} = \mathbf{w} \times \mathbf{u}$$

where $\mathbf{p}_i$ are the vertices of the triangle. Then, by definition, our vector in the appropriate coordinates is:

$$\mathbf{a} = \cos(2\pi\xi_1)\sqrt{\xi_2}\mathbf{u} + \sin(2\pi\xi_1)\sqrt{\xi_2}\mathbf{v} + \sqrt{1-\xi_2}\mathbf{w} \tag{19.3}$$

In pseudocode our algorithm for $p = 0.5$ and one luminaire is:

for *(Each of n particles)* ***do***
  RGB phi $= \Phi/n$
  compute uniform random point $\mathbf{a}$ *on luminaire*
  compute random direction $\mathbf{b}$ *with cosine density*
  done = false
  while *not done* ***do***
    if *(ray* $\mathbf{a} + t\mathbf{b}$ *hits at some point* $\mathbf{c}$ *)* ***then***
      add $n_t R\phi/(\pi A)$ *to appropriate texel*
      if $(\xi_1 > 0.5)$ ***then***
        $\phi = 2R\phi$
        $\mathbf{a} = \mathbf{c}$
        $\mathbf{b}$ = *random direction with cosine density*
    else
      done=true

Here ξ_i are cononical random numbers. Once this code has run, the texture maps store the radiance of each triangle and can be rendered directly for any viewpoint with no additional computation.

19.2 Path Tracing

While particle tracing is well-suited to precomputation of the radiances of diffuse scenes, it is problematic for creating images of scenes with general BRDFs or scenes that contain many objects. The most straightfoward way to create images of such scenes is to use *path tracing.* This is a probabilistic method that sends rays from the eye and traces them back to the light. Often path tracing is used only to compute the indirect lighting. Here we will present it in a way that captures all lighting, which can be inefficient. This is sometimes called *brute force* path tracing. In the next chapter, more efficient techniques for direct lighting can be added.

In path tracing, we start with the full transport equation:

$$L_s(\mathbf{k}_o) = L_e(\mathbf{k}_o) + \int_{\text{all } \mathbf{k}_i} \rho(\mathbf{k}_i, \mathbf{k}_o) L_f(\mathbf{k}_i) \cos\theta_i d\sigma_i.$$

We use Monte Carlo integration to approximate the solution to this equation for each viewing ray. Recall from Section 14.3, that we can use random samples to apprxoimate an integral:

$$\int_{x \in S} g(x) d\mu \approx \frac{1}{N} \sum_{i=1}^{N} \frac{g(x_i)}{p(x_i)},$$

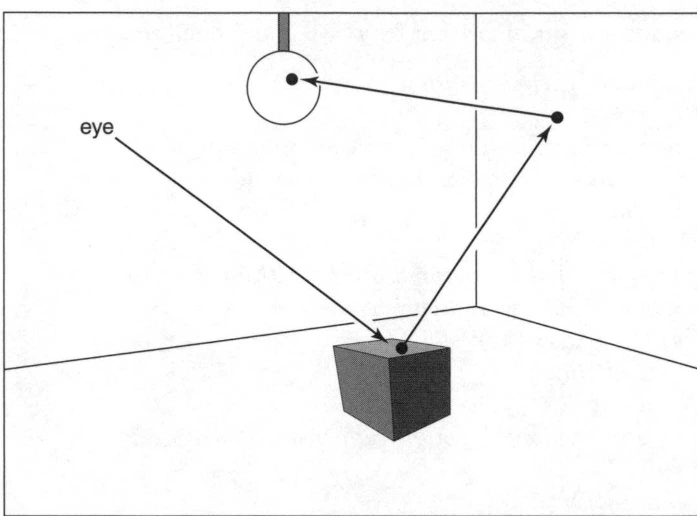

Figure 19.4. In path tracing, a ray is followed through a pixel from the eye and scattered through the scene until it hits a luminaire.

where the x_i are random points with probability density function p. If we apply this directly to the transport equation with $N = 1$ we get:

$$L_s(\mathbf{k}_o) \approx L_e(\mathbf{k}_o) + \frac{\rho(\mathbf{k}_i, \mathbf{k}_o) L_f(\mathbf{k}_i) \cos\theta_i d\sigma_i}{p(\mathbf{k}_i)}.$$

So if we have a way to select random directions $\mathbf{k}_i$ with a known density p, we can get an estimate. The catch is that $L_f(\mathbf{k}_i)$ is itself an unknown. Fortunately we can apply recursion and use a statistical estimate for $L_f(\mathbf{k}_i)$ by sending a ray in that direction to find the surface seen in that direction. We end when we hit a luminaire and L_e is nonzero (Figure 19.4). This method assumes lights have zero reflectance or we would continue to recurse.

In the case of a Lambertian BRDF ($\rho = R/\pi$), we can use a cosine density function:

$$p(\mathbf{k}_i) = \frac{\cos\theta_i}{\pi}$$

A direction with this density can be chosen according to Equation 19.3. This allows some cancellation of cosine terms in our estimate:

$$L_s(\mathbf{k}_o) \approx L_e(\mathbf{k}_o) + R L_f(\mathbf{k}_i).$$

In pseudocode such a path tracer for Lambertian surfaces would operate just like the ray tracers described in Chapter 9, but the *raycolor* fuction would be modified:

RGB raycolor(ray $\mathbf{a} + t\mathbf{b}$, *int depth)*
if *(ray hits at some point* $\mathbf{c}$ *)* ***then***
  RGB $c = L_e(-\mathbf{b})$
  if *(depth < maxdepth)* ***then***
    compute random direction $\mathbf{d}$
    return $c + R$ *raycolor(*$\mathbf{c} + s\mathbf{d}$*,depth+1)*
else
  return background color

This will result in a very noisy image unless either large luminaires or very large numbers of samples are used. Note the the color of the luminaires must be well above one (sometimes thousands or tens of thousands) to make the surfaces have final colors near one, because only those rays that hit a luminaire by chance will make a contribution, and most rays will contribute only a color near zero. To generate the random direction $\mathbf{d}$, we use the same technique as we do in particle tracing (see Equation 19.2).

In the general case we might want to use spectral colors or use a more general BRDF. In practice, we should have the material class contain member functions to compute a random direction as well as compute the p associated with that direction. This way materials can be added transparently to an implementation.

Frequently Asked Questions

• My pixel values are no longer in some sensible zero-to-one range. What should I display?

You should use one of the *tone reproduction* techniques described in the last chapter.

• What global illumination techniques are used in practice?

For batch rendering of complex scenes, path tracing with one level of reflection is often used. Path tracing is often augmented with a particle tracing preprocess as described in Jensen's book in the chapter notes. For walkthrough games, some form of world-space preprocess is often used, such as the particle tracing described in this chapter. For scenes with very complicated specular transport, a complex method described by Veach (*Metropolis Light Transport*, SIGGRAPH 96) may be the best choice.

• How does the ambient component relate to global illumination?

For diffuse scenes, the radiance of a surface is proportional to the product of the irradiance at the surface and the reflectance of the surface. The ambient component is just an approximation to the irradiance scaled by the inverse of π. So although it is a crude approximation, there can be some methodology to guessing it, and it is probably more accurate than doing nothing, i.e., using zero for the ambient term. Because the indirect irradiance can vary widely within a scene, using a different constant for each surface can be used for better results rather than using a global ambient term.

• Why do most algorithms compute direct lighting using traditional ray tracing?

Although global illumination algorithms automatically compute direct lighting, and it is in fact slightly more complicated to make them compute only indirect lighting, it is usually faster to compute direct lighting seperately. There are three reasons for this. First, indirect lighting tends to be smooth compared to direct lighting (see Figure 19.1) so coarser representations can be used, e.g., low-resolution texture maps for particle tracing. The second reason is that light sources tend to be small, and it is rare to hit them by chance in a "from the eye" method such as path tracing, while direct shadow rays are efficient. The third reason is that direct lighting allows stratified sampling so it converges rapidly compared to unstratified sampling. The issue of stratification is the eason that shadow rays are used in Metropolis Light Transport despite the stability of its default technique for dealing with direct lighting as just one type of path to handle.

• How artificial is it to assume ideal diffuse and specular behavior?

For environments that have only matte and mirrored surfaces, the Lambertian/specular assumption works well. A comparison between a rendering using that assumption and a photograph is shown in Figure 19.5.

Figure 19.5. A comparison between a rendering and a photo. Figure courtesy Sumant Pattanaik and the Cornell Program of Computer Graphics. (See also Plate X.)

Notes

Radiosity was introduced to computer graphics in *Modeling the Interaction of Light Between Diffuse Surfaces* (Goral et al., SIGGRAPH 84). There are several excellent books on radiosity: *Rasiosity and Realistic Image Synthesis* (Cohen and Wallace, Morgan Kaufmann Publishers, 1993), *Radiosity: A Programmer's Perspective* (Ashdown, John Wiley & Sons, 1994), and *Radiosity and Global Illumination* (Sillion and Puech, Morgan Kaufmann Publishers, 1994). Path tracing and the transport equation were introduced in *The Rendering Equation* (Kajiya, SIGGRAPH, 1986). Particle tracing for direct lighting was introduced in *Some Techniques for Shading Machine Renderings of Solids* (Appel, Proceedings of SJCC, 1968). Its modern form is described in *Realistic Image Synthesis Using Photon Mapping* (Jensen, A K Peters, Ltd, 2001). Many of the underpinnings of global illumination are covered in the two-volume *Principles of Digital Image Synthesis* (Glassner, Morgan Kaufmann Publishers, 1994).

Exercises

1. For a closed environment where every surface is a diffuse reflector and emittor with reflectance R and emitted radiance E, what is the total radiance at each point? *Hint: for* $R = 0.5$ *and* $E = 0.25$ *the answer is* 0.5. This is an excellent debugging case.

2. Using the definitions from Chapter 16, verify Equation 19.1.

3. If we want to take a typically-sized room with textures at centimater-square resolution, approximately how many particles should we send to get an average of about 1000 hits per texel?

Accurate Direct Lighting

This chapter presents a more physically-based method of direct lighting than Chapter 8. These methods will be useful in making the global illumination algorithms from the last chapter more efficient. The key idea is to send shadow rays to the luminaires as described in Chapter 9, but to do so with careful bookkeeping based on the transport equation from the previous chapter. The global illumination algorithms can be adjusted to make sure they compute the direct component exactly once. For example, in particle tracing, particles coming directly from the luminaire would not be logged, so the particles would only encode indirect lighting. This makes nice looking shadows much more efficiently than computing direct lighting in the context of global illumination.

20.1 Mathematical Framework

To calculate the direct light from one *luminaire* (light emitting object) onto a non-emitting surface, we solve a form of the transport equation from Section 16.2:

$$L_s(\mathbf{x}, \mathbf{k}_o) = \int_{\text{all } \mathbf{x}'} \frac{\rho(\mathbf{k}_i, \mathbf{k}_o) L_e(\mathbf{x}', -\mathbf{k}_i) v(\mathbf{x}, \mathbf{x}') \cos\theta_i \cos\theta'}{\|\mathbf{x} - \mathbf{x}'\|^2} \tag{20.1}$$

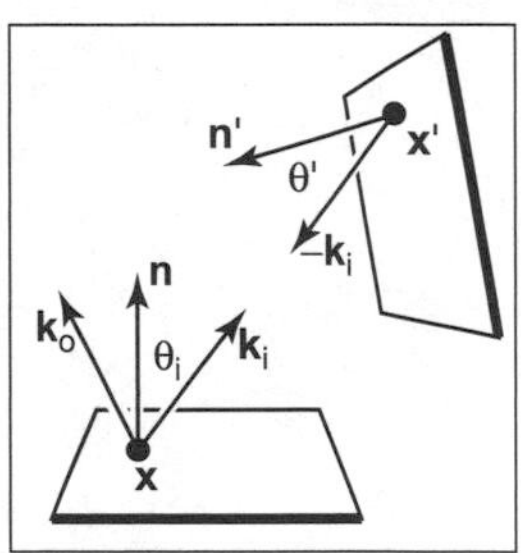

Figure 20.1. The direct lighting terms for Equation 20.1.

Recall that L_e is the emitted radiance of the source, v is a visibility function that is one if $\mathbf{x}$ "sees" $\mathbf{x}'$ and zero otherwise, and the other variables are as illustrated in Figure 20.1.

If we are to sample Equation 20.1 using Monte Carlo integration, we need to pick a random point $\mathbf{x}'$ on the surface of the luminaire with density function p (so $\mathbf{x}' \sim p$). Just plugging into the Equation 14.5 with one sample yields:

$$L_s(\mathbf{x}, \mathbf{k}_o) \approx \frac{\rho(\mathbf{k}_i, \mathbf{k}_o) L_e(\mathbf{x}', -\mathbf{k}_i) v(\mathbf{x}, \mathbf{x}') \cos\theta_i \cos\theta'}{p(\mathbf{x}') \|\mathbf{x} - \mathbf{x}'\|^2} \tag{20.2}$$

If we pick a uniform random point on the luminaire, then $p = 1/A$, where A is the area of the luminaire. This gives:

$$L_s(\mathbf{x}, \mathbf{k}_o) \approx \frac{\rho(\mathbf{k}_i, \mathbf{k}_o) L_e(\mathbf{x}', -\mathbf{k}_i) v(\mathbf{x}, \mathbf{x}') A \cos\theta_i \cos\theta'}{\|\mathbf{x} - \mathbf{x}'\|^2} \tag{20.3}$$

We can use Equation 20.3 to sample planar (e.g., rectangular) luminaires in a straightforward fashion. We simply pick a random point on each luminaire.

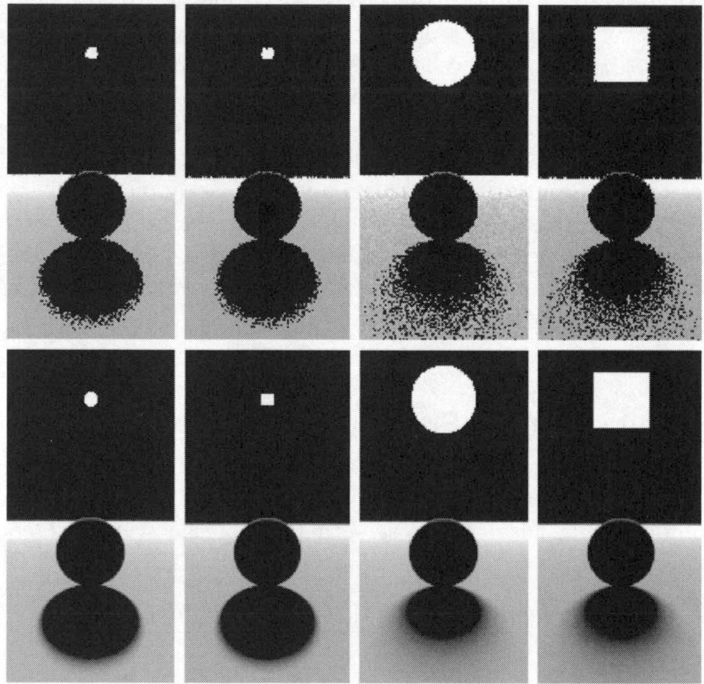

Figure 20.2. Various soft shadows on a backlit sphere with a square and an area light source. Top: 1 sample. Bottom: 100 samples. Note that the shape of the light source is less important than its size in determining shadow appearance.

The code for one luminaire is:

color directLight($\mathbf{x}$, $\mathbf{k}_o$, $\mathbf{n}$*)*
pick random point $\mathbf{x}'$ *with normal vector* $\mathbf{n}'$ *on light*
$\mathbf{d} = \mathbf{x}' - \mathbf{x}$
$\mathbf{k}_i = \mathbf{d}/\|d\|$
if *(ray* $\mathbf{x} + t\mathbf{d}$ *has no hits for* $t < 1 - \epsilon$*)* ***then***
  return $\rho(\mathbf{k}_i, \mathbf{k}_o) L_e(\mathbf{x}', -\mathbf{k}_i)(\mathbf{n} \cdot \mathbf{d})(-\mathbf{n}' \cdot \mathbf{d})/\|\mathbf{d}\|^4$
else
  return 0

The above code needs some extra tests such as clamping the cosines to zero if they are negative. Note that the term $\|\mathbf{d}\|^4$ comes from the distance squared term and the two cosines, e.g., $\mathbf{n} \cdot \mathbf{d} = \|\mathbf{d}\| \cos\theta$ because $\mathbf{d}$ is not necessarily a unit vector.

Several examples of soft shadows are shown in Figure 20.2.

20.1.1 Sampling a Spherical Luminaire

Although a sphere with center $\mathbf{c}$ and radius R can be sampled using Equation 20.3, this sampling will yield a very noisy image because many samples will be on the back of the sphere, and the $\cos\theta'$ term varies so much. Instead, we can use a more complex $p(\mathbf{x}')$ to reduce noise.

The first nonuniform density we might try is $p(\mathbf{x}') \propto \cos\theta'$. This turns out to be just as complicated as sampling with $p(\mathbf{x}') \propto \cos\theta'/\|\mathbf{x}' - \mathbf{x}\|^2$, so we instead discuss that here. We observe that sampling on the luminaire this way is the same as using a constant density function $q(\mathbf{k}_i) = \text{const}$ defined in the space of directions subtended by the luminaire as seen from $\mathbf{x}$. We now use a coordinate system defined with $\mathbf{x}$ at the origin, and a right-handed orthonormal basis with $\mathbf{w} = (\mathbf{c} - \mathbf{x})/\|\mathbf{c} - \mathbf{x}\|$, and $\mathbf{v} = (\mathbf{w} \times \mathbf{n})/\|(\mathbf{w} \times \mathbf{n})\|$ (see Figure 20.3). We also define (α, ϕ) to be the azimuthal and polar angles with respect to the uvw coordinate system.

The maximum α that includes the spherical luminaire is given by:

$$\alpha_{\max} = \arcsin\left(\frac{R}{\|\mathbf{x} - \mathbf{c}\|}\right) = \arccos\sqrt{1 - \left(\frac{R}{\|\mathbf{x} - \mathbf{c}\|}\right)^2}.$$

Thus a uniform density (with respect to solid angle) within the cone of directions subtended by the sphere is just the reciprocal of the solid angle $2\pi(1 - \cos\alpha_{\max})$ subtended by the sphere:

$$q(\mathbf{k}_i) = \frac{1}{2\pi\left(1 - \sqrt{1 - \left(\frac{R}{\|\mathbf{x} - \mathbf{c}\|}\right)^2}\right)}.$$

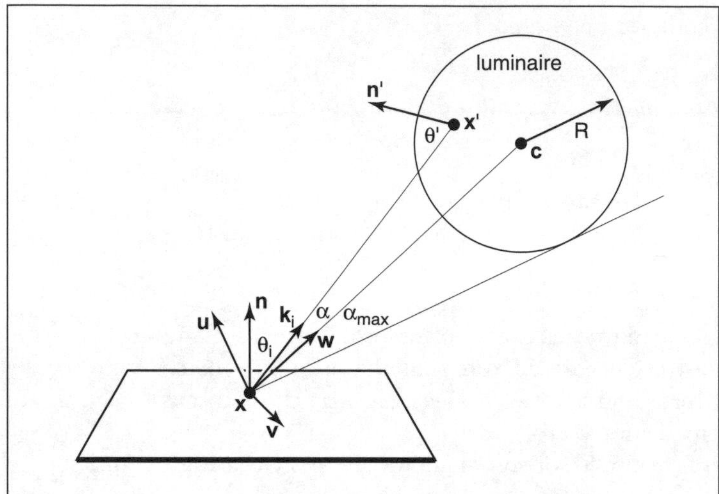

Figure 20.3. Geometry for direct lighting at point **x** from a spherical luminaire.

And we get

$$\begin{bmatrix} \cos\alpha \\ \phi \end{bmatrix} = \begin{bmatrix} 1 - \xi_1 + \xi_1 \sqrt{1 - \left(\frac{R}{\|\mathbf{x}-\mathbf{c}\|}\right)^2} \\ 2\pi\xi_2 \end{bmatrix}.$$

This gives us the direction $\mathbf{k}_i$. To find the actual point, we need to find the first point on the sphere in that direction. The ray in that direction is just $(\mathbf{x} + t\mathbf{k}_i)$, where $\mathbf{k}_i$ is given by:

$$\mathbf{k}_i = \begin{bmatrix} u_x & v_x & w_x \\ u_y & v_y & w_y \\ u_z & v_z & w_z \end{bmatrix} \begin{bmatrix} \cos\phi\sin\alpha \\ \sin\phi\sin\alpha \\ \cos\alpha \end{bmatrix}.$$

We must also calculate $p(\mathbf{x}')$, the probability density function with respect to the area measure (recall that the density function q is defined in solid angle space). Since we know that q is a valid probability density function using the ω measure, and we know that $d\Omega = dA(\mathbf{x}')\cos\theta'/\|\mathbf{x}' - \mathbf{x}\|^2$, we can relate any probability density function $q(\mathbf{k}_i)$ with its associated probability density function $p(\mathbf{x}')$:

$$q(\mathbf{k}_i) = \frac{p(\mathbf{x}')\cos\theta'}{\|\mathbf{x}' - \mathbf{x}\|^2}. \tag{20.4}$$

Figure 20.4. A sphere with $L_e = 1$ touching a sphere of reflectance 1. Where the two spheres touch, the reflective sphere should have $L(\mathbf{x}') = 1$. Left: 1 sample. Middle: 100 samples. Right: 100 samples, close-up.

So we can solve for $p(\mathbf{x}')$:

$$p(\mathbf{x}') = \frac{\cos\theta'}{2\pi\|\mathbf{x}' - \mathbf{x}\|^2 \left(1 - \sqrt{1 - \left(\frac{R}{\|\mathbf{x}-\mathbf{c}\|}\right)^2}\right)}.$$

A good debugging case for this is shown in Figure 20.4.

20.1.2 Non-Diffuse Luminaries

There is no reason the luminance of the luminaire cannot vary with both direction and position. For example, it can vary with position if the luminaire is a television. It can vary with direction for car headlights and other directional sources. Little in our analysis need change from the previous sections, except that $L_e(\mathbf{x}')$ must change to $L_e(\mathbf{x}', -\mathbf{k}_i)$. The simplest way to vary the intensity with direction is to use a Phong-like pattern with respect to the normal vector $\mathbf{n}'$. To avoid using an exponent in the term for the total light output, we can use the form:

$$L_e(\mathbf{x}', -\mathbf{k}_i) = \frac{(n+1)E(\mathbf{x}')}{2\pi} cos^{(n-1)}\theta',$$

where $E(\mathbf{x}')$ is the *radiant exitance* (power per unit area) at point $\mathbf{x}'$, and n is the Phong-exponent. You get a diffuse light for $n = 1$. If the light is non-uniform across its area, e.g., as a television set is, then E will not be a constant.

20.2 Direct Lighting from Many Luminaires

Traditionally, when N_L luminaires are in a scene, the direct lighting integral is broken into N_L separate integrals. This implies at least N_L samples must be taken to approximate the direct lighting, or some bias must be introduced. This is what you should probably do when you first implement your program. However, you can later leave the direct lighting integral intact and design a probability density function over all N_L luminaires.

As an example, suppose we have two luminaires, l_1 and l_2, and we devise two probability functions $p_1(\mathbf{x}')$ and $p_2(\mathbf{x}')$, where $p_i(\mathbf{x}') = 0$ for $\mathbf{x}'$ not on l_i and $p_i(\mathbf{x}')$ is found by a method such as one of those described previously for generating $\mathbf{x}'$ on l_i. These functions can be combined into a single density over both lights by applying a weighted average:

$$p(\mathbf{x}') = \alpha p_1(\mathbf{x}') + (1 - \alpha) p_2(\mathbf{x}'),$$

where $\alpha \in (0, 1)$. We can see that p is a probability density function because its integral over the two luminaires is one, and it is strictly positive at all points on the luminaires. Densities that are "mixed" from other densities are often called *mixture densities* and the coefficients α and $(1 - \alpha)$ are called the *mixing weights.*

To estimate $L = (L_1 + L_2)$, where L is the direct lighting and L_i is the lighting from luminaire l_i, we first choose a random canonical pair (ξ_1, ξ_2), and use it to decide which luminaire will be sampled. If $0 \le \xi_1 < \alpha$, we estimate L_1 with e_1 using the methods described previously to choose $\mathbf{x}'$ and to evaluate $p_1(\mathbf{x}')$, and we estimate L with e_1/α. If $\xi_1 \ge \alpha$ then we estimate L with $e_2/(1 - \alpha)$. In either case, once we decide which source to sample, we cannot use (ξ_1, ξ_2) directly because we have used some knowledge of ξ_1. So if we choose l_1 (so $\xi_1 < \alpha$), then we choose a point on l_1 using the random pair $(\xi_1/\alpha, \xi_2)$. If we sample l_2 (so $\xi_1 \ge \alpha$), then we use the pair $((\xi_1 - \alpha)/(1 - \alpha), \xi_2)$. This way a collection of stratified samples will remain stratified in some sense. This basic idea is illustrated in Figure 20.5 for nine samples and $\alpha = 0.7$.

This basic idea used to estimate $L = (L_1 + L_2)$ can be extended to N_L luminaires by mixing N_L densities

$$p(\mathbf{x}') = \alpha_1 p_1(\mathbf{x}') + \alpha_2 p_2(\mathbf{x}') + \cdots + \alpha_{N_L} p_{N_L}(\mathbf{x}'), \tag{20.5}$$

where the α_i's sum to one, and where each α_i is positive if l_i contributes to the direct lighting. The value of α_i is the probability of selecting a point on l_i, and p_i is then used to determine which point on l_i is chosen. If l_i is chosen, the we estimate L with $e_i/\alpha i$. Given a pair (ξ_1, ξ_2), we choose l_i by enforcing the conditions

$$\sum_{j=1}^{i-1} \alpha_j < \xi_1 < \sum_{j=1}^{i} \alpha_j.$$

And to sample the light, we can use the pair (ξ_1', ξ_2) where

$$\xi_1' = \frac{\xi_1 - \sum_{j=1}^{i-1} \alpha_j}{\alpha_i}.$$

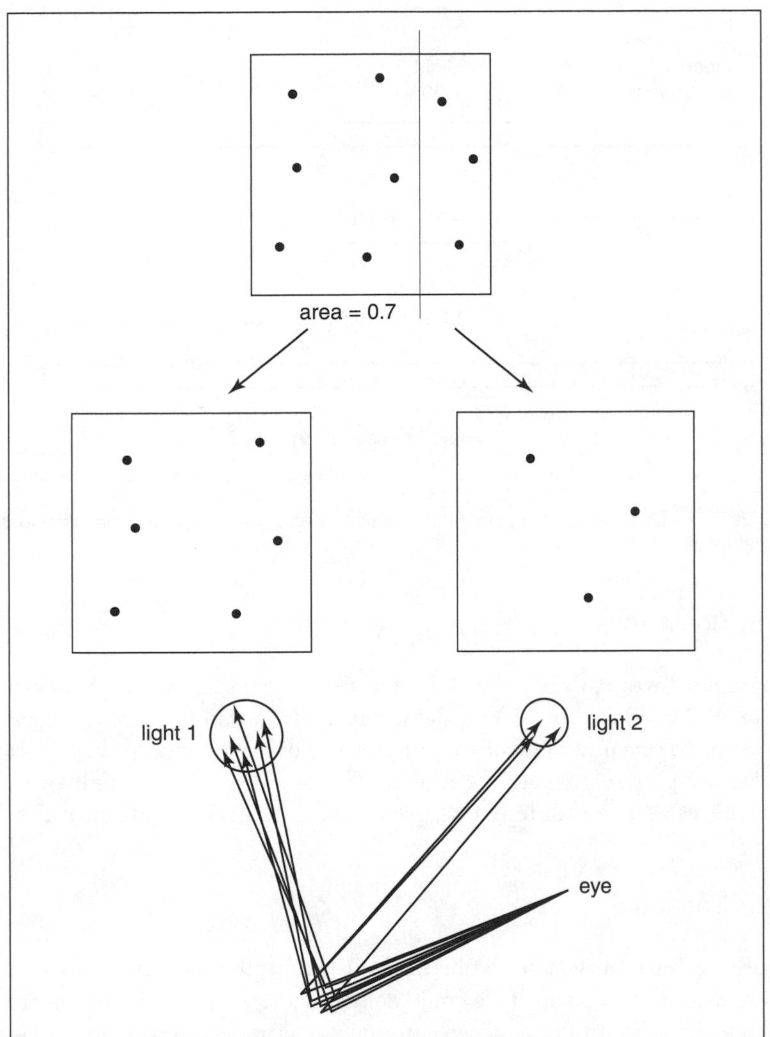

Figure 20.5. Each viewing ray generates exactly one shadow ray. A set of stratified samples on the unit square is mapped to luminaire locations, approximately 70% of which will go to the "more important" light because α = 0.7.

It cannot be over-stressed that it is important to "reuse" the random samples in this way to keep the variance low, in the same way we use stratified sampling (jittering) instead of random sampling in the space of the pixel. To choose the point on the luminaire l_i given (ξ_1', ξ_2), we can use the same types of p_i for luminaires as used in the last section (Figure 20.6). The question remaining is, "How to choose α_i".

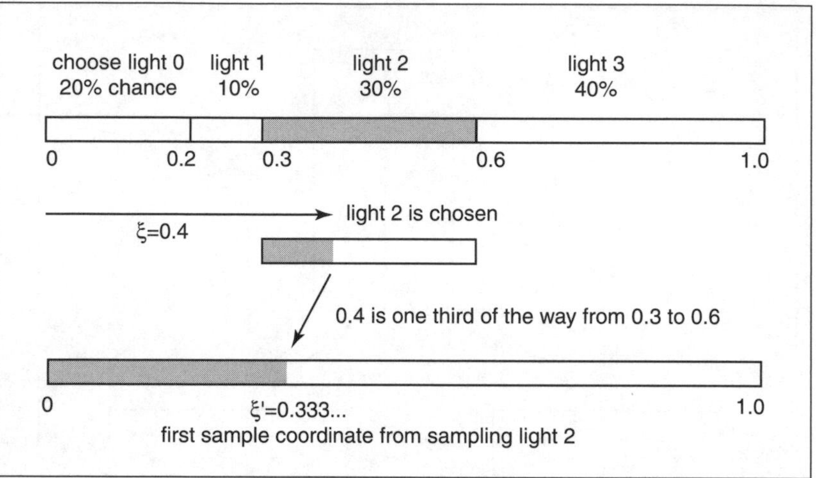

Figure 20.6. Diagram of mapping ξ_1 to choose l_i and the resulting remapping to new canonical sample ξ_1'.

20.2.1 Constant α_i

The simplest way to choose values for α_i is to make all weights equal: $\alpha_i = 1/N_L$ for all i. This would definitely make a valid estimator because the α_i sum to one and none of them is zero. This is a good debugging case. Unfortunately, in many scenes this estimate would produce a high variance (when the L_i are very different as occurs in most night "walkthroughs").

20.2.2 Linear α_i

Suppose we have perfect p_i defined for all the luminaires. A zero variance solution would then result if we could set $\alpha_i \propto L_i$, where L_i is the contribution from the ith luminaire. If we can make α_i approximately proportional to L_i, then we should have a fairly good estimator. This is called the *linear method* of setting α_i because the time used to choose one sample is linearly proportional to N_L, the number of luminaires.

To obtain such α_i, we get an estimated contribution e_i at $\mathbf{x}$ by approximating the rendering equation for l_i with the geometry term set to one. These e_is (from all luminaires) can be directly converted to α_i by scaling them so their sum is one:

$$\alpha_i = \frac{e_i}{e_1 + e_2 + \cdots + e_{N_L}}. \tag{20.6}$$

This method of choosing α_i will be valid because all potentially visible luminaires will end up with positive α_i. We should expect the highest variance in areas where shadowing occurs, because this is where setting the geometry term to one causes α_i to be a poor estimate of α_i.

Implementing the linear α_i method has several subtleties. If the entire luminaire is below the tangent plane at $\mathbf{x}$, then the estimate for e_i should be zero. An easy mistake to make is to set e_i to zero if the center of the luminaire is below the horizon. This will make α_i take on the one value that is not allowed: an incorrect zero. Such a bug will become obvious in pictures of spheres illuminated by luminaires that subtend large solid angles, but for many scenes such errors are not noticeable. To overcome this problem, we make sure that all of the vertices of a polygonal luminaire are below the horizon before it is given a zero probability of being sampled. For spherical luminaires, we check that the center of the luminaire is a distance greater than the sphere radius under the horizon plane before it is given a zero probability of being sampled.

Frequently Asked Questions

• How many shadow rays are needed per pixel?

Typically between 16 and 400. Using narrow penumbra, a large ambient term (or a large indirect component), and a masking texture can reduce the number needed.

• How do I sample something like a filament with a metal reflector where much of the light is reflected from the filament?

Typically the whole light is replaced by a simple source that approximates its aggregate behavior. For viewing rays, the complicated source is used. So a car headlight would look complex to the viewer, but the lighting code might see simple disk-shaped lights.

• Isn't something like the sky a luminaire?

Yes, and you can treat it as one. However, such large light sources may not be helped by direct lighting; the brute-force techniques from the last chapter are likely to work better.

Notes

Using Monte Carlo integration for computing direct lighting was introduced in *Distributed Ray Tracing* (Cook, SIGGRAPH, 1984). A deterministic method to reduce the number of shadow rays can be found in *Adaptive*

Shadow Testing for Ray Tracing, (Ward, Proceedings of the Second Eurographics Workshop on Rendering, 1991). The probabilistic methods discussed in this chapter are from *Monte Carlo Techniques for Direct Lighting Calculations*, (Shirley et al. ACM Transactions on Graphics, 15 (1), 1996).

Exercises

1. Develop a method to take random samples with uniform density from a disk.

2. Develop a method to take random samples with uniform density from a triangle.

3. Develop a method to take uniform random samples on a "sky dome" (the inside of a hemisphere).

Reflection Models

As we discussed in Chapter 16, the reflective properties of a surface can be summarized using the BRDF. In this chapter, we discuss some of the most visually important aspects of material properties, and a few fairly simple models that are useful in capturing these properties. There are many BRDF models in use in graphics, and the models presented here are meant to give just an idea of non-diffuse BRDFs.

21.1 Real-World Materials

Many real materials have a visible structure at normal viewing distances. For example, most carpets have easily visible pile that contributes to appearance. For our purposes, such structure is not part of the material property but is, instead, part of the geometric model. Structure whose details are invisible at normal viewing distances, but which do determine macroscopic material appearance, are part of the material property. For example, the fibers in paper have a complex appearance under magnification, but they are blurred together into an homogeneous appearance when viewed at arm's length. This distinction between microstructure that is folded into BRDF is somewhat arbitrary and depends on what one defines as "normal" viewing distance and visual acuity, but the distinction has proven quite useful in practice.

In this section we define some categories of materials. Later in the chapter, we present reflection models that target each type of material. In the notes at the end of the chapter some models that account for more exotic materials are also discussed.

21.1.1 Smooth Dielectrics and Metals

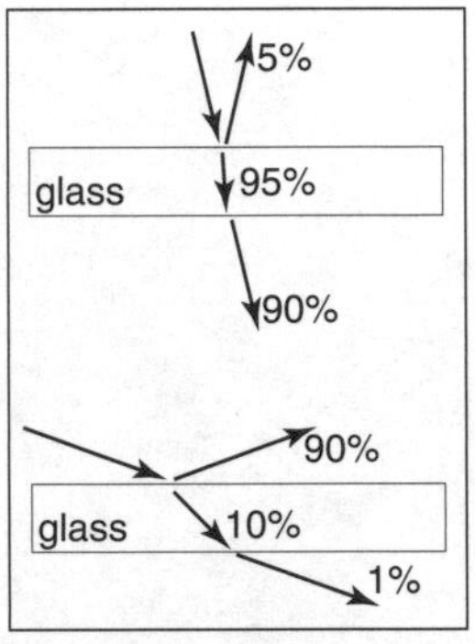

Figure 21.1. The amount of light reflected and transmitted by glass varies with the angle.

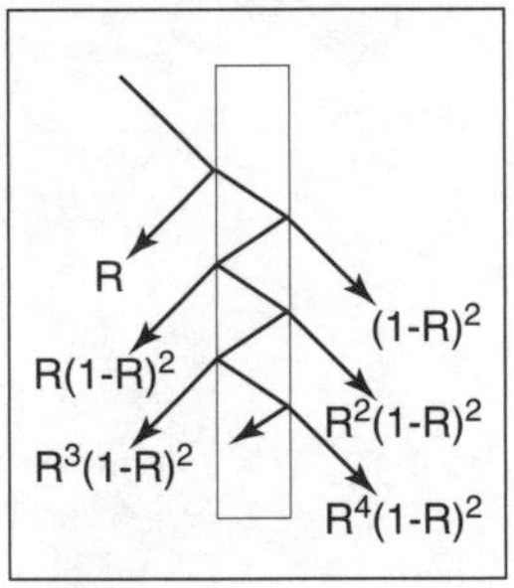

Figure 21.2. Light is repeatedly reflected and refracted by glass, with the fractions of energy shown.

Dielectrics are clear materials that refract light; their basic properties were summarized in Chapter 9. Metals reflect and refract light much like dielectrics, but they absorb light very, very quickly. Thus, only very thin metal sheets are transparent at all, e.g., the thin gold plating on some glass objects. For a smooth material, there are only two important properties:

1. How much light is reflected at each incident angle and wavelength;

2. What fraction of light is absorbed as it travels through the material for a given distance and wavelength.

The amount of light transmitted is whatever is not reflected (a result of energy conservation). For a metal, in practice, we can assume all the light is immediately absorbed. For a dielectric, the fraction is determined by the constant used in Beer's Law as discussed in Chapter 9.

The amount of light reflected is determined by the *Fresnel Equations* as discussed in Chapter 9. These equations are straightforward, but cumbersome. The main effect of the Fresnel Equations is to increase the reflectance as the incident angle increases, particularly near grazing angles. This effect works for transmitted light as well. These ideas are shown diagrammatically in Figure 21.1. Note that the light is repeatedly reflected and refracted as shown in Figure 21.2. Usually only one or two of the reflected images is easily visible.

21.1.2 Rough Surfaces

If a metal or dielectric is roughened to a small degree, but not so small that diffraction occurs, then we can think of it as a surface with *microfacets*. Such surfaces behave specularly at a closer distance, but viewed at a further distance seem to spread the light out in a distribution. For a metal, an example of this rough surface might be brushed steel, or the "cloudy" side of most aluminum foil.

For dielectrics, such as a sheet of glass, scratches or other irregular surface features make the glass blur the reflected and transmitted images that we can normally see clearly. If the surface is heavily scratched, we call it *translucent* rather than transparent. This is a somewhat arbitrary distinction, but it is usually clear whether we would consider a glass translucent or transparent.

21.1.3 Diffuse Materials

A material is *diffuse* if it is matte, i.e., not shiny. Many surfaces we see are diffuse, such as most stones, paper, and unfinished wood. To a first approximation, diffuse surfaces can be approximated with a Lambertian (constant) BRDF. Real diffuse materials usually become somewhat specular for grazing angles. This is a subtle effect, but can be important for realism.

21.1.4 Translucent Materials

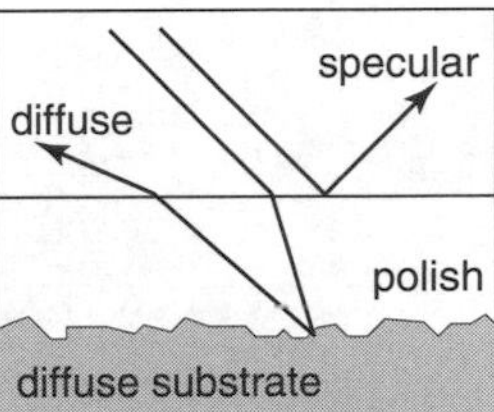

Figure 21.3. Light hitting a layered surface can be reflected specularly, or it can be transmitted and then scatter diffusely off the substrate.

Many thin objects, such as leaves and paper, both transmit and reflect light diffusely. For all practical purposes no clear image is transmitted by these objects. These surfaces can add a hue shift to the transmitted light. For example, red paper is red because it filters out non-red light, for light that penetrates a short distance into the paper, and then scatters back out. The paper also transmits light with a red hue because the same mechanisms apply, but the transmitted light makes it all the way through the paper. One implication of this property is that the transmitted coefficient should be the same in both directions.

21.1.5 Layered Materials

Many surfaces are composed of "layers" or are dielectrics with embedded particles that give the surface a diffuse property. The surface of such materials reflects specularly as shown in Figure 21.3, and thus obeys the Fresnel equations. The light that is transmitted is either absorbed or scattered back up to the dielectric surface where it may or may not be transmitted. That light that is transmitted, scattered, and then retransmitted in the opposite direction forms a diffuse "reflection" component.

Note that the diffuse component also is attenuated with the degree of the angle, because the Fresnel equations cause reflection back into the surface as the angle increases as shown in Figure 21.4. Thus instead of a constant diffuse BRDF, one that vanishes near the grazing angle is more appropriate.

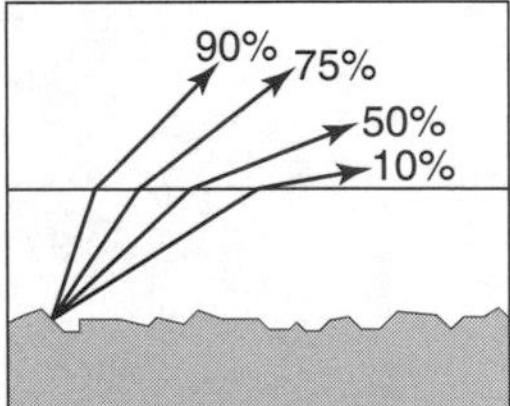

Figure 21.4. The light scattered by the substrate is less and less likely to make it out of the surface as the angle relative to the surface normal increases.

21.2 Implementing Reflection Models

A BRDF model, as described in Section 16.1.6, will produce a rendering which is more physially based than the rendering we get from point light sources and Phong-like models. Unfortunately, real BRDFs are typically quite complicated and cannot be deduced from first principles. Instead, they must either be measured and directly approximated from raw data, or they must be crudely approximated in an empirical fashion. The latter empirical strategy is what is usually done, and the development of such approximate models is still an area of research. This section discusses several desirable properties of such empirical models.

First, physical constraints imply two properties of a BRDF model. The first constraint is energy conservation:

$$\text{for all } \mathbf{k}_i, R(\mathbf{k}_i) = \int_{\text{all } \mathbf{k}_o} \rho(\mathbf{k}_i, \mathbf{k}_o) \cos\theta_o \, d\sigma_o \leq 1.$$

If you send a beam of light at a surface from any direction $\mathbf{k}_i$, then the total amount of light reflected over all directions will be at most the incident amount. The second physical property we expect all BRDFs to have is reciprocity:

$$\text{for all } \mathbf{k}_i,\, \mathbf{k}_o,\, \rho(\mathbf{k}_i, \mathbf{k}_o) = \rho(\mathbf{k}_o, \mathbf{k}_i).$$

Second, we want a clear separation between diffuse and specular components. The reason for this is that, although there is a mathematically-clean delta function formulation for ideal specular components, delta functions must be implemented as special cases in practice. Such special cases are only practical if the BRDF model clearly indicates what is specular and what is diffuse.

Third, we would like intuitive parameters. For example, one reason the Phong model has enjoyed such longevity is that its diffuse constant and exponent are both clearly related to the intuitive properties of the surface, namely surface color and highlight size.

Finally, we would like the BRDF function to be amenable to Monte Carlo sampling. Recall from Chapter 14 that an integral can be sampled by N random points $x_i \sim p$ where p is defined with the same measure as the integral:

$$\int f(x) d\mu \approx \frac{1}{N} \sum_{j=1}^{N} \frac{f(x_j)}{p(x_j)}.$$

Recall from Section 16.2 that the surface radiance in direction $\mathbf{k}_o$ is given by a transport equation:

$$L_s(\mathbf{k}_o) = \int_{\text{all } \mathbf{k}_i} \rho(\mathbf{k}_i, \mathbf{k}_o) L_f(\mathbf{k}_i) \cos\theta_i d\sigma_i.$$

If we sample directions with pdf $p(\mathbf{k}_i)$ as discussed in Chapter 19, then we can approximate the surface radiance with samples:

$$L_s(\mathbf{k}_o) \approx \frac{1}{N} \sum_{j=1}^{N} \frac{\rho(\mathbf{k}_j, \mathbf{k}_o) L_f(\mathbf{k}_j) \cos\theta_j}{p(\mathbf{k}_j)}.$$

This approximation will converge for any p that is non-zero wherever the integrand is non-zero. However, it will only converge well if the integrand is not very large relative to p. Ideally, $p(\mathbf{k})$ should be approximately shaped like the integrand $\rho(\mathbf{k}_j, \mathbf{k}_o)L_f(\mathbf{k}_j)\cos\theta_j$. In practice, L_f is complicated and the best we can accomplish is to have $p(\mathbf{k})$ shaped somewhat like $\rho(\mathbf{k}, \mathbf{k}_o)L_f(\mathbf{k})\cos\theta$.

For example, if the BRDF is Lambertian, then it is constant and the "ideal" $p(\mathbf{k})$ is proportional to $\cos\theta$. Because the integral of p must be one, we can deduce the leading constant:

$$\int_{\text{all } \mathbf{k} \text{ with } \theta < \pi/2} C\cos\theta d\sigma = 1.$$

This implies that $C = 1/\pi$, so we have:

$$p(\mathbf{k}) = \frac{1}{\pi}\cos\theta.$$

An acceptably efficient implementation will result as long as p doesn't get too small when the integrand is non-zero. Thus, the constant pdf will also suffice:

$$p(\mathbf{k}) = \frac{1}{2\pi}.$$

This emphasizes that many pdfs may be acceptable for a given BRDF model.

21.3 Specular Reflection Models

For a metal, we typically specify the reflectance at normal incidence $R_0(\lambda)$. The reflectance should vary according to the Fresnel equations, and a good approximation developed by Christophe Schlick is given by:

$$R(\theta, \lambda) = R_0(\lambda) + (1 - R_0(\lambda))(1 - cos\theta)^5$$

This approximation allows us to just set the normal reflectance of the metal either from data or by eye.

For a dielectric, the same formula works for reflectance. However, we can set $R_0(\lambda)$ in terms of the refractive index $n(\lambda)$:

$$R_0(\lambda) = \left(\frac{n(\lambda) - 1}{n(\lambda) + 1}\right)^2.$$

Typically, n does not vary with wavelength, but for applications where dispersion is important, n can vary. The refractive indices that are often useful include water ($n = 1.33$), glass ($n = 1.4$ to $n = 1.7$), and diamond ($n = 2.4$).

21.4 Smooth Layered Model

Reflection in matte/specular materials, such as plastics or polished woods, is governed by Fresnel equations at the surface and by scattering within the subsurface. An example of this reflection can be seen in the tiles in the photographs in Figure 21.5. Note that the blurring in the specular reflection is mostly vertical due to the compression of apparent bump spacing in the view direction. This effect causes the vertically-streaked reflections seen on lakes on windy days; it can either be modeled using explicit micro-geometry and a simple smooth-surface reflection model or by a more general model that accounts for this asymmetry.

We could use the traditional Lambertian-specular model for the tiles, which linearly mixes specular and Lambertian terms. In standard radiometric terms, this can be expressed as:

$$\rho(\theta, \phi, \theta', \phi' \lambda) = \frac{R_d(\lambda)}{\pi} + R_s \rho_s(\theta, \phi, \theta', \phi'),$$

where $R_d(\lambda)$ is the hemispherical reflectance of the matte term, R_s is the specular reflectance, and ρ_s is the normalized specular BRDF (a weighted Dirac delta function on the sphere). This equation is a simplified version of the BRDF where R_s is independent of wavelength. The independence of wavelength causes a highlight that is the color of the luminaire, so a polished rather than a metal appearance will be achieved. Ward suggests to set $R_d(\lambda) + R_s \leq 1$ in order to conserve energy. However, such models with constant R_s fail to show the increase in specularity for steep viewing angles. This is the key point: in the real world the relative proportions of matte and specular appearance change with the viewing angle.

Figure 21.5. Renderings of polished tiles using coupled model. These images were produced using a Monte Carlo path tracer. The sampling distribution for the diffuse term is $\cos\theta/\pi$.

One way to simulate the change in the matte appearance is to explicitly dampen $R_d(\lambda)$ as R_s increases:

$$\rho(\theta, \phi, \theta', \phi', \lambda) = R_f(\theta)\rho_s(\theta, \phi, \theta', \phi') + \frac{R_d(\lambda)(1 - R_f(\theta))}{\pi},$$

where $R_f(\theta)$ is the Fresnel reflectance for a polish-air interface. The problem with this equation is that it is not reciprocal, as can been seen by exchanging θ and θ'; this changes the value of the matte dampening factor because of the multiplication by $(1 - R_f(\theta))$. The specular term, a scaled Dirac delta function, is reciprocal, but this does not make up for the non-reciprocity of the matte term. Although this BRDF works well, its lack of reciprocity can cause some rendering methods to have ill-defined solutions.

We now present a model that produces the matte/specular tradeoff while remaining reciprocal and energy conserving. Because the key feature of the new model is that it couples the matte and specular scaling coefficients, it is called a *coupled* model.

Surfaces which have a glossy appearance are often a clear dielectric, such as polyurethane or oil, with some subsurface structure. The specular (mirror-like) component of the reflection is caused by the smooth dielectric surface and is independent of the structure below this surface. The magnitude of this specular term is governed by the Fresnel equations.

The light that is not reflected specularly at the surface is transmitted through the surface. There, either it is absorbed by the subsurface, or it is reflected from a pigment or a subsurface and transmitted back through the surface of the polish. This transmitted light forms the matte component of reflection. Since the matte component can only consist of the light that is transmitted, it will naturally decrease in total magnitude for increasing angle.

To avoid choosing between physically plausible models and models with good qualitative behavior over a range of incident angles, note that the Fresnel equations that account for the specular term, $R_f(\theta)$, are derived directly from the physics of the dielectric-air interface. Therefore, the problem must lie in the matte term. We could use a full-blown simulation of subsurface scattering as implemented, but this technique is both costly and requires detailed knowledge of subsurface structure, which is usually neither known nor easily measurable. Instead, we can modify the matte term to be a simple approximation that captures the important qualitative angular behavior shown in Figure 21.4.

Let us assume that the matte term is not Lambertian, but instead is some other function that depends only on θ, θ' and λ: $\rho_m(\theta, \theta', \lambda)$. We discard behavior that depends on ϕ or ϕ' in the interest of simplicity. We try to keep the formulas reasonably simple because the physics of the matte term is complicated and sometimes requires unknown parameters.

We expect the matte term to be close to constant, and roughly rotationally symmetric, as is argued in He's dissertation.

An obvious candidate for the matte component $\rho_m(\theta, \theta', \lambda)$ that will be reciprocal is the *separable* form $kR_m(\lambda)f(\theta)f(\theta')$ for some constant k and matte reflectance parameter $R_m(\lambda)$. We could merge k and $R_m(\lambda)$ into a single term, but we choose to keep them separated because this makes it more intuitive to set $R_m(\lambda)$—which must be between 0 and 1 for all wavelengths. Separable BRDFs have been shown to have several computational advantages, thus we use the separable model:

$$\rho(\theta, \phi, \theta', \phi', \lambda) = R_f(\theta)\rho_s(\theta, \phi, \theta', \phi') + kR_m(\lambda)f(\theta)f(\theta').$$

We know that the matte component can only contain energy not reflected in the surface (specular) component. This means that for $R_m(\lambda) = 1$, the incident and reflected energy are the same, which suggests the following constraint on the BRDF for each incident θ and λ:

$$R_f(\theta) + 2\pi k f(\theta) \int_0^{\frac{\pi}{2}} f(\theta') \cos\theta' \sin\theta' d\theta' = 1. \tag{21.1}$$

We can see that $f(\theta)$ must be proportional to $(1 - R_f(\theta))$. If we assume that matte components that absorb some energy have the same directional pattern as this ideal, we get a BRDF of the form:

$$\rho(\theta, \phi, \theta', \phi', \lambda) = R_f(\theta)\rho_s(\theta, \phi, \theta', \phi') + kR_m(\lambda)[1 - R_f(\theta)][1 - R_f(\theta')].$$

We could now insert the full form of the Fresnel equations to get $R_f(\theta)$, and then use energy conservation to solve for constraints on k. Instead, we will use the approximation discussed in Section 21.1.1 We find that

$$f(\theta) \propto (1 - (1 - \cos\theta)^5).$$

Applying Equation 21.1 yields

$$k = \frac{21}{20\pi(1 - R_0)}. \tag{21.2}$$

The full coupled BRDF is then

$$\begin{aligned}\rho(\theta, \phi, \theta', \phi', \lambda) = \\ &\left[R_0 + (1 - \cos\theta)^5(1 - R_0)\right] \rho_s(\theta, \phi, \theta', \phi') + \\ &kR_m(\lambda)\left[1 - (1 - \cos\theta)^5\right]\left[1 - (1 - \cos\theta')^5\right].\end{aligned} \tag{21.3}$$

The results of running the coupled model is shown in Figure 21.5. Note that for the high viewpoint, the specular reflection is almost invisible, but it is clearly visible in the low-angle photograph image, where the matte behavior is less obvious.

For reasonable values of refractive indices, R_0 is limited to approximately the range 0.03 to 0.06 (the value $R_0 = 0.05$ was used for Figure 21.0.5). The value of R_s in a traditional Phong model is harder to choose, because it typically must be tuned for viewpoint in static images and tuned for a particular camera sequence for animations. Thus, the coupled model is easier to use in a "hands-off" mode.

21.5 Rough Layered Model

The previous model is fine if the surface is smooth. However, if the surface is not ideal, some spread is needed in the specular component. An extension of the coupled model to this case is presented here. At a given point on a surface, the BRDF is a function of two directions, one in the direction towards the light and one in the direction towards the viewer. We would like to have a BRDF model that works for "common" surfaces, such as metal and plastic, and has the following characteristics:

1. **Plausible:** as defined by Lewis, this refers to the BRDF obeying energy conservation and reciprocity.

2. **Anisotropy:** the material should model simple anisotropy, such as seen on brushed metals.

3. **Intuitive parameters:** for material, such as plastics, there should be parameters R_d for the substrate and R_s for the normal specular reflectance as well as two roughness parameters n_u and n_v.

4. **Fresnel behavior:** specularity should increase as the incident angle decreases.

5. **Non-Lambertian diffuse term:** The material should allow for a diffuse term, but the component should be non-Lambertian to assure energy conservation in the presence of Fresnel behavior.

6. **Monte Carlo friendliness:** there should be some reasonable probability density function that allows straightforward Monte Carlo sample generation for the BRDF.

A BRDF with these properties is a Fresnel-weighted Phong-style cosine lobe model that is anisotropic.

We again decompose the BRDF into a specular component and a diffuse component (Figure 21.6). Accordingly, we write our BRDF as the classical sum of two parts:

$$\rho(\mathbf{k}_1, \mathbf{k}_2) = \rho_s(\mathbf{k}_1, \mathbf{k}_2) + \rho_d(\mathbf{k}_1, \mathbf{k}_2), \tag{21.4}$$

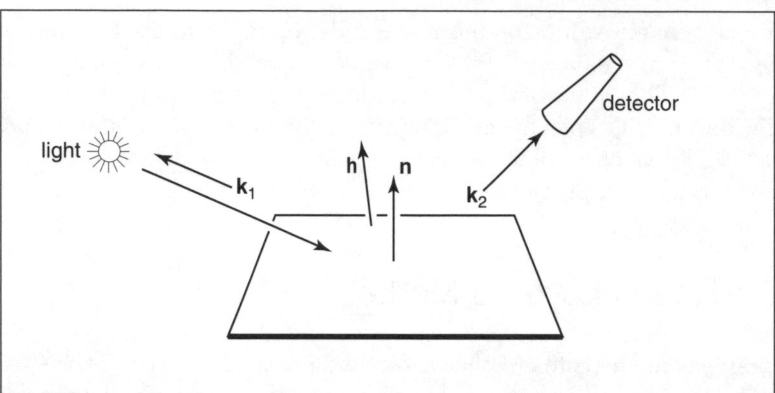

Figure 21.6. Geometry of reflection. Note that $\mathbf{k}_1$, $\mathbf{k}_2$, and $\mathbf{h}$ share a plane, which usually does not include $\mathbf{n}$.

where the first term accounts for the specular reflection (this will be presented in the next section). While it is possible to use the Lambertian BRDF for the diffuse term $\rho_d(\mathbf{k}_1, \mathbf{k}_2)$ in our model, we will discuss a better solution in Section 21.5.2. We discuss how to implement the model in Section 21.5.3. Readers who just want to implement the model should skip to that section.

21.5.1 Anisotropic Specular BRDF

To model the specular behavior, we use a Phong-style specular lobe but make this lobe anisotropic and incorporate Fresnel behavior while attempting to preserve the simplicity of the initial mode. This BRDF is

$$\rho(\mathbf{k}_1, \mathbf{k}_2) = \frac{\sqrt{(n_u+1)(n_v+1)}}{8\pi} \frac{(\mathbf{n}\cdot\mathbf{h})^{n_u \cos^2\phi + n_v \sin^2\phi}}{(\mathbf{h}\cdot\mathbf{k}_i)\max(\cos\theta_i, \cos\theta_o)} F(\mathbf{k}_i\cdot\mathbf{h}) \quad (21.5)$$

Again we use Schlick's approximation to the Fresnel equation:

$$F(\mathbf{k}_i\cdot\mathbf{h}) = R_s + (1-R_s)(1-(\mathbf{k}_i\cdot\mathbf{h}))^5, \quad (21.6)$$

where R_s is the material's reflectance for the normal incidence. Because $\mathbf{k}_i\cdot\mathbf{h} = \mathbf{k}_o\cdot\mathbf{h}$, this form is reciprocal. We have an empirical model whose terms are chosen to enforce energy conservation and reciprocity. A full rationaliztion for the terms is given in the paper by Ashikhmin, listed in the chapter notes.

The specular BRDF of Equation 21.5 is useful for representing metallic surfaces where the diffuse component of reflection is very small. Figure 21.7 shows a set of metal spheres on a texture-mapped Lambertian plane. As the

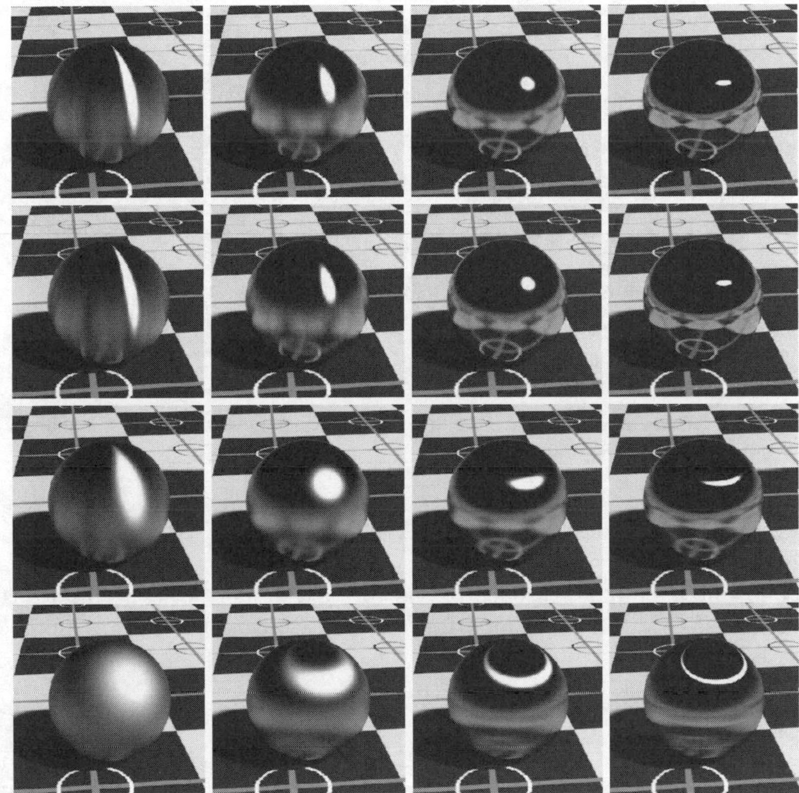

Figure 21.7. Metallic spheres for exponents 10, 100, 1000, 10000 increasing both left-to-right and top-to-bottom.

values of parameters n_u and n_v change, the appearence of the spheres shift from rough metal to almost perfect mirror, and from highly anisotropic to the more familiar Phong-like behavior.

21.5.2 Diffuse Term for the Anisotropic Phong Model

It is possible to use a Lambertian BRDF together with the anisotropic specular term; this is done for most models, but it does not necessarily conserve energy. A better approach is a simple angle-dependent form of the diffuse component which accounts for the fact that the amount of energy available for diffuse scattering varies due to the dependence of the specular term's total reflectance on the incident angle. In particular, diffuse color of a surface disappears near the grazing angle, because the total specular reflectance is close to one. This well-known effect cannot be reproduced

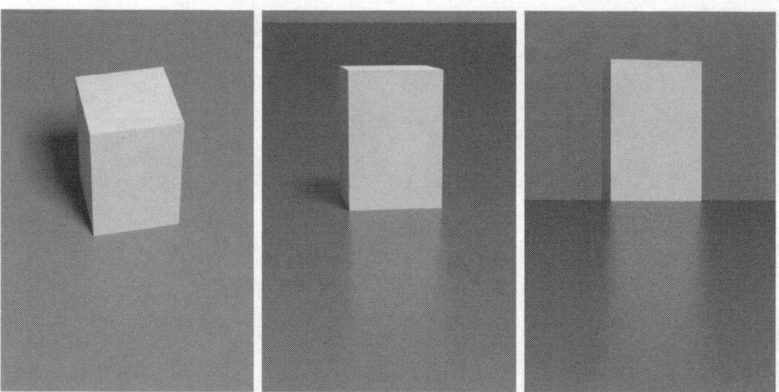

Figure 21.8. Three views for $n_u = n_v = 400$ and a diffuse substrate. Note the change in intensity of the specular reflection.

with a Lambertian diffuse term and is therefore missed by most reflection models.

Following a similar approach to the coupled model, we can find a form of the diffuse term that is compatible with the anisotropic Phong lobe:

$$\rho_d(\mathbf{k}_1, \mathbf{k}_2) = \frac{28R_d}{23\pi}(1 - R_s)\left(1 - \left(1 - \frac{\cos\theta_i}{2}\right)^5\right)\left(1 - \left(1 - \frac{\cos\theta_o}{2}\right)^5\right). \tag{21.7}$$

Here R_d is the diffuse reflectance for normal incidence, and R_s is the Phong lobe coefficient.

21.5.3 Implementing the Model

Recall the BRDF is a combination of diffuse and specular components:

$$\rho(\mathbf{k}_1, \mathbf{k}_2) = \rho_s(\mathbf{k}_1, \mathbf{k}_2) + \rho_d(\mathbf{k}_1, \mathbf{k}_2). \tag{21.8}$$

The diffuse component is given in Equation 21.7. The specular component is given in Equation 21.5. It is not necessary to call trigonometric functions

Figure 21.9. A closeup of the anisotropic phong model implemented in a path tracer with 9, 26, and 100 samples.

to compute the exponent, so the specular BRDF can be written:

$$\rho(\mathbf{k}_1, \mathbf{k}_2) = \frac{\sqrt{(n_u+1)(n_v+1)}}{8\pi} (\mathbf{n} \cdot \mathbf{h})^{\frac{(n_u(\mathbf{h}\cdot\mathbf{u})^2 + n_v(\mathbf{h}\cdot\mathbf{v})^2)/(1-(\mathbf{hn})^2)}{(\mathbf{h}\cdot\mathbf{k}_i)\max(\cos\theta_i, \cos\theta_o)}} F(\mathbf{k}_i \cdot \mathbf{h}). \tag{21.9}$$

In a Monte Carlo setting, we are interested in the following problem: given $\mathbf{k}_1$, generate samples of $\mathbf{k}_2$ with a distribution whose shape is similar to the cosine-weighted BRDF. Note that greatly undersampling a large value of the integrand is a serious error, while greatly oversampling a small value is acceptable in practice. The reader can verify that the densities suggested below have this property.

A suitable way to construct a pdf for sampling is to consider the distribution of half vectors that would give rise to our BRDF. Such a function is:

$$p_h(\mathbf{h}) = \frac{\sqrt{(n_u+1)(n_v+1)}}{2\pi} (\mathbf{nh})^{n_u \cos^2\phi + n_v \sin^2\phi}, \tag{21.10}$$

where the constants are chosen to ensure it is a valid pdf.

We can just use the probability density function $p_h(\mathbf{h})$ of Equation 21.10 to generate a random $\mathbf{h}$. However, to evaluate the rendering equation, we need both a reflected vector $\mathbf{k}_o$ and a probability density function $p(\mathbf{k}_o)$. It is important to note that if you generate $\mathbf{h}$ according to $p_h(\mathbf{h})$ and then transform to the resulting $\mathbf{k}_o$:

$$\mathbf{k}_o = -\mathbf{k}_i + 2(\mathbf{k}_i \cdot \mathbf{h})\mathbf{h}, \tag{21.11}$$

the density of the resulting $\mathbf{k}_o$ is **not** $p_h(\mathbf{k}_o)$. This is because of the difference in measures in $\mathbf{h}$ and $\mathbf{k}_o$. So the actual density $p(\mathbf{k}_o)$ is:

$$p(\mathbf{k}_o) = \frac{p_h(\mathbf{h})}{4(\mathbf{k}_i\mathbf{h})}. \tag{21.12}$$

Note that in an implementation where the BRDF is known to be this model, the estimate of the rendering equation is quite simple as many terms cancel out.

It is possible to generate a $\mathbf{h}$ vector whose corresponding vector $\mathbf{k}_o$ will point inside the surface, i.e., $\cos\theta_o < 0$. The weight of such a sample should be set to zero. This situation corresponds to the specular lobe going below the horizon and is the main source of energy loss in the model. Clearly, this problem becomes progressively less severe as n_u, n_v become larger.

The only thing left now is to describe how to generate $\mathbf{h}$ vectors with the pdf of Equation 21.10. We will start by generating $\mathbf{h}$ with its spherical angles in the range $(\theta, \phi) \in [0, \frac{\pi}{2}] \times [0, \frac{\pi}{2}]$. Note that this is only the first quadrant of the hemisphere. Given two random numbers (ξ_1, ξ_2) uniformly distributed in $[0, 1]$, we can choose

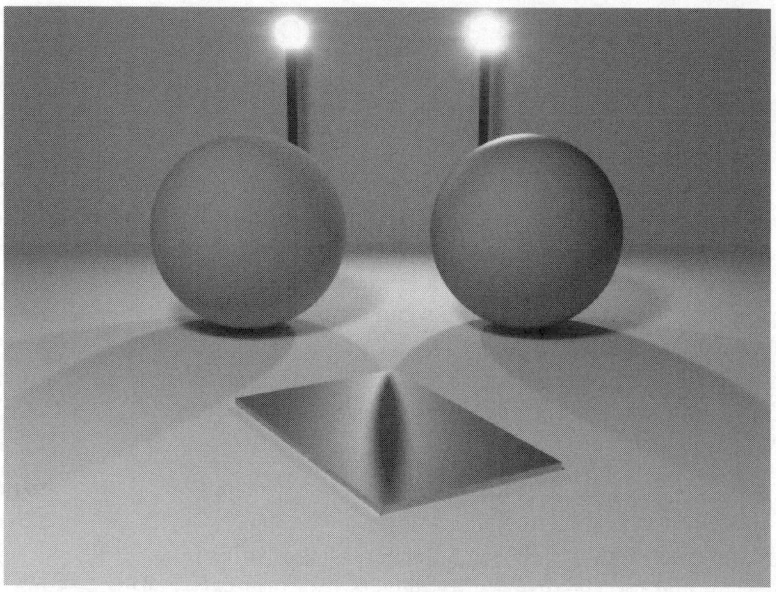

Figure 21.10. A rendering of a Lambertian ball (left), a anisotropic phong ball with $n_u = n_v = 5$ (right) and a metallic anisotropic phong plate. Based on a model by Eric Lafortune.

$$\phi = \arctan\left(\sqrt{\frac{n_u+1}{n_v+1}}\tan\left(\frac{\pi\xi_1}{2}\right)\right), \tag{21.13}$$

and then use this value of ϕ to obtain θ according to

$$\cos\theta = (1-\xi_2)^{1/(n_u\cos^2\phi+n_v\sin^2\phi+1)}. \tag{21.14}$$

To sample the entire hemisphere, we use the standard manipulation where ξ_1 is mapped to one of four possible functions depending on whether it is in $[0, 0.25)$, $[0.25, 0.5)$, $[0.5, 0.75)$, or $[0.75, 1.0)$. For example for $\xi_1 \in [0.25, 0.5)$, find $\phi(1 - 4(0.5 - \xi_1))$ via Equation 21.13, and then "flip" it about the $\phi = \pi/2$ axis. This ensures full coverage and stratification.

For the diffuse term, use a simpler approach and generate samples according to a cosine distribution. This is sufficiently close to the complete diffuse BRDF to substantially reduce variance of the Monte Carlo estimation.

An example of the model in a full scene is shown in Figure 21.10. Note the specular effects on the horizon of the right sphere which implements the model described here, and the absence of these effects on the left sphere which is Lambertian.

Frequently Asked Questions

• My images look too smooth, even with a complex BRDF. What am I doing wrong?

BRDFs only capture subpixel detail that is too small to be resolved by the eye. Most real surfaces also have some small variations, such as the wrinkles in skin, that can be seen. If you want true realism, some sort of texture or displacement map is needed.

• How do I integrate the BRDF with texture mapping?

Texture mapping can be used to control any parameter on a surface. So any kinds of colors or control parameters used by a BRDF should be programmable.

• I have very pretty code except for my material class. What am I doing wrong?

You are probably doing nothing wrong. Material classes tend to be the ugly thing in everybody's programs. If you find a nice way to deal with it, please let me know! My own code has a material class that just manages textures and how textures interact with the BRDF. When a viewing ray hits an object, a BRDF is created on the fly with $\mathbf{k}_o$ locked in, and specific values assigned for the control parameters. A destructor cleans up. This turns out to be efficient and allows a virtual function to evaluate the BRDF which only needs geometric information.

Notes

There are many BRDF models described in the literature, and only a few of them have been described here. Many of them, as well as more on the physics of surface reflection, are surveyed in Glassner's two-volume set *Principles of Digital Image Synthesis* (Morgan Kaufmann, 1994). The coupled model was introduced in *A Practitioners' Assessment of Light Reflection Models* (Shirley, Proceedings of Pacific Graphics, 1997). The anisotropic Phong model was presented in *An Anisotropic Phong Reflection Model* (Ashikhmin and Shirley,journal of graphics tools, 2000). The desired characteristics of BRDF models is discussed in *Making Shaders More Physically Plausible* (Lewis,Computer Graphics Forum,1994).

Exercises

1. Suppose that instead of the Lambertian BRDF we used a BRDF of the form $C \cos^a \theta_i$. What must C be to conserve energy?

2. The BRDF in Exercise 1 is not reciprocal. Can you modify it to be reciprocal?

3. Something like a highway sign is a *retroreflector*. This means that the BRDF is large when $\mathbf{k}_i$ and $\mathbf{k}_o$ are near each other. Make a model inspired by the Phong model that captures retroreflection behavior while being reciprocal and conserving energy.

22 Image-Based Rendering

A classic conflict in computer graphics is that between visual realism and the ability to interact. One attempt to deal with this problem is to use a set of captured or precomputed realistic images and to attempt to interpolate new images for novel viewpoints. This approach is called *image-based rendering*, abbreviated "IBR."

The basic idea of IBR idea is illustrated in 2D for a database of two images in Figure 22.1. Given two images, we approximate an image as seen from a novel viewpoint. The quality of this approximation depends on the

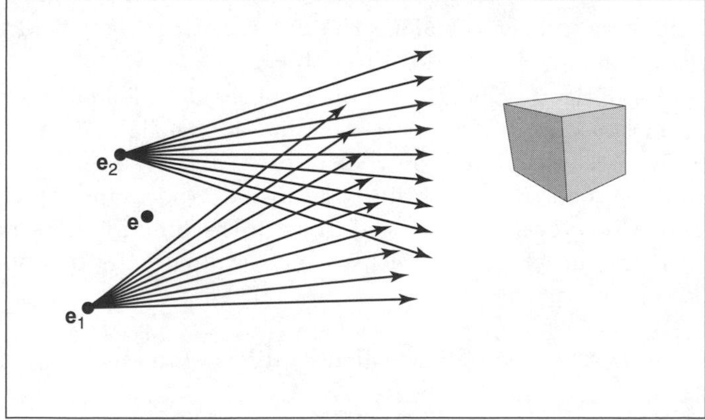

Figure 22.1. Given two images as seen from $\mathbf{e}_1$ and $\mathbf{e}_2$, image-based rendering can be used to make an approximation to the image that would be seen from a new viewpoint $\mathbf{e}$.

detail of the two source images, the underlying geometry of the object, and the relation of the three points. In this chapter, we discuss the most brute-force IBR method which uses very regular samples and straightforward interpolation.

22.1 The Light Field

For every point in space, light is passing through it in every direction. For a given point $\mathbf{a}$ and direction $\mathbf{d}$, the amount of light is quantified by the radiance (see Section 16.1.5). For the set of all points and all directions, we can describe the radiance at every location/direction pair as a function L that we evaluate to get the radiance:

$$L(\mathbf{a}, \mathbf{d}) \equiv \text{the radiance at point } \mathbf{a} \text{ in direction } \mathbf{d}.$$

An image is just a set of evaluations of this L function for a given eyepoint $\mathbf{a}$ and a structured set of directions $\mathbf{d}_i$. Technically, this function varies with wavelength (spectral radiance) and time. Usually we will think of RGB moments of the radiance and a steady-state in time. This L function has no standard name, but the most common one used in graphics is the *light field*.

There is a great deal of structure in the light field. Most importantly, L does not vary along a line for a fixed direction. This is illustrated in Figure 22.2, where

$$L(\mathbf{a}, \mathbf{d}) = L(\mathbf{b}, \mathbf{d}) = L(\mathbf{c}, \mathbf{d}) = L(\mathbf{e}, \mathbf{d}).$$

Note that if there in a object along the line, then the light field may be different for points on either side of the object.

Before we can try to approximate values of the light field at novel viewpoints, we must establish the dimensionality of the light field. At first glance it is 5D, because it varies over 3D position and 2D direction. Indeed, this is the dimensionality of the function inside a participating medium, such as smoke. However, because the value of the function does not vary along a line, we can create a *line-space* and evaluate the function for a directed line in 3D space:

$$L(\mathbf{A}) \equiv \text{the radiance along a directed line } \mathbf{A}.$$

A line in 3D is a 4D entity (see Section 14.1.3). This means we should be able to store radiance samples along rays as points in a 4D space. A way to do this is explored in the next section.

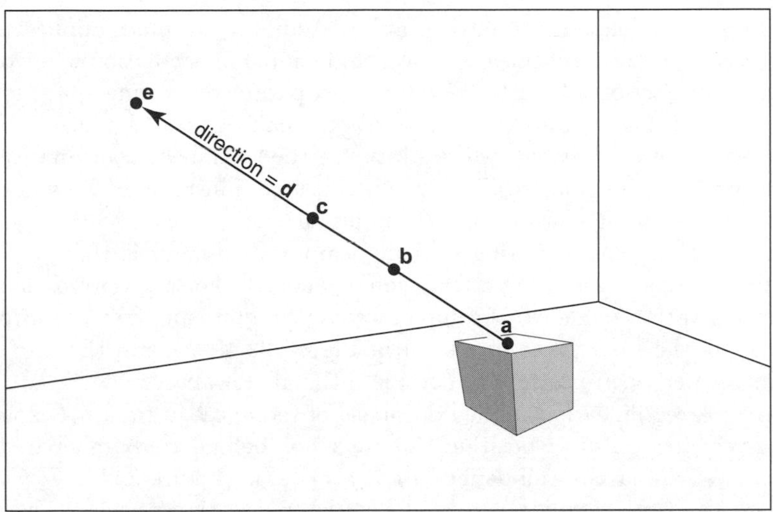

Figure 22.2. Several point/direction pairs in the light field. Because they lie along the same light ray, they have the same value.

22.2 Creating a Novel Image from a Set of Images

If we want to create an image from a novel viewpoint using only images from a precomputed set of images, then the key is to organize the data for this purpose. To simplify things, we create a space with dense samples

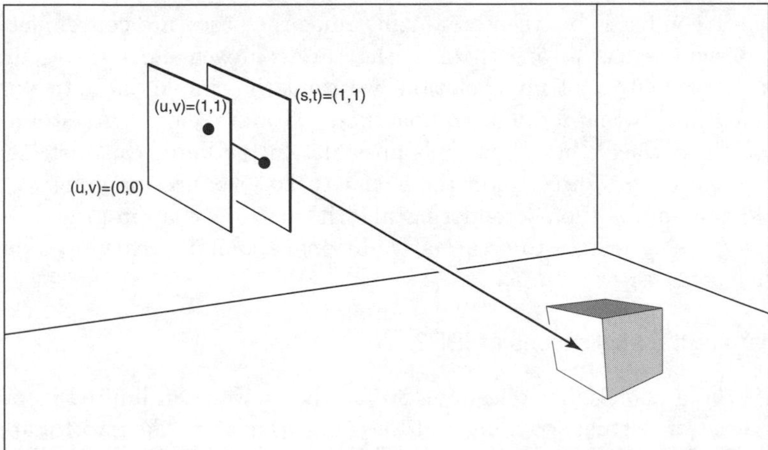

Figure 22.3. Any ray through the two rectangles can be parameterized by the two sets of texture coordinates, (u,v) and (s,t) of the hitpoints of the rays and the rectangle.

and do some simple form of interpolation. As in any graphics application, we first ask whether rectilinear samples and simple interpolation will work. Recall from Section 14.1.3 that one way to parameterize line space is to use two sets of 2D rectilinear coordinates on a pair of parallel planes. For a finite set of view directions, we can just use the rectilinear coordinates on a pair of parallel rectangles. This idea is illustrated in Figure 22.3 where a given ray is associated with a (u, v, s, t) quadruple.

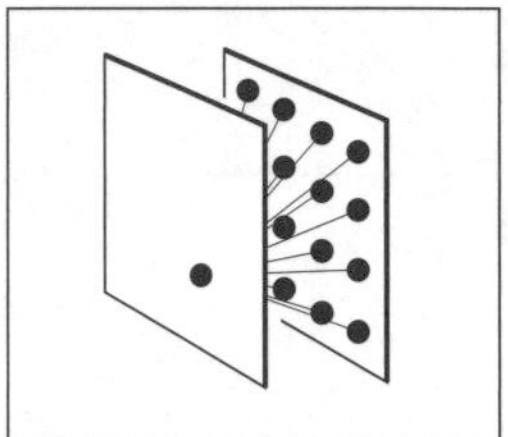

Figure 22.4. One (u,v) sample for all (s,t) values can be created with a single traditional rendering pass.

A nice thing about storing radiance samples this way is that we can assemble the database using a traditional renderer. For a given position $\mathbf{e}$ associated with a single (u, v) sample, we can compute an array of samples (pixels) on the (s, t) plane as shown in Figure 22.4. We can then render one image per (u, v) position to complete the 4D database.

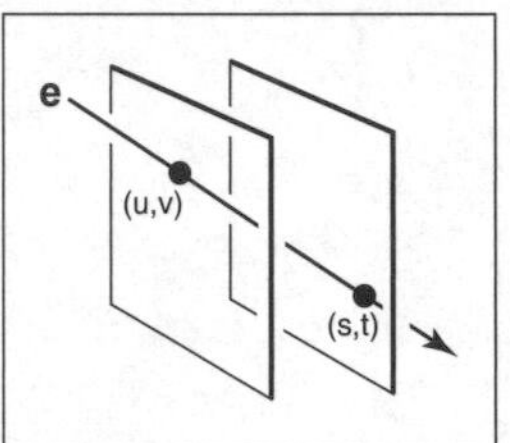

Figure 22.5. A ray from a new viewpoint that hits both planes will have a well-defined (u,v,s,t) value.

Given a rectilinearly sampled database of radiances in (u, v, s, t) space, and given a novel view position, all rays not behind or parallel to the two planes will have a well-defined (u, v, s, t) value (Figure 22.5). For rays through the two rectangles, we will have stored radiances near that 4D point and we can do some form of interpolation to compute a new value.

The interpolation scheme we use will determine the quality of the image. We could use full quadralinear interpolation between the nearest sixteen datapoints in (u, v, s, t) space. We could also use nearest-neighbor interpolation which will access less data, but will also result in blockier images.

Frequently Asked Questions

- What is the best place to store images?

The basic conflict is between organizing images so they are convenient for interpolation versus storing them so they are compact and yield accurate results. For convenient interpolation, we want the simple data structures described in this chapter. For compactness, we want the images stored as near to the surfaces they show as is possible. In the limit, this just means putting the images directly on the surfaces, i.e., texture mapping. Once you do this, a traditional rendering algorithm is most appropriate. The process of using images to create a traditional geometry/texture model is called *image-based modeling.*

- What are the applications of IBR?

This is the million-dollar question. So far they have been limited in practice. However, virtual shopping and web education seem like natural applications for IBR. In each of these, a set of photographs can be used to make compelling interactive experiences. For example, to browse homes for sale, the ability to move the viewpoint is essential to get a feel for the house.

Another natural application is sports. This has already been used in a professional football game with linear eye motion and nearest-neighbor (i.e., no) interpolation. In such applications brute-force techniques are likely to dominate, because there is little processing time available between image capture and image display.

- **Is the light field defined at surfaces?**

For a point on an opaque surface there is a well-defined radiance for each direction. The incoming directions will be incident radiance, and the outgoing directions will be outgoing radiance. These are sometimes called *field radiance* and *surface radiance*, respectively. . Thus, the light field is defined for such surfaces, although it is not continuous (it is zero inside the surface, and we define the light field on the surface as the limit function as taken from outside the surface). For dielectric surfaces, the light field is different for a full sphere of directions for both surface and field radiance, so the light field needs the sets of directions to be well-defined in that case.

- **What is depth correction?**

For matte scenes, we sometimes want to take advantage of approximate geometric information if it exists. Such a case is shown in Figure 22.6. Applying depth correction can give much crisper results, but it does complicate the interpolation scheme.

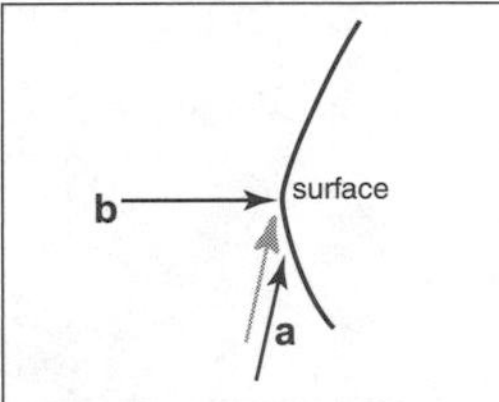

Figure 22.6. While the grey arrow is closer to **a**, it may be better to use the value for **b**, because the rays hit at a nearby point.

Notes

IBR was first introduced in *View Interpolation for Image Synthesis* (Chen and Williams, SIGGRAPH 93). The method described in this chapter was introduced in *The Lumigraph* (Gortler et al., SIGGRAPH 96), and *Light Field Rendering* (Levoy and Hanrahan, SIGGRAPH 96).

Exercises

1. Given a 5m × 5m × 3m room, how many texels are needed to have texture maps on the walls, floor, and ceiling at 1 square cm resolution? If we wanted to store a light field near the center of the room and use it to reconstruct images without depth correction, how many datapoints would be needed to reconstruct novel images with the same accuracy as the traditional texture maps?

2. How many operations are needed for nearest-neighbor interpolation in 4D line-space versus full 4D linear interpolation?

Visualization

One of the main application areas of computer graphics is *visualization*, where images are used to aid a user in understanding data. Sometimes this data has a natural geometric component, such as the elevation data for a region of the Earth. Other data has no obvious geometric meaning, such as trends in the stock market. This non-geometric data might nonetheless benefit from a visual representation, because the human visual system is so good at extracting information from images. The crucial part of visualizing non-geometric data is how the data is mapped to a spatial form. The general area of visualizing non-geometric data is called *information visualization* . This chapter will restrict itself to the more well-understood problems of visualizing 2D and 3D scalar fields, where a scalar data value is defined over a continuous region of space.

23.1 2D Scalar Fields

For simplicity, assume that our 2D scalar data is defined as

$$f(x,y) = \begin{cases} 1 - x^2 - y^2, & \text{if } x^2 + y^2 < 1, \\ 0 & \textit{otherwise}, \end{cases} \tag{23.1}$$

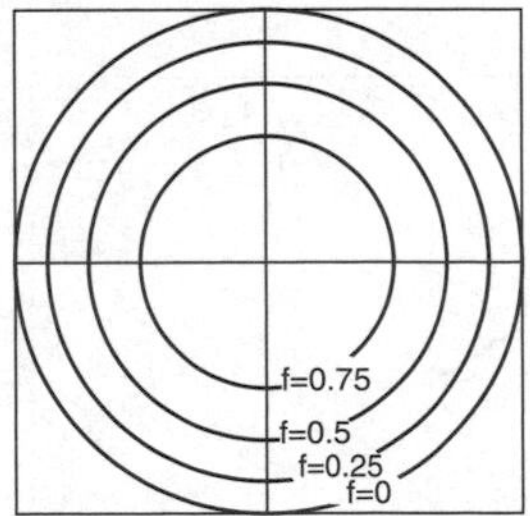

Figure 23.1. A contour plot for four levels of the function $1 - x^2 - y^2$.

over the square $(x, y) \in [-1, 1]^2$. In practice, we often have a sampled representation on a rectilinear grid that we interpolate to get a continuous field. We will ignore that issue in 2D for simplicity.

One way to visualize a 2D field is to draw lines at a finite set of values $f(x, y) = f_i$ (shown for the function in Equation 23.1 in Figure 23.1). This is done on many topographic maps to indicate elevation. Isocontours are excellent at communicating slope, but are hard to read "globally" to understand large trends and extrema in the data.

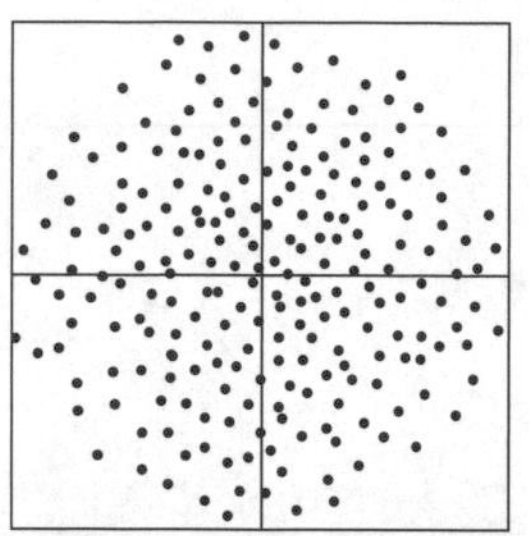

Figure 23.2. A random density plot for four levels of the function 1 - x² - y².

Another common way to visualize 2D data is to use small pseudorandom dots whose density is proportional to the value of the function. This is shown for our test function in Figure 23.2. Such random density plots are useful for display on black-and-white media, but are otherwise usually not a good choice for visualization. A generalization of random density plots takes the limit as the dot size goes to zero. This results in a greyscale continuous tone plot of the function. It is hard for humans to read such plots, because our ability to detect absolute intensity levels is poor. For this reason, colors or thresholding is often used. This is shown in greyscale in Figure 23.3. Formally, we can specify such a mapping with just a function g that maps scalar values to colors:

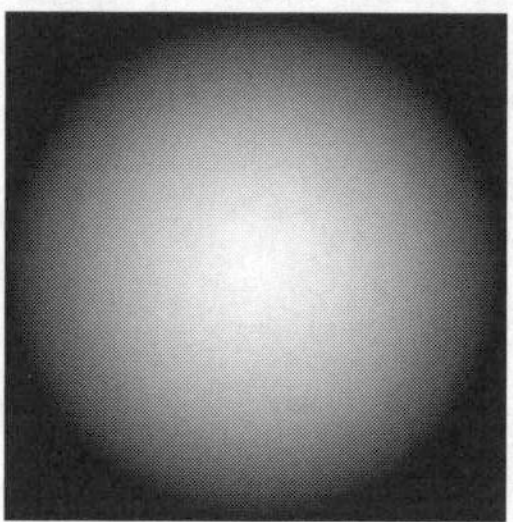

Figure 23.3. A greyscale density plot of the function 1 - x² - y².

$$g : \mathbb{R} \mapsto [0, 1]^3$$

Here $[0, 1]^3$ refers to the RGB cube. A common strategy is to specify a set of colors to which specific values map and linearly interpolate colors between them. A set of colors that increases in intensity and cycles in hue is often used. Such a set of colors for the domain $[0, 1]$ is:

$$\begin{aligned}
g(0.00) &= (0.0, 0.0, 0.0) \\
g(0.25) &= (0.0, 0.0, 1.0) \\
g(0.50) &= (1.0, 0.0, 0.0) \\
g(0.75) &= (1.0, 1.0, 0.0) \\
g(1.00) &= (1.0, 1.0, 1.0)
\end{aligned}$$

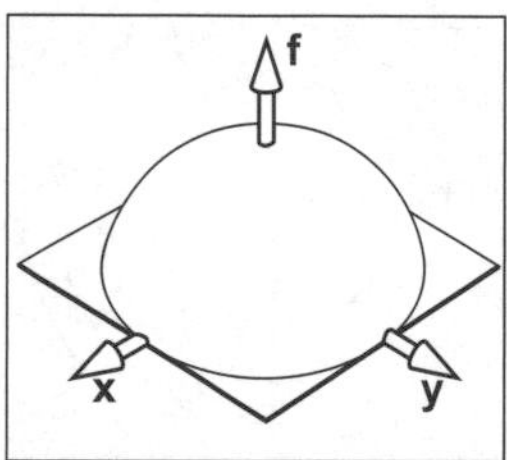

Figure 23.4. A height plot of the function.

These plots are often called *pseudocolor* displays. We can also display the function as a height plot as shown in Figure 23.4. This type of plot is good for showing the shape of a function. Note that this plot makes it more obvious that the function is spherical.

Often, more than one of these methods are used together in a single image, such as a colored or contoured height plot. Another hybrid technique that is often used is to shade the height plot and view it orthogonally from above. This is a *shaded relief map*, often used for geographical applications.

23.2 3D Scalar Fields

In 3D we can use some of the same techniques as in 2D. We can make a contour plot, where each contour is a 3D surface called an *isosurface*. We can also generalize a random density plot to 3D by scattering particles in 3D. If we take the limit, as we did in 2D to get a pesudocolor display, then we get *direct volume rendering*. These two methods are covered here. It is not clear how to generalize height plots, because we have run out of dimensions.

23.2.1 Isosurfaces

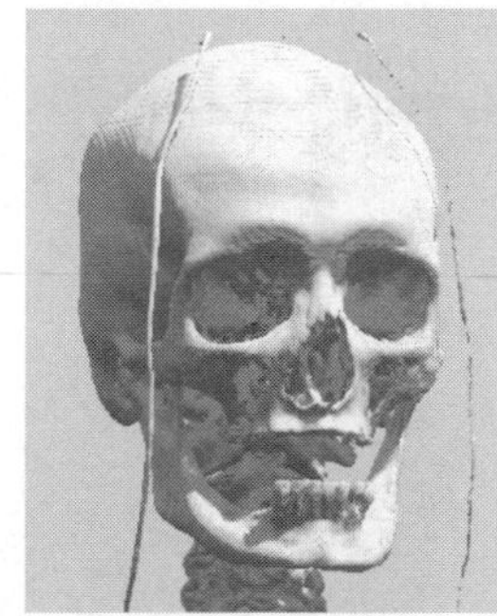

Figure 23.5. An isosurface from the NIH/NIM Visible Female dataset.

Given a 3D scalar field $f(x, y, z)$ we can create an isosurface for $f(x, y, z) = f_0$. In practice, we will have f defined in a 3D rectilinear table that we interpolate for intermediate values. An example image is shown in Figure 23.5.

There are two basic approaches to creating images of isosurfaces. The first is to explicitly create a polygonal representation of the isosurface and then render that representation using standard rendering techniques. The second is to use ray tracing to create an image by direct intersection calculation. In ray tracing, no explicit surface is computed. The explicit approach is better when we have small datasets, or we need the isosurface itself rather than just an image of it. The ray tracing approach is better for large datasets where we just need the image of the isosurface.

Creating polygonal isosurfaces

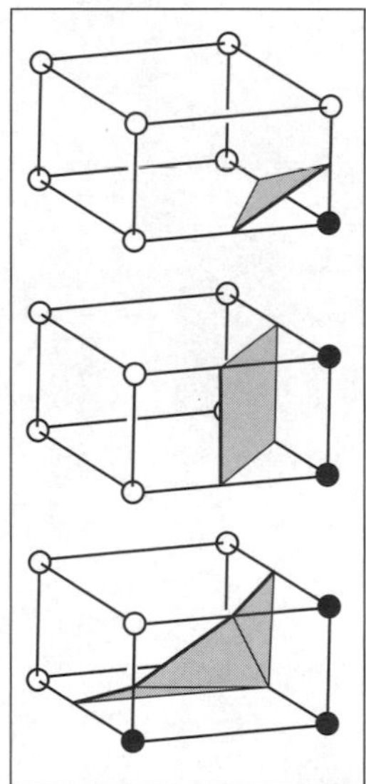

Figure 23.6. Three cases for polygonal isosurfacing. The black vertices are on one side of the isovalue, and the white on the other.

The basic idea of creating polygonal isosurfaces treats every rectilinear cell as a separate problem. Given an isovalue f_0, there is a surface in the cell if the minimum and maximum of the eight vertex values surround f_0. What surfaces occur depend on the arrangement of values above and below f_0. This is shown for three cases in Figure 23.6.

There are a total of $2^8 = 256$ cases for vertices above and below the isovalue. We can just enumerate all the cases in a table, and do a look-up. We can also take advantage of some symmetries to reduce the table size. For example, if we reverse above/below vertices, we can halve the table size. If we are willing to do flips and rotations, we can reduce the table to size 16, where only 15 of the cases have polygons.

Ray tracing

The algorithm for intersecting a ray with an isosurface has three phases: traversing a ray through cells which do not contain an isosurface, analytically computing the isosurface when intersecting a voxel containing the isosurface, shading the resulting intersection point. This process is repeated for each pixel on the screen.

To find an intersection, the ray $\mathbf{a} + t\mathbf{b}$ traverses cells in the volume checking each cell to see if its data range bounds an isovalue. If it does, an analytic computation is performed to solve for the ray parameter t at the intersection with the isosurface:

$$\rho(x_a + tx_b, y_a + ty_b, z_a + tz_b) - \rho_{\text{iso}} = 0.$$

When approximating ρ with a trilinear interpolation between discrete grid points, this equation will expand to a cubic polynomial in t. This cubic can then be solved in closed form to find the intersections of the ray with the isosurface in that cell. Only the roots of the polynomial which are contained in the cell are examined. There may be multiple roots corresponding to multiple intersection points. In this case, the smallest t (closest to the eye) is used. There may also be no roots of the polynomial, in which case the ray misses the isosurface in the cell.

A rectilinear volume is composed of a three-dimensional array of point samples that are aligned to the Cartesian axes and are equally spaced in a given dimension. A single cell from such a volume is shown in Figure 23.7. Other cells can be generated by exchanging indices (i, j, k) for the zeros and ones in the figure.

The density at a point within the cell is found using *trilinear* interpolation:

$$\begin{aligned}
\rho(u, v, w) \quad = \quad & (1-u)(1-v)(1-w)\rho_{000} \\
+ \; & (1-u)(1-v)(w)\rho_{001} \\
+ \; & (1-u)(v)(1-w)\rho_{010} \\
+ \; & (u)(1-v)(1-w)\rho_{100} \\
+ \; & (u)(1-v)(w)\rho_{101} \\
+ \; & (1-u)(v)(w)\rho_{011} \\
+ \; & (u)(v)(1-w)\rho_{110} \\
+ \; & (u)(v)(w)\rho_{111}
\end{aligned} \tag{23.2}$$

where

$$\begin{aligned}
u &= \frac{x - x_0}{x_1 - x_0} \\
v &= \frac{y - y_0}{y_1 - y_0} \\
w &= \frac{z - z_0}{z_1 - z_0}
\end{aligned} \tag{23.3}$$

Note that

$$\begin{aligned}
1 - u &= \frac{x_1 - x}{x_1 - x_0} \\
1 - v &= \frac{y_1 - y}{y_1 - y_0} \\
1 - w &= \frac{z_1 - z}{z_1 - z_0}
\end{aligned} \tag{23.4}$$

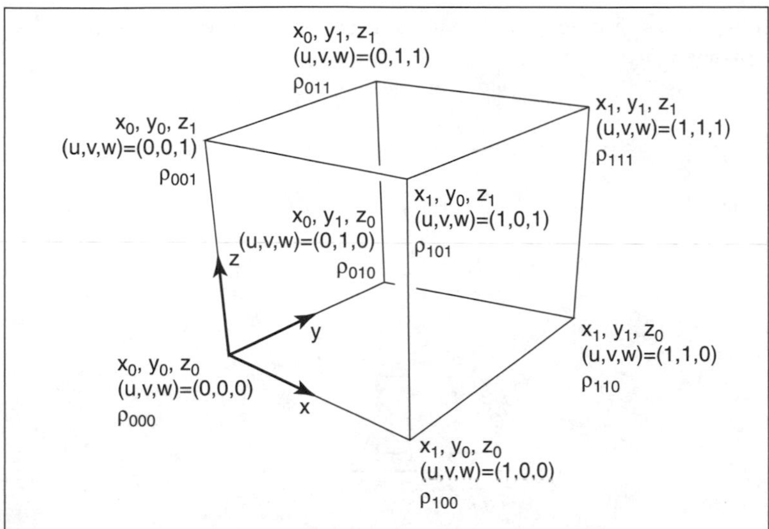

Figure 23.7. The geometry for a cell. A "nice" uvw coordinate system is used to make interpolation math cleaner.

If we redefine $u_0 = 1 - u$ and $u_1 = u$, and use similar definitions for v_0, v_1, w_0, w_1, then we get (Figure 23.8):

$$\rho = \sum_{i,j,k=0,1} u_i v_j w_k \rho_{ijk}.$$

It is interesting that the true trilinear isosurface can be fairly complex. The case where two opposite corners of the cube are on opposite sides of the isovalue from the other six vertices is shown in Figure 23.9. This is quite different from the two triangles given by polygonal isosurfacing for that case. One advantage of direct intersection with the trilinear surface is that ambiguous cases do not arise.

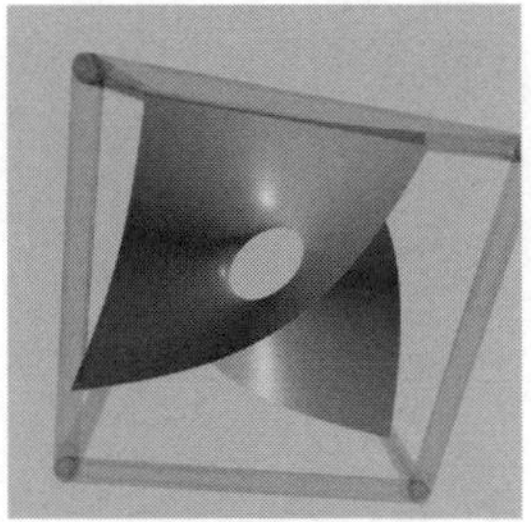

Figure 23.9. A true trilinear isosurface generated using direct ray tracing.

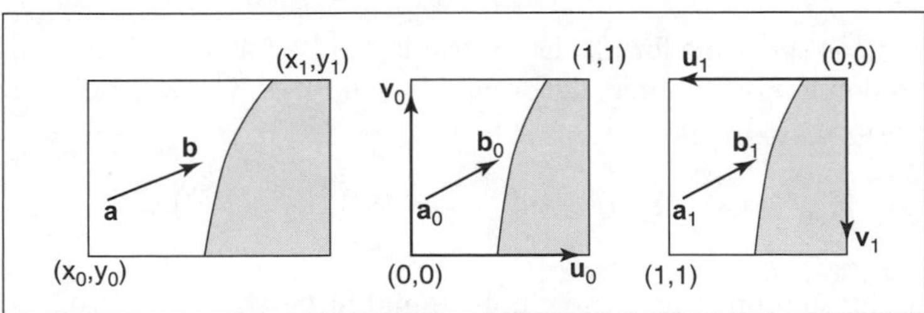

Figure 23.8. Various coordinate systems used for interpolation and intersection.

For a given point (x, y, z) in the cell, the surface normal is given by the gradient with respect to (x, y, z):

$$\mathbf{N} = \vec{\nabla}\rho = \left(\frac{\partial \rho}{\partial x}, \frac{\partial \rho}{\partial y}, \frac{\partial \rho}{\partial z}\right).$$

Thus, the normal vector of $(N_x, N_Y, N_z) = \vec{\nabla}\rho$ is

$$N_x = \sum_{i,j,k=0,1} \frac{(-1)^{i+1} v_j w_k}{x_1 - x_0} \rho_{ijk},$$

$$N_y = \sum_{i,j,k=0,1} \frac{(-1)^{j+1} u_i w_k}{y_1 - y_0} \rho_{ijk},$$

$$N_z = \sum_{i,j,k=0,1} \frac{(-1)^{k+1} u_i v_j}{z_1 - z_0} \rho_{ijk}.$$

Given a ray $\mathbf{p} = \mathbf{a} + t\mathbf{b}$, the intersection with the isosurface occurs when $\rho(\mathbf{p}) = \rho_{\text{iso}}$. We can convert this ray into coordinates defined by (u_0, v_0, w_0): $\mathbf{p}_0 = \mathbf{a}_0 + t\mathbf{b}_0$ and a second ray defined by $\mathbf{p}_1 = \mathbf{a}_1 + t\mathbf{b}_1$. Here the rays are in the two coordinate systems (Figure 23.8.):

$$\mathbf{a}_0 = (u_0^a, v_0^a, w_0^a) = \left(\frac{x_1 - x_a}{x_1 - x_0}, \frac{y_1 - y_a}{y_1 - y_0}, \frac{z_1 - z_a}{z_1 - z_0}\right),$$

and

$$\mathbf{b}_0 = (u_0^b, v_0^b, w_0^b) = \left(\frac{x_b}{x_1 - x_0}, \frac{y_b}{y_1 - y_0}, \frac{z_b}{z_1 - z_0}\right).$$

These equations are different because $\mathbf{a}_0$ is a location and $\mathbf{b}_0$ is a direction. The equations are similar for $\mathbf{a}_1$ and $\mathbf{b}_1$:

$$\mathbf{a}_1 = (u_1^a, v_1^a, w_1^a) = \left(\frac{x_a - x_0}{x_1 - x_0}, \frac{y_a - y_0}{y_1 - y_0}, \frac{z_a - z_0}{z_1 - z_0}\right),$$

and

$$\mathbf{b}_1 = (u_1^b, v_1^b, w_1^b) = \left(\frac{-x_b}{x_1 - x_0}, \frac{-y_b}{y_1 - y_0}, \frac{-z_b}{z_1 - z_0}\right).$$

Note that t is the same for all three rays; it can be found by traversing the cells and doing a brute-force algebraic solution for t. The intersection with the isosurface $\rho(\mathbf{p}) = \rho_{\text{iso}}$ occurs when:

$$\rho_{\text{iso}} = \sum_{i,j,k=0,1} \left(u_i^a + t u_i^b\right) \left(v_i^a + t v_i^b\right) \left(w_i^a + t w_i^b\right) \rho_{ijk}.$$

This can be simplified to a cubic polynomial in t:

$$At^3 + Bt^2 + Ct + D = 0$$

where

$$\begin{aligned} A &= \sum_{i,j,k=0,1} u_i^b v_i^b w_i^b \rho_{ijk}, \\ B &= \sum_{i,j,k=0,1} \left(u_i^a v_i^b w_i^b + u_i^b v_i^a w_i^b + u_i^b v_i^b w_i^a\right) \rho_{ijk}, \\ C &= \sum_{i,j,k=0,1} \left(u_i^b v_i^a w_i^a + u_i^a v_i^b w_i^a + u_i^a v_i^a w_i^b\right) \rho_{ijk}, \\ D &= -\rho_{\text{iso}} + \sum_{i,j,k=0,1} u_i^a v_i^a w_i^a \rho_{ijk}. \end{aligned}$$

The solution to a cubic polynomial is discussed in the article by Schwarze (Graphics Gems, Academic Press, 1990). His code is available on the web in several *Graphics Gems* archive sites. Two modifications are needed to use it: linear solutions (his code assumes A is non-zero), and the EQN_EPS parameter is set to 1.e-30 which provided for maximum stability for large coefficients.

23.2.2 Direct Volume Rendering

Another way to create a picture of a 3D scalar field is to do a 3D random density plot using small opaque spheres. To avoid complications, the spheres can be made a constant color and, in effect, they are light emitters with no reflectance. Such a random density plot can be implemented directly using ray tracing and small spheres, or with 3D points using a traditional graphics API. As in 2D, we can take the limit as the sphere size goes to zero. This yields a 3D analog of the pseudocolor display and is usually called *direct volume rendering*

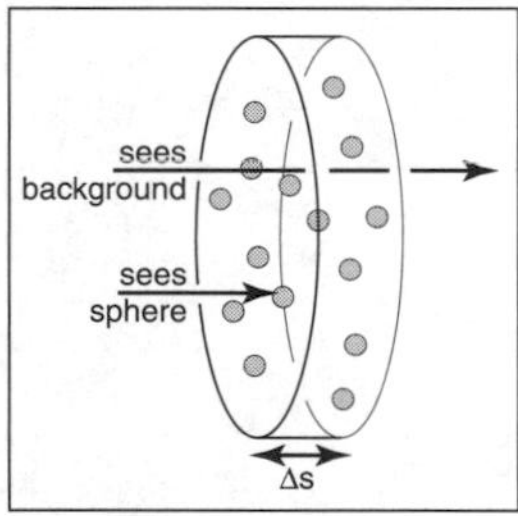

Figure 23.10. A thin slab filled with opaque spheres.

There are two parameters that affect the appearance of a volume rendering: sphere color, and sphere density. These are controlled by a user-specified *transfer function*:

$$\text{color} = c(\rho)$$

$$\text{number density} = d(\rho)$$

Here the *number density* is the number of spheres per unit volume. If we assume that the spheres have a small cross-sectional area a, and we consider a region along the line of sight that is of a small thickness Δs, such that no spheres appear to overlap (Figure 23.10), then the color is:

$$L(s + \Delta s) = (1 - F)L(s) + Fc$$

where F is the fraction of the disk that is covered by spheres as seen from the viewing direction. Because the disk is very thin, we can ignore spheres visually overlapping, so this fraction is just the total cross-sectional area of the spheres divided by the area A of the disk:

$$F = \frac{daA\,\Delta s}{A} = da\Delta s,$$

which yields

$$L(s + \Delta s) = (1 - da\,\Delta s)L(s) + da\Delta sc.$$

We can rearrange terms to give something like a definition of the derivative:

$$\frac{L(s + \Delta s) - L(s)}{\Delta s} = -daL(s) + dac.$$

If we take the limit $\Delta s \to 0$, we get a differential equation:

$$\frac{dL}{ds} = -daL(s) + dac.$$

For constant d and c this equation has the solution

$$L(s) = L(0)e^{-das} + c\left(1 - e^{-das}\right).$$

This would allow us to analytically compute color for constant density/color regions. However, in practice both d and c vary along the ray, and there is no analytic solution to the differential equation. So, in practice, we use a numerical technique. A simple way to proceed is to start at the back of the ray and incrementally step along the ray as shown in Figure 23.11.

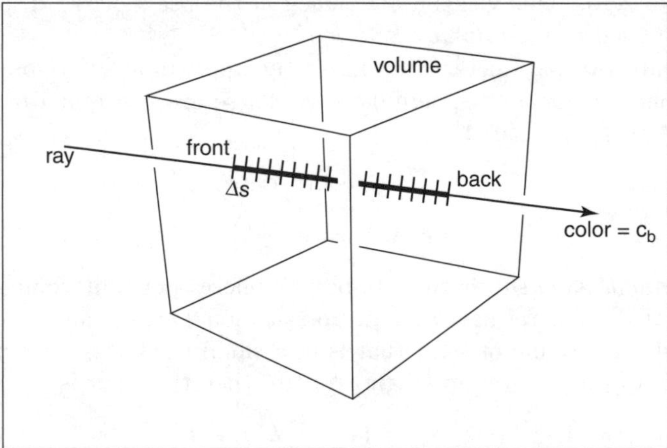

Figure 23.11. For direct volume rendering we can take constant size steps along the ray and numerically integrate.

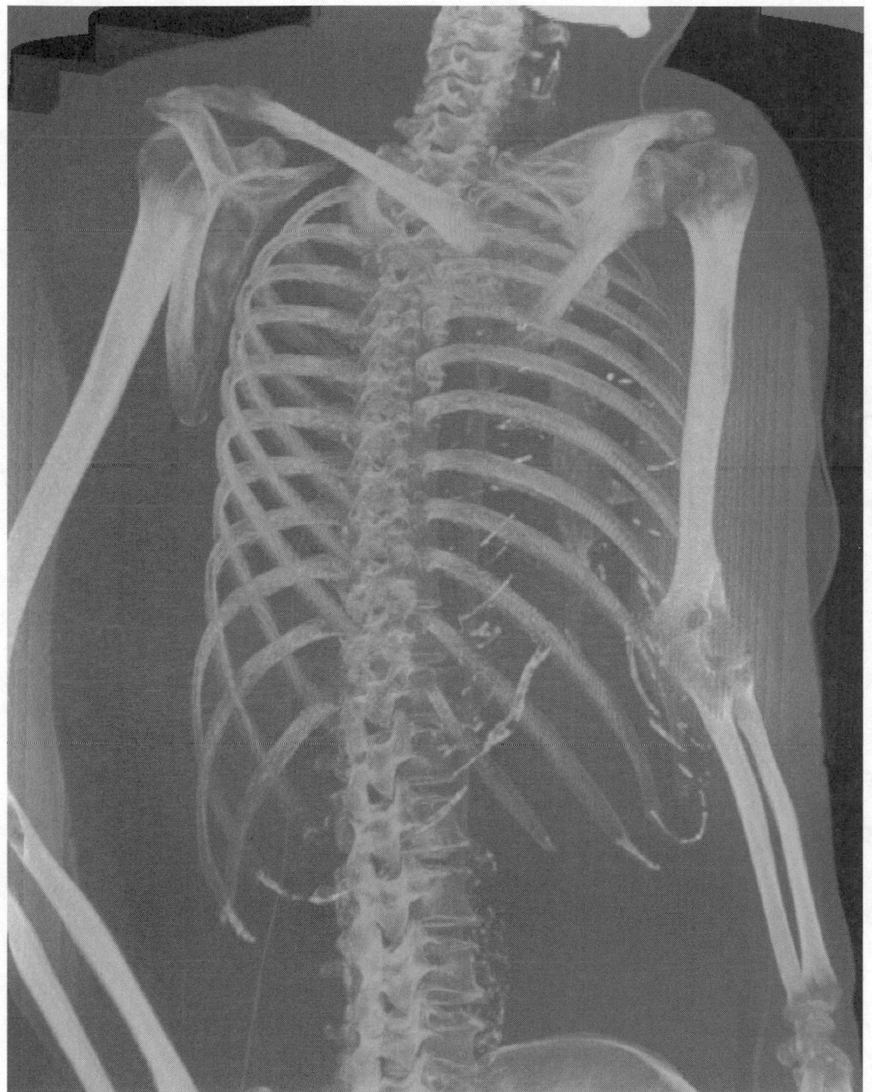

Figure 23.12. A maximum-intensity projection of the NIH/NIM Visible Female dataset. Each pixel contains a greyscale value that corresponds to the maximum density encountered along that ray. Image courtesy Steve Parker.

We can apply the original equation for each Δs slice:

$$L(s + \Delta s) = (1 - d(x, y, z)a\,\Delta s)L(s) + d(x, y, z)a\,\Delta s c(x, y, z).$$

In pseudocode, we initialize the color to the background color c_b and then traverse the volume from back to front:

find volume entry and exit points $\mathbf{a}$ *and* $\mathbf{b}$
$L = c_b$
$\Delta s =$ *distance(*$\mathbf{a}$, $\mathbf{b}$*)*
$\mathbf{p} = \mathbf{b}$
for $i = 1$ *to* N ***do***
  $\mathbf{p} = \mathbf{p} - \Delta s(\mathbf{b} - \mathbf{a})$
  $L = L + (1 - d(\mathbf{p})a\Delta sL + d(\mathbf{p})a\,\Delta s c(\mathbf{p})$

The step size Δs will determine the quality of the integration. To reduce the number of variables, we can use a new density function $g(\mathbf{p}) = d(\mathbf{p})a$.

In some applications direct volume rendering is used to render something similar to surfaces. In these cases the transfer function on density is "on" or "off" and the gradient of the number density is used to get a surface normal for shading. This can produce images of pseudosurfaces that are less sensitive to noise than traditional isosurfacing.

Another way to do volume rendering is *maximum-intensity projection.* Here, we set each pixel to the maximum density value encountered along a ray. This turns the ray integration into a search along the ray which is more efficient. Figure 23.12 shows an image generated using maximum-intensity projection.

Frequently Asked Questions

• What is the best transfer function for direct volume rendering?

The answer depends highly on the application and the characteristics of the data. Some empirical tests have been run and can be found in *The transfer function bake-off* (Pfister et al., IEEE Computer Graphics & Applications.21 (3),2001). Various optical models used in direct volume rendering are described in *Optical models for direct volume rendering* (Max,IEEE Transactions on Visualization and Computer Graphics,1 (2), 1995).

• What do I do to visualize vector or tensor data?

Vector data is often visualized using streamlines, arrows, and *line-integral convolution* (LIC). Such techniques are surveyed in *Visualizing 3D Flow* (Interrante and Grosch, IEEE Computer Graphics & Applications, 18 (4), 1998). Tensor data is more problematic. Even simple diffusion tensor data is hard to visualize effectively because you just run out of display dimensions for mpping of data dimensions. See *Strategies for Direct Volume Rendering of Diffusion Tensor Fields* (Kindlmann, Weinstein, and Hart. IEEE Transactions on Visualization and Computer Graphics. 6 (2),2000).

- **How do I interactively view a volume by changing isovalues?**

One way is to use ray tracing on a parallel machine. The other is to use polygonal isosurfacing with a preprocess that helps search for cells containing an isosurface. That search can be implemented using the data structure in *A near-optimal isosurface extraction algorithm using the span space* (Livnat, Shen, and Johnson, IEEE Transactions on Visualization and Computer Graphics, 2(1), 1996).

- **My volume data is unstructured tetrahedra. How do I do isosurfacing or direct volume rendering?**

Isosurfacing can still be done in a polygonal fashion, but there are fewer cases to preprocess. Ray tracing can also be used for isosurfacing or direct volume rendering, but the traversal algorithm must progress through the unstructured data using neighbor pointers.

- **What is "splatting" for direct volume rendering?**

Splatting refers to projecting semitransparent voxels onto the screen using some sort of painters' algorithm.

Notes

Efficient isosurfacing was developed in *Data Structure for Soft Objects* (Wyvill, McPheeters, and Wyvill, The Visual Computer, 1986) and *Marching Cubes: A High Resolution 3D Surface Construction Algorithm* (Lorensen and Cline, SIGGRAPH 87). Direct volume rendering was introduced in a variety of papers in 1988.

Exercises

1. If we have a tetrahedral data element with densities at each of the four vertices, how many "cases" are there for polygonal isosurfaces?
2. Suppose we have n^3 data elements in a volume. If the densities in the volume are "well-behaved," approximately how many cells will contain an isosurface for a particular isovalue?
3. Should we add shadowing to direct volume rendering? Why or why not?

Index

accommodation, 299
adaptation, 296
adjoint matrix, 77
aliasing, 65, 271
ambient shading, 143
angle, 20
    cosine, 20
    sine, 20
animation, 2
anti-umbra, 185
antialiasing, 65
API, 1, 3
application program interface, 3
arc-length parameterized curve, 37
array
    padded, 226
    tiling, 225
artistic shading, 147
assert(), 11
average, 251

B-spline, 241
    knots, 245
    nonuniform, 245
    rational, 245
Bézier curve
    control points, 233, 235
    cubic, 234
    quadratic, 233
backface elimination, 215
barycentric coordinates, 42–44, 60, 269
basis, 24
basis vectors, 24
bidirectional reflectance distribution function, 286, 337
bijection, 17
bilinear patch, 231
binary space partitioning (BSP) tree, 127, 187
blind spot, 296
bounding box, 168
bounding volume, 215
    hierarchy, 171
box filter, 64, 272
BRDF, 286, 337
    Lambertian, 287
bricking, 225
brightness, 298
BSP tree, 127, 189
    ray tracing, 181

CAD/CAM, 3
callbacks, 4

camera
    digital, 65, 302
candela, 290
canonical, 110
    view volume, 110
cardinal spline, 240
cardinality, 47
Cartesian coordinates, 24
Cartesian product, 16
Catmull-Rom spline, 239, 240
CCD, 65
chromaticity, 305
CIE scotopic sensitivity function, 308
circle, 20
clipping, 125, 209
    line segment, 214
    triangle, 214
closed interval, 17
CMOS, 65
cofactor matrix, 77
cofactors, 75
color, 301
    24 bit, 54
    additive, 53
    hue, 314
    opponent, 299, 310
    RGB, 49, 52, 301, 308, 309, 312
    saturation, 314
    trichromatic, 302
    value, 314
column vector, 73
compositing, 54
compression, 66
    lossless, 66
    lossy, 66
cones
    long, 295
    middle, 295
    short, 295
constructive solid geometry, 182
contrast, 298
control points, 233, 235
convex hull, 235
coordinate frame, 28
coordinates
    global, 224
    local, 224
    polar, 21
cosine, 20
Cramer's rule, 71, 78, 157
cross product, 26
CRT, 50
CSG (constructive solid geometry), 182
cube map, 205
cubic Bézier curve, 234
culling, 215
    backface elimination, 215
curve, 29
    arc-length parameterized, 37
    B-spline, 241
    cardinal, 240
    Catmull-Rom, 239, 240
    Hermite, 238
    implicit, 29
    interpolating, 238
    limit, 232
    parametric, 36, 40
    quadratic Bézier, 233
    spline, 235
    subdivision, 232
    tangent, 31
cycle (viewing), 128

debugging, 11
depth buffer, 135
    integer, 136
depth of field, 186
derivative, 31
determinant, 69, 75
    Laplace's expansion, 75
diagonal matrix, 73
diagonalization, 80
dielectric, 162
diffuse
    Lambertian, 287
digital camera, 65
direct lighting, 327
direct volume rendering, 365
Direct3D, 4
directional hemispherical reflectance, 286
directional light, 142
discriminant, 19
displacement map, 204

display
  CRT, 50
  LCD, 50
  raster, 49
  resolution, 49
display list, 217
distance
  signed, 35
distribution ray tracing, 183
domain, 16
dot product, 25
double, 9

efficiency, 7
eigenvalues, 79
eigenvectors, 79
environment maps, 205
expected value, 255, 257
eye
  retina, 302

field radiance, 284, 357
field-of-view, 123
fill-in, 296
filter
  box, 64, 272
  superable, 273
  support, 273
filtering, 271
float, 9
fovea, 295
frame of reference, 28
Fresnel Equations, 163, 338
function 15
  bijection, 17
  domain, 16
  inverse, 17, 29
  range, 16
  rational, 245
function inversion, 261

gamma, 51, 308
gamma correction, 52
gaze direction, 114
gif, 66
global coordinates, 28, 224
global illumination, 317
Gouraud color interpolation, 60
gradient, 31

hard shadow, 184
Hermite curve, 238
hidden surface elimination, 127
  BSP tree, 127
highlight, 144
homogeneous coordinate, 102, 117
homogenization, 119
hue, 305, 314
hypotenuse, 20

IBR, 353
identity matrix, 73
IEEE floating point, 5
illumination
  global, 317
image, 9
  compression, 66
image processing, 2
image-based modeling, 356
image-based rendering, 353
implicit curve, 29
  gradient, 31
importance sampling, 258
include guards, 10
incremental computation, 57
independent random variable, 255
indirect lighting, 317
information visualization, 3, 359
infrared light, 290
inline functions, 9
instancing, 165
integral geometry, 251
integration, 250
  Monte Carlo, 258, 321
  quasi-Monte Carlo, 260
intensity, 290
interpolation, 42, 238
  linear, 42
  normal vector, 147
intersection
  ray-bounding box, 168
  ray-implicit, 155
  ray-parametric, 156
  ray-sphere, 155
  ray-triangle, 156

interval, 17
  closed, 17
  open, 17
  set operations, 17
inverse function, 17, 29
inverse matrix, 74, 77
inversion
  function, 261
irradiance, 282
isosurface, 360

jaggies, 271
Java, 4
jittering, 184
jpeg, 66

knots, 245

Lambert's Law, 141
Lambertian, 141
  BRDF, 287
Law of Large Numbers, 258
LCD, 50
level-of-detail (LOD), 5
light
  directional, 142
  infrared, 290
  ultraviolet, 290
light field, 354
lighting, 215
  direct, 327
  indirect, 317
  two-sided, 142
lightness, 298, 314
limit curve, 232
line
  implicit, 33
  normal coordinates, 253
  parametric, 37, 40, 58
  slope, 33
  slope-intercept form, 33
  vector form, 40
line drawing, 55
  incremental, 57
line segment, 41
linear independence, 24
linear interpolation, 42
linear system
  solution, 78
    Cramer's rule, 71
local control, 243, 245
local coordinates, 28, 224
location, 23
LOD (level-of-detail), 5
logarithm, 18
  natural, 18
Loop subdivision, 245
luminaire, 317
  non-diffuse, 331
luminance, 290, 312
  scotopic, 308, 311
luminous efficiency function, 289

mappings, 15
material
  dielectric, 162
matrix, 71
  adjoint, 77
  cofactor, 77
  cofactors, 75
  determinant, 69
  diagonal, 73
  diagonal form, 80
  identity, 73
  inverse, 74, 77
  inversion using SVD, 104
  multiplication, 72
  product with scaler, 72
  projection, 122
  square, 71
  symmetric, 73
  transpose, 73
matrix stack, 225
maximum-intensity projection, 368
measure
  2D lines, 252
  3D lines, 253
  zero measure sets, 250
mesh, 199
metamer, 303
Metropolis sampling, 264
microfacets, 338
midpoint algorithm, 55
MIP-mapping, 207
mixture density, 332

modeling, 2, 4
Moire patterns, 184
monitor
  gamma, 51
  phosphors, 308
  tristimulus values, 309
  white point, 308
Monte Carlo integration, 258, 321
  importance sampling, 258
  stratified sampling, 259
motion blur, 188
mutual illumination, 317

nanometer, 280
natural logarithm, 18
non-photorealistic rendering, 147
nonuniform B-spline, 245
nonuniform rational B-spline (NURBS), 245
normal coordinates, 253
normal interpolation, 147
normal vector, 31, 99
  at vertices, 144
number density, 365
NURBS, 245

offset, 23
open interval, 17
OpenGL, 4
operators, 10
opponent color space, 310
opponent colors, 299
origin, 23
orthogonal, 24
orthographic projection, 114
orthographic view volume, 112
orthonormal, 24
orthonormal basis, 27

padded array, 226
painter's algorithm, 127
parallelepiped
  volume, 70
parallelogram
  area, 69, 75
parallelogram rule, 23
parametric curve, 36, 40
parametric line, 40
parametric surface, 41
particle tracing, 319
path tracing, 321
penumbra, 185
perspective
  three point, 116
perspective projection, 116
Phong exponent, 145
Phong normal interpolation, 147
Phong shading, 144
photometry, 279, 289
photon, 280
picking, 151, 190
pixel, 49
plane
  implicit, 38
point, 23
polar coordinates, 21
polygon
  ray intersection, 158
position, 23
power, 281
ppm, 66
probability, 254
  expected value, 255
probability density function, 254
projection
  orthographic, 114
projection matrix, 122
pseudocolor plot, 360
Pythagorean theorem, 20

quadratic Bézier curve, 233
quadratic equation, 19, 155
quasi-Monte Carlo integration, 260

radiance, 283, 354
  field, 284, 357
  surface, 284, 357
radiant exitance, 282
radiometry, 279
radiosity, 290, 318
random point density plot, 360
random sampling, 184
random variables 255
  independent identically distributed, 257
range, 16

raster display, 49
rasterization
  triangle, 60
rational function, 245
ray, 41
  shadow, 161
ray tracing, 151, 159
  distribution, 183
  instancing, 165
  object-oriented, 160
ray-polygon intersection, 158
reflect transform, 90
reflectance
  directional hemispherical, 286
reflection
  Lambertian, 141
  specular, 161
  total internal, 163
refraction, 165
regular sampling, 184
rejection method, 263
rendering, 2
  non-photorealistic, 147
rendering equation, 288
resolution, 49
retina, 295, 302
retroreflection, 352
RGB, 9
RGB color, 49, 52, 301
right-handed coordinates, 26
rigid body transforms, 103
Roberts, Larry, 12
rotation transform, 88
row vector, 73

sampling
  jittering, 184
  random, 184
  regular, 184
  stratified, 184
saturation, 314
scalar product, 25
scale transform, 86
Schlick approximation, 163
Seitz, Chuck, 12
set, 16
  Cartesian product, 16
set operations
  on intervals, 17
shading, 141, 215
  ambient, 143
  artistic, 147
  Phong, 144
shadow
  anti-umbra, 185
  hard, 184
  penumbra, 185
  soft, 184
  umbra, 185
shadow map, 206
shadow ray, 161
shear transform, 87
signed distance, 35
silhouettes, 147
sine, 20
singular value decomposition (SVD), 81, 94
  for matrix inversion, 104
singular values, 81
Sketchpad, 12
slope, 31
soft shadow, 184
software engineering, 8
solid texture
  turbulence, 197
space curve, 236
spectral energy, 281
specular reflection, 161
sphere
  implicit form, 155
  normal vector, 156
  vector form, 155
splatting, 369
spline, 235
  B-spline, 241
  cardinal, 240
  Catmull-Rom, 239, 240
  control points, 235
  control polygon, 235
  local control, 243, 245
  NURBS, 245
  trimming curve, 238
spot light, 207
square matrix, 71
steady state, 281